Divergence Measures: Mathematical Foundations and Applications in Information-Theoretic and Statistical Problems

Divergence Measures: Mathematical Foundations and Applications in Information-Theoretic and Statistical Problems

Editor

Igal Sason

MDPI • Basel • Beijing • Wuhan • Barcelona • Belgrade • Manchester • Tokyo • Cluj • Tianjin

Editor
Igal Sason
Andrew & Erna Viterbi
Faculty of Electrical and
Computer Engineering and
the Faculty of Mathematics
Technion – Israel Institute
of Technology
Haifa
Israel

Editorial Office
MDPI
St. Alban-Anlage 66
4052 Basel, Switzerland

This is a reprint of articles from the Special Issue published online in the open access journal *Entropy* (ISSN 1099-4300) (available at: www.mdpi.com/journal/entropy/special_issues/divergence).

For citation purposes, cite each article independently as indicated on the article page online and as indicated below:

LastName, A.A.; LastName, B.B.; LastName, C.C. Article Title. *Journal Name* **Year**, *Volume Number*, Page Range.

ISBN 978-3-0365-4332-1 (Hbk)
ISBN 978-3-0365-4331-4 (PDF)

© 2022 by the authors. Articles in this book are Open Access and distributed under the Creative Commons Attribution (CC BY) license, which allows users to download, copy and build upon published articles, as long as the author and publisher are properly credited, which ensures maximum dissemination and a wider impact of our publications.

The book as a whole is distributed by MDPI under the terms and conditions of the Creative Commons license CC BY-NC-ND.

Contents

About the Editor vii

Igal Sason
Divergence Measures: Mathematical Foundations and Applications in Information-Theoretic and Statistical Problems
Reprinted from: *Entropy* **2022**, 24, 712, doi:10.3390/e24050712 1

Frank Nielsen
On a Generalization of the Jensen–Shannon Divergence and the Jensen–Shannon Centroid
Reprinted from: *Entropy* **2020**, 22, 221, doi:10.3390/e22020221 7

Cédric Bleuler, Amos Lapidoth and Christoph Pfister
Conditional Rényi Divergences and Horse Betting
Reprinted from: *Entropy* **2020**, 22, 316, doi:10.3390/e22030316 31

Tomohiro Nishiyama and Igal Sason
On Relations Between the Relative Entropy and χ^2-Divergence, Generalizations and Applications
Reprinted from: *Entropy* **2020**, 22, 563, doi:10.3390/e22050563 71

Galen Reeves
A Two-Moment Inequality with Applications to Rényi Entropy and Mutual Information
Reprinted from: *Entropy* **2020**, 22, 1244, doi:10.3390/e22111244 107

James Melbourne
Strongly Convex Divergences
Reprinted from: *Entropy* **2020**, 22, 1327, doi:10.3390/e22111327 133

Michel Broniatowski
Minimum Divergence Estimators, Maximum Likelihood and the Generalized Bootstrap
Reprinted from: *Entropy* **2021**, 23, 185, doi:10.3390/e23020185 153

Sergio Verdú
Error Exponents and α-Mutual Information
Reprinted from: *Entropy* **2021**, 23, 199, doi:10.3390/e23020199 169

Anmol Dwivedi, Sihui Wang and Ali Tajer
Discriminant Analysis under f-Divergence Measures
Reprinted from: *Entropy* **2022**, 24, 188, doi:10.3390/e24020188 221

About the Editor

Igal Sason

Igal Sason received his B.Sc. and Ph.D. degrees in electrical engineering from the Technion —Israel Institute of Technology, Haifa, Israel, in 1992 and 2001, respectively. During 1993–1997, he worked in Israel as a communication engineer. During 2001–2003, he was a scientific collaborator at the School of Computer and Communication Sciences at EPFL, Lausanne, Switzerland. Since 2003, he has been a faculty member at the Andrew and Erna Viterbi Faculty of Electrical and Computer Engineering of the Technion, where he is currently a professor. Since 2021, he is also a Professor at the Faculty of Mathematics of the Technion. His research interests are in information theory, and its aspects in combinatorics and probability theory. He served at the editorial board of the IEEE Transactions on Information Theory for overall 10 years, including terms as the Executive Editor and Editor-in-Chief. He also served as a Guest Editor of two Special Issues of the *Entropy* journal (MDPI) during 2019–2022. I. Sason has been a member of the IEEE since 1998, and he is an IEEE Fellow of the Information Theory Society (effective from 2019) for contributions to the achievable rate region of the Gaussian interference channel, and the analysis of low-complexity capacity-achieving linear codes.

Editorial

Divergence Measures: Mathematical Foundations and Applications in Information-Theoretic and Statistical Problems

Igal Sason [1,2]

[1] Andrew & Erna Viterbi Faculty of Electrical and Computer Engineering, Technion—Israel Institute of Technology, Haifa 3200003, Israel; eeigal@technion.ac.il; Tel.: +972-4-8294699
[2] Faculty of Mathematics, Technion—Israel Institute of Technology, Haifa 3200003, Israel

Citation: Sason, I. Divergence Measures: Mathematical Foundations and Applications in Information-Theoretic and Statistical Problems. *Entropy* **2022**, *24*, 712. https://doi.org/10.3390/e24050712

Received: 3 May 2022
Accepted: 13 May 2022
Published: 16 May 2022

Publisher's Note: MDPI stays neutral with regard to jurisdictional claims in published maps and institutional affiliations.

Copyright: © 2022 by the author. Licensee MDPI, Basel, Switzerland. This article is an open access article distributed under the terms and conditions of the Creative Commons Attribution (CC BY) license (https://creativecommons.org/licenses/by/4.0/).

Data science, information theory, probability theory, statistical learning, statistical signal processing, and other related disciplines greatly benefit from non-negative measures of dissimilarity between pairs of probability measures. These are known as divergence measures, and exploring their mathematical foundations and diverse applications is of significant interest (see, e.g., [1–10] and references therein).

The present Special Issue, entitled *Divergence Measures: Mathematical Foundations and Applications in Information-Theoretic and Statistical Problems*, is focused on the study of the mathematical properties and applications of classical and generalized divergence measures from an information-theoretic perspective. It includes eight original contributions on the subject, which mainly deal with two key generalizations of the relative entropy: namely, the Rényi divergence and the important class of f-divergences. The Rényi divergence was introduced by Rényi as a generalization of relative entropy (relative entropy is a.k.a. the Kullback–Leibler divergence [11]), and it found numerous applications in information theory, statistics, and other related fields [12,13]. The notion of an f-divergence, which was independently introduced by Ali-Silvey [14], Csiszár [15–17], and Morimoto [18], is a useful generalization of some well-known divergence measures, retaining some of their major properties, including data-processing inequalities. It should be noted that, although the Rényi divergence of an arbitrary order is not an f-divergence, it is a one-to-one transformation of a subclass of f-divergences, so it inherits some of the key properties of f-divergences. We next describe the eight contributions in this Special Issue, and their relation to the literature.

Relative entropy is a well-known asymmetric and unbounded divergence measure [11], whereas the Jensen-Shannon divergence [19,20] (a.k.a. the capacitory discrimination [21]) is a bounded symmetrization of relative entropy, which does not require the pair of probability measures to have matching supports. It has the pleasing property that its square root is a distance metric, and it also belongs to the class of f-divergences. The latter implies, in particular, that the Jensen–Shannon divergence satisfies data-processing inequalities. The first paper in this Special Issue [22], authored by Nielsen, studies generalizations of the Jensen–Shannon divergence and the Jensen–Shannon centroid. The work in [22] further suggests an iterative algorithm for the numerical computation of the Jensen–Shannon-type centroids for a set of probability densities belonging to a mixture family in information geometry. This includes the case of calculating the Jensen–Shannon centroid of a set of categorical distributions or normalized histograms.

Many of Shannon's information measures appear naturally in the context of horse gambling, when the gambler's utility function is the expected log-wealth. The second paper [23], coauthored by Bleuler, Lapidoth, and Pfister, shows that, under a more general family of utility functions, gambling also provides a context for some of Rényi's information measures. Motivated by a horse betting problem in the setting where the gambler has side information, a new conditional Rényi divergence is introduced in [23]. It is compared with the conditional Rényi divergences by Csiszár and Sibson, and the properties of all the three are studied in depth by the authors, with an emphasis on the behavior of these conditional divergence measures under data processing. In the same way that Csiszár's and Sibson's conditional divergences lead to the respective dependence measures, so does the new conditional divergence in [23] lead to the Lapidoth–Pfister mutual information. The authors further demonstrate that their new conditional divergence measure is also related to the Arimoto–Rényi conditional entropy and to Arimoto's measure of dependence. In the second part of [23], the horse betting problem is analyzed where, instead of Kelly's expected log-wealth criterion, a more general family of power-mean utility functions is considered. The key role in the analysis is played by the Rényi divergence, and the setting where the gambler has access to side information provides an operational meaning to the Lapidoth–Pfister mutual information. Finally, a universal strategy for independent and identically distributed races is presented in [23] which, without knowing the winning probabilities or the parameter of the utility function, asymptotically maximizes the gambler's utility function.

The relative entropy [11] and the chi-squared divergence [24] are classical divergence measures which play a key role in information theory, statistical machine learning, signal processing, statistics, probability theory, and many other branches of mathematics. These divergence measures are fundamental in problems pertaining to source and channel coding, large deviations theory, tests of goodness-of-fit and independence in statistics, expectation–maximization iterative algorithms for estimating a distribution from an incomplete data, and other sorts of problems. They also belong to the generalized class of f-divergences. The third paper [25], by Nishiyama and Sason, studies integral relations between the relative entropy and chi-squared divergence, the implications of these relations, their information-theoretic applications, and some generalizations pertaining to the rich class of f-divergences. Applications that are studied in [25] include lossless compression, the method of types and large deviations, strong data-processing inequalities, bounds on contraction coefficients and maximal correlation, and the convergence rate to the stationarity of a type of discrete-time Markov chain.

The interesting interplay between inequalities and information theory has a rich history, with notable examples that include the relationship between the Brunn–Minkowski inequality and the entropy power inequality, transportation-cost inequalities and their tight connections to information theory, logarithmic Sobolev inequalities and the entropy method, inequalities for matrices obtained from the nonnegativity of relative entropy, connections between information inequalities and finite groups, combinatorics, and other fields of mathematics (see, e.g., [26–30]). The fourth paper by Reeves [31] considers applications of a two-moment inequality for the integral of fractional power of a function between zero and one. The first contribution of this paper provides an upper bound on the Rényi entropy of a random vector, expressed in terms of the two different moments. This also recovers some previous results based on maximum entropy distributions under a single moment constraint. The second contribution in [31] is a method for upper bounding mutual information in terms of certain integrals with respect to the variance of the conditional density.

Basic properties of an f-divergence are its non-negativity, convexity in the pair of probability measures, and the satisfiability of data-processing inequalities as a result of the convexity of the function f (and by the requirement that f vanishes at 1). These properties lead to f-divergence inequalities, and to information-theoretic applications (see, e.g., [4,10,32–37]). Furthermore, tightened (strong) data-processing inequalities for f-divergences have been of recent interest (see, e.g., [38–42]). The fifth paper [43], authored by Melbourne, is focused on the study of how stronger convexity properties of the function f imply improvements of classical f-divergence inequalities. It provides a systematic study of strongly convex divergences, and it quantifies how the convexity of a divergence generator f influences the behavior of the f-divergence. It proves that every (so-called) strongly convex divergence dominates the square of the total variation, which extends the classical bound provided by the chi-squared divergence. Its analysis also yields improvements of Bayes risk f-divergence inequalities, consequently achieving a sharpening of Pinsker's inequality.

Divergences between probability measures are often used in statistics and data science in order to perform inference under models of various types. The corresponding methods extend the likelihood paradigm, and suggest inference in settings of minimum distance or minimum divergence, while allowing some tradeoff between efficiency and robustness. The sixth paper [44], authored by Broniatowski, considers a subclass of f-divergences, which contains most of the classical inferential tools, and which is indexed by a single scalar parameter. This class belongs to the family of f-divergences, and is usually referred to as the power divergence class, which has been considered by Cressie and Read [7,45]. The work in [44] states that the most commonly used minimum divergence estimators are maximum-likelihood estimators for suitably generalized bootstrapped sampling schemes. It also considers optimality of associated goodness-of-fit tests under such sampling schemes.

The seventh paper by Verdú [46] is a research and tutorial paper on error exponents and α-mutual information. Similarly to [23] (the second paper in this Special Issue), it relates to Rényi's generalization of the relative entropy and mutual information. In light of the landmark paper by Shannon [47], it is well known that the analysis of the fundamental limits of noisy communication channels in the regime of vanishing error probability (by letting the blocklength of the code tend to infinity) leads to the introduction of the channel capacity as the maximal rate which enables to obtain reliable communication. The channel capacity is expressed in terms of a basic information measure: the input–output mutual information maximized over the input distribution. Furthermore, in the regime of fixed nonzero error probability, the asymptotic fundamental limit is a function of not only the channel capacity but the channel dispersion, which is expressible in terms of an information measure: the variance of the information density obtained with the capacity-achieving distribution [48]. In the regime of exponentially decreasing error probability, at fixed code rate below capacity, the analysis of the fundamental limits has gone through three distinct phases: (1) the early days of information theory and the error exponents analysis at MIT; (2) expressions for the error exponent functions by incorporating the relative entropy; and (3) the error exponent research with Rényi information measures. Thanks to Csiszár's realization of the relevance of Rényi's information measures to this problem [32], the third phase has found a way to express the error exponent functions as a function of generalized information measures, and also to solve the associated optimization problems in a systematic way. While in the absence of cost constraints, the problem reduces to finding the maximal α-mutual information, cost constraints make the problem significantly more challenging. The remained gaps in the interrelationships between three approaches, in the general case of cost-constrained encoding, motivated the present study in [46]. Furthermore, no systematic approach has been suggested so far for solving the attendant optimization problems by exploiting the specific structure of the information functions. The work by Verdú in [46] closes those gaps, while proposing a simple method to maximize the Augustin–Csiszár mutual information of order α under cost constraints [32,49], by means of the maximization of the α-mutual information subject to an exponential average constraint.

In statistical inference, the information-theoretic performance limits can often be expressed in terms of a statistical divergence measure between the underlying statistical models (see, e.g., [50] and references therein). As the data dimension grows, computing the statistics involved in decision making and the attendant performance limits (divergence measures) face complexity and stability challenges. Dimensionality reduction addresses these challenges at the expense of compromising performance because of the attendant loss of information. The eighth and last paper in the present Special Issue [51] considers linear dimensionality reduction, such that the divergence between the models is maximally preserved. Specifically, this work is focused on Gaussian models where discriminant analysis under several f-divergence measures are considered. The optimal design of the linear transformation of the data onto a lower-dimensional subspace is characterized for zero-mean Gaussian models, and numerical algorithms are employed to find the design for general Gaussian models with non-zero means.

It is our hope that the reader will find interest in the eight original contributions of this Special Issue, and that these works will stimulate further research in the study of the mathematical foundations and applications of divergence measures.

Acknowledgments: The Guest Editor is grateful to all the authors for their contributions to this Special Issue, to the anonymous peer-reviewers for their timely reports and constructive feedback.

Conflicts of Interest: The author declares no conflict of interest.

References

1. Basseville, M. Divergence measures for statistical data processing—An annotated bibliography. *Signal Process.* **2013**, *93*, 621–633. [CrossRef]
2. Broniatowski, M.; Stummer, W. Some universal insights on divergences for statistics, machine learning and artificial intelligence. In *Geometric Structures of Information*; Nielsen, F., Ed.; Springer: Berlin/Heidelberg, Germany, 2019; pp. 149–211. [CrossRef]
3. Csiszár, I.; Shields, P.C. Information Theory and Statistics: A Tutorial. *Found. Trends Commun. Inf. Theory* **2004**, *1*, 417–528. [CrossRef]
4. Esposito, A.R.; Gastpar, M.; Issa, I. Generalization error bounds via Rényi-, f-divergences and maximal leakage. *IEEE Trans. Inf. Theory* **2021**, *67*, 4986–5004. [CrossRef]
5. Liese, F.; Vajda, I. *Convex Statistical Distances*; Teubner-Texte Zur Mathematik: Leipzig, Germany, 1987; Volume 95.
6. Liese, F.; Vajda, I. On divergences and informations in statistics and information theory. *IEEE Trans. Inf. Theory* **2006**, *52*, 4394–4412. [CrossRef]
7. Pardo, L. *Statistical Inference Based on Divergence Measures*; Chapman and Hall/CRC: Boca Raton, FL, USA, 2006.
8. Stummer W.; Vajda, I. On divergences of finite measures and their applicability in statistics and information theory. *Statistics* **2010**, *44*, 169–187. [CrossRef]
9. Vajda, I. *Theory of Statistical Inference and Information*; Kluwer Academic Publishers: Dordrecht, The Netherlands, 1989.
10. Zakai, M.; Ziv, J. A generalization of the rate-distortion theory and applications. In *Information Theory—New Trends and Open Problems*; Longo, G., Ed.; Springer: Berlin/Heidelberg, Germany, 1975; pp. 87–123. [CrossRef]
11. Kullback, S.; Leibler, R.A. On information and sufficiency. *Ann. Math. Stat.* **1951**, *22*, 79–86. [CrossRef]
12. Rényi, A. On measures of entropy and information. In *Proceedings of the Fourth Berkeley Symposium on Mathematical Statistics and Probability, Volume 1: Contributions to the Theory of Statistics*; University of California Press: Berkeley, CA, USA, 1961; pp. 547–561. Available online: https://digitalassets.lib.berkeley.edu/math/ucb/text/math_s4_v1_article-27.pdf (accessed on 12 May 2022).
13. Van Erven, T.; Harremoës, P. Rényi divergence and Kullback–Leibler divergence. *IEEE Trans. Inf. Theory* **2014**, *60*, 3797–3820. [CrossRef]
14. Ali, S.M.; Silvey, S.D. A general class of coefficients of divergence of one distribution from another. *J. R. Stat. Soc.* **1966**, *28*, 131–142. [CrossRef]
15. Csiszár, I. Eine Informationstheoretische Ungleichung und ihre Anwendung auf den Bewis der Ergodizität von Markhoffschen Ketten. *Publ. Math. Inst. Hungar. Acad. Sci.* **1963**, *8*, 85–108.
16. Csiszár, I. Information-type measures of difference of probability distributions and indirect observations. *Stud. Sci. Math. Hung.* **1967**, *2*, 299–318.
17. Csiszár, I. On topological properties of f-divergences. *Stud. Sci. Math. Hung.* **1967**, *2*, 329–339.
18. Morimoto, T. Markov processes and the H-theorem. *J. Phys. Soc. Jpn.* **1963**, *18*, 328–331. [CrossRef]
19. Lin, J. Divergence measures based on the Shannon entropy. *IEEE Trans. Inf. Theory* **1991**, *37*, 145–151. [CrossRef]
20. Menéndez, M.L.; Pardo, J.A.; Pardo, L.; Pardo, M.C. The Jensen–Shannon divergence. *J. Frankl. Inst.* **1997**, *334*, 307–318. [CrossRef]
21. Topsøe, F. Some inequalities for information divergence and related measures of discrimination. *IEEE Trans. Inf. Theory* **2000**, *46*, 1602–1609. [CrossRef]
22. Nielsen, F. On a generalization of the Jensen–Shannon divergence and the Jensen–Shannon centroid. *Entropy* **2020**, *22*, 221. [CrossRef]
23. Bleuler, C.; Lapidoth, A.; Pfister, C. Conditional Rényi divergences and horse betting. *Entropy* **2020**, *22*, 316. 10.3390/e22030316. [CrossRef]
24. Pearson, K. On the criterion that a given system of deviations from the probable in the case of a correlated system of variables is such that it can be reasonably supposed to have arisen from random sampling. *Lond. Edinb. Dublin Philos. Mag. J. Sci.* **1900**, *50*, 157–175. [CrossRef]
25. Nishiyama, T.; Sason, I. On relations between the relative entropy and χ^2-divergence, generalizations and applications. *Entropy* **2020**, *22*, 563. [CrossRef]
26. Dembo, A.; Cover, T.M.; Thomas, J.A. Information theoretic inequalities. *IEEE Trans. Inf. Theory* **1991**, *37*, 1501–1518. [CrossRef]

27. Madiman, M.; Mellbourne, J.; Xeng, P. Forward and reverse entropy power inequalities in convex geometry. In *Convexity and Concentration*; Carlen, E., Madiman, M., Werner, E.M., Eds.; IMA Volumes in Mathematics and Its Applications; Springer: Berlin/Heidelberg, Germany, 2017, Volume 161, pp. 427–485. [CrossRef]
28. Marton, K. Distance-divergence inequalities. *IEEE Inf. Theory Soc. Newsl.* **2014**, *64*, 9–13.
29. Boucheron, S.; Lugosi, G.; Massart, P. *Concentration Inequalities—A Nonasymptotic Theory of Independence*; Oxford University Press: Oxford, UK, 2013.
30. Raginsky, M.; Sason, I. *Concentration of Measure Inequalities in Information Theory, Communications and Coding*, 3rd ed.; Now Publishers: Delft, The Netherlands, 2018. [CrossRef]
31. Reeves, G. A two-moment inequality with applications to Rényi entropy and mutual information. *Entropy* **2020**, *22*, 1244. [CrossRef] [PubMed]
32. Csiszár, I. A class of measures of informativity of observation channels. *Period. Mat. Hung.* **1972**, *2*, 191–213. [CrossRef]
33. Guntuboyina, A.; Saha, S.; Schiebinger, G. Sharp inequalities for f-divergences. *IEEE Trans. Inf. Theory* **2014**, *60*, 104–121. [CrossRef]
34. Harremoës, P.; Vajda, I. On pairs of f-divergences and their joint range. *IEEE Trans. Inf. Theory* **2011**, *57*, 3230–3235. [CrossRef]
35. Merhav, N. Data processing theorems and the second law of thermodynamics. *IEEE Trans. Inf. Theory* **2011**, *57*, 4926–4939. [CrossRef]
36. Sason, I.; Verdú, S. f-divergence inequalities. *IEEE Trans. Inf. Theory* **2016**, *62*, 5973–6006. [CrossRef]
37. Sason, I. On f-divergences: Integral representations, local behavior, and inequalities. *Entropy* **2018**, *20*, 383. [CrossRef]
38. Calmon, F.P.; Polyanskiy, Y.; Wu, Y. Strong data processing inequalities for input constrained additive noise channels. *IEEE Trans. Inf. Theory* **2018**, *64*, 1879–1892. [CrossRef]
39. Raginsky, M. Strong data processing inequalities and Φ-Sobolev inequalities for discrete channels. *IEEE Trans. Inf. Theory* **2016**, *62*, 3355–3389. [CrossRef]
40. Polyanskiy, Y.; Wu, Y. Strong data processing inequalities for channels and Bayesian networks. In *Convexity and Concentration*; Carlen, E., Madiman, M., Werner, E.M., Eds.; Springer: Berlin/Heidelberg, Germany, 2017; Volume 161, pp. 211–249. [CrossRef]
41. Makur, A.; Zheng, L. Linear bounds between contraction coefficients for f-divergences. *Probl. Inf. Transm.* **2020**, *56*, 103–156. [CrossRef]
42. Sason, I. On data-processing and majorization inequalities for f-divergences with applications. *Entropy* **2019**, *21*, 1022. [CrossRef]
43. Melbourne, J. Strongly convex divergences. *Entropy* **2020**, *22*, 1327. [CrossRef] [PubMed]
44. Broniatowski, M. Minimum divergence estimators, maximum likelihood and the generalized bootstrap. *Entropy* **2021**, *23*, 185. [CrossRef] [PubMed]
45. Cressie, N.; Read, T.R.C. Multinomial Goodness-of-Fit Tests. *J. R. Stat. Soc. Ser. (Methodol.)* **1984**, *46*, 440–464. [CrossRef]
46. Verdú, S. Error Exponents and α-Mutual Information. *Entropy* **2021**, *23*, 199. [CrossRef]
47. Shannon, C.E. A Mathematical Theory of Communication. *Bell Syst. Tech. J.* **1948**, *27*, 379–423. 623–656. [CrossRef]
48. Polyanskiy, Y.; Poor, H.V.; Verdú, S. Channel coding rate in the finite blocklength regime. *IEEE Trans. Inf. Theory* **2010**, *56*, 2307–2359. [CrossRef]
49. Augustin, U. Noisy Channels. Ph.D. Thesis, Universität Erlangen-Nürnberg, Erlangen, Germany, 1978. Available online: http://libgen.rs/book/index.php?md5=4431004A794657A85AA356F111AA52FE (accessed on 12 May 2022).
50. Sason, I.; Verdú, S. Arimoto-Rényi conditional entropy and Bayesian M-ary hypothesis testing. *IEEE Trans. Inf. Theory* **2018**, *64*, 4–25. [CrossRef]
51. Dwivedi, A.; Wang, S.; Tajer, A. Discriminant analysis under f-divergence measures. *Entropy* **2022**, *24*, 188. [CrossRef]

Article

On a Generalization of the Jensen–Shannon Divergence and the Jensen–Shannon Centroid

Frank Nielsen

Sony Computer Science Laboratories, Tokyo 141-0022, Japan; Frank.Nielsen@acm.org

Received: 5 December 2019; Accepted: 14 February 2020; Published: 16 February 2020

Abstract: The Jensen–Shannon divergence is a renown bounded symmetrization of the Kullback–Leibler divergence which does not require probability densities to have matching supports. In this paper, we introduce a vector-skew generalization of the scalar α-Jensen–Bregman divergences and derive thereof the vector-skew α-Jensen–Shannon divergences. We prove that the vector-skew α-Jensen–Shannon divergences are f-divergences and study the properties of these novel divergences. Finally, we report an iterative algorithm to numerically compute the Jensen–Shannon-type centroids for a set of probability densities belonging to a mixture family: This includes the case of the Jensen–Shannon centroid of a set of categorical distributions or normalized histograms.

Keywords: Bregman divergence; f-divergence; Jensen–Bregman divergence; Jensen diversity; Jensen–Shannon divergence; capacitory discrimination; Jensen–Shannon centroid; mixture family; information geometry; difference of convex (DC) programming

1. Introduction

Let $(\mathcal{X}, \mathcal{F}, \mu)$ be a measure space [1] where $\mathcal{X}$ denotes the sample space, $\mathcal{F}$ the σ-algebra of measurable events, and μ a positive measure; for example, the measure space defined by the Lebesgue measure μ_L with Borel σ-algebra $\mathcal{B}(\mathbb{R}^d)$ for $\mathcal{X} = \mathbb{R}^d$ or the measure space defined by the counting measure μ_c with the power set σ-algebra $2^\mathcal{X}$ on a finite alphabet $\mathcal{X}$. Denote by $L_1(\mathcal{X}, \mathcal{F}, \mu)$ the Lebesgue space of measurable functions, $\mathcal{P}_1$ the subspace of *positive* integrable functions f such that $\int_\mathcal{X} f(x) \mathrm{d}\mu(x) = 1$ and $f(x) > 0$ for all $x \in \mathcal{X}$, and $\overline{\mathcal{P}}_1$ the subspace of *non-negative* integrable functions f such that $\int_\mathcal{X} f(x) \mathrm{d}\mu(x) = 1$ and $f(x) \geq 0$ for all $x \in \mathcal{X}$.

We refer to the book of Deza and Deza [2] and the survey of Basseville [3] for an introduction to the many types of statistical divergences met in information sciences and their justifications. The *Kullback–Leibler Divergence* (KLD) $\mathrm{KL} : \mathcal{P}_1 \times \mathcal{P}_1 \to [0, \infty]$ is an oriented statistical distance (commonly called the relative entropy in information theory [4]) defined between two densities p and q (i.e., the Radon–Nikodym densities of μ-absolutely continuous probability measures P and Q) by

$$\mathrm{KL}(p:q) := \int p \log \frac{p}{q} \mathrm{d}\mu. \qquad (1)$$

Although $\mathrm{KL}(p:q) \geq 0$ with equality iff. $p = q$ μ-a. e. (Gibb's inequality [4]), the KLD may diverge to infinity depending on the underlying densities. Since the KLD is asymmetric, several symmetrizations [5] have been proposed in the literature.

A well-grounded symmetrization of the KLD is the *Jensen–Shannon Divergence* [6] (JSD), also called *capacitory discrimination* in the literature (e.g., see [7]):

$$\mathrm{JS}(p,q) := \frac{1}{2}\left(\mathrm{KL}\left(p:\frac{p+q}{2}\right)+\mathrm{KL}\left(q:\frac{p+q}{2}\right)\right), \tag{2}$$

$$= \frac{1}{2}\int\left(p\log\frac{2p}{p+q}+q\log\frac{2q}{p+q}\right)d\mu = \mathrm{JS}(q,p). \tag{3}$$

The Jensen–Shannon divergence can be interpreted as the *total KL divergence to the average distribution* $\frac{p+q}{2}$. The Jensen–Shannon divergence was historically implicitly introduced in [8] (Equation (19)) to calculate distances between random graphs. A nice feature of the Jensen–Shannon divergence is that this divergence can be applied to densities with *arbitrary* support (i.e., $p,q \in \overline{\mathcal{P}}_1$ with the convention that $0\log 0 = 0$ and $\log\frac{0}{0} = 0$); moreover, the JSD is *always* upper bounded by $\log 2$. Let $\mathcal{X}_p = \mathrm{supp}(p)$ and $\mathcal{X}_q = \mathrm{supp}(q)$ denote the supports of the densities p and q, respectively, where $\mathrm{supp}(p) := \{x \in \mathcal{X} : p(x) > 0\}$. The JSD saturates to $\log 2$ whenever the supports $\mathcal{X}_p$ and $\mathcal{X}_p$ are disjoints. We can rewrite the JSD as

$$\mathrm{JS}(p,q) = h\left(\frac{p+q}{2}\right) - \frac{h(p)+h(q)}{2}, \tag{4}$$

where $h(p) = -\int p\log p\, d\mu$ denotes Shannon's entropy. Thus, the JSD can also be interpreted as the *entropy of the average distribution minus the average of the entropies*.

The square root of the JSD is a metric [9] satisfying the triangle inequality, but the square root of the JD is not a metric (nor any positive power of the Jeffreys divergence, see [10]). In fact, the JSD can be interpreted as a Hilbert metric distance, meaning that there exists some isometric embedding of $(\mathcal{X}, \sqrt{\mathrm{JS}})$ into a Hilbert space [11,12]. Other principled symmetrizations of the KLD have been proposed in the literature: For example, Naghshvar et al. [13] proposed the *extrinsic Jensen–Shannon divergence* and demonstrated its use for variable-length coding over a discrete memoryless channel (DMC).

Another symmetrization of the KLD sometimes met in the literature [14–16] is the *Jeffreys divergence* [17,18] (JD) defined by

$$J(p,q) := \mathrm{KL}(p:q) + \mathrm{KL}(q:p) = \int (p-q)\log\frac{p}{q}d\mu = J(q,p). \tag{5}$$

However, we point out that this Jeffreys divergence lacks sound information-theoretical justifications.

For two positive but not necessarily normalized densities $\tilde{p}$ and $\tilde{q}$, we define the *extended Kullback–Leibler divergence* as follows:

$$\mathrm{KL}^+(\tilde{p}:\tilde{q}) := \mathrm{KL}(\tilde{p}:\tilde{q}) + \int \tilde{q}d\mu - \int \tilde{p}d\mu, \tag{6}$$

$$= \int \left(\tilde{p}\log\frac{\tilde{p}}{\tilde{q}} + \tilde{q} - \tilde{p}\right)d\mu. \tag{7}$$

The Jensen–Shannon divergence and the Jeffreys divergence can both be extended to positive (unnormalized) densities without changing their formula expressions:

$$\mathrm{JS}^+(\tilde{p},\tilde{q}) := \frac{1}{2}\left(\mathrm{KL}^+\left(\tilde{p}:\frac{\tilde{p}+\tilde{q}}{2}\right)+\mathrm{KL}^+\left(\tilde{q}:\frac{\tilde{p}+\tilde{q}}{2}\right)\right), \tag{8}$$

$$= \frac{1}{2}\left(\mathrm{KL}\left(\tilde{p}:\frac{\tilde{p}+\tilde{q}}{2}\right)+\mathrm{KL}\left(\tilde{q}:\frac{\tilde{p}+\tilde{q}}{2}\right)\right) = \mathrm{JS}(\tilde{p},\tilde{q}), \tag{9}$$

$$J^+(\tilde{p},\tilde{q}) := \mathrm{KL}^+(\tilde{p}:\tilde{q}) + \mathrm{KL}^+(\tilde{p}:\tilde{q}) = \int (\tilde{p}-\tilde{q})\log\frac{\tilde{p}}{\tilde{q}}d\mu = J(\tilde{p},\tilde{q}). \tag{10}$$

However, the extended JS^+ divergence is upper-bounded by $(\frac{1}{2}\log 2)(\int(\tilde{p}+\tilde{q})d\mu) = \frac{1}{2}(\mu(p)+\mu(q))\log 2$ instead of $\log 2$ for normalized densities (i.e., when $\mu(p)+\mu(q) = 2$).

Let $(pq)_\alpha(x) := (1-\alpha)p(x) + \alpha q(x)$ denote the statistical weighted mixture with component densities p and q for $\alpha \in [0,1]$. The asymmetric α-skew Jensen–Shannon divergence can be defined for a scalar parameter $\alpha \in (0,1)$ by considering the weighted mixture $(pq)_\alpha$ as follows:

$$JS_a^\alpha(p:q) := (1-\alpha)\mathrm{KL}(p:(pq)_\alpha) + \alpha\mathrm{KL}(q:(pq)_\alpha), \tag{11}$$

$$= (1-\alpha)\int p\log\frac{p}{(pq)_\alpha}d\mu + \alpha\int q\log\frac{q}{(pq)_\alpha}d\mu. \tag{12}$$

Let us introduce the *α-skew K-divergence* [6,19] $K_\alpha(p:q)$ by:

$$K_\alpha(p:q) := \mathrm{KL}(p:(1-\alpha)p + \alpha q) = \mathrm{KL}(p:(pq)_\alpha). \tag{13}$$

Then, both the Jensen–Shannon divergence and the Jeffreys divergence can be rewritten [20] using K_α as follows:

$$JS(p,q) = \frac{1}{2}\left(K_{\frac{1}{2}}(p:q) + K_{\frac{1}{2}}(q:p)\right), \tag{14}$$

$$J(p,q) = K_1(p:q) + K_1(q:p), \tag{15}$$

since $(pq)_1 = q$, $\mathrm{KL}(p:q) = K_1(p:q)$ and $(pq)_{\frac{1}{2}} = (qp)_{\frac{1}{2}}$.

We can thus define the *symmetric α-skew Jensen–Shannon divergence* [20] for $\alpha \in (0,1)$ as follows:

$$JS^\alpha(p,q) := \frac{1}{2}K_\alpha(p:q) + \frac{1}{2}K_\alpha(q:p) = JS^\alpha(q,p). \tag{16}$$

The ordinary Jensen–Shannon divergence is recovered for $\alpha = \frac{1}{2}$.

In general, skewing divergences (e.g., using the divergence K_α instead of the KLD) have been experimentally shown to perform better in applications like in some natural language processing (NLP) tasks [21].

The α-Jensen–Shannon divergences are Csiszár f-divergences [22–24]. An f-divergence is defined for a convex function f, strictly convex at 1, and satisfies $f(1) = 0$ as:

$$I_f(p:q) = \int q(x)f\left(\frac{p(x)}{q(x)}\right)dx \geq f(1) = 0. \tag{17}$$

We can always symmetrize f-divergences by taking the *conjugate* convex function $f^*(x) = xf(\frac{1}{x})$ (related to the perspective function): $I_{f+f^*}(p,q)$ is a symmetric divergence. The f-divergences are convex statistical distances which are provably the only separable invariant divergences in information geometry [25], except for binary alphabets $\mathcal{X}$ (see [26]).

The Jeffreys divergence is an f-divergence for the generator $f(x) = (x-1)\log x$, and the α-Jensen–Shannon divergences are f-divergences for the generator family $f_\alpha(x) = -\log((1-\alpha) + \alpha x) - x\log((1-\alpha) + \frac{\alpha}{x})$. The f-divergences are upper-bounded by $f(0) + f^*(0)$. Thus, the f-divergences are finite when $f(0) + f^*(0) < \infty$.

The main contributions of this paper are summarized as follows:

- First, we generalize the Jensen–Bregman divergence by skewing a weighted separable Jensen–Bregman divergence with a k-dimensional *vector* $\alpha \in [0,1]^k$ in Section 2. This yields a generalization of the symmetric skew α-Jensen–Shannon divergences to a vector-skew parameter. This extension retains the key properties for being upper-bounded and for application to densities with potentially different supports. The proposed generalization also allows one to grasp a better understanding of the "mechanism" of the Jensen–Shannon divergence itself. We also show how to

directly obtain the weighted vector-skew Jensen–Shannon divergence from the decomposition of the KLD as the difference of the cross-entropy minus the entropy (i.e., KLD as the relative entropy).
- Second, we prove that weighted vector-skew Jensen–Shannon divergences are f-divergences (Theorem 1), and show how to build families of symmetric Jensen–Shannon-type divergences which can be controlled by a vector of parameters in Section 2.3, generalizing the work of [20] from scalar skewing to vector skewing. This may prove useful in applications by providing additional tuning parameters (which can be set, for example, by using cross-validation techniques).
- Third, we consider the calculation of the *Jensen–Shannon centroids* in Section 3 for densities belonging to mixture families. Mixture families include the family of categorical distributions and the family of statistical mixtures sharing the same prescribed components. Mixture families are well-studied manifolds in information geometry [25]. We show how to compute the Jensen–Shannon centroid using a concave–convex numerical iterative optimization procedure [27]. The experimental results graphically compare the Jeffreys centroid with the Jensen–Shannon centroid for grey-valued image histograms.

2. Extending the Jensen–Shannon Divergence

2.1. Vector-Skew Jensen–Bregman Divergences and Jensen Diversities

Recall our notational shortcut: $(ab)_\alpha := (1-\alpha)a + \alpha b$. For a k-dimensional vector $\alpha \in [0,1]^k$, a weight vector w belonging to the $(k-1)$-dimensional open simplex Δ_k, and a scalar $\gamma \in (0,1)$, let us define the following vector *skew α-Jensen–Bregman divergence* (α-JBD) following [28]:

$$JB_F^{\alpha,\gamma,w}(\theta_1:\theta_2) := \sum_{i=1}^k w_i B_F\left((\theta_1\theta_2)_{\alpha_i} : (\theta_1\theta_2)_\gamma\right) \geq 0, \tag{18}$$

where B_F is the *Bregman divergence* [29] induced by a strictly convex and smooth generator F:

$$B_F(\theta_1:\theta_2) := F(\theta_1) - F(\theta_2) - \langle \theta_1 - \theta_2, \nabla F(\theta_2) \rangle, \tag{19}$$

with $\langle \cdot,\cdot \rangle$ denoting the Euclidean inner product $\langle x,y \rangle = x^\top y$ (dot product). Expanding the Bregman divergence formulas in the expression of the α-JBD and using the fact that

$$(\theta_1\theta_2)_{\alpha_i} - (\theta_1\theta_2)_\gamma = (\gamma - \alpha_i)(\theta_1 - \theta_2), \tag{20}$$

we get the following expression:

$$JB_F^{\alpha,\gamma,w}(\theta_1:\theta_2) = \left(\sum_{i=1}^k w_i F\left((\theta_1\theta_2)_{\alpha_i}\right)\right) - F((\theta_1\theta_2)_\gamma) - \left\langle \sum_{i=1}^k w_i(\gamma - \alpha_i)(\theta_1 - \theta_2), \nabla F((\theta_1\theta_2)_\gamma) \right\rangle. \tag{21}$$

The inner product term of Equation (21) vanishes when

$$\gamma = \sum_{i=1}^k w_i \alpha_i := \bar{\alpha}. \tag{22}$$

Thus, when $\gamma = \bar{\alpha}$ (assuming at least two distinct components in α so that $\gamma \in (0,1)$), we get the simplified formula for the vector-skew α-JBD:

$$\boxed{JB_F^{\alpha,w}(\theta_1:\theta_2) = \left(\sum_{i=1}^k w_i F\left((\theta_1\theta_2)_{\alpha_i}\right)\right) - F((\theta_1\theta_2)_{\bar{\alpha}}).} \tag{23}$$

This vector-skew Jensen–Bregman divergence is always finite and amounts to a *Jensen diversity* [30] J_F induced by Jensen's inequality gap:

$$\mathrm{JB}_F^{\alpha,w}(\theta_1:\theta_2) = J_F((\theta_1\theta_2)_{\alpha_1},\ldots,(\theta_1\theta_2)_{\alpha_k};w_1,\ldots,w_k) := \sum_{i=1}^k w_i F((\theta_1\theta_2)_{\alpha_i}) - F((\theta_1\theta_2)_{\bar{\alpha}}) \geq 0. \quad (24)$$

The Jensen diversity is a quantity which arises as a generalization of the cluster variance when clustering with Bregman divergences instead of the ordinary squared Euclidean distance; see [29,30] for details. In the context of Bregman clustering, the Jensen diversity has been called the *Bregman information* [29] and motivated by rate distortion theory: Bregman information measures the minimum expected loss when encoding a set of points using a single point when the loss is measured using a Bregman divergence. In general, a k-point measure is called a diversity measure (for $k > 2$), while a distance/divergence is the special case of a 2-point measure.

Conversely, in 1D, we may start from Jensen's inequality for a strictly convex function F:

$$\sum_{i=1}^k w_i F(\theta_i) \geq F\left(\sum_{i=1}^k w_i \theta_i\right). \quad (25)$$

Let us notationally write $[k] := \{1,\ldots,k\}$, and define $\theta_m := \min_{i\in[k]}\{\theta_i\}_i$ and $\theta_M := \max_{i\in[k]}\{\theta_i\}_i > \theta_m$ (i.e., assuming at least two distinct values). We have the barycenter $\bar{\theta} = \sum_i w_i \theta_i =: (\theta_m\theta_M)_\gamma$ which can be interpreted as the linear interpolation of the extremal values for some $\gamma \in (0,1)$. Let us write $\theta_i = (\theta_m\theta_M)_{\alpha_i}$ for $i \in [k]$ and proper values of the α_is. Then, it comes that

$$\bar{\theta} = \sum_i w_i \theta_i, \quad (26)$$

$$= \sum_i w_i (\theta_m\theta_M)_{\alpha_i}, \quad (27)$$

$$= \sum_i w_i((1-\alpha_i)\theta_m + \alpha_i\theta_M), \quad (28)$$

$$= \left(1 - \sum_i w_i\alpha_i\right)\theta_m + \sum_i \alpha_i w_i \theta_M, \quad (29)$$

$$= (\theta_m\theta_M)_{\sum_i w_i\alpha_i} = (\theta_m\theta_M)_\gamma, \quad (30)$$

so that $\gamma = \sum_i w_i \alpha_i = \bar{\alpha}$.

2.2. Vector-Skew Jensen–Shannon Divergences

Let $f(x) = x\log x - x$ be a strictly smooth convex function on $(0,\infty)$. Then, the Bregman divergence induced by this univariate generator is

$$B_f(p:q) = p\log\frac{p}{q} + q - p = \mathrm{kl}_+(p:q), \quad (31)$$

the *extended scalar Kullback–Leibler divergence*.

We extend the scalar-skew Jensen–Shannon divergence as follows: $\mathrm{JS}^{\alpha,w}(p:q) := \mathrm{JB}_{-h}^{\alpha,\bar{\alpha},w}(p:q)$ for h, the Shannon's entropy [4] (a strictly concave function [4]).

Definition 1 (Weighted vector-skew (α,w)-Jensen–Shannon divergence). *For a vector $\alpha \in [0,1]^k$ and a unit positive weight vector $w \in \Delta_k$, the (α,w)-Jensen–Shannon divergence between two densities $p,q \in \bar{\mathcal{P}}_1$ is defined by:*

$$\boxed{\mathrm{JS}^{\alpha,w}(p:q) := \sum_{i=1}^k w_i \mathrm{KL}((pq)_{\alpha_i}:(pq)_{\bar{\alpha}}) = h((pq)_{\bar{\alpha}}) - \sum_{i=1}^k w_i h((pq)_{\alpha_i}),}$$

with $\bar{\alpha} = \sum_{i=1}^{k} w_i \alpha_i$, where $h(p) = -\int p(x) \log p(x) d\mu(x)$ denotes the Shannon entropy [4] (i.e., $-h$ is strictly convex).

This definition generalizes the ordinary JSD; we recover the ordinary Jensen–Shannon divergence when $k = 2$, $\alpha_1 = 0$, $\alpha_2 = 1$, and $w_1 = w_2 = \frac{1}{2}$ with $\bar{\alpha} = \frac{1}{2}$: $\mathrm{JS}(p,q) = \mathrm{JS}^{(0,1),(\frac{1}{2},\frac{1}{2})}(p:q)$.

Let $\mathrm{KL}_{\alpha,\beta}(p:q) := \mathrm{KL}((pq)_\alpha : (pq)_\beta)$. Then, we have $\mathrm{KL}_{\alpha,\beta}(q:p) = \mathrm{KL}_{1-\alpha,1-\beta}(p:q)$. Using this (α,β)-KLD, we have the following identity:

$$\mathrm{JS}^{\alpha,w}(p:q) = \sum_{i=1}^{k} w_i \mathrm{KL}_{\alpha_i,\bar{\alpha}}(p:q), \tag{32}$$

$$= \sum_{i=1}^{k} w_i \mathrm{KL}_{1-\alpha_i,1-\bar{\alpha}}(q:p) = \mathrm{JS}^{1_k-\alpha,w}(q:p), \tag{33}$$

since $\sum_{i=1}^{k} w_i(1-\alpha_i) = \overline{1_k - \alpha} = 1 - \bar{\alpha}$, where $1_k = (1,\ldots,1)$ is a k-dimensional vector of ones.

A very interesting property is that the vector-skew Jensen–Shannon divergences are f-divergences [22].

Theorem 1. *The vector-skew Jensen–Shannon divergences $\mathrm{JS}^{\alpha,w}(p:q)$ are f-divergences for the generator $f_{\alpha,w}(u) = \sum_{i=1}^{k} w_i(\alpha_i u + (1-\alpha_i)) \log \frac{(1-\alpha_i)+\alpha_i u}{(1-\bar{\alpha})+\bar{\alpha} u}$ with $\bar{\alpha} = \sum_{i=1}^{k} w_i \alpha_i$.*

Proof. First, let us observe that the positively weighted sum of f-divergences is an f-divergence: $\sum_{i=1}^{k} w_i I_{f_i}(p:q) = I_f(p:q)$ for the generator $f(u) = \sum_{i=1}^{k} w_i f_i(u)$.

Now, let us express the divergence $\mathrm{KL}_{\alpha,\beta}(p:q)$ as an f-divergence:

$$\mathrm{KL}_{\alpha,\beta}(p:q) = I_{f_{\alpha,\beta}}(p:q), \tag{34}$$

with generator

$$f_{\alpha,\beta}(u) = (\alpha u + 1 - \alpha) \log \frac{(1-\alpha)+\alpha u}{(1-\beta)+\beta u}. \tag{35}$$

Thus, it follows that

$$\mathrm{JS}^{\alpha,w}(p:q) = \sum_{i=1}^{k} w_i \mathrm{KL}((pq)_{\alpha_i} : (pq)_{\bar{\alpha}}), \tag{36}$$

$$= \sum_{i=1}^{k} w_i I_{f_{\alpha_i,\bar{\alpha}}}(p:q), \tag{37}$$

$$= I_{\sum_{i=1}^{k} w_i f_{\alpha_i,\bar{\alpha}}}(p:q). \tag{38}$$

Therefore, the vector-skew Jensen–Shannon divergence is an f-divergence for the following generator:

$$\boxed{f_{\alpha,w}(u) = \sum_{i=1}^{k} w_i(\alpha_i u + (1-\alpha_i)) \log \frac{(1-\alpha_i)+\alpha_i u}{(1-\bar{\alpha})+\bar{\alpha} u},} \tag{39}$$

where $\bar{\alpha} = \sum_{i=1}^{k} w_i \alpha_i$.

When $\alpha = (0,1)$ and $w = (\frac{1}{2},\frac{1}{2})$, we recover the f-divergence generator for the JSD:

$$f_{\mathrm{JS}}(u) = \frac{1}{2} \log \frac{1}{\frac{1}{2}+\frac{1}{2}u} + \frac{1}{2} u \log \frac{u}{\frac{1}{2}+\frac{1}{2}u}, \tag{40}$$

$$= \frac{1}{2}\left(\log \frac{2}{1+u} + u \log \frac{2u}{1+u}\right). \tag{41}$$

Observe that $f^*_{\alpha,w}(u) = u f_{\alpha,w}(1/u) = f_{1-\alpha,w}(u)$, where $1 - \alpha := (1 - \alpha_1, \ldots, 1 - \alpha_k)$.

We also refer the reader to Theorem 4.1 of [31], which defines skew f-divergences from any f-divergence. □

Remark 1. *Since the vector-skew Jensen divergence is an f-divergence, we easily obtain Fano and Pinsker inequalities following [32], or reverse Pinsker inequalities following [33,34] (i.e., upper bounds for the vector-skew Jensen divergences using the total variation metric distance), data processing inequalities using [35], etc.*

Next, we show that $\mathrm{KL}_{\alpha,\beta}$ (and $\mathrm{JS}^{\alpha,w}$) are separable convex divergences. Since the f-divergences are separable convex, the $\mathrm{KL}_{\alpha,\beta}$ divergences and the $\mathrm{JS}^{\alpha,w}$ divergences are separable convex. For the sake of completeness, we report a simplex explicit proof below.

Theorem 2 (Separable convexity). *The divergence $\mathrm{KL}_{\alpha,\beta}(p:q)$ is strictly separable convex for $\alpha \neq \beta$ and $x \in \mathcal{X}_p \cap \mathcal{X}_q$.*

Proof. Let us calculate the second partial derivative of $\mathrm{KL}_{\alpha,\beta}(x:y)$ with respect to x, and show that it is strictly positive:

$$\frac{\partial^2}{\partial x^2} \mathrm{KL}_{\alpha,\beta}(x:y) = \frac{(\beta - \alpha)^2 y^2}{(xy)_\alpha (xy)_\beta^2} > 0, \tag{42}$$

for $x, y > 0$. Thus, $\mathrm{KL}_{\alpha,\beta}$ is strictly convex on the left argument. Similarly, since $\mathrm{KL}_{\alpha,\beta}(y:x) = \mathrm{KL}_{1-\alpha, 1-\beta}(x:y)$, we deduce that $\mathrm{KL}_{\alpha,\beta}$ is strictly convex on the right argument. Therefore, the divergence $\mathrm{KL}_{\alpha,\beta}$ is separable convex. □

It follows that the divergence $\mathrm{JS}^{\alpha,w}(p:q)$ is strictly separable convex, since it is a convex combination of weighted $\mathrm{KL}_{\alpha_i,\bar\alpha}$ divergences.

Another way to derive the vector-skew JSD is to decompose the KLD as the difference of the cross-entropy $h^\times$ minus the entropy h (i.e., KLD is also called the relative entropy):

$$\mathrm{KL}(p:q) = h^\times(p:q) - h(p), \tag{43}$$

where $h^\times(p:q) := -\int p \log q \, d\mu$ and $h(p) := h^\times(p:p)$ (self cross-entropy). Since $\alpha_1 h^\times(p_1:q) + \alpha_2 h^\times(p_2:q) = h^\times(\alpha_1 p_1 + \alpha_2 p_2 : q)$ (for $\alpha_2 = 1 - \alpha_1$), it follows that

$$\mathrm{JS}^{\alpha,w}(p:q) := \sum_{i=1}^k w_i \mathrm{KL}((pq)_{\alpha_i} : (pq)_\gamma), \tag{44}$$

$$= \sum_{i=1}^k w_i \left(h^\times((pq)_{\alpha_i} : (pq)_\gamma) - h((pq)_{\alpha_i}) \right), \tag{45}$$

$$= h^\times \left(\sum_{i=1}^k w_i (pq)_{\alpha_i} : (pq)_\gamma \right) - \sum_{i=1}^k w_i h((pq)_{\alpha_i}). \tag{46}$$

Here, the "trick" is to choose $\gamma = \bar\alpha$ in order to "convert" the cross-entropy into an entropy: $h^\times(\sum_{i=1}^k w_i (pq)_{\alpha_i} : (pq)_\gamma) = h((pq)_{\bar\alpha})$ when $\gamma = \bar\alpha$. Then, we end up with

$$\boxed{\mathrm{JS}^{\alpha,w}(p:q) = h((pq)_{\bar\alpha}) - \sum_{i=1}^k w_i h((pq)_{\alpha_i}).} \tag{47}$$

When $\alpha = (\alpha_1, \alpha_2)$ with $\alpha_1 = 0$ and $\alpha_2 = 0$ and $w = (w_1, w_2) = (\frac{1}{2}, \frac{1}{2})$, we have $\bar{\alpha} = \frac{1}{2}$, and we recover the Jensen–Shannon divergence:

$$\mathrm{JS}(p:q) = h\left(\frac{p+q}{2}\right) - \frac{h(p)+h(q)}{2}. \tag{48}$$

Notice that Equation (13) is the usual definition of the Jensen–Shannon divergence, while Equation (48) is the reduced formula of the JSD, which can be interpreted as a Jensen gap for Shannon entropy, hence its name: The *Jensen–Shannon divergence*.

Moreover, if we consider the cross-entropy/entropy extended to positive densities $\tilde{p}$ and $\tilde{q}$:

$$h_+^\times(\tilde{p}:\tilde{q}) = -\int (\tilde{p}\log\tilde{q} + \tilde{q})d\mu, \quad h_+(\tilde{p}) = h_+^\times(\tilde{p}:\tilde{p}) = -\int (\tilde{p}\log\tilde{p} + \tilde{p})d\mu, \tag{49}$$

we get:

$$\mathrm{JS}_+^{\alpha,w}(\tilde{p}:\tilde{q}) = \sum_{i=1}^k w_i \mathrm{KL}_+((\tilde{p}\tilde{q})_{\alpha_i} : (\tilde{p}\tilde{q})_\gamma) = h_+((\tilde{p}\tilde{q})_{\bar{\alpha}}) - \sum_{i=1}^k w_i h_+((\tilde{p}\tilde{q})_{\alpha_i}). \tag{50}$$

Next, we shall prove that our generalization of the skew Jensen–Shannon divergence to vector-skewing is always bounded. We first start by a lemma bounding the KLD between two mixtures sharing the same components:

Lemma 1 (KLD between two w-mixtures). *For $\alpha \in [0,1]$ and $\beta \in (0,1)$, we have:*

$$\mathrm{KL}_{\alpha,\beta}(p:q) = \mathrm{KL}\left((pq)_\alpha : (pq)_\beta\right) \leq \log\max\left\{\frac{1-\alpha}{1-\beta}, \frac{\alpha}{\beta}\right\}.$$

Proof. For $p(x), q(x) > 0$, we have

$$\frac{(1-\alpha)p(x) + \alpha q(x)}{(1-\beta)p(x) + \beta q(x)} \leq \max\left\{\frac{1-\alpha}{1-\beta}, \frac{\alpha}{\beta}\right\}. \tag{51}$$

Indeed, by considering the two cases $\alpha \geq \beta$ (or equivalently, $1-\alpha \leq 1-\beta$) and $\alpha \leq \beta$ (or equivalently, $1-\alpha \geq 1-\beta$), we check that $(1-\alpha)p(x) \leq \max\left\{\frac{1-\alpha}{1-\beta}, \frac{\alpha}{\beta}\right\}(1-\beta)p(x)$ and $\alpha q(x) \leq \max\left\{\frac{1-\alpha}{1-\beta}, \frac{\alpha}{\beta}\right\}\beta q(x)$. Thus, we have $\frac{(1-\alpha)p(x)+\alpha q(x)}{(1-\beta)p(x)+\beta q(x)} \leq \max\left\{\frac{1-\alpha}{1-\beta}, \frac{\alpha}{\beta}\right\}$. Therefore, it follows that:

$$\mathrm{KL}\left((pq)_\alpha : (pq)_\beta\right) \leq \int (pq)_\alpha \log\max\left\{\frac{1-\alpha}{1-\beta}, \frac{\alpha}{\beta}\right\} d\mu = \log\max\left\{\frac{1-\alpha}{1-\beta}, \frac{\alpha}{\beta}\right\}. \tag{52}$$

Notice that we can interpret $\log\max\left\{\frac{1-\alpha}{1-\beta}, \frac{\alpha}{\beta}\right\} = \max\{\log\frac{1-\alpha}{1-\beta}, \log\frac{\alpha}{\beta}\}$ as the ∞-Rényi divergence [36,37] between the following two two-point distributions: $(\alpha, 1-\alpha)$ and $(\beta, 1-\beta)$. See Theorem 6 of [36].

A weaker upper bound is $\mathrm{KL}((pq)_\alpha : (pq)_\beta) \leq \log\frac{1}{\beta(1-\beta)}$. Indeed, let us form a partition of the sample space $\mathcal{X}$ into two dominance regions:

- $R_p := \{x \in \mathcal{X} : q(x) \leq p(x)\}$ and
- $R_q := \{x \in \mathcal{X} : q(x) > p(x)\}$.

We have $(pq)_\alpha(x) = (1-\alpha)p(x) + \alpha q(x) \leq p(x)$ for $x \in R_p$ and $(pq)_\alpha(x) \leq q(x)$ for $x \in R_q$. It follows that

$$\mathrm{KL}\left((pq)_\alpha : (pq)_\beta\right) \leq \int_{R_p} (pq)_\alpha(x) \log\frac{p(x)}{(1-\beta)p(x)} d\mu(x) + \int_{R_q} (pq)_\alpha(x) \log\frac{q(x)}{\beta q(x)} d\mu(x).$$

That is, $\mathrm{KL}((pq)_\alpha : (pq)_\beta) \leq -\log(1-\beta) - \log \beta = \log \frac{1}{\beta(1-\beta)}$. Notice that we allow $\alpha \in \{0,1\}$ but not β to take the extreme values (i.e., $\beta \in (0,1)$). □

In fact, it is known that for both $\alpha, \beta \in (0,1)$, $\mathrm{KL}\left((pq)_\alpha : (pq)_\beta\right)$ amount to compute a Bregman divergence for the Shannon negentropy generator, since $\{(pq)_\gamma : \gamma \in (0,1)\}$ defines a *mixture family* [38] of order 1 in information geometry. Hence, it is always finite, as Bregman divergences are always finite (but not necessarily bounded).

By using the fact that

$$\mathrm{JS}^{\alpha,w}(p:q) = \sum_{i=1}^{k} w_i \mathrm{KL}\left((pq)_{\alpha_i} : (pq)_{\bar{\alpha}}\right), \tag{53}$$

we conclude that the vector-skew Jensen–Shannon divergence is upper-bounded:

Lemma 2 (Bounded (w,α)-Jensen–Shannon divergence). $\mathrm{JS}^{\alpha,w}$ *is bounded by* $\log \frac{1}{\bar{\alpha}(1-\bar{\alpha})}$ *where* $\bar{\alpha} = \sum_{i=1}^{k} w_i \alpha_i \in (0,1)$.

Proof. We have $\mathrm{JS}^{\alpha,w}(p:q) = \sum_i w_i \mathrm{KL}\left((pq)_{\alpha_i} : (pq)_{\bar{\alpha}}\right)$. Since $0 \leq \mathrm{KL}\left((pq)_{\alpha_i} : (pq)_{\bar{\alpha}}\right) \leq \log \frac{1}{\bar{\alpha}(1-\bar{\alpha})}$, it follows that we have

$$0 \leq \mathrm{JS}^{\alpha,w}(p:q) \leq \log \frac{1}{\bar{\alpha}(1-\bar{\alpha})}.$$

Notice that we also have

$$\mathrm{JS}^{\alpha,w}(p:q) \leq \sum_i w_i \log \max\left\{\frac{1-\alpha_i}{1-\bar{\alpha}}, \frac{\alpha_i}{\bar{\alpha}}\right\}.$$

□

The vector-skew Jensen–Shannon divergence is symmetric if and only if for each index $i \in [k]$ there exists a matching index $\sigma(i)$ such that $\alpha_{\sigma(i)} = 1 - \alpha_i$ and $w_{\sigma(i)} = w_i$.

For example, we may define the *symmetric scalar α-skew Jensen–Shannon divergence* as

$$\mathrm{JS}^{\alpha}_s(p,q) = \frac{1}{2}\mathrm{KL}((pq)_\alpha : (pq)_{\frac{1}{2}}) + \frac{1}{2}\mathrm{KL}((pq)_{1-\alpha} : (pq)_{\frac{1}{2}}), \tag{54}$$

$$= \frac{1}{2}\int (pq)_\alpha \log \frac{(pq)_\alpha}{(pq)_{\frac{1}{2}}} d\mu + \frac{1}{2}\int (pq)_{1-\alpha} \log \frac{(pq)_{1-\alpha}}{(pq)_{\frac{1}{2}}} d\mu, \tag{55}$$

$$= \frac{1}{2}\int (qp)_{1-\alpha} \log \frac{(qp)_{1-\alpha}}{(qp)_{\frac{1}{2}}} d\mu + + \frac{1}{2}\int (qp)_\alpha \log \frac{(qp)_\alpha}{(qp)_{\frac{1}{2}}} d\mu, \tag{56}$$

$$= h((pq)_{\frac{1}{2}}) - \frac{h((pq)_\alpha) + h((pq)_{1-\alpha})}{2}, \tag{57}$$

$$=: \mathrm{JS}^{\alpha}_s(q,p), \tag{58}$$

since it holds that $(ab)_c = (ba)_{1-c}$ for any $a,b,c \in \mathbb{R}$. Note that $\mathrm{JS}^{\alpha}_s(p,q) \neq \mathrm{JS}^{\alpha}(p,q)$.

Remark 2. *We can always symmetrize a vector-skew Jensen–Shannon divergence by doubling the dimension of the skewing vector. Let $\alpha = (\alpha_1, \ldots, \alpha_k)$ and w be the vector parameters of an asymmetric vector-skew JSD, and consider $\alpha' = (1-\alpha_1, \ldots, 1-\alpha_k)$ and w to be the parameters of $\mathrm{JS}^{\alpha',w}$. Then, $\mathrm{JS}^{(\alpha,\alpha'),(\frac{w}{2},\frac{w}{2})}$ is a symmetric skew-vector JSD:*

$$\mathrm{JS}^{(\alpha,\alpha'),(\frac{w}{2},\frac{w}{2})}(p:q) := \frac{1}{2}\mathrm{JS}^{\alpha,w}(p:q) + \frac{1}{2}\mathrm{JS}^{\alpha',w}(p:q), \tag{59}$$

$$= \frac{1}{2}\mathrm{JS}^{\alpha,w}(p:q) + \frac{1}{2}\mathrm{JS}^{\alpha,w}(q:p) = \mathrm{JS}^{(\alpha,\alpha'),(\frac{w}{2},\frac{w}{2})}(q:p). \tag{60}$$

Since the vector-skew Jensen–Shannon divergence is an f-divergence for the generator $f_{\alpha,w}$ (Theorem 1), we can take generator $f^S_{w,\alpha}(u) = \frac{f_{w,\alpha}(u) + f^*_{w,\alpha}(u)}{2}$ to define the symmetrized f-divergence, where $f^*_{w,\alpha}(u) = u f_{w,\alpha}(\frac{1}{u})$ denotes the convex conjugate function. When $f_{\alpha,w}$ yields a symmetric f-divergence $I_{f_{\alpha,w}}$, we can apply the generic upper bound of f-divergences (i.e., $I_f \leq f(0) + f^*(0)$) to get the upper bound on the symmetric vector-skew Jensen–Shannon divergences:

$$I_{f_{\alpha,w}}(p:q) \leq f_{\alpha,w}(0) + f^*_{\alpha,w}(0), \tag{61}$$

$$\leq \sum_{i=1}^{k} w_i \left((1-\alpha_i) \log \frac{1-\alpha_i}{1-\bar{\alpha}} + \alpha_i \log \frac{\alpha_i}{\bar{\alpha}} \right), \tag{62}$$

since

$$f^*_{\alpha,w}(u) = u f_{\alpha,w}\left(\frac{1}{u}\right), \tag{63}$$

$$= \sum_{i=1}^{k} w_i ((1-\alpha_i)u + \alpha_i) \log \frac{(1-\alpha_i)u + \alpha_i}{(1-\bar{\alpha})u + \bar{\alpha}}. \tag{64}$$

For example, consider the ordinary Jensen–Shannon divergence with $w = \left(\frac{1}{2}, \frac{1}{2}\right)$ and $\alpha = (0,1)$. Then, we find $\mathrm{JS}(p:w) = I_{f_{(0,1),(\frac{1}{2},\frac{1}{2})}}(p:q) \leq \frac{1}{2}\log 2 + \frac{1}{2}\log 2 = \log 2$, the usual upper bound of the JSD.

As a side note, let us notice that our notation $(pq)_\alpha$ allows one to compactly write the following property:

Property 1. *We have $q = (qq)_\lambda$ for any $\lambda \in [0,1]$, and $((p_1 p_2)_\lambda (q_1 q_2)_\lambda)_\alpha = ((p_1 q_1)_\alpha (p_2 q_2)_\alpha)_\lambda$ for any $\alpha, \lambda \in [0,1]$.*

Proof. Clearly, $q = (1-\lambda)q + \lambda q =: ((qq)_\lambda)$ for any $\lambda \in [0,1]$. Now, we have

$$((p_1 p_2)_\lambda (q_1 q_2)_\lambda)_\alpha = (1-\alpha)(p_1 p_2)_\lambda + \alpha (q_1 q_2)_\lambda, \tag{65}$$

$$= (1-\alpha)((1-\lambda)p_1 + \lambda p_2) + \alpha((1-\lambda)q_1 + \lambda q_2), \tag{66}$$

$$= (1-\lambda)((1-\alpha)p_1 + \alpha q_1) + \lambda((1-\alpha)p_2 + \alpha q_2), \tag{67}$$

$$= (1-\lambda)(p_1 q_1)_\alpha + \lambda (p_2 q_2)_\alpha, \tag{68}$$

$$= ((p_1 q_1)_\alpha (p_2 q_2)_\alpha)_\lambda. \tag{69}$$

□

2.3. Building Symmetric Families of Vector-Skewed Jensen–Shannon Divergences

We can build infinitely many vector-skew Jensen–Shannon divergences. For example, consider $\alpha = \left(0, 1, \frac{1}{3}\right)$ and $w = \left(\frac{1}{3}, \frac{1}{3}, \frac{1}{3}\right)$. Then, $\bar{\alpha} = \frac{1}{3} + \frac{1}{9} = \frac{4}{9}$, and

$$\mathrm{JS}^{\alpha,w}(p:q) = h\left((pq)_{\frac{4}{9}}\right) - \frac{h(p) + h(q) + h\left((pq)_{\frac{1}{3}}\right)}{3} \neq \mathrm{JS}^{\alpha,w}(q:p). \tag{70}$$

Interestingly, we can also build infinitely many families of *symmetric* vector-skew Jensen–Shannon divergences. For example, consider these two examples that illustrate the construction process:

- Consider $k = 2$. Let $(w, 1-w)$ denote the weight vector, and $\alpha = (\alpha_1, \alpha_2)$ the skewing vector. We have $\bar{\alpha} = w\alpha_1 + (1-w)\alpha_2 = \alpha_2 + w(\alpha_1 - \alpha_2)$. The vector-skew JSD is symmetric iff. $w =$

$1 - w = \frac{1}{2}$ (with $\bar{\alpha} = \frac{\alpha_1 + \alpha_2}{2}$) and $\alpha_2 = 1 - \alpha_1$. In that case, we have $\bar{\alpha} = \frac{1}{2}$, and we obtain the following family of symmetric Jensen–Shannon divergences:

$$JS^{(\alpha, 1-\alpha),(\frac{1}{2},\frac{1}{2})}(p,q) = h\left((pq)_{\frac{1}{2}}\right) - \frac{h((pq)_\alpha) + h((pq)_{1-\alpha})}{2}, \tag{71}$$

$$= h\left((pq)_{\frac{1}{2}}\right) - \frac{h((pq)_\alpha) + h((qp)_\alpha)}{2} = JS^{(\alpha, 1-\alpha),(\frac{1}{2},\frac{1}{2})}(q,p). \tag{72}$$

- Consider $k = 4$, weight vector $w = \left(\frac{1}{3}, \frac{1}{3}, \frac{1}{6}, \frac{1}{6}\right)$, and skewing vector $\alpha = (\alpha_1, 1 - \alpha_1, \alpha_2, 1 - \alpha_2)$ for $\alpha_1, \alpha_2 \in (0,1)$. Then, $\bar{\alpha} = \frac{1}{2}$, and we get the following family of symmetric vector-skew JSDs:

$$JS^{(\alpha_1, \alpha_2)}(p,q) = h\left((pq)_{\frac{1}{2}}\right) - \frac{2h((pq)_{\alpha_1}) + 2h((pq)_{1-\alpha_1}) + h((pq)_{\alpha_2}) + h((pq)_{1-\alpha_2})}{6}, \tag{73}$$

$$= h\left((pq)_{\frac{1}{2}}\right) - \frac{2h((pq)_{\alpha_1}) + 2h((qp)_{\alpha_1}) + h((pq)_{\alpha_2}) + h((qp)_{\alpha_2})}{6}, \tag{74}$$

$$= JS^{(\alpha_1, \alpha_2)}(q,p). \tag{75}$$

- We can similarly carry on the construction of such symmetric JSDs by increasing the dimensionality of the skewing vector.

In fact, we can define

$$JS_s^{\alpha,w}(p,q) := h\left((pq)_{\frac{1}{2}}\right) - \sum_{i=1}^k w_i \frac{h((pq)_{\alpha_i}) + h((pq)_{1-\alpha_i})}{2} = \sum_{i=1}^k w_i JS_s^{\alpha_i}(p,q), \tag{76}$$

with

$$JS_s^\alpha(p,q) := h\left((pq)_{\frac{1}{2}}\right) - \frac{h((pq)_\alpha) + h((pq)_{1-\alpha})}{2}. \tag{77}$$

3. Jensen–Shannon Centroids on Mixture Families

3.1. Mixture Families and Jensen–Shannon Divergences

Consider a mixture family in information geometry [25]. That is, let us give a prescribed set of $D + 1$ linearly independent probability densities $p_0(x), \ldots, p_D(x)$ defined on the sample space $\mathcal{X}$. A *mixture family* $\mathcal{M}$ of order D consists of all *strictly* convex combinations of these component densities:

$$\mathcal{M} := \left\{ m(x; \theta) := \sum_{i=1}^D \theta^i p_i(x) + \left(1 - \sum_{i=1}^D \theta^i\right) p_0(x) \; : \; \theta^i > 0, \sum_{i=1}^D \theta^i < 1 \right\}. \tag{78}$$

For example, the family of categorical distributions (sometimes called "multinouilli" distributions) is a mixture family [25]:

$$\mathcal{M} = \left\{ m_\theta(x) = \sum_{i=1}^D \theta_i \delta(x - x_i) + \left(1 - \sum_{i=1}^D \theta_i\right) \delta(x - x_0) \right\}, \tag{79}$$

where $\delta(x)$ is the Dirac distribution (i.e., $\delta(x) = 1$ for $x = 0$ and $\delta(x) = 0$ for $x \neq 0$). Note that the mixture family of categorical distributions can also be interpreted as an exponential family.

Notice that the linearly independent assumption on probability densities is to ensure to have an identifiable model: $\theta \leftrightarrow m(x; \theta)$.

The KL divergence between two densities of a mixture family $\mathcal{M}$ amounts to a Bregman divergence for the Shannon negentropy generator $F(\theta) = -h(m_\theta)$ (see [38]):

$$KL(m_{\theta_1} : m_{\theta_2}) = B_F(\theta_1 : \theta_2) = B_{-h(m_\theta)}(\theta_1 : \theta_2). \tag{80}$$

On a mixture manifold $\mathcal{M}$, the mixture density $(1-\alpha)m_{\theta_1} + \alpha m_{\theta_2}$ of two mixtures m_{θ_1} and m_{θ_2} of $\mathcal{M}$ also belongs to $\mathcal{M}$:

$$(1-\alpha)m_{\theta_1} + \alpha m_{\theta_2} = m_{(\theta_1\theta_2)_\alpha} \in \mathcal{M}, \tag{81}$$

where we extend the notation $(\theta_1\theta_2)_\alpha := (1-\alpha)\theta_1 + \alpha\theta_2$ to vectors θ_1 and θ_2: $(\theta_1\theta_2)^i_\alpha = (\theta_1^i \theta_2^i)_\alpha$.

Thus, the vector-skew JSD amounts to a vector-skew Jensen diversity for the Shannon negentropy convex function $F(\theta) = -h(m_\theta)$:

$$\begin{aligned}
\mathrm{JS}^{\alpha,w}(m_{\theta_1} : m_{\theta_2}) &= \sum_{i=1}^{k} w_i \mathrm{KL}\left((m_{\theta_1} m_{\theta_2})_{\alpha_i} : (m_{\theta_1} m_{\theta_2})_{\bar{\alpha}}\right), & (82)\\
&= \sum_{i=1}^{k} w_i \mathrm{KL}\left(m_{(\theta_1\theta_2)_{\alpha_i}} : m_{(\theta_1\theta_2)_{\bar{\alpha}}}\right), & (83)\\
&= \sum_{i=1}^{k} w_i B_F\left((\theta_1\theta_2)_{\alpha_i} : (\theta_1\theta_2)_{\bar{\alpha}}\right), & (84)\\
&= \mathrm{JB}_F^{\alpha,\bar{\alpha},w}(\theta_1 : \theta_2), & (85)\\
&= \sum_{i=1}^{k} w_i F\left((\theta_1\theta_2)_{\alpha_i}\right) - F\left((\theta_1\theta_2)_{\bar{\alpha}}\right), & (86)\\
&= h(m_{(\theta_1\theta_2)_{\bar{\alpha}}}) - \sum_{i=1}^{k} w_i h\left(m_{(\theta_1\theta_2)_{\alpha_i}}\right). & (87)
\end{aligned}$$

3.2. Jensen–Shannon Centroids

Given a set of n mixture densities $m_{\theta_1}, \ldots, m_{\theta_n}$ of $\mathcal{M}$, we seek to calculate the *skew-vector Jensen–Shannon centroid* (or barycenter for non-uniform weights) defined as m_{θ^*}, where θ^* is the minimizer of the following objective function (or loss function):

$$L(\theta) := \sum_{j=1}^{n} \omega_j \mathrm{JS}^{\alpha,w}(m_{\theta_k} : m_\theta), \tag{88}$$

where $\omega \in \Delta_n$ is the weight vector of densities (uniform weight for the centroid and non-uniform weight for a barycenter). This definition of the skew-vector Jensen–Shannon centroid is a generalization of the *Fréchet mean* (the Fréchet mean may not be unique, as it is the case on the sphere for two antipodal points for which their Fréchet means with respect to the geodesic metric distance form a great circle) [39] to non-metric spaces. Since the divergence $\mathrm{JS}^{\alpha,w}$ is strictly separable convex, it follows that the Jensen–Shannon-type centroids are unique when they exist.

Plugging Equation (86) into Equation (88), we get that the calculation of the Jensen–Shannon centroid amounts to the following minimization problem:

$$L(\theta) = \sum_{j=1}^{n} \omega_j \left(\sum_{i=1}^{k} w_i F((\theta_j\theta)_{\alpha_i}) - F\left((\theta_j\theta)_{\bar{\alpha}}\right)\right). \tag{89}$$

This optimization is a *Difference of Convex* (DC) programming optimization, for which we can use the ConCave–Convex procedure [27,40] (CCCP). Indeed, let us define the following two convex functions:

$$\begin{aligned}
A(\theta) &= \sum_{j=1}^{n} \sum_{i=1}^{k} \omega_j w_i F((\theta_j\theta)_{\alpha_i}), & (90)\\
B(\theta) &= \sum_{j=1}^{n} \omega_j F\left((\theta_j\theta)_{\bar{\alpha}}\right). & (91)
\end{aligned}$$

Both functions $A(\theta)$ and $B(\theta)$ are convex since F is convex. Then, the minimization problem of Equation (89) to solve can be rewritten as:

$$\min_{\theta} A(\theta) - B(\theta). \tag{92}$$

This is a DC programming optimization problem which can be solved iteratively by initializing θ to an arbitrary value $\theta^{(0)}$ (say, the centroid of the θ_is), and then by updating the parameter at step t using the CCCP [27] as follows:

$$\theta^{(t+1)} = (\nabla B)^{-1}(\nabla A(\theta^{(t)})). \tag{93}$$

Compared to a gradient descent local optimization, there is no required step size (also called "learning" rate) in CCCP.

We have $\nabla A(\theta) = \sum_{j=1}^{n} \sum_{i=1}^{k} w_j w_i \alpha_i \nabla F((\theta_j \theta)_{\alpha_i})$ and $\nabla B(\theta) = \sum_{j=1}^{n} w_j \bar{\alpha} \nabla F((\theta_j \theta)_{\bar{\alpha}})$.

The CCCP converges to a local optimum θ^* where the support hyperplanes of the function graphs of A and B at θ^* are parallel to each other, as depicted in Figure 1. The set of stationary points is $\{\theta : \nabla A(\theta) = \nabla B(\theta)\}$. In practice, the delicate step is to invert ∇B. Next, we show how to implement this algorithm for the Jensen–Shannon centroid of a set of categorical distributions (i.e., normalized histograms with all non-empty bins).

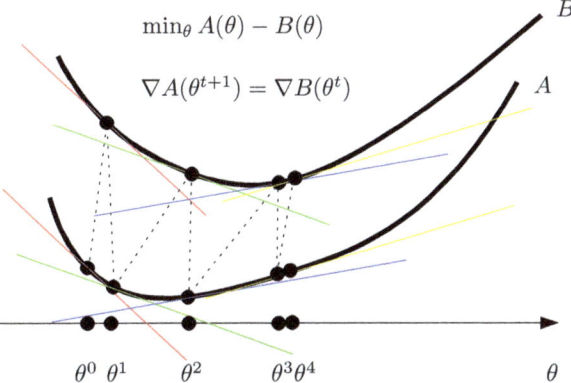

Figure 1. The Convex–ConCave Procedure (CCCP) iteratively updates the parameter θ by aligning the support hyperplanes at θ. In the limit case of convergence to θ^*, the support hyperplanes at θ^* are parallel to each other. CCCP finds a local minimum.

3.2.1. Jensen–Shannon Centroids of Categorical Distributions

To illustrate the method, let us consider the mixture family of categorical distributions [25]:

$$\mathcal{M} = \left\{ m_\theta(x) = \sum_{i=1}^{D} \theta_i \delta(x - x_i) + \left(1 - \sum_{i=1}^{D} \theta_i\right) \delta(x - x_0) \right\}. \tag{94}$$

The Shannon negentropy is

$$F(\theta) = -h(m_\theta) = \sum_{i=1}^{D} \theta_i \log \theta_i + \left(1 - \sum_{i=1}^{D} \theta_i\right) \log \left(1 - \sum_{i=1}^{D} \theta_i\right). \tag{95}$$

We have the partial derivatives

$$\nabla F(\theta) = \left[\frac{\partial}{\partial \theta_i}\right]_i, \quad \frac{\partial}{\partial \theta_i} F(\theta) = \log \frac{\theta_i}{1 - \sum_{j=1}^{D} \theta_j}. \tag{96}$$

Inverting the gradient ∇F requires us to solve the equation $\nabla F(\theta) = \eta$ so that we get $\theta = (\nabla F)^{-1}(\eta)$. We find that

$$\nabla F^*(\eta) = (\nabla F)^{-1}(\eta) = \frac{1}{1 + \sum_{j=1}^{D} \exp(\eta_j)} [\exp(\eta_i)]_i, \quad \theta_i = (\nabla F^{-1}(\eta))_i = \frac{\exp(\eta_i)}{1 + \sum_{j=1}^{D} \exp(\eta_j)}, \quad \forall i \in [D]. \quad (97)$$

Table 1 summarizes the dual view of the family of categorical distributions, either interpreted as an exponential family or as a mixture family.

We have $JS(p_1, p_2) = J_F(\theta_1, \theta_2)$ for $p_1 = m_{\theta_1}$ and $p_2 = m_{\theta_2}$, where

$$J_F(\theta_1 : \theta_2) = \frac{F(\theta_1) + F(\theta_2)}{2} - F\left(\frac{\theta_1 + \theta_2}{2}\right), \quad (98)$$

is the Jensen divergence [40]. Thus, to compute the Jensen–Shannon centroid of a set of n densities $p_1, \ldots, p_n$ of a mixture family (with $p_i = m_{\theta_i}$), we need to solve the following optimization problem for a density $p = m_\theta$:

$$\min_p \sum_i JS(p_i, p), \quad (99)$$

$$\min_\theta \sum_i J_F(\theta_i, \theta), \quad (100)$$

$$\min_\theta \sum_i \frac{F(\theta_i) + F(\theta)}{2} - F\left(\frac{\theta_i + \theta}{2}\right), \quad (101)$$

$$\equiv \min_\theta \frac{1}{2} F(\theta) - \frac{1}{n} \sum_i F\left(\frac{\theta_i + \theta}{2}\right) := E(\theta). \quad (102)$$

The CCCP algorithm for the Jensen–Shannon centroid proceeds by initializing $\theta^{(0)} = \frac{1}{n} \sum_i \theta_i$ (center of mass of the natural parameters), and iteratively updates as follows:

$$\theta^{(t+1)} = (\nabla F)^{-1} \left(\frac{1}{n} \sum_i \nabla F\left(\frac{\theta_i + \theta^{(t)}}{2}\right) \right). \quad (103)$$

We iterate until the absolute difference $|E(\theta^{(t)}) - E(\theta^{(t+1)})|$ between two successive $\theta^{(t)}$ and $\theta^{(t+1)}$ goes below a prescribed threshold value. The convergence of the CCCP algorithm is linear [41] to a local minimum that is a fixed point of the equation

$$\theta = M_H\left(\frac{\theta_1 + \theta}{2}, \ldots, \frac{\theta_n + \theta}{2}\right), \quad (104)$$

where $M_H(v_1, \ldots, v_n) := H^{-1}(\sum_{i=1}^{n} H(v_i))$ is a vector generalization of the formula of the quasi-arithmetic means [30,40] obtained for the generator $H = \nabla F$. Algorithm 1 summarizes the method for approximating the Jensen–Shannon centroid of a given set of categorical distributions (given a prescribed number of iterations). In the pseudo-code, we used the notation $^{(t+1)}\theta$ instead of $\theta^{(t+1)}$ in order to highlight the conversion procedures of the natural parameters to/from the mixture weight parameters by using superscript notations for coordinates.

Table 1. Two views of the family of categorical distributions with d choices: An exponential family or a mixture family of order $D = d - 1$. Note that the Bregman divergence associated to the exponential family view corresponds to the reverse Kullback–Leibler (KL) divergence, while the Bregman divergence associated to the mixture family view corresponds to the KL divergence.

	Exponential Family	Mixture Family
pdf	$p_\theta(x) = \prod_{i=1}^d p_i^{t_i(x)}$, $p_i = \Pr(x = e_i)$, $t_i(x) \in \{0,1\}$, $\sum_{i=1}^d t_i(x) = 1$	$m_\theta(x) = \sum_{i=1}^d p_i \delta_{e_i}(x)$
primal θ	$\theta_i = \log \frac{p_i}{p_d}$	$\theta_i = p_i$
$F(\theta)$	$\log(1 + \sum_{i=1}^D \exp(\theta_i))$	$\theta_i \log \theta_i + (1 - \sum_{i=1}^D \theta_i) \log(1 - \sum_{i=1}^D \theta_i)$
dual $\eta = \nabla F(\theta)$	$\frac{e^{\theta_i}}{1 + \sum_{j=1}^D \exp(\theta_j)}$	$\log \frac{\theta_i}{1 - \sum_{j=1}^D \theta_j}$
primal $\theta = \nabla F^*(\eta)$	$\log \frac{\eta_i}{1 - \sum_{j=1}^D \eta_j}$	$\frac{\exp(\eta_i)}{1 + \sum_{j=1}^D \exp(\eta_j)}$
$F^*(\eta)$	$\sum_{i=1}^D \eta_i \log \eta_i + (1 - \sum_{j=1}^D \eta_j) \log(1 - \sum_{j=1}^D \eta_j)$	$\log(1 + \sum_{i=1}^D \exp(\eta_i))$
Bregman divergence	$B_F(\theta : \theta') = \mathrm{KL}^*(p_\theta : p_{\theta'})$ $= \mathrm{KL}(p_{\theta'} : p_\theta)$	$B_F(\theta : \theta') = \mathrm{KL}(m_\theta : m_{\theta'})$

Algorithm 1: The CCCP algorithm for computing the Jensen–Shannon centroid of a set of categorical distributions.

Input: A set $\{p_i = (p_i^1, \ldots, p_i^d)\}_{i \in [n]}$ of n categorical distributions belonging to the $(d-1)$-dimensional probability simplex Δ_{d-1}
Input: T: The number of CCCP iterations
Output: An approximation $^{(T)}\bar{p}$ of the Jensen–Shannon centroid $\bar{p}$

/* Convert the categorical distributions to their natural parameters by dropping the last coordinate */
$\theta_i^j = p_i^j$ for $j \in \{1, \ldots, d-1\}$; /* Initialize the JS centroid */
$t \leftarrow 0$; $^{(0)}\bar{\theta} = \frac{1}{n} \sum_{i=1}^n \theta_i$; /* Convert the initial natural parameter of the JS centroid to a categorical distribution */
$^{(0)}\bar{p}^j = {}^{(0)}\bar{\theta}^j$ for $j \in \{1, \ldots, d-1\}$; $^{(0)}\bar{p}^d = 1 - \sum_{i=1}^d {}^{(0)}\bar{p}^i$;
/* Perform the ConCave-Convex Procedure (CCCP) */
while $t \leq T$ **do**
    /* Use Equation (96) for ∇F and Equation (97) for $\nabla F^* = (\nabla F)^{-1}$ */
    $^{(t+1)}\theta = (\nabla F)^{-1}\left(\frac{1}{n}\sum_i \nabla F\left(\frac{\theta_i + {}^{(t)}\theta}{2}\right)\right)$; $t \leftarrow t + 1$;
end
$^{(T)}\bar{p}^j = {}^{(T)}\bar{\theta}^j$ for $j \in \{1, \ldots, d-1\}$; $^{(T)}\bar{p}^d = 1 - \sum_{i=1}^d {}^{(T)}\bar{p}^i$; **return** $^{(T)}\bar{p}$;

Figure 2 displays the results of the calculations of the Jeffreys centroid [18] and the Jensen–Shannon centroid for two normalized histograms obtained from grey-valued images of Lena and Barbara. Figure 3 show the Jeffreys centroid and the Jensen–Shannon centroid for the Barbara image and its negative image. Figure 4 demonstrates that the Jensen–Shannon centroid is well defined even if the input histograms do not have coinciding supports. Notice that on the parts of the support where only one distribution is defined, the JS centroid is a scaled copy of that defined distribution.

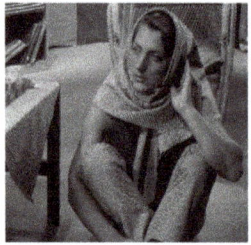
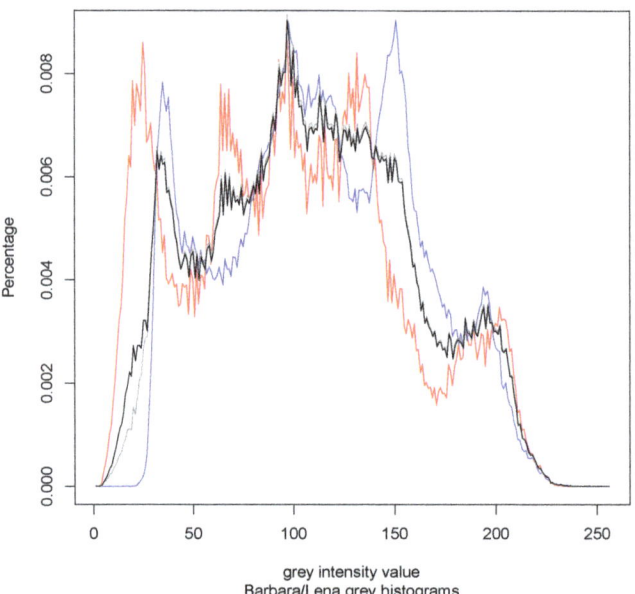

Figure 2. The Jeffreys centroid (grey histogram) and the Jensen–Shannon centroid (black histogram) for two grey normalized histograms of the Lena image (red histogram) and the Barbara image (blue histogram). Although these Jeffreys and Jensen–Shannon centroids look quite similar, observe that there is a major difference between them in the range $[0, 20]$ where the blue histogram is zero.

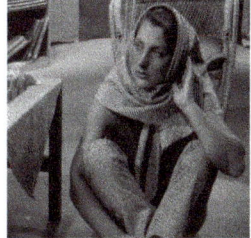

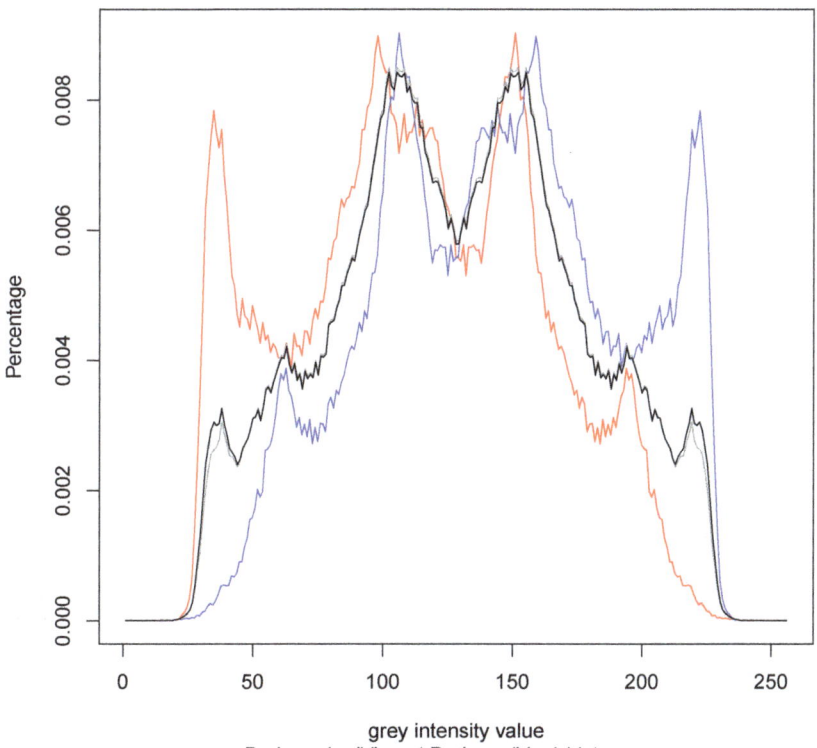

Figure 3. The Jeffreys centroid (grey histogram) and the Jensen–Shannon centroid (black histogram) for the grey normalized histogram of the Barbara image (red histogram) and its negative image (blue histogram which corresponds to the reflection around the vertical axis $x = 128$ of the red histogram).

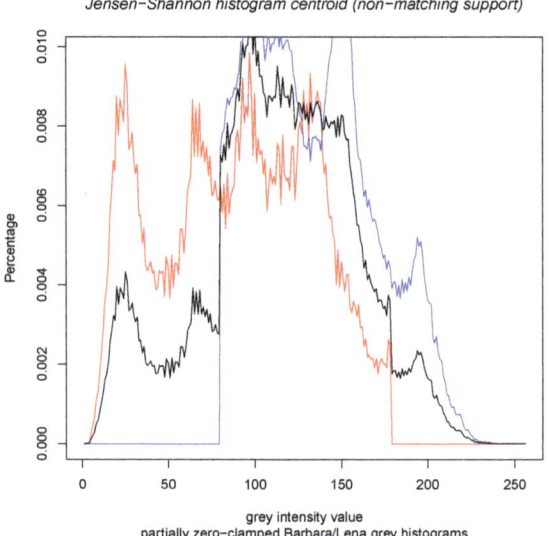

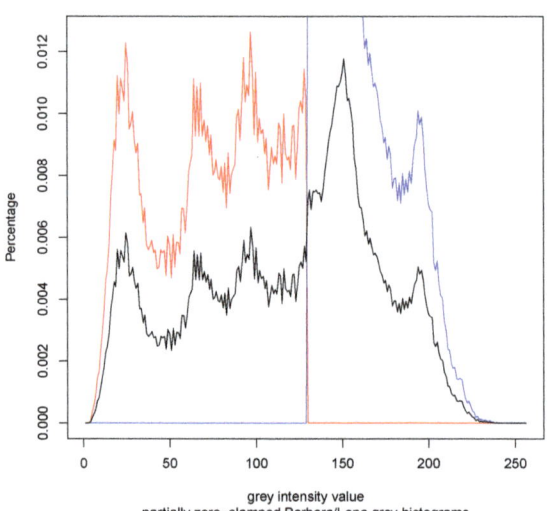

Figure 4. Jensen–Shannon centroid (black histogram) for the clamped grey normalized histogram of the Lena image (red histograms) and the clamped gray normalized histogram of Barbara image (blue histograms). Notice that on the part of the sample space where only one distribution is non-zero, the JS centroid scales that histogram portion.

3.2.2. Special Cases

Let us now consider two special cases:

- For the special case of $D = 1$, the categorical family is the Bernoulli family, and we have $F(\theta) = \theta \log \theta + (1-\theta) \log(1-\theta)$ (binary negentropy), $F'(\theta) = \log \frac{\theta}{1-\theta}$ (and $F''(\theta) = \frac{1}{\theta(1-\theta)} > 0$)

and $(F')^{-1}(\eta) = \frac{e^\eta}{1+e^\eta}$. The CCCP update rule to compute the binary Jensen–Shannon centroid becomes

$$\theta^{(t+1)} = (F')^{-1}\left(\sum_i w_i F'\left(\frac{\theta^{(t)} + \theta_i}{2}\right)\right). \quad (105)$$

- Since the skew-vector Jensen–Shannon divergence formula holds for positive densities:

$$\begin{aligned}
\mathrm{JS}^{+\alpha,w}(\tilde{p}:\tilde{q}) &= \sum_{i=1}^k w_i \mathrm{KL}^+((\tilde{p}\tilde{q})_{\alpha_i} : ((\tilde{p}\tilde{q})_{\bar{\alpha}}), \quad (106) \\
&= \sum_{i=1}^k w_i \left(\mathrm{KL}((\tilde{p}\tilde{q})_{\alpha_i} : ((\tilde{p}\tilde{q})_{\bar{\alpha}}) + \int (\tilde{p}\tilde{q})_{\bar{\alpha}} d\mu - \underbrace{\sum_{i=1}^k w_i \int (\tilde{p}\tilde{q})_{\alpha_i} d\mu}_{=\int (\tilde{p}\tilde{q})_{\bar{\alpha}} d\mu} \right), \quad (107) \\
&= \mathrm{JS}^{\alpha,w}(\tilde{p}:\tilde{q}), \quad (108)
\end{aligned}$$

we can *relax* the computation of the Jensen–Shannon centroid by considering 1D separable minimization problems. We then normalize the positive JS centroids to get an approximation of the probability JS centroids. This approach was also considered when dealing with the Jeffreys' centroid [18]. In 1D, we have $F(\theta) = \theta \log \theta - \theta$, $F'(\theta) = \log \theta$ and $(F')^{-1}(\eta) = e^\eta$.

In general, calculating the negentropy for a mixture family with continuous densities sharing the same support is not tractable because of the log-sum term of the differential entropy. However, the following remark emphasizes an extension of the mixture family of categorical distributions:

3.2.3. Some Remarks and Properties

Remark 3. *Consider a mixture family $m(\theta) = \sum_{i=1}^D \theta_i p_i(x) + \left(1 - \sum_{i=1}^D \theta_i\right) p_0(x)$ (for a parameter θ belonging to the D-dimensional standard simplex) of probability densities $p_0(x), \ldots, p_D(x)$ defined respectively on the supports $\mathcal{X}_0, \mathcal{X}_1, \ldots, \mathcal{X}_D$. Let $\theta_0 := 1 - \sum_{i=1}^D \theta_i$. Assume that the support $\mathcal{X}_i$s of the p_is are mutually non-intersecting ($\mathcal{X}_i \cap \mathcal{X}_j = \emptyset$ for all $i \neq j$ implying that the $D + 1$ densities are linearly independent) so that $m_\theta(x) = \theta_i p_i(x)$ for all $x \in \mathcal{X}_i$, and let $\mathcal{X} = \cup_i \mathcal{X}_i$. Consider Shannon negative entropy $F(\theta) = -h(m_\theta)$ as a strictly convex function. Then, we have*

$$\begin{aligned}
F(\theta) &= -h(m_\theta) = \int_\mathcal{X} m_\theta(x) \log m_\theta(x), \quad (109) \\
&= \sum_{i=0}^D \theta_i \int_{\mathcal{X}_i} p_i(x) \log(\theta_i p_i(x)) d\mu(x), \quad (110) \\
&= \sum_{i=0}^D \theta_i \log \theta_i - \sum_{i=0}^D \theta_i h(p_i). \quad (111)
\end{aligned}$$

Note that the term $\sum_i \theta_i h(p_i)$ is affine in θ, and Bregman divergences are defined up to affine terms so that the Bregman generator F is equivalent to the Bregman generator of the family of categorical distributions. This example generalizes the ordinary mixture family of categorical distributions where the p_is are distinct Dirac distributions. Note that when the support of the component distributions are not pairwise disjoint, the (neg)entropy may not be analytic [42] (e.g., mixture of the convex weighting of two prescribed distinct Gaussian distributions). This contrasts with the fact that the cumulant function of an exponential family is always real-analytic [43]. Observe that the term $\sum_i \theta_i h(p_i)$ can be interpreted as a conditional entropy: $\sum_i \theta_i h(p_i) = h(X|\Theta)$ where $\Pr(\Theta = i) = \theta_i$ and $\Pr(X \in S|\Theta = i) = \int_S p_i(x) d\mu(x)$.

Notice that we can truncate an exponential family [25] to get a (potentially non-regular [44]) exponential family for defining the p_is on mutually non-intersecting domains $\mathcal{X}_i$s. The entropy of a natural exponential family $\{e(x:\theta) = \exp(x^\top \theta - \psi(\theta)) : \theta \in \Theta\}$ with cumulant function $\psi(\theta)$ and natural parameter space Θ is $-\psi^*(\eta)$, where $\eta = \nabla \psi(\theta)$, and ψ^* is the Legendre convex conjugate [45]: $h(e(x:\theta)) = -\psi^*(\nabla \psi(\theta))$.

In general, the entropy and cross-entropy between densities of a mixture family (whether the distributions have disjoint supports or not) can be calculated in closed-form.

Property 2. *The entropy of a density belonging to a mixture family $\mathcal{M}$ is $h(m_\theta) = -F(\theta)$, and the cross-entropy between two mixture densities m_{θ_1} and m_{θ_2} is $h^\times(m_{\theta_1} : m_{\theta_2}) = -F(\theta_2) - (\theta_1 - \theta_2)^\top \eta_2 = F^*(\eta_2) - \theta_1^\top \eta_2$.*

Proof. Let us write the KLD as the difference between the cross-entropy minus the entropy [4]:

$$\begin{align}
\mathrm{KL}(m_{\theta_1} : m_{\theta_2}) &= h^\times(m_{\theta_1} : m_{\theta_2}) - h(m_{\theta_1}), \tag{112}\\
&= B_F(\theta_1 : \theta_2), \tag{113}\\
&= F(\theta_1) - F(\theta_2) - (\theta_1 - \theta_2)^\top \nabla F(\theta_2). \tag{114}
\end{align}$$

Following [45], we deduce that $h(m_\theta) = -F(\theta) + c$ and $h^\times(m_{\theta_1} : m_{\theta_2}) = -F(\theta_2) - (\theta_1 - \theta_2)^\top \eta_2 - c$ for a constant c. Since $F(\theta) = -h(m_\theta)$ by definition, it follows that $c = 0$ and that $h^\times(m_{\theta_1} : m_{\theta_2}) = -F(\theta_2) - (\theta_1 - \theta_2)^\top \eta_2 = F^*(\eta_2) - \theta_1^\top \eta_2$ where $\eta = \nabla F(\theta)$. □

Thus, we can numerically compute the Jensen–Shannon centroids (or barycenters) of a set of densities belonging to a mixture family. This includes the case of categorical distributions and the case of Gaussian Mixture Models (GMMs) with prescribed Gaussian components [38] (although in this case, the negentropy needs to be stochastically approximated using Monte Carlo techniques [46]). When the densities do not belong to a mixture family (say, the Gaussian family, which is an exponential family [25]), we face the problem that the mixture of two densities does not belong to the family anymore. One way to tackle this problem is to project the mixture onto the Gaussian family. This corresponds to an m-projection (mixture projection) which can be interpreted as a Maximum Entropy projection of the mixture [25,47]).

Notice that we can perform fast k-means clustering without centroid calculations using a generalization of the k-means++ probabilistic initialization [48,49]. See [50] for details of the generalized k-means++ probabilistic initialization defined according to an arbitrary divergence.

Finally, let us notice some decompositions of the Jensen–Shannon divergence and the skew Jensen divergences.

Remark 4. *We have the following decomposition for the Jensen–Shannon divergence:*

$$\begin{align}
\mathrm{JS}(p_1, p_2) &= h\left(\frac{p_1 + p_2}{2}\right) - \frac{h(p_1) + h(p_2)}{2}, \tag{115}\\
&= h_{\mathrm{JS}}^\times(p_1 : p_2) - h_{\mathrm{JS}}(p_2) \geq 0, \tag{116}
\end{align}$$

where

$$h_{\mathrm{JS}}^\times(p_1 : p_2) = h\left(\frac{p_1 + p_2}{2}\right) - \frac{1}{2} h(p_1), \tag{117}$$

and $h_{\mathrm{JS}}(p_2) = h_{\mathrm{JS}}^\times(p_2 : p_2) = h(p_2) - \frac{1}{2} h(p_2) = \frac{1}{2} h(p_2)$. This decomposition bears some similarity with the KLD decomposition viewed as the cross-entropy minus the entropy (with the cross-entropy always upper-bounding the entropy).

Similarly, the α-skew Jensen divergence

$$J_F^\alpha(\theta_1 : \theta_2) := (F(\theta_1)F(\theta_2))_\alpha - F((\theta_1\theta_2)_\alpha), \quad \alpha \in (0,1) \tag{118}$$

can be decomposed as the sum of the information $I_F^\alpha(\theta_1) = (1-\alpha)F(\theta_1)$ minus the cross-information $C_F^\alpha(\theta_1 : \theta_2) := F((\theta_1\theta_2)_\alpha) - \alpha F(\theta_2)$:

$$J_F^\alpha(\theta_1 : \theta_2) = I_F^\alpha(\theta_1) - C_F^\alpha(\theta_1 : \theta_2) \geq 0. \tag{119}$$

Notice that the information $I_F^\alpha(\theta_1)$ is the self cross-information: $I_F^\alpha(\theta_1) = C_F^\alpha(\theta_1 : \theta_1) = (1-\alpha)F(\theta_1)$. Recall that the convex information is the negentropy where the entropy is concave. For the Jensen–Shannon divergence on the mixture family of categorical distributions, the convex generator $F(\theta) = -h(m_\theta) = \sum_{i=1}^{D} \theta^i \log \theta^i$ is the Shannon negentropy.

Finally, let us briefly mention the *Jensen–Shannon diversity* [30] which extends the Jensen–Shannon divergence to a weighted set of densities as follows:

$$\mathrm{JS}(p_1, \ldots, p_k; w_1, \ldots, w_k) := \sum_{i=1}^{k} w_i \mathrm{KL}(p_i : \bar{p}), \tag{120}$$

where $\bar{p} = \sum_{i=1}^{k} w_i p_i$. The Jensen–Shannon diversity plays the role of the variance of a cluster with respect to the KLD. Indeed, let us state the compensation identity [51]: For any q, we have

$$\sum_{i=1}^{k} w_i \mathrm{KL}(p_i : q) = \sum_{i=1}^{k} w_i \mathrm{KL}(p_i : \bar{p}) + \mathrm{KL}(\bar{p} : q). \tag{121}$$

Thus, the cluster center defined as the minimizer of $\sum_{i=1}^{k} w_i \mathrm{KL}(p_i : q)$ is the centroid $\bar{p}$, and

$$\sum_{i=1}^{k} w_i \mathrm{KL}(p_i : \bar{p}) = \mathrm{JS}(p_1, \ldots, p_k; w_1, \ldots, w_k). \tag{122}$$

4. Conclusions and Discussion

The Jensen–Shannon divergence [6] is a renown symmetrization of the Kullback–Leibler oriented divergence that enjoys the following three essential properties:

1. It is always bounded,
2. it applies to densities with potentially different supports, and
3. it extends to unnormalized densities while enjoying the same formula expression.

This JSD plays an important role in machine learning and in deep learning for studying Generative Adversarial Networks (GANs) [52]. Traditionally, the JSD has been skewed with a scalar parameter [19,53] $\alpha \in (0,1)$. In practice, it has been experimentally demonstrated that skewing divergences may significantly improve the performance of some tasks (e.g., [21,54]).

In general, we can symmetrize the KLD $\mathrm{KL}(p : q)$ by taking an *abstract mean* (we require a symmetric mean $M(x,y) = M(y,x)$ with the in-betweenness property: $\min\{x,y\} \leq M(x,y) \leq \max\{x,y\}$) M between the two orientations $\mathrm{KL}(p : q)$ and $\mathrm{KL}(q : p)$:

$$\mathrm{KL}_M(p,q) := M(\mathrm{KL}(p : q), \mathrm{KL}(q : p)). \tag{123}$$

We recover the Jeffreys divergence by taking the arithmetic mean twice (i.e., $J(p,q) = 2A(\mathrm{KL}(p : q), \mathrm{KL}(q : p))$ where $A(x,y) = \frac{x+y}{2}$), and the resistor average divergence [55] by taking the harmonic mean (i.e., $R_{\text{KL}}(p,q) = H(\text{KL}(p:q), \text{KL}(q:p)) = \frac{2\text{KL}(p:q)\text{KL}(q:p)}{\text{KL}(p:q)+\text{KL}(q:p)}$ where $H(x,y) = \frac{2}{\frac{1}{x}+\frac{1}{y}}$). When we take the limit of Hölder power means, we get the following extremal symmetrizations of the KLD:

$$\text{KL}^{\min}(p:q) = \min\{\text{KL}(p:q), \text{KL}(q:p)\} = \text{KL}^{\min}(q:p), \quad (124)$$
$$\text{KL}^{\max}(p:q) = \max\{\text{KL}(p:q), \text{KL}(q:p)\} = \text{KL}^{\max}(q:p). \quad (125)$$

In this work, we showed how to *vector-skew* the JSD while preserving the above three properties. These new families of *weighted vector-skew Jensen–Shannon divergences* may allow one to fine-tune the dissimilarity in applications by replacing the skewing scalar parameter of the JSD by a vector parameter (informally, adding some "knobs" for tuning a divergence). We then considered computing the Jensen–Shannon centroids of a set of densities belonging to a mixture family [25] by using the convex–concave procedure [27].

In general, we can vector-skew any arbitrary divergence D by using two k-dimensional vectors $\alpha \in [0,1]^k$ and $\beta \in [0,1]^k$ (with $\alpha \neq \beta$) by building a weighted separable divergence as follows:

$$D^{\alpha,\beta,w}(p:q) := \sum_{i=1}^{k} w_i D\left((pq)_{\alpha_i} : (pq)_{\beta_i}\right) = D^{1_k-\alpha, 1_k-\beta, w}(q:p), \quad \alpha \neq \beta. \quad (126)$$

This bi-vector-skew divergence unifies the Jeffreys divergence with the Jensen–Shannon α-skew divergence by setting the following parameters:

$$\text{KL}^{(0,1),(1,0),(1,1)}(p:q) = \text{KL}(p:q) + \text{KL}(q:p) = J(p,q), \quad (127)$$
$$\text{KL}^{(0,\alpha),(1,1-\alpha),(\frac{1}{2},\frac{1}{2})}(p:q) = \frac{1}{2}\text{KL}(p:(pq)_\alpha) + \frac{1}{2}\text{KL}(q:(pq)_\alpha). \quad (128)$$

We have shown in this paper that interesting properties may occur when the skewing vector β is purposely correlated to the skewing vector α: Namely, for the bi-vector-skew Bregman divergences with $\beta = (\bar{\alpha}, \ldots, \bar{\alpha})$ and $\bar{\alpha} = \sum_i w_i \alpha_i$, we obtain an equivalent Jensen diversity for the Jensen–Bregman divergence, and, as a byproduct, a vector-skew generalization of the Jensen–Shannon divergence.

Funding: This research received no external funding.

Acknowledgments: The author is very grateful to the two Reviewers and the Academic Editor for their careful reading, helpful comments, and suggestions which led to this improved manuscript. In particular, Reviewer 2 kindly suggested the stronger bound of Lemma 1 and hinted at Theorem 1. .

Conflicts of Interest: The authors declare no conflict of interest.

References

1. Billingsley, P. *Probability and Measure*; John Wiley & Sons: Hoboken, NJ, USA, 2008.
2. Deza, M.M.; Deza, E. *Encyclopedia of Distances*; Springer: Berlin/Heidelberg, Germany, 2009.
3. Basseville, M. Divergence measures for statistical data processing—An annotated bibliography. *Signal Process.* **2013**, *93*, 621–633. [CrossRef]
4. Cover, T.M.; Thomas, J.A. *Elements of information theory*; John Wiley & Sons: Hoboken, NJ, USA, 2012.
5. Nielsen, F. On the Jensen–Shannon Symmetrization of Distances Relying on Abstract Means. *Entropy* **2019**, *21*, 485. [CrossRef]
6. Lin, J. Divergence measures based on the Shannon entropy. *IEEE Trans. Inf. Theory* **1991**, *37*, 145–151. [CrossRef]
7. Sason, I. Tight bounds for symmetric divergence measures and a new inequality relating f-divergences. In Proceedings of the 2015 IEEE Information Theory Workshop (ITW), Jerusalem, Israel, 26 April–1 May 2015; pp. 1–5.
8. Wong, A.K.; You, M. Entropy and distance of random graphs with application to structural pattern recognition. *IEEE Trans. Pattern Anal. Mach. Intell.* **1985**, *7*, 599–609. [CrossRef]

9. Endres, D.M.; Schindelin, J.E. A new metric for probability distributions. *IEEE Trans. Inf. Theory* **2003**, *49*, 1858–1860. [CrossRef]
10. Kafka, P.; Österreicher, F.; Vincze, I. On powers of f-divergences defining a distance. *Stud. Sci. Math. Hung.* **1991**, *26*, 415–422.
11. Fuglede, B. Spirals in Hilbert space: With an application in information theory. *Expo. Math.* **2005**, *23*, 23–45. [CrossRef]
12. Acharyya, S.; Banerjee, A.; Boley, D. Bregman divergences and triangle inequality. In Proceedings of the 2013 SIAM International Conference on Data Mining, Austin, TX, USA, 2–4 May 2013; pp. 476–484.
13. Naghshvar, M.; Javidi, T.; Wigger, M. Extrinsic Jensen–Shannon divergence: Applications to variable-length coding. *IEEE Trans. Inf. Theory* **2015**, *61*, 2148–2164. [CrossRef]
14. Bigi, B. Using Kullback-Leibler distance for text categorization. In *European Conference on Information Retrieval*; Springer: Berlin/Heidelberg, Germany, 2003; pp. 305–319.
15. Chatzisavvas, K.C.; Moustakidis, C.C.; Panos, C. Information entropy, information distances, and complexity in atoms. *J. Chem. Phys.* **2005**, *123*, 174111. [CrossRef]
16. Yurdakul, B. Statistical Properties of Population Stability Index. Ph.D. Thesis, Western Michigan University, Kalamazoo, MI, USA, 2018.
17. Jeffreys, H. An invariant form for the prior probability in estimation problems. *Proc. R. Soc. Lond. A* **1946**, *186*, 453–461.
18. Nielsen, F. Jeffreys centroids: A closed-form expression for positive histograms and a guaranteed tight approximation for frequency histograms. *IEEE Signal Process. Lett.* **2013**, *20*, 657–660. [CrossRef]
19. Lee, L. Measures of Distributional Similarity. In *Proceedings of the 37th Annual Meeting of the Association for Computational Linguistics on Computational Linguistics, ACL '99*; Association for Computational Linguistics: Stroudsburg, PA, USA, 1999; pp. 25–32. doi:10.3115/1034678.1034693. [CrossRef]
20. Nielsen, F. A family of statistical symmetric divergences based on Jensen's inequality. *arXiv* **2010**, arXiv:1009.4004.
21. Lee, L. On the effectiveness of the skew divergence for statistical language analysis. In Proceedings of the 8th International Workshop on Artificial Intelligence and Statistics (AISTATS 2001), Key West, FL, USA, 4–7 January 2001.
22. Csiszár, I. Information-type measures of difference of probability distributions and indirect observation. *Stud. Sci. Math. Hung.* **1967**, *2*, 229–318.
23. Ali, S.M.; Silvey, S.D. A general class of coefficients of divergence of one distribution from another. *J. R. Stat. Soc. Ser. B (Methodol.)* **1966**, *28*, 131–142. [CrossRef]
24. Sason, I. On f-divergences: Integral representations, local behavior, and inequalities. *Entropy* **2018**, *20*, 383. [CrossRef]
25. Amari, S.I. *Information Geometry and Its Applications*; Springer: Berlin/Heidelberg, Germany, 2016.
26. Jiao, J.; Courtade, T.A.; No, A.; Venkat, K.; Weissman, T. Information measures: The curious case of the binary alphabet. *IEEE Trans. Inf. Theory* **2014**, *60*, 7616–7626. [CrossRef]
27. Yuille, A.L.; Rangarajan, A. The concave-convex procedure (CCCP). In Proceedings of the Neural Information Processing Systems 2002, Vancouver, BC, Canada, 9–14 December 2002; pp. 1033–1040.
28. Nielsen, F.; Nock, R. Skew Jensen-Bregman Voronoi diagrams. In *Transactions on Computational Science XIV*; Springer: Berlin/Heidelberg, Germany, 2011; pp. 102–128.
29. Banerjee, A.; Merugu, S.; Dhillon, I.S.; Ghosh, J. Clustering with Bregman divergences. *J. Mach. Learn. Res.* **2005**, *6*, 1705–1749.
30. Nielsen, F.; Nock, R. Sided and symmetrized Bregman centroids. *IEEE Trans. Inf. Theory* **2009**, *55*, 2882–2904. [CrossRef]
31. Melbourne, J.; Talukdar, S.; Bhaban, S.; Madiman, M.; Salapaka, M.V. On the Entropy of Mixture distributions. Availabline online: http://box5779.temp.domains/~jamesmel/publications/ (accesse on 16 February 2020).
32. Guntuboyina, A. Lower bounds for the minimax risk using f-divergences, and applications. *IEEE Trans. Inf. Theory* **2011**, *57*, 2386–2399. [CrossRef]
33. Sason, I.; Verdu, S. f-divergence Inequalities. *IEEE Trans. Inf. Theory* **2016**, *62*, 5973–6006. [CrossRef]
34. Melbourne, J.; Madiman, M.; Salapaka, M.V. Relationships between certain f-divergences. In Proceeding of the 57th Annual Allerton Conference on Communication, Control, and Computing (Allerton), Monticello, IL, USA, 24–27 September 2019; pp. 1068–1073.

35. Sason, I. On Data-Processing and Majorization Inequalities for f-Divergences with Applications. *Entropy* **2019**, *21*, 1022. [CrossRef]
36. Van Erven, T.; Harremos, P. Rényi divergence and Kullback-Leibler divergence. *IEEE Trans. Inf. Theory* **2014**, *60*, 3797–3820. [CrossRef]
37. Xu, P.; Melbourne, J.; Madiman, M. Infinity-Rényi entropy power inequalities. In Proceedings of the 2017 IEEE International Symposium on Information Theory (ISIT), Aachen, Germany, 25–30 June 2017; pp. 2985–2989.
38. Nielsen, F.; Nock, R. On the geometry of mixtures of prescribed distributions. In Proceedings of the 2018 IEEE International Conference on Acoustics, Speech and Signal Processing (ICASSP), Calgary, AB, Canada, 15–20 April 2018; pp. 2861–2865.
39. Fréchet, M. Les éléments aléatoires de nature quelconque dans un espace distancié. *Ann. De L'institut Henri PoincarÉ* **1948**, *10*, 215–310.
40. Nielsen, F.; Boltz, S. The Burbea-Rao and Bhattacharyya centroids. *IEEE Trans. Inf. Theory* **2011**, *57*, 5455–5466. [CrossRef]
41. Lanckriet, G.R.; Sriperumbudur, B.K. On the convergence of the concave-convex procedure. In Proceedings of the Advances in Neural Information Processing Systems 22 (NIPS 2009), Vancouver, BC, Canada, 7–10 December 2009; pp. 1759–1767.
42. Nielsen, F.; Sun, K. Guaranteed bounds on information-theoretic measures of univariate mixtures using piecewise log-sum-exp inequalities. *Entropy* **2016**, *18*, 442. [CrossRef]
43. Springer Verlag GmbH, European Mathematical Society. Encyclopedia of Mathematics. Available online: https://www.encyclopediaofmath.org/ (accessed on 19 December 2019).
44. Del Castillo, J. The singly truncated normal distribution: A non-steep exponential family. *Ann. Inst. Stat. Math.* **1994**, *46*, 57–66. [CrossRef]
45. Nielsen, F.; Nock, R. Entropies and cross-entropies of exponential families. In Proceedings of the 2010 IEEE International Conference on Image Processing, Hong Kong, China, 26–29 September 2010; pp. 3621–3624.
46. Nielsen, F.; Hadjeres, G. Monte Carlo information geometry: The dually flat case. *arXiv* **2018**, arXiv:1803.07225.
47. Schwander, O.; Nielsen, F. Learning mixtures by simplifying kernel density estimators. In *Matrix Information Geometry*; Springer: Berlin/Heidelberg, Germany, 2013; pp. 403–426.
48. Arthur, D.; Vassilvitskii, S. k-means++: The advantages of careful seeding. In Proceedings of the Eighteenth Annual ACM-SIAM Symposium on Discrete Algorithms (SODA'07), New Orleans LA, USA, 7–9 January 2007; pp. 1027–1035.
49. Nielsen, F.; Nock, R.; Amari, S.i. On clustering histograms with k-means by using mixed α-divergences. *Entropy* **2014**, *16*, 3273–3301. [CrossRef]
50. Nielsen, F.; Nock, R. Total Jensen divergences: Definition, properties and clustering. In Proceedings of the 2015 IEEE International Conference on Acoustics, Speech and Signal Processing (ICASSP), Brisbane, QLD, Australia, 19–24 April 2015; pp. 2016–2020.
51. Topsøe, F. Basic concepts, identities and inequalities-the toolkit of information theory. *Entropy* **2001**, *3*, 162–190. [CrossRef]
52. Goodfellow, I.; Pouget-Abadie, J.; Mirza, M.; Xu, B.; Warde-Farley, D.; Ozair, S.; Courville, A.; Bengio, Y. Generative adversarial nets. In Proceedings of the Advances in Neural Information Processing Systems 27 (NIPS 2014), Montreal, QC, Canada 8–13 December 2014; pp. 2672–2680.
53. Yamano, T. Some bounds for skewed α-Jensen-Shannon divergence. *Results Appl. Math.* **2019**, *3*, 100064. [CrossRef]
54. Kotlerman, L.; Dagan, I.; Szpektor, I.; Zhitomirsky-Geffet, M. Directional distributional similarity for lexical inference. *Nat. Lang. Eng.* **2010**, *16*, 359–389. [CrossRef]
55. Johnson, D.; Sinanovic, S. Symmetrizing the Kullback-Leibler distance. *IEEE Trans. Inf. Theory* **2001**, 1–8.

© 2020 by the authors. Licensee MDPI, Basel, Switzerland. This article is an open access article distributed under the terms and conditions of the Creative Commons Attribution (CC BY) license (http://creativecommons.org/licenses/by/4.0/).

Article

Conditional Rényi Divergences and Horse Betting

Cédric Bleuler, Amos Lapidoth and Christoph Pfister *

Signal and Information Processing Laboratory, ETH Zurich, 8092 Zurich, Switzerland;
cedric.bleuler@gmail.com (C.B.); lapidoth@isi.ee.ethz.ch (A.L.)
* Correspondence: pfister@isi.ee.ethz.ch

Received: 17 December 2019; Accepted: 9 March 2020; Published: 11 March 2020

Abstract: Motivated by a horse betting problem, a new conditional Rényi divergence is introduced. It is compared with the conditional Rényi divergences that appear in the definitions of the dependence measures by Csiszár and Sibson, and the properties of all three are studied with emphasis on their behavior under data processing. In the same way that Csiszár's and Sibson's conditional divergence lead to the respective dependence measures, so does the new conditional divergence lead to the Lapidoth–Pfister mutual information. Moreover, the new conditional divergence is also related to the Arimoto–Rényi conditional entropy and to Arimoto's measure of dependence. In the second part of the paper, the horse betting problem is analyzed where, instead of Kelly's expected log-wealth criterion, a more general family of power-mean utility functions is considered. The key role in the analysis is played by the Rényi divergence, and in the setting where the gambler has access to side information, the new conditional Rényi divergence is key. The setting with side information also provides another operational meaning to the Lapidoth–Pfister mutual information. Finally, a universal strategy for independent and identically distributed races is presented that—without knowing the winning probabilities or the parameter of the utility function—asymptotically maximizes the gambler's utility function.

Keywords: conditional Rényi divergence; horse betting; Kelly gambling; Rényi divergence; Rényi mutual information

1. Introduction

As shown by Kelly [1,2], many of Shannon's information measures appear naturally in the context of horse gambling when the gambler's utility function is expected log-wealth. Here, we show that under a more general family of utility functions, gambling also provides a context for some of Rényi's information measures. Moreover, the setting where the gambler has side information motivates a new Rényi-like conditional divergence, which we study and compare to other conditional divergences. The proposed family of utility functions in the context of gambling with side information also provides another operational meaning to the Rényi-like mutual information that was recently proposed by Lapidoth and Pfister [3]: it measures the gambler's gain from the side information as measured by the increase in the minimax value of the two-player zero-sum game in which the bookmaker picks the odds and the gambler then places the bets based on these odds and her side information.

Deferring the gambling-based motivation to the second part of the paper, we first describe the different conditional divergences and study some of their properties with emphasis on their behavior under data processing. We also show that the new conditional Rényi divergence relates to the Lapidoth–Pfister mutual information in much the same way that Csiszár's and Sibson's conditional divergences relate to their corresponding mutual informations. Before discussing the conditional divergences, we first recall other information measures.

The Kullback–Leibler divergence (or relative entropy) is an important concept in information theory and statistics [2,4–6]. It is defined between two probability mass functions (PMFs) P and Q over a finite set $\mathcal{X}$ as

$$D(P\|Q) \triangleq \sum_{x \in \mathcal{X}} P(x) \log \frac{P(x)}{Q(x)}, \tag{1}$$

where $\log(\cdot)$ denotes the base-2 logarithm. Defining a conditional Kullback–Leibler divergence is straightforward because, as simple algebra shows, the two natural approaches lead to the same result:

$$D(P_{Y|X}\|Q_{Y|X}|P_X) \triangleq \sum_{x \in \text{supp}(P_X)} P(x) D(P_{Y|X=x}\|Q_{Y|X=x}) \tag{2}$$

$$= D(P_X P_{Y|X} \| P_X Q_{Y|X}), \tag{3}$$

where $\text{supp}(P) \triangleq \{x \in \mathcal{X} : P(x) > 0\}$ denotes the support of P, and in (3) and throughout $P_X P_{Y|X}$ denotes the PMF on $\mathcal{X} \times \mathcal{Y}$ that assigns (x,y) the probability $P_X(x) P_{Y|X}(y|x)$.

The Rényi divergence of order α [7,8] between two PMFs P and Q is defined for all positive α's other than one as

$$D_\alpha(P\|Q) \triangleq \frac{1}{\alpha - 1} \log \sum_{x \in \mathcal{X}} P(x)^\alpha Q(x)^{1-\alpha}. \tag{4}$$

A conditional Rényi divergence can be defined in more than one way. In this paper, we consider the following three definitions, two classic and one new:

$$D_\alpha^c(P_{Y|X}\|Q_{Y|X}|P_X) \triangleq \sum_{x \in \text{supp}(P_X)} P(x) D_\alpha(P_{Y|X=x}\|Q_{Y|X=x}), \tag{5}$$

$$D_\alpha^s(P_{Y|X}\|Q_{Y|X}|P_X) \triangleq D_\alpha(P_X P_{Y|X} \| P_X Q_{Y|X}), \tag{6}$$

$$D_\alpha^1(P_{Y|X}\|Q_{Y|X}|P_X) \triangleq \frac{\alpha}{\alpha - 1} \log \sum_{x \in \text{supp}(P_X)} P(x) 2^{\frac{\alpha-1}{\alpha} D_\alpha(P_{Y|X=x}\|Q_{Y|X=x})}, \tag{7}$$

where (5) is inspired by Csiszár [9]; (6) is inspired by Sibson [10]; and (7) is motivated by the horse betting problem discussed in Section 9. The first two conditional Rényi divergences were used to define the Rényi measures of dependence of Csiszár $I_\alpha^c(X;Y)$ [9] and of Sibson $I_\alpha^s(X;Y)$ [10]:

$$I_\alpha^c(X;Y) \triangleq \min_{Q_Y} D_\alpha^c(P_{Y|X}\|Q_Y|P_X), \tag{8}$$

$$I_\alpha^s(X;Y) \triangleq \min_{Q_Y} D_\alpha^s(P_{Y|X}\|Q_Y|P_X), \tag{9}$$

where the minimization is over all PMFs on the set $\mathcal{Y}$. (Gallager's E_0 function [11] and $I_\alpha^s(X;Y)$ are in one-to-one correspondence; see (65) below.) The analogous minimization of $D_\alpha^1(\cdot)$ leads to the Lapidoth–Pfister mutual information $J_\alpha(X;Y)$ [3]:

$$J_\alpha(X;Y) \triangleq \min_{Q_X, Q_Y} D_\alpha(P_{XY}\|Q_X Q_Y) \tag{10}$$

$$= \min_{Q_Y} D_\alpha^1(P_{Y|X}\|Q_Y|P_X), \tag{11}$$

where (11) is proved in Proposition 5.

The first part of the paper is structured as follows: In Section 2, we discuss some preliminaries. In Sections 3–5, we study the properties of the three conditional Rényi divergences and their associated measure of dependence. In Section 6, we express the Arimoto–Rényi conditional entropy $H_\alpha(X|Y)$ and the Arimoto measure of dependence $I_\alpha^a(X;Y)$ [12] in terms of $D_\alpha^1(P_{X|Y}\|U_X|P_Y)$. In Section 7, we relate the conditional Rényi divergences to each other and discuss the relations between the Rényi dependence measures.

The second part of the paper deals with horse gambling under our proposed family of power-mean utility functions. It is in this context that the Rényi divergence (Theorem 9) and the conditional Rényi divergence $D_\alpha^1(\cdot)$ (Theorem 10) appear naturally.

More specifically, consider a horse race with a finite nonempty set of horses $\mathcal{X}$, where a bookmaker offers odds $o(x)$-for-1 on each horse $x \in \mathcal{X}$, where $o\colon \mathcal{X} \to (0, \infty)$ [2] (Section 6.1). A gambler spends all her wealth placing bets on the horses. The fraction of her wealth that she bets on Horse $x \in \mathcal{X}$ is denoted $b(x) \geq 0$, which sums up to 1 over $x \in \mathcal{X}$, and the PMF b is her "betting strategy." The winning horse, which we denote X, is drawn according to the PMF p, where we assume $p(x) > 0$ for all $x \in \mathcal{X}$. The wealth relative (or end-to-beginning wealth ratio) is the random variable

$$S \triangleq b(X)o(X). \tag{12}$$

Hence, given an initial wealth γ, the gambler's wealth after the race is γS. We seek betting strategies that maximize the utility function

$$U_\beta \triangleq \begin{cases} \frac{1}{\beta} \log \mathrm{E}[S^\beta] & \text{if } \beta \neq 0, \\ \mathrm{E}[\log S] & \text{if } \beta = 0, \end{cases} \tag{13}$$

where $\beta \in \mathbb{R}$ is a parameter that accounts for the risk sensitivity. This optimization generalizes the following cases:

(a) In the limit as β tends to $-\infty$, we optimize the worst-case return. The optimal strategy is risk-free in the sense that S does not depend on the winning horse (see Proposition 8).

(b) If $\beta = 0$, then we optimize $\mathrm{E}[\log S]$, which is known as the doubling rate [2] (Section 6.1). The optimal strategy is proportional betting, i.e., to choose $b = p$ (see Remark 4).

(c) If $\beta = 1$, then we optimize $\mathrm{E}[S]$, the expected return. The optimal strategy is to put all the money on a horse that maximizes $p(x)o(x)$ (see Proposition 9).

(d) In general, if $\beta \geq 1$, then it is optimal to put all the money on one horse (see Proposition 9). This is risky: if that horse loses, the gambler will go broke.

(e) In the limit as β tends to $+\infty$, we optimize the best-case return. The optimal strategy is to put all the money on a horse that maximizes $o(x)$ (see Proposition 10).

Note that, for $\beta \neq 0$ and $\eta \triangleq 1 - \beta$, maximizing U_β is equivalent to maximizing

$$\mathrm{E}\left[\frac{S^{1-\eta}}{1-\eta}\right], \tag{14}$$

which is known in the finance literature as Constant Relative Risk Aversion (CRRA) [13,14].

We refer to our utility function as "power mean" because it can be written as the logarithm of a weighted power mean [15,16]:

$$U_\beta = \log\left[\sum_x p(x)\left(b(x)o(x)\right)^\beta\right]^{\frac{1}{\beta}}. \tag{15}$$

Because the power mean tends to the geometric mean as β tends to zero [15] (Problem 8.1), U_β is continuous at $\beta = 0$:

$$\lim_{\beta \to 0} U_\beta = \log \prod_x \left(b(x)o(x)\right)^{p(x)} \tag{16}$$

$$= \mathrm{E}[\log S]. \tag{17}$$

Campbell [17,18] used an exponential cost function with a similar structure to (15) to provide an operational meaning to the Rényi entropy in source coding. Other information-theoretic applications of exponential moments were studied in [19].

The second part of the paper is structured as follows: In Section 8, we relate the utility function U_β to the Rényi divergence (Theorem 9) and derive its optimal gambling strategy. In Section 9, we consider the situation where the gambler observes side information prior to betting, a situation that leads to the conditional Rényi divergence $D_\alpha^1(\cdot)$ (Theorem 10) and to a new operational meaning for the measure of dependence $J_\alpha(X;Y)$ (Theorem 11). In Section 10, we consider the situation where the gambler invests only part of her money. In Section 11, we present a universal strategy for independent and identically distributed (IID) races that requires neither knowledge of the winning probabilities nor of the parameter β of the utility function and yet asymptotically maximizes the utility function for all PMFs p and all $\beta \in \mathbb{R}$.

2. Preliminaries

Throughout the paper, $\log(\cdot)$ denotes the base-2 logarithm, $\mathcal{X}$ and $\mathcal{Y}$ are finite sets, P_{XY} denotes a joint PMF over $\mathcal{X} \times \mathcal{Y}$, Q_X denotes a PMF over $\mathcal{X}$, and Q_Y denotes a PMF over $\mathcal{Y}$. An expression of the form $P_X P_{Y|X}$ denotes the PMF on $\mathcal{X} \times \mathcal{Y}$ that assigns (x,y) the probability $P_X(x) P_{Y|X}(y|x)$. We use P and Q as generic PMFs over a finite set $\mathcal{X}$. We denote by $\mathrm{supp}(P) \triangleq \{x \in \mathcal{X} : P(x) > 0\}$ the support of P, and by $\mathcal{P}(\mathcal{X})$ the set of all PMFs over $\mathcal{X}$. When clear from the context, we often omit sets and subscripts: for example, we write $\sum_x$ for $\sum_{x \in \mathcal{X}}$, $\min_{Q_X, Q_Y}$ for $\min_{(Q_X, Q_Y) \in \mathcal{P}(\mathcal{X}) \times \mathcal{P}(\mathcal{Y})}$, $P(x)$ for $P_X(x)$, and $P(y|x)$ for $P_{Y|X}(y|x)$. When $P(x)$ is 0, we define the conditional probability $P(y|x)$ as $1/|\mathcal{Y}|$. The conditional distribution of Y given $X = x$ is denoted by $P_{Y|X=x}$, thus

$$P_{Y|X=x}(y) = P(y|x). \tag{18}$$

We denote by $\mathbb{1}\{\text{condition}\}$ the indicator function that is one if the condition is satisfied and zero otherwise.

In the definition of the Kullback–Leibler divergence in (1), we use the conventions

$$0 \log \frac{0}{q} = 0 \quad \forall q \geq 0, \qquad p \log \frac{p}{0} = \infty \quad \forall p > 0. \tag{19}$$

In the definition of the Rényi divergence in (4), we read $P(x)^\alpha Q(x)^{1-\alpha}$ as $P(x)^\alpha / Q(x)^{\alpha-1}$ for $\alpha > 1$ and use the conventions

$$\frac{0}{0} = 0, \qquad \frac{p}{0} = \infty \quad \forall p > 0. \tag{20}$$

For α being zero, one, or infinity, we define by continuous extension of (4)

$$D_0(P\|Q) \triangleq -\log \sum_{x \in \mathrm{supp}(P)} Q(x), \tag{21}$$

$$D_1(P\|Q) \triangleq D(P\|Q), \tag{22}$$

$$D_\infty(P\|Q) \triangleq \log \max_x \frac{P(x)}{Q(x)}. \tag{23}$$

The Rényi divergence for negative α is defined as

$$D_\alpha(P\|Q) \triangleq \frac{1}{\alpha - 1} \log \sum_x \frac{Q(x)^{1-\alpha}}{P(x)^{-\alpha}}. \tag{24}$$

(We use negative α in the proof of Proposition 1 (e) below and in Remark 6. More about negative orders can be found in [8] (Section V). For other applications of negative orders, see [20] (Proof of Theorem 1 and Example 1).)

The Rényi divergence satisfies the following basic properties:

Proposition 1. *Let P and Q be PMFs. Then, the Rényi divergence $D_\alpha(P\|Q)$ satisfies the following:*

(a) *For all $\alpha \in [0,\infty]$, $D_\alpha(P\|Q) \geq 0$. If $\alpha \in (0,\infty]$, then $D_\alpha(P\|Q) = 0$ if and only if $P = Q$.*

(b) *For all $\alpha \in [0,1)$, $D_\alpha(P\|Q)$ is finite if and only if $|\mathrm{supp}(P) \cap \mathrm{supp}(Q)| > 0$. For all $\alpha \in [1,\infty]$, $D_\alpha(P\|Q)$ is finite if and only if $\mathrm{supp}(P) \subseteq \mathrm{supp}(Q)$.*

(c) *The mapping $\alpha \mapsto D_\alpha(P\|Q)$ is continuous on $[0,\infty]$.*

(d) *The mapping $\alpha \mapsto D_\alpha(P\|Q)$ is nondecreasing on $[0,\infty]$.*

(e) *The mapping $\alpha \mapsto \frac{1-\alpha}{\alpha} D_\alpha(P\|Q)$ is nonincreasing on $(0,\infty)$.*

(f) *The mapping $\alpha \mapsto (1-\alpha) D_\alpha(P\|Q)$ is concave on $[0,\infty)$.*

(g) *The mapping $\alpha \mapsto (\alpha-1) D_{1/\alpha}(P\|Q)$ is concave on $(0,\infty)$.*

(h) *(Data-processing inequality.) Let $A_{X'|X}$ be a conditional PMF, and define the PMFs*

$$P'(x') \triangleq \sum_x P(x) A_{X'|X}(x'|x), \tag{25}$$

$$Q'(x') \triangleq \sum_x Q(x) A_{X'|X}(x'|x). \tag{26}$$

Then, for all $\alpha \in [0,\infty]$,

$$D_\alpha(P'\|Q') \leq D_\alpha(P\|Q). \tag{27}$$

Proof. See Appendix A. □

All three conditional Rényi divergences reduce to the unconditional Rényi divergence when both $P_{Y|X}$ and $Q_{Y|X}$ are independent of X:

Remark 1. *Let P_Y, Q_Y, and P_X be PMFs. Then, for all $\alpha \in [0,\infty]$,*

$$D_\alpha^{\mathrm{c}}(P_Y\|Q_Y|P_X) = D_\alpha^{\mathrm{s}}(P_Y\|Q_Y|P_X) = D_\alpha^{\mathrm{1}}(P_Y\|Q_Y|P_X) = D_\alpha(P_Y\|Q_Y). \tag{28}$$

Proof. This follows from the definitions of $D_\alpha^{\mathrm{c}}(\cdot)$, $D_\alpha^{\mathrm{s}}(\cdot)$, and $D_\alpha^{\mathrm{1}}(\cdot)$ in (5)–(7). □

3. Csiszár's Conditional Rényi Divergence

For a PMF P_X and conditional PMFs $P_{Y|X}$ and $Q_{Y|X}$, Csiszár's conditional Rényi divergence $D_\alpha^{\mathrm{c}}(\cdot)$ is defined for every $\alpha \in [0,\infty]$ as

$$D_\alpha^{\mathrm{c}}(P_{Y|X}\|Q_{Y|X}|P_X) \triangleq \sum_{x \in \mathrm{supp}(P_X)} P(x) D_\alpha(P_{Y|X=x}\|Q_{Y|X=x}). \tag{29}$$

For $\alpha \in (0,1) \cup (1,\infty)$,

$$D_\alpha^{\mathrm{c}}(P_{Y|X}\|Q_{Y|X}|P_X) = \frac{1}{\alpha-1} \sum_{x \in \mathrm{supp}(P_X)} P(x) \log \sum_y P(y|x)^\alpha Q(y|x)^{1-\alpha}, \tag{30}$$

which follows from the definition of the Rényi divergence in (4). For α being zero, one, or infinity, we obtain from (21)–(23) and (2)

$$D_0^c(P_{Y|X}\|Q_{Y|X}|P_X) = -\sum_{x\in\mathrm{supp}(P_X)} P(x)\log \sum_{y\in\mathrm{supp}(P_{Y|X=x})} Q(y|x), \tag{31}$$

$$D_1^c(P_{Y|X}\|Q_{Y|X}|P_X) = D(P_{Y|X}\|Q_{Y|X}|P_X), \tag{32}$$

$$D_\infty^c(P_{Y|X}\|Q_{Y|X}|P_X) = \sum_{x\in\mathrm{supp}(P_X)} P(x)\log\max_y \frac{P(y|x)}{Q(y|x)}. \tag{33}$$

Augustin [21] and later Csiszár [9] defined the measure of dependence

$$I_\alpha^c(X;Y) \triangleq \min_{Q_Y} D_\alpha^c(P_{Y|X}\|Q_Y|P_X). \tag{34}$$

Augustin used this measure to study the error exponents for channel coding with input constraints, while Csiszár used it to study generalized cutoff rates for channel coding with composition constraints. Nakiboğlu [22] studied more properties of $I_\alpha^c(X;Y)$. Inter alia, he analyzed the minimax properties of the Augustin capacity

$$\sup_{P_X\in\mathcal{A}} I_\alpha^c(P_X, P_{Y|X}) = \sup_{P_X\in\mathcal{A}} \min_{Q_Y} D_\alpha^c(P_{Y|X}\|Q_Y|P_X), \tag{35}$$

where $\mathcal{A} \subseteq \mathcal{P}(\mathcal{X})$ is a constraint set. The Augustin capacity is used in [23] to establish the sphere packing bound for memoryless channels with cost constraints.

The rest of the section presents some properties of $D_\alpha^c(\cdot)$. Being an average of Rényi divergences (see (29)), $D_\alpha^c(\cdot)$ inherits many properties from the Rényi divergence:

Proposition 2. *Let P_X be a PMF, and let $P_{Y|X}$ and $Q_{Y|X}$ be conditional PMFs. Then,*

(a) *For all $\alpha \in [0,\infty]$, $D_\alpha^c(P_{Y|X}\|Q_{Y|X}|P_X) \geq 0$. If $\alpha \in (0,\infty]$, then $D_\alpha^c(P_{Y|X}\|Q_{Y|X}|P_X) = 0$ if and only if $(P_{Y|X=x} = Q_{Y|X=x}$ for all $x \in \mathrm{supp}(P_X))$.*

(b) *For all $\alpha \in [0,1)$, $D_\alpha^c(P_{Y|X}\|Q_{Y|X}|P_X)$ is finite if and only if $(|\mathrm{supp}(P_{Y|X=x}) \cap \mathrm{supp}(Q_{Y|X=x})| > 0$ for all $x \in \mathrm{supp}(P_X))$. For all $\alpha \in [1,\infty]$, $D_\alpha^c(P_{Y|X}\|Q_{Y|X}|P_X)$ is finite if and only if $(\mathrm{supp}(P_{Y|X=x}) \subseteq \mathrm{supp}(Q_{Y|X=x})$ for all $x \in \mathrm{supp}(P_X))$.*

(c) *The mapping $\alpha \mapsto D_\alpha^c(P_{Y|X}\|Q_{Y|X}|P_X)$ is continuous on $[0,\infty]$.*

(d) *The mapping $\alpha \mapsto D_\alpha^c(P_{Y|X}\|Q_{Y|X}|P_X)$ is nondecreasing on $[0,\infty]$.*

(e) *The mapping $\alpha \mapsto \frac{1-\alpha}{\alpha} D_\alpha^c(P_{Y|X}\|Q_{Y|X}|P_X)$ is nonincreasing on $(0,\infty)$.*

(f) *The mapping $\alpha \mapsto (1-\alpha) D_\alpha^c(P_{Y|X}\|Q_{Y|X}|P_X)$ is concave on $[0,\infty)$.*

(g) *The mapping $\alpha \mapsto (\alpha-1) D_{1/\alpha}^c(P_{Y|X}\|Q_{Y|X}|P_X)$ is concave on $(0,\infty)$.*

Proof. These follow from (29) and the properties of the Rényi divergence (Proposition 1). For Parts (f) and (g), recall that a nonnegative weighted sum of concave functions is concave. □

We next consider data-processing inequalities for $D_\alpha^c(\cdot)$. We distinguish between processing Y and processing X. The data-processing inequality for processing Y follows from the data-processing inequality for the (unconditional) Rényi divergence:

Theorem 1. *Let P_X be a PMF, and let $P_{Y|X}$ and $Q_{Y|X}$ be conditional PMFs. For a conditional PMF $A_{Y'|XY}$, define*

$$P_{Y'|X}(y'|x) \triangleq \sum_y P_{Y|X}(y|x) A_{Y'|XY}(y'|x,y), \tag{36}$$

$$Q_{Y'|X}(y'|x) \triangleq \sum_y Q_{Y|X}(y|x) A_{Y'|XY}(y'|x,y). \tag{37}$$

Then, for all $\alpha \in [0,\infty]$,

$$D_\alpha^c(P_{Y'|X} \| Q_{Y'|X} | P_X) \leq D_\alpha^c(P_{Y|X} \| Q_{Y|X} | P_X). \tag{38}$$

Proof. See Appendix B. □

The following data-processing inequality for processing X holds for $\alpha \in [0,1]$ (as shown in Example 1 below, it does not extend to $\alpha \in (1,\infty]$):

Theorem 2. *Let P_X be a PMF, and let $P_{Y|X}$ and $Q_{Y|X}$ be conditional PMFs. For a conditional PMF $B_{X'|X}$, define the PMFs*

$$P_{X'}(x') \triangleq \sum_x P_X(x) B_{X'|X}(x'|x), \tag{39}$$

$$B_{X|X'}(x|x') \triangleq \begin{cases} P_X(x) B_{X'|X}(x'|x)/P_{X'}(x') & \text{if } P_{X'}(x') > 0, \\ 1/|\mathcal{X}| & \text{otherwise,} \end{cases} \tag{40}$$

$$P_{Y|X'}(y|x') \triangleq \sum_x B_{X|X'}(x|x') P_{Y|X}(y|x), \tag{41}$$

$$Q_{Y|X'}(y|x') \triangleq \sum_x B_{X|X'}(x|x') Q_{Y|X}(y|x). \tag{42}$$

Then, for all $\alpha \in [0,1]$,

$$D_\alpha^c(P_{Y|X'} \| Q_{Y|X'} | P_{X'}) \leq D_\alpha^c(P_{Y|X} \| Q_{Y|X} | P_X). \tag{43}$$

Note that $P_{X'}$, $P_{Y|X'}$, and $Q_{Y|X'}$ in Theorem 2 can be obtained from the following marginalizations:

$$P_{X'}(x') P_{Y|X'}(y|x') = \sum_x P_X(x) B_{X'|X}(x'|x) P_{Y|X}(y|x), \tag{44}$$

$$P_{X'}(x') Q_{Y|X'}(y|x') = \sum_x P_X(x) B_{X'|X}(x'|x) Q_{Y|X}(y|x). \tag{45}$$

Proof of Theorem 2. See Appendix C. □

As a special case of Theorem 2, we obtain the following relation between the conditional and the unconditional Rényi divergence:

Corollary 1. *For a PMF P_X and conditional PMFs $P_{Y|X}$ and $Q_{Y|X}$, define the marginal PMFs*

$$P_Y(y) \triangleq \sum_x P_X(x) P_{Y|X}(y|x), \tag{46}$$

$$Q_Y(y) \triangleq \sum_x P_X(x) Q_{Y|X}(y|x). \tag{47}$$

Then, for all $\alpha \in [0,1]$,

$$D_\alpha(P_Y \| Q_Y) \leq D_\alpha^c(P_{Y|X} \| Q_{Y|X} | P_X). \tag{48}$$

Proof. See Appendix D. □

Consider next $\alpha \in (1, \infty]$. It turns out that Corollary 1, and hence Theorem 2, cannot be extended to these values of α (not even if $Q_{Y|X}$ is restricted to be independent of X, i.e., if $Q_{Y|X} = Q_Y$):

Example 1. *Let $\mathcal{X} = \mathcal{Y} = \{0, 1\}$. For $\epsilon \in (0, 1)$, define the PMFs P_X, $Q_Y^{(\epsilon)}$, and $P_{Y|X}^{(\epsilon)}$ as*

$$P_X(0) = 0.5, \qquad P_X(1) = 0.5, \tag{49}$$

$$Q_Y^{(\epsilon)}(0) = 1 - \epsilon, \qquad Q_Y^{(\epsilon)}(1) = \epsilon, \tag{50}$$

$$P_{Y|X}^{(\epsilon)}(0|0) = 1 - \epsilon, \qquad P_{Y|X}^{(\epsilon)}(1|0) = \epsilon, \tag{51}$$

$$P_{Y|X}^{(\epsilon)}(0|1) = \epsilon, \qquad P_{Y|X}^{(\epsilon)}(1|1) = 1 - \epsilon. \tag{52}$$

Then, for every $\alpha \in (1, \infty]$, there exists an $\epsilon \in (0, 1)$ such that

$$D_\alpha(P_Y \| Q_Y^{(\epsilon)}) > D_\alpha^c(P_{Y|X}^{(\epsilon)} \| Q_Y^{(\epsilon)} | P_X), \tag{53}$$

where the PMF P_Y is defined by (46) and, irrespective of ϵ, satisfies $P_Y(0) = P_Y(1) = 0.5$.

Proof. See Appendix E. □

4. Sibson's Conditional Rényi Divergence

For a PMF P_X and conditional PMFs $P_{Y|X}$ and $Q_{Y|X}$, Sibson's conditional Rényi divergence $D_\alpha^s(\cdot)$ is defined for every $\alpha \in [0, \infty]$ as

$$D_\alpha^s(P_{Y|X} \| Q_{Y|X} | P_X) \triangleq D_\alpha(P_X P_{Y|X} \| P_X Q_{Y|X}). \tag{54}$$

For $\alpha \in (0, 1) \cup (1, \infty)$,

$$D_\alpha^s(P_{Y|X} \| Q_{Y|X} | P_X) = \frac{1}{\alpha - 1} \log \sum_{x \in \text{supp}(P_X)} P(x) \sum_y P(y|x)^\alpha Q(y|x)^{1-\alpha} \tag{55}$$

$$= \frac{1}{\alpha - 1} \log \sum_{x \in \text{supp}(P_X)} P(x) 2^{(\alpha-1) D_\alpha(P_{Y|X=x} \| Q_{Y|X=x})}, \tag{56}$$

where (55) and (56) follow from the definition of the Rényi divergence in (4). For α being zero, one, or infinity, we obtain from (21)–(23) and (3)

$$D_0^s(P_{Y|X} \| Q_{Y|X} | P_X) = -\log \sum_{x \in \text{supp}(P_X)} P(x) \sum_{y \in \text{supp}(P_{Y|X=x})} Q(y|x), \tag{57}$$

$$D_1^s(P_{Y|X} \| Q_{Y|X} | P_X) = D(P_{Y|X} \| Q_{Y|X} | P_X), \tag{58}$$

$$D_\infty^s(P_{Y|X} \| Q_{Y|X} | P_X) = \log \max_{x \in \text{supp}(P_X)} \max_y \frac{P(y|x)}{Q(y|x)}. \tag{59}$$

Sibson [10] defined the measure of dependence

$$I_\alpha^s(X; Y) \triangleq \min_{Q_Y} D_\alpha^s(P_{Y|X} \| Q_Y | P_X). \tag{60}$$

This minimum can be computed explicitly [10] (Corollary 2.3): For $\alpha \in (0, 1) \cup (1, \infty)$,

$$I_\alpha^s(X; Y) = \frac{\alpha}{\alpha - 1} \log \sum_y \left[\sum_x P(x) P(y|x)^\alpha \right]^{\frac{1}{\alpha}}, \tag{61}$$

and for α being one or infinity,

$$I_1^s(X;Y) = I(X;Y), \tag{62}$$
$$I_\infty^s(X;Y) = \log \sum_y \max_x P(y|x), \tag{63}$$

where $I(X;Y)$ denotes Shannon's mutual information.

The concavity and convexity properties of $D_\alpha^s(\cdot)$ and $I_\alpha^s(X;Y)$ were studied by Ho–Verdú [24]. More properties of $I_\alpha^s(X;Y)$ were collected by Verdú [25]. The maximization of $I_\alpha^s(X;Y)$ with respect to P_X and the minimax properties of $D_\alpha^s(\cdot)$ were studied by Nakiboğlu [26] and Cai–Verdú [27].

The conditional Rényi divergence $D_\alpha^s(\cdot)$ was used by Fong and Tan [28] to establish strong converse theorems for multicast networks. Yu and Tan [29] analyzed channel resolvability, among other measures, in terms of $D_\alpha^s(\cdot)$.

From (61) we see that Gallager's E_0 function [11], which is defined as

$$E_0(\rho, P_X, P_{Y|X}) \triangleq -\log \sum_y \left[\sum_x P(x) P(y|x)^{\frac{1}{1+\rho}} \right]^{1+\rho}, \tag{64}$$

is in one-to-one correspondence to Sibson's measure of dependence:

$$I_\alpha^s(X;Y) = \frac{\alpha}{1-\alpha} E_0\left(\frac{1-\alpha}{\alpha}, P_X, P_{Y|X}\right). \tag{65}$$

Gallager's E_0 function is important in channel coding: it appears in the random coding exponent [30] and in the sphere packing exponent [31,32] (see also Gallager [11]). The exponential strong converse theorem proved by Arimoto [33] also uses the E_0 function. Polyanskiy and Verdú [34] extended the exponential strong converse theorem to channels with feedback. Augustin [21] and Nakiboğlu [35,36] extended the sphere packing bound to channels with feedback.

The rest of the section presents some properties of $D_\alpha^s(\cdot)$. Because $D_\alpha^s(\cdot)$ can be written as an (unconditional) Rényi divergence (see (54)), it inherits many properties from the Rényi divergence:

Proposition 3. *Let P_X be a PMF, and let $P_{Y|X}$ and $Q_{Y|X}$ be conditional PMFs. Then,*

(a) *For all $\alpha \in [0,\infty]$, $D_\alpha^s(P_{Y|X}\|Q_{Y|X}|P_X) \geq 0$. If $\alpha \in (0,\infty]$, then $D_\alpha^s(P_{Y|X}\|Q_{Y|X}|P_X) = 0$ if and only if $\bigl(P_{Y|X=x} = Q_{Y|X=x}$ for all $x \in \mathrm{supp}(P_X)\bigr)$.*

(b) *For all $\alpha \in [0,1)$, $D_\alpha^s(P_{Y|X}\|Q_{Y|X}|P_X)$ is finite if and only if $\bigl($there exists an $x \in \mathrm{supp}(P_X)$ such that $|\mathrm{supp}(P_{Y|X=x}) \cap \mathrm{supp}(Q_{Y|X=x})| > 0\bigr)$. For all $\alpha \in [1,\infty]$, $D_\alpha^s(P_{Y|X}\|Q_{Y|X}|P_X)$ is finite if and only if $\bigl(\mathrm{supp}(P_{Y|X=x}) \subseteq \mathrm{supp}(Q_{Y|X=x})$ for all $x \in \mathrm{supp}(P_X)\bigr)$.*

(c) *The mapping $\alpha \mapsto D_\alpha^s(P_{Y|X}\|Q_{Y|X}|P_X)$ is continuous on $[0,\infty]$.*

(d) *The mapping $\alpha \mapsto D_\alpha^s(P_{Y|X}\|Q_{Y|X}|P_X)$ is nondecreasing on $[0,\infty]$.*

(e) *The mapping $\alpha \mapsto \frac{1-\alpha}{\alpha} D_\alpha^s(P_{Y|X}\|Q_{Y|X}|P_X)$ is nonincreasing on $(0,\infty)$.*

(f) *The mapping $\alpha \mapsto (1-\alpha) D_\alpha^s(P_{Y|X}\|Q_{Y|X}|P_X)$ is concave on $[0,\infty)$.*

(g) *The mapping $\alpha \mapsto (\alpha - 1) D_{1/\alpha}^s(P_{Y|X}\|Q_{Y|X}|P_X)$ is concave on $(0,\infty)$.*

Proof. These follow from (54) and the properties of the Rényi divergence (Proposition 1). □

We next consider data-processing inequalities for $D_\alpha^s(\cdot)$. We distinguish between processing Y and processing X. The data-processing inequality for processing Y follows from the data-processing inequality for the (unconditional) Rényi divergence:

Theorem 3. Let P_X be a PMF, and let $P_{Y|X}$ and $Q_{Y|X}$ be conditional PMFs. For a conditional PMF $A_{Y'|XY}$, define

$$P_{Y'|X}(y'|x) \triangleq \sum_y P_{Y|X}(y|x) A_{Y'|XY}(y'|x,y), \tag{66}$$

$$Q_{Y'|X}(y'|x) \triangleq \sum_y Q_{Y|X}(y|x) A_{Y'|XY}(y'|x,y). \tag{67}$$

Then, for all $\alpha \in [0,\infty]$,

$$D_\alpha^{\mathsf{s}}(P_{Y'|X} \| Q_{Y'|X} | P_X) \leq D_\alpha^{\mathsf{s}}(P_{Y|X} \| Q_{Y|X} | P_X). \tag{68}$$

Proof. See Appendix F. □

The data-processing inequality for processing X similarly follows from the data-processing inequality for the (unconditional) Rényi divergence:

Theorem 4. Let P_X be a PMF, and let $P_{Y|X}$ and $Q_{Y|X}$ be conditional PMFs. For a conditional PMF $B_{X'|X}$, define the PMFs

$$P_{X'}(x') \triangleq \sum_x P_X(x) B_{X'|X}(x'|x), \tag{69}$$

$$B_{X|X'}(x|x') \triangleq \begin{cases} P_X(x) B_{X'|X}(x'|x)/P_{X'}(x') & \text{if } P_{X'}(x') > 0, \\ 1/|\mathcal{X}| & \text{otherwise,} \end{cases} \tag{70}$$

$$P_{Y|X'}(y|x') \triangleq \sum_x B_{X|X'}(x|x') P_{Y|X}(y|x), \tag{71}$$

$$Q_{Y|X'}(y|x') \triangleq \sum_x B_{X|X'}(x|x') Q_{Y|X}(y|x). \tag{72}$$

Then, for all $\alpha \in [0,\infty]$,

$$D_\alpha^{\mathsf{s}}(P_{Y|X'} \| Q_{Y|X'} | P_{X'}) \leq D_\alpha^{\mathsf{s}}(P_{Y|X} \| Q_{Y|X} | P_X). \tag{73}$$

Proof. See Appendix G. □

As a special case of Theorem 4, we obtain the following relation between the conditional and the unconditional Rényi divergence:

Corollary 2. Let P_X be a PMF, and let $P_{Y|X}$ and $Q_{Y|X}$ be conditional PMFs. Define the marginal PMFs

$$P_Y(y) \triangleq \sum_x P_X(x) P_{Y|X}(y|x), \tag{74}$$

$$Q_Y(y) \triangleq \sum_x P_X(x) Q_{Y|X}(y|x). \tag{75}$$

Then, for all $\alpha \in [0,\infty]$,

$$D_\alpha(P_Y \| Q_Y) \leq D_\alpha^{\mathsf{s}}(P_{Y|X} \| Q_{Y|X} | P_X). \tag{76}$$

Proof. This follows from Theorem 4 in the same way that Corollary 1 followed from Theorem 2. □

5. New Conditional Rényi Divergence

Let P_X be a PMF, and let $P_{Y|X}$ and $Q_{Y|X}$ be conditional PMFs. For $\alpha \in (0,1) \cup (1, \infty)$, define

$$D_\alpha^1(P_{Y|X}\|Q_{Y|X}|P_X) \triangleq \frac{\alpha}{\alpha-1} \log \sum_{x \in \mathrm{supp}(P_X)} P(x) 2^{\frac{\alpha-1}{\alpha} D_\alpha(P_{Y|X=x}\|Q_{Y|X=x})} \tag{77}$$

$$= \frac{\alpha}{\alpha-1} \log \sum_{x \in \mathrm{supp}(P_X)} P(x) \left[\sum_y P(y|x)^\alpha Q(y|x)^{1-\alpha}\right]^{\frac{1}{\alpha}}, \tag{78}$$

where (78) follows from the definition of the Rényi divergence in (4). (Except for the sign, the exponential averaging in (77) is very similar to the one of the Arimoto–Rényi conditional entropy; compare with (147) below.) For α being zero, one, or infinity, we define by continuous extension of (77)

$$D_0^1(P_{Y|X}\|Q_{Y|X}|P_X) \triangleq -\log \max_{x \in \mathrm{supp}(P_X)} \sum_{y \in \mathrm{supp}(P_{Y|X=x})} Q(y|x), \tag{79}$$

$$D_1^1(P_{Y|X}\|Q_{Y|X}|P_X) \triangleq D(P_{Y|X}\|Q_{Y|X}|P_X), \tag{80}$$

$$D_\infty^1(P_{Y|X}\|Q_{Y|X}|P_X) \triangleq \log \sum_{x \in \mathrm{supp}(P_X)} P(x) \max_y \frac{P(y|x)}{Q(y|x)}. \tag{81}$$

This conditional Rényi divergence has an operational meaning in horse betting with side information (see Theorem 10 below). Before discussing the measure of dependence associated with $D_\alpha^1(\cdot)$, we establish the following alternative characterization of $D_\alpha^1(\cdot)$:

Proposition 4. *Let P_X be a PMF, and let $P_{Y|X}$ and $Q_{Y|X}$ be conditional PMFs. Then, for all $\alpha \in [0, \infty]$,*

$$D_\alpha^1(P_{Y|X}\|Q_{Y|X}|P_X) = \min_{Q_X} D_\alpha(P_X P_{Y|X}\|Q_X Q_{Y|X}). \tag{82}$$

Proof. We first treat the case $\alpha \in (0,1) \cup (1,\infty)$. Some algebra reveals that, for every PMF Q_X,

$$D_\alpha(P_X P_{Y|X}\|Q_X Q_{Y|X}) = D_\alpha(Q_X^{*(\alpha)}\|Q_X) + \frac{\alpha}{\alpha-1} \log \sum_{x \in \mathrm{supp}(P_X)} P(x) \left[\sum_y P(y|x)^\alpha Q(y|x)^{1-\alpha}\right]^{\frac{1}{\alpha}}, \tag{83}$$

where the PMF $Q_X^{*(\alpha)}$ is defined as

$$Q_X^{*(\alpha)}(x) \triangleq \frac{P(x)\left[\sum_y P(y|x)^\alpha Q(y|x)^{1-\alpha}\right]^{1/\alpha}}{\sum_{x' \in \mathrm{supp}(P_X)} P(x')\left[\sum_y P(y|x')^\alpha Q(y|x')^{1-\alpha}\right]^{1/\alpha}}. \tag{84}$$

The right-hand side (RHS) of (82) is thus equal to the minimum over Q_X of the RHS of (83). Since $D_\alpha(Q_X^{*(\alpha)}\|Q_X) \geq 0$ with equality if $Q_X = Q_X^{*(\alpha)}$ (Proposition 1 (a)), this minimum is equal to the second term on the RHS of (83), which, by (78), equals $D_\alpha^1(P_{Y|X}\|Q_{Y|X}|P_X)$.

For $\alpha = 1$ and $\alpha = \infty$, (82) follows from the same argument using that, for every PMF Q_X,

$$D_1(P_X P_{Y|X}\|Q_X Q_{Y|X}) = D(P_X\|Q_X) + D(P_{Y|X}\|Q_{Y|X}|P_X), \tag{85}$$

$$D_\infty(P_X P_{Y|X}\|Q_X Q_{Y|X}) = D_\infty(Q_X^{*(\infty)}\|Q_X) + \log \sum_{x \in \mathrm{supp}(P_X)} P(x) \max_y \frac{P(y|x)}{Q(y|x)}, \tag{86}$$

where the PMF $Q_X^{*(\infty)}$ is defined as

$$Q_X^{*(\infty)}(x) \triangleq \frac{P(x) \max_y [P(y|x)/Q(y|x)]}{\sum_{x' \in \mathrm{supp}(P_X)} P(x') \max_y [P(y|x')/Q(y|x')]}. \tag{87}$$

For $\alpha = 0$, (82) holds because

$$\min_{Q_X} D_0(P_X P_{Y|X} \| Q_X Q_{Y|X}) = \min_{Q_X} -\log \sum_{x \in \mathrm{supp}(P_X)} Q(x) \sum_{y \in \mathrm{supp}(P_{Y|X=x})} Q(y|x) \tag{88}$$

$$= -\log \max_{Q_X} \sum_{x \in \mathrm{supp}(P_X)} Q(x) \sum_{y \in \mathrm{supp}(P_{Y|X=x})} Q(y|x) \tag{89}$$

$$= -\log \max_{x \in \mathrm{supp}(P_X)} \sum_{y \in \mathrm{supp}(P_{Y|X=x})} Q(y|x) \tag{90}$$

$$= D_0^1(P_{Y|X} \| Q_{Y|X} | P_X), \tag{91}$$

where (88) follows from the definition of $D_0(P \| Q)$ in (21), and (91) follows from (79). □

Tomamichel and Hayashi [37] and Lapidoth and Pfister [3] independently introduced and studied the dependence measure

$$J_\alpha(X;Y) \triangleq \min_{Q_X, Q_Y} D_\alpha(P_{XY} \| Q_X Q_Y). \tag{92}$$

(For some measure-theoretic properties of $J_\alpha(X;Y)$, see Aishwarya–Madiman [38].) The measure $J_\alpha(X;Y)$ can be related to the error exponents in a hypothesis testing problem where the samples are either from a known joint distribution or an unknown product distribution (see [37] (Equation (57)) and [39]). It also appears in horse betting with side information (see Theorem 11 below).

Similar to $I_\alpha^c(X;Y)$ in (34) and $I_\alpha^s(X;Y)$ in (60), the measure $J_\alpha(X;Y)$ can be expressed as a minimization involving the new conditional Rényi divergence:

Proposition 5. *Let P_{XY} be a joint PMF. Denote its marginal PMFs by P_X and P_Y and its conditional PMFs by $P_{Y|X}$ and $P_{X|Y}$, so $P_{XY} = P_X P_{Y|X} = P_Y P_{X|Y}$. Then, for all $\alpha \in [0, \infty]$,*

$$J_\alpha(X;Y) = \min_{Q_Y} D_\alpha^1(P_{Y|X} \| Q_Y | P_X) \tag{93}$$

$$= \min_{Q_X} D_\alpha^1(P_{X|Y} \| Q_X | P_Y). \tag{94}$$

Proof. Equation (93) holds because

$$\min_{Q_Y} D_\alpha^1(P_{Y|X} \| Q_Y | P_X) = \min_{Q_Y} \min_{Q_X} D_\alpha(P_X P_{Y|X} \| Q_X Q_Y) \tag{95}$$

$$= J_\alpha(X;Y), \tag{96}$$

where (95) follows from Proposition 4, and (96) follows from (92). Swapping the roles of X and Y establishes (94):

$$\min_{Q_X} D_\alpha^1(P_{X|Y} \| Q_X | P_Y) = \min_{Q_X} \min_{Q_Y} D_\alpha(P_Y P_{X|Y} \| Q_Y Q_X) \tag{97}$$

$$= J_\alpha(X;Y), \tag{98}$$

where (97) follows from Proposition 4, and (98) follows from (92). □

The rest of the section presents some properties of $D_\alpha^1(\cdot)$.

Proposition 6. Let P_X be a PMF, and let $P_{Y|X}$ and $Q_{Y|X}$ be conditional PMFs. Then,

(a) For all $\alpha \in [0, \infty]$, $D_\alpha^1(P_{Y|X} \| Q_{Y|X} | P_X) \geq 0$. If $\alpha \in (0, \infty]$, then $D_\alpha^1(P_{Y|X} \| Q_{Y|X} | P_X) = 0$ if and only if $(P_{Y|X=x} = Q_{Y|X=x}$ for all $x \in \text{supp}(P_X))$.

(b) For all $\alpha \in [0, 1)$, $D_\alpha^1(P_{Y|X} \| Q_{Y|X} | P_X)$ is finite if and only if (there exists an $x \in \text{supp}(P_X)$ such that $|\text{supp}(P_{Y|X=x}) \cap \text{supp}(Q_{Y|X=x})| > 0$). For all $\alpha \in [1, \infty]$, $D_\alpha^1(P_{Y|X} \| Q_{Y|X} | P_X)$ is finite if and only if $(\text{supp}(P_{Y|X=x}) \subseteq \text{supp}(Q_{Y|X=x})$ for all $x \in \text{supp}(P_X))$.

(c) The mapping $\alpha \mapsto D_\alpha^1(P_{Y|X} \| Q_{Y|X} | P_X)$ is continuous on $[0, \infty]$.

(d) The mapping $\alpha \mapsto D_\alpha^1(P_{Y|X} \| Q_{Y|X} | P_X)$ is nondecreasing on $[0, \infty]$.

(e) The mapping $\alpha \mapsto \frac{1-\alpha}{\alpha} D_\alpha^1(P_{Y|X} \| Q_{Y|X} | P_X)$ is nonincreasing on $(0, \infty)$.

(f) The mapping $\alpha \mapsto (1-\alpha) D_\alpha^1(P_{Y|X} \| Q_{Y|X} | P_X)$ is concave on $[0, 1]$.

(g) The mapping $\alpha \mapsto (\alpha - 1) D_{1/\alpha}^1(P_{Y|X} \| Q_{Y|X} | P_X)$ is concave on $[1, \infty)$.

Proof. We prove these properties as follows:

(a) For all $\alpha \in [0, \infty]$, Proposition 4 implies

$$D_\alpha^1(P_{Y|X} \| Q_{Y|X} | P_X) = \min_{Q_X} D_\alpha(P_X P_{Y|X} \| Q_X Q_{Y|X}). \tag{99}$$

The nonnegativity of $D_\alpha^1(\cdot)$ now follows from the nonnegativity of the Rényi divergence (Proposition 1 (a)). If $(P_{Y|X=x} = Q_{Y|X=x}$ for all $x \in \text{supp}(P_X))$, then $P_X P_{Y|X} = P_X Q_{Y|X}$. Hence, using $Q_X = P_X$ on the RHS of (99), $D_\alpha^1(P_{Y|X} \| Q_{Y|X} | P_X)$ equals zero. Conversely, if $\alpha \in (0, \infty]$ and $D_\alpha^1(\cdot) = 0$, then $P_X P_{Y|X} = Q_X Q_{Y|X}$ for some Q_X by Proposition 1 (a), which implies $(P_{Y|X=x} = Q_{Y|X=x}$ for all $x \in \text{supp}(P_X))$.

(b) This follows from the definitions in (77) and (79)–(81) and the conventions in (20).

(c) For $\alpha \in (0, 1) \cup (1, \infty)$, $D_\alpha^1(\cdot)$ is continuous because it is, by its definition in (77), a composition of continuous functions. The continuity at $\alpha = 1$ follows from a careful application of L'Hôpital's rule.

We next consider the continuity at $\alpha = 0$. Define $\tau \triangleq \min_{x \in \text{supp}(P_X)} P(x)$. Then, for all $\alpha \in (0, 1)$,

$$(\alpha - 1) D_\alpha^1(P_{Y|X} \| Q_{Y|X} | P_X) = \alpha \log \sum_{x \in \text{supp}(P_X)} P(x) 2^{\frac{\alpha-1}{\alpha} D_\alpha(P_{Y|X=x} \| Q_{Y|X=x})} \tag{100}$$

$$\geq \alpha \log \sum_{x \in \text{supp}(P_X)} \tau 2^{\frac{\alpha-1}{\alpha} D_\alpha(P_{Y|X=x} \| Q_{Y|X=x})} \tag{101}$$

$$\geq \alpha \log \max_{x \in \text{supp}(P_X)} \tau 2^{\frac{\alpha-1}{\alpha} D_\alpha(P_{Y|X=x} \| Q_{Y|X=x})} \tag{102}$$

$$= \alpha \log \tau + \max_{x \in \text{supp}(P_X)} (\alpha - 1) D_\alpha(P_{Y|X=x} \| Q_{Y|X=x}), \tag{103}$$

where (100) follows from the definition in (77). On the other hand, for all $\alpha \in (0, 1)$,

$$(\alpha - 1) D_\alpha^1(P_{Y|X} \| Q_{Y|X} | P_X) = \alpha \log \sum_{x \in \text{supp}(P_X)} P(x) 2^{\frac{\alpha-1}{\alpha} D_\alpha(P_{Y|X=x} \| Q_{Y|X=x})} \tag{104}$$

$$\leq \alpha \log \max_{x \in \text{supp}(P_X)} 2^{\frac{\alpha-1}{\alpha} D_\alpha(P_{Y|X=x} \| Q_{Y|X=x})} \tag{105}$$

$$= \max_{x \in \text{supp}(P_X)} (\alpha - 1) D_\alpha(P_{Y|X=x} \| Q_{Y|X=x}). \tag{106}$$

Because $\lim_{\alpha \to 0} \alpha \log \tau = 0$, it follows from (103) and (106) and the sandwich theorem that

$$\lim_{\alpha \downarrow 0} D_\alpha^1(P_{Y|X} \| Q_{Y|X} | P_X) = \lim_{\alpha \downarrow 0} \frac{1}{\alpha - 1} \max_{x \in \text{supp}(P_X)} (\alpha - 1) D_\alpha(P_{Y|X=x} \| Q_{Y|X=x}) \tag{107}$$

$$= -\log \max_{x \in \text{supp}(P_X)} \sum_{y \in \text{supp}(P_{Y|X=x})} Q(y|x), \tag{108}$$

where (108) follows from the continuity of the Rényi divergence (Proposition 1 (c)) and the definition of $D_0(P\|Q)$ in (21).

We conclude with the continuity at $\alpha = \infty$. Observe that

$$\lim_{\alpha \to \infty} D_\alpha^1(P_{Y|X} \| Q_{Y|X} | P_X) = \lim_{\alpha \to \infty} \frac{\alpha}{\alpha - 1} \log \sum_{x \in \text{supp}(P_X)} P(x) 2^{\frac{\alpha - 1}{\alpha} D_\alpha(P_{Y|X=x} \| Q_{Y|X=x})} \tag{109}$$

$$= \log \sum_{x \in \text{supp}(P_X)} P(x) 2^{\lim_{\alpha \to \infty} D_\alpha(P_{Y|X=x} \| Q_{Y|X=x})} \tag{110}$$

$$= \log \sum_{x \in \text{supp}(P_X)} P(x) \max_y \frac{P(y|x)}{Q(y|x)}, \tag{111}$$

where (109) follows from the definition in (77), and (111) follows from the continuity of the Rényi divergence (Proposition 1 (c)) and the definition of $D_\infty(P\|Q)$ in (23).

(d) For all $\alpha \in [0, \infty]$, Proposition 4 implies

$$D_\alpha^1(P_{Y|X} \| Q_{Y|X} | P_X) = \min_{Q_X} D_\alpha(P_X P_{Y|X} \| Q_X Q_{Y|X}). \tag{112}$$

Because $\alpha \mapsto D_\alpha(P\|Q)$ is nonincreasing on $[0, \infty]$ (Proposition 1 (d)) and because the pointwise minimum preserves the monotonicity, the mapping $\alpha \mapsto D_\alpha^1(\cdot)$ is nonincreasing on $[0, \infty]$.

(e) By Proposition 4,

$$\frac{1-\alpha}{\alpha} D_\alpha^1(P_{Y|X} \| Q_{Y|X} | P_X) = \begin{cases} \min_{Q_X} \frac{1-\alpha}{\alpha} D_\alpha(P_X P_{Y|X} \| Q_X Q_{Y|X}) & \text{if } \alpha \in (0, 1], \\ \max_{Q_X} \frac{1-\alpha}{\alpha} D_\alpha(P_X P_{Y|X} \| Q_X Q_{Y|X}) & \text{if } \alpha \in (1, \infty). \end{cases} \tag{113}$$

By the nonnegativity of the Rényi divergence (Proposition 1 (a)), the RHS of (113) is nonnegative for $\alpha \in (0, 1]$ and nonpositive for $\alpha \in (1, \infty)$. Hence, it suffices to show separately that the mapping $\alpha \mapsto \frac{1-\alpha}{\alpha} D_\alpha^1(P_{Y|X} \| Q_{Y|X} | P_X)$ is nonincreasing on $(0, 1]$ and on $(1, \infty)$. This is indeed the case: the mapping $\alpha \mapsto \frac{1-\alpha}{\alpha} D_\alpha(P_X P_{Y|X} \| Q_X Q_{Y|X})$ on the RHS of (113) is nonincreasing on $(0, \infty)$ (Proposition 1 (e)), and the monotonicity is preserved by the pointwise minimum and maximum, respectively.

(f) For $\alpha \in [0, 1]$, Proposition 4 implies that

$$(1 - \alpha) D_\alpha^1(P_{Y|X} \| Q_{Y|X} | P_X) = \min_{Q_X} [(1 - \alpha) D_\alpha(P_X P_{Y|X} \| Q_X Q_{Y|X})]. \tag{114}$$

Because $\alpha \mapsto (1 - \alpha) D_\alpha(P_X P_{Y|X} \| Q_X Q_{Y|X})$ is concave on $[0, 1]$ (Proposition 1 (f)) and because the pointwise minimum preserves the concavity, the mapping $\alpha \mapsto (1 - \alpha) D_\alpha^1(P_{Y|X} \| Q_{Y|X} | P_X)$ is concave on $[0, 1]$.

(g) This follows from Proposition 1 (g) in the same way that Part (f) followed from Proposition 1 (f). □

We next consider data-processing inequalities for $D_\alpha^1(\cdot)$. We distinguish between processing Y and processing X. The data-processing inequality for processing Y follows from the data-processing inequality for the (unconditional) Rényi divergence:

Theorem 5. Let P_X be a PMF, and let $P_{Y|X}$ and $Q_{Y|X}$ be conditional PMFs. For a conditional PMF $A_{Y'|XY}$, define

$$P_{Y'|X}(y'|x) \triangleq \sum_y P_{Y|X}(y|x) A_{Y'|XY}(y'|x,y), \tag{115}$$

$$Q_{Y'|X}(y'|x) \triangleq \sum_y Q_{Y|X}(y|x) A_{Y'|XY}(y'|x,y). \tag{116}$$

Then, for all $\alpha \in [0,\infty]$,

$$D_\alpha^1(P_{Y'|X}\|Q_{Y'|X}|P_X) \leq D_\alpha^1(P_{Y|X}\|Q_{Y|X}|P_X). \tag{117}$$

Proof. We prove (117) for $\alpha \in (0,1) \cup (1,\infty)$; the claim will then extend to $\alpha \in [0,\infty]$ by the continuity of $D_\alpha^1(\cdot)$ in α (Proposition 6 (c)). For every $x \in \mathrm{supp}(P_X)$, we can apply Proposition 1 (h) with the substitution of $A_{Y'|Y,X=x}$ for $A_{Y'|Y}$ to obtain

$$D_\alpha(P_{Y'|X=x}\|Q_{Y'|X=x}) \leq D_\alpha(P_{Y|X=x}\|Q_{Y|X=x}). \tag{118}$$

For $\alpha \in (0,1) \cup (1,\infty)$, (117) now follows from (77) and (118). □

Processing X is different. Consider first $Q_{Y|X}$ that does not depend on X. Then, writing $Q_{Y|X} = Q_Y$, we have the following result (which, as shown in Example 2 below, does not extend to general $Q_{Y|X}$):

Theorem 6. Let P_X and Q_Y be PMFs, and let $P_{Y|X}$ be a conditional PMF. For a conditional PMF $B_{X'|X}$, define the PMFs

$$P_{X'}(x') \triangleq \sum_x P_X(x) B_{X'|X}(x'|x), \tag{119}$$

$$B_{X|X'}(x|x') \triangleq \begin{cases} P_X(x) B_{X'|X}(x'|x)/P_{X'}(x') & \text{if } P_{X'}(x') > 0, \\ 1/|\mathcal{X}| & \text{otherwise,} \end{cases} \tag{120}$$

$$P_{Y|X'}(y|x') \triangleq \sum_x B_{X|X'}(x|x') P_{Y|X}(y|x). \tag{121}$$

Then, for all $\alpha \in [0,\infty]$,

$$D_\alpha^1(P_{Y|X'}\|Q_Y|P_{X'}) \leq D_\alpha^1(P_{Y|X}\|Q_Y|P_X). \tag{122}$$

Once we provide the operational meaning of $D_\alpha^1(\cdot)$ in horse betting with side information (Theorem 10 below), Theorem 6 will become very intuitive: it expresses the fact that preprocessing the side information cannot increase the gambler's utility; see Remark 8. Note that $P_{X'}$ and $P_{Y|X'}$ in Theorem 6 can be obtained from the following marginalization:

$$P_{X'}(x') P_{Y|X'}(y|x') = \sum_x P_X(x) B_{X'|X}(x'|x) P_{Y|X}(y|x). \tag{123}$$

Proof of Theorem 6. We show (122) for $\alpha \in (0,1) \cup (1,\infty)$; the claim will then extend to $\alpha \in [0,\infty]$ by the continuity of $D_\alpha^1(\cdot)$ in α (Proposition 6 (c)). Consider first $\alpha \in (1,\infty)$. Then, (122) holds because

$$\frac{\alpha-1}{\alpha} D_\alpha^1(P_{Y|X'}\|Q_Y|P_{X'})$$

$$= \log \sum_{x' \in \mathrm{supp}(P_{X'})} P_{X'}(x') \left[\sum_y P_{Y|X'}(y|x')^\alpha Q_Y(y)^{1-\alpha}\right]^{\frac{1}{\alpha}} \tag{124}$$

$$= \log \sum_{x' \in \text{supp}(P_{X'})} P_{X'}(x') \left[\sum_y \left[\sum_x B_{X|X'}(x|x') P_{Y|X}(y|x) Q_Y(y)^{\frac{1-\alpha}{\alpha}} \right]^\alpha \right]^{\frac{1}{\alpha}} \qquad (125)$$

$$= \log \sum_{x' \in \text{supp}(P_{X'})} \left[\sum_y \left[\sum_{x \in \text{supp}(P_X)} P_X(x) B_{X'|X}(x'|x) P_{Y|X}(y|x) Q_Y(y)^{\frac{1-\alpha}{\alpha}} \right]^\alpha \right]^{\frac{1}{\alpha}} \qquad (126)$$

$$\leq \log \sum_{x' \in \text{supp}(P_{X'})} \sum_{x \in \text{supp}(P_X)} \left[\sum_y \left[P_X(x) B_{X'|X}(x'|x) P_{Y|X}(y|x) Q_Y(y)^{\frac{1-\alpha}{\alpha}} \right]^\alpha \right]^{\frac{1}{\alpha}} \qquad (127)$$

$$= \log \sum_{x \in \text{supp}(P_X)} P_X(x) \left[\sum_{x' \in \text{supp}(P_{X'})} B_{X'|X}(x'|x) \right] \left[\sum_y P_{Y|X}(y|x)^\alpha Q_Y(y)^{1-\alpha} \right]^{\frac{1}{\alpha}} \qquad (128)$$

$$= \log \sum_{x \in \text{supp}(P_X)} P_X(x) \left[\sum_y P_{Y|X}(y|x)^\alpha Q_Y(y)^{1-\alpha} \right]^{\frac{1}{\alpha}} \qquad (129)$$

$$= \frac{\alpha - 1}{\alpha} D_\alpha^1(P_{Y|X} \| Q_Y | P_X), \qquad (130)$$

where (124) follows from (78); (125) follows from (121); (126) follows from (120); (127) follows from the Minkowski inequality [16] (III 2.4 Theorem 9); (129) holds because $P_X(x) > 0$ and $P_{X'}(x') = 0$ imply $B_{X'|X}(x'|x) = 0$, hence the first expression in square brackets on the left-hand side (LHS) of (129) equals one; and (130) follows from (78).

The proof for $\alpha \in (0,1)$ is very similar: (124)–(126) and (128)–(130) continue to hold, and (127) is reversed [16] (III 2.4 Theorem 9). Because now $\frac{\alpha-1}{\alpha} < 0$, (122) continues to hold for $\alpha \in (0,1)$. □

As a special case of Theorem 6, we obtain the following relation between the conditional and the unconditional Rényi divergence:

Corollary 3. *Let P_X and Q_Y be PMFs, and let $P_{Y|X}$ be a conditional PMF. Define the marginal PMF*

$$P_Y(y) \triangleq \sum_x P_X(x) P_{Y|X}(y|x). \qquad (131)$$

Then, for all $\alpha \in [0, \infty]$,

$$D_\alpha(P_Y \| Q_Y) \leq D_\alpha^1(P_{Y|X} \| Q_Y | P_X). \qquad (132)$$

Proof. This follows from Theorem 6 in the same way that Corollary 1 followed from Theorem 2. □

Consider next $Q_{Y|X}$ that does depend on X. It turns out that Corollary 3, and hence Theorem 6, cannot be extended to this setting:

Example 2. *Let $\mathcal{X} = \{0,1\}$ and $\mathcal{Y} = \{0,1,2\}$. Define the PMFs P_X, $P_{Y|X}$, and $Q_{Y|X}$ as*

$$P_X(0) = 0.5, \qquad P_X(1) = 0.5, \qquad (133)$$
$$P_{Y|X}(0|0) = 0.96, \qquad P_{Y|X}(1|0) = 0.02, \qquad P_{Y|X}(2|0) = 0.02, \qquad (134)$$
$$P_{Y|X}(0|1) = 0.12, \qquad P_{Y|X}(1|1) = 0.02, \qquad P_{Y|X}(2|1) = 0.86, \qquad (135)$$
$$Q_{Y|X}(0|0) = 0.06, \qquad Q_{Y|X}(1|0) = 0.92, \qquad Q_{Y|X}(2|0) = 0.02, \qquad (136)$$
$$Q_{Y|X}(0|1) = 0.02, \qquad Q_{Y|X}(1|1) = 0.16, \qquad Q_{Y|X}(2|1) = 0.82. \qquad (137)$$

Then, for $\alpha = 0.5$ and for $\alpha = 2$,

$$D_\alpha(P_Y \| Q_Y) > D_\alpha^1(P_{Y|X} \| Q_{Y|X} | P_X), \qquad (138)$$

where the PMFs P_Y and Q_Y are given by

$$P_Y(y) \triangleq \sum_x P_X(x) P_{Y|X}(y|x), \tag{139}$$

$$Q_Y(y) \triangleq \sum_x P_X(x) Q_{Y|X}(y|x). \tag{140}$$

Proof. Numerically, $D_{0.5}(P_Y \| Q_Y) \approx 1.11$ bits, which is larger than $D_{0.5}^1(P_{Y|X} \| Q_{Y|X} | P_X) \approx 0.93$ bits. Similarly, $D_2(P_Y \| Q_Y) \approx 2.95$ bits, which is larger than $D_2^1(P_{Y|X} \| Q_{Y|X} | P_X) \approx 2.75$ bits. □

6. Relation to Arimoto's Measures

Before discussing Arimoto's measures, we first recall the definition of the Rényi entropy. The Rényi entropy of order α [7] is defined for all positive α's other than one as

$$H_\alpha(X) \triangleq \frac{1}{1-\alpha} \log \sum_x P(x)^\alpha. \tag{141}$$

For α being zero, one, or infinity, we define by continuous extension of (141)

$$H_0(X) \triangleq \log |\mathrm{supp}(P_X)|, \tag{142}$$

$$H_1(X) \triangleq H(X), \tag{143}$$

$$H_\infty(X) \triangleq -\log \max_x P(x), \tag{144}$$

where $H(X)$ denotes Shannon's entropy. The Rényi entropy can be related to the Rényi divergence as follows:

$$H_\alpha(X) = \log |\mathcal{X}| - D_\alpha(P_X \| U_X), \tag{145}$$

where U_X denotes the uniform distribution over $\mathcal{X}$.

There are different ways to define a conditional Rényi entropy [40]; we use Arimoto's proposal. The Arimoto–Rényi conditional entropy of order α [12,38,40,41] is defined for positive α other than one as

$$H_\alpha(X|Y) \triangleq \frac{\alpha}{1-\alpha} \log \sum_{y \in \mathrm{supp}(P_Y)} P(y) \left[\sum_x P(x|y)^\alpha \right]^{\frac{1}{\alpha}} \tag{146}$$

$$= \frac{\alpha}{1-\alpha} \log \sum_{y \in \mathrm{supp}(P_Y)} P(y) 2^{\frac{1-\alpha}{\alpha} H_\alpha(P_{X|Y=y})}, \tag{147}$$

where (147) follows from the definition of the Rényi entropy in (141). The Arimoto–Rényi conditional entropy plays a key role in guessing with side information [20,42–44] and in task encoding with side information [45]; and it can be related to hypothesis testing [41]. For α being zero, one, or infinity, we define by continuous extension of (146)

$$H_0(X|Y) \triangleq \log \max_{y \in \mathrm{supp}(P_Y)} |\mathrm{supp}(P_{X|Y=y})|, \tag{148}$$

$$H_1(X|Y) \triangleq H(X|Y), \tag{149}$$

$$H_\infty(X|Y) \triangleq -\log \sum_{y \in \mathrm{supp}(P_Y)} P(y) \max_x P(x|y), \tag{150}$$

where $H(X|Y)$ denotes Shannon's conditional entropy. The analog of (145) for $H_\alpha(X|Y)$ is:

Remark 2. *For all $\alpha \in [0, \infty]$,*

$$H_\alpha(X|Y) = \log|\mathcal{X}| - D_\alpha^1(P_{X|Y}\|U_X|P_Y) \tag{151}$$

$$= \log|\mathcal{X}| - \min_{Q_Y} D_\alpha(P_Y P_{X|Y}\|Q_Y U_X). \tag{152}$$

Proof. Equation (151) follows, using some algebra, from the definition of $D_\alpha^1(\cdot)$ in (78)–(81); and (152) follows from Proposition 4. (The characterization in (152) previously appeared as [40] (Theorem 4).) □

Arimoto [12] also defined the following measure of dependence:

$$I_\alpha^a(X;Y) \triangleq H_\alpha(X) - H_\alpha(X|Y) \tag{153}$$

$$= \frac{\alpha}{\alpha - 1} \log \sum_y \left[\sum_x \frac{P(x)^\alpha}{\sum_{x' \in \mathcal{X}} P(x')^\alpha} P(y|x)^\alpha \right]^{\frac{1}{\alpha}}, \tag{154}$$

where (154) follows from (141) and (146). Using Remark 2, we can express $I_\alpha^a(X;Y)$ in terms of $D_\alpha^1(\cdot)$:

Remark 3. *For all $\alpha \in [0, \infty]$,*

$$I_\alpha^a(X;Y) = D_\alpha^1(P_{X|Y}\|U_X|P_Y) - D_\alpha(P_X\|U_X). \tag{155}$$

Proof. This follows from (145), (151), and (153). □

7. Relations Between the Conditional Rényi Divergences and the Rényi Dependence Measures

In this section, we first establish the greater-or-equal-than order between the conditional Rényi divergences, where the order depends on whether $\alpha \in [0,1]$ or $\alpha \in [1,\infty]$. We then show that this implies the same order between the dependence measures derived from the conditional Rényi divergences. Finally, we remark that many of the dependence measures coincide when they are maximized over all PMFs P_X.

Proposition 7. *For all $\alpha \in [0, \infty]$,*

$$D_\alpha^1(P_{Y|X}\|Q_{Y|X}|P_X) \leq D_\alpha^s(P_{Y|X}\|Q_{Y|X}|P_X). \tag{156}$$

Proof. This holds because

$$D_\alpha^1(P_{Y|X}\|Q_{Y|X}|P_X) = \min_{Q_X} D_\alpha(P_X P_{Y|X}\|Q_X Q_{Y|X}) \tag{157}$$

$$\leq D_\alpha(P_X P_{Y|X}\|P_X Q_{Y|X}) \tag{158}$$

$$= D_\alpha^s(P_{Y|X}\|Q_{Y|X}|P_X), \tag{159}$$

where (157) follows from Proposition 4, and (159) follows from the definition of $D_\alpha^s(\cdot)$ in (54). □

Theorem 7. *For all $\alpha \in [0, 1]$,*

$$D_\alpha^1(P_{Y|X}\|Q_{Y|X}|P_X) \leq D_\alpha^s(P_{Y|X}\|Q_{Y|X}|P_X) \leq D_\alpha^c(P_{Y|X}\|Q_{Y|X}|P_X). \tag{160}$$

For all $\alpha \in [1, \infty]$,

$$D_\alpha^c(P_{Y|X}\|Q_{Y|X}|P_X) \leq D_\alpha^1(P_{Y|X}\|Q_{Y|X}|P_X) \leq D_\alpha^s(P_{Y|X}\|Q_{Y|X}|P_X). \tag{161}$$

Proof. For both $\alpha \in [0,1]$ and $\alpha \in [1,\infty]$, the relation $D_\alpha^1(\cdot) \leq D_\alpha^s(\cdot)$ follows from Proposition 7.

We next show that $D^s_\alpha(\cdot) \leq D^c_\alpha(\cdot)$ for $\alpha \in [0,1]$. We show this for $\alpha \in (0,1)$; the claim will then extend to $\alpha \in [0,1]$ by the continuity in α of $D^s_\alpha(\cdot)$ and $D^c_\alpha(\cdot)$ (Proposition 3 (c) and Proposition 2 (c)). For $\alpha \in (0,1)$,

$$(\alpha - 1) D^s_\alpha(P_{Y|X} \| Q_{Y|X} | P_X) = \log \sum_{x \in \text{supp}(P_X)} P(x) \sum_y P(y|x)^\alpha Q(y|x)^{1-\alpha} \tag{162}$$

$$\geq \sum_{x \in \text{supp}(P_X)} P(x) \log \sum_y P(y|x)^\alpha Q(y|x)^{1-\alpha} \tag{163}$$

$$= (\alpha - 1) D^c_\alpha(P_{Y|X} \| Q_{Y|X} | P_X), \tag{164}$$

where (162) follows from (55); (163) follows from Jensen's inequality because $\log(\cdot)$ is a concave function; and (164) follows from (30). The proof of the claim for $\alpha \in (0,1)$ is finished by dividing (162)–(164) by $\alpha - 1$, which reverses the inequality because $\alpha - 1 < 0$.

We conclude by showing that $D^c_\alpha(\cdot) \leq D^1_\alpha(\cdot)$ for $\alpha \in [1,\infty]$. We show this for $\alpha \in (1,\infty)$; the claim will then extend to $\alpha \in [1,\infty]$ by the continuity of $D^c_\alpha(\cdot)$ and $D^1_\alpha(\cdot)$ in α (Proposition 2 (c) and Proposition 6 (c)). For $\alpha \in (1,\infty)$,

$$D^c_\alpha(P_{Y|X} \| Q_{Y|X} | P_X) = \sum_{x \in \text{supp}(P_X)} P(x) \frac{1}{\alpha - 1} \log \sum_y P(y|x)^\alpha Q(y|x)^{1-\alpha} \tag{165}$$

$$= \frac{\alpha}{\alpha - 1} \sum_{x \in \text{supp}(P_X)} P(x) \log \left[\sum_y P(y|x)^\alpha Q(y|x)^{1-\alpha} \right]^{\frac{1}{\alpha}} \tag{166}$$

$$\leq \frac{\alpha}{\alpha - 1} \log \sum_{x \in \text{supp}(P_X)} P(x) \left[\sum_y P(y|x)^\alpha Q(y|x)^{1-\alpha} \right]^{\frac{1}{\alpha}} \tag{167}$$

$$= D^1_\alpha(P_{Y|X} \| Q_{Y|X} | P_X), \tag{168}$$

where (165) follows from (30); (167) follows from Jensen's inequality because $\log(\cdot)$ is a concave function; and (168) follows from (78). □

Corollary 4. *For all $\alpha \in [0,1]$,*

$$J_\alpha(X;Y) \leq I^s_\alpha(X;Y) \leq I^c_\alpha(X;Y). \tag{169}$$

For all $\alpha \in [1,\infty]$,

$$I^c_\alpha(X;Y) \leq J_\alpha(X;Y) \leq I^s_\alpha(X;Y). \tag{170}$$

Proof. By (34) and (60) and Proposition 5, respectively,

$$I^c_\alpha(X;Y) = \min_{Q_Y} D^c_\alpha(P_{Y|X} \| Q_Y | P_X), \tag{171}$$

$$I^s_\alpha(X;Y) = \min_{Q_Y} D^s_\alpha(P_{Y|X} \| Q_Y | P_X), \tag{172}$$

$$J_\alpha(X;Y) = \min_{Q_Y} D^1_\alpha(P_{Y|X} \| Q_Y | P_X). \tag{173}$$

The corollary now follows from (171)–(173) and Theorem 7. □

Despite $I^c_\alpha(X;Y)$, $I^s_\alpha(X;Y)$, $I^a_\alpha(X;Y)$, and $J_\alpha(X;Y)$ being different measures, they often coincide when maximized over all PMFs P_X:

Theorem 8. *For every conditional PMF $P_{Y|X}$ and every $\alpha \in (0,1) \cup (1,\infty)$,*

$$\max_{P_X} I_\alpha^c(P_X, P_{Y|X}) = \max_{P_X} I_\alpha^s(P_X, P_{Y|X}) \tag{174}$$

$$= \max_{P_X} I_\alpha^a(P_X, P_{Y|X}). \tag{175}$$

In addition, for every conditional PMF $P_{Y|X}$ and every $\alpha \in [\frac{1}{2}, 1) \cup (1, \infty)$,

$$\max_{P_X} J_\alpha(P_X, P_{Y|X}) = \max_{P_X} I_\alpha^s(P_X, P_{Y|X}). \tag{176}$$

For $\alpha \in (0, \frac{1}{2})$, the situation is different: there exists a conditional PMF $P_{Y|X}$ such that, for every $\alpha \in (0, \frac{1}{2})$,

$$\max_{P_X} J_\alpha(P_X, P_{Y|X}) < \max_{P_X} I_\alpha^s(P_X, P_{Y|X}). \tag{177}$$

Proof. Equation (174) follows from [9] (Proposition 1); (175) follows from [12] (Lemma 1); and (176) follows from [38] (Theorem V.1) for $\alpha \in (1, \infty)$.

We next establish (176) for $\alpha \in [\frac{1}{2}, 1)$. Observe that, for $\alpha \in [\frac{1}{2}, 1)$, (176) is equivalent to

$$\max_{P_X} -2^{\frac{\alpha-1}{\alpha} J_\alpha(P_X, P_{Y|X})} = \max_{P_X} -2^{\frac{\alpha-1}{\alpha} I_\alpha^s(P_X, P_{Y|X})}. \tag{178}$$

For $\alpha \in [\frac{1}{2}, 1)$, (178) holds because

$$\max_{P_X} -2^{\frac{\alpha-1}{\alpha} J_\alpha(P_X, P_{Y|X})} = \max_{P_X} \min_{Q_Y} -2^{\frac{\alpha-1}{\alpha} D_\alpha^1(P_{Y|X} \| Q_Y | P_X)} \tag{179}$$

$$= -\min_{P_X} \max_{Q_Y} \sum_x P_X(x) \left[\sum_y P(y|x)^\alpha Q_Y(y)^{1-\alpha} \right]^{\frac{1}{\alpha}} \tag{180}$$

$$= -\max_{Q_Y} \min_{P_X} \sum_x P_X(x) \left[\sum_y P(y|x)^\alpha Q_Y(y)^{1-\alpha} \right]^{\frac{1}{\alpha}} \tag{181}$$

$$= -\max_{Q_Y} \min_x \left[\sum_y P(y|x)^\alpha Q_Y(y)^{1-\alpha} \right]^{\frac{1}{\alpha}} \tag{182}$$

$$= -\left[\max_{Q_Y} \min_x \sum_y P(y|x)^\alpha Q_Y(y)^{1-\alpha} \right]^{\frac{1}{\alpha}} \tag{183}$$

$$= -\left[\max_{Q_Y} \min_{P_X} \sum_x P_X(x) \sum_y P(y|x)^\alpha Q_Y(y)^{1-\alpha} \right]^{\frac{1}{\alpha}} \tag{184}$$

$$= -\left[\min_{P_X} \max_{Q_Y} \sum_x P_X(x) \sum_y P(y|x)^\alpha Q_Y(y)^{1-\alpha} \right]^{\frac{1}{\alpha}} \tag{185}$$

$$= -\min_{P_X} \max_{Q_Y} \left[\sum_x P_X(x) \sum_y P(y|x)^\alpha Q_Y(y)^{1-\alpha} \right]^{\frac{1}{\alpha}} \tag{186}$$

$$= \max_{P_X} \min_{Q_Y} -2^{\frac{\alpha-1}{\alpha} D_\alpha^s(P_{Y|X} \| Q_Y | P_X)} \tag{187}$$

$$= \max_{P_X} -2^{\frac{\alpha-1}{\alpha} I_\alpha^s(P_X, P_{Y|X})}, \tag{188}$$

where (179) follows from Proposition 5; (180) follows from (78); (181) and (185) follow from a minimax theorem and are justified below; (187) follows from (55); and (188) follows from (60).

To justify (181), we apply the minimax theorem [46] (Corollary 37.3.2) to the function $f\colon \mathcal{P}(\mathcal{Y}) \times \mathcal{P}(\mathcal{X}) \to \mathbb{R}$,

$$f(Q_Y, P_X) = \sum_x P_X(x) \left[\sum_y P(y|x)^\alpha Q_Y(y)^{1-\alpha}\right]^{\frac{1}{\alpha}}. \tag{189}$$

The sets of all PMFs over $\mathcal{X}$ and over $\mathcal{Y}$ are convex and compact; the function f is jointly continuous in the pair (Q_Y, P_X) because it is a composition of continuous functions; for every $Q_Y \in \mathcal{P}(\mathcal{Y})$, the function f is linear and hence convex in P_X; and it only remains to show that the function f is concave in Q_Y for every $P_X \in \mathcal{P}(\mathcal{X})$. Indeed, for every $\lambda, \lambda' \in [0,1]$ with $\lambda + \lambda' = 1$, every $Q_Y, Q'_Y \in \mathcal{P}(\mathcal{Y})$, and every $P_X \in \mathcal{P}(\mathcal{X})$,

$$f(\lambda Q_Y + \lambda' Q'_Y, P_X) \tag{190}$$

$$= \sum_x P_X(x) \left[\sum_y P(y|x)^\alpha [\lambda Q_Y(y) + \lambda' Q'_Y(y)]^{1-\alpha}\right]^{\frac{1}{\alpha}} \tag{191}$$

$$= \sum_x P_X(x) \left[\sum_y [\lambda P(y|x)^{\frac{\alpha}{1-\alpha}} Q_Y(y) + \lambda' P(y|x)^{\frac{\alpha}{1-\alpha}} Q'_Y(y)]^{1-\alpha}\right]^{\frac{1}{1-\alpha}\cdot\frac{1-\alpha}{\alpha}} \tag{192}$$

$$\geq \sum_x P_X(x) \left\{\left[\sum_y [\lambda P(y|x)^{\frac{\alpha}{1-\alpha}} Q_Y(y)]^{1-\alpha}\right]^{\frac{1}{1-\alpha}} + \left[\sum_y [\lambda' P(y|x)^{\frac{\alpha}{1-\alpha}} Q'_Y(y)]^{1-\alpha}\right]^{\frac{1}{1-\alpha}}\right\}^{\frac{1-\alpha}{\alpha}} \tag{193}$$

$$= \sum_x P_X(x) \left\{\lambda \left[\sum_y P(y|x)^\alpha Q_Y(y)^{1-\alpha}\right]^{\frac{1}{1-\alpha}} + \lambda' \left[\sum_y P(y|x)^\alpha Q'_Y(y)^{1-\alpha}\right]^{\frac{1}{1-\alpha}}\right\}^{\frac{1-\alpha}{\alpha}} \tag{194}$$

$$\geq \sum_x P_X(x) \left\{\lambda \left[\sum_y P(y|x)^\alpha Q_Y(y)^{1-\alpha}\right]^{\frac{1}{\alpha}} + \lambda' \left[\sum_y P(y|x)^\alpha Q'_Y(y)^{1-\alpha}\right]^{\frac{1}{\alpha}}\right\} \tag{195}$$

$$= \lambda f(Q_Y, P_X) + \lambda' f(Q'_Y, P_X), \tag{196}$$

where (193) follows from the reverse Minkowski inequality [16] (III 2.4 Theorem 9) because $\alpha \in [\frac{1}{2}, 1)$; and (195) holds because the function $z \mapsto z^{(1-\alpha)/\alpha}$ is concave for $\alpha \in [\frac{1}{2}, 1)$.

The justification of (185) is very similar to that of (181); here, we apply the minimax theorem to the function $g\colon \mathcal{P}(\mathcal{Y}) \times \mathcal{P}(\mathcal{X}) \to \mathbb{R}$,

$$g(Q_Y, P_X) = \sum_x P_X(x) \sum_y P(y|x)^\alpha Q_Y(y)^{1-\alpha}. \tag{197}$$

Compared to the justification of (181), the only essential difference lies in showing that the function g is concave in Q_Y for every $P_X \in \mathcal{P}(\mathcal{X})$: here, this follows easily from the concavity of the function $z \mapsto z^{1-\alpha}$ for $\alpha \in [\frac{1}{2}, 1)$.

We conclude the proof by establishing (177). Let $\mathcal{X} = \mathcal{Y} = \{0,1\}$, and let the conditional PMF $P_{Y|X}$ be given by $P_{Y|X}(y|x) = \mathbb{1}\{y = x\}$. (This corresponds to a binary noiseless channel.) Then, denoting by U_X the uniform distribution over $\mathcal{X}$,

$$\max_{P_X} I_\alpha^s(P_X, P_{Y|X}) \geq I_\alpha^s(U_X, P_{Y|X}) \tag{198}$$

$$= \log 2, \tag{199}$$

where (199) follows from (61). On the other hand, for every $\alpha \in (0, \tfrac{1}{2})$ and every PMF P_X,

$$J_\alpha(P_X, P_{Y|X}) = \frac{\alpha}{1-\alpha} H_\infty(P_X) \tag{200}$$

$$\leq \frac{\alpha}{1-\alpha} \log 2 \tag{201}$$

$$< \log 2, \tag{202}$$

where (200) follows from [3] (Lemma 11); (201) follows from (144); and (202) holds because $\alpha \in (0, \tfrac{1}{2})$. Inequality (177) now follows from (199) and (202). □

8. Horse Betting

In this section, we analyze horse betting with a gambler investing all her money. Recall from the introduction that the winning horse X is distributed according to the PMF p, where we assume $p(x) > 0$ for all $x \in \mathcal{X}$; that the odds offered by the bookmaker are denoted by $o \colon \mathcal{X} \to (0, \infty)$; that the fraction of her wealth that the gambler bets on Horse $x \in \mathcal{X}$ is denoted $b(x) \geq 0$; that the wealth relative is the random variable $S \triangleq b(X) o(X)$; and that we seek betting strategies that maximize the utility function

$$U_\beta \triangleq \begin{cases} \frac{1}{\beta} \log \mathbb{E}[S^\beta] & \text{if } \beta \neq 0, \\ \mathbb{E}[\log S] & \text{if } \beta = 0. \end{cases} \tag{203}$$

Because the gambler invests all her money, b is a PMF. As in [47] (Section 10.3), define the constant

$$c \triangleq \left[\sum_x \frac{1}{o(x)} \right]^{-1} \tag{204}$$

and the PMF

$$r(x) \triangleq \frac{c}{o(x)}. \tag{205}$$

Using these definitions, the utility function U_β can be decomposed as follows:

Theorem 9. *Let $\beta \in (-\infty, 1)$, and let b be a PMF. Then,*

$$U_\beta = \log c + D_{\frac{1}{1-\beta}}(p \| r) - D_{1-\beta}(g^{(\beta)} \| b), \tag{206}$$

where the PMF $g^{(\beta)}$ is given by

$$g^{(\beta)}(x) \triangleq \frac{p(x)^{\frac{1}{1-\beta}} o(x)^{\frac{\beta}{1-\beta}}}{\sum_{x' \in \mathcal{X}} p(x')^{\frac{1}{1-\beta}} o(x')^{\frac{\beta}{1-\beta}}}. \tag{207}$$

Thus, choosing $b = g^{(\beta)}$ uniquely maximizes U_β among all PMFs b.

The three terms in (206) can be interpreted as follows:

1. The first term, $\log c$, depends only on the odds and is related to the fairness of the odds. The odds are called subfair if $c < 1$, fair if $c = 1$, and superfair if $c > 1$.
2. The second term, $D_{1/(1-\beta)}(p \| r)$, is related to the bookmaker's estimate of the winning probabilities. It is zero if and only if the odds are inversely proportional to the winning probabilities.

3. The third term, $-D_{1-\beta}(g^{(\beta)}\|b)$, is related to the gambler's estimate of the winning probabilities. It is zero if and only if b is equal to $g^{(\beta)}$.

Remark 4. *For $\beta = 0$, (206) reduces to the following decomposition of the doubling rate $\mathrm{E}[\log S]$:*

$$\mathrm{E}[\log S] = \log c + D(p\|r) - D(p\|b). \tag{208}$$

(This decomposition appeared previously in [47] (Section 10.3).) Equation (208) implies that the doubling rate is maximized by proportional gambling, i.e., that $\mathrm{E}[\log S]$ is maximized if and only if b is equal to p.

Remark 5. *Considering the limits $\beta \to -\infty$ and $\beta \uparrow 1$, the PMF $g^{(\beta)}$ satisfies, for every $x \in \mathcal{X}$,*

$$\lim_{\beta \to -\infty} g^{(\beta)}(x) = \frac{c}{o(x)}, \tag{209}$$

$$\lim_{\beta \uparrow 1} g^{(\beta)}(x) = \frac{p(x)\mathbb{1}\{x \in \mathcal{S}\}}{\sum_{x' \in \mathcal{X}} p(x')\mathbb{1}\{x' \in \mathcal{S}\}}, \tag{210}$$

where the set $\mathcal{S}$ is defined as $\mathcal{S} \triangleq \{x' \in \mathcal{X} : p(x')o(x') = \max_x[p(x)o(x)]\}$. It follows from Proposition 8 below that the RHS of (209) is the unique maximizer of $\lim_{\beta \to -\infty} U_\beta$; and it follows from the proof of Proposition 9 below that the RHS of (210) is a maximizer (not necessarily unique) of U_1.

Proof of Remark 5. Recall that we assume $p(x) > 0$ for every $x \in \mathcal{X}$. Then, (209) follows from (207) and the definition of c in (204). To establish (210), define $\tau \triangleq \max_x[p(x)o(x)]$ and observe that, for every $x \in \mathcal{X}$,

$$\lim_{\beta \uparrow 1} g^{(\beta)}(x) = \lim_{\beta \uparrow 1} \frac{p(x)\left[p(x)o(x)/\tau\right]^{\frac{\beta}{1-\beta}}}{\sum_{x' \in \mathcal{X}} p(x')\left[p(x')o(x')/\tau\right]^{\frac{\beta}{1-\beta}}} \tag{211}$$

$$= \frac{p(x)\mathbb{1}\{x \in \mathcal{S}\}}{\sum_{x' \in \mathcal{X}} p(x')\mathbb{1}\{x' \in \mathcal{S}\}}, \tag{212}$$

where (211) follows from (207) and some algebra; and (212) is justified as follows: if $x \in \mathcal{S}$, then $[p(x)o(x)/\tau]^{\beta/(1-\beta)}$ equals one; and if $x \notin \mathcal{S}$, then $[p(x)o(x)/\tau]^{\beta/(1-\beta)}$ tends to zero as $\beta \uparrow 1$ because $p(x)o(x)/\tau < 1$ and because $\lim_{\beta \uparrow 1} \frac{\beta}{1-\beta} = +\infty$. □

Remark 6. *Using the definition in (24) for the Rényi divergence of negative orders, it is not difficult to see from the proof of Theorem 9 below that (206) also holds for $\beta > 1$. However, because the Rényi divergence of negative orders is nonpositive instead of nonnegative, the above interpretation is not valid anymore; in particular, for $\beta > 1$, choosing $b = g^{(\beta)}$ is in general not optimal.*

Proof of Theorem 9. We first show the maximization claim. The only term on the RHS of (206) that depends on b is $-D_{1-\beta}(g^{(\beta)}\|b)$. Because $1 - \beta > 0$, this term is maximized if and only if $b = g^{(\beta)}$ (Proposition 1 (a)).

We now establish (206) for $\beta \in (-\infty, 0) \cup (0, 1)$; we omit the proof for $\beta = 0$, which can be found in [47] (Section 10.3). For $\beta \in (-\infty, 0) \cup (0, 1)$,

$$U_\beta = \frac{1}{\beta} \log \sum_x p(x) b(x)^\beta o(x)^\beta. \tag{213}$$

For every $x \in \mathcal{X}$,

$$p(x)b(x)^\beta o(x)^\beta = \left[\sum_{x' \in \mathcal{X}} p(x')^{\frac{1}{1-\beta}} o(x')^{\frac{\beta}{1-\beta}} \right]^{1-\beta} \cdot g^{(\beta)}(x)^{1-\beta} b(x)^\beta, \qquad (214)$$

which follows from (207). Now, (206) holds because

$$U_\beta = \frac{1-\beta}{\beta} \log \sum_{x' \in \mathcal{X}} p(x')^{\frac{1}{1-\beta}} o(x')^{\frac{\beta}{1-\beta}} + \frac{1}{\beta} \log \sum_x g^{(\beta)}(x)^{1-\beta} b(x)^\beta \qquad (215)$$

$$= \frac{1-\beta}{\beta} \log \sum_{x' \in \mathcal{X}} p(x')^{\frac{1}{1-\beta}} o(x')^{\frac{\beta}{1-\beta}} - D_{1-\beta}(g^{(\beta)} \| b) \qquad (216)$$

$$= \log c + \frac{1-\beta}{\beta} \log \sum_{x' \in \mathcal{X}} p(x')^{\frac{1}{1-\beta}} r(x')^{\frac{-\beta}{1-\beta}} - D_{1-\beta}(g^{(\beta)} \| b) \qquad (217)$$

$$= \log c + D_{\frac{1}{1-\beta}}(p \| r) - D_{1-\beta}(g^{(\beta)} \| b), \qquad (218)$$

where (215) follows from (213) and (214); (216) follows from identifying the Rényi divergence (recall that $g^{(\beta)}$ and b are PMFs); (217) follows from (205); and (218) follows from identifying the Rényi divergence (recall that r is a PMF). □

The rest of the section presents the cases $\beta \to -\infty$, $\beta \geq 1$, and $\beta \to +\infty$.

Proposition 8. *Let b be a PMF. Then,*

$$\lim_{\beta \to -\infty} U_\beta = \log \min_x [b(x) o(x)] \qquad (219)$$

$$\leq \log c. \qquad (220)$$

Inequality (220) holds with equality if and only if $b(x) = c/o(x)$ for all $x \in \mathcal{X}$.

Observe that if $b(x) = c/o(x)$ for all $x \in \mathcal{X}$, then $S = c$ with probability one, i.e., S does not depend on the winning horse.

Proof of Proposition 8. Equation (219) holds because

$$\lim_{\beta \to -\infty} U_\beta = \lim_{\beta \to -\infty} \log \left[\sum_x p(x) \left(b(x) o(x) \right)^\beta \right]^{\frac{1}{\beta}} \qquad (221)$$

$$= \log \min_x [b(x) o(x)], \qquad (222)$$

where (222) holds because, in the limit as β tends to $-\infty$, the power mean tends to the minimum (since p is a PMF with $p(x) > 0$ for all $x \in \mathcal{X}$ [15] (Chapter 8)).

We show (220) by contradiction. Assume that there exists a PMF b that does not satisfy (220), thus

$$b(x) o(x) > c \qquad (223)$$

for all $x \in \mathcal{X}$. Then,

$$1 = \sum_x b(x) \qquad (224)$$

$$> \sum_x \frac{c}{o(x)} \qquad (225)$$

$$= 1, \qquad (226)$$

where (224) holds because b is a PMF; (225) follows from (223); and (226) follows from the definition of c in (204). Because $1 > 1$ is impossible, such a b cannot exist, which establishes (220).

It is not difficult to see that (220) holds with equality if $b(x) = c/o(x)$ for all $x \in \mathcal{X}$. We therefore focus on establishing that if (220) holds with equality, then $b(x) = c/o(x)$ for all $x \in \mathcal{X}$. Observe first that, if (220) holds with equality, then, for all $x \in \mathcal{X}$,

$$b(x) o(x) \geq c. \tag{227}$$

We now claim that (227) holds with equality for all $x \in \mathcal{X}$. Indeed, if this were not the case, then there would exist an $x' \in \mathcal{X}$ for which $b(x')o(x') > c$, thus (224)–(226) would hold, which would lead to a contradiction. Hence, if (220) holds with equality, then $b(x) = c/o(x)$ for all $x \in \mathcal{X}$. □

Proposition 9. *Let $\beta \geq 1$, and let b be a PMF. Then,*

$$U_\beta \leq \log \max_x \left[p(x)^{1/\beta} o(x) \right]. \tag{228}$$

Equality in (228) can be achieved by choosing $b(x) = \mathbb{1}\{x = x'\}$ for some $x' \in \mathcal{X}$ satisfying

$$p(x')^{1/\beta} o(x') = \max_x \left[p(x)^{1/\beta} o(x) \right]. \tag{229}$$

Remark 7. *Proposition 9 implies that if $\beta \geq 1$, then it is optimal to bet on a single horse. Unless $|\mathcal{X}| = 1$, this is not the case when $\beta < 1$: When $\beta < 1$, an optimal betting strategy requires placing a bet on every horse. This follows from Theorem 9 and our assumption that $p(x)$ and $o(x)$ are all positive.*

Proof of Proposition 9. Inequality (228) holds because

$$U_\beta = \frac{1}{\beta} \log \sum_x p(x) b(x)^\beta o(x)^\beta \tag{230}$$

$$\leq \frac{1}{\beta} \log \sum_x p(x) b(x) o(x)^\beta \tag{231}$$

$$\leq \frac{1}{\beta} \log \sum_x b(x) \cdot \max_{x' \in \mathcal{X}} \left[p(x') o(x')^\beta \right] \tag{232}$$

$$= \frac{1}{\beta} \log \max_{x' \in \mathcal{X}} \left[p(x') o(x')^\beta \right] \tag{233}$$

$$= \log \max_{x' \in \mathcal{X}} \left[p(x')^{1/\beta} o(x') \right], \tag{234}$$

where (231) holds because $b(x) \in [0,1]$ and $\beta \geq 1$, and (233) holds because b is a PMF. It is not difficult to see that (228) holds with equality if $b(x) = \mathbb{1}\{x = x'\}$ for some $x' \in \mathcal{X}$ satisfying (229). □

Proposition 10. *Let b be a PMF. Then,*

$$\lim_{\beta \to +\infty} U_\beta = \log \max_x \left[b(x) o(x) \right] \tag{235}$$

$$\leq \log \max_x o(x). \tag{236}$$

Equality in (236) can be achieved by choosing $b(x) = \mathbb{1}\{x = x'\}$ for some $x' \in \mathcal{X}$ satisfying

$$o(x') = \max_x o(x). \tag{237}$$

Proof. Equation (235) holds because

$$\lim_{\beta \to +\infty} U_\beta = \lim_{\beta \to +\infty} \log \left[\sum_x p(x) \left(b(x) o(x) \right)^\beta \right]^{\frac{1}{\beta}} \tag{238}$$

$$= \log \max_x [b(x) o(x)], \tag{239}$$

where (239) holds because in the limit as β tends to $+\infty$, the power mean tends to the maximum (since p is a PMF with $p(x) > 0$ for all $x \in \mathcal{X}$ [15] (Chapter 8)). Inequality (236) holds because $b(x) \leq 1$ for all $x \in \mathcal{X}$. It is not difficult to see that (236) holds with equality if $b(x) = \mathbb{1}\{x = x'\}$ for some $x' \in \mathcal{X}$ satisfying (237). □

9. Horse Betting with Side Information

In this section, we study the horse betting problem where the gambler observes some side information Y before placing her bets. This setting leads to the conditional Rényi divergence $D_\alpha^1(\cdot)$ discussed in Section 5 (see Theorem 10). In addition, it provides a new operational meaning to the dependence measure $J_\alpha(X; Y)$ (see Theorem 11).

We adapt our notation as follows: The joint PMF of X and Y is denoted p_{XY}. (Recall that X denotes the winning horse.) We drop the assumption that the winning probabilities $p(x)$ are positive, but we assume that $p(y) > 0$ for all $y \in \mathcal{Y}$. We continue to assume that the gambler invests all her wealth, so a betting strategy is now a conditional PMF $b_{X|Y}$, and the wealth relative S is

$$S \triangleq b(X|Y) o(X). \tag{240}$$

As in Section 8, define the constant

$$c \triangleq \left[\sum_x \frac{1}{o(x)} \right]^{-1} \tag{241}$$

and the PMF

$$r_X(x) \triangleq \frac{c}{o(x)}. \tag{242}$$

The following decomposition of the utility function U_β parallels that of Theorem 9:

Theorem 10. Let $\beta \in (-\infty, 1)$. Then,

$$U_\beta = \log c + D_{\frac{1}{1-\beta}}^1 (p_{X|Y} \| r_X | p_Y) - D_{1-\beta}(g_{X|Y}^{(\beta)} g_Y^{(\beta)} \| b_{X|Y} g_Y^{(\beta)}), \tag{243}$$

where the conditional PMF $g_{X|Y}^{(\beta)}$ and the PMF $g_Y^{(\beta)}$ are given by

$$g_{X|Y}^{(\beta)}(x|y) \triangleq \frac{p(x|y)^{\frac{1}{1-\beta}} o(x)^{\frac{\beta}{1-\beta}}}{\sum_{x'} p(x'|y)^{\frac{1}{1-\beta}} o(x')^{\frac{\beta}{1-\beta}}}, \tag{244}$$

$$g_Y^{(\beta)}(y) \triangleq \frac{p(y) \left[\sum_{x'} p(x'|y)^{\frac{1}{1-\beta}} o(x')^{\frac{\beta}{1-\beta}} \right]^{1-\beta}}{\sum_{y'} p(y') \left[\sum_{x'} p(x'|y')^{\frac{1}{1-\beta}} o(x')^{\frac{\beta}{1-\beta}} \right]^{1-\beta}}. \tag{245}$$

Thus, choosing $b_{X|Y} = g_{X|Y}^{(\beta)}$ uniquely maximizes U_β among all conditional PMFs $b_{X|Y}$.

Proof. We first show that U_β is uniquely maximized by $g_{X|Y}^{(\beta)}$. The only term on the RHS of (243) that depends on $b_{X|Y}$ is $-D_{1-\beta}(g_{X|Y}^{(\beta)}g_Y^{(\beta)}\|b_{X|Y}g_Y^{(\beta)})$. Because $1-\beta > 0$, this term is maximized if and only if $b_{X|Y}g_Y^{(\beta)} = g_{X|Y}^{(\beta)}g_Y^{(\beta)}$ (Proposition 1 (a)). By our assumptions that $p(y) > 0$ for all $y \in \mathcal{Y}$ and $o(x) > 0$ for all $x \in \mathcal{X}$, we have $g_Y^{(\beta)}(y) > 0$ for all $y \in \mathcal{Y}$. Consequently, $b_{X|Y}g_Y^{(\beta)} = g_{X|Y}^{(\beta)}g_Y^{(\beta)}$ if and only if $b_{X|Y} = g_{X|Y}^{(\beta)}$.

Consider now (243) for $\beta = 0$. For $\beta = 0$, (243) reduces to

$$\mathrm{E}[\log S] = \log c + D(p_{X|Y}p_Y \| r_X p_Y) - D(p_{X|Y}p_Y \| b_{X|Y}p_Y), \tag{246}$$

and some algebra reveals that (246) holds.

We conclude with establishing (243) for $\beta \in (-\infty, 0) \cup (0, 1)$. For $\beta \in (-\infty, 0) \cup (0, 1)$,

$$U_\beta = \frac{1}{\beta} \log \sum_{x,y} p(x,y) b(x|y)^\beta o(x)^\beta. \tag{247}$$

For every $x \in \mathcal{X}$ and every $y \in \mathcal{Y}$,

$$p(x,y)b(x|y)^\beta o(x)^\beta = \sum_{y' \in \mathcal{Y}} p(y') \left[\sum_{x' \in \mathcal{X}} p(x'|y')^{\frac{1}{1-\beta}} o(x')^{\frac{\beta}{1-\beta}} \right]^{1-\beta} \cdot g_Y^{(\beta)}(y) g_{X|Y}^{(\beta)}(x|y)^{1-\beta} b(x|y)^\beta, \tag{248}$$

which follows from (244) and (245). Now, (243) holds because

$$U_\beta = \frac{1}{\beta} \log \sum_{y' \in \mathcal{Y}} p(y') \left[\sum_{x' \in \mathcal{X}} p(x'|y')^{\frac{1}{1-\beta}} o(x')^{\frac{\beta}{1-\beta}} \right]^{1-\beta}$$
$$+ \frac{1}{\beta} \log \sum_{x,y} [g_{X|Y}^{(\beta)}(x|y) g_Y^{(\beta)}(y)]^{1-\beta} [b(x|y) g_Y^{(\beta)}(y)]^\beta \tag{249}$$

$$= \frac{1}{\beta} \log \sum_{y' \in \mathcal{Y}} p(y') \left[\sum_{x' \in \mathcal{X}} p(x'|y')^{\frac{1}{1-\beta}} o(x')^{\frac{\beta}{1-\beta}} \right]^{1-\beta} - D_{1-\beta}(g_{X|Y}^{(\beta)}g_Y^{(\beta)} \| b_{X|Y}g_Y^{(\beta)}) \tag{250}$$

$$= \log c + \frac{1}{\beta} \log \sum_{y' \in \mathcal{Y}} p(y') \left[\sum_{x' \in \mathcal{X}} p(x'|y')^{\frac{1}{1-\beta}} r_X(x')^{\frac{-\beta}{1-\beta}} \right]^{1-\beta} - D_{1-\beta}(g_{X|Y}^{(\beta)}g_Y^{(\beta)} \| b_{X|Y}g_Y^{(\beta)}) \tag{251}$$

$$= \log c + D_{\frac{1}{1-\beta}}(p_{X|Y} \| r_X | p_Y) - D_{1-\beta}(g_{X|Y}^{(\beta)}g_Y^{(\beta)} \| b_{X|Y}g_Y^{(\beta)}), \tag{252}$$

where (249) follows from (247) and (248) and the fact that $g_Y^{(\beta)}(y) = g_Y^{(\beta)}(y)^{1-\beta} g_Y^{(\beta)}(y)^\beta$; (250) follows by identifying the Rényi divergence; (251) follows from (242); and (252) follows by identifying the conditional Rényi divergence using (78). □

Remark 8. *It follows from Theorem 10 that, if the gambler gambles optimally, then, for $\beta \in (-\infty, 1)$,*

$$U_\beta = \log c + D_{\frac{1}{1-\beta}}(p_{X|Y} \| r_X | p_Y). \tag{253}$$

Operationally, it is clear that preprocessing the side information cannot increase the gambler's utility, i.e., that, for every conditional PMF $p_{Y'|Y}$,

$$D_{\frac{1}{1-\beta}}(p_{X|Y'} \| r_X | p_{Y'}) \leq D_{\frac{1}{1-\beta}}(p_{X|Y} \| r_X | p_Y), \tag{254}$$

where $p_{X|Y'}$ and $p_{Y'}$ are derived from the joint PMF $p_{XYY'}$ given by

$$p_{XYY'}(x,y,y') = p_Y(y) p_{X|Y}(x|y) p_{Y'|Y}(y'|y). \tag{255}$$

This provides the intuition for Theorem 6, where (254) is shown directly.

The extreme case is when the preprocessing maps the side information to a constant and hence leads to the case where the side information is absent. In this case, Y' is deterministic and $p_{X|Y'}$ equals p_X. Theorem 9 and Theorem 10 then lead to the following relation between the conditional and unconditional Rényi divergence:

$$D_{\frac{1}{1-\beta}}(p_X \| r_X) \leq D^1_{\frac{1}{1-\beta}}(p_{X|Y} \| r_X | p_Y), \tag{256}$$

where the marginal PMF p_X is given by

$$p_X(x) = \sum_y p_{XY}(x,y). \tag{257}$$

This motivates Corollary 3, where (256) is derived from (254).

The last result of this section provides a new operational meaning to the Lapidoth–Pfister mutual information $J_\alpha(X;Y)$: assuming that $\beta \in (-\infty, 1)$ and that the gambler knows the winning probabilities, $J_{1/(1-\beta)}(X;Y)$ measures how much the side information that is available to the gambler but not the bookmaker increases the gambler's smallest guaranteed utility for a fixed level of fairness c. To see this, consider first the setting without side information. By Theorem 9, the gambler chooses $b = g^{(\beta)}$ to maximize her utility, where $g^{(\beta)}$ is defined in (207). Then, using the nonnegativity of the Rényi divergence (Proposition 1 (a)), the following lower bound on the gambler's utility follows from (206):

$$U_\beta \geq \log c. \tag{258}$$

We call the RHS of (258) the smallest guaranteed utility for a fixed level of fairness c because (258) holds with equality if the bookmaker chooses the odds inversely proportional to the winning probabilities. Comparing (258) with (259) below, we see that the difference due to the side information is $J_{1/(1-\beta)}(X;Y)$. Note that $J_{1/(1-\beta)}(X;Y)$ is typically not the difference between the utility with and without side information; this is because the odds for which (258) and (259) hold with equality are typically not the same.

Theorem 11. Let $\beta \in (-\infty, 1)$. If $b_{X|Y}$ is equal to $g^{(\beta)}_{X|Y}$ from Theorem 10, then

$$U_\beta \geq \log c + J_{\frac{1}{1-\beta}}(X;Y). \tag{259}$$

Moreover, for every $c > 0$, there exist odds $o: \mathcal{X} \to (0, \infty)$ such that (259) holds with equality.

Proof. For this choice of $b_{X|Y}$, (259) holds because

$$U_\beta = \log c + D^1_{\frac{1}{1-\beta}}(p_{X|Y} \| r_X | p_Y) \tag{260}$$

$$\geq \log c + \min_{\tilde{r}_X \in \mathcal{P}(\mathcal{X})} D^1_{\frac{1}{1-\beta}}(p_{X|Y} \| \tilde{r}_X | p_Y) \tag{261}$$

$$= \log c + J_{\frac{1}{1-\beta}}(X;Y), \tag{262}$$

where (260) follows from Theorem 10, and (262) follows from Proposition 5.

Fix now $c > 0$, let $\tilde{r}_X^*$ achieve the minimum on the RHS of (261), and choose the odds

$$o(x) = \frac{c}{\tilde{r}_X^*(x)}. \tag{263}$$

Then, (261) holds with equality because $r_X = \tilde{r}_X^*$ by (241) and (242). □

10. Horse Betting with Part of the Money

In this section, we treat the possibility that the gambler does not invest all her wealth. We restrict ourselves to the setting without side information and to $\beta \in (-\infty, 0) \cup (0, 1)$. (For the case $\beta = 0$, see [47] (Section 10.5).) We assume that $p(x) > 0$ and $o(x) > 0$ for all $x \in \mathcal{X}$. Denote by $b(0)$ the fraction of her wealth that the gambler does not use for betting. (We assume $0 \notin \mathcal{X}$.) Then, $b \colon \mathcal{X} \cup \{0\} \to [0, 1]$ is a PMF, and the wealth relative S is the random variable

$$S \triangleq b(0) + b(X)o(X). \tag{264}$$

As in Section 8, define the constant

$$c \triangleq \left[\sum_x \frac{1}{o(x)} \right]^{-1}. \tag{265}$$

We treat the cases $c < 1$ and $c \geq 1$ separately, starting with the latter. If $c \geq 1$, then it is optimal to invest all the money:

Proposition 11. *Assume $c \geq 1$, let $\beta \in \mathbb{R}$, and let b be a PMF on $\mathcal{X} \cup \{0\}$ with utility U_β. Then, there exists a PMF b' on $\mathcal{X} \cup \{0\}$ with $b'(0) = 0$ and utility $U'_\beta \geq U_\beta$.*

Proof. Choose the PMF b' as follows:

$$b'(x) = \begin{cases} \frac{c}{o(x)} \cdot b(0) + b(x) & \text{if } x \in \mathcal{X}, \\ 0 & \text{if } x = 0. \end{cases} \tag{266}$$

Then, for every $x \in \mathcal{X}$,

$$b'(0) + b'(x)o(x) = c \cdot b(0) + b(x)o(x) \tag{267}$$
$$\geq b(0) + b(x)o(x), \tag{268}$$

where (268) holds because $c \geq 1$ by assumption. For $\beta > 0$, $U'_\beta \geq U_\beta$ holds because (268) implies $E[S'^\beta] \geq E[S^\beta]$. For $\beta < 0$ and $\beta = 0$, $U'_\beta \geq U_\beta$ follows similarly from (268). □

On the other hand, if $\beta < 1$ and the odds are subfair, i.e., if $c < 1$, then Claim (c) of the following theorem shows that investing all the money is not optimal:

Theorem 12. *Assume $c < 1$, let $\beta \in (-\infty, 0) \cup (0, 1)$, and let b^* be a PMF on $\mathcal{X} \cup \{0\}$ that maximizes U_β among all PMFs b. Defining*

$$\mathcal{S} \triangleq \{x \in \mathcal{X} : b^*(x) > 0\}, \tag{269}$$

$$\Gamma \triangleq \frac{1 - \sum_{x \in \mathcal{S}} p(x)}{1 - \sum_{x \in \mathcal{S}} \frac{1}{o(x)}}, \tag{270}$$

$$\gamma(x) \triangleq \max\left\{0, \Gamma^{\frac{1}{\beta-1}} p(x)^{\frac{1}{1-\beta}} o(x)^{\frac{\beta}{1-\beta}} - \frac{1}{o(x)}\right\} \quad \forall x \in \mathcal{X}, \tag{271}$$

the following claims hold:

(a) Both the numerator and denominator on the RHS of (270) are positive, so Γ is well-defined and positive.
(b) For every $x \in \mathcal{X}$,

$$b^*(x) = \gamma(x) b^*(0). \tag{272}$$

(c) The quantity $b^*(0)$ satisfies

$$b^*(0) = \frac{1}{1 + \sum_{x \in \mathcal{X}} \gamma(x)}. \tag{273}$$

In particular, $b^*(0) > 0$.

Claim (b) implies that for every $x \in \mathcal{X}$, $b^*(x) > 0$ if and only if $p(x)o(x) > \Gamma$. Ordering the elements $x_1, x_2, \ldots$ of $\mathcal{X}$ such that $p(x_1)o(x_1) \geq p(x_2)o(x_2) \geq \ldots$, the set $\mathcal{S}$ thus has a special structure: it is either empty or equal to $\{x_1, x_2, \ldots, x_k\}$ for some integer k. To maximize U_β, the following procedure can be used: for every $\mathcal{S}$ with the above structure, compute the corresponding b according to (270)–(273); and from these b's, take one that maximizes U_β. This procedure leads to an optimal solution: an optimal solution b^* exists because we are optimizing a continuous function over a compact set, and b^* corresponds to a set $\mathcal{S}$ that will be considered by the procedure.

Proof of Theorem 12. The proof is based on the Karush–Kuhn–Tucker conditions. By separately considering the cases $\beta \in (0,1)$ and $\beta < 0$, we first show that, for $\beta \in (-\infty, 0) \cup (0, 1)$, a strategy $b(\cdot)$ is optimal if and only if the following conditions are satisfied for some $\mu \in \mathbb{R}$:

$$\sum_{x \in \mathcal{X}} p(x) \left(b(0) + b(x) o(x) \right)^{\beta-1} \begin{cases} = \mu & \text{if } b(0) > 0, \\ \leq \mu & \text{if } b(0) = 0, \end{cases} \tag{274}$$

and, for every $x \in \mathcal{X}$,

$$p(x) o(x) \left(b(0) + b(x) o(x) \right)^{\beta-1} \begin{cases} = \mu & \text{if } b(x) > 0, \\ \leq \mu & \text{if } b(x) = 0. \end{cases} \tag{275}$$

Consider first $\beta \in (0,1)$, and define the function $\tau \colon \mathcal{P}(\mathcal{X} \cup \{0\}) \to \mathbb{R}$,

$$\tau(b) \triangleq \sum_{x \in \mathcal{X}} p(x) \left(b(0) + b(x) o(x) \right)^\beta. \tag{276}$$

Since $\beta > 0$ and since the logarithm is an increasing function, maximizing $U_\beta = \frac{1}{\beta} \log \mathrm{E}[S^\beta]$ over b is equivalent to maximizing $\tau(b)$. Observe that τ is concave, thus, by the Karush–Kuhn–Tucker conditions [11] (Theorem 4.4.1), it is maximized by a PMF b if and only if there exists a $\lambda \in \mathbb{R}$ such that (i) for all $x \in \mathcal{X} \cup \{0\}$ with $b(x) > 0$,

$$\frac{\partial \tau}{\partial b(x)}(b) = \lambda, \tag{277}$$

and (ii) for all $x \in \mathcal{X} \cup \{0\}$ with $b(x) = 0$,

$$\frac{\partial \tau}{\partial b(x)}(b) \leq \lambda. \tag{278}$$

Henceforth, we use the following notation: to designate that (i) and (ii) both hold, we write

$$\frac{\partial \tau}{\partial b(x)}(b) \begin{cases} = \lambda & \text{if } b(x) > 0, \\ \leq \lambda & \text{if } b(x) = 0. \end{cases} \quad (279)$$

Dividing both sides of (279) by $\beta > 0$ and defining $\mu \triangleq \frac{\lambda}{\beta}$, we obtain that (279) is equivalent to

$$\frac{1}{\beta} \cdot \frac{\partial \tau}{\partial b(x)}(b) \begin{cases} = \mu & \text{if } b(x) > 0, \\ \leq \mu & \text{if } b(x) = 0. \end{cases} \quad (280)$$

Now, (280) translates to (274) for $x = 0$ and to (275) for $x \in \mathcal{X}$.

Consider now $\beta < 0$, and define τ as in (276). Then, because $\beta < 0$, maximizing $U_\beta = \frac{1}{\beta} \log \mathbb{E}[S^\beta]$ is equivalent to minimizing τ. The function τ is convex, thus Inequality (278) is reversed. Dividing by $\beta < 0$ again reverses the inequalities, thus (280), (274), and (275) continue to hold for $\beta < 0$.

Having established that, for all $\beta \in (-\infty, 0) \cup (0, 1)$, a strategy b is optimal if and only if (274) and (275) hold, we next continue with the proof. Let $\beta \in (-\infty, 0) \cup (0, 1)$, and let b^* be a PMF on $\mathcal{X} \cup \{0\}$ that maximizes U_β. By the above discussion, (274) and (275) are satisfied by b^* for some $\mu \in \mathbb{R}$. The LHS of (274) is positive, so $\mu > 0$. We now show that for all $x \in \mathcal{X}$,

$$b^*(x) = \max\left\{0, \left[\frac{p(x)o(x)^\beta}{\mu}\right]^{\frac{1}{1-\beta}} - \frac{b^*(0)}{o(x)}\right\}. \quad (281)$$

To this end, fix $x \in \mathcal{X}$. If $b^*(x) > 0$, then (275) implies

$$b^*(x) = \left[\frac{p(x)o(x)^\beta}{\mu}\right]^{\frac{1}{1-\beta}} - \frac{b^*(0)}{o(x)}, \quad (282)$$

and the RHS of (282) is equal to the RHS of (281) because, being equal to $b^*(x)$, it is positive. If $b^*(x) = 0$, then (275) implies

$$\left[\frac{p(x)o(x)^\beta}{\mu}\right]^{\frac{1}{1-\beta}} - \frac{b^*(0)}{o(x)} \leq 0, \quad (283)$$

so the RHS of (281) is zero and (281) hence holds.

Having established (281), we next show that $b^*(\hat{x}) = 0$ for some $\hat{x} \in \mathcal{X}$. For a contradiction, assume that $b^*(x) > 0$ for all $x \in \mathcal{X}$. Then,

$$\sum_{x \in \mathcal{X}} p(x) \left(b^*(0) + b^*(x)o(x)\right)^{\beta-1} = \mu \sum_{x \in \mathcal{X}} \frac{1}{o(x)} \quad (284)$$

$$> \mu, \quad (285)$$

where (284) follows from (275), and (285) holds because $c < 1$ by assumption. However, this is impossible: (285) contradicts (274).

Let now $\hat{x} \in \mathcal{X}$ be such that $b^*(\hat{x}) = 0$. Then, by (281),

$$\left[\frac{p(\hat{x})o(\hat{x})^\beta}{\mu}\right]^{\frac{1}{1-\beta}} - \frac{b^*(0)}{o(\hat{x})} \leq 0. \quad (286)$$

Because $p(\hat{x})$ and $o(\hat{x})$ are positive, this implies $b^*(0) > 0$. Thus, by (274),

$$\sum_{x \in \mathcal{X}} p(x) \left(b^*(0) + b^*(x)o(x)\right)^{\beta-1} = \mu. \quad (287)$$

Splitting the sum on the LHS of (287) depending on whether $b^*(x) > 0$ or $b^*(x) = 0$, we obtain

$$\mu = \sum_{x \in S} p(x) \left(b^*(0) + b^*(x) o(x)\right)^{\beta-1} + \sum_{x \notin S} p(x) \left(b^*(0) + b^*(x) o(x)\right)^{\beta-1} \tag{288}$$

$$= \sum_{x \in S} \frac{\mu}{o(x)} + \sum_{x \notin S} p(x) b^*(0)^{\beta-1} \tag{289}$$

$$= \mu \sum_{x \in S} \frac{1}{o(x)} + b^*(0)^{\beta-1} \left[1 - \sum_{x \in S} p(x)\right], \tag{290}$$

where (289) follows from (275). Rearranging (290), we obtain

$$\mu \left[1 - \sum_{x \in S} \frac{1}{o(x)}\right] = b^*(0)^{\beta-1} \left[1 - \sum_{x \in S} p(x)\right]. \tag{291}$$

Recall that $\mu > 0$ and $b^*(0) > 0$. In addition, $1 - \sum_{x \in S} p(x) > 0$ because $b^*(\hat{x}) = 0$ and hence $\hat{x} \notin S$. Thus, $1 - \sum_{x \in S} \frac{1}{o(x)} > 0$, so both the numerator and denominator in the definition of Γ in (270) are positive, which establishes Claim (a), namely that Γ is well-defined and positive.

To establish Claim (b), note that (291) and (270) imply that μ is given by

$$\mu = b^*(0)^{\beta-1} \Gamma, \tag{292}$$

which, when substituted into (281), yields (272).

We conclude by proving Claim (c). Because b^* is a PMF on $\mathcal{X} \cup \{0\}$,

$$1 = b^*(0) + \sum_{x \in \mathcal{X}} b^*(x) \tag{293}$$

$$= b^*(0) \left[1 + \sum_{x \in \mathcal{X}} \gamma(x)\right], \tag{294}$$

where (294) follows from (272). Rearranging (294) yields (273). □

11. Universal Betting for IID Races

In this section, we present a universal gambling strategy for IID races that requires neither knowledge of the winning probabilities nor of the parameter β of the utility function and yet asymptotically maximizes the utility function for all PMFs p and all $\beta \in \mathbb{R}$. Consider n consecutive horse races, where the winning horse in the ith race is denoted X_i for $i \in \{1, \ldots, n\}$. We assume that $X_1, \ldots, X_n$ are IID according to the PMF p, where $p(x) > 0$ for all $x \in \mathcal{X}$. In every race, the bookmaker offers the same odds $o \colon \mathcal{X} \to (0, \infty)$, and the gambler spends all her wealth placing bets on the horses. The gambler plays race-after-race, i.e., before placing bets for a race, she is revealed the winning horse of the previous race and receives the money from the bookmaker. Her betting strategy is hence a sequence of conditional PMFs $(b_{X_1}, b_{X_2|X_1}, b_{X_3|X_1 X_2}, \ldots, b_{X_n|X_1 X_2 \cdots X_{n-1}})$. The wealth relative is the random variable

$$S_n \triangleq \prod_{i=1}^{n} b(X_i|X_1, \ldots, X_{i-1}) o(X_i). \tag{295}$$

We seek betting strategies that maximize the utility function

$$U_{\beta,n} \triangleq \begin{cases} \frac{1}{\beta} \log \mathrm{E}[S_n^\beta] & \text{if } \beta \neq 0, \\ \mathrm{E}[\log S_n] & \text{if } \beta = 0. \end{cases} \tag{296}$$

We first establish that to maximize $U_{\beta,n}$ for a fixed $\beta \in \mathbb{R}$, it suffices to use the same betting strategy in every race; see Theorem 13. We then show that the individual-sequence-universal strategy by Cover–Ordentlich [48] allows to asymptotically achieve the same normalized utility without knowing p or β (see Theorem 14).

For a fixed $\beta \in \mathbb{R}$, let the PMF b^* be a betting strategy that maximizes the single-race utility U_β discussed in Section 8, and denote by U_β^* the utility associated with b^*. Using the same betting strategy b^* over n races leads to the utility $U_{\beta,n}$, and it follows from (295) and (296) that

$$U_{\beta,n} = n U_\beta^*. \tag{297}$$

As we show next, $n U_\beta^*$ is the maximum utility that can be achieved among all betting strategies:

Theorem 13. *Let $\beta \in \mathbb{R}$, and let $(b_{X_1}, b_{X_2|X_1}, b_{X_3|X_1X_2}, \ldots, b_{X_n|X_1X_2\cdots X_{n-1}})$ be a sequence of conditional PMFs. Then,*

$$U_{\beta,n} \leq n U_\beta^*. \tag{298}$$

Proof. We show (298) for $\beta > 0$; analogous arguments establish (298) for $\beta < 0$ and $\beta = 0$. We prove (298) by induction on n. For $n = 1$, (298) holds because U_β^* is the maximum single-race utility. Assume now $n \geq 2$ and that (298) is valid for $n-1$. For $\beta > 0$, (298) holds because

$$U_{\beta,n} = \frac{1}{\beta} \log \mathbb{E}[S_n^\beta] \tag{299}$$

$$= \frac{1}{\beta} \log \sum_{x_1, \ldots, x_n} P(x_1) \cdots P(x_n) \prod_{i=1}^{n} b(x_i|x^{i-1})^\beta o(x_i)^\beta \tag{300}$$

$$= \frac{1}{\beta} \log \sum_{x_1, \ldots, x_{n-1}} P(x_1) \cdots P(x_{n-1}) \left[\prod_{i=1}^{n-1} b(x_i|x^{i-1})^\beta o(x_i)^\beta\right] \sum_{x_n} P(x_n) b(x_n|x^{n-1})^\beta o(x_n)^\beta \tag{301}$$

$$\leq \frac{1}{\beta} \log \sum_{x_1, \ldots, x_{n-1}} P(x_1) \cdots P(x_{n-1}) \left[\prod_{i=1}^{n-1} b(x_i|x^{i-1})^\beta o(x_i)^\beta\right] \max_{b \in \mathcal{P}(\mathcal{X})} \sum_{x_n} P(x_n) b(x_n)^\beta o(x_n)^\beta \tag{302}$$

$$= \frac{1}{\beta} \log \sum_{x_1, \ldots, x_{n-1}} P(x_1) \cdots P(x_{n-1}) \left[\prod_{i=1}^{n-1} b(x_i|x^{i-1})^\beta o(x_i)^\beta\right] \sum_{x_n} P(x_n) b^*(x_n)^\beta o(x_n)^\beta \tag{303}$$

$$= U_{\beta,n-1} + U_\beta^* \tag{304}$$

$$\leq (n-1) U_\beta^* + U_\beta^* \tag{305}$$

$$= n U_\beta^*, \tag{306}$$

where (303) holds because b^* maximizes the single-race utility U_β, and (305) holds because (298) is valid for $n-1$. □

In portfolio theory, Cover–Ordentlich [48] (Definition 1) proposed a universal strategy. Adapted to our setting, it leads to the following sequence of conditional PMFs:

$$\hat{b}(x_i|x^{i-1}) = \frac{\int_{b \in \mathcal{P}(\mathcal{X})} b(x_i) S_{i-1}(b, x^{i-1}) d\mu(b)}{\int_{b \in \mathcal{P}(\mathcal{X})} S_{i-1}(b, x^{i-1}) d\mu(b)}, \tag{307}$$

where $i \in \{1, 2, \ldots\}$; μ is the Dirichlet$(1/2, \ldots, 1/2)$ distribution on $\mathcal{P}(\mathcal{X})$; $S_0(b, x^0) \triangleq 1$; and

$$S_i(b, x^i) \triangleq \prod_{j=1}^{i} b(x_j) o(x_j). \tag{308}$$

This strategy depends neither on the winning probabilities p nor on the parameter β. Denoting the utility (296) associated with the strategy $\hat{b}(x_i|x^{i-1})$ by $\hat{U}_{\beta,n}$, we have the following result:

Theorem 14. *For every $\beta \in \mathbb{R}$,*

$$nU_\beta^* - \log 2 - \frac{|\mathcal{X}|-1}{2}\log(n+1) \leq \hat{U}_{\beta,n} \tag{309}$$

$$\leq nU_\beta^*. \tag{310}$$

Hence,

$$\lim_{n\to\infty} \frac{1}{n} \hat{U}_{\beta,n} = U_\beta^*. \tag{311}$$

Proof. Inequality (310) follows from Theorem 13; and (311) follows from (309) and (310) and the sandwich theorem. It thus remains to establish (309): We do so for $\beta > 0$; analogous arguments establish (309) for $\beta < 0$ and $\beta = 0$. For a fixed sequence $x^n \in \mathcal{X}^n$, let $\tilde{b}$ be a PMF on $\mathcal{X}$ that maximizes $S_n(b, x^n)$, and denote the wealth relative in (295) associated with using $\tilde{b}$ in every race by $\tilde{S}_n(x^n)$, thus

$$\tilde{S}_n(x^n) = \max_{b \in \mathcal{P}(\mathcal{X})} \prod_{i=1}^n b(x_i)o(x_i). \tag{312}$$

Let $\hat{S}_n(x^n)$ denote the wealth relative in (295) associated with the strategy $\hat{b}(x_i|x^{i-1})$ and the sequence x^n. Using [48] (Theorem 2) it follows that, for every $x^n \in \mathcal{X}^n$,

$$\hat{S}_n(x^n) \geq \frac{1}{2(n+1)^{(|\mathcal{X}|-1)/2}} \tilde{S}_n(x^n). \tag{313}$$

This implies that (309) holds for $\beta > 0$ because

$$\hat{U}_{\beta,n} = \frac{1}{\beta}\log \mathrm{E}[\hat{S}_n(X^n)^\beta] \tag{314}$$

$$\geq \frac{1}{\beta}\log \mathrm{E}[\tilde{S}_n(X^n)^\beta] - \log 2 - \frac{|\mathcal{X}|-1}{2}\log(n+1) \tag{315}$$

$$\geq \frac{1}{\beta}\log \sum_{x_1,\ldots,x_n} P(x_1)\cdots P(x_n)\prod_{i=1}^n b^*(x_i)^\beta o(x_i)^\beta - \log 2 - \frac{|\mathcal{X}|-1}{2}\log(n+1) \tag{316}$$

$$= nU_\beta^* - \log 2 - \frac{|\mathcal{X}|-1}{2}\log(n+1), \tag{317}$$

where (315) follows from (313), and (316) follows from (312). □

Remark 9. *As discussed in Section 8, the optimal single-race betting strategy varies significantly with different values of β, thus it might be a bit surprising that the Cover–Ordentlich strategy is not only universal with respect to the winning probabilities, but also with respect to β. This is due to the following two reasons: First, for fixed winning probabilities and a fixed β, it is optimal to use the same betting strategy in every race (see Theorem 13). Second, for every $x^n \in \mathcal{X}^n$, the wealth relative of the Cover–Ordentlich strategy is not much worse than that of using the same strategy $b(\cdot)$ in every race, irrespective of $b(\cdot)$ (see (313)). Hence, irrespective of the optimal single-race betting strategy, the Cover–Ordentlich strategy is able to asymptotically achieve the same normalized utility.*

Author Contributions: Writing—original draft preparation, C.B., A.L., and C.P.; and writing—review and editing, C.B., A.L., and C.P. All authors have read and agreed to the published version of the manuscript

Funding: This research received no external funding.

Conflicts of Interest: The authors declare no conflict of interest.

Appendix A. Proof of Proposition 1

These properties mostly follow from van Erven–Harremoës [8]:

(a) See [8] (Theorem 8).
(b) This follows from the definitions in (4) and (21)–(23) and the conventions in (20).
(c) This follows from [8] (Theorem 7) and the fact that $\lim_{\alpha \to 1} D_\alpha(P\|Q) = D(P\|Q)$ by L'Hôpital's rule. (Note that $\alpha \mapsto D_\alpha(P\|Q)$ does not need to be continuous at $\alpha = 1$ when the alphabets are not finite; see the discussion after [8] (Equation (18)).)
(d) See [8] (Theorem 3).
(e) Let $\alpha, \alpha' \in (0, \infty)$ satisfy $\alpha \leq \alpha'$. Then,

$$\frac{1-\alpha}{\alpha} D_\alpha(P\|Q) = D_{1-\alpha}(Q\|P) \tag{A1}$$

$$\geq D_{1-\alpha'}(Q\|P) \tag{A2}$$

$$= \frac{1-\alpha'}{\alpha'} D_{\alpha'}(P\|Q), \tag{A3}$$

where (A1) and (A3) follow from [8] (Lemma 10), and (A2) holds because the Rényi divergence, extended to negative orders, is nondecreasing ([8] (Theorem 39)).

(f) See [8] (Corollary 2).
(g) For $\alpha \in (0, \infty)$,

$$(\alpha - 1) D_{1/\alpha}(P\|Q) = \alpha \left(1 - \frac{1}{\alpha}\right) D_{1/\alpha}(P\|Q) \tag{A4}$$

$$= \alpha \inf_R \left[\frac{1}{\alpha} D(R\|P) + \left(1 - \frac{1}{\alpha}\right) D(R\|Q)\right] \tag{A5}$$

$$= \inf_R \left[D(R\|P) + (\alpha - 1) D(R\|Q)\right], \tag{A6}$$

where (A5) follows from [8] (Theorem 30). Hence, $(\alpha - 1) D_{1/\alpha}(P\|Q)$ is concave in α because the expression in square brackets on the RHS of (A6) is concave in α for every R and because the pointwise infimum preserves the concavity.

(h) See [8] (Theorem 9).

Appendix B. Proof of Theorem 1

Beginning with (29),

$$D_\alpha^c(P_{Y'|X}\|Q_{Y'|X}|P_X) = \sum_{x \in \mathrm{supp}(P_X)} P(x) D_\alpha(P_{Y'|X=x}\|Q_{Y'|X=x}) \tag{A7}$$

$$\leq \sum_{x \in \mathrm{supp}(P_X)} P(x) D_\alpha(P_{Y|X=x}\|Q_{Y|X=x}) \tag{A8}$$

$$= D_\alpha^c(P_{Y|X}\|Q_{Y|X}|P_X), \tag{A9}$$

where (A8) follows by applying, separately for every $x \in \mathrm{supp}(P_X)$, Proposition 1 (h) with the conditional PMF $A_{Y'|Y, X=x}$.

Appendix C. Proof of Theorem 2

We show (43) for $\alpha \in (0,1)$; the claim then extends to $\alpha \in [0,1]$ by the continuity of $D_\alpha^c(\cdot)$ in α (Proposition 2 (c)). Let $\alpha \in (0,1)$. Keeping in mind that $\alpha - 1 < 0$, (43) holds because

$$(\alpha - 1) D_\alpha^c(P_{Y|X'} \| Q_{Y|X'} | P_{X'})$$
$$= \sum_{x' \in \mathrm{supp}(P_{X'})} P_{X'}(x') \log \sum_y P_{Y|X'}(y|x')^\alpha Q_{Y|X'}(y|x')^{1-\alpha} \qquad \text{(A10)}$$

$$= \sum_{x' \in \mathrm{supp}(P_{X'})} P_{X'}(x') \log \sum_y \left[\sum_x B_{X|X'}(x|x') P_{Y|X}(y|x)\right]^\alpha \left[\sum_x B_{X|X'}(x|x') Q_{Y|X}(y|x)\right]^{1-\alpha} \qquad \text{(A11)}$$

$$\geq \sum_{x' \in \mathrm{supp}(P_{X'})} P_{X'}(x') \log \sum_y \sum_x B_{X|X'}(x|x') P_{Y|X}(y|x)^\alpha Q_{Y|X}(y|x)^{1-\alpha} \qquad \text{(A12)}$$

$$= \sum_{x' \in \mathrm{supp}(P_{X'})} P_{X'}(x') \log \sum_{x \in \mathrm{supp}(P_X)} B_{X|X'}(x|x') \sum_y P_{Y|X}(y|x)^\alpha Q_{Y|X}(y|x)^{1-\alpha} \qquad \text{(A13)}$$

$$\geq \sum_{x' \in \mathrm{supp}(P_{X'})} P_{X'}(x') \sum_{x \in \mathrm{supp}(P_X)} B_{X|X'}(x|x') \log \sum_y P_{Y|X}(y|x)^\alpha Q_{Y|X}(y|x)^{1-\alpha} \qquad \text{(A14)}$$

$$= \sum_{x \in \mathrm{supp}(P_X)} P_X(x) \left[\sum_{x' \in \mathrm{supp}(P_{X'})} B_{X'|X}(x'|x)\right] \log \sum_y P_{Y|X}(y|x)^\alpha Q_{Y|X}(y|x)^{1-\alpha} \qquad \text{(A15)}$$

$$= \sum_{x \in \mathrm{supp}(P_X)} P_X(x) \log \sum_y P_{Y|X}(y|x)^\alpha Q_{Y|X}(y|x)^{1-\alpha} \qquad \text{(A16)}$$

$$= (\alpha - 1) D_\alpha^c(P_{Y|X} \| Q_{Y|X} | P_X), \qquad \text{(A17)}$$

where (A10) follows from (30); (A11) follows from (41) and (42); (A12) follows from Hölder's inequality; (A13) holds because $B_{X|X'}(x|x') = 0$ if $P_{X'}(x') > 0$ and $P_X(x) = 0$; (A14) follows from Jensen's inequality because $\log(\cdot)$ is concave; (A15) follows from (40); (A16) holds because $P_X(x) > 0$ and $P_{X'}(x') = 0$ imply $B_{X'|X}(x'|x) = 0$, hence the expression in square brackets on the LHS of (A16) equals one; and (A17) follows from (30).

Appendix D. Proof of Corollary 1

Applying Theorem 2 with $\mathcal{X}' \triangleq \{1\}$ and the conditional PMF $B_{X'|X}(x'|x) \triangleq 1$, we obtain

$$D_\alpha^c(P_{Y|X'} \| Q_{Y|X'} | P_{X'}) \leq D_\alpha^c(P_{Y|X} \| Q_{Y|X} | P_X). \qquad \text{(A18)}$$

To complete the proof of (48), observe that

$$D_\alpha^c(P_{Y|X'} \| Q_{Y|X'} | P_{X'}) = D_\alpha^c(P_Y \| Q_Y | P_{X'}) \qquad \text{(A19)}$$
$$= D_\alpha(P_Y \| Q_Y), \qquad \text{(A20)}$$

where (A19) holds because (41) and (46) imply $P_{Y|X'}(y|x') = P_Y(y)$ and because (42) and (47) imply $Q_{Y|X'}(y|x') = Q_Y(y)$; and (A20) follows from Remark 1.

Appendix E. Proof of Example 1

If $\alpha = \infty$, then it can be verified numerically that (53) holds for $\epsilon = 0.1$. Fix now $\alpha \in (1, \infty)$. Then, for all $\epsilon \in (0,1)$,

$$D_\alpha(P_Y \| Q_Y^{(\epsilon)}) = \frac{1}{\alpha - 1} \log\left[0.5^\alpha (1-\epsilon)^{1-\alpha} + 0.5^\alpha \epsilon^{1-\alpha}\right] \qquad \text{(A21)}$$

$$\geq \frac{1}{\alpha - 1} \log\left[0.5^\alpha \epsilon^{1-\alpha}\right] \qquad \text{(A22)}$$

$$= \frac{\alpha}{\alpha - 1} \log 0.5 + \log \frac{1}{\epsilon}. \tag{A23}$$

The RHS of (53) satisfies, for sufficiently small ϵ,

$$D_\alpha^c(P_{Y|X}^{(\epsilon)} \| Q_Y^{(\epsilon)} | P_X) = 0.5 \cdot 0 + 0.5 \cdot D_\alpha(P_{Y|X=1}^{(\epsilon)} \| Q_Y^{(\epsilon)}) \tag{A24}$$

$$= \frac{0.5}{\alpha - 1} \log \left[\epsilon^\alpha (1-\epsilon)^{1-\alpha} + (1-\epsilon)^\alpha \epsilon^{1-\alpha} \right] \tag{A25}$$

$$= \frac{0.5}{\alpha - 1} \log \left[\epsilon^{1-\alpha} \left((1-\epsilon)^\alpha + \epsilon^{2\alpha-1}(1-\epsilon)^{1-\alpha} \right) \right] \tag{A26}$$

$$\leq \frac{0.5}{\alpha - 1} \log \left[2\epsilon^{1-\alpha} \right] \tag{A27}$$

$$= \frac{0.5}{\alpha - 1} \log 2 + 0.5 \log \frac{1}{\epsilon}, \tag{A28}$$

where (A27) holds for sufficiently small ϵ because $\lim_{\epsilon \downarrow 0} ((1-\epsilon)^\alpha + \epsilon^{2\alpha-1}(1-\epsilon)^{1-\alpha}) = 1$. Because $\lim_{\epsilon \downarrow 0} \log \frac{1}{\epsilon} = \infty$, (53) follows from (A23) and (A28) for sufficiently small ϵ.

Appendix F. Proof of Theorem 3

Observe that, for all $x' \in \mathcal{X}$ and all $y' \in \mathcal{Y}'$,

$$P_X(x') P_{Y'|X}(y'|x') = \sum_{x,y} P_X(x) P_{Y|X}(y|x) \mathbb{1}\{x' = x\} A_{Y'|XY}(y'|x,y), \tag{A29}$$

$$P_X(x') Q_{Y'|X}(y'|x') = \sum_{x,y} P_X(x) Q_{Y|X}(y|x) \mathbb{1}\{x' = x\} A_{Y'|XY}(y'|x,y). \tag{A30}$$

Hence, (68) follows from (54) and

$$D_\alpha(P_X P_{Y'|X} \| P_X Q_{Y'|X}) \leq D_\alpha(P_X P_{Y|X} \| P_X Q_{Y|X}), \tag{A31}$$

which follows from the data-processing inequality for the Rényi divergence by substituting $\mathbb{1}_{X'=X} A_{Y'|XY}$ for $A_{X'Y'|XY}$ in Proposition 1 (h).

Appendix G. Proof of Theorem 4

Observe that, for all $x' \in \mathcal{X}'$ and all $y' \in \mathcal{Y}$,

$$P_{X'}(x') P_{Y|X'}(y'|x') = \sum_{x,y} P_X(x) P_{Y|X}(y|x) B_{X'|X}(x'|x) \mathbb{1}\{y' = y\}, \tag{A32}$$

$$P_{X'}(x') Q_{Y|X'}(y'|x') = \sum_{x,y} P_X(x) Q_{Y|X}(y|x) B_{X'|X}(x'|x) \mathbb{1}\{y' = y\}. \tag{A33}$$

Hence, (73) follows from (54) and

$$D_\alpha(P_{X'} P_{Y|X'} \| P_{X'} Q_{Y|X'}) \leq D_\alpha(P_X P_{Y|X} \| P_X Q_{Y|X}), \tag{A34}$$

which follows from the data-processing inequality for the Rényi divergence by substituting $B_{X'|X} \mathbb{1}_{Y'=Y}$ for $A_{X'Y'|XY}$ in Proposition 1 (h).

References

1. Kelly, J.L., Jr. A new interpretation of information rate. *Bell Syst. Tech. J.* **1956**, *35*, 917–926. [CrossRef]
2. Cover, T.M.; Thomas, J.A. *Elements of Information Theory*, 2nd ed.; John Wiley & Sons: Hoboken, NJ, USA, 2006; ISBN 978-0-471-24195-9.
3. Lapidoth, A.; Pfister, C. Two measures of dependence. *Entropy* **2019**, *21*, 778. [CrossRef]

4. Kullback, S.; Leibler, R.A. On information and sufficiency. *Ann. Math. Stat.* **1951**, *22*, 79–86. [CrossRef]
5. Csiszár, I.; Körner, J. *Information Theory: Coding Theorems for Discrete Memoryless Systems*, 2nd ed.; Cambridge University Press: Cambridge, UK, 2011; ISBN 978-0-521-19681-9.
6. Csiszár, I.; Shields, P.C. *Information Theory and Statistics: A Tutorial*; now Publishers: Hanover, MA, USA, 2004; ISBN 978-1-933019-05-5.
7. Rényi, A. On measures of entropy and information. In Proceedings of the Fourth Berkeley Symposium on Mathematical Statistics and Probability, Berkeley, CA, USA, 20 June–30 July 1960; Volume 1, pp. 547–561.
8. van Erven, T.; Harremoës, P. Rényi divergence and Kullback–Leibler divergence. *IEEE Trans. Inf. Theory* **2014**, *60*, 3797–3820. [CrossRef]
9. Csiszár, I. Generalized cutoff rates and Rényi's information measures. *IEEE Trans. Inf. Theory* **1995**, *41*, 26–34. [CrossRef]
10. Sibson, R. Information radius. *Z. Wahrscheinlichkeitstheorie verw. Geb.* **1969**, *14*, 149–160. [CrossRef]
11. Gallager, R.G. *Information Theory and Reliable Communication*; John Wiley & Sons: Hoboken, NJ, USA, 1968; ISBN 978-0-471-29048-3.
12. Arimoto, S. Information measures and capacity of order α for discrete memoryless channels. In *Topics in Information Theory*; Csiszár, I., Elias, P., Eds.; North-Holland Publishing Company: Amsterdam, The Netherlands, 1977; pp. 41–52, ISBN 0-7204-0699-4.
13. Eeckhoudt, L.; Gollier, C.; Schlesinger, H. *Economic and Financial Decisions under Risk*; Princeton University Press: Princeton, NJ, USA, 2005; ISBN 978-0-691-12215-1.
14. Soklakov, A.N. Economics of disagreement – financial intuition for the Rényi divergence. *arXiv* **2018**, arXiv:1811.08308.
15. Steele, J.M. *The Cauchy–Schwarz Master Class: An Introduction to the Art of Mathematical Inequalities*; Cambridge University Press: Cambridge, UK, 2004; ISBN 978-0-521-54677-5.
16. Bullen, P.S. *Handbook of Means and Their Inequalities*; Kluwer Academic Publishers: Dordrecht, The Netherlands, 2003; ISBN 978-1-4020-1522-9.
17. Campbell, L.L. A coding theorem and Rényi's entropy. *Inf. Control* **1965**, *8*, 423–429. [CrossRef]
18. Campbell, L.L. Definition of entropy by means of a coding problem. *Z. Wahrscheinlichkeitstheorie verw. Geb.* **1966**, *6*, 113–118. [CrossRef]
19. Merhav, N. On optimum strategies for minimizing the exponential moments of a loss function. *Commun. Inf. Syst.* **2011**, *11*, 343–368. [CrossRef]
20. Sason, I.; Verdú, S. Improved bounds on lossless source coding and guessing moments via Rényi measures. *IEEE Trans. Inf. Theory* **2018**, *64*, 4323–4346. [CrossRef]
21. Augustin, U. Noisy Channels. Habilitation Thesis, Universität Erlangen–Nürnberg, Erlangen, Germany, 1978.
22. Nakiboğlu, B. The Augustin capacity and center. *Probl. Inf. Transm.* **2019**, *55*, 299–342. [CrossRef]
23. Nakiboğlu, B. The sphere packing bound for memoryless channels. *arXiv* **2018**, arXiv:1804.06372.
24. Ho, S.-W.; Verdú, S. Convexity/concavity of Rényi entropy and α-mutual information. In Proceedings of the 2015 IEEE International Symposium on Information Theory (ISIT), Hong Kong, China, 14–19 June 2015; pp. 745–749. [CrossRef]
25. Verdú, S. α-mutual information. In Proceedings of the 2015 Information Theory and Applications Workshop (ITA), San Diego, CA, USA, 1–6 February 2015; pp. 1–6. [CrossRef]
26. Nakiboğlu, B. The Rényi capacity and center. *IEEE Trans. Inf. Theory* **2019**, *65*, 841–860. [CrossRef]
27. Cai, C.; Verdú, S. Conditional Rényi divergence saddlepoint and the maximization of α-mutual information. *Entropy* **2019**, *21*, 969. [CrossRef]
28. Fong, S.L.; Tan, V.Y.F. Strong converse theorems for classes of multimessage multicast networks: A Rényi divergence approach. *IEEE Trans. Inf. Theory* **2016**, *62*, 4953–4967. [CrossRef]
29. Yu, L.; Tan, V.Y.F. Rényi resolvability and its applications to the wiretap channel. *IEEE Trans. Inf. Theory* **2019**, *65*, 1862–1897. [CrossRef]
30. Gallager, R.G. A simple derivation of the coding theorem and some applications. *IEEE Trans. Inf. Theory* **1965**, *11*, 3–18. [CrossRef]
31. Shannon, C.E.; Gallager, R.G.; Berlekamp, E.R. Lower bounds to error probability for coding on discrete memoryless channels. I. *Inf. Control* **1967**, *10*, 65–103. [CrossRef]
32. Shannon, C.E.; Gallager, R.G.; Berlekamp, E.R. Lower bounds to error probability for coding on discrete memoryless channels. II. *Inf. Control* **1967**, *10*, 522–552. [CrossRef]

33. Arimoto, S. On the converse to the coding theorem for discrete memoryless channels. *IEEE Trans. Inf. Theory* **1973**, *19*, 357–359. [CrossRef]
34. Polyanskiy, Y.; Verdú, S. Arimoto channel coding converse and Rényi divergence. In Proceedings of the 2010 48th Annual Allerton Conference on Communication, Control, and Computing (Allerton), Allerton, IL, USA, 29 September–1 October 2010; pp. 1327–1333. [CrossRef]
35. Nakiboğlu, B. The sphere packing bound via Augustin's method. *IEEE Trans. Inf. Theory* **2019**, *65*, 816–840. [CrossRef]
36. Nakiboğlu, B. The sphere packing bound for DSPCs with feedback à la Augustin. *IEEE Trans. Commun.* **2019**, *67*, 7456–7467. [CrossRef]
37. Tomamichel, M.; Hayashi, M. Operational interpretation of Rényi information measures via composite hypothesis testing against product and Markov distributions. *IEEE Trans. Inf. Theory* **2018**, *64*, 1064–1082. [CrossRef]
38. Aishwarya, G.; Madiman, M. Remarks on Rényi versions of conditional entropy and mutual information. In Proceedings of the 2019 IEEE International Symposium on Information Theory (ISIT), Paris, France, 7–12 July 2019; pp. 1117–1121. [CrossRef]
39. Lapidoth, A.; Pfister, C. Testing against independence and a Rényi information measure. In Proceedings of the 2018 IEEE Information Theory Workshop (ITW), Guangzhou, China, 25–29 November 2018; pp. 1–5. [CrossRef]
40. Fehr, S.; Berens, S. On the conditional Rényi entropy. *IEEE Trans. Inf. Theory* **2014**, *60*, 6801–6810. [CrossRef]
41. Sason, I.; Verdú, S. Arimoto–Rényi conditional entropy and Bayesian M-ary hypothesis testing. *IEEE Trans. Inf. Theory* **2018**, *64*, 4–25. [CrossRef]
42. Arıkan, E. An inequality on guessing and its application to sequential decoding. *IEEE Trans. Inf. Theory* **1996**, *42*, 99–105. [CrossRef]
43. Sundaresan, R. Guessing under source uncertainty. *IEEE Trans. Inf. Theory* **2007**, *53*, 269–287. [CrossRef]
44. Bracher, A.; Lapidoth, A.; Pfister, C. Guessing with distributed encoders. *Entropy* **2019**, *21*, 298. [CrossRef]
45. Bunte, C.; Lapidoth, A. Encoding tasks and Rényi entropy. *IEEE Trans. Inf. Theory* **2014**, *60*, 5065–5076. [CrossRef]
46. Rockafellar, R.T. *Convex Analysis*; Princeton University Press: Princeton, NJ, USA, 1970; ISBN 978-0-691-01586-6.
47. Moser, S.M. Information Theory (Lecture Notes), version 6.6. 2018. Available online: http://moser-isi.ethz.ch/scripts.html (accessed on 8 March 2020).
48. Cover, T.M.; Ordentlich, E. Universal portfolios with side information. *IEEE Trans. Inf. Theory* **1996**, *42*, 348–363. [CrossRef]

© 2020 by the authors. Licensee MDPI, Basel, Switzerland. This article is an open access article distributed under the terms and conditions of the Creative Commons Attribution (CC BY) license (http://creativecommons.org/licenses/by/4.0/).

Article

On Relations Between the Relative Entropy and χ^2-Divergence, Generalizations and Applications

Tomohiro Nishiyama [1] and Igal Sason [2],*

[1] Independent Researcher, Tokyo 206–0003, Japan; htam0ybboh@gmail.com
[2] Faculty of Electrical Engineering, Technion—Israel Institute of Technology, Technion City, Haifa 3200003, Israel
* Correspondence: sason@ee.technion.ac.il; Tel.: +972-4-8294699

Received: 22 April 2020; Accepted: 17 May 2020; Published: 18 May 2020

Abstract: The relative entropy and the chi-squared divergence are fundamental divergence measures in information theory and statistics. This paper is focused on a study of integral relations between the two divergences, the implications of these relations, their information-theoretic applications, and some generalizations pertaining to the rich class of f-divergences. Applications that are studied in this paper refer to lossless compression, the method of types and large deviations, strong data–processing inequalities, bounds on contraction coefficients and maximal correlation, and the convergence rate to stationarity of a type of discrete-time Markov chains.

Keywords: relative entropy; chi-squared divergence; f-divergences; method of types; large deviations; strong data–processing inequalities; information contraction; maximal correlation; Markov chains

1. Introduction

The relative entropy (also known as the Kullback–Leibler divergence [1]) and the chi-squared divergence [2] are divergence measures which play a key role in information theory, statistics, learning, signal processing, and other theoretical and applied branches of mathematics. These divergence measures are fundamental in problems pertaining to source and channel coding, combinatorics and large deviations theory, goodness-of-fit and independence tests in statistics, expectation–maximization iterative algorithms for estimating a distribution from an incomplete data, and other sorts of problems (the reader is referred to the tutorial paper by Csiszár and Shields [3]). They both belong to an important class of divergence measures, defined by means of convex functions f, and named f-divergences [4–8]. In addition to the relative entropy and the chi-squared divergence, this class unifies other useful divergence measures such as the total variation distance in functional analysis, and it is also closely related to the Rényi divergence which generalizes the relative entropy [9,10]. In general, f-divergences (defined in Section 2) are attractive since they satisfy pleasing features such as the data–processing inequality, convexity, (semi)continuity, and duality properties, and they therefore find nice applications in information theory and statistics (see, e.g., [6,8,11,12]).

In this work, we study integral relations between the relative entropy and the chi-squared divergence, implications of these relations, and some of their information-theoretic applications. Some generalizations which apply to the class of f-divergences are also explored in detail. In this context, it should be noted that integral representations of general f-divergences, expressed as a function of either the DeGroot statistical information [13], the E_γ-divergence (a parametric sub-class of f-divergences, which generalizes the total variation distance [14] [p. 2314]) and the relative information spectrum, have been derived in [12] [Section 5], [15] [Section 7.B], and [16] [Section 3], respectively.

Applications in this paper are related to lossless source compression, large deviations by the method of types, and strong data–processing inequalities. The relevant background for each of these applications is provided to make the presentation self contained.

We next outline the paper contributions and the structure of our manuscript.

1.1. Paper Contributions

This work starts by introducing integral relations between the relative entropy and the chi-squared divergence, and some inequalities which relate these two divergences (see Theorem 1, its corollaries, and Proposition 1). It continues with a study of the implications and generalizations of these relations, pertaining to the rich class of f-divergences. One implication leads to a tight lower bound on the relative entropy between a pair of probability measures, expressed as a function of the means and variances under these measures (see Theorem 2). A second implication of Theorem 1 leads to an upper bound on a skew divergence (see Theorem 3 and Corollary 3). Due to the concavity of the Shannon entropy, let the concavity deficit of the entropy function be defined as the non-negative difference between the entropy of a convex combination of distributions and the convex combination of the entropies of these distributions. Then, Corollary 4 provides an upper bound on this deficit, expressed as a function of the pairwise relative entropies between all pairs of distributions. Theorem 4 provides a generalization of Theorem 1 to the class of f-divergences. It recursively constructs non-increasing sequences of f-divergences and as a consequence of Theorem 4 followed by the usage of polylogairthms, Corollary 5 provides a generalization of the useful integral relation in Theorem 1 between the relative entropy and the chi-squared divergence. Theorem 5 relates probabilities of sets to f-divergences, generalizing a known and useful result by Csiszár for the relative entropy. With respect to Theorem 1, the integral relation between the relative entropy and the chi-squared divergence has been independently derived in [17], which also derived an alternative upper bound on the concavity deficit of the entropy as a function of total variational distances (differing from the bound in Corollary 4, which depends on pairwise relative entropies). The interested reader is referred to [17], with a preprint of the extended version in [18], and to [19] where the connections in Theorem 1 were originally discovered in the quantum setting.

The second part of this work studies information-theoretic applications of the above results. These are ordered by starting from the relatively simple applications, and ending at the more complicated ones. The first one includes a bound on the redundancy of the Shannon code for universal lossless compression with discrete memoryless sources, used in conjunction with Theorem 3 (see Section 4.1). An application of Theorem 2 in the context of the method of types and large deviations analysis is then studied in Section 4.2, providing non-asymptotic bounds which lead to a closed-form expression as a function of the Lambert W function (see Proposition 2). Strong data–processing inequalities with bounds on contraction coefficients of skew divergences are provided in Theorem 6, Corollary 7 and Proposition 3. Consequently, non-asymptotic bounds on the convergence to stationarity of time-homogeneous, irreducible, and reversible discrete-time Markov chains with finite state spaces are obtained by relying on our bounds on the contraction coefficients of skew divergences (see Theorem 7). The exact asymptotic convergence rate is also obtained in Corollary 8. Finally, a property of maximal correlations is obtained in Proposition 4 as an application of our starting point on the integral relation between the relative entropy and the chi-squared divergence.

1.2. Paper Organization

This paper is structured as follows. Section 2 presents notation and preliminary material which is necessary for, or otherwise related to, the exposition of this work. Section 3 refers to the developed relations between divergences, and Section 4 studies information-theoretic applications. Proofs of the results in Sections 3 and 4 (except for short proofs) are deferred to Section 5.

2. Preliminaries and Notation

This section provides definitions of divergence measures which are used in this paper, and it also provides relevant notation.

Definition 1. *[12] [p. 4398] Let P and Q be probability measures, let μ be a dominating measure of P and Q (i.e., $P, Q \ll \mu$), and let $p := \frac{dP}{d\mu}$ and $q := \frac{dQ}{d\mu}$ be the densities of P and Q with respect to μ. The f-divergence from P to Q is given by*

$$D_f(P\|Q) := \int q f\left(\frac{p}{q}\right) d\mu, \tag{1}$$

where

$$f(0) := \lim_{t \to 0^+} f(t), \quad 0f\left(\frac{0}{0}\right) := 0, \tag{2}$$

$$0f\left(\frac{a}{0}\right) := \lim_{t \to 0^+} tf\left(\frac{a}{t}\right) = a \lim_{u \to \infty} \frac{f(u)}{u}, \quad a > 0. \tag{3}$$

It should be noted that the right side of (1) does not depend on the dominating measure μ.

Throughout the paper, we denote by 1{relation} the indicator function; it is equal to 1 if the relation is true, and it is equal to 0 otherwise. Throughout the paper, unless indicated explicitly, logarithms have an arbitrary common base (that is larger than 1), and $\exp(\cdot)$ indicates the inverse function of the logarithm with that base.

Definition 2. *[1] The* relative entropy *is the f-divergence with $f(t) := t \log t$ for $t > 0$,*

$$D(P\|Q) := D_f(P\|Q) \tag{4}$$
$$= \int p \log \frac{p}{q} d\mu. \tag{5}$$

Definition 3. *The* total variation distance *between probability measures P and Q is the f-divergence from P to Q with $f(t) := |t - 1|$ for all $t \geq 0$. It is a symmetric f-divergence, denoted by $|P - Q|$, which is given by*

$$|P - Q| := D_f(P\|Q) \tag{6}$$
$$= \int |p - q| d\mu. \tag{7}$$

Definition 4. *[2] The* chi-squared divergence *from P to Q is defined to be the f-divergence in (1) with $f(t) := (t - 1)^2$ or $f(t) := t^2 - 1$ for all $t > 0$,*

$$\chi^2(P\|Q) := D_f(P\|Q) \tag{8}$$
$$= \int \frac{(p-q)^2}{q} d\mu = \int \frac{p^2}{q} d\mu - 1. \tag{9}$$

The Rényi divergence, a generalization of the relative entropy, was introduced by Rényi [10] in the special case of finite alphabets. Its general definition is given as follows (see, e.g., [9]).

Definition 5. *[10] Let P and Q be probability measures on $\mathcal{X}$ dominated by μ, and let their densities be respectively denoted by $p = \frac{dP}{d\mu}$ and $q = \frac{dQ}{d\mu}$. The* Rényi divergence *of order $\alpha \in [0, \infty]$ is defined as follows:*

- If $\alpha \in (0,1) \cup (1, \infty)$, then

$$D_\alpha(P\|Q) = \frac{1}{\alpha - 1} \log \mathbb{E}\left[p^\alpha(Z) q^{1-\alpha}(Z)\right] \tag{10}$$

$$= \frac{1}{\alpha - 1} \log \sum_{x \in \mathcal{X}} P^\alpha(x) Q^{1-\alpha}(x), \tag{11}$$

where $Z \sim \mu$ in (10), and (11) holds if $\mathcal{X}$ is a discrete set.
- By the continuous extension of $D_\alpha(P\|Q)$,

$$D_0(P\|Q) = \max_{\mathcal{A}: P(\mathcal{A}) = 1} \log \frac{1}{Q(\mathcal{A})}, \tag{12}$$

$$D_1(P\|Q) = D(P\|Q), \tag{13}$$

$$D_\infty(P\|Q) = \log \operatorname{ess\,sup} \frac{p(Z)}{q(Z)}. \tag{14}$$

The second-order Rényi divergence and the chi-squared divergence are related as follows:

$$D_2(P\|Q) = \log(1 + \chi^2(P\|Q)), \tag{15}$$

and the relative entropy and the chi-squared divergence satisfy (see, e.g., [20] [Theorem 5])

$$D(P\|Q) \leq \log(1 + \chi^2(P\|Q)). \tag{16}$$

Inequality (16) readily follows from (13), (15), and since $D_\alpha(P\|Q)$ is monotonically increasing in $\alpha \in (0, \infty)$ (see [9] [Theorem 3]). A tightened version of (16), introducing an improved and locally-tight upper bound on $D(P\|Q)$ as a function of $\chi^2(P\|Q)$ and $\chi^2(Q\|P)$, is introduced in [15] [Theorem 20]. Another sharpened version of (16) is derived in [15] [Theorem 11] under the assumption of a bounded relative information. Furthermore, under the latter assumption, tight upper and lower bounds on the ratio $\frac{D(P\|Q)}{\chi^2(P\|Q)}$ are obtained in [15] [(169)].

Definition 6. *[21] The* Györfi–Vajda divergence *of order $s \in [0,1]$ is an f-divergence with*

$$f(t) = \phi_s(t) := \frac{(t-1)^2}{s + (1-s)t}, \quad t \geq 0. \tag{17}$$

Vincze–Le Cam distance (also known as the triangular discrimination) ([22,23]) is a special case with $s = \frac{1}{2}$.

In view of (1), (9) and (17), it can be verified that the Györfi–Vajda divergence is related to the chi-squared divergence as follows:

$$D_{\phi_s}(P\|Q) = \begin{cases} \frac{1}{s^2} \cdot \chi^2(P \| (1-s)P + sQ), & s \in (0,1], \\ \chi^2(Q\|P), & s = 0. \end{cases} \tag{18}$$

Hence,

$$D_{\phi_1}(P\|Q) = \chi^2(P\|Q), \tag{19}$$

$$D_{\phi_0}(P\|Q) = \chi^2(Q\|P). \tag{20}$$

3. Relations between Divergences

We introduce in this section results on the relations between the relative entropy and the chi-squared divergence, their implications, and generalizations. Information–theoretic applications are studied in the next section.

3.1. Relations between the Relative Entropy and the Chi-Squared Divergence

The following result relates the relative entropy and the chi-squared divergence, which are two fundamental divergence measures in information theory and statistics. This result was recently obtained in an equivalent form in [17] [(12)] (it is noted that this identity was also independently derived by the coauthors in two separate un-published works in [24] [(16)] and [25]). It should be noted that these connections between divergences in the quantum setting were originally discovered in [19] [Theorem 6]. Beyond serving as an interesting relation between these two fundamental divergence measures, it is introduced here for the following reasons:

(a) New consequences and applications of it are obtained, including new shorter proofs of some known results;
(b) An interesting extension provides new relations between f-divergences (see Section 3.3).

Theorem 1. *Let P and Q be probability measures defined on a measurable space $(\mathcal{X}, \mathscr{F})$, and let*

$$R_\lambda := (1 - \lambda)P + \lambda Q, \quad \lambda \in [0,1] \tag{21}$$

be the convex combination of P and Q. Then, for all $\lambda \in [0,1]$,

$$\tfrac{1}{\log e} D(P\|R_\lambda) = \int_0^\lambda \chi^2(P\|R_s) \, \frac{ds}{s}, \tag{22}$$

$$\tfrac{1}{2} \lambda^2 \chi^2(R_{1-\lambda}\|Q) = \int_0^\lambda \chi^2(R_{1-s}\|Q) \, \frac{ds}{s}. \tag{23}$$

Proof. See Section 5.1. □

A specialization of Theorem 1 by letting $\lambda = 1$ gives the following identities.

Corollary 1.

$$\tfrac{1}{\log e} D(P\|Q) = \int_0^1 \chi^2(P \| (1-s)P + sQ) \, \frac{ds}{s}, \tag{24}$$

$$\tfrac{1}{2} \chi^2(P\|Q) = \int_0^1 \chi^2(sP + (1-s)Q \| Q) \, \frac{ds}{s}. \tag{25}$$

Remark 1. *The substitution $s := \frac{1}{1+t}$ transforms (24) to [26] [Equation (31)], i.e.,*

$$\tfrac{1}{\log e} D(P\|Q) = \int_0^\infty \chi^2\left(P \, \Big\| \, \frac{tP+Q}{1+t}\right) \frac{dt}{1+t}. \tag{26}$$

In view of (18) and (21), an equivalent form of (22) and (24) is given as follows:

Corollary 2. *For $s \in [0,1]$, let $\phi_s \colon [0,\infty) \to \mathbb{R}$ be given in (17). Then,*

$$\tfrac{1}{\log e} D(P\|R_\lambda) = \int_0^\lambda s D_{\phi_s}(P\|Q) \, ds, \quad \lambda \in [0,1], \tag{27}$$

$$\tfrac{1}{\log e} D(P\|Q) = \int_0^1 s D_{\phi_s}(P\|Q) \, ds. \tag{28}$$

By Corollary 1, we obtain original and simple proofs of new and old f-divergence inequalities.

Proposition 1. (*f-divergence inequalities*).

(a) *Pinsker's inequality:*

$$D(P\|Q) \geq \tfrac{1}{2} |P-Q|^2 \log e. \tag{29}$$

(b)

$$\tfrac{1}{\log e} D(P\|Q) \leq \tfrac{1}{3} \chi^2(P\|Q) + \tfrac{1}{6} \chi^2(Q\|P). \tag{30}$$

Furthermore, let $\{P_n\}$ be a sequence of probability measures that is defined on a measurable space $(\mathcal{X}, \mathscr{F})$, and which converges to a probability measure P in the sense that

$$\lim_{n \to \infty} \operatorname{ess\,sup} \frac{dP_n}{dP}(X) = 1, \tag{31}$$

with $X \sim P$. Then, (30) is locally tight in the sense that its both sides converge to 0, and

$$\lim_{n \to \infty} \frac{\tfrac{1}{3} \chi^2(P_n\|P) + \tfrac{1}{6} \chi^2(P\|P_n)}{\tfrac{1}{\log e} D(P_n\|P)} = 1. \tag{32}$$

(c) *For all $\theta \in (0,1)$,*

$$D(P\|Q) \geq (1-\theta) \log\left(\frac{1}{1-\theta}\right) D_{\phi_\theta}(P\|Q). \tag{33}$$

Moreover, under the assumption in (31), for all $\theta \in [0,1]$

$$\lim_{n \to \infty} \frac{D(P\|P_n)}{D_{\phi_\theta}(P\|P_n)} = \tfrac{1}{2} \log e. \tag{34}$$

(d) *[15] [Theorem 2]:*

$$\tfrac{1}{\log e} D(P\|Q) \leq \tfrac{1}{2} \chi^2(P\|Q) + \tfrac{1}{4} |P-Q|. \tag{35}$$

Proof. See Section 5.2. □

Remark 2. *Inequality (30) is locally tight in the sense that (31) yields (32). This property, however, is not satisfied by (16) since the assumption in (31) implies that*

$$\lim_{n \to \infty} \frac{\log(1 + \chi^2(P_n\|P))}{D(P_n\|P)} = 2. \tag{36}$$

Remark 3. *Inequality (30) readily yields*

$$D(P\|Q) + D(Q\|P) \leq \tfrac{1}{2} \left(\chi^2(P\|Q) + \chi^2(Q\|P) \right) \log e, \tag{37}$$

which is proved by a different approach in [27] [Proposition 4]. It is further shown in [15] [Theorem 2 b)] that

$$\sup \frac{D(P\|Q) + D(Q\|P)}{\chi^2(P\|Q) + \chi^2(Q\|P)} = \tfrac{1}{2} \log e, \tag{38}$$

where the supremum is over $P \ll \gg Q$ and $P \neq Q$.

3.2. Implications of Theorem 1

We next provide two implications of Theorem 1. The first implication, which relies on the Hammersley–Chapman–Robbins (HCR) bound for the chi-squared divergence [28,29], gives the following tight lower bound on the relative entropy $D(P\|Q)$ as a function of the means and variances under P and Q.

Theorem 2. *Let P and Q be probability measures defined on the measurable space $(\mathbb{R}, \mathscr{B})$, where $\mathbb{R}$ is the real line and $\mathscr{B}$ is the Borel σ–algebra of subsets of $\mathbb{R}$. Let m_P, m_Q, σ_P^2, and σ_Q^2 denote the expected values and variances of $X \sim P$ and $Y \sim Q$, i.e.,*

$$\mathbb{E}[X] =: m_P, \quad \mathbb{E}[Y] =: m_Q, \quad \text{Var}(X) =: \sigma_P^2, \quad \text{Var}(Y) =: \sigma_Q^2. \tag{39}$$

(a) *If $m_P \neq m_Q$, then*

$$D(P\|Q) \geq d(r\|s), \tag{40}$$

where $d(r\|s) := r \log \frac{r}{s} + (1-r) \log \frac{1-r}{1-s}$, for $r,s \in [0,1]$, denotes the binary relative entropy (with the convention that $0 \log \frac{0}{0} = 0$), and

$$r := \frac{1}{2} + \frac{b}{4av} \in [0,1], \tag{41}$$

$$s := r - \frac{a}{2v} \in [0,1], \tag{42}$$

$$a := m_P - m_Q, \tag{43}$$

$$b := a^2 + \sigma_Q^2 - \sigma_P^2, \tag{44}$$

$$v := \sqrt{\sigma_P^2 + \frac{b^2}{4a^2}}. \tag{45}$$

(b) *The lower bound on the right side of (40) is attained for P and Q which are defined on the two-element set $\mathcal{U} := \{u_1, u_2\}$, and*

$$P(u_1) = r, \quad Q(u_1) = s, \tag{46}$$

with r and s in (41) and (42), respectively, and for $m_P \neq m_Q$

$$u_1 := m_P + \sqrt{\frac{(1-r)\sigma_P^2}{r}}, \quad u_2 := m_P - \sqrt{\frac{r\sigma_P^2}{1-r}}. \tag{47}$$

(c) *If $m_P = m_Q$, then*

$$\inf_{P,Q} D(P\|Q) = 0, \tag{48}$$

where the infimum on the left side of (48) is taken over all P and Q which satisfy (39).

Proof. See Section 5.3. □

Remark 4. *Consider the case of the non-equal means in Items (a) and (b) of Theorem 2. If these means are fixed, then the infimum of $D(P\|Q)$ is zero by choosing arbitrarily large equal variances. Suppose now that the non-equal means m_P and m_Q are fixed, as well as one of the variances (either σ_P^2 or σ_Q^2). Numerical experimentation shows that, in this case, the achievable lower bound in (40) is monotonically decreasing as a function of the other variance, and it tends to zero as we let the free variance tend to infinity.*

This asymptotic convergence to zero can be justified by assuming, for example, that $m_P, m_Q,$ and σ_Q^2 are fixed, and $m_P > m_Q$ (the other cases can be justified in a similar way). Then, it can be verified from (41)–(45) that

$$r = \frac{(m_P - m_Q)^2}{\sigma_P^2} + O\left(\frac{1}{\sigma_P^4}\right), \quad s = O\left(\frac{1}{\sigma_P^4}\right), \tag{49}$$

which implies that $d(r\|s) \to 0$ as we let $\sigma_P \to \infty$. The infimum of the relative entropy $D(P\|Q)$ is therefore equal to zero since the probability measures P and Q in (46) and (47), which are defined on a two-element set and attain the lower bound on the relative entropy under the constraints in (39), have a vanishing relative entropy in this asymptotic case.

Remark 5. The proof of Item (c) in Theorem 2 suggests explicit constructions of sequences of pairs probability measures $\{(P_n, Q_n)\}$ such that

(a) The means under P_n and Q_n are both equal to m (independently of n);
(b) The variance under P_n is equal to σ_P^2, and the variance under Q_n is equal to σ_Q^2 (independently of n);
(c) The relative entropy $D(P_n\|Q_n)$ vanishes as we let $n \to \infty$.

This yields in particular (48).

A second consequence of Theorem 1 gives the following result. Its first part holds due to the concavity of $\exp(-D(P\|\cdot))$ (see [30] [Problem 4.2]). The second part is new, and its proof relies on Theorem 1. As an educational note, we provide an alternative proof of the first part by relying on Theorem 1.

Theorem 3. Let $P \ll Q$, and $F \colon [0,1] \to [0, \infty)$ be given by

$$F(\lambda) := D(P \| (1-\lambda)P + \lambda Q), \quad \forall \lambda \in [0,1]. \tag{50}$$

Then, for all $\lambda \in [0,1]$,

$$F(\lambda) \leq \log\left(\frac{1}{1 - \lambda + \lambda \exp(-D(P\|Q))}\right), \tag{51}$$

with an equality if $\lambda = 0$ or $\lambda = 1$. Moreover, F is monotonically increasing, differentiable, and it satisfies

$$F'(\lambda) \geq \frac{1}{\lambda}\bigl[\exp(F(\lambda)) - 1\bigr] \log e, \quad \forall \lambda \in (0,1], \tag{52}$$

$$\lim_{\lambda \to 0^+} \frac{F'(\lambda)}{\lambda} = \chi^2(Q\|P) \log e, \tag{53}$$

so the limit in (53) is twice as large as the value of the lower bound on this limit as it follows from the right side of (52).

Proof. See Section 5.4. □

Remark 6. By the convexity of the relative entropy, it follows that $F(\lambda) \leq \lambda D(P\|Q)$ for all $\lambda \in [0,1]$. It can be verified, however, that the inequality $1 - \lambda + \lambda \exp(-x) \geq \exp(-\lambda x)$ holds for all $x \geq 0$ and $\lambda \in [0,1]$. Letting $x := D(P\|Q)$ implies that the upper bound on $F(\lambda)$ on the right side of (51) is tighter than or equal to the upper bound $\lambda D(P\|Q)$ (with an equality if and only if either $\lambda \in \{0,1\}$ or $P \equiv Q$).

Corollary 3. Let $\{P_j\}_{j=1}^m$, with $m \in \mathbb{N}$, be probability measures defined on a measurable space $(\mathcal{X}, \mathscr{F})$, and let $\{\alpha_j\}_{j=1}^m$ be a sequence of non-negative numbers that sum to 1. Then, for all $i \in \{1, \ldots, m\}$,

$$D\left(P_i \,\|\, \sum_{j=1}^{m} \alpha_j P_j\right) \leq -\log\left(\alpha_i + (1-\alpha_i)\exp\left(-\tfrac{1}{1-\alpha_i}\sum_{j\neq i}\alpha_j D(P_i\|P_j)\right)\right). \tag{54}$$

Proof. For an arbitrary $i \in \{1,\ldots,m\}$, apply the upper bound on the right side of (51) with $\lambda := 1 - \alpha_i$, $P := P_i$ and $Q := \tfrac{1}{1-\alpha_i}\sum_{j\neq i}\alpha_j P_j$. The right side of (54) is obtained from (51) by invoking the convexity of the relative entropy, which gives $D(P_i\|Q) \leq \tfrac{1}{1-\alpha_i}\sum_{j\neq i}\alpha_j D(P_i\|P_j)$. □

The next result provides an upper bound on the non-negative difference between the entropy of a convex combination of distributions and the respective convex combination of the individual entropies (it is also termed as the concavity deficit of the entropy function in [17] [Section 3]).

Corollary 4. *Let $\{P_j\}_{j=1}^{m}$, with $m \in \mathbb{N}$, be probability measures defined on a measurable space $(\mathcal{X}, \mathcal{F})$, and let $\{\alpha_j\}_{j=1}^{m}$ be a sequence of non-negative numbers that sum to 1. Then,*

$$0 \leq H\left(\sum_{j=1}^{m}\alpha_j P_j\right) - \sum_{j=1}^{m}\alpha_j H(P_j) \leq -\sum_{i=1}^{m}\alpha_i \log\left(\alpha_i + (1-\alpha_i)\exp\left(-\tfrac{1}{1-\alpha_i}\sum_{j\neq i}\alpha_j D(P_i\|P_j)\right)\right). \tag{55}$$

Proof. The lower bound holds due to the concavity of the entropy function. The upper bound readily follows from Corollary 3, and the identity

$$H\left(\sum_{j=1}^{m}\alpha_j P_j\right) - \sum_{j=1}^{m}\alpha_j H(P_j) = \sum_{i=1}^{m}\alpha_i D\left(P_i \,\|\, \sum_{j=1}^{m}\alpha_j P_j\right). \tag{56}$$

□

Remark 7. *The upper bound in (55) refines the known bound (see, e.g., [31] [Lemma 2.2])*

$$H\left(\sum_{j=1}^{m}\alpha_j P_j\right) - \sum_{j=1}^{m}\alpha_j H(P_j) \leq \sum_{j=1}^{m}\alpha_j \log\frac{1}{\alpha_j} = H(\underline{\alpha}), \tag{57}$$

by relying on all the $\tfrac{1}{2}m(m-1)$ pairwise relative entropies between the individual distributions $\{P_j\}_{j=1}^{m}$. Another refinement of (57), expressed in terms of total variation distances, has been recently provided in [17] [Theorem 3.1].

3.3. Monotonic Sequences of f-Divergences and an Extension of Theorem 1

The present subsection generalizes Theorem 1, and it also provides relations between f-divergences which are defined in a recursive way.

Theorem 4. *Let P and Q be probability measures defined on a measurable space $(\mathcal{X}, \mathcal{F})$. Let R_λ, for $\lambda \in [0,1]$, be the convex combination of P and Q as in (21). Let $f_0 : (0,\infty) \to \mathbb{R}$ be a convex function with $f_0(1) = 0$, and let $\{f_k(\cdot)\}_{k=0}^{\infty}$ be a sequence of functions that are defined on $(0,\infty)$ by the recursive equation*

$$f_{k+1}(x) := \int_{0}^{1-x} f_k(1-s)\,\frac{ds}{s}, \quad x > 0, \ k \in \{0,1,\ldots\}. \tag{58}$$

Then,

(a) $\{D_{f_k}(P\|Q)\}_{k=0}^{\infty}$ *is a non-increasing (and non-negative) sequence of f-divergences.*

(b) For all $\lambda \in [0,1]$ and $k \in \{0,1,\ldots\}$,

$$D_{f_{k+1}}(R_\lambda \| P) = \int_0^\lambda D_{f_k}(R_s \| P) \, \frac{ds}{s}. \tag{59}$$

Proof. See Section 5.5. □

We next use the polylogarithm functions, which satisfy the recursive equation [32] [Equation (7.2)]:

$$\mathrm{Li}_k(x) := \begin{cases} \dfrac{x}{1-x}, & \text{if } k = 0, \\ \displaystyle\int_0^x \dfrac{\mathrm{Li}_{k-1}(s)}{s} \, ds, & \text{if } k \geq 1. \end{cases} \tag{60}$$

This gives $\mathrm{Li}_1(x) = -\log_e(1-x)$, $\mathrm{Li}_2(x) = -\int_0^x \frac{1}{s} \log_e(1-s) \, ds$ and so on, which are real-valued and finite for $x < 1$.

Corollary 5. Let

$$f_k(x) := \mathrm{Li}_k(1-x), \quad x > 0, \quad k \in \{0,1,\ldots\}. \tag{61}$$

Then, (59) holds for all $\lambda \in [0,1]$ and $k \in \{0,1,\ldots\}$. Furthermore, setting $k = 0$ in (59) yields (22) as a special case.

Proof. See Section 5.6. □

3.4. On Probabilities and f-Divergences

The following result relates probabilities of sets to f-divergences.

Theorem 5. Let $(\mathcal{X}, \mathscr{F}, \mu)$ be a probability space, and let $\mathcal{C} \in \mathscr{F}$ be a measurable set with $\mu(\mathcal{C}) > 0$. Define the conditional probability measure

$$\mu_\mathcal{C}(\mathcal{E}) := \frac{\mu(\mathcal{C} \cap \mathcal{E})}{\mu(\mathcal{C})}, \quad \forall \mathcal{E} \in \mathscr{F}. \tag{62}$$

Let $f \colon (0,\infty) \to \mathbb{R}$ be an arbitrary convex function with $f(1) = 0$, and assume (by continuous extension of f at zero) that $f(0) := \lim_{t \to 0^+} f(t) < \infty$. Furthermore, let $\tilde{f} \colon (0,\infty) \to \mathbb{R}$ be the convex function which is given by

$$\tilde{f}(t) := t f\!\left(\frac{1}{t}\right), \quad \forall\, t > 0. \tag{63}$$

Then,

$$D_f(\mu_\mathcal{C} \| \mu) = \tilde{f}(\mu(\mathcal{C})) + (1 - \mu(\mathcal{C})) f(0). \tag{64}$$

Proof. See Section 5.7. □

Connections of probabilities to the relative entropy, and to the chi-squared divergence, are next exemplified as special cases of Theorem 5.

Corollary 6. In the setting of Theorem 5,

$$D(\mu_\mathcal{C}\|\mu) = \log \frac{1}{\mu(\mathcal{C})}, \qquad (65)$$

$$\chi^2(\mu_\mathcal{C}\|\mu) = \frac{1}{\mu(\mathcal{C})} - 1, \qquad (66)$$

so (16) is satisfied in this case with equality. More generally, for all $\alpha \in (0, \infty)$,

$$D_\alpha(\mu_\mathcal{C}\|\mu) = \log \frac{1}{\mu(\mathcal{C})}. \qquad (67)$$

Proof. See Section 5.7. □

Remark 8. *In spite of its simplicity, (65) proved very useful in the seminal work by Marton on transportation–cost inequalities, proving concentration of measures by information-theoretic tools [33,34] (see also [35] [Chapter 8] and [36] [Chapter 3]). As a side note, the simple identity (65) was apparently first explicitly used by Csiszár (see [37] [Equation (4.13)]).*

4. Applications

This section provides applications of our results in Section 3. These include universal lossless compression, method of types and large deviations, and strong data–processing inequalities (SDPIs).

4.1. Application of Corollary 3: Shannon Code for Universal Lossless Compression

Consider $m > 1$ discrete, memoryless, and stationary sources with probability mass functions $\{P_i\}_{i=1}^m$, and assume that the symbols are emitted by one of these sources with an *a priori* probability α_i for source no. i, where $\{\alpha_i\}_{i=1}^m$ are positive and sum to 1.

For lossless data compression by a universal source code, suppose that a single source code is designed with respect to the average probability mass function $P := \sum_{j=1}^m \alpha_j P_j$.

Assume that the designer uses a Shannon code, where the code assignment for a symbol $x \in \mathcal{X}$ is of length $\ell(x) = \left\lceil \log \frac{1}{P(x)} \right\rceil$ bits (logarithms are on base 2). Due to the mismatch in the source distribution, the average codeword length ℓ_{avg} satisfies (see [38] [Proposition 3.B])

$$\sum_{i=1}^m \alpha_i H(P_i) + \sum_{i=1}^m \alpha_i D(P_i\|P) \le \ell_{\text{avg}} \le \sum_{i=1}^m \alpha_i H(P_i) + \sum_{i=1}^m \alpha_i D(P_i\|P) + 1. \qquad (68)$$

The fractional penalty in the average codeword length, denoted by ν, is defined to be equal to the ratio of the penalty in the average codeword length as a result of the source mismatch, and the average codeword length in case of a perfect matching. From (68), it follows that

$$\frac{\sum_{i=1}^m \alpha_i D(P_i\|P)}{1 + \sum_{i=1}^m \alpha_i H(P_i)} \le \nu \le \frac{1 + \sum_{i=1}^m \alpha_i D(P_i\|P)}{\sum_{i=1}^m \alpha_i H(P_i)}. \qquad (69)$$

We next rely on Corollary 3 to obtain an upper bound on ν which is expressed as a function of the $m(m-1)$ relative entropies $D(P_i\|P_j)$ for all $i \neq j$ in $\{1, \ldots, m\}$. This is useful if, e.g., the m relative entropies on the left and right sides of (69) do not admit closed-form expressions, in contrast to the $m(m-1)$ relative entropies $D(P_i\|P_j)$ for $i \neq j$. We next exemplify this case.

For $i \in \{1, \ldots, m\}$, let P_i be a Poisson distribution with parameter $\lambda_i > 0$. For all $i, j \in \{1, \ldots, m\}$, the relative entropy from P_i to P_j admits the closed-form expression

$$D(P_i \| P_j) = \lambda_i \log\left(\frac{\lambda_i}{\lambda_j}\right) + (\lambda_j - \lambda_i) \log e. \tag{70}$$

From (54) and (70), it follows that

$$D(P_i \| P) \leq -\log\left(\alpha_i + (1 - \alpha_i) \exp\left(-\frac{f_i(\underline{\alpha}, \underline{\lambda})}{1 - \alpha_i}\right)\right), \tag{71}$$

where

$$f_i(\underline{\alpha}, \underline{\lambda}) := \sum_{j \neq i} \alpha_j\, D(P_i \| P_j) \tag{72}$$

$$= \sum_{j \neq i} \left\{ \alpha_j \left[\lambda_i \log\left(\frac{\lambda_i}{\lambda_j}\right) + (\lambda_j - \lambda_i) \log e \right] \right\}. \tag{73}$$

The entropy of a Poisson distribution, with parameter λ_i, is given by the integral representation [39–41]

$$H(P_i) = \lambda_i \log\left(\frac{e}{\lambda_i}\right) + \int_0^\infty \left(\lambda_i - \frac{1 - e^{-\lambda_i(1-e^{-u})}}{1 - e^{-u}}\right) \frac{e^{-u}}{u}\, du\, \log e. \tag{74}$$

Combining (69), (71) and (74) finally gives an upper bound on ν in the considered setup.

Example 1. *Consider five discrete memoryless sources where the probability mass function of source no. i is given by $P_i = \mathrm{Poisson}(\lambda_i)$ with $\underline{\lambda} = [16, 20, 24, 28, 32]$. Suppose that the symbols are emitted from one of the sources with equal probability, so $\underline{\alpha} = \left[\frac{1}{5}, \frac{1}{5}, \frac{1}{5}, \frac{1}{5}, \frac{1}{5}\right]$. Let $P := \frac{1}{5}(P_1 + \ldots + P_5)$ be the average probability mass function of the five sources. The term $\sum_i \alpha_i\, D(P_i \| P)$, which appears in the numerators of the upper and lower bounds on ν (see (69)), does not lend itself to a closed-form expression, and it is not even an easy task to calculate it numerically due to the need to compute an infinite series which involves factorials. We therefore apply the closed-form upper bound in (71) to get that $\sum_i \alpha_i\, D(P_i \| P) \leq 1.46$ bits, whereas the upper bound which follows from the convexity of the relative entropy (i.e., $\sum_i \alpha_i f_i(\underline{\alpha}, \underline{\lambda})$) is equal to 1.99 bits (both upper bounds are smaller than the trivial bound $\log_2 5 \approx 2.32$ bits). From (69), (74), and the stronger upper bound on $\sum_i \alpha_i\, D(P_i \| P)$, the improved upper bound on ν is equal to 57.0% (as compared to a looser upper bound of 69.3%, which follows from (69), (74), and the looser upper bound on $\sum_i \alpha_i\, D(P_i \| P)$ that is equal to 1.99 bits).*

4.2. Application of Theorem 2 in the Context of the Method of Types and Large Deviations Theory

Let $X^n = (X_1, \ldots, X_n)$ be a sequence of i.i.d. random variables with $X_1 \sim Q$, where Q is a probability measure defined on a finite set $\mathcal{X}$, and $Q(x) > 0$ for all $x \in \mathcal{X}$. Let $\mathscr{P}$ be a set of probability measures on $\mathcal{X}$ such that $Q \notin \mathscr{P}$, and suppose that the closure of $\mathscr{P}$ coincides with the closure of its interior. Then, by Sanov's theorem (see, e.g., [42] [Theorem 11.4.1] and [43] [Theorem 3.3]), the probability that the empirical distribution $\widehat{P}_{X^n}$ belongs to $\mathscr{P}$ vanishes exponentially at the rate

$$\lim_{n \to \infty} \frac{1}{n} \log \frac{1}{\mathbb{P}[\widehat{P}_{X^n} \in \mathscr{P}]} = \inf_{P \in \mathscr{P}} D(P \| Q). \tag{75}$$

Furthermore, for finite n, the method of types yields the following upper bound on this rare event:

$$\mathbb{P}[\widehat{P}_{X^n} \in \mathscr{P}] \leq \binom{n + |\mathcal{X}| - 1}{|\mathcal{X}| - 1} \exp\left(-n \inf_{P \in \mathscr{P}} D(P \| Q)\right) \tag{76}$$

$$\leq (n+1)^{|\mathcal{X}|-1} \exp\left(-n \inf_{P \in \mathscr{P}} D(P \| Q)\right), \tag{77}$$

whose exponential decay rate coincides with the exact asymptotic result in (75).

Suppose that Q is not fully known, but its mean m_Q and variance σ_Q^2 are available. Let $m_1 \in \mathbb{R}$ and $\delta_1, \varepsilon_1, \sigma_1 > 0$ be fixed, and let $\mathscr{P}$ be the set of all probability measures P, defined on the finite set $\mathcal{X}$, with mean $m_P \in [m_1 - \delta_1, m_1 + \delta_1]$ and variance $\sigma_P^2 \in [\sigma_1^2 - \varepsilon_1, \sigma_1^2 + \varepsilon_1]$, where $|m_1 - m_Q| > \delta_1$. Hence, $\mathscr{P}$ coincides with the closure of its interior, and $Q \notin \mathscr{P}$.

The lower bound on the relative entropy in Theorem 2, used in conjunction with the upper bound in (77), can serve to obtain an upper bound on the probability of the event that the empirical distribution of X^n belongs to the set $\mathscr{P}$, regardless of the uncertainty in Q. This gives

$$\mathbb{P}[\widehat{P}_{X^n} \in \mathscr{P}] \leq (n+1)^{|\mathcal{X}|-1} \exp(-nd^*), \tag{78}$$

where

$$d^* := \inf_{m_P, \sigma_P^2} d(r\|s), \tag{79}$$

and, for fixed $(m_P, m_Q, \sigma_P^2, \sigma_Q^2)$, the parameters r and s are given in (41) and (42), respectively.

Standard algebraic manipulations that rely on (78) lead to the following result, which is expressed as a function of the Lambert W function [44]. This function, which finds applications in various engineering and scientific fields, is a standard built–in function in mathematical software tools such as Mathematica, Matlab, and Maple. Applications of the Lambert W function in information theory and coding are briefly surveyed in [45].

Proposition 2. *For $\varepsilon \in (0,1)$, let $n^* := n^*(\varepsilon)$ denote the minimal value of $n \in \mathbb{N}$ such that the upper bound on the right side of (78) does not exceed $\varepsilon \in (0,1)$. Then, n^* admits the following closed-form expression:*

$$n^* = \max\left\{\left\lceil -\frac{(|\mathcal{X}|-1) W_{-1}(\eta) \log e}{d^*} \right\rceil - 1, 1\right\}, \tag{80}$$

with

$$\eta := -\frac{d^* \left(\varepsilon \exp(-d^*)\right)^{1/(|\mathcal{X}|-1)}}{(|\mathcal{X}|-1) \log e} \in [-\tfrac{1}{e}, 0), \tag{81}$$

and $W_{-1}(\cdot)$ on the right side of (80) denotes the secondary real–valued branch of the Lambert W function (i.e., $x := W_{-1}(y)$ where $W_{-1}\colon [-\tfrac{1}{e}, 0) \to (-\infty, -1]$ is the inverse function of $y := xe^x$).

Example 2. *Let Q be an arbitrary probability measure, defined on a finite set $\mathcal{X}$, with mean $m_Q = 40$ and variance $\sigma_Q^2 = 20$. Let $\mathscr{P}$ be the set of all probability measures P, defined on $\mathcal{X}$, whose mean m_P and variance σ_P^2 lie in the intervals $[43, 47]$ and $[18, 22]$, respectively. Suppose that it is required that, for all probability measures Q as above, the probability that the empirical distribution of the i.i.d. sequence $X^n \sim Q^n$ be included in the set $\mathscr{P}$ is at most $\varepsilon = 10^{-10}$. We rely here on the upper bound in (78), and impose the stronger condition where it should not exceed ε. By this approach, it is obtained numerically from (79) that $d^* = 0.203$ nats. We next examine two cases:*

(i) *If $|\mathcal{X}| = 2$, then it follows from (80) that $n^* = 138$.*
(ii) *Consider a richer alphabet size of the i.i.d. samples where, e.g., $|\mathcal{X}| = 100$. By relying on the same universal lower bound d^*, which holds independently of the value of $|\mathcal{X}|$ ($\mathcal{X}$ can possibly be an infinite set), it follows from (80) that $n^* = 4170$ is the minimal value such that the upper bound in (78) does not exceed 10^{-10}.*

We close this discussion by providing numerical experimentation of the lower bound on the relative entropy in Theorem 2, and comparing this attainable lower bound (see Item (b) of Theorem 2) with the following closed-form expressions for relative entropies:

(a) The relative entropy between real-valued Gaussian distributions is given by

$$D\bigl(\mathcal{N}(m_P, \sigma_P^2) \,\|\, \mathcal{N}(m_Q, \sigma_Q^2)\bigr) = \log \frac{\sigma_Q}{\sigma_P} + \frac{1}{2}\left[\frac{(m_P - m_Q)^2 + \sigma_P^2}{\sigma_Q^2} - 1\right] \log e. \tag{82}$$

(b) Let E_μ denote a random variable which is exponentially distributed with mean $\mu > 0$; its probability density function is given by

$$e_\mu(x) = \frac{1}{\mu} e^{-x/\mu} \, 1\{x \geq 0\}. \tag{83}$$

Then, for $a_1, a_2 > 0$ and $d_1, d_2 \in \mathbb{R}$,

$$D(E_{a_1} + d_1 \| E_{a_2} + d_2) = \begin{cases} \log \dfrac{a_2}{a_1} + \dfrac{d_1 + a_1 - d_2 - a_2}{a_2} \log e, & d_1 \geq d_2, \\ \infty, & d_1 < d_2. \end{cases} \tag{84}$$

In this case, the means under P and Q are $m_P = d_1 + a_1$ and $m_Q = d_2 + a_2$, respectively, and the variances are $\sigma_P^2 = a_1^2$ and $\sigma_Q^2 = a_2^2$. Hence, for obtaining the required means and variances, set

$$a_1 = \sigma_P, \quad a_2 = \sigma_Q, \quad d_1 = m_P - \sigma_P, \quad d_2 = m_Q - \sigma_Q. \tag{85}$$

Example 3. *We compare numerically the attainable lower bound on the relative entropy, as it is given in (40), with the two relative entropies in (82) and (84):*

(i) *If $(m_P, m_Q, \sigma_P^2, \sigma_Q^2) = (45, 40, 20, 20)$, then the lower bound in (40) is equal to 0.521 nats, and the two relative entropies in (82) and (84) are equal to 0.625 and 1.118 nats, respectively.*
(ii) *If $(m_P, m_Q, \sigma_P^2, \sigma_Q^2) = (50, 35, 10, 20)$, then the lower bound in (40) is equal to 2.332 nats, and the two relative entropies in (82) and (84) are equal to 5.722 and 3.701 nats, respectively.*

4.3. Strong Data–Processing Inequalities and Maximal Correlation

The information contraction is a fundamental concept in information theory. The contraction of f-divergences through channels is captured by data–processing inequalities, which can be further tightened by the derivation of SDPIs with channel-dependent or source-channel dependent contraction coefficients (see, e.g., [26,46–52]).

We next provide necessary definitions which are relevant for the presentation in this subsection.

Definition 7. *Let Q_X be a probability distribution which is defined on a set $\mathcal{X}$, and that is not a point mass, and let $W_{Y|X} \colon \mathcal{X} \to \mathcal{Y}$ be a stochastic transformation. The contraction coefficient for f-divergences is defined as*

$$\mu_f(Q_X, W_{Y|X}) := \sup_{P_X \colon D_f(P_X \| Q_X) \in (0, \infty)} \frac{D_f(P_Y \| Q_Y)}{D_f(P_X \| Q_X)}, \tag{86}$$

where, for all $y \in \mathcal{Y}$,

$$P_Y(y) = (P_X W_{Y|X})(y) := \int_\mathcal{X} \mathrm{d}P_X(x) \, W_{Y|X}(y|x), \tag{87}$$

$$Q_Y(y) = (Q_X W_{Y|X})(y) := \int_\mathcal{X} \mathrm{d}Q_X(x) \, W_{Y|X}(y|x). \tag{88}$$

The notation in (87) and (88) is consistent with the standard notation used in information theory (see, e.g., the first displayed equation after (3.2) in [53]).

The derivation of good upper bounds on contraction coefficients for f-divergences, which are strictly smaller than 1, lead to SDPIs. These inequalities find their applications, e.g., in studying the exponential convergence rate of an irreducible, time-homogeneous and reversible discrete-time Markov chain to its unique invariant distribution over its state space (see, e.g., [49] [Section 2.4.3] and [50] [Section 2]). It is in sharp contrast to DPIs which do not yield convergence to stationarity at any rate. We return to this point later in this subsection, and determine the exact convergence rate to stationarity under two parametric families of f-divergences.

We next rely on Theorem 1 to obtain upper bounds on the contraction coefficients for the following f-divergences.

Definition 8. *For $\alpha \in (0,1]$, the α-skew K-divergence is given by*

$$K_\alpha(P\|Q) := D(P \| (1-\alpha)P + \alpha Q), \tag{89}$$

and, for $\alpha \in [0,1]$, let

$$S_\alpha(P\|Q) := \alpha D(P \| (1-\alpha)P + \alpha Q) + (1-\alpha) D(Q \| (1-\alpha)P + \alpha Q) \tag{90}$$

$$= \alpha K_\alpha(P\|Q) + (1-\alpha) K_{1-\alpha}(Q\|P), \tag{91}$$

with the convention that $K_0(P\|Q) \equiv 0$ (by a continuous extension at $\alpha = 0$ in (89)). These divergence measures are specialized to the relative entropies:

$$K_1(P\|Q) = D(P\|Q) = S_1(P\|Q), \quad S_0(P\|Q) = D(Q\|P), \tag{92}$$

and $S_{\frac{1}{2}}(P\|Q)$ is the Jensen–Shannon divergence [54–56] (also known as the capacitory discrimination [57]):

$$S_{\frac{1}{2}}(P\|Q) = \tfrac{1}{2} D(P \| \tfrac{1}{2}(P+Q)) + \tfrac{1}{2} D(Q \| \tfrac{1}{2}(P+Q)) \tag{93}$$

$$= H(\tfrac{1}{2}(P+Q)) - \tfrac{1}{2} H(P) - \tfrac{1}{2} H(Q) := \mathrm{JS}(P\|Q). \tag{94}$$

It can be verified that the divergence measures in (89) and (90) are f-divergences:

$$K_\alpha(P\|Q) = D_{k_\alpha}(P\|Q), \quad \alpha \in (0,1], \tag{95}$$

$$S_\alpha(P\|Q) = D_{s_\alpha}(P\|Q), \quad \alpha \in [0,1], \tag{96}$$

with

$$k_\alpha(t) := t \log t - t \log(\alpha + (1-\alpha)t), \quad t > 0, \ \alpha \in (0,1], \tag{97}$$

$$s_\alpha(t) := \alpha t \log t - (\alpha t + 1 - \alpha) \log(\alpha + (1-\alpha)t) \tag{98}$$

$$= \alpha k_\alpha(t) + (1-\alpha) t \, k_{1-\alpha}\!\left(\frac{1}{t}\right), \quad t > 0, \ \alpha \in [0,1], \tag{99}$$

where $k_\alpha(\cdot)$ and $s_\alpha(\cdot)$ are strictly convex functions on $(0,\infty)$, and vanish at 1.

Remark 9. *The α-skew K-divergence in (89) is considered in [55] and [58] [(13)] (including pointers in the latter paper to its utility). The divergence in (90) is akin to Lin's measure in [55] [(4.1)], the asymmetric α-skew Jensen–Shannon divergence in [58] [(11)–(12)], the symmetric α-skew Jensen–Shannon divergence in [58] [(16)], and divergence measures in [59] which involve arithmetic and geometric means of two probability distributions. Properties and applications of quantum skew divergences are studied in [19] and references therein.*

Theorem 6. *The f-divergences in (89) and (90) satisfy the following integral identities, which are expressed in terms of the Györfi–Vajda divergence in (17):*

$$\frac{1}{\log e} K_\alpha(P\|Q) = \int_0^\alpha s D_{\phi_s}(P\|Q) \, ds, \qquad \alpha \in (0,1], \tag{100}$$

$$\frac{1}{\log e} S_\alpha(P\|Q) = \int_0^1 g_\alpha(s) \, D_{\phi_s}(P\|Q) \, ds, \qquad \alpha \in [0,1], \tag{101}$$

with

$$g_\alpha(s) := \alpha s\, 1\{s \in (0,\alpha]\} + (1-\alpha)(1-s)\, 1\{s \in [\alpha,1)\}, \quad (\alpha,s) \in [0,1] \times [0,1]. \tag{102}$$

Moreover, the contraction coefficients for these f-divergences are related as follows:

$$\mu_{\chi^2}(Q_X, W_{Y|X}) \leq \mu_{k_\alpha}(Q_X, W_{Y|X}) \leq \sup_{s \in (0,\alpha]} \mu_{\phi_s}(Q_X, W_{Y|X}), \quad \alpha \in (0,1], \tag{103}$$

$$\mu_{\chi^2}(Q_X, W_{Y|X}) \leq \mu_{s_\alpha}(Q_X, W_{Y|X}) \leq \sup_{s \in (0,1)} \mu_{\phi_s}(Q_X, W_{Y|X}), \quad \alpha \in [0,1], \tag{104}$$

where $\mu_{\chi^2}(Q_X, W_{Y|X})$ denotes the contraction coefficient for the chi-squared divergence.

Proof. See Section 5.8. □

Remark 10. *The upper bounds on the contraction coefficients for the parametric f-divergences in (89) and (90) generalize the upper bound on the contraction coefficient for the relative entropy in [51] [Theorem III.6] (recall that $K_1(P\|Q) = D(P\|Q) = S_1(P\|Q)$), so the upper bounds in Theorem 6 are specialized to the latter bound at $\alpha = 1$.*

Corollary 7. *Let*

$$\mu_{\chi^2}(W_{Y|X}) := \sup_Q \mu_{\chi^2}(Q_X, W_{Y|X}), \tag{105}$$

where the supremum on the right side is over all probability measures Q_X defined on $\mathcal{X}$. Then,

$$\mu_{\chi^2}(Q_X, W_{Y|X}) \leq \mu_{k_\alpha}(Q_X, W_{Y|X}) \leq \mu_{\chi^2}(W_{Y|X}), \quad \alpha \in (0,1], \tag{106}$$

$$\mu_{\chi^2}(Q_X, W_{Y|X}) \leq \mu_{s_\alpha}(Q_X, W_{Y|X}) \leq \mu_{\chi^2}(W_{Y|X}), \quad \alpha \in [0,1]. \tag{107}$$

Proof. See Section 5.9. □

Example 4. *Let $Q_X = \text{Bernoulli}(\frac{1}{2})$, and let $W_{Y|X}$ correspond to a binary symmetric channel (BSC) with crossover probability ε. Then, $\mu_{\chi^2}(Q_X, W_{Y|X}) = \mu_{\chi^2}(W_{Y|X}) = (1-2\varepsilon)^2$. The upper and lower bounds on $\mu_{k_\alpha}(Q_X, W_{Y|X})$ and $\mu_{s_\alpha}(Q_X, W_{Y|X})$ in (106) and (107) match for all α, and they are all equal to $(1-2\varepsilon)^2$.*

The upper bound on the contraction coefficients in Corollary 7 is given by $\mu_{\chi^2}(W_{Y|X})$, whereas the lower bound is given by $\mu_{\chi^2}(Q_X, W_{Y|X})$, which depends on the input distribution Q_X. We next provide alternative upper bounds on the contraction coefficients for the considered (parametric) f-divergences, which, similarly to the lower bound, scale like $\mu_{\chi^2}(Q_X, W_{Y|X})$. Although the upper bound in Corollary 7 may be tighter in some cases than the alternative upper bounds which are next presented in Proposition 3 (and in fact, the former upper bound may be even achieved with equality as in Example 4), the bounds in Proposition 3 are used shortly to determine the exponential rate of the convergence to stationarity of a type of Markov chains.

Proposition 3. *For all $\alpha \in (0,1]$,*

$$\mu_{\chi^2}(Q_X, W_{Y|X}) \leq \mu_{k_\alpha}(Q_X, W_{Y|X}) \leq \frac{1}{\alpha \, Q_{\min}} \cdot \mu_{\chi^2}(Q_X, W_{Y|X}), \tag{108}$$

$$\mu_{\chi^2}(Q_X, W_{Y|X}) \leq \mu_{s_\alpha}(Q_X, W_{Y|X}) \leq \frac{(1-\alpha)\log_e\left(\frac{1}{\alpha}\right) + 2\alpha - 1}{(1 - 3\alpha + 3\alpha^2) \, Q_{\min}} \cdot \mu_{\chi^2}(Q_X, W_{Y|X}), \tag{109}$$

where $Q_{\min}$ denotes the minimal positive mass of the input distribution Q_X.

Proof. See Section 5.10. □

Remark 11. *In view of (92), at $\alpha = 1$, (108) and (109) specialize to an upper bound on the contraction coefficient of the relative entropy (KL divergence) as a function of the contraction coefficient of the chi-squared divergence. In this special case, both (108) and (109) give*

$$\mu_{\chi^2}(Q_X, W_{Y|X}) \leq \mu_{\mathrm{KL}}(Q_X, W_{Y|X}) \leq \frac{1}{Q_{\min}} \cdot \mu_{\chi^2}(Q_X, W_{Y|X}), \tag{110}$$

which then coincides with [48] [Theorem 10].

We next apply Proposition 3 to consider the convergence rate to stationarity of Markov chains by the introduced f-divergences in Definition 8. The next result follows [49] [Section 2.4.3], and it provides a generalization of the result there.

Theorem 7. *Consider a time-homogeneous, irreducible, and reversible discrete-time Markov chain with a finite state space $\mathcal{X}$, let W be its probability transition matrix, and Q_X be its unique stationary distribution (reversibility means that $Q_X(x)[W]_{x,y} = Q_X(y)[W]_{y,x}$ for all $x, y \in \mathcal{X}$). Let P_X be an initial probability distribution over $\mathcal{X}$. Then, for all $\alpha \in (0,1]$ and $n \in \mathbb{N}$,*

$$K_\alpha(P_X W^n \| Q_X) \leq \mu_{k_\alpha}(Q_X, W^n) \, K_\alpha(P_X \| Q_X), \tag{111}$$

$$S_\alpha(P_X W^n \| Q_X) \leq \mu_{s_\alpha}(Q_X, W^n) \, S_\alpha(P_X \| Q_X), \tag{112}$$

and the contraction coefficients on the right sides of (111) and (112) scale like the n-th power of the contraction coefficient for the chi-squared divergence as follows:

$$\left(\mu_{\chi^2}(Q_X, W)\right)^n \leq \mu_{k_\alpha}(Q_X, W^n) \leq \frac{1}{\alpha \, Q_{\min}} \cdot \left(\mu_{\chi^2}(Q_X, W)\right)^n, \tag{113}$$

$$\left(\mu_{\chi^2}(Q_X, W)\right)^n \leq \mu_{s_\alpha}(Q_X, W^n) \leq \frac{(1-\alpha)\log_e\left(\frac{1}{\alpha}\right) + 2\alpha - 1}{(1 - 3\alpha + 3\alpha^2) \, Q_{\min}} \cdot \left(\mu_{\chi^2}(Q_X, W)\right)^n. \tag{114}$$

Proof. Inequalities (111) and (112) hold since $Q_X W^n = Q_X$, for all $n \in \mathbb{N}$, and due to Definition 7 and (95) and (96). Inequalities (113) and (114) hold by Proposition 3, and due to the reversibility of the Markov chain which implies that (see [49] [Equation (2.92)])

$$\mu_{\chi^2}(Q_X, W^n) = \left(\mu_{\chi^2}(Q_X, W)\right)^n, \quad n \in \mathbb{N}. \tag{115}$$

□

In view of (113) and (114), Theorem 7 readily gives the following result on the exponential decay rate of the upper bounds on the divergences on the left sides of (111) and (112).

Corollary 8. *For all* $\alpha \in (0,1]$,

$$\lim_{n\to\infty} \left(\mu_{k_\alpha}(Q_X, W^n)\right)^{1/n} = \mu_{\chi^2}(Q_X, W) = \lim_{n\to\infty} \left(\mu_{s_\alpha}(Q_X, W^n)\right)^{1/n}. \tag{116}$$

Remark 12. *Theorem 7 and Corollary 8 generalize the results in [49] [Section 2.4.3], which follow as a special case at $\alpha = 1$ (see (92)).*

We end this subsection by considering maximal correlations, which are closely related to the contraction coefficient for the chi-squared divergence.

Definition 9. *The* maximal correlation *between two random variables X and Y is defined as*

$$\rho_m(X;Y) := \sup_{f,g} \mathbb{E}[f(X)g(Y)], \tag{117}$$

where the supremum is taken over all real-valued functions f and g such that

$$\mathbb{E}[f(X)] = \mathbb{E}[g(Y)] = 0, \quad \mathbb{E}[f^2(X)] \leq 1, \ \mathbb{E}[g^2(Y)] \leq 1. \tag{118}$$

It is well-known [60] that, if $X \sim Q_X$ and $Y \sim Q_Y = Q_X W_{Y|X}$, then the contraction coefficient for the chi-squared divergence $\mu_{\chi^2}(Q_X, W_{Y|X})$ is equal to the square of the maximal correlation between the random variables X and Y, i.e.,

$$\rho_m(X;Y) = \sqrt{\mu_{\chi^2}(Q_X, W_{Y|X})}. \tag{119}$$

A simple application of Corollary 1 and (119) gives the following result.

Proposition 4. *In the setting of Definition 7, for $s \in [0,1]$, let $X_s \sim (1-s)P_X + sQ_X$ and $Y_s \sim (1-s)P_Y + sQ_Y$ with $P_X \neq Q_X$ and $P_X \ll \gg Q_X$. Then, the following inequality holds:*

$$\sup_{s\in[0,1]} \rho_m(X_s; Y_s) \geq \max\left\{ \sqrt{\frac{D(P_Y\|Q_Y)}{D(P_X\|Q_X)}}, \sqrt{\frac{D(Q_Y\|P_Y)}{D(Q_X\|P_X)}} \right\}. \tag{120}$$

Proof. See Section 5.11. □

5. Proofs

This section provides proofs of the results in Sections 3 and 4.

5.1. Proof of Theorem 1

Proof of (22): We rely on an integral representation of the logarithm function (on base e):

$$\log_e x = \int_0^1 \frac{x-1}{x + (1-x)v} \, dv, \quad \forall x > 0. \tag{121}$$

Let μ be a dominating measure of P and Q (i.e., $P, Q \ll \mu$), and let $p := \frac{dP}{d\mu}$, $q := \frac{dQ}{d\mu}$, and

$$r_\lambda := \frac{dR_\lambda}{d\mu} = (1-\lambda)p + \lambda q, \quad \forall \lambda \in [0,1], \tag{122}$$

where the last equality is due to (21). For all $\lambda \in [0,1]$,

$$\frac{1}{\log e} D(P\|R_\lambda) = \int p \log_e\left(\frac{p}{r_\lambda}\right) d\mu \qquad (123)$$

$$= \int_0^1 \int \frac{p(p - r_\lambda)}{p + v(r_\lambda - p)} d\mu \, dv, \qquad (124)$$

where (124) holds due to (121) with $x := \frac{p}{r_\lambda}$, and by swapping the order of integration. The inner integral on the right side of (124) satisfies, for all $v \in (0, 1]$,

$$\int \frac{p(p - r_\lambda)}{p + v(r_\lambda - p)} d\mu = \int (p - r_\lambda)\left(1 + \frac{v(p - r_\lambda)}{p + v(r_\lambda - p)}\right) d\mu \qquad (125)$$

$$= \int (p - r_\lambda) d\mu + v \int \frac{(p - r_\lambda)^2}{p + v(r_\lambda - p)} d\mu \qquad (126)$$

$$= v \int \frac{(p - r_\lambda)^2}{(1 - v)p + v r_\lambda} d\mu \qquad (127)$$

$$= \frac{1}{v} \int \frac{(p - [(1 - v)p + v r_\lambda])^2}{(1 - v)p + v r_\lambda} d\mu \qquad (128)$$

$$= \frac{1}{v} \chi^2(P \| (1 - v)P + v R_\lambda), \qquad (129)$$

where (127) holds since $\int p \, d\mu = 1$, and $\int r_\lambda \, d\mu = 1$. From (21), for all $(\lambda, v) \in [0, 1] \times [0, 1]$,

$$(1 - v)P + v R_\lambda = (1 - \lambda v)P + \lambda v Q = R_{\lambda v}. \qquad (130)$$

The substitution of (130) into the right side of (129) gives that, for all $(\lambda, v) \in [0, 1] \times (0, 1]$,

$$\int \frac{p(p - r_\lambda)}{p + v(r_\lambda - p)} d\mu = \frac{1}{v} \chi^2(P\|R_{\lambda v}). \qquad (131)$$

Finally, substituting (131) into the right side of (124) gives that, for all $\lambda \in (0, 1]$,

$$\frac{1}{\log e} D(P\|R_\lambda) = \int_0^1 \frac{1}{v} \chi^2(P\|R_{\lambda v}) \, dv \qquad (132)$$

$$= \int_0^\lambda \frac{1}{s} \chi^2(P\|R_s) \, ds, \qquad (133)$$

where (133) holds by the transformation $s := \lambda v$. Equality (133) also holds for $\lambda = 0$ since we have $D(P\|R_0) = D(P\|P) = 0$.

Proof of (23): For all $s \in (0, 1]$,

$$\chi^2(P\|Q) = \int \frac{(p - q)^2}{q} d\mu$$

$$= \frac{1}{s^2} \int \frac{[(sp + (1 - s)q) - q]^2}{q} d\mu \qquad (134)$$

$$= \frac{1}{s^2} \int \frac{(r_{1-s} - q)^2}{q} d\mu \qquad (135)$$

$$= \frac{1}{s^2} \chi^2(R_{1-s} \| Q), \qquad (136)$$

where (135) holds due to (122). From (136), it follows that for all $\lambda \in [0,1]$,

$$\int_0^\lambda \frac{1}{s} \chi^2(R_{1-s} \| Q) \, ds = \int_0^\lambda s \, ds \, \chi^2(P\|Q) = \tfrac{1}{2} \lambda^2 \chi^2(P\|Q). \tag{137}$$

5.2. Proof of Proposition 1

(a) *Simple Proof of Pinsker's Inequality*: By [61] or [62] [(58)],

$$\chi^2(P\|Q) \geq \begin{cases} |P-Q|^2, & \text{if } |P-Q| \in [0,1], \\ \dfrac{|P-Q|}{2-|P-Q|}, & \text{if } |P-Q| \in (1,2]. \end{cases} \tag{138}$$

We need the weaker inequality $\chi^2(P\|Q) \geq |P-Q|^2$, proved by the Cauchy–Schwarz inequality:

$$\chi^2(P\|Q) = \int \frac{(p-q)^2}{q} \, d\mu \int q \, d\mu \tag{139}$$

$$\geq \left(\int \frac{|p-q|}{\sqrt{q}} \cdot \sqrt{q} \, d\mu \right)^2 \tag{140}$$

$$= |P-Q|^2. \tag{141}$$

By combining (24) and (139)–(141), it follows that

$$\frac{1}{\log e} D(P\|Q) = \int_0^1 \chi^2(P \| (1-s)P + sQ) \, \frac{ds}{s} \tag{142}$$

$$\geq \int_0^1 |P - ((1-s)P + sQ)|^2 \, \frac{ds}{s} \tag{143}$$

$$= \int_0^1 s |P-Q|^2 \, ds \tag{144}$$

$$= \tfrac{1}{2} |P-Q|^2. \tag{145}$$

(b) *Proof of (30) and its local tightness*:

$$\frac{1}{\log e} D(P\|Q) = \int_0^1 \chi^2(P \| (1-s)P + sQ) \, \frac{ds}{s} \tag{146}$$

$$= \int_0^1 \left(\int \frac{[p - ((1-s)p + sq)]^2}{(1-s)p + sq} \, d\mu \right) \frac{ds}{s} \tag{147}$$

$$= \int_0^1 \int \frac{s(p-q)^2}{(1-s)p + sq} \, d\mu \, ds \tag{148}$$

$$\leq \int_0^1 \int s(p-q)^2 \left(\frac{1-s}{p} + \frac{s}{q} \right) d\mu \, ds \tag{149}$$

$$= \int_0^1 s^2 \, ds \int \frac{(p-q)^2}{q} \, d\mu + \int_0^1 s(1-s) \, ds \int \frac{(p-q)^2}{p} \, d\mu \tag{150}$$

$$= \tfrac{1}{3} \chi^2(P\|Q) + \tfrac{1}{6} \chi^2(Q\|P), \tag{151}$$

where (146) is (24), and (149) holds due to Jensen's inequality and the convexity of the hyperbola.

We next show the local tightness of inequality (30) by proving that (31) yields (32). Let $\{P_n\}$ be a sequence of probability measures, defined on a measurable space $(\mathcal{X}, \mathscr{F})$, and assume that $\{P_n\}$

converges to a probability measure P in the sense that (31) holds. In view of [16] [Theorem 7] (see also [15] [Section 4.F] and [63]), it follows that

$$\lim_{n \to \infty} D(P_n \| P) = \lim_{n \to \infty} \chi^2(P_n \| P) = 0, \tag{152}$$

and

$$\lim_{n \to \infty} \frac{D(P_n \| P)}{\chi^2(P_n \| P)} = \tfrac{1}{2} \log e, \tag{153}$$

$$\lim_{n \to \infty} \frac{\chi^2(P_n \| P)}{\chi^2(P \| P_n)} = 1, \tag{154}$$

which therefore yields (32).

(c) *Proof of (33) and (34):* The proof of (33) relies on (28) and the following lemma.

Lemma 1. *For all $s, \theta \in (0,1)$,*

$$\frac{D_{\phi_s}(P \| Q)}{D_{\phi_\theta}(P \| Q)} \geq \min\left\{\frac{1-\theta}{1-s}, \frac{\theta}{s}\right\}. \tag{155}$$

Proof.

$$D_{\phi_s}(P \| Q) = \int \frac{(p-q)^2}{(1-s)p + sq} \, d\mu \tag{156}$$

$$= \int \frac{(p-q)^2}{(1-\theta)p + \theta q} \cdot \frac{(1-\theta)p + \theta q}{(1-s)p + sq} \, d\mu \tag{157}$$

$$\geq \min\left\{\frac{1-\theta}{1-s}, \frac{\theta}{s}\right\} \int \frac{(p-q)^2}{(1-\theta)p + \theta q} \, d\mu \tag{158}$$

$$= \min\left\{\frac{1-\theta}{1-s}, \frac{\theta}{s}\right\} D_{\phi_\theta}(P \| Q). \tag{159}$$

☐

From (28) and (155), for all $\theta \in (0,1)$,

$$\frac{1}{\log e} D(P \| Q) = \int_0^\theta s D_{\phi_s}(P \| Q) \, ds + \int_\theta^1 s D_{\phi_s}(P \| Q) \, ds \tag{160}$$

$$\geq \int_0^\theta \frac{s(1-\theta)}{1-s} \cdot D_{\phi_\theta}(P \| Q) \, ds + \int_\theta^1 \theta \, D_{\phi_\theta}(P \| Q) \, ds \tag{161}$$

$$= \left[-\theta + \log_e\left(\frac{1}{1-\theta}\right)\right](1-\theta) D_{\phi_\theta}(P \| Q) + \theta(1-\theta) D_{\phi_\theta}(P \| Q) \tag{162}$$

$$= (1-\theta) \log_e\left(\frac{1}{1-\theta}\right) D_{\phi_\theta}(P \| Q). \tag{163}$$

This proves (33). Furthermore, under the assumption in (31), for all $\theta \in [0,1]$,

$$\lim_{n \to \infty} \frac{D(P \| P_n)}{D_{\phi_\theta}(P \| P_n)} = \lim_{n \to \infty} \frac{D(P \| P_n)}{\chi^2(P \| P_n)} \lim_{n \to \infty} \frac{\chi^2(P \| P_n)}{D_{\phi_\theta}(P \| P_n)} \tag{164}$$

$$= \tfrac{1}{2} \log e \cdot \frac{2}{\phi_\theta''(1)} \tag{165}$$

$$= \tfrac{1}{2} \log e, \tag{166}$$

where (165) holds due to (153) and the local behavior of f-divergences [63], and (166) holds due to (17) which implies that $\phi''_\theta(1) = 2$ for all $\theta \in [0,1]$. This proves (34).

(d) *Proof of (35):* From (24), we get

$$\frac{1}{\log e} D(P\|Q) = \int_0^1 \chi^2(P \| (1-s)P + sQ) \frac{ds}{s} \tag{167}$$

$$= \int_0^1 [\chi^2(P \| (1-s)P + sQ) - s^2 \chi^2(P\|Q)] \frac{ds}{s} + \int_0^1 s\,ds\, \chi^2(P\|Q) \tag{168}$$

$$= \int_0^1 [\chi^2(P \| (1-s)P + sQ) - s^2 \chi^2(P\|Q)] \frac{ds}{s} + \tfrac{1}{2}\chi^2(P\|Q). \tag{169}$$

Referring to the integrand of the first term on the right side of (169), for all $s \in (0,1]$,

$$\frac{1}{s} [\chi^2(P \| (1-s)P + sQ) - s^2 \chi^2(P\|Q)]$$

$$= s \int (p-q)^2 \left[\frac{1}{(1-s)p + sq} - \frac{1}{q} \right] d\mu \tag{170}$$

$$= s(1-s) \int \frac{(q-p)^3}{q[(1-s)p + sq]} d\mu \tag{171}$$

$$= s(1-s) \int |q-p| \cdot \underbrace{\frac{|q-p|}{q} \cdot \frac{q-p}{p + s(q-p)}}_{\leq \frac{1}{s} 1\{q \geq p\}} d\mu \tag{172}$$

$$\leq (1-s) \int (q-p) \, 1\{q \geq p\} \, d\mu \tag{173}$$

$$= \tfrac{1}{2}(1-s) |P - Q|, \tag{174}$$

where the last equality holds since the equality $\int (q-p) \, d\mu = 0$ implies that

$$\int (q-p) 1\{q \geq p\} d\mu = \int (p-q) 1\{p \geq q\} d\mu \tag{175}$$

$$= \tfrac{1}{2} \int |p-q| d\mu = \tfrac{1}{2} |P-Q|. \tag{176}$$

From (170)–(174), an upper bound on the right side of (169) results. This gives

$$\tfrac{1}{\log e} D(P\|Q) \leq \tfrac{1}{2} \int_0^1 (1-s)\,ds\, |P-Q| + \tfrac{1}{2} \chi^2(P\|Q) \tag{177}$$

$$= \tfrac{1}{4} |P-Q| + \tfrac{1}{2} \chi^2(P\|Q). \tag{178}$$

It should be noted that [15] [Theorem 2(a)] shows that inequality (35) is tight. To that end, let $\varepsilon \in (0,1)$, and define probability measures P_ε and Q_ε on the set $\mathcal{A} = \{0,1\}$ with $P_\varepsilon(1) = \varepsilon^2$ and $Q_\varepsilon(1) = \varepsilon$. Then,

$$\lim_{\varepsilon \downarrow 0} \frac{\tfrac{1}{\log e} D(P_\varepsilon\|Q_\varepsilon)}{\tfrac{1}{4}|P_\varepsilon - Q_\varepsilon| + \tfrac{1}{2}\chi^2(P_\varepsilon\|Q_\varepsilon)} = 1. \tag{179}$$

5.3. Proof of Theorem 2

We first prove Item (a) in Theorem 2. In view of the Hammersley–Chapman–Robbins lower bound on the χ^2 divergence, for all $\lambda \in [0,1]$

$$\chi^2(P\|(1-\lambda)P+\lambda Q) \geq \frac{(\mathbb{E}[X]-\mathbb{E}[Z_\lambda])^2}{\mathrm{Var}(Z_\lambda)}, \tag{180}$$

where $X \sim P$, $Y \sim Q$ and $Z_\lambda \sim R_\lambda := (1-\lambda)P + \lambda Q$ is defined by

$$Z_\lambda := \begin{cases} X, & \text{with probability } 1-\lambda, \\ Y, & \text{with probability } \lambda. \end{cases} \tag{181}$$

For $\lambda \in [0,1]$,

$$\mathbb{E}[Z_\lambda] = (1-\lambda)m_P + \lambda m_Q, \tag{182}$$

and it can be verified that

$$\mathrm{Var}(Z_\lambda) = (1-\lambda)\sigma_P^2 + \lambda\sigma_Q^2 + \lambda(1-\lambda)(m_P-m_Q)^2. \tag{183}$$

We now rely on (24)

$$\frac{1}{\log e} D(P\|Q) = \int_0^1 \chi^2(P\|(1-\lambda)P+\lambda Q) \frac{d\lambda}{\lambda} \tag{184}$$

to get a lower bound on the relative entropy. Combining (180), (183) and (184) yields

$$\frac{1}{\log e} D(P\|Q) \geq (m_P - m_Q)^2 \int_0^1 \frac{\lambda}{(1-\lambda)\sigma_P^2 + \lambda\sigma_Q^2 + \lambda(1-\lambda)(m_P-m_Q)^2} \, d\lambda. \tag{185}$$

From (43) and (44), we get

$$\int_0^1 \frac{\lambda}{(1-\lambda)\sigma_P^2 + \lambda\sigma_Q^2 + \lambda(1-\lambda)(m_P-m_Q)^2} \, d\lambda = \int_0^1 \frac{\lambda}{(\alpha - a\lambda)(\beta + a\lambda)} \, d\lambda, \tag{186}$$

where

$$\alpha := \sqrt{\sigma_P^2 + \frac{b^2}{4a^2}} + \frac{b}{2a}, \tag{187}$$

$$\beta := \sqrt{\sigma_P^2 + \frac{b^2}{4a^2}} - \frac{b}{2a}. \tag{188}$$

By using the partial fraction decomposition of the integrand on the right side of (186), we get (after multiplying both sides of (185) by $\log e$)

$$D(P\|Q) \geq \frac{(m_P-m_Q)^2}{a^2} \left[\frac{\alpha}{\alpha+\beta} \log\left(\frac{\alpha}{\alpha-a}\right) + \frac{\beta}{\alpha+\beta} \log\left(\frac{\beta}{\beta+a}\right) \right] \tag{189}$$

$$= \frac{\alpha}{\alpha+\beta} \log\left(\frac{\alpha}{\alpha-a}\right) + \frac{\beta}{\alpha+\beta} \log\left(\frac{\beta}{\beta+a}\right) \tag{190}$$

$$= d\left(\frac{\alpha}{\alpha+\beta} \Big\| \frac{\alpha-a}{\alpha+\beta}\right), \tag{191}$$

where (189) holds by integration since $\alpha - a\lambda$ and $\beta + a\lambda$ are both non-negative for all $\lambda \in [0,1]$. To verify the latter claim, it should be noted that (43) and the assumption that $m_P \neq m_Q$ imply that $a \neq 0$. Since $\alpha, \beta > 0$, it follows that, for all $\lambda \in [0,1]$, either $\alpha - a\lambda > 0$ or $\beta + a\lambda > 0$ (if $a < 0$, then the former is positive, and, if $a > 0$, then the latter is positive). By comparing the denominators of both integrands on the left and right sides of (186), it follows that $(\alpha - a\lambda)(\beta + a\lambda) \geq 0$ for all $\lambda \in [0,1]$. Since the product of $\alpha - a\lambda$ and $\beta + a\lambda$ is non-negative and at least one of these terms is positive, it follows that $\alpha - a\lambda$ and $\beta + a\lambda$ are both non-negative for all $\lambda \in [0,1]$. Finally, (190) follows from (43).

If $m_P - m_Q \to 0$ and $\sigma_P \neq \sigma_Q$, then it follows from (43) and (44) that $a \to 0$ and $b \to \sigma_P^2 - \sigma_Q^2 \neq 0$. Hence, from (187) and (188), $\alpha \geq \left|\frac{b}{a}\right| \to \infty$ and $\beta \to 0$, which implies that the lower bound on $D(P\|Q)$ in (191) tends to zero.

Letting $r := \frac{\alpha}{\alpha+\beta}$ and $s := \frac{\alpha-a}{\alpha+\beta}$, we obtain that the lower bound on $D(P\|Q)$ in (40) holds. This bound is consistent with the expressions of r and s in (41) and (42) since, from (45), (187) and (188),

$$r = \frac{\alpha}{\alpha+\beta} = \frac{v+\frac{b}{2a}}{2v} = \frac{1}{2} + \frac{b}{4av}, \qquad (192)$$

$$s = \frac{\alpha-a}{\alpha+\beta} = r - \frac{a}{\alpha+\beta} = r - \frac{a}{2v}. \qquad (193)$$

It should be noted that $r, s \in [0,1]$. First, from (187) and (188), α and β are positive if $\sigma_P \neq 0$, which yields $r = \frac{\alpha}{\alpha+\beta} \in (0,1)$. We next show that $s \in [0,1]$. Recall that $\alpha - a\lambda$ and $\beta + a\lambda$ are both non-negative for all $\lambda \in [0,1]$. Setting $\lambda = 1$ yields $\alpha \geq a$, which (from (193)) implies that $s \geq 0$. Furthermore, from (193) and the positivity of $\alpha + \beta$, it follows that $s \leq 1$ if and only if $\beta \geq -a$. The latter holds since $\beta + a\lambda \geq 0$ for all $\lambda \in [0,1]$ (in particular, for $\lambda = 1$). If $\sigma_P = 0$, then it follows from (41)–(45) that $v = \frac{b}{2|a|}$, $b = a^2 + \sigma_Q^2$, and (recall that $a \neq 0$)

(i) If $a > 0$, then $v = \frac{b}{2a}$ implies that $r = \frac{1}{2} + \frac{b}{4av} = 1$, and $s = r - \frac{a}{2v} = 1 - \frac{a^2}{b} = \frac{\sigma_Q^2}{\sigma_Q^2+a^2} \in [0,1]$;

(ii) if $a < 0$, then $v = -\frac{b}{2a}$ implies that $r = 0$, and $s = r - \frac{a}{2v} = \frac{a^2}{b} = \frac{a^2}{a^2+\sigma_Q^2} \in [0,1]$.

We next prove Item (b) in Theorem 2 (i.e., the achievability of the lower bound in (40)). To that end, we provide a technical lemma, which can be verified by the reader.

Lemma 2. *Let r, s be given in (41)–(45), and let $u_{1,2}$ be given in (47). Then,*

$$(s-r)(u_1 - u_2) = m_Q - m_P, \qquad (194)$$

$$u_1 + u_2 = m_P + m_Q + \frac{\sigma_Q^2 - \sigma_P^2}{m_Q - m_P}. \qquad (195)$$

Let $X \sim P$ and $Y \sim Q$ be defined on a set $\mathcal{U} = \{u_1, u_2\}$ (for the moment, the values of u_1 and u_2 are not yet specified) with $P[X = u_1] = r$, $P[X = u_2] = 1-r$, $Q[Y = u_1] = s$, and $Q[Y = u_2] = 1-s$. We now calculate u_1 and u_2 such that $\mathbb{E}[X] = m_P$ and $\text{Var}(X) = \sigma_P^2$. This is equivalent to

$$r u_1 + (1-r) u_2 = m_P, \qquad (196)$$
$$r u_1^2 + (1-r) u_2^2 = m_P^2 + \sigma_P^2. \qquad (197)$$

Substituting (196) into the right side of (197) gives

$$r u_1^2 + (1-r) u_2^2 = [r u_1 + (1-r) u_2]^2 + \sigma_P^2, \qquad (198)$$

which, by rearranging terms, also gives

$$u_1 - u_2 = \pm \sqrt{\frac{\sigma_P^2}{r(1-r)}}. \tag{199}$$

Solving simultaneously (196) and (199) gives

$$u_1 = m_P \pm \sqrt{\frac{(1-r)\sigma_P^2}{r}}, \tag{200}$$

$$u_2 = m_P \mp \sqrt{\frac{r\sigma_P^2}{1-r}}. \tag{201}$$

We next verify that, by setting $u_{1,2}$ as in (47), one also gets (as desired) that $\mathbb{E}[Y] = m_Q$ and $\text{Var}(Y) = \sigma_Q^2$. From Lemma 2, and, from (196) and (197), we have

$$\mathbb{E}[Y] = su_1 + (1-s)u_2 \tag{202}$$

$$= \big(ru_1 + (1-r)u_2\big) + (s-r)(u_1 - u_2) \tag{203}$$

$$= m_P + (s-r)(u_1 - u_2) = m_Q, \tag{204}$$

$$\mathbb{E}[Y^2] = su_1^2 + (1-s)u_2^2 \tag{205}$$

$$= ru_1^2 + (1-r)u_2^2 + (s-r)(u_1^2 - u_2^2) \tag{206}$$

$$= \mathbb{E}[X^2] + (s-r)(u_1 - u_2)(u_1 + u_2) \tag{207}$$

$$= m_P^2 + \sigma_P^2 + (m_Q - m_P)\left(m_P + m_Q + \frac{\sigma_Q^2 - \sigma_P^2}{m_Q - m_P}\right) \tag{208}$$

$$= m_Q^2 + \sigma_Q^2. \tag{209}$$

By combining (204) and (209), we obtain $\text{Var}(Y) = \sigma_Q^2$. Hence, the probability mass functions P and Q defined on $\mathcal{U} = \{u_1, u_2\}$ (with u_1 and u_2 in (47)) such that

$$P(u_1) = 1 - P(u_2) = r, \quad Q(u_1) = 1 - Q(u_2) = s \tag{210}$$

satisfy the equality constraints in (39), while also achieving the lower bound on $D(P\|Q)$ that is equal to $d(r\|s)$. It can be also verified that the second option where

$$u_1 = m_P - \sqrt{\frac{(1-r)\sigma_P^2}{r}}, \quad u_2 = m_P + \sqrt{\frac{r\sigma_P^2}{1-r}} \tag{211}$$

does *not* yield the satisfiability of the conditions $\mathbb{E}[Y] = m_Q$ and $\text{Var}(Y) = \sigma_Q^2$, so there is only a unique pair of probability measures P and Q, defined on a two-element set that achieves the lower bound in (40) under the equality constraints in (39).

We finally prove Item (c) in Theorem 2. Let $m \in \mathbb{R}$, σ_P^2, and σ_Q^2 be selected arbitrarily such that $\sigma_Q^2 \geq \sigma_P^2$. We construct probability measures P_ε and Q_ε, depending on a free parameter ε, with means $m_P = m_Q := m$ and variances σ_P^2 and σ_Q^2, respectively (means and variances are independent of ε), and which are defined on a three-element set $\mathcal{U} := \{u_1, u_2, u_3\}$ as follows:

$$P_\varepsilon(u_1) = r, \quad P_\varepsilon(u_2) = 1 - r, \quad P_\varepsilon(u_3) = 0, \tag{212}$$

$$Q_\varepsilon(u_1) = s, \quad Q_\varepsilon(u_2) = 1 - s - \varepsilon, \quad Q_\varepsilon(u_3) = \varepsilon, \tag{213}$$

with $\varepsilon > 0$. We aim to set the parameters r, s, u_1, u_2 and u_3 (as a function of m, σ_P, σ_Q and ε) such that

$$\lim_{\varepsilon \to 0^+} D(P_\varepsilon \| Q_\varepsilon) = 0. \tag{214}$$

Proving (214) yields (48), while it also follows that the infimum on the left side of (48) can be restricted to probability measures which are defined on a three-element set.

In view of the constraints on the means and variances in (39), with equal means m, we get the following set of equations from (212) and (213):

$$\begin{cases} ru_1 + (1-r)u_2 = m, \\ su_1 + (1-s-\varepsilon)u_2 + \varepsilon u_3 = m, \\ ru_1^2 + (1-r)u_2^2 = m^2 + \sigma_P^2, \\ su_1^2 + (1-s-\varepsilon)u_2^2 + \varepsilon u_3^2 = m^2 + \sigma_Q^2. \end{cases} \tag{215}$$

The first and second equations in (215) refer to the equal means under P and Q, and the third and fourth equations in (215) refer to the second moments in (39). Furthermore, in view of (212) and (213), the relative entropy is given by

$$D(P_\varepsilon \| Q_\varepsilon) = r \log \frac{r}{s} + (1-r) \log \frac{1-r}{1-s-\varepsilon}. \tag{216}$$

Subtracting the square of the first equation in (215) from its third equation gives the equivalent set of equations

$$\begin{cases} ru_1 + (1-r)u_2 = m, \\ su_1 + (1-s-\varepsilon)u_2 + \varepsilon u_3 = m, \\ r(1-r)(u_1 - u_2)^2 = \sigma_P^2, \\ su_1^2 + (1-s-\varepsilon)u_2^2 + \varepsilon u_3^2 = m^2 + \sigma_Q^2. \end{cases} \tag{217}$$

We next select u_1 and u_2 such that $u_1 - u_2 := 2\sigma_P$. Then, the third equation in (217) gives $r(1-r) = \frac{1}{4}$, so $r = \frac{1}{2}$. Furthermore, the first equation in (217) gives

$$u_1 = m + \sigma_P, \tag{218}$$
$$u_2 = m - \sigma_P. \tag{219}$$

Since r, u_1, and u_2 are independent of ε, so is the probability measure $P_\varepsilon := P$. Combining the second equation in (217) with (218) and (219) gives

$$u_3 = m - \left(1 + \frac{2s-1}{\varepsilon}\right) \sigma_P. \tag{220}$$

Substituting (218)–(220) into the fourth equation of (217) gives a quadratic equation for s, whose selected solution (such that s and $r = \frac{1}{2}$ be close for small $\varepsilon > 0$) is equal to

$$s = \frac{1}{2} \left[1 - \varepsilon + \sqrt{\left(\frac{\sigma_Q^2}{\sigma_P^2} - 1 + \varepsilon\right) \varepsilon} \right]. \tag{221}$$

Hence, $s = \frac{1}{2} + O(\sqrt{\varepsilon})$, which implies that $s \in (0, 1-\varepsilon)$ for sufficiently small $\varepsilon > 0$ (as it is required in (213)). In view of (216), it also follows that $D(P \| Q_\varepsilon)$ vanishes as we let ε tend to zero.

We finally outline an alternative proof, which refers to the case of equal means with arbitrarily selected σ_P^2 and σ_Q^2. Let $(\sigma_P^2, \sigma_Q^2) \in (0, \infty)^2$. We next construct a sequence of pairs of probability measures $\{(P_n, Q_n)\}$ with zero mean and respective variances (σ_P^2, σ_Q^2) for which $D(P_n \| Q_n) \to 0$ as $n \to \infty$ (without any loss of generality, one can assume that the equal means are equal to zero). We start by assuming $(\sigma_P^2, \sigma_Q^2) \in (1, \infty)^2$. Let

$$\mu_n := \sqrt{1 + n(\sigma_Q^2 - 1)}, \tag{222}$$

and define a sequence of quaternary real-valued random variables with probability mass functions

$$Q_n(a) := \begin{cases} \frac{1}{2} - \frac{1}{2n} & a = \pm 1, \\ \frac{1}{2n} & a = \pm \mu_n. \end{cases} \tag{223}$$

It can be verified that, for all $n \in \mathbb{N}$, Q_n has zero mean and variance σ_Q^2. Furthermore, let

$$P_n(a) := \begin{cases} \frac{1}{2} - \frac{\xi}{2n} & a = \pm 1, \\ \frac{\xi}{2n} & a = \pm \mu_n, \end{cases} \tag{224}$$

with

$$\xi := \frac{\sigma_P^2 - 1}{\sigma_Q^2 - 1}. \tag{225}$$

If $\xi > 1$, for $n = 1, \ldots, \lceil \xi \rceil$, we choose P_n arbitrarily with mean 0 and variance σ_P^2. Then,

$$\operatorname{Var}(P_n) = 1 - \frac{\xi}{n} + \frac{\xi}{n} \mu_n^2 = \sigma_P^2, \tag{226}$$

$$D(P_n \| Q_n) = d\left(\frac{\xi}{n} \middle\| \frac{1}{n}\right) \to 0. \tag{227}$$

Next, suppose $\min\{\sigma_P^2, \sigma_Q^2\} := \sigma^2 < 1$, then construct P'_n and Q'_n as before with variances $\frac{2\sigma_P^2}{\sigma^2} > 1$ and $\frac{2\sigma_Q^2}{\sigma^2} > 1$, respectively. If P_n and Q_n denote the random variables P'_n and Q'_n scaled by a factor of $\frac{\sigma}{\sqrt{2}}$, then their variances are σ_P^2, σ_Q^2, respectively, and $D(P_n \| Q_n) = D(P'_n \| Q'_n) \to 0$ as we let $n \to \infty$.

To conclude, it should be noted that the sequences of probability measures in the latter proof are defined on a four-element set. Recall that, in the earlier proof, specialized to the case of (equal means with) $\sigma_P^2 \leq \sigma_Q^2$, the introduced probability measures are defined on a three-element set, and the reference probability measure P is fixed while referring to an equiprobable binary random variable.

5.4. Proof of Theorem 3

We first prove (52). Differentiating both sides of (22) gives that, for all $\lambda \in (0, 1]$,

$$F'(\lambda) = \frac{1}{\lambda} \chi^2(P \| R_\lambda) \log e \tag{228}$$

$$\geq \frac{1}{\lambda} \left[\exp(D(P \| R_\lambda)) - 1 \right] \log e \tag{229}$$

$$= \frac{1}{\lambda} \left[\exp(F(\lambda)) - 1 \right] \log e, \tag{230}$$

where (228) holds due to (21), (22) and (50); (229) holds by (16) and (230) is due to (21) and (50). This gives (52).

We next prove (53), and the conclusion which appears after it. In view of [16] [Theorem 8], applied to $f(t) := -\log t$ for all $t > 0$, we get (it should be noted that, by the definition of F in (50), the result in [16] [(195)–(196)] is used here by swapping P and Q)

$$\lim_{\lambda \to 0^+} \frac{F(\lambda)}{\lambda^2} = \tfrac{1}{2} \chi^2(Q\|P) \log e. \tag{231}$$

Since $\lim_{\lambda \to 0^+} F(\lambda) = 0$, it follows by L'Hôpital's rule that

$$\lim_{\lambda \to 0^+} \frac{F'(\lambda)}{\lambda} = 2 \lim_{\lambda \to 0^+} \frac{F(\lambda)}{\lambda^2} = \chi^2(Q\|P) \log e, \tag{232}$$

which gives (53). A comparison of the limit in (53) with a lower bound which follows from (52) gives

$$\lim_{\lambda \to 0^+} \frac{F'(\lambda)}{\lambda} \geq \lim_{\lambda \to 0^+} \frac{1}{\lambda^2} \bigl[\exp(F(\lambda)) - 1\bigr] \log e \tag{233}$$

$$= \lim_{\lambda \to 0^+} \frac{F(\lambda)}{\lambda^2} \lim_{\lambda \to 0^+} \frac{\exp(F(\lambda)) - 1}{F(\lambda)} \cdot \log e \tag{234}$$

$$= \lim_{\lambda \to 0^+} \frac{F(\lambda)}{\lambda^2} \lim_{u \to 0} \frac{e^u - 1}{u} \tag{235}$$

$$= \tfrac{1}{2} \chi^2(Q\|P) \log e, \tag{236}$$

where (236) relies on (231). Hence, the limit in (53) is twice as large as its lower bound on the right side of (236). This proves the conclusion which comes right after (53).

We finally prove the known result in (51), by showing an alternative proof which is based on (52). The function F is non-negative on $[0,1]$, and it is strictly positive on $(0,1]$ if $P \neq Q$. Let $P \neq Q$ (otherwise, (51) is trivial). Rearranging terms in (52) and integrating both sides over the interval $[\lambda, 1]$, for $\lambda \in (0,1]$, gives that

$$\int_\lambda^1 \frac{F'(t)}{\exp(F(t)) - 1} \, dt \geq \int_\lambda^1 \frac{dt}{t} \log e \tag{237}$$

$$= \log \frac{1}{\lambda}, \quad \forall \lambda \in (0,1]. \tag{238}$$

The left side of (237) satisfies

$$\int_\lambda^1 \frac{F'(t)}{\exp(F(t)) - 1} \, dt = \int_\lambda^1 \frac{F'(t) \exp(-F(t))}{1 - \exp(-F(t))} \, dt \tag{239}$$

$$= \int_\lambda^1 \frac{d}{dt}\bigl\{\log\bigl(1 - \exp(-F(t))\bigr)\bigr\} \, dt \tag{240}$$

$$= \log\left(\frac{1 - \exp(-D(P\|Q))}{1 - \exp(-F(\lambda))}\right), \tag{241}$$

where (241) holds since $F(1) = D(P\|Q)$ (see (50)). Combining (237)–(241) gives

$$\frac{1 - \exp(-D(P\|Q))}{1 - \exp(-F(\lambda))} \geq \frac{1}{\lambda}, \quad \forall \lambda \in (0,1], \tag{242}$$

which, due to the non-negativity of F, gives the right side inequality in (51) after rearrangement of terms in (242).

5.5. Proof of Theorem 4

Lemma 3. *Let $f_0 \colon (0, \infty) \to \mathbb{R}$ be a convex function with $f_0(1) = 0$, and let $\{f_k(\cdot)\}_{k=0}^{\infty}$ be defined as in (58). Then, $\{f_k(\cdot)\}_{k=0}^{\infty}$ is a sequence of convex functions on $(0, \infty)$, and*

$$f_k(x) \geq f_{k+1}(x), \quad \forall x > 0, \ k \in \{0, 1, \ldots\}. \tag{243}$$

Proof. We prove the convexity of $\{f_k(\cdot)\}$ on $(0, \infty)$ by induction. Suppose that $f_k(\cdot)$ is a convex function with $f_k(1) = 0$ for a fixed integer $k \geq 0$. The recursion in (58) yields $f_{k+1}(1) = 0$ and, by the change of integration variable $s := (1-x)s'$,

$$f_{k+1}(x) = \int_0^1 f_k(s'x - s' + 1) \frac{ds'}{s'}, \quad x > 0. \tag{244}$$

Consequently, for $t \in (0,1)$ and $x \neq y$ with $x, y > 0$, applying (244) gives

$$f_{k+1}((1-t)x + ty) = \int_0^1 f_k\bigl(s'[(1-t)x + ty] - s' + 1\bigr) \frac{ds'}{s'} \tag{245}$$

$$= \int_0^1 f_k\bigl((1-t)(s'x - s' + 1) + t(s'y - s' + 1)\bigr) \frac{ds'}{s'} \tag{246}$$

$$\leq (1-t) \int_0^1 f_k(s'x - s' + 1) \frac{ds'}{s'} + t \int_0^1 f_k(s'y - s' + 1) \frac{ds'}{s'} \tag{247}$$

$$= (1-t) f_{k+1}(x) + t f_{k+1}(y), \tag{248}$$

where (247) holds since $f_k(\cdot)$ is convex on $(0, \infty)$ (by assumption). Hence, from (245)–(248), $f_{k+1}(\cdot)$ is also convex on $(0, \infty)$ with $f_{k+1}(1) = 0$. By mathematical induction and our assumptions on f_0, it follows that $\{f_k(\cdot)\}_{k=0}^{\infty}$ is a sequence of convex functions on $(0, \infty)$ which vanish at 1.

We next prove (243). For all $x, y > 0$ and $k \in \{0, 1, \ldots\}$,

$$f_{k+1}(y) \geq f_{k+1}(x) + f'_{k+1}(x)(y - x) \tag{249}$$

$$= f_{k+1}(x) + \frac{f_k(x)}{x - 1}(y - x), \tag{250}$$

where (249) holds since $f_k(\cdot)$ is convex on $(0, \infty)$, and (250) relies on the recursive equation in (58). Substituting $y = 1$ into (249)–(250), and using the equality $f_{k+1}(1) = 0$, gives (243). $\square$

We next prove Theorem 4. From Lemma 3, it follows that $D_{f_k}(P \| Q)$ is an f-divergence for all integers $k \geq 0$, and the non-negative sequence $\{D_{f_k}(P \| Q)\}_{k=0}^{\infty}$ is monotonically non-increasing. From (21) and (58), it also follows that, for all $\lambda \in [0,1]$ and integer $k \in \{0, 1, \ldots\}$,

$$D_{f_{k+1}}(R_\lambda \| P) = \int p f_{k+1}\left(\frac{r_\lambda}{p}\right) d\mu \tag{251}$$

$$= \int p \int_0^{(p-q)\lambda/p} f_k(1 - s) \frac{ds}{s} d\mu \tag{252}$$

$$= \int p \int_0^{\lambda} f_k\left(1 + \frac{(q-p)s'}{p}\right) \frac{ds'}{s'} d\mu \tag{253}$$

$$= \int_0^\lambda \int p f_k\left(\frac{r_{s'}}{p}\right) d\mu \, \frac{ds'}{s'} \tag{254}$$

$$= \int_0^\lambda D_{f_k}(R_{s'} \| P) \frac{ds'}{s'}, \tag{255}$$

where the substitution $s := \frac{(p-q)s'}{p}$ is invoked in (253), and then (254) holds since $\frac{rs'}{p} = 1 + \frac{(q-p)s'}{p}$ for $s' \in [0,1]$ (this follows from (21)) and by interchanging the order of the integrations.

5.6. Proof of Corollary 5

Combining (60) and (61) yields (58); furthermore, $f_0 \colon (0, \infty) \to \mathbb{R}$, given by $f_0(x) = \frac{1}{x} - 1$ for all $x > 0$, is convex on $(0, \infty)$ with $f_0(1) = 0$. Hence, Theorem 4 holds for the selected functions $\{f_k(\cdot)\}_{k=0}^{\infty}$ in (61), which therefore are all convex on $(0, \infty)$ and vanish at 1. This proves that (59) holds for all $\lambda \in [0,1]$ and $k \in \{0, 1, \ldots\}$. Since $f_0(x) = \frac{1}{x} - 1$ and $f_1(x) = -\log_e(x)$ for all $x > 0$ (see (60) and (61)), then, for every pair of probability measures P and Q:

$$D_{f_0}(P\|Q) = \chi^2(Q\|P), \quad D_{f_1}(P\|Q) = \tfrac{1}{\log e} D(Q\|P). \tag{256}$$

Finally, combining (59), for $k = 0$, together with (256), gives (22) as a special case.

5.7. Proof of Theorem 5 and Corollary 6

For an arbitrary measurable set $\mathcal{E} \subseteq \mathcal{X}$, we have from (62)

$$\mu_{\mathcal{C}}(\mathcal{E}) = \int_{\mathcal{E}} \frac{1_{\mathcal{C}}(x)}{\mu(\mathcal{C})} \, d\mu(x), \tag{257}$$

where $1_{\mathcal{C}} \colon \mathcal{X} \to \{0,1\}$ is the indicator function of $\mathcal{C} \subseteq \mathcal{X}$, i.e., $1_{\mathcal{C}}(x) := 1\{x \in \mathcal{C}\}$ for $x \in \mathcal{X}$. Hence,

$$\frac{d\mu_{\mathcal{C}}}{d\mu}(x) = \frac{1_{\mathcal{C}}(x)}{\mu(\mathcal{C})}, \quad \forall x \in \mathcal{X}, \tag{258}$$

and

$$D(\mu_{\mathcal{C}}\|\mu) = \int_{\mathcal{X}} f\left(\frac{d\mu_{\mathcal{C}}}{d\mu}\right) d\mu \tag{259}$$

$$= \int_{\mathcal{C}} f\left(\frac{1}{\mu(\mathcal{C})}\right) d\mu(x) + \int_{\mathcal{X} \setminus \mathcal{C}} f(0) \, d\mu(x) \tag{260}$$

$$= \mu(\mathcal{C}) \, f\left(\frac{1}{\mu(\mathcal{C})}\right) + \mu(\mathcal{X} \setminus \mathcal{C}) \, f(0) \tag{261}$$

$$= \tilde{f}(\mu(\mathcal{C})) + (1 - \mu(\mathcal{C})) \, f(0), \tag{262}$$

where the last equality holds by the definition of $\tilde{f}$ in (63). This proves Theorem 5. Corollary 6 is next proved by first proving (67) for the Rényi divergence. For all $\alpha \in (0,1) \cup (1,\infty)$,

$$D_\alpha(\mu_{\mathcal{C}}\|\mu) = \frac{1}{\alpha - 1} \log \int_{\mathcal{X}} \left(\frac{d\mu_{\mathcal{C}}}{d\mu}\right)^\alpha d\mu \tag{263}$$

$$= \frac{1}{\alpha - 1} \log \int_{\mathcal{C}} \left(\frac{1}{\mu(\mathcal{C})}\right)^\alpha d\mu \tag{264}$$

$$= \frac{1}{\alpha - 1} \log\left(\left(\frac{1}{\mu(\mathcal{C})}\right)^\alpha \mu(\mathcal{C})\right) \tag{265}$$

$$= \log \frac{1}{\mu(\mathcal{C})}. \tag{266}$$

The justification of (67) for $\alpha = 1$ is due to the continuous extension of the order-α Rényi divergence at $\alpha = 1$, which gives the relative entropy (see (13)). Equality (65) is obtained from (67) at $\alpha = 1$. Finally, (66) is obtained by combining (15) and (67) with $\alpha = 2$.

5.8. Proof of Theorem 6

(100) is an equivalent form of (27). From (91) and (100), for all $\alpha \in [0,1]$,

$$\frac{1}{\log e} S_\alpha(P\|Q) = \alpha \frac{1}{\log e} K_\alpha(P\|Q) + (1-\alpha) \frac{1}{\log e} K_{1-\alpha}(Q\|P) \tag{267}$$

$$= \alpha \int_0^\alpha s D_{\phi_s}(P\|Q)\, ds + (1-\alpha) \int_0^{1-\alpha} s D_{\phi_s}(Q\|P)\, ds \tag{268}$$

$$= \alpha \int_0^\alpha s D_{\phi_s}(P\|Q)\, ds + (1-\alpha) \int_\alpha^1 (1-s) D_{\phi_{1-s}}(Q\|P)\, ds. \tag{269}$$

Regarding the integrand of the second term in (269), in view of (18), for all $s \in (0,1)$

$$D_{\phi_{1-s}}(Q\|P) = \frac{1}{(1-s)^2} \cdot \chi^2(Q \| (1-s)P + sQ) \tag{270}$$

$$= \frac{1}{s^2} \cdot \chi^2(P \| (1-s)P + sQ) \tag{271}$$

$$= D_{\phi_s}(P\|Q), \tag{272}$$

where (271) readily follows from (9). Since we also have $D_{\phi_1}(P\|Q) = \chi^2(P\|Q) = D_{\phi_0}(Q\|P)$ (see (18)), it follows that

$$D_{\phi_{1-s}}(Q\|P) = D_{\phi_s}(P\|Q), \quad s \in [0,1]. \tag{273}$$

By using this identity, we get from (269) that, for all $\alpha \in [0,1]$

$$\frac{1}{\log e} S_\alpha(P\|Q) = \alpha \int_0^\alpha s D_{\phi_s}(P\|Q)\, ds + (1-\alpha) \int_\alpha^1 (1-s) D_{\phi_s}(P\|Q)\, ds \tag{274}$$

$$= \int_0^1 g_\alpha(s) D_{\phi_s}(P\|Q)\, ds, \tag{275}$$

where the function $g_\alpha \colon [0,1] \to \mathbb{R}$ is defined in (102). This proves the integral identity (101).

The lower bounds in (103) and (104) hold since, if $f \colon (0,\infty) \to \mathbb{R}$ is convex, continuously twice differentiable and strictly convex at 1, then

$$\mu_{\chi^2}(Q_X, W_{Y|X}) \leq \mu_f(Q_X, W_{Y|X}), \tag{276}$$

(see, e.g., [46] [Proposition II.6.5] and [50] [Theorem 2]). Hence, this holds in particular for the f-divergences in (95) and (96) (since the required properties are satisfied by the parametric functions in (97) and (98), respectively). We next prove the upper bound on the contraction coefficients in (103) and (104) by relying on (100) and (101), respectively. In the setting of Definition 7, if $P_X \neq Q_X$, then it follows from (100) that for $\alpha \in (0,1]$,

$$\frac{K_\alpha(P_Y\|Q_Y)}{K_\alpha(P_X\|Q_X)} = \frac{\int_0^\alpha s D_{\phi_s}(P_Y\|Q_Y)\, ds}{\int_0^\alpha s D_{\phi_s}(P_X\|Q_X)\, ds} \tag{277}$$

$$\leq \frac{\int_0^\alpha s \mu_{\phi_s}(Q_X, W_{Y|X}) D_{\phi_s}(P_X\|Q_X)\, ds}{\int_0^\alpha s D_{\phi_s}(P_X\|Q_X)\, ds} \tag{278}$$

$$\leq \sup_{s \in (0,\alpha]} \mu_{\phi_s}(Q_X, W_{Y|X}). \tag{279}$$

Finally, taking the supremum of the left-hand side of (277) over all probability measures P_X such that $0 < K_\alpha(P_X\|Q_X) < \infty$ gives the upper bound on $\mu_{k_\alpha}(Q_X, W_{Y|X})$ in (103). The proof of the upper bound on $\mu_{s_\alpha}(Q_X, W_{Y|X})$, for all $\alpha \in [0,1]$, follows similarly from (101), since the function $g_\alpha(\cdot)$ as defined in (102) is positive over the interval $(0,1)$.

5.9. Proof of Corollary 7

The upper bounds in (106) and (107) rely on those in (103) and (104), respectively, by showing that

$$\sup_{s \in (0,1]} \mu_{\phi_s}(Q_X, W_{Y|X}) \leq \mu_{\chi^2}(W_{Y|X}). \tag{280}$$

Inequality (280) is obtained as follows, similarly to the concept of the proof of [51] [Remark 3.8]. For all $s \in (0,1]$ and $P_X \neq Q_X$,

$$\frac{D_{\phi_s}(P_X W_{Y|X} \| Q_X W_{Y|X})}{D_{\phi_s}(P_X \| Q_X)}$$

$$= \frac{\chi^2(P_X W_{Y|X} \| (1-s)P_X W_{Y|X} + sQ_X W_{Y|X})}{\chi^2(P_X \| (1-s)P_X + sQ_X)} \tag{281}$$

$$\leq \mu_{\chi^2}((1-s)P_X + sQ_X, W_{Y|X}) \tag{282}$$

$$\leq \mu_{\chi^2}(W_{Y|X}), \tag{283}$$

where (281) holds due to (18), and (283) is due to the definition in (105).

5.10. Proof of Proposition 3

The lower bound on the contraction coefficients in (108) and (109) is due to (276). The derivation of the upper bounds relies on [49] [Theorem 2.2], which states the following. Let $f \colon [0, \infty) \to \mathbb{R}$ be a three–times differentiable, convex function with $f(1) = 0$, $f''(1) > 0$, and let the function $z \colon (0, \infty) \to \mathbb{R}$ defined as $z(t) := \frac{f(t) - f(0)}{t}$, for all $t > 0$, be concave. Then,

$$\mu_f(Q_X, W_{Y|X}) \leq \frac{f'(1) + f(0)}{f''(1) Q_{\min}} \cdot \mu_{\chi^2}(Q_X, W_{Y|X}). \tag{284}$$

For $\alpha \in (0,1]$, let $z_{\alpha,1} \colon (0, \infty) \to \mathbb{R}$ and $z_{\alpha,2} \colon (0, \infty) \to \mathbb{R}$ be given by

$$z_{\alpha,1}(t) := \frac{k_\alpha(t) - k_\alpha(0)}{t}, \quad t > 0, \tag{285}$$

$$z_{\alpha,2}(t) := \frac{s_\alpha(t) - s_\alpha(0)}{t}, \quad t > 0, \tag{286}$$

with k_α and s_α in (97) and (98). Straightforward calculus shows that, for $\alpha \in (0,1]$ and $t > 0$,

$$\frac{1}{\log e} z''_{\alpha,1}(t) = -\frac{\alpha^2 + 2\alpha(1-\alpha)t}{t^2 [\alpha + (1-\alpha)t]^2} < 0, \tag{287}$$

$$\frac{1}{\log e} z''_{\alpha,2}(t) = -\frac{\alpha^2 [\alpha + 2(1-\alpha)t]}{t^2 [\alpha + (1-\alpha)t]^2}$$

$$- \frac{2(1-\alpha)}{t^3} \left[\log_e \left(1 + \frac{(1-\alpha)t}{\alpha} \right) - \frac{(1-\alpha)t}{\alpha + (1-\alpha)t} - \frac{(1-\alpha)^2 t^2}{2[\alpha + (1-\alpha)t]^2} \right]. \tag{288}$$

The first term on the right side of (288) is negative. For showing that the second term is also negative, we rely on the power series expansion $\log_e(1+u) = u - \frac{1}{2}u^2 + \frac{1}{3}u^3 - \ldots$ for $u \in (-1, 1]$. Setting $u := -\frac{x}{1+x}$, for $x > 0$, and using Leibnitz theorem for alternating series yields

$$\log_e(1+x) = -\log_e\left(1 - \frac{x}{1+x}\right) > \frac{x}{1+x} + \frac{x^2}{2(1+x)^2}, \quad x > 0. \tag{289}$$

Consequently, setting $x := \frac{(1-\alpha)t}{\alpha} \in [0, \infty)$ in (289), for $t > 0$ and $\alpha \in (0,1]$, proves that the second term on the right side of (288) is negative. Hence, $z''_{\alpha,1}(t), z''_{\alpha,2}(t) < 0$, so both $z_{\alpha,1}, z_{\alpha,2} \colon (0,\infty) \to \mathbb{R}$ are concave functions.

In view of the satisfiability of the conditions of [49] [Theorem 2.2] for the f-divergences with $f = k_\alpha$ or $f = s_\alpha$, the upper bounds in (108) and (109) follow from (284), and also since

$$k_\alpha(0) = 0, \qquad k'_\alpha(1) = \alpha \log e, \qquad k''_\alpha(1) = \alpha^2 \log e, \tag{290}$$

$$s_\alpha(0) = -(1-\alpha)\log\alpha, \quad s'_\alpha(1) = (2\alpha - 1)\log e, \quad s''_\alpha(1) = (1 - 3\alpha + 3\alpha^2)\log e. \tag{291}$$

5.11. Proof of Proposition 4

In view of (24), we get

$$\frac{D(P_Y\|Q_Y)}{D(P_X\|Q_X)} = \frac{\int_0^1 \chi^2(P_Y \| (1-s)P_Y + sQ_Y)\frac{ds}{s}}{\int_0^1 \chi^2(P_X \| (1-s)P_X + sQ_X)\frac{ds}{s}} \tag{292}$$

$$\leq \frac{\int_0^1 \mu_{\chi^2}((1-s)P_X + sQ_X, W_{Y|X})\, \chi^2(P_X \| (1-s)P_X + sQ_X)\frac{ds}{s}}{\int_0^1 \chi^2(P_X \| (1-s)P_X + sQ_X)\frac{ds}{s}} \tag{293}$$

$$\leq \sup_{s\in[0,1]} \mu_{\chi^2}((1-s)P_X + sQ_X, W_{Y|X}). \tag{294}$$

In view of (119), the distributions of X_s and Y_s, and since $((1-s)P_X + sQ_X)W_{Y|X} = (1-s)P_Y + sQ_Y$ holds for all $s \in [0,1]$, it follows that

$$\rho_\mathrm{m}(X_s; Y_s) = \sqrt{\mu_{\chi^2}((1-s)P_X + sQ_X, W_{Y|X})}, \quad s \in [0,1], \tag{295}$$

which, from (292)–(295), implies that

$$\sup_{s\in[0,1]} \rho_\mathrm{m}(X_s; Y_s) \geq \sqrt{\frac{D(P_Y\|Q_Y)}{D(P_X\|Q_X)}}. \tag{296}$$

Switching P_X and Q_X in (292)–(294) and using the mapping $s \mapsto 1-s$ in (294) gives (due to the symmetry of the maximal correlation)

$$\sup_{s\in[0,1]} \rho_\mathrm{m}(X_s; Y_s) \geq \sqrt{\frac{D(Q_Y\|P_Y)}{D(Q_X\|P_X)}}, \tag{297}$$

and, finally, taking the maximal lower bound among those in (296) and (297) gives (120).

Author Contributions: Both coauthors contributed to this research work, and to the writing and proofreading of this article. The starting point of this work was in independent derivations of preliminary versions of Theorems 1 and 2 in two separate un-published works [24,25]. All authors have read and agreed to the published version of the manuscript.

Funding: This research received no external funding.

Acknowledgments: Sergio Verdú is gratefully acknowledged for a careful reading, and well-appreciated feedback on the submitted version of this paper.

Conflicts of Interest: The authors declare no conflict of interest.

References

1. Kullback, S.; Leibler, R.A. On information and sufficiency. *Ann. Math. Stat.* **1951**, *22*, 79–86. [CrossRef]

2. Pearson, K. On the criterion that a given system of deviations from the probable in the case of a correlated system of variables is such that it can be reasonably supposed to have arisen from random sampling. *Lond. Edinb. Dublin Philos. Mag. J. Sci.* **1900**, *50*, 157–175. [CrossRef]
3. Csiszár, I.; Shields, P.C. Information Theory and Statistics: A Tutorial. *Found. Trends Commun. Inf. Theory* **2004**, *1*, 417–528. [CrossRef]
4. Ali, S.M.; Silvey, S.D. A general class of coefficients of divergence of one distribution from another. *J. R. Stat. Soc.* **1966**, *28*, 131–142. [CrossRef]
5. Csiszár, I. Eine Informationstheoretische Ungleichung und ihre Anwendung auf den Bewis der Ergodizität von Markhoffschen Ketten. *Publ. Math. Inst. Hungar. Acad. Sci.* **1963**, *8*, 85–108.
6. Csiszár, I. Information-type measures of difference of probability distributions and indirect observations. *Stud. Sci. Math. Hung.* **1967**, *2*, 299–318.
7. Csiszár, I. On topological properties of f-divergences. *Stud. Sci. Math. Hung.* **1967**, *2*, 329–339.
8. Csiszár, I. A class of measures of informativity of observation channels. *Period. Math. Hung.* **1972**, *2*, 191–213. [CrossRef]
9. van Erven, T.; Harremoës, P. Rényi divergence and Kullback–Leibler divergence. *IEEE Trans. Inf. Theory* **2014**, *60*, 3797–3820. [CrossRef]
10. Rényi, A. On measures of entropy and information. In *Proceedings of the Fourth Berkeley Symposium on Mathematical Statistics and Probability, Volume 1: Contributions to the Theory of Statistics*; University of California Press: Berkeley, CA, USA, 1961; pp. 547–561.
11. Liese, F.; Vajda, I. *Convex Statistical Distances*; Teubner-Texte Zur Mathematik: Leipzig, Germany, 1987.
12. Liese, F.; Vajda, I. On divergences and informations in statistics and information theory. *IEEE Trans. Inf. Theory* **2006**, *52*, 4394–4412. [CrossRef]
13. DeGroot, M.H. Uncertainty, information and sequential experiments. *Ann. Math. Stat.* **1962**, *33*, 404–419. [CrossRef]
14. Polyanskiy, Y.; Poor, H.V.; Verdú, S. Channel coding rate in the finite blocklength regime. *IEEE Trans. Inf. Theory* **2010**, *56*, 2307–2359. [CrossRef]
15. Sason, I.; Verdú, S. f-divergence inequalities. *IEEE Trans. Inf. Theory* **2016**, *62*, 5973–6006. [CrossRef]
16. Sason, I. On f-divergences: Integral representations, local behavior, and inequalities. *Entropy* **2018**, *20*, 383. [CrossRef]
17. Melbourne, J.; Madiman, M.; Salapaka, M.V. Relationships between certain f-divergences. In Proceedings of the 57th Annual Allerton Conference on Communication, Control and Computing, Urbana, IL, USA, 24–27 September 2019; pp. 1068–1073.
18. Melbourne, J.; Talukdar, S.; Bhaban, S.; Madiman, M.; Salapaka, M.V. The Differential Entropy of Mixtures: New Bounds and Applications. Available online: https://arxiv.org/pdf/1805.11257.pdf (accessed on 22 April 2020).
19. Audenaert, K.M.R. Quantum skew divergence. *J. Math. Phys.* **2014**, *55*, 112202. [CrossRef]
20. Gibbs, A.L.; Su, F.E. On choosing and bounding probability metrics. *Int. Stat. Rev.* **2002**, *70*, 419–435. [CrossRef]
21. Györfi, L.; Vajda, I. A class of modified Pearson and Neyman statistics. *Stat. Decis.* **2001**, *19*, 239–251. [CrossRef]
22. Le Cam, L. *Asymptotic Methods in Statistical Decision Theory*; Series in Statistics; Springer: New York, NY, USA, 1986.
23. Vincze, I. On the concept and measure of information contained in an observation. In *Contributions to Probability*; Gani, J., Rohatgi, V.K., Eds.; Academic Press: New York, NY, USA, 1981; pp. 207–214.
24. Nishiyama, T. A New Lower Bound for Kullback–Leibler Divergence Based on Hammersley-Chapman-Robbins Bound. Available online: https://arxiv.org/abs/1907.00288v3 (accessed on 2 November 2019).
25. Sason, I. On Csiszár's f-divergences and informativities with applications. In *Workshop on Channels, Statistics, Information, Secrecy and Randomness for the 80th birthday of I. Csiszár*; The Rényi Institute of Mathematics, Hungarian Academy of Sciences: Budapest, Hungary, 2018.
26. Makur, A.; Polyanskiy, Y. Comparison of channels: Criteria for domination by a symmetric channel. *IEEE Trans. Inf. Theory* **2018**, *64*, 5704–5725. [CrossRef]
27. Simic, S. On a new moments inequality. *Stat. Probab. Lett.* **2008**, *78*, 2671–2678. [CrossRef]
28. Chapman, D.G.; Robbins, H. Minimum variance estimation without regularity assumptions. *Ann. Math. Stat.* **1951**, *22*, 581–586. [CrossRef]
29. Hammersley, J.M. On estimating restricted parameters. *J. R. Stat. Soc. Ser. B* **1950**, *12*, 192–240. [CrossRef]
30. Verdú, S. *Information Theory*; in preparation.

31. Wang, L.; Madiman, M. Beyond the entropy power inequality, via rearrangments. *IEEE Trans. Inf. Theory* **2014**, *60*, 5116–5137. [CrossRef]
32. Lewin, L. *Polylogarithms and Associated Functions*; Elsevier North Holland: Amsterdam, The Netherlands, 1981.
33. Marton, K. Bounding $\bar{d}$-distance by informational divergence: A method to prove measure concentration. *Ann. Probab.* **1996**, *24*, 857–866. [CrossRef]
34. Marton, K. Distance-divergence inequalities. *IEEE Inf. Theory Soc. Newsl.* **2014**, *64*, 9–13.
35. Boucheron, S.; Lugosi, G.; Massart, P. *Concentration Inequalities—A Nonasymptotic Theory of Independence*; Oxford University Press: Oxford, UK, 2013.
36. Raginsky, M.; Sason, I. Concentration of Measure Inequalities in Information Theory, Communications and Coding: Third Edition. In *Foundations and Trends in Communications and Information Theory*; NOW Publishers: Boston, MA, USA; Delft, The Netherlands, 2018.
37. Csiszár, I. Sanov property, generalized I-projection and a conditional limit theorem. *Ann. Probab.* **1984**, *12*, 768–793. [CrossRef]
38. Clarke, B.S.; Barron, A.R. Information-theoretic asymptotics of Bayes methods. *IEEE Trans. Inf. Theory* **1990**, *36*, 453–471. [CrossRef]
39. Evans, R.J.; Boersma, J.; Blachman, N.M.; Jagers, A.A. The entropy of a Poisson distribution. *SIAM Rev.* **1988**, *30*, 314–317. [CrossRef]
40. Knessl, C. Integral representations and asymptotic expansions for Shannon and Rényi entropies. *Appl. Math. Lett.* **1998**, *11*, 69–74. [CrossRef]
41. Merhav, N.; Sason, I. An integral representation of the logarithmic function with applications in information theory. *Entropy* **2020**, *22*, 51. [CrossRef]
42. Cover, T.M.; Thomas, J.A. *Elements of Information Theory*, 2nd ed.; John Wiley & Sons: Hoboken, NJ, USA, 2006.
43. Csiszár, I. The method of types. *IEEE Trans. Inf. Theory* **1998**, *44*, 2505–2523. [CrossRef]
44. Corless, R.M.; Gonnet, G.H.; Hare, D.E.G.; Jeffrey, D.J.; Knuth, D.E. On the Lambert W function. *Adv. Comput. Math.* **1996**, *5*, 329–359. [CrossRef]
45. Tamm, U. Some refelections about the Lambert W function as inverse of $x \cdot \log(x)$. In Proceedings of the 2014 IEEE Information Theory and Applications Workshop, San Diego, CA, USA, 9–14 February 2014.
46. Cohen, J.E.; Kemperman, J.H.B.; Zbăganu, G. *Comparison of Stochastic Matrices with Applications in Information Theory, Statistics, Economics and Population Sciences*; Birkhäuser: Boston, MA, USA, 1998.
47. Cohen, J.E.; Iwasa, Y.; Rautu, G.; Ruskai, M.B.; Seneta, E.; Zbăganu, G. Relative entropy under mappings by stochastic matrices. *Linear Algebra Its Appl.* **1993**, *179*, 211–235. [CrossRef]
48. Makur, A.; Zheng, L. Bounds between contraction coefficients. In Proceedings of the 53rd Annual Allerton Conference on Communication, Control and Computing, Urbana, IL, USA, 29 September–2 October 2015; pp. 1422–1429.
49. Makur, A. Information Contraction and Decomposition. Ph.D. Thesis, MIT, Cambridge, MA, USA, May 2019.
50. Polyanskiy, Y.; Wu, Y. Strong data processing inequalities for channels and Bayesian networks. In *Convexity and Concentration*; The IMA Volumes in Mathematics and its Applications; Carlen, E., Madiman, M., Werner, E.M., Eds.; Springer: New York, NY, USA, 2017; Volume 161, pp. 211–249.
51. Raginsky, M. Strong data processing inequalities and Φ-Sobolev inequalities for discrete channels. *IEEE Trans. Inf. Theory* **2016**, *62*, 3355–3389. [CrossRef]
52. Sason, I. On data-processing and majorization inequalities for f-divergences with applications. *Entropy* **2019**, *21*, 1022. [CrossRef]
53. Csiszár, I.; Körner, J. *Information Theory: Coding Theorems for Discrete Memoryless Systems*, 2nd ed.; Cambridge University Press: Cambridge, UK, 2011.
54. Burbea, J.; Rao, C.R. On the convexity of some divergence measures based on entropy functions. *IEEE Trans. Inf. Theory* **1982**, *28*, 489–495. [CrossRef]
55. Lin, J. Divergence measures based on the Shannon entropy. *IEEE Trans. Inf. Theory* **1991**, *37*, 145–151. [CrossRef]
56. Menéndez, M.L.; Pardo, J.A.; Pardo, L.; Pardo, M.C. The Jensen–Shannon divergence. *J. Frankl. Inst.* **1997**, *334*, 307–318. [CrossRef]
57. Topsøe, F. Some inequalities for information divergence and related measures of discrimination. *IEEE Trans. Inf. Theory* **2000**, *46*, 1602–1609. [CrossRef]

58. Nielsen, F. On a generalization of the Jensen–Shannon divergence and the Jensen–Shannon centroids. *Entropy* **2020**, *22*, 221. [CrossRef]
59. Asadi, M.; Ebrahimi, N.; Karazmi, O.; Soofi, E.S. Mixture models, Bayes Fisher information, and divergence measures. *IEEE Trans. Inf. Theory* **2019**, *65*, 2316–2321. [CrossRef]
60. Sarmanov, O.V. Maximum correlation coefficient (non-symmetric case). *Sel. Transl. Math. Stat. Probab.* **1962**, *2*, 207–210. (In Russian)
61. Gilardoni, G.L. Corrigendum to the note on the minimum f-divergence for given total variation. *Comptes Rendus Math.* **2010**, *348*, 299. [CrossRef]
62. Reid, M.D.; Williamson, R.C. Information, divergence and risk for binary experiments. *J. Mach. Learn. Res.* **2011**, *12*, 731–817.
63. Pardo, M.C.; Vajda, I. On asymptotic properties of information-theoretic divergences. *IEEE Trans. Inf. Theory* **2003**, *49*, 1860–1868. [CrossRef]

© 2020 by the authors. Licensee MDPI, Basel, Switzerland. This article is an open access article distributed under the terms and conditions of the Creative Commons Attribution (CC BY) license (http://creativecommons.org/licenses/by/4.0/).

Article

A Two-Moment Inequality with Applications to Rényi Entropy and Mutual Information

Galen Reeves [1,2]

[1] Department of Electrical and Computer Engineering, Duke University, Durham, NC 27708, USA; galen.reeves@duke.edu
[2] Department of Statistical Science, Duke University, Durham, NC 27708, USA

Received: 14 September 2020; Accepted: 6 October 2020; Published: 1 November 2020

Abstract: This paper explores some applications of a two-moment inequality for the integral of the rth power of a function, where $0 < r < 1$. The first contribution is an upper bound on the Rényi entropy of a random vector in terms of the two different moments. When one of the moments is the zeroth moment, these bounds recover previous results based on maximum entropy distributions under a single moment constraint. More generally, evaluation of the bound with two carefully chosen nonzero moments can lead to significant improvements with a modest increase in complexity. The second contribution is a method for upper bounding mutual information in terms of certain integrals with respect to the variance of the conditional density. The bounds have a number of useful properties arising from the connection with variance decompositions.

Keywords: information inequalities; mutual information; Rényi entropy; Carlson–Levin inequality

1. Introduction

The interplay between inequalities and information theory has a rich history, with notable examples including the relationship between the Brunn–Minkowski inequality and the entropy power inequality as well as the matrix determinant inequalities obtained from differential entropy [1]. In this paper, the focus is on a "two-moment" inequality that provides an upper bound on the integral of the rth power of a function. Specifically, if f is a nonnegative function defined on $\mathbb{R}^n$ and p, q, r are real numbers satisfying $0 < r < 1$ and $p < 1/r - 1 < q$, then

$$\left(\int f(x)^r \, dx\right)^{\frac{1}{r}} \leq C_{n,p,q,r} \left(\int \|x\|^{np} f(x) \, dx\right)^{\frac{qr+r-1}{(q-p)r}} \left(\int \|x\|^{nq} f(x) \, dx\right)^{\frac{1-r-pr}{(q-p)r}}, \quad (1)$$

where the best possible constant $C_{n,p,q,r}$ is given exactly; see Propositions 2 and 3 ahead. The one-dimensional version of this inequality is a special case of the classical Carlson–Levin inequality [2–4], and the multidimensional version is a special case of a result presented by Barza et al. [5]. The particular formulation of the inequality used in this paper was derived independently in [6], where the proof follows from a direct application of Hölder's inequality and Jensen's inequality.

In the context of information theory and statistics, a useful property of the two-moment inequality is that it provides a bound on a nonlinear functional, namely the r-quasi-norm $\|\cdot\|_r$, in terms of integrals that are linear in f. Consequently, this inequality is well suited to settings where f is a mixture of simple functions whose moments can be evaluated. We note that this reliance on moments to bound a nonlinear functional is closely related to bounds obtained from variational characterizations such as the Donsker–Varadhan representation of Kullback divergence [7] and its generalizations to Rényi divergence [8,9].

The first application considered in this paper concerns the relationship between the entropy of a probability measure and its moments. This relationship is fundamental to the principle of maximum entropy, which originated in statistical physics and has since been applied to statistical inference problems [10]. It also plays a prominent role in information theory and estimation theory where the fact that the Gaussian distribution maximizes differential entropy under second moment constraints ([11], [Theorem 8.6.5]) plays a prominent role. Moment–entropy inequalities for Rényi entropy were studied in a series of works by Lutwak et al. [12–14], as well as related works by Costa et al. [15,16] and Johonson and Vignat [17], in which it is shown that, under a single moment constraint, Rényi entropy is maximized by a family of generalized Gaussian distributions. The connection between these moment–entropy inequalities and the Carlson–Levin inequality was noted recently by Nguyen [18].

In this direction, one of the contributions of this paper is a new family of moment–entropy inequalities. This family of inequalities follows from applying Inequality (1) in the setting where f is a probability density function, and thus there is a one-to-one correspondence between the integral of the rth power and the Rényi entropy of order r. In the special case where one of the moments is the zeroth moment, this approach recovers the moment–entropy inequalities given in previous work. More generally, the additional flexibility provided by considering two different moments can lead to stronger results. For example, in Proposition 6, it is shown that if f is the standard Gaussian density function defined on $\mathbb{R}^n$, then the difference between the Rényi entropy and the upper bound given by the two-moment inequality (equivalently, the ratio between the left- and right-hand sides of (1)) is bounded uniformly with respect to n under the following specification of the moments:

$$p_n = \frac{1-r}{r} - \frac{1}{r}\sqrt{\frac{2(1-r)}{n+1}}, \qquad q_n = \frac{1-r}{r} + \frac{1}{r}\sqrt{\frac{2(1-r)}{n+1}}. \tag{2}$$

Conversely, if one of the moments is restricted to be equal to zero, as is the case in the usual moment–entropy inequalities, then the difference between the Rényi entropy and the upper bound diverges with n.

The second application considered in this paper is the problem of bounding mutual information. In conjunction with Fano's inequality and its extensions, bounds on mutual information play a prominent role in establishing minimax rates of statistical estimation [19] as well as the information-theoretic limits of detection in high-dimensional settings [20]. In many cases, one of the technical challenges is to provide conditions under which the dependence between the observations and an underlying signal or model parameters converges to zero in the limit of high dimension.

This paper introduces a new method for bounding mutual information, which can be described as follows. Let $P_{X,Y}$ be a probability measure on $\mathcal{X} \times \mathcal{Y}$ such that $P_{Y|X=x}$ and P_Y have densities $f(y \mid x)$ and $f(y)$ with respect to the Lebesgue measure on $\mathbb{R}^n$. We begin by showing that the mutual information between X and Y satisfies the upper bound

$$I(X;Y) \leq \int \sqrt{\text{Var}(f(y \mid X))}\, dy, \tag{3}$$

where $\text{Var}(p(y \mid X)) = \int (f(y \mid x) - f(y))^2\, dP_X(x)$ is the variance of $f(y \mid X)$; see Proposition 8 ahead. In view of (3), an application of the two-moment Inequality (1) with $r = 1/2$ leads to an upper bound with respect to the moments of the variance of the density:

$$\int \|y\|^{ns} \text{Var}(f(y \mid X))\, dy \tag{4}$$

where this expression is evaluated at $s \in \{p, q\}$ with $p < 1 < q$. A useful property of this bound is that the integrated variance is quadratic in P_X, and thus Expression (4) can be evaluated by swapping the integration over y and with the expectation of over two independent copies of X. For example, when $P_{X,Y}$ is a Gaussian scale mixture, this approach provides closed-form upper bounds in terms of the moments of the Gaussian density. An early version of this technique is used to prove Gaussian approximations for random projections [21] arising in the analysis of a random linear estimation problem appearing in wireless communications and compressed sensing [22,23].

2. Moment Inequalities

Let $L^p(S)$ be the space of Lebesgue measurable functions from S to $\mathbb{R}$ whose pth power is absolutely integrable, and for $p \neq 0$, define

$$\|f\|_p := \left(\int_S |f(x)|^p \, dx \right)^{1/p}.$$

Recall that $\|\cdot\|_p$ is a norm for $p \geq 1$ but only a quasi-norm for $0 < p < 1$ because it does not satisfy the triangle inequality. The sth moment of f is defined as

$$\mathcal{M}_s(f) := \int_S \|x\|^s |f(x)| \, dx,$$

where $\|\cdot\|$ denotes the standard Euclidean norm on vectors.

The two-moment Inequality (1) can be derived straightforwardly using the following argument. For $r \in (0,1)$, the mapping $f \mapsto \|f\|_r$ is concave on the subset of nonnegative functions and admits the variational representation

$$\|f\|_r = \inf \left\{ \frac{\|fg\|_1}{\|g\|_{r^*}} : g \in L^{r^*} \right\}, \qquad (5)$$

where $r^* = r/(r-1) \in (-\infty, 0)$ is the Hölder conjugate of r. Consequently, each $g \in L^{r^*}$ leads to an upper bound on $\|f\|_r$. For example, if f has bounded support S, choosing g to be the indicator function of S leads to the basic inequality $\|f\|_r \leq (\mathrm{Vol}(S))^{(1-r)/r} \|f\|_1$. The upper bound on $\|f\|_r$ given in Inequality (1) can be obtained by restricting the minimum in Expression (5) to the parametric class of functions of the form $g(x) = \nu_1 \|x\|^{np} + \nu_2 \|x\|^{nq}$ with $\nu_1, \nu_2 > 0$ and then optimizing over the parameters (ν_1, ν_2). Here, the constraints on p, q are necessary and sufficient to ensure that $g \in L^{r^*}(\mathbb{R}^n)$.

In the following sections, we provide a more detailed derivation, starting with the problem of maximizing $\|f\|_r$ under multiple moment constraints and then specializing to the case of two moments. For a detailed account of the history of the Carlson type inequalities as well as some further extensions, see [4].

2.1. Multiple Moments

Consider the following optimization problem:

$$\begin{aligned}
\text{maximize} \quad & \|f\|_r \\
\text{subject to} \quad & f(x) \geq 0 \quad \text{for all } x \in S \\
& \mathcal{M}_{s_i}(f) \leq m_i \quad \text{for } 1 \leq i \leq k.
\end{aligned}$$

For $r \in (0,1)$, this is a convex optimization problem because $\|\cdot\|_r^r$ is concave and the moment constraints are linear. By standard theory in convex optimization (e.g., [24]), it can be shown that if the problem is feasible and the maximum is finite, then the maximizer has the form

$$f^*(x) = \left(\sum_{i=1}^k \nu_i^* \|x\|^{s_i} \right)^{\frac{1}{r-1}}, \quad \text{for all } x \in S.$$

The parameters $v_1^*, \cdots, v_k^*$ are nonnegative and the ith moment constraint holds with equality for all i such that v_i^* is strictly positive—that is, $v_i^* > 0 \implies \mu_{s_i}(f^*) = m_i$. Consequently, the maximum can be expressed in terms of a linear combination of the moments:

$$\|f^*\|_r^r = \|(f^*)^r\|_1 = \|f^*(f^*)^{r-1}\|_1 = \sum_{i=1}^{k} v_i^* m_i.$$

For the purposes of this paper, it is useful to consider a relative inequality in terms of the moments of the function itself. Given a number $0 < r < 1$ and vectors $s \in \mathbb{R}^k$ and $v \in \mathbb{R}_+^k$, the function $c_r(v,s)$ is defined according to

$$c_r(v,s) = \left(\int_0^\infty \left(\sum_{i=1}^{k} v_i x^{s_i} \right)^{-\frac{r}{1-r}} dx \right)^{\frac{1-r}{r}},$$

if the integral exists. Otherwise, $c_r(v,s)$ is defined to be positive infinity. It can be verified that $c_r(v,s)$ is finite provided that there exists i, j such that v_i and v_j are strictly positive and $s_i < (1-r)/r < s_j$.

The following result can be viewed as a consequence of the constrained optimization problem described above. We provide a different and very simple proof that depends only on Hölder's inequality.

Proposition 1. *Let f be a nonnegative Lebesgue measurable function defined on the positive reals $\mathbb{R}_+$. For any number $0 < r < 1$ and vectors $s \in \mathbb{R}^k$ and $v \in \mathbb{R}_+^k$, we have*

$$\|f\|_r \le c_r(v,s) \sum_{i=1}^{k} v_i \mathcal{M}_{s_i}(f).$$

Proof. Let $g(x) = \sum_{i=1}^{k} v_i x^{s_i}$. Then, we have

$$\|f\|_r^r = \|g^{-r}(fg)^r\|_1 \le \|g^{-r}\|_{\frac{1}{1-r}} \|(gf)^r\|_{\frac{1}{r}} = \|g^{\frac{-r}{1-r}}\|_1^{1-r} \|gf\|_1^r = \left(c_r(v,s) \sum_{i=1}^{k} v_i \mathcal{M}_{s_i}(f) \right)^r,$$

where the second step is Hölder's inequality with conjugate exponents $1/(1-r)$ and $1/r$. □

2.2. Two Moments

For $a, b > 0$, the beta function $B(a,b)$ and gamma function $\Gamma(a)$ are given by

$$B(a,b) = \int_0^1 t^{a-1}(1-t)^{b-1} dt$$

$$\Gamma(a) = \int_0^\infty t^{a-1} e^{-t} dt,$$

and satisfy the relation $B(a,b) = \Gamma(a)\Gamma(b)/\Gamma(a+b)$, $a,b > 0$. To lighten the notation, we define the normalized beta function

$$\widetilde{B}(a,b) = B(a,b)(a+b)^{a+b} a^{-a} b^{-b}. \tag{6}$$

Properties of these functions are provided in Appendix A.

The next result follows from Proposition 1 for the case of two moments.

Proposition 2. *Let f be a nonnegative Lebesgue measurable function defined on $[0, \infty)$. For any numbers p, q, r with $0 < r < 1$ and $p < 1/r - 1 < q$,*

$$\|f\|_r \le [\psi_r(p,q)]^{\frac{1-r}{r}} [\mathcal{M}_p(f)]^\lambda [\mathcal{M}_q(f)]^{1-\lambda},$$

where $\lambda = (q + 1 - 1/r)/(q - p)$ and

$$\psi_r(p, q) = \frac{1}{(q-p)} \widetilde{B}\left(\frac{r\lambda}{1-r}, \frac{r(1-\lambda)}{1-r}\right),\qquad(7)$$

where $\widetilde{B}(\cdot, \cdot)$ is defined in Equation (6).

Proof. Letting $s = (p, q)$ and $\nu = (\gamma^{1-\lambda}, \gamma^{-\lambda})$ with $\lambda > 0$, we have

$$[c_r(\nu, s)]^{\frac{r}{1-r}} = \int_0^\infty \left(\gamma^{1-\lambda} x^p + \gamma^{-\lambda} x^q\right)^{-\frac{r}{1-r}} dx.$$

Making the change of variable $x \mapsto (\gamma u)^{\frac{1}{q-p}}$ leads to

$$[c_r(\nu, s)]^{\frac{r}{1-r}} = \frac{1}{q-p} \int_0^\infty \frac{u^{b-1}}{(1+u)^{a+b}} du = \frac{B(a,b)}{q-p},$$

where $a = \frac{r}{1-r}\lambda$ and $b = \frac{r}{1-r}(1-\lambda)$ and the second step follows from recognizing the integral representation of the beta function given in Equation (A3). Therefore, by Proposition 1, the inequality

$$\|f\|_r \leq \left(\frac{B(a,b)}{q-p}\right)^{\frac{1-r}{r}} \left(\gamma^{1-\lambda} \mathcal{M}_p(f) + \gamma^{-\lambda} \mathcal{M}_q(f)\right),$$

holds for all $\gamma > 0$. Evaluating this inequality with

$$\gamma = \frac{\lambda \mathcal{M}_q(f)}{(1-\lambda)\mathcal{M}_p(f)},$$

leads to the stated result. □

The special case $r = 1/2$ admits the simplified expression

$$\psi_{1/2}(p, q) = \frac{\pi \lambda^{-\lambda}(1-\lambda)^{-(1-\lambda)}}{(q-p)\sin(\pi\lambda)},\qquad(8)$$

where we have used Euler's reflection formula for the beta function ([25], [Theorem 1.2.1]).

Next, we consider an extension of Proposition 2 for functions defined on $\mathbb{R}^n$. Given any measurable subset S of $\mathbb{R}^n$, we define

$$\omega(S) = \text{Vol}(B^n \cap \text{cone}(S)),\qquad(9)$$

where $B^n = \{u \in \mathbb{R}^n : \|u\| \leq 1\}$ is the n-dimensional Euclidean ball of radius one and

$$\text{cone}(S) = \{x \in \mathbb{R}^n : tx \in S \text{ for some } t > 0\}.$$

The function $\omega(S)$ is proportional to the surface measure of the projection of S on the Euclidean sphere and satisfies

$$\omega(S) \leq \omega(\mathbb{R}^n) = \frac{\pi^{\frac{n}{2}}}{\Gamma(\frac{n}{2}+1)},\qquad(10)$$

for all $S \subseteq \mathbb{R}^n$. Note that $\omega(\mathbb{R}_+) = 1$ and $\omega(\mathbb{R}) = 2$.

Proposition 3. Let f be a nonnegative Lebesgue measurable function defined on a subset S of $\mathbb{R}^n$. For any numbers p, q, r with $0 < r < 1$ and $p < 1/r - 1 < q$,

$$\|f\|_r \leq [\omega(S)\, \psi_r(p,q)]^{\frac{1-r}{r}} [\mathcal{M}_{np}(f)]^{\lambda} [\mathcal{M}_{nq}(f)]^{1-\lambda},$$

where $\lambda = (q + 1 - 1/r)/(q - p)$ and $\psi_r(p,q)$ is given by Equation (7).

Proof. Let f be extended to $\mathbb{R}^n$ using the rule $f(x) = 0$ for all x outside of S and let $g: \mathbb{R}_+ \to \mathbb{R}_+$ be defined according to

$$g(y) = \frac{1}{n} \int_{\mathbb{S}^{n-1}} f(y^{1/n} u)\, d\sigma(u),$$

where $\mathbb{S}^{n-1} = \{u \in \mathbb{R}^n : \|u\| = 1\}$ is the Euclidean sphere of radius one and $\sigma(u)$ is the surface measure of the sphere. In the following, we will show that

$$\|f\|_r \leq (\omega(S))^{\frac{1-r}{r}} \|g\|_r \tag{11}$$

$$\mathcal{M}_{ns}(f) = \mathcal{M}_s(g). \tag{12}$$

Then, the stated inequality then follows from applying Proposition 2 to the function g.

To prove Inequality (11), we begin with a transformation into polar coordinates:

$$\|f\|_r^r = \int_0^\infty \int_{\mathbb{S}^{n-1}} |f(tu)|^r t^{n-1} d\sigma(u)\, dt. \tag{13}$$

Letting $\mathbf{1}_{\text{cone}(S)}(x)$ denote the indicator function of the set $\text{cone}(S)$, the integral over the sphere can be bounded using:

$$\int_{\mathbb{S}^{n-1}} |f(tu)|^r d\sigma(u) = \int_{\mathbb{S}^{n-1}} \mathbf{1}_{\text{cone}(S)}(u)\, |f(tu)|^r d\sigma(u)$$

$$\overset{(a)}{\leq} \left(\int_{\mathbb{S}^{n-1}} \mathbf{1}_{\text{cone}(S)}(u)\, d\sigma(u) \right)^{1-r} \left(\int_{\mathbb{S}^{n-1}} |f(tu)|\, d\sigma(u) \right)^r$$

$$\overset{(b)}{=} n\, (\omega(S))^{1-r}\, g^r(t^n), \tag{14}$$

where: (a) follows from Hölder's inequality with conjugate exponents $\frac{1}{1-r}$ and $\frac{1}{r}$, and (b) follows from the definition of g and the fact that

$$\omega(S) = \int_0^1 \int_{\mathbb{S}^{n-1}} \mathbf{1}_{\text{cone}(S)}(u)\, t^{n-1} d\sigma(u)\, dt$$

$$= \frac{1}{n} \int_{\mathbb{S}^{n-1}} \mathbf{1}_{\text{cone}(S)}(u)\, d\sigma(u).$$

Plugging Inequality (14) back into Equation (13) and then making the change of variable $t \to y^{\frac{1}{n}}$ yields

$$\|f\|_r^r \leq n\, (\omega(S))^{1-r} \int_0^\infty g^r(t^n) t^{n-1} dt = (\omega(S))^{1-r} \|g\|_r^r.$$

The proof of Equation (12) follows along similar lines. We have

$$\mathcal{M}_{ns}(f) \overset{(a)}{=} \int_0^\infty \int_{\mathbb{S}^{n-1}} t^{ns} f(tu)\, t^{n-1} d\sigma(u)\, dt$$

$$\overset{(b)}{=} \frac{1}{n} \int_0^\infty \int_{\mathbb{S}^{n-1}} y^s f(y^{\frac{1}{n}} u)\, d\sigma(u)\, dy$$

$$= \mathcal{M}_s(g)$$

where (a) follows from a transformation into polar coordinates and (b) follows from the change of variable $t \mapsto y^{\frac{1}{n}}$.

Having established Inequality (11) and Equation (12), an application of Proposition 2 completes the proof. □

3. Rényi Entropy Bounds

Let X be a random vector that has a density $f(x)$ with respect to the Lebesgue measure on $\mathbb{R}^n$. The differential Rényi entropy of order $r \in (0,1) \cup (1,\infty)$ is defined according to [11]:

$$h_r(X) = \frac{1}{1-r} \log \left(\int_{\mathbb{R}^n} f^r(x) \, dx \right).$$

Throughout this paper, it is assumed that the logarithm is defined with respect to the natural base and entropy is measured in nats. The Rényi entropy is continuous and nonincreasing in r. If the support set $S = \{x \in \mathbb{R}^n : f(x) > 0\}$ has finite measure, then the limit as r converges to zero is given by $h_0(X) = \log \text{Vol}(S)$. If the support does not have finite measure, then $h_r(X)$ increases to infinity as r decreases to zero. The case $r = 1$ is given by the Shannon differential entropy:

$$h_1(X) = -\int_S f(x) \log f(x) \, dx.$$

Given a random variable X that is not identical to zero and numbers p, q, r with $0 < r < 1$ and $p < 1/r - 1 < q$, we define the function

$$L_r(X; p, q) = \frac{r\lambda}{1-r} \log \mathbb{E}\left[|X|^p\right] + \frac{r(1-\lambda)}{1-r} \log \mathbb{E}\left[|X|^q\right],$$

where $\lambda = (q + 1 - 1/r)/(q - p)$.

The next result, which follows directly from Proposition 3, provides an upper bound on the Rényi entropy.

Proposition 4. *Let X be a random vector with a density on $\mathbb{R}^n$. For any numbers p, q, r with $0 < r < 1$ and $p < 1/r - 1 < q$, the Rényi entropy satisfies*

$$h_r(X) \leq \log \omega(S) + \log \psi_r(p, q) + L_r(\|X\|^n; p, q), \tag{15}$$

where $\omega(S)$ is defined in Equation (9) and $\psi_r(p, q)$ is defined in Equation (7).

Proof. This result follows immediately from Proposition 3 and the definition of Rényi entropy. □

The relationship between Proposition 4 and previous results depends on whether the moment p is equal to zero:

- *One-moment inequalities:* If $p = 0$, then there exists a distribution such that Inequality (15) holds with equality. This is because the zero-moment constraint ensures that the function that maximizes the Rényi entropy integrates to one. In this case, Proposition 4 is equivalent to previous results that focused on distributions that maximize Rényi entropy subject to a single moment constraint [12,13,15]. With some abuse of terminology, we refer to these bounds as one-moment inequalities. (A more accurate name would be two-moment inequalities under the constraint that one of the moments is the zeroth moment.)
- *Two-moment inequalities:* If $p \neq 0$, then the right-hand side of Inequality (15) corresponds to the Rényi entropy of a nonnegative function that might not integrate to one. Nevertheless, the expression provides an upper bound on the Rényi entropy for any density with the same moments. We refer to the bounds obtained using a general pair (p, q) as two-moment inequalities.

The contribution of two-moment inequalities is that they lead to tighter bounds. To quantify the tightness, we define $\Delta_r(X; p, q)$ to be the gap between the right-hand side and left-hand side of Inequality (15) corresponding to the pair (p, q)—that is,

$$\Delta_r(X; p, q) = \log \omega(S) + \log \psi_r(p, q) + L_r(\|X\|^n; p, q) - h_r(X).$$

The gaps corresponding to the optimal two-moment and one-moment inequalities are defined according to

$$\Delta_r(X) = \inf_{p,q} \Delta_r(X; p, q)$$
$$\widetilde{\Delta}_r(X) = \inf_{q} \Delta_r(X; 0, q).$$

3.1. Some Consequences of These Bounds

By Lyapunov's inequality, the mapping $s \mapsto \frac{1}{s} \log \mathbb{E}\left[|X|^s\right]$ is nondecreasing on $[0, \infty)$, and thus

$$L_r(X; p, q) \leq L_r(X; 0, q) = \frac{1}{q} \log \mathbb{E}\left[|X|^q\right], \quad p \geq 0. \tag{16}$$

In other words, the case $p = 0$ provides an upper bound on $L_r(X; p, q)$ for nonnegative p. Alternatively, we also have the lower bound

$$L_r(X; p, q) \geq \frac{r}{1-r} \log \mathbb{E}\left[|X|^{\frac{1-r}{r}}\right], \tag{17}$$

which follows from the convexity of $\log \mathbb{E}\left[|X|^s\right]$.

A useful property of $L_r(X; p, q)$ is that it is additive with respect to the product of independent random variables. Specifically, if X and Y are independent, then

$$L_r(XY; p, q) = L_r(X; p, q) + L_r(Y; p, q). \tag{18}$$

One consequence is that multiplication by a bounded random variable cannot increase the Rényi entropy by an amount that exceeds the gap of the two-moment inequality with nonnegative moments.

Proposition 5. *Let Y be a random vector on $\mathbb{R}^n$ with finite Rényi entropy of order $0 < r < 1$, and let X be an independent random variable that satisfies $0 < X \leq t$. Then,*

$$h_r(XY) \leq h_r(tY) + \Delta_r(Y; p, q),$$

for all $0 < p < 1/r - 1 < q$.

Proof. Let $Z = XY$ and let S_Z and S_Y denote the support sets of Z and Y, respectively. The assumption that X is nonnegative means that $\mathrm{cone}(S_Z) = \mathrm{cone}(S_Y)$. We have

$$h_r(Z) \stackrel{(a)}{\leq} \log \omega(S_Z) + \log \psi_r(p, q) + L_r(\|Z\|^n; p, q)$$
$$\stackrel{(b)}{=} h_r(Y) + L_r(|X|^n; p, q) + \Delta_r(Y; p, q)$$
$$\stackrel{(c)}{\leq} h_r(Y) + n \log t + \Delta_r(Y; p, q),$$

where (a) follows from Proposition 4, (b) follows from Equation (18) and the definition of $\Delta_r(Y; p, q)$, and (c) follows from Inequality (16) and the assumption $|X| \leq t$. Finally, recalling that $h_r(tY) = h_r(Y) + n \log t$ completes the proof. □

3.2. Example with Log-Normal Distribution

If $W \sim \mathcal{N}(\mu, \sigma^2)$, then the random variable $X = \exp(W)$ has a log-normal distribution with parameters (μ, σ^2). The Rényi entropy is given by

$$h_r(X) = \mu + \frac{1}{2}\left(\frac{1-r}{r}\right)\sigma^2 + \frac{1}{2}\log(2\pi r^{\frac{1}{r-1}}\sigma^2),$$

and the logarithm of the sth moment is given by

$$\log \mathbb{E}\left[|X|^s\right] = \mu s + \frac{1}{2}\sigma^2 s^2.$$

With a bit of work, it can be shown that the gap of the optimal two-moment inequality does not depend on the parameters (μ, σ^2) and is given by

$$\Delta_r(X) = \log\left(\widetilde{B}\left(\frac{r}{2(1-r)}, \frac{r}{2(1-r)}\right)\sqrt{\frac{r}{4(1-r)}}\right) + \frac{1}{2} - \frac{1}{2}\log(2\pi r^{\frac{1}{r-1}}). \tag{19}$$

The details of this derivation are given in Appendix B.1. Meanwhile, the gap of the optimal one-moment inequality is given by

$$\widetilde{\Delta}_r(X) = \inf_q \left[\log\left(\widetilde{B}\left(\frac{r}{1-r} - \frac{1}{q}, \frac{1}{q}\right)\frac{1}{q}\right) + \frac{1}{2}q\sigma^2\right] - \frac{1}{2}\left(\frac{1-r}{r}\right)\sigma^2 - \frac{1}{2}\log(2\pi r^{\frac{1}{r-1}}\sigma^2). \tag{20}$$

The functions $\Delta_r(X)$ and $\widetilde{\Delta}_r(X)$ are illustrated in Figure 1 as a function of r for various σ^2. The function $\Delta_r(X)$ is bounded uniformly with respect to r and converges to zero as r increases to one. The tightness of the two-moment inequality in this regime follows from the fact that the log-normal distribution maximizes Shannon entropy subject to a constraint on $\mathbb{E}[\log X]$. By contrast, the function $\widetilde{\Delta}_r(X)$ varies with the parameter σ^2. For any fixed $r \in (0,1)$, it can be shown that $\widetilde{\Delta}_r(X)$ increases to infinity if σ^2 converges to zero or infinity.

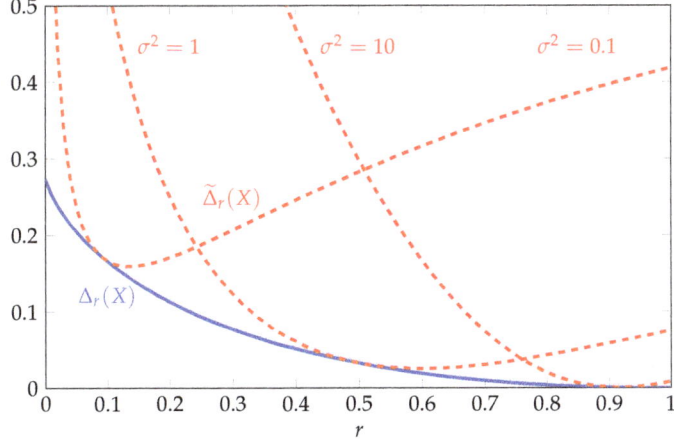

Figure 1. Comparison of upper bounds on Rényi entropy in nats for the log-normal distribution as a function of the order r for various σ^2.

3.3. Example with Multivariate Gaussian Distribution

Next, we consider the case where $Y \sim \mathcal{N}(0, I_n)$ is an n-dimensional Gaussian vector with mean zero and identity covariance. The Rényi entropy is given by

$$h_r(Y) = \frac{n}{2} \log(2\pi r^{\frac{1}{r-1}}),$$

and the sth moment of the magnitude $\|Y\|$ is given by

$$\mathbb{E}\left[\|Y\|^s\right] = \frac{2^{\frac{s}{2}} \Gamma(\frac{n+s}{2})}{\Gamma(\frac{n}{2})}.$$

The next result shows that as the dimension n increases, the gap of the optimal two-moment inequality converges to the gap for the log-normal distribution. Moreover, for each $r \in (0,1)$, the following choice of moments is optimal in the large-n limit:

$$p_n = \frac{1-r}{r} - \frac{1}{r}\sqrt{\frac{2(1-r)}{n+1}}, \qquad q_n = \frac{1-r}{r} + \frac{1}{r}\sqrt{\frac{2(1-r)}{n+1}}. \tag{21}$$

The proof is given in Appendix B.3.

Proposition 6. *If $Y \sim \mathcal{N}(0, I_n)$, then, for each $r \in (0,1)$,*

$$\lim_{n \to \infty} \Delta_r(Y) = \lim_{n \to \infty} \Delta_r(Y; p_n, q_n) = \Delta_r(X),$$

where X has a log-normal distribution and (p_n, q_n) are given by (21).

Figure 2 provides a comparison of $\Delta_r(Y)$, $\Delta_r(Y; p_n, q_n)$, and $\tilde{\Delta}_r(Y)$ as a function of n for $r = 0.1$. Here, we see that both $\Delta_r(Y)$ and $\Delta_r(Y; p_n, q_n)$ converge rapidly to the asymptotic limit given by the gap of the log-normal distribution. By contrast, the gap of the optimal one-moment inequality $\tilde{\Delta}_r(Y)$ increases without bound.

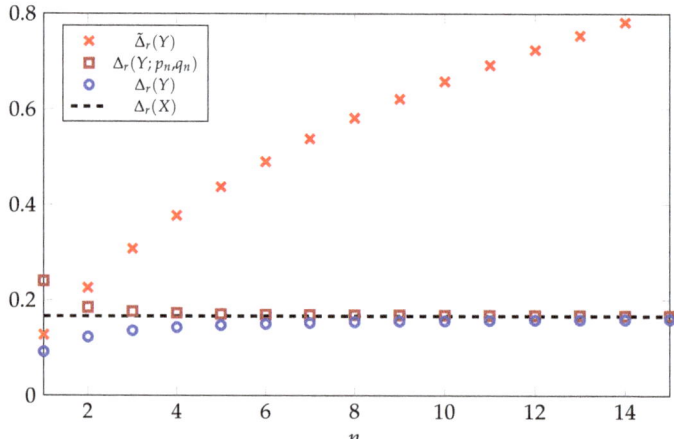

Figure 2. Comparison of upper bounds on Rényi entropy in nats for the multivariate Gaussian distribution $\mathcal{N}(0, I_n)$ as a function of the dimension n with $r = 0.1$. The solid black line is the gap of the optimal two-moment inequality for the log-normal distribution.

3.4. Inequalities for Differential Entropy

Proposition 4 can also be used to recover some known inequalities for differential entropy by considering the limiting behavior as r converges to one. For example, it is well known that the differential entropy of an n-dimensional random vector X with finite second moment satisfies

$$h(X) \leq \frac{1}{2} \log \left(2\pi e \, \mathbb{E}\left[\tfrac{1}{n}\|X\|^2\right] \right), \tag{22}$$

with equality if and only if the entries of X are i.i.d. zero-mean Gaussian. A generalization of this result in terms of an arbitrary positive moment is given by

$$h(X) \leq \log \frac{\Gamma\left(\frac{n}{s}+1\right)}{\Gamma\left(\frac{n}{2}+1\right)} + \frac{n}{2} \log \pi + \frac{n}{s} \log \left(es \, \mathbb{E}\left[\tfrac{1}{n}\|X\|^s\right] \right), \tag{23}$$

for all $s > 0$. Note that Inequality (22) corresponds to the case $s = 2$.

Inequality (23) can be proved as an immediate consequence of Proposition 4 and the fact that $h_r(X)$ is nonincreasing in r. Using properties of the beta function given in Appendix A, it is straightforward to verify that

$$\lim_{r \to 1} \psi_r(0, q) = (eq)^{\frac{1}{q}} \Gamma\left(\frac{1}{q}+1\right), \quad \text{for all } q > 0.$$

Combining this result with Proposition 4 and Inequality (16) leads to

$$h(X) \leq \log \omega(S) + \log \Gamma\left(\frac{1}{q}+1\right) + \frac{1}{q} \log \left(eq \mathbb{E}\left[\|X\|^{nq}\right] \right).$$

Using Inequality (10) and making the substitution $s = nq$ leads to Inequality (23).

Another example follows from the fact that the log-normal distribution maximizes the differential entropy of a positive random variable X subject to constraints on the mean and variance of $\log(X)$, and hence

$$h(X) \leq \mathbb{E}[\log(X)] + \frac{1}{2} \log \left(2\pi e \, \text{Var}(\log(X)) \right), \tag{24}$$

with equality if and only if X is log-normal. In Appendix B.4, it is shown how this inequality can be proved using our two-moment inequalities by studying the behavior as both p and q converge to zero as r increases to one.

4. Bounds on Mutual Information

4.1. Relative Entropy and Chi-Squared Divergence

Let P and Q be distributions defined on a common probability space that have densities p and q with respect to a dominating measure μ. The relative entropy (or Kullback–Leibler divergence) is defined according to

$$D(P \| Q) = \int p \log \left(\frac{p}{q}\right) d\mu,$$

and the chi-squared divergence is defined as

$$\chi^2(P \| Q) = \int \frac{(p-q)^2}{q} d\mu.$$

Both of these divergences can be seen as special cases of the general class of f-divergence measures and there exists a rich literature on comparisons between different divergences [8,26–32]. The chi-squared divergence can also be viewed as the squared L_2 distance between $p/\sqrt{q}$ and $\sqrt{q}$. The chi-square can also be interpreted as the first non-zero term in the power series expansion of the relative entropy ([26], [Lemma 4]). More generally, the chi-squared divergence provides an upper bound on the relative entropy via

$$D(P \| Q) \leq \log(1 + \chi^2(P\|Q)). \tag{25}$$

The proof of this inequality follows straightforwardly from Jensen's inequality and the concavity of the logarithm; see [27,31,32] for further refinements.

Given a random pair (X, Y), the mutual information between X and Y is defined according to

$$I(X; Y) = D(P_{X,Y} \| P_X P_Y).$$

From Inequality (25), we see that the mutual information can always be upper bounded using

$$I(X; Y) \leq \log(1 + \chi^2(P_{X,Y}\|P_X P_Y)). \tag{26}$$

The next section provides bounds on the mutual information that can improve upon this inequality.

4.2. Mutual Information and Variance of Conditional Density

Let (X, Y) be a random pair such that the conditional distribution of Y given X has a density $f_{Y|X}(y|x)$ with respect to the Lebesgue measure on $\mathbb{R}^n$. Note that the marginal density of Y is given by $f_Y(y) = \mathbb{E}\left[f_{Y|X}(y|X)\right]$. To simplify notation, we will write $f(y|x)$ and $f(y)$ where the subscripts are implicit. The support set of Y is denoted by S_Y.

The measure of the dependence between X and Y that is used in our bounds can be understood in terms of the variance of the conditional density. For each y, the conditional density $f(y|X)$ evaluated with a random realization of X is a random variable. The variance of this random variable is given by

$$\mathrm{Var}(f(y|X)) = \mathbb{E}\left[(f(y|X) - f(y))^2\right], \tag{27}$$

where we have used the fact that the marginal density $f(y)$ is the expectation of $f(y|X)$. The sth moment of the variance of the conditional density is defined according to

$$V_s(Y|X) = \int_{S_Y} \|y\|^s \, \mathrm{Var}(f(y|X)) \, dy. \tag{28}$$

The variance moment $V_s(Y|X)$ is nonnegative and equal to zero if and only if X and Y are independent.

The function $\kappa(t)$ is defined according to

$$\kappa(t) = \sup_{u \in (0,\infty)} \frac{\log(1+u)}{u^t}, \qquad t \in (0,1]. \tag{29}$$

The proof of the following result is given in Appendix C. The behavior of $\kappa(t)$ is illustrated in Figure 3.

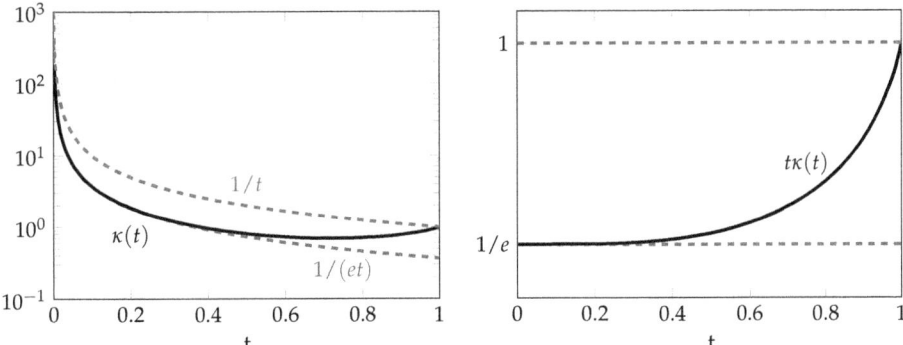

Figure 3. Graphs of $\kappa(t)$ and $t\kappa(t)$ as a function of t.

Proposition 7. *The function $\kappa(t)$ defined in Equation (29) can be expressed as*

$$\kappa(t) = \frac{\log(1+u)}{u^t}, \quad t \in (0,1]$$

where

$$u = \exp\left(W\left(-\tfrac{1}{t}\exp\left(-\tfrac{1}{t}\right)\right) + \tfrac{1}{t}\right) - 1,$$

and $W(\cdot)$ denotes Lambert's W-function, i.e., $W(z)$ is the unique solution to the equation $z = w\exp(w)$ on the interval $[-1, \infty)$. Furthermore, the function $g(t) = t\kappa(t)$ is strictly increasing on $(0,1]$ with $\lim_{t \to 0} g(t) = 1/e$ and $g(1) = 1$, and thus

$$\frac{1}{et} \leq \kappa(t) \leq \frac{1}{t}, \quad t \in (0,1],$$

where the lower bound $1/(et)$ is tight for small values of $t \in (0,1)$ and the upper bound $1/t$ is tight for values of t close to 1.

We are now ready to give the main results of this section, which are bounds on the mutual information. We begin with a general upper bound in terms of the variance of the conditional density.

Proposition 8. *For any $0 < t \leq 1$, the mutual information satisfies*

$$I(X;Y) \leq \kappa(t) \int_{S_Y} [f(y)]^{1-2t} \left[\mathsf{Var}(f(y \mid X))\right]^t \, dy.$$

Proof. We use the following series of inequalities:

$$I(X;Y) \stackrel{(a)}{=} \int f(y) D\left(P_{X|Y=y} \,\middle\|\, P_X\right) dy$$

$$\stackrel{(b)}{\leq} \int f(y) \log\left(1 + \chi^2(P_{X|Y=y} \| P_X)\right) dy$$

$$\stackrel{(c)}{=} \int f(y) \log\left(1 + \frac{\mathsf{Var}(f(y \mid X))}{f^2(y)}\right) dy$$

$$\stackrel{(d)}{\leq} \kappa(t) \int f(y) \left(\frac{\mathsf{Var}(f(y \mid X))}{f^2(y)}\right)^t dy,$$

where (a) follows from the definition of mutual information, (b) follows from Inequality (25), and (c) follows from Bayes' rule, which allows us to write the chi-square in terms of the variance of the conditional density:

$$\chi^2(P_{X|Y=y}\|P_X) = \mathbb{E}\left[\left(\frac{f(y|X)}{f(y)}-1\right)^2\right] = \frac{\mathsf{Var}(f(y|X))}{f^2(y)}.$$

Inequality (d) follows from the nonnegativity of the variance and the definition of $\kappa(t)$. □

Evaluating Proposition 8 with $t = 1$ recovers the well-known inequality $I(X;Y) \leq \chi^2(P_{X,Y}\|P_X P_Y)$. The next two results follow from the cases $0 < t < \frac{1}{2}$ and $t = \frac{1}{2}$, respectively.

Proposition 9. *For any $0 < r < 1$, the mutual information satisfies*

$$I(X;Y) \leq \kappa(t)\left(e^{h_r(Y)} V_0(Y|X)\right)^t,$$

where $t = (1-r)/(2-r)$.

Proof. Starting with Proposition 8 and applying Hölder's inequality with conjugate exponents $1/(1-t)$ and $1/t$ leads to

$$I(X;Y) \leq \kappa(t)\left(\int f^r(y)\,dy\right)^{1-t}\left(\int \mathsf{Var}(f(y\mid X))\,dy\right)^t = \kappa(t)\,e^{t\,h_r(Y)}V_0^t(Y|X),$$

where we have used the fact that $r = (1-2t)/(1-t)$. □

Proposition 10. *For any $p < 1 < q$, the mutual information satisfies*

$$I(X;Y) \leq C(\lambda)\sqrt{\frac{\omega(S_Y)V_{np}^{\lambda}(Y|X)V_{nq}^{1-\lambda}(Y|X)}{(q-p)}},$$

where $\lambda = (q-1)/(q-p)$ and

$$C(\lambda) = \kappa(\tfrac{1}{2})\sqrt{\frac{\pi\lambda^{-\lambda}(1-\lambda)^{-(1-\lambda)}}{\sin(\pi\lambda)}},$$

with $\kappa(\tfrac{1}{2}) = 0.80477\ldots$.

Proof. Evaluating Proposition 8 with $t = 1/2$ gives

$$I(X;Y) \leq \kappa(\tfrac{1}{2})\int_{S_Y}\sqrt{\mathsf{Var}(f(y\mid X))}\,dy.$$

Evaluating Proposition 3 with $r = \tfrac{1}{2}$ leads to

$$\left(\int_{S_Y}\sqrt{\mathsf{Var}(f(y\mid X))}\,dy\right)^2 \leq \omega(S_Y)\,\psi_{1/2}(p,q)V_{np}^{\lambda}(Y|X)V_{nq}^{1-\lambda}(Y|X).$$

Combining these inequalities with the expression for $\psi_{1/2}(p,q)$ given in Equation (8) completes the proof. □

The contribution of Propositions 9 and 10 is that they provide bounds on the mutual information in terms of quantities that can be easy to characterize. One application of these bounds is to establish conditions under which the mutual information corresponding to a sequence of random pairs (X_k, Y_k) converges to zero. In this case, Proposition 9 provides a sufficient condition in terms of the Rényi entropy of Y_n and the function $V_0(Y_n|X_n)$, while Proposition 10 provides a sufficient condition in terms of $V_s(Y_n|X_n)$ evaluated with two difference values of s. These conditions are summarized in the following result.

Proposition 11. *Let (X_k, Y_k) be a sequence of random pairs such that the conditional distribution of Y_k given X_k has a density on $\mathbb{R}^n$. The following are sufficient conditions under which the mutual information of $I(X_k; Y_k)$ converges to zero as k increases to infinity:*

1. *There exists $0 < r < 1$ such that*

$$\lim_{k \to \infty} e^{h_r(Y_k)} V_0(Y_k|X_k) = 0.$$

2. *There exists $p < 1 < q$ such that*

$$\lim_{k \to \infty} V_{np}^{q-1}(Y_k|X_k) V_{nq}^{1-p}(Y_k|X_k) = 0.$$

4.3. Properties of the Bounds

The variance moment $V_s(Y|X)$ has a number of interesting properties. The variance of the conditional density can be expressed in terms of an expectation with respect to two independent random variables X_1 and X_2 with the same distribution as X via the decomposition:

$$\mathrm{Var}(f(y|X)) = \mathbb{E}\left[f(y|X)f(y|X) - f(y|X_1)f(y|X_2)\right].$$

Consequently, by swapping the order of the integration and expectation, we obtain

$$V_s(Y|X) = \mathbb{E}\left[K_s(X, X) - K_s(X_1, X_2)\right], \tag{30}$$

where

$$K_s(x_1, x_2) = \int \|y\|^s f(y|x_1) f(y|x_2)\, dy.$$

The function $K_s(x_1, x_2)$ is a positive definite kernel that does not depend on the distribution of X. For $s = 0$, this kernel has been studied previously in the machine learning literature [33], where it is referred to as the expected likelihood kernel.

The variance of the conditional density also satisfies a data processing inequality. Suppose that $U \to X \to Y$ forms a Markov chain. Then, the square of the conditional density of Y given U can be expressed as

$$f_{Y|U}^2(y|u) = \mathbb{E}\left[f_{Y|X}(y|X_1') f_{Y|X}(y|X_2') \mid U = u\right],$$

where $(U, X_1', X_2') \sim P_U P_{X_1|U} P_{X_2|U}$. Combining this expression with Equation (30) yields

$$V_s(Y|U) = \mathbb{E}\left[K_s(X_1', X_2') - K_s(X_1, X_2)\right], \tag{31}$$

where we recall that (X_1, X_2) are independent copies of X.

Finally, it is easy to verify that the function $V_s(Y)$ satisfies

$$V_s(aY|X) = |a|^{s-n} V_s(Y|X), \quad \text{for all } a \neq 0.$$

Using this scaling relationship, we see that the sufficient conditions in Proposition 11 are invariant to scaling of Y.

4.4. Example with Additive Gaussian Noise

We now provide a specific example of our bounds on the mutual information. Let $X \in \mathbb{R}^n$ be a random vector with distribution P_X and let Y be the output of a Gaussian noise channel

$$Y = X + W, \tag{32}$$

where $W \sim \mathcal{N}(0, I_n)$ is independent of X. If $\|X\|$ has finite second moment, then the mutual information satisfies

$$I(X;Y) \leq \frac{n}{2} \log\left(1 + \frac{1}{n}\mathbb{E}\left[\|X\|^2\right]\right), \tag{33}$$

where equality is attained if and only if X has zero-mean isotropic Gaussian distribution. This inequality follows straightforwardly from the fact that the Gaussian distribution maximizes differential entropy subject to a second moment constraint [11]. One of the limitations of this bound is that it can be loose when the second moment is dominated by events that have small probability. In fact, it is easy to construct examples for which $\|X\|$ does not have a finite second moment, and yet $I(X;Y)$ is arbitrarily close to zero.

Our results provide bounds on $I(X;Y)$ that are less sensitive to the effects of rare events. Let $\phi_n(x) = (2\pi)^{-n/2} \exp(-\|x\|^2/2)$ denote the density of the standard Gaussian distribution on $\mathbb{R}^n$. The product of the conditional densities can be factored according to

$$f(y \mid x_1)f(y \mid x_2) = \phi_{2n}\left(\begin{bmatrix} y - x_1 \\ y - x_2 \end{bmatrix}\right) = \phi_{2n}\left(\begin{bmatrix} \sqrt{2}y - (x_1 + x_2)/\sqrt{2} \\ (x_1 - x_2)/\sqrt{2} \end{bmatrix}\right)$$

$$= \phi_n\left(\sqrt{2}y - \frac{x_1 + x_2}{\sqrt{2}}\right) \phi_n\left(\frac{x_1 - x_2}{\sqrt{2}}\right),$$

where the second step follows because $\phi_{2n}(\cdot)$ is invariant to orthogonal transformations. Integrating with respect to y leads to

$$K_s(x_1, x_2) = 2^{-\frac{n+s}{2}} \mathbb{E}\left[\left\|W + \frac{x_1 + x_2}{\sqrt{2}}\right\|^s\right] \phi_n\left(\frac{x_1 - x_2}{\sqrt{2}}\right),$$

where we recall that $W \sim \mathcal{N}(0, I_n)$. For the case $s = 0$, we see that $K_0(x_1, x_2)$ is a Gaussian kernel, thus

$$V_0(Y|X) = (4\pi)^{-\frac{n}{2}} \left[1 - \mathbb{E}\left[e^{-\frac{1}{4}\|X_1 - X_2\|^2}\right]\right]. \tag{34}$$

A useful property of $V_0(Y|X)$ is that the conditions under which it converges to zero are weaker than the conditions needed for other measures of dependence. Observe that the expectation in Equation (34) is bounded uniformly with respect to (X_1, X_2). In particular, for every $\epsilon > 0$ and $x \in \mathbb{R}$, we have

$$1 - \mathbb{E}\left[e^{-\frac{1}{4}(X_1 - X_2)^2}\right] \leq \epsilon^2 + 2\mathbb{P}\left[|X - x| \geq \epsilon\right],$$

where we have used the inequality $1 - e^{-x} \leq x$ and the fact that $\mathbb{P}\left[|X_1 - X_2| \geq 2\epsilon\right] \leq 2\mathbb{P}\left[|X - x| \geq \epsilon\right]$. Consequently, $V_0(Y|X)$ converges to zero whenever X converges to a constant value x in probability.

To study some further properties of these bounds, we now focus on the case where X is a Gaussian scalar mixture generated according to

$$X = A\sqrt{U}, \quad A \sim \mathcal{N}(0, 1), \quad U \geq 0, \tag{35}$$

with A and U independent. In this case, the expectations with respect to the kernel $K_s(x_1, x_2)$ can be computed explicitly, leading to

$$V_s(Y|X) = \frac{\Gamma(\frac{1+s}{2})}{2\pi} \mathbb{E}\left[(1+2U)^{\frac{s}{2}} - \frac{(1+U_1)^{\frac{s}{2}}(1+U_2)^{\frac{s}{2}}}{(1+\frac{1}{2}(U_1+U_2))^{\frac{s+1}{2}}}\right], \qquad (36)$$

where (U_1, U_2) are independent copies of U. It can be shown that this expression depends primarily on the magnitude of U. This is not surprising given that X converges to a constant if and only if U converges to zero.

Our results can also be used to bound the mutual information $I(U;Y)$ by noting that $U \to X \to Y$ forms a Markov chain, and taking advantage of the characterization provided in Equation (31). Letting $X_1' = A_1\sqrt{U}$ and $X_2' = A_2\sqrt{U}$ with (A_1, A_2, U) be mutually independent leads to

$$V_s(Y|U) = \frac{\Gamma(\frac{1+s}{2})}{2\pi} \mathbb{E}\left[(1+U)^{\frac{s-1}{2}} - \frac{(1+U_1)^{\frac{s}{2}}(1+U_2)^{\frac{s}{2}}}{(1+\frac{1}{2}(U_1+U_2))^{\frac{s+1}{2}}}\right], \qquad (37)$$

In this case, $V_s(Y|U)$ is a measure of the variation in U. To study its behavior, we consider the simple upper bound

$$V_s(Y|U) \leq \frac{\Gamma(\frac{1+s}{2})}{2\pi} \mathbb{P}[U_1 \neq U_2] \mathbb{E}\left[(1+U)^{\frac{s-1}{2}}\right], \qquad (38)$$

which follows from noting that the term inside the expectation in Equation (37) is zero on the event $U_1 = U_2$. This bound shows that if $s \leq 1$ then $V_s(Y|U)$ is bounded uniformly with respect to distributions on U, and if $s > 1$, then $V_s(Y|U)$ is bounded in terms of the $(\frac{s-1}{2})$th moment of U.

In conjunction with Propositions 9 and 10, the function $V_s(Y|U)$ provides bounds on the mutual information $I(U;Y)$ that can be expressed in terms of simple expectations involving two independent copies of U. Figure 4 provides an illustration of the upper bound in Proposition 10 for the case where U is a discrete random variable supported on two points, and X and Y are generated according to Equations (32) and (35). This example shows that there exist sequences of distributions for which our upper bounds on the mutual information converge to zero while the chi-squared divergence between P_{XY} and $P_X P_Y$ is bounded away from zero.

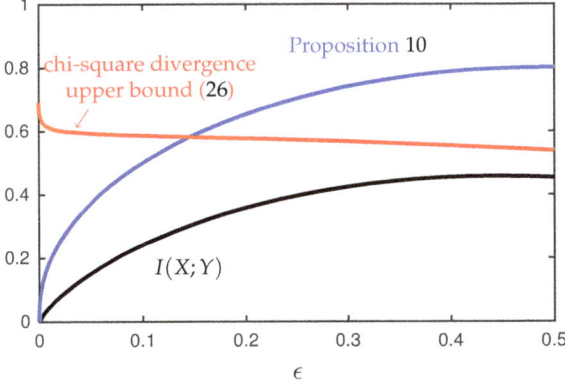

Figure 4. Bounds on the mutual information $I(U;Y)$ in nats when $U \sim (1-\epsilon)\delta_1 + \epsilon\delta_{a(\epsilon)}$, with $a(\epsilon) = 1 + 1/\sqrt{\epsilon}$, and X and Y are generated according to Equations (32) and (35). The bound from Proposition 10 is evaluated with $p = 0$ and $q = 2$.

5. Conclusions

This paper provides bounds on Rényi entropy and mutual information that are based on a relatively simple two-moment inequality. Extensions to inequalities with more moments are worth exploring. Another potential application is to provide a refined characterization of the "all-or-nothing" behavior seen in a sparse linear regression problem [34,35], where the current methods of analysis depend on a complicated conditional second moment method.

Funding: This research was supported in part by the National Science Foundation under Grant 1750362 and in part by the Laboratory for Analytic Sciences (LAS). Any opinions, findings, conclusions, and recommendations expressed in this material are those of the author and do not necessarily reflect the views of the sponsors.

Conflicts of Interest: The author declares no conflict of interest. The funders had no role in the design of the study; in the collection, analyses, or interpretation of data; in the writing of the manuscript, or in the decision to publish the results.

Appendix A. The Gamma and Beta Functions

This section reviews some properties of the gamma and beta functions. For $x > 0$, the gamma function is defined according to $\Gamma(x) = \int_0^\infty t^{x-1} e^{-t} \, dt$. Binet's formula for the logarithm for the gamma function ([25], [Theorem 1.6.3]) gives

$$\log \Gamma(x) = \left(x - \frac{1}{2}\right) \log x - x + \frac{1}{2} \log(2\pi) + \theta(x), \tag{A1}$$

where the remainder term $\theta(x)$ is convex and nonincreasing with $\lim_{x \to 0} \theta(x) = \infty$ and $\lim_{x \to \infty} \theta(x) = 0$. Euler's reflection formula ([25], [Theorem 1.2.1]) gives

$$\Gamma(x)\Gamma(1-x) = \frac{\pi}{\sin(\pi x)}, \quad 0 < x < 1. \tag{A2}$$

For $x, y > 0$, the beta function can be expressed as follows

$$B(x,y) = \frac{\Gamma(x)\Gamma(y)}{\Gamma(x+y)} = \int_0^1 t^{x-1} (1-t)^{y-1} \, dt = \int_0^\infty \frac{u^{a-1}}{(1+u)^{a+b}} \, du, \tag{A3}$$

where the second integral expression follows from the change of variables $t \mapsto u/(1+u)$. Recall that $\widetilde{B}(x,y) = B(x,y)(x+y)^{x+y} x^{-x} y^{-y}$. Using Equation (A1) leads to

$$\log\left(\widetilde{B}(x,y) \sqrt{\frac{xy}{2\pi(x+y)}}\right) = \theta(x) + \theta(y) - \theta(x+y). \tag{A4}$$

It can also be shown that ([36], [Equation (2), pg. 2])

$$\widetilde{B}(x,y) \geq \frac{x+y}{xy}. \tag{A5}$$

Appendix B. Details for Rényi Entropy Examples

This appendix studies properties of the two-moment inequalities for Rényi entropy described in Section 3.

Appendix B.1. Log-Normal Distribution

Let X be a log-normal random variable with parameters (μ, σ^2) and consider the parametrization

$$p = \frac{1-r}{r} - (1-\lambda)\sqrt{\frac{(1-r)u}{r\lambda(1-\lambda)}}$$

$$q = \frac{1-r}{r} + \lambda\sqrt{\frac{(1-r)u}{r\lambda(1-\lambda)}}.$$

where $\lambda \in (0,1)$ and $u \in (0, \infty)$. Then, we have

$$\psi_r(p,q) = \widetilde{B}\left(\frac{r\lambda}{1-r}, \frac{r(1-\lambda)}{1-r}\right)\sqrt{\frac{r\lambda(1-\lambda)}{(1-r)u}}$$

$$L_r(X; p, q) = \mu + \frac{1}{2}\left(\frac{1-r}{r}\right)\sigma^2 + \frac{1}{2}u\sigma^2.$$

Combining these expressions with Equation (A4) leads to

$$\Delta_r(X; p, q) = \theta\left(\frac{r\lambda}{1-r}\right) + \theta\left(\frac{r(1-\lambda)}{1-r}\right) - \theta\left(\frac{r}{1-r}\right) + \frac{1}{2}u\sigma^2 - \frac{1}{2}\log\left(u\sigma^2\right) - \frac{1}{2}\log(r^{\frac{1}{r-1}}). \quad (A6)$$

We now characterize the minimum with respect to the parameters (λ, u). Note that the mapping $\lambda \mapsto \theta(\frac{r\lambda}{1-r}) + \theta(\frac{r(1-\lambda)}{1-r})$ is convex and symmetric about the point $\lambda = 1/2$. Therefore, the minimum with respect to λ is attained at $\lambda = 1/2$. Meanwhile, mapping $u \mapsto u\sigma^2 - \log(u\sigma^2)$ is convex and attains its minimum at $u = 1/\sigma^2$. Evaluating Equation (A6) with these values, we see that the optimal two-moment inequality can be expressed as

$$\Delta_r(X) = 2\theta\left(\frac{r}{2(1-r)}\right) - \theta\left(\frac{r}{1-r}\right) + \frac{1}{2}\log\left(e\, r^{\frac{1}{1-r}}\right).$$

By Equation (A4), this expression is equivalent to Equation (A1). Moreover, the fact that $\Delta_r(X)$ decreases to zero as r increases to one follows from the fact that $\theta(x)$ decreases to zero and x increases to infinity.

Next, we express the gap in terms of the pair (p, q). Comparing the difference between $\Delta_r(X; p, q)$ and $\Delta_r(X)$ leads to

$$\Delta_r(X; p, q) = \Delta_r(X) + \frac{1}{2}\varphi\left(\frac{r\lambda(1-\lambda)}{1-r}(q-p)^2\sigma^2\right) + \theta\left(\frac{r\lambda}{1-r}\right) + \theta\left(\frac{r(1-\lambda)}{1-r}\right) - 2\theta\left(\frac{r}{2(1-r)}\right),$$

where $\varphi(x) = x - \log(x) - 1$. In particular, if $p = 0$, then we obtain the simplified expression

$$\Delta_r(X; 0, q) = \Delta_r(X) + \frac{1}{2}\varphi\left(\left(q - \frac{1-r}{r}\right)\sigma^2\right) + \theta\left(\frac{r}{1-r} - \frac{1}{q}\right) + \theta\left(\frac{1}{q}\right) - 2\theta\left(\frac{r}{2(1-r)}\right).$$

This characterization shows that the gap of the optimal one-moment inequality $\widetilde{\Delta}_r(X)$ increases to infinity in the limit as either $\sigma^2 \to 0$ or $\sigma^2 \to \infty$.

Appendix B.2. Multivariate Gaussian Distribution

Let $Y \sim \mathcal{N}(0, I_n)$ be an n-dimensional Gaussian vector and consider the parametrization

$$p = \frac{1-r}{r} - \frac{1-\lambda}{r}\sqrt{\frac{2(1-r)z}{\lambda(1-\lambda)n}}$$

$$q = \frac{1-r}{r} + \frac{\lambda}{r}\sqrt{\frac{2(1-r)z}{\lambda(1-\lambda)n}}.$$

where $\lambda \in (0,1)$ and $z \in (0,\infty)$. We can write

$$\log \omega(S_Y) = \frac{n}{2}\log \pi - \log\left(\frac{n}{2}\right) - \log \Gamma\left(\frac{n}{2}\right)$$

$$\psi_r(p,q) = \widetilde{B}\left(\frac{r\lambda}{1-r}, \frac{r(1-\lambda)}{1-r}\right)\sqrt{\frac{r\lambda(1-\lambda)}{(1-r)}}\sqrt{\frac{nr}{2z}}.$$

Furthermore, if

$$(1-\lambda)\sqrt{\frac{2(1-r)z}{\lambda(1-\lambda)n}} < 1, \qquad (A7)$$

then $L_r(\|Y\|^n; p, q)$ is finite and is given by

$$L_r(\|Y\|^n; p, q) = Q_{r,n}(\lambda, z) + \frac{n}{2}\log 2 + \frac{r}{1-r}\left[\log \Gamma\left(\frac{n}{2r}\right) - \log \Gamma\left(\frac{n}{2}\right)\right],$$

where

$$Q_{r,n}(\lambda, z) = \frac{r\lambda}{1-r}\log \Gamma\left(\frac{n}{2r} - \frac{1-\lambda}{r}\sqrt{\frac{(1-r)nz}{2\lambda(1-\lambda)}}\right) + \frac{r(1-\lambda)}{1-r}\log \Gamma\left(\frac{n}{2r} + \frac{\lambda}{r}\sqrt{\frac{(1-r)nz}{2\lambda(1-\lambda)}}\right)$$
$$- \frac{r}{1-r}\log \Gamma\left(\frac{n}{2r}\right). \qquad (A8)$$

Here, we note that the scaling in Equation (21) corresponds to $\lambda = 1/2$ and $z = n/(n+1)$, and thus the condition Inequality (A7) is satisfied for all $n \geq 1$. Combining the above expressions and then using Equations (A1) and (A4) leads to

$$\Delta_r(Y; p, q) = \theta\left(\frac{r\lambda}{1-r}\right) + \theta\left(\frac{r(1-\lambda)}{1-r}\right) - \theta\left(\frac{r}{1-r}\right) + Q_{r,n}(z, \lambda) - \frac{1}{2}\log z - \frac{1}{2}\log\left(r^{\frac{1}{r-1}}\right)$$
$$+ \frac{r}{1-r}\theta\left(\frac{n}{2r}\right) - \frac{1}{1-r}\theta\left(\frac{n}{2}\right). \qquad (A9)$$

Next, we study some properties of $Q_{r,n}(\lambda, z)$. By Equation (A1), the logarithm of the gamma function can be expressed as the sum of convex functions:

$$\log \Gamma(x) = \varphi(x) + \frac{1}{2}\log\left(\frac{1}{x}\right) + \frac{1}{2}\log(2\pi) - 1 + \theta(x),$$

where $\varphi(x) = x \log x + 1 - x$. Starting with the definition of $Q(\lambda, z)$ and then using Jensen's inequality yields

$$Q_{r,n}(z, \lambda) \geq \frac{r\lambda}{1-r} \varphi\left(\frac{n}{2r} - \frac{1-\lambda}{r}\sqrt{\frac{(1-r)nz}{2\lambda(1-\lambda)}}\right)$$

$$+ \frac{r(1-\lambda)}{1-r} \varphi\left(\frac{n}{2r} + \frac{\lambda}{r}\sqrt{\frac{(1-r)nz}{2\lambda(1-\lambda)}}\right) - \frac{r}{1-r} \varphi\left(\frac{n}{2r}\right)$$

$$= \frac{\lambda}{a} \varphi\left(1 - \sqrt{\left(\frac{1-\lambda}{\lambda}\right) az}\right) + \frac{(1-\lambda)}{a} \varphi\left(1 + \sqrt{\left(\frac{\lambda}{1-\lambda}\right) az}\right),$$

where $a = 2(1-r)/n$. Using the inequality $\varphi(x) \geq (3/2)(x-1)^2/(x+2)$ leads to

$$Q_{r,n}(\lambda, z) \geq \frac{z}{2}\left[\left(1 - \sqrt{\left(\frac{1-\lambda}{\lambda}\right) bz}\right)\left(1 + \sqrt{\left(\frac{\lambda}{1-\lambda}\right) bz}\right)\right]^{-1}$$

$$\geq \frac{z}{2}\left(1 + \sqrt{\left(\frac{\lambda}{1-\lambda}\right) bz}\right)^{-1}, \qquad (A10)$$

where $b = 2(1-r)/(9n)$.

Observe that the right-hand side of Inequality (A10) converges to $z/2$ as n increases to infinity. It turns out this limiting behavior is tight. Using Equation (A1), it is straightforward to show that $Q_n(\lambda, z)$ converges pointwise to $z/2$ as n increases to infinity—that is,

$$\lim_{n \to \infty} Q_{r,n}(\lambda, z) = \frac{1}{2}z, \qquad (A11)$$

for any fixed pair $(\lambda, z) \in (0, 1) \times (0, \infty)$.

Appendix B.3. Proof of Proposition 6

Let $D = (0, 1) \times (0, \infty)$. For fixed $r \in (0, 1)$, we use $Q_n(\lambda, z)$ to denote the function $Q_{r,n}(\lambda, z)$ defined in Equation (A8) and we use $G_n(\lambda, z)$ to denote the right-hand side of Equation (A9). These functions are defined to be equal to positive infinity for any pair $(\lambda, z) \in D$ such that Inequality (A7) does not hold.

Note that the terms $\theta(n/(2r))$ and $\theta(n/2)$ converge to zero in the limit as n increases to infinity. In conjunction with Equation (A11), this shows that $G_n(\lambda, z)$ converges pointwise to a limit $G(\lambda, z)$ given by

$$G(\lambda, z) = \theta\left(\frac{r\lambda}{1-r}\right) + \theta\left(\frac{r(1-\lambda)}{1-r}\right) - \theta\left(\frac{r}{1-r}\right) + \frac{1}{2}z - \frac{1}{2}\log(z) - \frac{1}{2}\log(r^{\frac{1}{r-1}}).$$

At this point, the correspondence with the log-normal distribution can be seen from the fact that $G(\lambda, z)$ is equal to the right-hand side of Equation (A6) evaluated with $u\sigma^2 = z$.

To show that the gap corresponding to the log-normal distribution provides an upper bound on the limit, we use

$$\limsup_{n \to \infty} \Delta_r(Y) = \limsup_{n \to \infty} \inf_{(\lambda, z) \in D} G_n(\lambda, z)$$

$$\leq \inf_{(\lambda, z) \in D} \limsup_{n \to \infty} G_n(\lambda, z)$$

$$= \inf_{(\lambda, z) \in D} G(\lambda, z)$$

$$= \Delta_r(X). \qquad (A12)$$

Here, the last equality follows from the analysis in Appendix B.1, which shows that the minimum of $G(\lambda, z)$ is a attained at $\lambda = 1/2$ and $z = 1$.

To prove the lower bound requires a bit more work. Fix any $\epsilon \in (0, 1)$ and let $D_\epsilon = (0, 1 - \epsilon] \times (0, \infty)$. Using the lower bound on $Q_n(\lambda, z)$ given in Inequality (A10), it can be verified that

$$\liminf_{n \to \infty} \inf_{(\lambda, z) \in D_\epsilon} \left[Q_{r,n}(z, \lambda) - \frac{1}{2} \log z \right] \geq \frac{1}{2}.$$

Consequently, we have

$$\liminf_{n \to \infty} \inf_{(\lambda, z) \in D_\epsilon} G_n(\lambda, z) = \inf_{(\lambda, z) \in D_\epsilon} G(\lambda, z) \geq \Delta_r(X). \tag{A13}$$

To complete the proof we will show that for any sequence λ_n that converges to one as n increases to infinity, we have

$$\liminf_{n \to \infty} \inf_{z \in (0, \infty)} G_n(\lambda_n, z) = \infty. \tag{A14}$$

To see why this is the case, note that by Equation (A4) and Inequality (A5),

$$\theta\left(\frac{r\lambda}{1-r}\right) + \theta\left(\frac{r(1-\lambda)}{1-r}\right) - \theta\left(\frac{r}{1-r}\right) \geq \frac{1}{2} \log \left(\frac{1-r}{2\pi r \lambda (1-\lambda)} \right).$$

Therefore, we can write

$$G_n(\lambda, z) \geq Q_n(\lambda, z) - \frac{1}{2} \log\left(\lambda(1-\lambda)z\right) + c_n, \tag{A15}$$

where c_n is bounded uniformly for all n. Making the substitution $u = \lambda(1 - \lambda)z$, we obtain

$$\inf_{z > 0} G_n(\lambda, z) \geq \inf_{u > 0} \left[Q_n\left(\lambda, \frac{u}{\lambda(1-\lambda)}\right) - \frac{1}{2} \log u \right] + c_n.$$

Next, let $b_n = 2(1 - r)/(9n)$. The lower bound in Inequality (A10) leads to

$$\inf_{u > 0} \left[Q_n\left(\lambda, \frac{u}{\lambda(1-\lambda)}\right) - \frac{1}{2} \log u \right] \geq \inf_{u > 0} \left[\frac{u}{2\lambda} \left(\frac{1}{1 - \lambda + \sqrt{b_n u}} \right) - \frac{1}{2} \log u \right]. \tag{A16}$$

The limiting behavior in Equation (A14) can now be seen as a consequence of Inequality (A15) and the fact that, for any sequence λ_n converging to one, the right-hand side of Inequality (A16) increases without bound as n increases. Combining Inequality (A12), Inequality (A13), and Equation (A14) establishes that the large n limit of $\Delta_r(Y)$ exists and is equal to $\Delta_r(X)$. This concludes the proof of Proposition 6.

Appendix B.4. Proof of Inequality (24)

Given any $\lambda \in (0, 1)$ and $u \in (0, \infty)$ let

$$p(r) = \frac{1-r}{r} - \sqrt{\frac{1-r}{r} \left(\frac{1-\lambda}{\lambda}\right) u}$$

$$q(r) = \frac{1-r}{r} + \sqrt{\frac{1-r}{r} \left(\frac{\lambda}{1-\lambda}\right) u}.$$

We need the following results, which characterize the terms in Proposition 4 in the limit as r increases to one.

Lemma A1. *The function $\psi_r(p(r), q(r))$ satisfies*

$$\lim_{r \to 1} \psi_r(p(r), q(r)) = \sqrt{\frac{2\pi}{u}}.$$

Proof. Starting with Equation (A4), we can write

$$\psi_r(p,q) = \frac{1}{q-p} \sqrt{\frac{2\pi(1-r)}{r\lambda(1-\lambda)}} \exp\left(\theta\left(\frac{r\lambda}{1-r}\right) + \theta\left(\frac{r(1-\lambda)}{1-r}\right) - \theta\left(\frac{r}{1-r}\right)\right).$$

As r converges to one, the terms in the exponent converge to zero. Note that $q(r) - p(r) = \sqrt{r\lambda(1-\lambda)/(1-r)}$ completes the proof. □

Lemma A2. *If X is a random variable such that $s \mapsto \mathbb{E}[|X|^s]$ is finite in a neighborhood of zero, then $\mathbb{E}[\log(X)]$ and $\mathrm{Var}(\log(X))$ are finite, and*

$$\lim_{r \to 1} L_r(X; p(r), q(r)) = \mathbb{E}[\log|X|] + \frac{u}{2} \mathrm{Var}(\log|X|).$$

Proof. Let $\Lambda(s) = \log(\mathbb{E}[|X|^s])$. The assumption that $\mathbb{E}[|X|^s]$ is finite in a neighborhood of zero means that $\mathbb{E}[(\log|X|)^m]$ is finite for all positive integers m, and thus $\Lambda(s)$ is real analytic in a neighborhood of zero. Hence, there exist constants $\delta > 0$ and $C < \infty$, depending on the distribution of X, such that

$$\left|\Lambda(s) - as + bs^2\right| \leq C|s|^3, \quad \text{for all } |s| \leq \delta,$$

where $a = \mathbb{E}[\log|X|]$ and $b = \frac{1}{2}\mathrm{Var}(|X|)$. Consequently, for all r such that $1 - \delta < p(r) < (1-r)/r < q(r) < 1 + \delta$, it follows that

$$\left|L_r(X; p(r), q(r)) - a - \left(\frac{1-r}{r} + u\right)b\right| \leq C \frac{r}{1-r} \left(\lambda |p(r)|^3 + (1-\lambda)|q(r)|^3\right).$$

Taking the limit as r increases to one completes the proof. □

We are now ready to prove Inequality (24). Combining Proposition 4 with Lemma A1 and Lemma A2 yields

$$\limsup_{r \to \infty} h_r(X) \leq \frac{1}{2} \log\left(\frac{2\pi}{u}\right) + \mathbb{E}[\log X] + \frac{u}{2} \mathrm{Var}(\log X).$$

The stated inequality follows from evaluating the right-hand side with $u = 1/\mathrm{Var}(\log X)$, recalling that $h(X)$ corresponds to the limit of $h_r(X)$ as r increases to one.

Appendix C. Proof of Proposition 7

The function $\kappa \colon (0,1] \to \mathbb{R}_+$ can be expressed as

$$\kappa(t) = \sup_{u \in (0,\infty)} \rho_t(u), \tag{A17}$$

where $\rho_t(u) = \log(1+u)/u^t$. For $t = 1$, the bound $\log(1+u) \leq u$ implies that $\rho_1(u) \leq 1$. Noting that $\lim_{u \to 0} \rho_1(u) = 1$, we conclude that $\kappa(1) = 1$.

Next, we consider the case $t \in (0,1)$. The function ρ_t is continuously differentiable on $(0,\infty)$ with

$$\mathrm{sgn}(\rho'_t(u)) = \mathrm{sgn}\left(u - t(1+u)\log(1+u)\right). \tag{A18}$$

Under the assumption $t \in (0,1)$, we see that $\rho_t(u)$ is increasing for all u sufficiently close to zero and decreasing for all u sufficiently large, and thus the supremum is attained at a stationary point of $\rho_t(u)$ on $(0, \infty)$. Making the substitution $w = \log(1+u) - 1/t$ leads to

$$\rho'_t(u) = 0 \iff we^w = -\frac{1}{t}e^{-\frac{1}{t}}.$$

For $t \in (0,1)$, it follows that $-\frac{1}{t}e^{-\frac{1}{t}} \in (-e^{-1}, 0)$, and thus $\rho'_t(u)$ has a unique root that can be expressed as

$$u_t^* = \exp\left(W\left(-\frac{1}{t}\exp\left(-\frac{1}{t}\right)\right) + \frac{1}{t}\right) - 1,$$

where Lambert's function $W(z)$ is the solution to the equation $z = we^w$ on the interval on $[-1, \infty)$.

Lemma A3. *The function $g(t) = t\kappa(t)$ is strictly increasing on $(0,1]$ with $\lim_{t\to 0} g(t) = 1/e$ and $g(1) = 1$.*

Proof. The fact that $g(1) = 1$ follows from $\kappa(1) = 1$. By the envelope theorem [37], the derivative of $g(t)$ can be expressed as

$$g'(t) = \frac{d}{dt} t\rho_t(u)\bigg|_{u=u_t^*} = \frac{\log(1+u_t^*)}{(u_t^*)^t} - t\log(u_t^*)\frac{\log(1+u_t^*)}{(u_t^*)^t}$$

In view of Equation (A18), it follows that $\rho'_t(u_t^*) = 0$ can be expressed equivalently as

$$\frac{u_t^*}{(1+u_t^*)\log(1+u_t^*)} = t, \tag{A19}$$

and thus

$$\operatorname{sgn}(g'(t)) = \operatorname{sgn}\left(1 - \frac{u_t^* \log u_t^*}{(1+u_t^*)\log(1+u_t^*)}\right). \tag{A20}$$

Noting that $u\log u < (1+u)\log(1+u)$ for all $u \in (0, \infty)$, it follows that $g'(t) > 0$ is strictly positive, and thus $g(t)$ is strictly increasing.

To prove the small t limit, we use Equation (A19) to write

$$\log(g(t)) = \log\left(\frac{u_t^*}{1+u_t^*}\right) - \frac{u_t^* \log u_t^*}{(1+u_t^*)\log(1+u_t^*)}. \tag{A21}$$

Now, as t decreases to zero, Equation (A19) shows that u_t^* increases to infinity. By Equation (A21), it then follows that $\log(g(t))$ converges to negative one, which proves the desired limit. □

References

1. Dembo, A.; Cover, T.M.; Thomas, J.A. Information Theoretic Inequalities. *IEEE Trans. Inf. Theory* **1991**, *37*, 1501–1518. [CrossRef]
2. Carslon, F. Une inégalité. *Ark. Mat. Astron. Fys.* **1934**, *25*, 1–5.
3. Levin, V.I. Exact constants in inequalities of the Carlson type. *Doklady Akad. Nauk. SSSR (N. S.)* **1948**, *59*, 635–638.
4. Larsson, L.; Maligranda, L.; Persson, L.E.; Pečarić, J. *Multiplicative Inequalities of Carlson Type and Interpolation*; World Scientific Publishing Company: Singapore, 2006.
5. Barza, S.; Burenkov, V.; Pečarić, J.E.; Persson, L.E. Sharp multidimensional multiplicative inequalities for weighted L_p spaces with homogeneous weights. *Math. Inequalities Appl.* **1998**, *1*, 53–67. [CrossRef]
6. Reeves, G. Two-Moment Inequailties for Rényi Entropy and Mutual Information. In Proceedings of the IEEE International Symposium on Information Theory (ISIT), Aachen, Germany, 25–30 June 2017; pp. 664–668.

7. Gray, R.M. *Entropy and Information Theory*; Springer-Verlag: Berlin/Heidelberg, Germany, 2013.
8. van Erven, T.; Harremoës, P. Rényi Divergence and Kullback–Liebler Divergence. *IEEE Trans. Inf. Theory* **2014**, *60*, 3937–3820. [CrossRef]
9. Atar, R.; Chowdharry, K.; Dupuis, P. Abstract. Robust Bounds on Risk-Sensitive Functionals via Rényi Divergence. *SIAM/ASA J. Uncertain. Quantif.* **2015**, *3*, 18–33. [CrossRef]
10. Rosenkrantz, R. (Ed.) *E. T. Jaynes: Papers on Probability, Staistics and Statistical Physics*; Springer: Berlin/Heidelberg, Germany, 1989.
11. Cover, T.M.; Thomas, J.A. *Elements of Information Theory*, 2nd ed.; Wiley-Interscience: Hoboken, NJ, USA, 2006.
12. Lutwak, E.; Yang, D.; Zhang, G. Moment-entropy inequalities. *Ann. Probab.* **2004**, *32*, 757–774. [CrossRef]
13. Lutwak, E.; Yang, D.; Zhang, G. Moment-Entropy Inequalities for a Random Vector. *IEEE Trans. Inf. Theory* **2007**, *53*, 1603–1607. [CrossRef]
14. Lutwak, E.; Lv, S.; Yang, D.; Zhang, G. Affine Moments of a Random Vector. *IEEE Trans. Inf. Theory* **2013**, *59*, 5592–5599. [CrossRef]
15. Costa, J.A.; Hero, A.O.; Vignat, C. A Characterization of the Multivariate Distributions Maximizing Rényi Entropy. In Proceedings of the IEEE International Symposium on Information Theory (ISIT), Lausanne, Switzerland, 30 June–5 July 2002. [CrossRef]
16. Costa, J.A.; Hero, A.O.; Vignat, C. A Geometric Characterization of Maximum Rényi Entropy Distributions. In Proceedings of the IEEE International Symposium on Information Theory (ISIT), Seattle, WA, USA, 9–14 July 2006; pp. 1822–1826.
17. Johnson, O.; Vignat, C. Some results concerning maximum Rényi entropy distributions. *Ann. de l'Institut Henri Poincaré (B) Probab. Stat.* **2007**, *43*, 339–351. [CrossRef]
18. Nguyen, V.H. A simple proof of the Moment-Entropy inequalities. *Adv. Appl. Math.* **2019**, *108*, 31–44. [CrossRef]
19. Barron, A.; Yang, Y. Information-theoretic determination of minimax rates of convergence. *Ann. Stat.* **1999**, *27*, 1564–1599. [CrossRef]
20. Wu, Y.; Xu, J. Statistical problems with planted structures: Information-theoretical and computational limits. In *Information-Theoretic Methods in Data Science*; Rodrigues, M.R.D.; Eldar, Y.C., Eds.; Cambridge University Press: Cambridge, UK, 2020; Chapter 13.
21. Reeves, G. Conditional Central Limit Theorems for Gaussian Projections. In Proceedings of the IEEE International Symposium on Information Theory (ISIT), Aachen, Germany, 25–30 June 2017; pp. 3055–3059.
22. Reeves, G.; Pfister, H.D. The Replica-Symmetric Prediction for Random Linear Estimation with Gaussian Matrices is Exact. *IEEE Trans. Inf. Theory* **2019**, *65*, 2252–2283. [CrossRef]
23. Reeves, G.; Pfister, H.D. Understanding Phase Transitions via Mutual Information and MMSE. In *Information-Theoretic Methods in Data Science*; Rodrigues, M.R.D.; Eldar, Y.C., Eds.; Cambridge University Press: Cambridge, UK, 2020; Chapter 7.
24. Rockafellar, R.T. *Convex Analysis*; Princeton University Press: Princeton, NJ, USA, 1970.
25. Andrews, G.E.; Askey, R.; Roy, R. *Special Functions*; Vol. 71, Encyclopedia of Mathematics and its Applications, Cambridge University Press: Cambridge, UK, 1999.
26. Nielsen, F.; Nock, R. On the Chi Square and Higher-Order Chi Distances for Approximationg f-Divergences. *IEEE Signal Process. Lett.* **1014**, *1*, 10–13.
27. Sason, I.; Verdú, S. f-Divergence Inequalities. *IEEE Trans. Inf. Theory* **2016**, *62*, 5973–6006. [CrossRef]
28. Sason, I. On the Rényi Divergence, Joint Range of Relative Entropy, and a Channel Coding Theorem. *IEEE Trans. Inf. Theory* **2016**, *62*, 23–34. [CrossRef]
29. Sason, I.; Verdú, S. Improved Bounds on Lossless Source Coding and Guessing Moments via Rényi Measures. *IEEE Trans. Inf. Theory* **2018**, *64*, 4323–4326. [CrossRef]
30. Sason, I. On f-divergences: Integral representations, local behavior, and inequalities. *Entropy* **2018**, *20*, 383. [CrossRef]
31. Melbourne, J.; Madiman, M.; Salapaka, M.V. Relationships between certain f-divergences. In Proceedings of the Allerton Conference on Communication, Control, and Computing, Monticello, IL, USA, 24–27 September 2019; pp. 1068–1073.
32. Nishiyama, T.; Sason, I. On Relations Between the Relative Entropy and χ^2-Divergence, Generalizations and Applications. *Entropy* **2020**, *22*, 563. [CrossRef]
33. Jebara, T.; Kondor, R.; Howard, A. Probability Product Kernels. *J. Mach. Learn. Res.* **2004**, *5*, 818–844.

34. Reeves, G.; Xu, J.; Zadik, I. The All-or-Nothing Phenomenon in Sparse Linear Regression. In Proceedings of the Conference On Learning Theory (COLT), Phoenix, AZ, USA, 25–28 June 2019.
35. Reeves, G.; Xu, J.; Zadik, I. All-or-nothing phenomena from single-letter to high dimensions. In Proceedings of the IEEE International Workshop on Computational Advances in Multi-Sensor Adaptive Processing (CAMSAP), Guadeloupe, France, 15–18 December 2019.
36. Grenié, L.; Molteni, G. Inequalities for the beta function. *Math. Inequalities Appl.* **2015**, *18*, 1427–1442. [CrossRef]
37. Milgrom, P.; Segal, I. Envelope Theorems for Arbitrary Choice Sets. *Econometrica* **2002**, *70*, 583–601. [CrossRef]

© 2020 by the authors. Licensee MDPI, Basel, Switzerland. This article is an open access article distributed under the terms and conditions of the Creative Commons Attribution (CC BY) license (http://creativecommons.org/licenses/by/4.0/).

Article
Strongly Convex Divergences

James Melbourne

Department of Electrical and Computer Engineering, University of Minnesota-Twin Cities, Minneapolis, MN 55455, USA; melbo013@umn.edu

Received: 2 September 2020; Accepted: 9 November 2020; Published: 21 November 2020

Abstract: We consider a sub-class of the f-divergences satisfying a stronger convexity property, which we refer to as strongly convex, or κ-convex divergences. We derive new and old relationships, based on convexity arguments, between popular f-divergences.

Keywords: information measures; f-divergence; hypothesis testing; total variation; skew-divergence; convexity; Pinsker's inequality; Bayes risk; Jensen–Shannon divergence

1. Introduction

The concept of an f-divergence, introduced independently by Ali-Silvey [1], Morimoto [2], and Csiszár [3], unifies several important information measures between probability distributions, as integrals of a convex function f, composed with the Radon–Nikodym of the two probability distributions. (An additional assumption can be made that f is strictly convex at 1, to ensure that $D_f(\mu||\nu) > 0$ for $\mu \neq \nu$. This obviously holds for any $f''(1) > 0$, and can hold for some f-divergences without classical derivatives at 0, for instance the total variation is strictly convex at 1. An example of an f-divergence not strictly convex is provided by the so-called "hockey-stick" divergence, where $f(x) = (x - \gamma)_+$, see [4–6].) For a convex function $f : (0, \infty) \to \mathbb{R}$ such that $f(1) = 0$, and measures P and Q such that $P \ll Q$, the f-divergence from P to Q is given by $D_f(P||Q) := \int f\left(\frac{dP}{dQ}\right) dQ$. The canonical example of an f-divergence, realized by taking $f(x) = x \log x$, is the relative entropy (often called the KL-divergence), which we denote with the subscript f omitted. f-divergences inherit many properties enjoyed by this special case; non-negativity, joint convexity of arguments, and a data processing inequality. Other important examples include the total variation, the χ^2-divergence, and the squared Hellinger distance. The reader is directed to Chapter 6 and 7 of [7] for more background.

We are interested in how stronger convexity properties of f give improvements of classical f-divergence inequalities. More explicitly, we consider consequences of f being κ-convex, in the sense that the map $x \mapsto f(x) - \kappa x^2/2$ is convex. This is in part inspired by the work of Sason [8], who demonstrated that divergences that are κ-convex satisfy "stronger than χ^2" data-processing inequalities.

Perhaps the most well known example of an f-divergence inequality is Pinsker's inequality, which bounds the square of the total variation above by a constant multiple of the relative entropy. That is for probability measures P and Q, $|P - Q|^2_{TV} \leq c\, D(P||Q)$. The optimal constant is achieved for Bernoulli measures, and under our conventions for total variation, $c = 1/2 \log e$. Many extensions and sharpenings of Pinsker's inequality exist (for examples, see [9–11]). Building on the work of Guntuboyina [9] and Topsøe [11], we achieve a further sharpening of Pinsker's inequality in Theorem 9.

Aside from the total variation, most divergences of interest have stronger than affine convexity, at least when f is restricted to a sub-interval of the real line. This observation is especially relevant to the situation in which one wishes to study $D_f(P||Q)$ in the existence of a bounded Radon–Nikodym derivative $\frac{dP}{dQ} \in (a, b) \subsetneq (0, \infty)$. One naturally obtains such bounds for skew divergences. That is divergences of the form $(P, Q) \mapsto D_f((1-t)P + tQ||(1-s)P + sQ)$ for $t, s \in [0, 1]$, as in this case,

$\frac{(1-t)P+tQ}{(1-s)P+sQ} \leq \max\left\{\frac{1-t}{1-s}, \frac{t}{s}\right\}$. Important examples of skew-divergences include the skew divergence [12] based on the relative entropy and the Vincze–Le Cam divergence [13,14], called the triangular discrimination in [11] and its generalization due to Györfi and Vajda [15] based on the χ^2-divergence. The Jensen–Shannon divergence [16] and its recent generalization [17] give examples of f-divergences realized as linear combinations of skewed divergences.

Let us outline the paper. In Section 2, we derive elementary results of κ-convex divergences and give a table of examples of κ-convex divergences. We demonstrate that κ-convex divergences can be lower bounded by the χ^2-divergence, and that the joint convexity of the map $(P,Q) \mapsto D_f(P||Q)$ can be sharpened under κ-convexity conditions on f. As a consequence, we obtain bounds between the mean square total variation distance of a set of distributions from its barycenter, and the average f-divergence from the set to the barycenter.

In Section 3, we investigate general skewing of f-divergences. In particular, we introduce the skew-symmetrization of an f-divergence, which recovers the Jensen–Shannon divergence and the Vincze–Le Cam divergences as special cases. We also show that a scaling of the Vincze–Le Cam divergence is minimal among skew-symmetrizations of κ-convex divergences on $(0,2)$. We then consider linear combinations of skew divergences and show that a generalized Vincze–Le Cam divergence (based on skewing the χ^2-divergence) can be upper bounded by the generalized Jensen–Shannon divergence introduced recently by Nielsen [17] (based on skewing the relative entropy), reversing the classical convexity bounds $D(P||Q) \leq \log(1 + \chi^2(P||Q)) \leq \log e \, \chi^2(P||Q)$. We also derive upper and lower total variation bounds for Nielsen's generalized Jensen–Shannon divergence.

In Section 4, we consider a family of densities $\{p_i\}$ weighted by λ_i, and a density q. We use the Bayes estimator $T(x) = \arg\max_i \lambda_i p_i(x)$ to derive a convex decomposition of the barycenter $p = \sum_i \lambda_i p_i$ and of q, each into two auxiliary densities. (Recall, a Bayes estimator is one that minimizes the expected value of a loss function. By the assumptions of our model, that $\mathbb{P}(\theta = i) = \lambda_i$, and $\mathbb{P}(X \in A | \theta = i) = \int_A p_i(x) dx$, we have $\mathbb{E}\ell(\theta, \hat{\theta}) = 1 - \int \lambda_{\hat{\theta}(x)} p_{\hat{\theta}(x)}(x) dx$ for the loss function $\ell(i,j) = 1 - \delta_i(j)$ and any estimator $\hat{\theta}$. It follows that $\mathbb{E}\ell(\theta, \hat{\theta}) \geq \mathbb{E}\ell(\theta, T)$ by $\lambda_{\hat{\theta}(x)} p_{\hat{\theta}(x)}(x) \leq \lambda_{T(x)} p_{T(x)}(x)$. Thus, T is a Bayes estimator associated to ℓ.) We use this decomposition to sharpen, for κ-convex divergences, an elegant theorem of Guntuboyina [9] that generalizes Fano and Pinsker's inequality to f-divergences. We then demonstrate explicitly, using an argument of Topsøe, how our sharpening of Guntuboyina's inequality gives a new sharpening of Pinsker's inequality in terms of the convex decomposition induced by the Bayes estimator.

Notation

Throughout, f denotes a convex function $f : (0, \infty) \to \mathbb{R} \cup \{\infty\}$, such that $f(1) = 0$. For a convex function defined on $(0, \infty)$, we define $f(0) := \lim_{x \to 0} f(x)$. We denote by f^*, the convex function $f^* : (0, \infty) \to \mathbb{R} \cup \{\infty\}$ defined by $f^*(x) = xf(x^{-1})$. We consider Borel probability measures P and Q on a Polish space $\mathcal{X}$ and define the f-divergence from P to Q, via densities p for P and q for Q with respect to a common reference measure μ as

$$D_f(p||q) = \int_{\mathcal{X}} f\left(\frac{p}{q}\right) q \, d\mu$$
$$= \int_{\{pq>0\}} qf\left(\frac{p}{q}\right) d\mu + f(0)Q(\{p=0\}) + f^*(0)P(\{q=0\}). \quad (1)$$

We note that this representation is independent of μ, and such a reference measure always exists, take $\mu = P + Q$ for example.

For $t, s \in [0, 1]$, define the binary f-divergence

$$D_f(t||s) := sf\left(\frac{t}{s}\right) + (1-s)f\left(\frac{1-t}{1-s}\right) \quad (2)$$

with the conventions, $f(0) = \lim_{t \to 0^+} f(t)$, $0f(0/0) = 0$, and $0f(a/0) = a \lim_{t \to \infty} f(t)/t$. For a random variable X and a set A, we denote the probability that X takes a value in A by $\mathbb{P}(X \in A)$, the expectation of the random variable by $\mathbb{E}X$, and the variance by $\text{Var}(X) := \mathbb{E}|X - \mathbb{E}X|^2$. For a probability measure μ satisfying $\mu(A) = \mathbb{P}(X \in A)$ for all Borel A, we write $X \sim \mu$, and, when there exists a probability density function such that $\mathbb{P}(X \in A) = \int_A f(x) d\gamma(x)$ for a reference measure γ, we write $X \sim f$. For a probability measure μ on $\mathcal{X}$, and an L^2 function $f : \mathcal{X} \to \mathbb{R}$, we denote $\text{Var}_\mu(f) := \text{Var}(f(X))$ for $X \sim \mu$.

2. Strongly Convex Divergences

Definition 1. *A $\mathbb{R} \cup \{\infty\}$-valued function f on a convex set $K \subseteq \mathbb{R}$ is κ-convex when $x, y \in K$ and $t \in [0, 1]$ implies*

$$f((1-t)x + ty) \leq (1-t)f(x) + tf(y) - \kappa t(1-t)(x-y)^2/2. \tag{3}$$

For example, when f is twice differentiable, (3) is equivalent to $f''(x) \geq \kappa$ for $x \in K$. Note that the case $\kappa = 0$ is just usual convexity.

Proposition 1. *For $f : K \to \mathbb{R} \cup \{\infty\}$ and $\kappa \in [0, \infty)$, the following are equivalent:*

1. *f is κ-convex.*
2. *The function $f - \kappa(t-a)^2/2$ is convex for any $a \in \mathbb{R}$.*
3. *The right handed derivative, defined as $f'_+(t) := \lim_{h \downarrow 0} \frac{f(t+h) - f(t)}{h}$ satisfies,*

$$f'_+(t) \geq f'_+(s) + \kappa(t - s)$$

for $t \geq s$.

Proof. Observe that it is enough to prove the result when $\kappa = 0$, where the proposition is reduced to the classical result for convex functions. □

Definition 2. *An f-divergence D_f is κ-convex on an interval K for $\kappa \geq 0$ when the function f is κ-convex on K.*

Table 1 lists some κ-convex f-divergences of interest to this article.

Table 1. Examples of Strongly Convex Divergences.

Divergence	f	κ	Domain
relative entropy (KL)	$t \log t$	$\frac{1}{M}$	$(0, M]$
total variation	$\frac{|t-1|}{2}$	0	$(0, \infty)$
Pearson's χ^2	$(t-1)^2$	2	$(0, \infty)$
squared Hellinger	$2(1 - \sqrt{t})$	$M^{-\frac{3}{2}}/2$	$(0, M]$
reverse relative entropy	$-\log t$	$1/M^2$	$(0, M]$
Vincze- Le Cam	$\frac{(t-1)^2}{t+1}$	$\frac{8}{(M+1)^3}$	$(0, M]$
Jensen–Shannon	$(t+1) \log \frac{2}{t+1} + t \log t$	$\frac{1}{M(M+1)}$	$(0, M]$
Neyman's χ^2	$\frac{1}{t} - 1$	$2/M^3$	$(0, M]$
Sason's s	$\log(s+t)^{(s+t)^2} - \log(s+1)^{(s+1)^2}$	$2 \log(s + M) + 3$	$[M, \infty), s > e^{-3/2}$
α-divergence	$\frac{4\left(1 - t^{\frac{1+\alpha}{2}}\right)}{1 - \alpha^2}, \alpha \neq \pm 1$	$M^{\frac{\alpha-3}{2}}$	$\begin{cases} [M, \infty), & \alpha > 3 \\ (0, M], & \alpha < 3 \end{cases}$

Observe that we have taken the normalization convention on the total variation (the total variation for a signed measure μ on a space X can be defined through the Hahn-Jordan decomposition of the measure into non-negative measures μ^+ and μ^- such that $\mu = \mu^+ - \mu^-$, as $\|\mu\| = \mu^+(X) + \mu^-(X)$

(see [18]); in our notation, $|\mu|_{TV} = \|\mu\|/2$) which we denote by $|P - Q|_{TV}$, such that $|P - Q|_{TV} = \sup_A |P(A) - Q(A)| \leq 1$. In addition, note that the α-divergence interpolates Pearson's χ^2-divergence when $\alpha = 3$, one half Neyman's χ^2-divergence when $\alpha = -3$, the squared Hellinger divergence when $\alpha = 0$, and has limiting cases, the relative entropy when $\alpha = 1$ and the reverse relative entropy when $\alpha = -1$. If f is κ-convex on $[a, b]$, then recalling its dual divergence $f^*(x) := xf(x^{-1})$ is κa^3-convex on $[\frac{1}{b}, \frac{1}{a}]$. Recall that f^* satisfies the equality $D_{f^*}(P||Q) = D_f(Q||P)$. For brevity, we use χ^2-divergence to refer to the Pearson χ^2-divergence, and we articulate Neyman's χ^2 explicitly when necessary.

The next lemma is a restatement of Jensen's inequality.

Lemma 1. *If f is κ-convex on the range of X,*

$$\mathbb{E}f(X) \geq f(\mathbb{E}(X)) + \frac{\kappa}{2}\operatorname{Var}(X).$$

Proof. Apply Jensen's inequality to $f(x) - \kappa x^2/2$. □

For a convex function f such that $f(1) = 0$ and $c \in \mathbb{R}$, the function $\tilde{f}(t) = f(t) + c(t-1)$ remains a convex function, and what is more satisfies

$$D_f(P||Q) = D_{\tilde{f}}(P||Q)$$

since $\int c(p/q - 1)q d\mu = 0$.

Definition 3 (χ^2-divergence). *For $f(t) = (t-1)^2$, we write*

$$\chi^2(P||Q) := D_f(P||Q).$$

We pursue a generalization of the following bound on the total variation by the χ^2-divergence [19–21].

Theorem 1 ([19–21]). *For measures P and Q,*

$$|P - Q|_{TV}^2 \leq \frac{\chi^2(P||Q)}{2}. \tag{4}$$

We mention the work of Harremos and Vadja [20], in which it is shown, through a characterization of the extreme points of the joint range associated to a pair of f-divergences (valid in general), that the inequality characterizes the "joint range", that is, the range of the function $(P, Q) \mapsto (|P - Q|_{TV}, \chi^2(P||Q))$. We use the following lemma, which shows that every strongly convex divergence can be lower bounded, up to its convexity constant $\kappa > 0$, by the χ^2-divergence,

Lemma 2. *For a κ-convex f,*

$$D_f(P||Q) \geq \frac{\kappa}{2}\chi^2(P||Q).$$

Proof. Define a $\tilde{f}(t) = f(t) - f'_+(1)(t-1)$ and note that $\tilde{f}$ defines the same κ-convex divergence as f. Thus, we may assume without loss of generality that f'_+ is uniquely zero when $t = 1$. Since f is

κ-convex $\phi: t \mapsto f(t) - \kappa(t-1)^2/2$ is convex, and, by $f'_+(1) = 0$, $\phi'_+(1) = 0$ as well. Thus, ϕ takes its minimum when $t = 1$ and hence $\phi \geq 0$ so that $f(t) \geq \kappa(t-1)^2/2$. Computing,

$$\begin{aligned}D_f(P||Q) &= \int f\left(\frac{dP}{dQ}\right) dQ \\ &\geq \frac{\kappa}{2} \int \left(\frac{dP}{dQ} - 1\right)^2 dQ \\ &= \frac{\kappa}{2} \chi^2(P||Q).\end{aligned}$$

□

Based on a Taylor series expansion of f about 1, Nielsen and Nock ([22], [Corollary 1]) gave the estimate

$$D_f(P||Q) \approx \frac{f''(1)}{2} \chi^2(P||Q) \qquad (5)$$

for divergences with a non-zero second derivative and P close to Q. Lemma 2 complements this estimate with a lower bound, when f is κ-concave. In particular, if $f''(1) = \kappa$, it shows that the approximation in (5) is an underestimate.

Theorem 2. *For measures P and Q, and a κ convex divergence D_f,*

$$|P - Q|_{TV}^2 \leq \frac{D_f(P||Q)}{\kappa}. \qquad (6)$$

Proof. By Lemma 2 and then Theorem 1,

$$\frac{D_f(P||Q)}{\kappa} \geq \frac{\chi^2(P||Q)}{2} \geq |P - Q|_{TV}. \qquad (7)$$

□

The proof of Lemma 2 uses a pointwise inequality between convex functions to derive an inequality between their respective divergences. This simple technique was shown to have useful implications by Sason and Verdu in [6], where it appears as Theorem 1 and is used to give sharp comparisons in several f-divergence inequalities.

Theorem 3 (Sason–Verdu [6]). *For divergences defined by g and f with $cf(t) \geq g(t)$ for all t, then*

$$D_g(P||Q) \leq cD_f(P||Q).$$

Moreover, if $f'(1) = g'(1) = 0$, then

$$\sup_{P \neq Q} \frac{D_g(P||Q)}{D_f(P||Q)} = \sup_{t \neq 1} \frac{g(t)}{f(t)}.$$

Corollary 1. *For a smooth κ-convex divergence f, the inequality*

$$D_f(P||Q) \geq \frac{\kappa}{2} \chi^2(P||Q) \qquad (8)$$

is sharp multiplicatively in the sense that

$$\inf_{P \neq Q} \frac{D_f(P||Q)}{\chi^2(P||Q)} = \frac{\kappa}{2}. \qquad (9)$$

if $f''(1) = \kappa$.

In information geometry, a standard f-divergence is defined as an f-divergence satisfying the normalization $f(1) = f'(1) = 0, f''(1) = 1$ (see [23]). Thus, Corollary 1 shows that $\frac{1}{2}\chi^2$ provides a sharp lower bound on every standard f-divergence that is 1-convex. In particular, the lower bound in Lemma 2 complimenting the estimate (5) is shown to be sharp.

Proof. Without loss of generality, we assume that $f'(1) = 0$. If $f''(1) = \kappa + 2\varepsilon$ for some $\varepsilon > 0$, then taking $g(t) = (t-1)^2$ and applying Theorem 3 and Lemma 2

$$\sup_{P \neq Q} \frac{D_g(P||Q)}{D_f(P||Q)} = \sup_{t \neq 1} \frac{g(t)}{f(t)} \leq \frac{2}{\kappa}. \tag{10}$$

Observe that, after two applications of L'Hospital,

$$\lim_{\varepsilon \to 0} \frac{g(1+\varepsilon)}{f(1+\varepsilon)} = \lim_{\varepsilon \to 0} \frac{g'(1+\varepsilon)}{f'(1+\varepsilon)} = \frac{g''(1)}{f''(1)} = \frac{2}{\kappa} \leq \sup_{t \neq 1} \frac{g(t)}{f(t)}.$$

Thus, (9) follows. □

Proposition 2. *When D_f is an f divergence such that f is κ-convex on $[a, b]$ and that P_θ and Q_θ are probability measures indexed by a set Θ such that $a \leq \frac{dP_\theta}{dQ_\theta}(x) \leq b$, holds for all θ and $P := \int_\Theta P_\theta d\mu(\theta)$ and $Q := \int_\Theta Q_\theta d\mu(\theta)$ for a probability measure μ on Θ, then*

$$D_f(P||Q) \leq \int_\Theta D_f(P_\theta||Q_\theta) d\mu(\theta) - \frac{\kappa}{2} \int_\Theta \int_\mathcal{X} \left(\frac{dP_\theta}{dQ_\theta} - \frac{dP}{dQ} \right)^2 dQ d\mu, \tag{11}$$

In particular, when $Q_\theta = Q$ for all θ

$$D_f(P||Q)$$
$$\leq \int_\Theta D_f(P_\theta||Q) d\mu(\theta) - \frac{\kappa}{2} \int_\Theta \int_\mathcal{X} \left(\frac{dP_\theta}{dQ} - \frac{dP}{dQ} \right)^2 dQ d\mu(\theta) \tag{12}$$
$$\leq \int_\Theta D_f(P_\theta||Q) d\mu(\theta) - \kappa \int_\Theta |P_\theta - P|^2_{TV} d\mu(\theta)$$

Proof. Let $d\theta$ denote a reference measure dominating μ so that $d\mu = \varphi(\theta)d\theta$ then write $\nu_\theta = \nu(\theta, x) = \frac{dQ_\theta}{dQ}(x)\varphi(\theta)$.

$$D_f(P||Q) = \int_\mathcal{X} f\left(\frac{dP}{dQ}\right) dQ$$
$$= \int_\mathcal{X} f\left(\int_\Theta \frac{dP_\theta}{dQ} d\mu(\theta) \right) dQ \tag{13}$$
$$= \int_\mathcal{X} f\left(\int_\Theta \frac{dP_\theta}{dQ_\theta} \nu(\theta, x) d\theta \right) dQ$$

By Jensen's inequality, as in Lemma 1

$$f\left(\int_\Theta \frac{dP_\theta}{dQ_\theta} \nu_\theta d\theta \right) \leq \int_\theta f\left(\frac{dP_\theta}{dQ_\theta} \right) \nu_\theta d\theta - \frac{\kappa}{2} \int_\Theta \left(\frac{dP_\theta}{dQ_\theta} - \int_\Theta \frac{dP_\theta}{dQ_\theta} \nu_\theta d\theta \right)^2 \nu_\theta d\theta$$

Integrating this inequality gives

$$D_f(P||Q) \leq \int_{\mathcal{X}} \left(\int_\Theta f\left(\frac{dP_\theta}{dQ_\theta}\right) v_\theta d\theta - \frac{\kappa}{2} \int_\Theta \left(\frac{dP_\theta}{dQ_\theta} - \int_\Theta \frac{dP_\theta}{dQ_\theta} v_\theta d\theta\right)^2 v_\theta d\theta \right) dQ \tag{14}$$

Note that

$$\int_{\mathcal{X}} \int_\Theta \left(\frac{dP_\theta}{dQ_\theta} dQ - \int_\Theta \frac{dP_\theta}{dQ_{\theta_0}} v_{\theta_0} d\theta_0\right)^2 v_\theta d\theta dQ = \int_\Theta \int_{\mathcal{X}} \left(\frac{dP_\theta}{dQ_\theta} - \frac{dP}{dQ}\right)^2 dQ d\mu,$$

and

$$\int_{\mathcal{X}} \int_\Theta f\left(\frac{dP_\theta}{dQ_\theta}\right) v(\theta, x) d\theta dQ = \int_\Theta \int_{\mathcal{X}} f\left(\frac{dP_\theta}{dQ_\theta}\right) v(\theta, x) dQ d\theta$$
$$= \int_\Theta \int_{\mathcal{X}} f\left(\frac{dP_\theta}{dQ_\theta}\right) dQ_\theta d\mu(\theta) \tag{15}$$
$$= \int_\Theta D(P_\theta||Q_\theta) d\mu(\theta)$$

Inserting these equalities into (14) gives the result.

To obtain the total variation bound, one needs only to apply Jensen's inequality,

$$\int_{\mathcal{X}} \left(\frac{dP_\theta}{dQ} - \frac{dP}{dQ}\right)^2 dQ \geq \left(\int_{\mathcal{X}} \left|\frac{dP_\theta}{dQ} - \frac{dP}{dQ}\right| dQ\right)^2 \tag{16}$$
$$= |P_\theta - P|_{TV}^2.$$

□

Observe that, taking $Q = P = \int_\Theta P_\theta d\mu(\theta)$ in Proposition 2, one obtains a lower bound for the average f-divergence from the set of distribution to their barycenter, by the mean square total variation of the set of distributions to the barycenter,

$$\kappa \int_\Theta |P_\theta - P|_{TV}^2 d\mu(\theta) \leq \int_\Theta D_f(P_\theta||P) d\mu(\theta). \tag{17}$$

An alternative proof of this can be obtained by applying $|P_\theta - P|_{TV}^2 \leq D_f(P_\theta||P)/\kappa$ from Theorem 2 pointwise.

The next result shows that, for f strongly convex, Pinsker type inequalities can never be reversed,

Proposition 3. *Given f strongly convex and $M > 0$, there exists P, Q measures such that*

$$D_f(P||Q) \geq M|P - Q|_{TV}. \tag{18}$$

Proof. By κ-convexity $\phi(t) = f(t) - \kappa t^2/2$ is a convex function. Thus, $\phi(t) \geq \phi(1) + \phi'_+(1)(t-1) = (f'_+(1) - \kappa)(t-1)$ and hence $\lim_{t\to\infty} \frac{f(t)}{t} \geq \lim_{t\to\infty} \kappa t/2 + (f'_+(1) - \kappa)\left(1 - \frac{1}{t}\right) = \infty$. Taking measures on the two points space $P = \{1/2, 1/2\}$ and $Q = \{1/2t, 1 - 1/2t\}$ gives $D_f(P||Q) \geq \frac{1}{2}\frac{f(t)}{t}$ which tends to infinity with $t \to \infty$, while $|P - Q|_{TV} \leq 1$. □

In fact, building on the work of Basu-Shioya-Park [24] and Vadja [25], Sason and Verdu proved [6] that, for any f divergence, $\sup_{P \neq Q} \frac{D_f(P||Q)}{|P-Q|_{TV}} = f(0) + f^*(0)$. Thus, an f-divergence can be bounded above by a constant multiple of a the total variation, if and only if $f(0) + f^*(0) < \infty$. From this perspective, Proposition 3 is simply the obvious fact that strongly convex functions have super linear (at least quadratic) growth at infinity.

3. Skew Divergences

If we denote $Cvx(0,\infty)$ to be quotient of the cone of convex functions f on $(0,\infty)$ such that $f(1) = 0$ under the equivalence relation $f_1 \sim f_2$ when $f_1 - f_2 = c(x-1)$ for $c \in \mathbb{R}$, then the map $f \mapsto D_f$ gives a linear isomorphism between $Cvx(0,\infty)$ and the space of all f-divergences. The mapping $\mathcal{T} : Cvx(0,\infty) \to Cvx(0,\infty)$ defined by $\mathcal{T}f = f^*$, where we recall $f^*(t) = tf(t^{-1})$, gives an involution of $Cvx(0,\infty)$. Indeed, $D_{\mathcal{T}f}(P||Q) = D_f(Q||P)$, so that $D_{\mathcal{T}(\mathcal{T}(f))}(P||Q) = D_f(P||Q)$. Mathematically, skew divergences give an interpolation of this involution as

$$(P,Q) \mapsto D_f((1-t)P + tQ||(1-s)P + sQ)$$

gives $D_f(P||Q)$ by taking $s = 1$ and $t = 0$ or yields $D_{f^*}(P||Q)$ by taking $s = 0$ and $t = 1$.

Moreover, as mentioned in the Introduction, skewing imposes boundedness of the Radon–Nikodym derivative $\frac{dP}{dQ}$, which allows us to constrain the domain of f-divergences and leverage κ-convexity to obtain f-divergence inequalities in this section.

The following appears as Theorem III.1 in the preprint [26]. It states that skewing an f-divergence preserves its status as such. This guarantees that the generalized skew divergences of this section are indeed f-divergences. A proof is given in the Appendix A for the convenience of the reader.

Theorem 4 (Melbourne et al [26]). *For $t, s \in [0,1]$ and a divergence D_f, then*

$$S_f(P||Q) := D_f((1-t)P + tQ||(1-s)P + sQ) \tag{19}$$

is an f-divergence as well.

Definition 4. *For an f-divergence, its skew symmetrization,*

$$\Delta_f(P||Q) := \frac{1}{2}D_f\left(P\left\|\frac{P+Q}{2}\right.\right) + \frac{1}{2}D_f\left(Q\left\|\frac{P+Q}{2}\right.\right).$$

Δ_f is determined by the convex function

$$x \mapsto \frac{1+x}{2}\left(f\left(\frac{2x}{1+x}\right) + f\left(\frac{2}{1+x}\right)\right). \tag{20}$$

Observe that $\Delta_f(P||Q) = \Delta_f(Q||P)$, and when $f(0) < \infty$, $\Delta_f(P||Q) \leq \sup_{x \in [0,2]} f(x) < \infty$ for all P, Q since $\frac{dP}{d(P+Q)/2}, \frac{dQ}{d(P+Q)/2} \leq 2$. When $f(x) = x \log x$, the relative entropy's skew symmetrization is the Jensen–Shannon divergence. When $f(x) = (x-1)^2$ up to a normalization constant the χ^2-divergence's skew symmetrization is the Vincze–Le Cam divergence which we state below for emphasis. The work of Topsøe [11] provides more background on this divergence, where it is referred to as the triangular discrimination.

Definition 5. *When $f(t) = \frac{(t-1)^2}{t+1}$, denote the Vincze–Le Cam divergence by*

$$\Delta(P||Q) := D_f(P||Q).$$

If one denotes the skew symmetrization of the χ^2-divergence by Δ_{χ^2}, one can compute easily from (20) that $\Delta_{\chi^2}(P||Q) = \Delta(P||Q)/2$. We note that although skewing preserves 0-convexity, by the above example, it does not preserve κ-convexity in general. The skew symmetrization of the χ^2-divergence a 2-convex divergence while $f(t) = (t-1)^2/(t+1)$ corresponding to the Vincze–Le Cam divergence satisfies $f''(t) = \frac{8}{(t+1)^3}$, which cannot be bounded away from zero on $(0,\infty)$.

Corollary 2. *For an f-divergence such that f is a κ-convex on $(0, 2)$,*

$$\Delta_f(P||Q) \geq \frac{\kappa}{4}\Delta(P||Q) = \frac{\kappa}{2}\Delta_{\chi^2}(P||Q), \tag{21}$$

with equality when the $f(t) = (t-1)^2$ corresponding the the χ^2-divergence, where Δ_f denotes the skew symmetrized divergence associated to f and Δ is the Vincze-Le Cam divergence.

Proof. Applying Proposition 2

$$\begin{aligned}
0 &= D_f\left(\frac{P+Q}{2} \middle\| \frac{Q+P}{2}\right) \\
&\leq \frac{1}{2}D_f\left(P \middle\| \frac{Q+P}{2}\right) + \frac{1}{2}D_f\left(Q \middle\| \frac{Q+P}{2}\right) - \frac{\kappa}{8}\int\left(\frac{2P}{P+Q} - \frac{2Q}{P+Q}\right)^2 d(P+Q)/2 \\
&= \Delta_f(P||Q) - \frac{\kappa}{4}\Delta(P||Q).
\end{aligned}$$

□

When $f(x) = x \log x$, we have $f''(x) \geq \frac{\log e}{2}$ on $[0,2]$, which demonstrates that up to a constant $\frac{\log e}{8}$ the Jensen–Shannon divergence bounds the Vincze–Le Cam divergence (see [11] for improvement of the inequality in the case of the Jensen–Shannon divergence, called the "capacitory discrimination" in the reference, by a factor of 2).

We now investigate more general, non-symmetric skewing in what follows.

Proposition 4. *For $\alpha, \beta \in [0, 1]$, define*

$$C(\alpha) := \begin{cases} 1 - \alpha & \text{when } \alpha \leq \beta \\ \alpha & \text{when } \alpha > \beta, \end{cases} \tag{22}$$

and

$$S_{\alpha,\beta}(P||Q) := D((1-\alpha)P + \alpha Q || (1-\beta)P + \beta Q). \tag{23}$$

Then,

$$S_{\alpha,\beta}(P||Q) \leq C(\alpha) D_\infty(\alpha||\beta) |P - Q|_{TV}, \tag{24}$$

where $D_\infty(\alpha||\beta) := \log\left(\max\left\{\frac{\alpha}{\beta}, \frac{1-\alpha}{1-\beta}\right\}\right)$ is the binary ∞-Rényi divergence [27].

We need the following lemma originally proved by Audenart in the quantum setting [28]. It is based on a differential relationship between the skew divergence [12] and the [15] (see [29,30]).

Lemma 3 (Theorem III.1 [26]). *For P and Q probability measures and $t \in [0, 1]$,*

$$S_{0,t}(P||Q) \leq -\log t |P - Q|_{TV}. \tag{25}$$

Proof of Theorem 4. If $\alpha \leq \beta$, then $D_\infty(\alpha||\beta) = \log\frac{1-\alpha}{1-\beta}$ and $C(\alpha) = 1 - \alpha$. In addition,

$$(1-\beta)P + \beta Q = t((1-\alpha)P + \alpha Q) + (1-t)Q \tag{26}$$

with $t = \frac{1-\beta}{1-\alpha}$, thus

$$\begin{aligned}
S_{\alpha,\beta}(P||Q) &= S_{0,t}((1-\alpha)P + \alpha Q||Q) \\
&\leq (-\log t)\,|((1-\alpha)P + \alpha Q) - Q|_{TV} \\
&= C(\alpha)\,D_\infty(\alpha||\beta)\,|P - Q|_{TV},
\end{aligned} \tag{27}$$

where the inequality follows from Lemma 3. Following the same argument for $\alpha > \beta$, so that $C(\alpha) = \alpha$, $D_\infty(\alpha||\beta) = \log \frac{\alpha}{\beta}$, and

$$(1-\beta)P + \beta Q = t\left((1-\alpha)P + \alpha Q\right) + (1-t)P \tag{28}$$

for $t = \frac{\beta}{\alpha}$ completes the proof. Indeed,

$$\begin{aligned} S_{\alpha,\beta}(P||Q) &= S_{0,t}((1-\alpha)P + \alpha Q||P) \\ &\leq -\log t \, |((1-\alpha)P + \alpha Q) - P|_{TV} \\ &= C(\alpha)\, D_\infty(\alpha||\beta)\, |P - Q|_{TV}. \end{aligned} \tag{29}$$

□

We recover the classical bound [11,16] of the Jensen–Shannon divergence by the total variation.

Corollary 3. *For probability measure P and Q,*

$$\mathrm{JSD}(P||Q) \leq \log 2 \, |P - Q|_{TV} \tag{30}$$

Proof. Since $\mathrm{JSD}(P||Q) = \frac{1}{2} S_{0,\frac{1}{2}}(P||Q) + \frac{1}{2} S_{1,\frac{1}{2}}(P||Q)$. □

Proposition 4 gives a sharpening of Lemma 1 of Nielsen [17], who proved $S_{\alpha,\beta}(P||Q) \leq D_\infty(\alpha||\beta)$, and used the result to establish the boundedness of a generalization of the Jensen–Shannon Divergence.

Definition 6 (Nielsen [17]). *For p and q densities with respect to a reference measure μ, $w_i > 0$, such that $\sum_{i=1}^n w_i = 1$ and $\alpha_i \in [0,1]$, define*

$$JS^{\alpha,w}(p:q) = \sum_{i=1}^n w_i\, D((1-\alpha_i)p + \alpha_i q||(1-\bar{\alpha})p + \bar{\alpha}q) \tag{31}$$

where $\sum_{i=1}^n w_i \alpha_i = \bar{\alpha}$.

Note that, when $n = 2$, $\alpha_1 = 1$, $\alpha_2 = 0$ and $w_i = \frac{1}{2}$, $JS^{\alpha,w}(p:q) = \mathrm{JSD}(p||q)$, the usual Jensen–Shannon divergence. We now demonstrate that Nielsen's generalized Jensen–Shannon Divergence can be bounded by the total variation distance just as the ordinary Jensen–Shannon Divergence.

Theorem 5. *For p and q densities with respect to a reference measure μ, $w_i > 0$, such that $\sum_{i=1}^n w_i = 1$ and $\alpha_i \in (0,1)$,*

$$\log e\, \mathrm{Var}_w(\alpha)\, |p-q|_{TV}^2 \leq JS^{\alpha,w}(p:q) \leq \mathcal{A}\, H(w)\, |p-q|_{TV} \tag{32}$$

where $H(w) := -\sum_i w_i \log w_i \geq 0$ and $\mathcal{A} = \max_i |\alpha_i - \tilde{\alpha}_i|$ with $\tilde{\alpha}_i = \sum_{j \neq i} \frac{w_j \alpha_j}{1-w_i}$.

Note that, since $\tilde{\alpha}_i$ is the w average of the α_j terms with α_i removed, $\tilde{\alpha}_i \in [0,1]$ and thus $\mathcal{A} \leq 1$. We need the following Theorem from Melbourne et al. [26] for the upper bound.

Theorem 6 ([26] Theorem 1.1). *For f_i densities with respect to a common reference measure γ and $\lambda_i > 0$ such that $\sum_{i=1}^n \lambda_i = 1$,*

$$h_\gamma\left(\sum_i \lambda_i f_i\right) - \sum_i \lambda_i h_\gamma(f_i) \leq \mathcal{T} H(\lambda), \tag{33}$$

where $h_\gamma(f_i) := -\int f_i(x) \log f_i(x) d\gamma(x)$ and $\mathcal{T} = \sup_i |f_i - \tilde{f}_i|_{TV}$ with $\tilde{f}_i = \sum_{j \neq i} \frac{\lambda_j}{1-\lambda_i} f_j$.

Proof of Theorem 5. We apply Theorem 6 with $f_i = (1-\alpha_i)p + \alpha_i q$, $\lambda_i = w_i$, and noticing that in general

$$h_\gamma(\sum_i \lambda_i f_i) - \sum_i \lambda_i h_\gamma(f_i) = \sum_i \lambda_i D(f_i \| f), \tag{34}$$

we have

$$JS^{\alpha,w}(p:q) = \sum_{i=1}^n w_i D((1-\alpha_i)p + \alpha_i q \| (1-\bar{\alpha})p + \bar{\alpha}q) \tag{35}$$
$$\leq \mathcal{T} H(w).$$

It remains to determine $\mathcal{T} = \max_i |f_i - \tilde{f}_i|_{TV}$,

$$\begin{aligned}
\tilde{f}_i - f_i &= \frac{f - f_i}{1 - \lambda_i} \\
&= \frac{((1-\bar{\alpha})p + \bar{\alpha}q) - ((1-\alpha_i)p + \alpha_i q)}{1 - w_i} \\
&= \frac{(\alpha_i - \bar{\alpha})(p - q)}{1 - w_i} \\
&= (\alpha_i - \bar{\alpha}_i)(p - q).
\end{aligned} \tag{36}$$

Thus, $\mathcal{T} = \max_i (\alpha_i - \bar{\alpha}_i)|p - q|_{TV} = \mathcal{A}|p - q|_{TV}$, and the proof of the upper bound is complete.

To prove the lower bound, we apply Pinsker's inequality, $2\log e |P - Q|_{TV}^2 \leq D(P\|Q)$,

$$\begin{aligned}
JS^{\alpha,w}(p:q) &= \sum_{i=1}^n w_i D((1-\alpha_i)p + \alpha_i q \| (1-\bar{\alpha})p + \bar{\alpha}q) \\
&\geq \frac{1}{2} \sum_{i=1}^n w_i 2\log e \, |((1-\alpha_i)p + \alpha_i q) - ((1-\bar{\alpha})p + \bar{\alpha}q)|_{TV}^2 \\
&= \log e \sum_{i=1}^n w_i (\alpha_i - \bar{\alpha})^2 |p - q|_{TV}^2 \\
&= \log e \, \mathrm{Var}_w(\alpha) \, |p - q|_{TV}^2.
\end{aligned} \tag{37}$$

□

Definition 7. *Given an f-divergence, densities p and q with respect to common reference measure, $\alpha \in [0,1]^n$ and $w \in (0,1)^n$ such that $\sum_i w_i = 1$ define its generalized skew divergence*

$$D_f^{\alpha,w}(p:q) = \sum_{i=1}^n w_i D_f((1-\alpha_i)p + \alpha_i q \| (1-\bar{\alpha})p + \bar{\alpha}q). \tag{38}$$

where $\bar{\alpha} = \sum_i w_i \alpha_i$.

Note that, by Theorem 4, $D_f^{\alpha,w}$ is an f-divergence. The generalized skew divergence of the relative entropy is the generalized Jensen–Shannon divergence $JS^{\alpha,w}$. We denote the generalized skew divergence of the χ^2-divergence from p to q by

$$\chi^2_{\alpha,w}(p:q) := \sum_i w_i \chi^2((1-\alpha_i)p + \alpha_i q \| (1-\bar{\alpha}p + \bar{\alpha}q) \tag{39}$$

Note that, when $n = 2$ and $\alpha_1 = 0$, $\alpha_2 = 1$ and $w_i = \frac{1}{2}$, we recover the skew symmetrized divergence in Definition 4

$$D_f^{(0,1),(1/2,1/2)}(p:q) = \Delta_f(p||q) \tag{40}$$

The following theorem shows that the usual upper bound for the relative entropy by the χ^2-divergence can be reversed up to a factor in the skewed case.

Theorem 7. *For p and q with a common dominating measure μ,*

$$\chi^2_{\alpha,w}(p:q) \leq N_\infty(\alpha,w) JS^{\alpha,w}(p:q).$$

Writing $N_\infty(\alpha,w) = \max_i \max\left\{\frac{1-\alpha_i}{1-\bar{\alpha}}, \frac{\alpha_i}{\bar{\alpha}}\right\}$. *For $\alpha \in [0,1]^n$ and $w \in (0,1)^n$ such that $\sum_i w_i = 1$, we use the notation $N_\infty(\alpha,w) := \max_i e^{D_\infty(\alpha_i||\bar{\alpha})}$ where $\bar{\alpha} := \sum_i w_i \alpha_i$.*

Proof. By definition,

$$JS^{\alpha,w}(p:q) = \sum_{i=1}^n w_i D((1-\alpha_i)p + \alpha_i q || (1-\bar{\alpha})p + \bar{\alpha}q).$$

Taking P_i to be the measure associated to $(1-\alpha_i)p + \alpha_i q$ and Q given by $(1-\bar{\alpha})p + \bar{\alpha}q$, then

$$\frac{dP_i}{dQ} = \frac{(1-\alpha_i)p + \alpha_i q}{(1-\bar{\alpha})p + \bar{\alpha}q} \leq \max\left\{\frac{1-\alpha_i}{1-\bar{\alpha}}, \frac{\alpha_i}{\bar{\alpha}}\right\} = e^{D_\infty(\alpha_i||\bar{\alpha})} \leq N_\infty(\alpha,w). \tag{41}$$

Since $f(x) = x \log x$, the convex function associated to the usual KL divergence, satisfies $f''(x) = \frac{1}{x}$, f is $e^{-D_\infty(\alpha)}$-convex on $[0, \sup_{x,i} \frac{dP_i}{dQ}(x)]$, applying Proposition 2, we obtain

$$D\left(\sum_i w_i P_i \,\Big|\Big|\, Q\right) \leq \sum_i w_i D(P_i||Q) - \frac{\sum_i w_i \int_\mathcal{X} \left(\frac{dP_i}{dQ} - \frac{dP}{dQ}\right)^2 dQ}{2 N_\infty(\alpha,w)}. \tag{42}$$

Since $Q = \sum_i w_i P_i$, the left hand side of (42) is zero, while

$$\sum_i w_i \int_\mathcal{X} \left(\frac{dP_i}{dQ} - \frac{dP}{dQ}\right)^2 dQ = \sum_i w_i \int_\mathcal{X} \left(\frac{dP_i}{dP} - 1\right)^2 dP$$
$$= \sum_i w_i \chi^2(P_i||P) \tag{43}$$
$$= \chi^2_{\alpha,w}(p:q).$$

Rearranging gives,

$$\frac{\chi^2_{\alpha,w}(p:q)}{2 N_\infty(\alpha,w)} \leq JS^{\alpha,w}(p:q), \tag{44}$$

which is our conclusion. □

4. Total Variation Bounds and Bayes Risk

In this section, we derive bounds on the Bayes risk associated to a family of probability measures with a prior distribution λ. Let us state definitions and recall basic relationships. Given probability densities $\{p_i\}_{i=1}^n$ on a space $\mathcal{X}$ with respect a reference measure μ and $\lambda_i \geq 0$ such that $\sum_{i=1}^n \lambda_i = 1$, define the Bayes risk,

$$R := R_\lambda(p) := 1 - \int_\mathcal{X} \max_i \{\lambda_i p_i(x)\} d\mu(x) \tag{45}$$

If $\ell(x,y) = 1 - \delta_x(y)$, and we define $T(x) := \arg\max_i \lambda_i p_i(x)$ then observe that this definition is consistent with, the usual definition of the Bayes risk associated to the loss function ℓ. Below, we consider θ to be a random variable on $\{1, 2, \ldots, n\}$ such that $\mathbb{P}(\theta = i) = \lambda_i$, and x to be a variable with conditional distribution $\mathbb{P}(X \in A | \theta = i) = \int_A p_i(x) d\mu(x)$. The following result shows that the Bayes risk gives the probability of the categorization error, under an optimal estimator.

Proposition 5. *The Bayes risk satisfies*

$$R = \min_{\hat{\theta}} \mathbb{E}\ell(\theta, \hat{\theta}(X)) = \mathbb{E}\ell(\theta, T(X))$$

where the minimum is defined over $\hat{\theta} : \mathcal{X} \to \{1, 2, \ldots, n\}$.

Proof. Observe that $R = 1 - \int_{\mathcal{X}} \lambda_{T(x)} p_{T(x)}(x) d\mu(x) = \mathbb{E}\ell(\theta, T(X))$. Similarly,

$$\mathbb{E}\ell(\theta, \hat{\theta}(X)) = 1 - \int_{\mathcal{X}} \lambda_{\hat{\theta}(x)} p_{\hat{\theta}(x)}(x) d\mu(x)$$
$$\geq 1 - \int_{\mathcal{X}} \lambda_{T(x)} p_{T(x)}(x) d\mu(x) = R,$$

which gives our conclusion. □

It is known (see, for example, [9,31]) that the Bayes risk can also be tied directly to the total variation in the following special case, whose proof we include for completeness.

Proposition 6. *When $n = 2$ and $\lambda_1 = \lambda_2 = \frac{1}{2}$, the Bayes risk associated to the densities p_1 and p_2 satisfies*

$$2R = 1 - |p_1 - p_2|_{TV} \tag{46}$$

Proof. Since $p_T = \frac{|p_1 - p_2| + p_1 + p_2}{2}$, integrating gives $\int_{\mathcal{X}} p_T(x) d\mu(x) = |p_1 - p_2|_{TV} + 1$ from which the equality follows. □

Information theoretic bounds to control the Bayes and minimax risk have an extensive literature (see, for example, [9,32–35]). Fano's inequality is the seminal result in this direction, and we direct the reader to a survey of such techniques in statistical estimation (see [36]). What follows can be understood as a sharpening of the work of Guntuboyina [9] under the assumption of a κ-convexity.

The function $T(x) = \arg\max_i \{\lambda_i p_i(x)\}$ induces the following convex decompositions of our densities. The density q can be realized as a convex combination of $q_1 = \frac{\lambda_T q}{1-Q}$ where $Q = 1 - \int \lambda_T q d\mu$ and $q_2 = \frac{(1-\lambda_T)q}{Q}$,

$$q = (1-Q)q_1 + Qq_2.$$

If we take $p := \sum_i \lambda_i p_i$, then p can be decomposed as $\rho_1 = \frac{\lambda_T p_T}{1-R}$ and $\rho_2 = \frac{p - \lambda_T p_T}{R}$ so that

$$p = (1-R)\rho_1 + R\rho_2.$$

Theorem 8. *When f is κ-convex, on (a,b) with $a = \inf_{i,x} \frac{p_i(x)}{q(x)}$ and $b = \sup_{i,x} \frac{p_i(x)}{q(x)}$*

$$\sum_i \lambda_i D_f(p_i \| q) \geq D_f(R \| Q) + \frac{\kappa W}{2}$$

where

$$W := W(\lambda_i, p_i, q) := \frac{(1-R)^2}{1-Q} \chi^2(\rho_1 \| q_1) + \frac{R^2}{Q} \chi^2(\rho_2 \| q_2) + W_0$$

for $W_0 \geq 0$.

W_0 can be expressed explicitly as

$$W_0 = \int (1-\lambda_T) Var_{\lambda_i \neq T}\left(\frac{p_i}{q}\right) d\mu = \int \sum_{i \neq T} \lambda_i \frac{|p_i - \sum_{j \neq T} \frac{\lambda_j}{1-\lambda_T} p_j|^2}{q} d\mu,$$

where for fixed x, we consider the variance $Var_{\lambda_i \neq T}\left(\frac{p_i}{q}\right)$ to be the variance of a random variable taking values $p_i(x)/q(x)$ with probability $\lambda_i/(1-\lambda_{T(x)})$ for $i \neq T(x)$. Note this term is a non-zero term only when $n > 2$.

Proof. For a fixed x, we apply Lemma 1

$$\sum_i \lambda_i f\left(\frac{p_i}{q}\right) = \lambda_T f\left(\frac{p_T}{q}\right) + (1-\lambda_T) \sum_{i \neq T} \frac{\lambda_i}{1-\lambda_T} f\left(\frac{p_i}{q}\right)$$

$$\geq \lambda_T f\left(\frac{p_T}{q}\right) + (1-\lambda_T) \left[f\left(\frac{p - \lambda_T p_T}{q(1-\lambda_T)}\right) + \frac{\kappa}{2} Var_{\lambda_i \neq T}\left(\frac{p_i}{q}\right)\right] \quad (47)$$

Integrating,

$$\sum_i \lambda_i D_f(p_i || q) \geq \int \lambda_T f\left(\frac{p_T}{q}\right) q + \int (1-\lambda_T) f\left(\frac{-\lambda_T p_T + \sum_i \lambda_i p_i}{q(1-\lambda_T)}\right) q + \frac{\kappa}{2} W_0, \quad (48)$$

where

$$W_0 = \int \sum_{i \neq T(x)} \frac{\lambda_i}{1-\lambda_T(x)} \frac{|p_i - \sum_{j \neq T} \frac{\lambda_j}{1-\lambda_T} p_j|^2}{q} d\mu. \quad (49)$$

Applying the κ-convexity of f,

$$\int \lambda_T f\left(\frac{p_T}{q}\right) q = (1-Q) \int q_1 f\left(\frac{p_T}{q}\right)$$

$$\geq (1-Q) \left(f\left(\frac{\int \lambda_T p_T}{1-Q}\right) + \frac{\kappa}{2} Var_{q_1}\left(\frac{p_T}{q}\right)\right) \quad (50)$$

$$= (1-Q)f((1-R)/(1-Q)) + \frac{Q\kappa}{2} W_1,$$

with

$$W_1 := Var_{q_1}\left(\frac{p_T}{q}\right)$$

$$= \left(\frac{1-R}{1-Q}\right)^2 Var_{q_1}\left(\frac{\lambda_T p_T}{\lambda_T q} \frac{1-Q}{1-R}\right)$$

$$= \left(\frac{1-R}{1-Q}\right)^2 Var_{q_1}\left(\frac{p_1}{q_1}\right) \quad (51)$$

$$= \left(\frac{1-R}{1-Q}\right)^2 \chi^2(p_1 || q_1)$$

Similarly,

$$\int (1-\lambda_T) f\left(\frac{p-\lambda_T p_T}{q(1-\lambda_T)}\right) q = Q\int q_2 f\left(\frac{p-\lambda_T p_T}{q(1-\lambda_T)}\right)$$
$$\geq Qf\left(\int q_2 \frac{p-\lambda_T p_T}{q(1-\lambda_T)}\right) + \frac{Q\kappa}{2}W_2 \quad (52)$$
$$= Qf\left(\frac{R}{1-Q}\right) + \frac{Q\kappa}{2}W_2$$

where

$$W_2 := \operatorname{Var}_{q_2}\left(\frac{p-\lambda_T p_T}{q(1-\lambda_T)}\right)$$
$$= \left(\frac{R}{Q}\right)^2 \operatorname{Var}_{q_2}\left(\frac{p-\lambda_T p_T}{q(1-\lambda_T)}\frac{Q}{R}\right)$$
$$= \left(\frac{R}{Q}\right)^2 \operatorname{Var}_{q_2}\left(\frac{p-\lambda_T p_T}{q(1-\lambda_T)} - \frac{R}{Q}\right)^2 \quad (53)$$
$$= \left(\frac{R}{Q}\right)^2 \int q_2 \left(\frac{p_2}{q_2}-1\right)^2$$
$$= \left(\frac{R}{Q}\right)^2 \chi^2(p_2\|q_2)$$

Writing $W = W_0 + W_1 + W_2$, we have our result. □

Corollary 4. *When* $\lambda_i = \frac{1}{n}$, *and* f *is* κ-*convex on* $(\inf_{i,x} p_i/q, \sup_{i,x} p_i/q)$

$$\frac{1}{n}\sum_i D_f(p_i\|q)$$
$$\geq D_f(R\|(n-1)/n) + \frac{\kappa}{2}\left(n^2(1-R)^2\chi^2(\rho_1\|q) + \left(\frac{nR}{n-1}\right)^2\chi^2(\rho_2\|q) + W_0\right) \quad (54)$$

further when $n=2$,

$$\frac{D_f(p_1\|q) + D_f(p_2\|q)}{2} \geq D_f\left(\frac{1-|p_1-p_2|_{TV}}{2}\bigg\|\frac{1}{2}\right)$$
$$+ \frac{\kappa}{2}\left((1+|p_1-p_2|_{TV})^2\chi^2(\rho_1\|q) + (1-|p_1-p_2|_{TV})^2\chi^2(\rho_2\|q)\right). \quad (55)$$

Proof. Note that $q_1 = q_2 = q$, since $\lambda_i = \frac{1}{n}$ implies $\lambda_T = \frac{1}{n}$ as well. In addition, $Q = 1 - \int \lambda_T q d\mu = \frac{n-1}{n}$ so that applying Theorem 8 gives

$$\sum_{i=1}^n D_f(p_i\|q) \geq nD_f(R\|(n-1)/n) + \frac{\kappa n W(\lambda_i, p_i, q)}{2}. \quad (56)$$

The term W can be simplified as well. In the notation of the proof of Theorem 8,

$$W_1 = n^2(1-R)^2\chi^2(\rho_1,q)$$
$$W_2 = \left(\frac{nR}{n-1}\right)^2\chi^2(\rho_2||q) \tag{57}$$
$$W_0 = \int \frac{\frac{1}{n-1}\sum_{i\neq T}(p_i - \frac{1}{n-1}\sum_{j\neq T}p_j)^2}{q}d\mu.$$

For the special case, one needs only to recall $R = \frac{1-|p_1-p_2|_{TV}}{2}$ while inserting 2 for n. □

Corollary 5. *When $p_i \leq q/t^*$ for $t^* > 0$, and $f(x) = x\log x$*

$$\sum_i \lambda_i D(p_i||q) \geq D(R||Q) + \frac{t^* W(\lambda_i, p_i, q)}{2}$$

for $D(p_i||q)$ the relative entropy. In particular,

$$\sum_i \lambda_i D(p_i||q) \geq D(p||q) + D(R||P) + \frac{t^* W(\lambda_i, p_i, p)}{2}$$

where $P = 1 - \int \lambda_T p d\mu$ for $p = \sum_i \lambda_i p_i$ and $t^* = \min \lambda_i$.

Proof. For the relative entropy, $f(x) = x\log x$ is $\frac{1}{M}$-convex on $[0,M]$ since $f''(x) = 1/x$. When $p_i \leq q/t^*$ holds for all i, then we can apply Theorem 8 with $M = \frac{1}{t^*}$. For the second inequality, recall the compensation identity, $\sum_i \lambda_i D(p_i||q) = \sum_i \lambda_i D(p_i||p) + D(p||q)$, and apply the first inequality to $\sum_i D(p_i||p)$ for the result.
□

This gives an upper bound on the Jensen–Shannon divergence, defined as $JSD(\mu||\nu) = \frac{1}{2}D(\mu||\mu/2 + \nu/2) + \frac{1}{2}D(\nu||\mu/2 + \nu/2)$. Let us also note that through the compensation identity $\sum_i \lambda_i D(p_i||q) = \sum_i \lambda_i D(p_i||p) + D(p||q)$, $\sum_i \lambda_i D(p_i||q) \geq \sum_i \lambda_i D(p_i||p)$ where $p = \sum_i \lambda_i p_i$. In the case that $\lambda_i = \frac{1}{N}$,

$$\sum_i \lambda_i D(p_i||q)$$
$$\geq \sum_i \lambda_i D(p_i||p) \tag{58}$$
$$\geq Qf\left(\frac{1-R}{Q}\right) + (1-Q)f\left(\frac{R}{1-Q}\right) + \frac{t^* W}{2}$$

Corollary 6. *For two densities p_1 and p_2, the Jensen–Shannon divergence satisfies the following,*

$$JSD(p_1||p_2) \geq D\left(\frac{1-|p_1-p_2|_{TV}}{2}\bigg|\bigg|1/2\right)$$
$$+ \frac{1}{4}\left((1+|p_1-p_2|_{TV})^2\chi^2(\rho_1||p) + (1-|p_1-p_2|_{TV})^2\chi^2(\rho_2||p)\right) \tag{59}$$

with $\rho(i)$ defined above and $p = p_1/2 + p_2/2$.

Proof. Since $\frac{p_i}{(p_1+p_2)/2} \leq 2$ and $f(x) = x\log x$ satisfies $f''(x) \geq \frac{1}{2}$ on $(0,2)$. Taking $q = \frac{p_1+p_2}{2}$, in the $n = 2$ example of Corollary 4 with $\kappa = \frac{1}{2}$ yields the result. □

Note that $2D((1+V)/2||1/2) = (1+V)\log(1+V) + (1-V)\log(1-V) \geq V^2 \log e$, we see that a further bound,

$$\text{JSD}(p_1||p_2) \geq \frac{\log e}{2} V^2 + \frac{(1+V)^2 \chi^2(\rho_1||p) + (1-V)^2 \chi^2(\rho_2||p)}{4}, \tag{60}$$

can be obtained for $V = |p_1 - p_2|_{TV}$.

On Topsøe's Sharpening of Pinsker's Inequality

For P_i, Q probability measures with densities p_i and q with respect to a common reference measure, $\sum_{i=1}^{n} t_i = 1$, with $t_i > 0$, denote $P = \sum_i t_i P_i$, with density $p = \sum_i t_i p_i$, the compensation identity is

$$\sum_{i=1}^{n} t_i D(P_i||Q) = D(P||Q) + \sum_{i=1}^{n} t_i D(P_i||P). \tag{61}$$

Theorem 9. *For P_1 and P_2, denote $M_k = 2^{-k} P_1 + (1 - 2^{-k}) P_2$, and define*

$$\mathcal{M}_1(k) = \frac{M_k \mathbb{1}_{\{P_1 > P_2\}} + P_2 \mathbb{1}_{\{P_1 \leq P_2\}}}{M_k \{P_1 > P_2\} + P_2 \{P_1 \leq P_2\}} \qquad \mathcal{M}_2(k) = \frac{M_k \mathbb{1}_{\{P_1 \leq P_2\}} + P_2 \mathbb{1}_{\{P_1 > P_2\}}}{M_k \{P_1 \leq P_2\} + P_2 \{P_1 > P_2\}},$$

then the following sharpening of Pinsker's inequality can be derived,

$$D(P_1||P_2) \geq (2 \log e)|P_1 - P_2|_{TV}^2 + \sum_{k=0}^{\infty} 2^k \left(\frac{\chi^2(\mathcal{M}_1(k), M_{k+1})}{2} + \frac{\chi^2(\mathcal{M}_2(k), M_{k+1})}{2} \right).$$

Proof. When $n = 2$ and $t_1 = t_2 = \frac{1}{2}$, if we denote $M = \frac{P_1 + P_2}{2}$, then (61) reads as

$$\frac{1}{2} D(P_1||Q) + \frac{1}{2} D(P_2||Q) = D(M||Q) + \text{JSD}(P_1||P_2). \tag{62}$$

Taking $Q = P_2$, we arrive at

$$D(P_1||P_2) = 2D(M||P_2) + 2\text{JSD}(P_1||P_2) \tag{63}$$

Iterating and writing $M_k = 2^{-k} P_1 + (1 - 2^{-k}) P_2$, we have

$$D(P_1||P_2) = 2^n \left(D(M_n||P_2) + 2 \sum_{k=0}^{n} \text{JSD}(M_n||P_2) \right) \tag{64}$$

It can be shown (see [11]) that $2^n D(M_n||P_2) \to 0$ with $n \to \infty$, giving the following series representation,

$$D(P_1||P_2) = 2 \sum_{k=0}^{\infty} 2^k \text{JSD}(M_k||P_2). \tag{65}$$

Note that the ρ-decomposition of M_k is exactly $\rho_i = \mathcal{M}_k(i)$, thus, by Corollary 6,

$$D(P_1||P_2) = 2 \sum_{k=0}^{\infty} 2^k \text{JSD}(M_k||P_2)$$

$$\geq \sum_{k=0}^{\infty} 2^k \left(|M_k - P_2|_{TV}^2 \log e + \frac{\chi^2(\mathcal{M}_1(k), M_{k+1})}{2} + \frac{\chi^2(\mathcal{M}_2(k), M_{k+1})}{2} \right) \tag{66}$$

$$= (2 \log e)|P_1 - P_2|_{TV}^2 + \sum_{k=0}^{\infty} 2^k \left(\frac{\chi^2(\mathcal{M}_1(k), M_{k+1})}{2} + \frac{\chi^2(\mathcal{M}_2(k), M_{k+1})}{2} \right).$$

Thus, we arrive at the desired sharpening of Pinsker's inequality. □

Observe that the $k = 0$ term in the above series is equivalent to

$$2^0 \left(\frac{\chi^2(\mathcal{M}_1(0), M_{0+1})}{2} + \frac{\chi^2(\mathcal{M}_2(0), M_{0+1})}{2} \right) = \frac{\chi^2(\rho_1, p)}{2} + \frac{\chi^2(\rho_2, p)}{2}, \qquad (67)$$

where ρ_i is the convex decomposition of $p = \frac{p_1 + p_2}{2}$ in terms of $T(x) = \arg\max\{p_1(x), p_2(x)\}$.

5. Conclusions

In this article, we begin a systematic study of strongly convex divergences, and how the strength of convexity of a divergence generator f, quantified by the parameter κ, influences the behavior of the divergence D_f. We prove that every strongly convex divergence dominates the square of the total variation, extending the classical bound provided by the χ^2-divergence. We also study a general notion of a skew divergence, providing new bounds, in particular for the generalized skew divergence of Nielsen. Finally, we show how κ-convexity can be leveraged to yield improvements of Bayes risk f-divergence inequalities, and as a consequence achieve a sharpening of Pinsker's inequality.

Funding: This research was funded by NSF grant CNS 1809194.

Conflicts of Interest: The authors declare no conflict of interest.

Appendix A

Theorem A1. *The class of f-divergences is stable under skewing. That is, if f is convex, satisfying $f(1) = 0$, then*

$$\hat{f}(x) := (tx + (1-t)) f\left(\frac{rx + (1-r)}{tx + (1-t)} \right) \qquad (A1)$$

is convex with $\hat{f}(1) = 0$ as well.

Proof. If μ and ν have respective densities u and v with respect to a reference measure γ, then $r\mu + (1-r)\nu$ and $t\mu + 1 - t\nu$ have densities $ru + (1-r)v$ and $tu + (1-t)v$

$$S_{f,r,t}(\mu\|\nu) = \int f\left(\frac{ru + (1-r)v}{tu + (1-t)v} \right) (tu + (1-t)v) d\gamma \qquad (A2)$$

$$= \int f\left(\frac{r\frac{u}{v} + (1-r)}{t\frac{u}{v} + (1-t)} \right) (t\frac{u}{v} + (1-t)) v \, d\gamma \qquad (A3)$$

$$= \int \hat{f}\left(\frac{u}{v} \right) v \, d\gamma. \qquad (A4)$$

Since $\hat{f}(1) = f(1) = 0$, we need only prove $\hat{f}$ convex. For this, recall that the conic transform g of a convex function f defined by $g(x, y) = yf(x/y)$ for $y > 0$ is convex, since

$$\frac{y_1 + y_2}{2} f\left(\frac{x_1 + x_2}{2} \Big/ \frac{y_1 + y_2}{2} \right) = \frac{y_1 + y_2}{2} f\left(\frac{y_1}{y_1 + y_2} \frac{x_1}{y_1} + \frac{y_2}{y_1 + y_2} \frac{x_2}{y_2} \right) \qquad (A5)$$

$$\leq \frac{y_1}{2} f(x_1/y_1) + \frac{y_2}{2} f(x_2/y_2). \qquad (A6)$$

Our result follows since $\hat{f}$ is the composition of the affine function $A(x) = (rx + (1-r), tx + (1-t))$ with the conic transform of f,

$$\hat{f}(x) = g(A(x)). \qquad (A7)$$

□

References

1. Ali, S.M.; Silvey, S.D. A general class of coefficients of divergence of one distribution from another. *J. Roy. Statist. Soc. Ser. B* **1966**, *28*, 131–142. [CrossRef]
2. Morimoto, T. Markov processes and the H-theorem. *J. Phys. Soc. Jpn.* **1963**, *18*, 328–331. [CrossRef]
3. Csiszár, I. Eine informationstheoretische Ungleichung und ihre Anwendung auf den Beweis der Ergodizität von Markoffschen Ketten. *Magyar Tud. Akad. Mat. Kutató Int. Közl.* **1963**, *8*, 85–108.
4. Csiszár, I. Information-type measures of difference of probability distributions and indirect observation. *Stud. Sci. Math. Hung.* **1967**, *2*, 229–318.
5. Polyanskiy, Y.; Poor, H.V.; Verdú, S. Channel coding rate in the finite blocklength regime. *IEEE Trans. Inf. Theory* **2010**, *56*, 2307–2359. [CrossRef]
6. Sason, I.; Verdú, S. f-divergence inequalities. *IEEE Trans. Inf. Theory* **2016**, *62*, 5973–6006,. [CrossRef]
7. Polyanskiy, Y.; Wu, Y. Lecture Notes on Information Theory. Available online: http://people.lids.mit.edu/yp/homepage/data/itlectures_v5.pdf (accessed on 13 November 2019).
8. Sason, I. On data-processing and majorization inequalities for f-divergences with applications. *Entropy* **2019**, *21*, 1022. [CrossRef]
9. Guntuboyina, A. Lower bounds for the minimax risk using f-divergences, and applications. *IEEE Trans. Inf. Theory* **2011**, *57*, 2386–2399. [CrossRef]
10. Reid, M.; Williamson, R. Generalised Pinsker inequalities. *arXiv* **2009**, arXiv:0906.1244.
11. Topsøe, F. Some inequalities for information divergence and related measures of discrimination. *IEEE Trans. Inf. Theory* **2000**, *46*, 1602–1609. [CrossRef]
12. Lee, L. Measures of distributional similarity. In *Proceedings of the 37th Annual Meeting of the Association For Computational Linguistics on Computational Linguistics*; Association for Computational Linguistics: Stroudsburg, PA, USA, 1999; pp. 25–32 .
13. Le Cam, L. *Asymptotic Methods in Statistical Decision Theory*; Springer Series in Statistics; Springer: New York, NY, USA, 1986.
14. Vincze, I. On the concept and measure of information contained in an observation. *Contrib. Probab.* **1981**, 207–214. [CrossRef]
15. Györfi, L.; Vajda, I. A class of modified Pearson and Neyman statistics. *Stat. Decis.* **2001**, *19*, 239–251. [CrossRef]
16. Lin, J. Divergence measures based on the Shannon entropy. *IEEE Trans. Inf. Theory* **1991**, *37*, 145–151. [CrossRef]
17. Nielsen, F. On a generalization of the Jensen–Shannon divergence and the Jensen–Shannon centroid. *Entropy* **2020**, *22*, 221. [CrossRef]
18. Folland, G. *Real Analysis: Modern Techniques and Their Applications*; John Wiley & Sons: Hoboken, NJ, USA, 1999.
19. Gibbs, A.L.; Su, F.E. On choosing and bounding probability metrics. *Int. Stat. Rev.* **2002**, *70*, 419–435. [CrossRef]
20. Harremoës, P.; Vajda, I. On pairs of f-divergences and their joint range. *IEEE Trans. Inf. Theory* **2011**, *57*, 3230–3235. [CrossRef]
21. Reiss, R. *Approximate Distributions of Order Statistics: With Applications to Nonparametric Statistics*; Springer: Berlin/Heidelberg, Germany, 2012.
22. Nielsen, F.; Nock, R. On the chi square and higher-order chi distances for approximating f-divergences. *IEEE Signal Process. Lett.* **2013**, *21*, 10–13. [CrossRef]
23. Amari, S. *Information Geometry and Its Applications*; Springer: Berlin/Heidelberg, Germany, 2016; p. 194.
24. Basu, A.; Shioya, H.; Park, C. *Statistical Inference: The Minimum Distance Approach*; CRC Press: Boca Raton, FL, USA, 2011.
25. Vajda, I. On the f-divergence and singularity of probability measures. *Period. Math. Hung.* **1972**, *2*, 223–234. [CrossRef]
26. Melbourne, J.; Talukdar, S.; Bhaban, S.; Madiman, M.; Salapaka, M.V. The differential entropy of mixtures: new bounds and applications. *arXiv* **2020**, arXiv:1805.11257.
27. Erven, T.V.; Harremos, P. Rényi divergence and Kullback-Leibler divergence. *IEEE Trans. Inf. Theory* **2014**, *60*, 3797–3820. [CrossRef]

28. Audenaert, K.M.R. Quantum skew divergence. *J. Math. Phys.* **2014**, *55*, 112202. [CrossRef]
29. Melbourne, J.; Madiman, M.; Salapaka, M.V. Relationships between certain f-divergences. In Proceedings of the 2019 57th Annual Allerton Conference on Communication, Control, and Computing (Allerton), Monticello, IL, USA, 24–27 September 2019; pp. 1068–1073.
30. Nishiyama, T.; Sason, I. On relations between the relative entropy and χ^2-divergence, generalizations and applications. *Entropy* **2020**, *22*, 563. [CrossRef]
31. Nielsen, F. Generalized Bhattacharyya and Chernoff upper bounds on Bayes error using quasi-arithmetic means. *Pattern Recognit. Lett.* **2014**, *42*, 25–34. [CrossRef]
32. Birgé, L. A new lower bound for multiple hypothesis testing. *IEEE Trans. Inf. Theory* **2005**, *51*, 1611–1615. [CrossRef]
33. Chen, X.; Guntuboyina, A.; Zhang, Y. On Bayes risk lower bounds. *J. Mach. Learn. Res.* **2016**, *17*, 7687–7744.
34. Xu, A.; Raginsky, M. Information-theoretic lower bounds on Bayes risk in decentralized estimation. *IEEE Trans. Inf. Theory* **2016**, *63*, 1580–1600. [CrossRef]
35. Yang, Y.; Barron, A. Information-theoretic determination of minimax rates of convergence. *Ann. Statist.* **1999**, *27*, 1564–1599.
36. Scarlett, J.; Cevher, V. An introductory guide to Fano's inequality with applications in statistical estimation. *arXiv* **2019**, arXiv:1901.00555.

© 2020 by the authors. Licensee MDPI, Basel, Switzerland. This article is an open access article distributed under the terms and conditions of the Creative Commons Attribution (CC BY) license (http://creativecommons.org/licenses/by/4.0/).

Article

Minimum Divergence Estimators, Maximum Likelihood and the Generalized Bootstrap

Michel Broniatowski

Faculté de Mathématiques, Laboratoire de Probabilité, Statistique et Modélisation, Université Pierre et Marie Curie (Sorbonne Université), 4 Place Jussieu, CEDEX 05, 75252 Paris, France; michel.broniatowski@sorbonne-universite.fr

Abstract: This paper states that most commonly used minimum divergence estimators are MLEs for suited generalized bootstrapped sampling schemes. Optimality in the sense of Bahadur for associated tests of fit under such sampling is considered.

Keywords: statistical divergences; minimum divergence estimator; maximum likelihood; bootstrap; conditional limit theorem; Bahadur efficiency

1. Motivation and Context

Divergences between probability measures are widely used in statistics and data science in order to perform inference under models of various kinds; parametric or semi-parametric, or even in non-parametric settings. The corresponding methods extend the likelihood paradigm and insert inference in some minimum "distance" framing, which provides a convenient description for the properties of the resulting estimators and tests, under the model or under misspecification. Furthermore, they pave the way to a large number of competitive methods, which allows to trade-off between efficiency and robustness, among other things. Many families of such divergences have been proposed, some of them stemming from classical statistics (such as the Chi-square divergence), while others have their origin in other fields, such as information theory. Some measures of discrepancy involve regularity of the corresponding probability measures while others seem to be restricted to measures on finite or countable spaces, at least when using them as inferential tools, henceforth in situations when the elements of a model have to be confronted with a dataset. The choice of a specific discrepancy measure in specific context is somehow arbitrary in many cases, although the resulting conclusion of the inference might differ accordingly, above all under misspecification.

The goal of this paper is explained shortly. The current literature on risks, seen from a statistical standpoint, has developed in two main directions, from basic definitions and principles, following the seminal papers [1,2].

A first stream of papers aims to describe classes of discrepancy indices (divergences) associated with invariance under classes of transformations and similar properties; see [3–5] for a review.

The second flow aims at making use of these indices for practical purposes under various models, from parametric models to semi-parametric ones, mostly. Also the literature in learning procedures makes extensive use of divergence-based risks, with a strong accent on the implementation issues. Following the standard approach, their properties are mainly considered under i.i.d. sampling, providing limit results, confidence areas, etc; see [6,7] and references therein for review and developments, and the monographs [8,9]. Also comparison among discrepancy indices are considered in terms of performances either under the model, or with respect to robustness (aiming at minimizing the role of outliers in the inference by providing estimators with redescending influence function), or

with respect to misspecification, hence focusing on the loss in estimation or testing with respect to the distance from the assumed model to the true one.

This literature, however, rarely considers the rationale for specific choices of indices in relation with the concepts which define statistics, such as the Bayesian paradigm or the maximum likelihood (ML) one; for a contribution in this direction for inference in models defined by linear constraints, see [10]. In [11], we could prove that minimum divergence estimators (in the class of the ones considered in the present paper) coincide with MLEs under i.i.d. sampling in regular exponential models (but need not, even in common models such as mixtures). Here it is proved that minimum divergence estimators are indeed MLEs under weighted sampling, instead of standard i.i.d. one, commonly met in bootstrap procedures which aim at providing finite sample properties of estimators through simulation.

This paper considers a specific class of divergences, which contains most of the classical inferential tools, and which is indexed by a single scalar parameter. This class of divergences belongs to the Csiszar-Ali-Silvey-Arimoto family of divergences (see [4]), and is usually referred to as the power divergence class, which has been considered by Cressie and Read [12]; however this denomination is also shared by other discrepancy measures of some different nature [13]. We will use the acronym CR for the class of divergences under consideration in this paper.

Section 2 recalls that the MLE is obtained as a proxy of the minimizer of the Kullback-Leibler divergence between the generic law of the observed variable and the model, which is the large deviation limit for the empirical distribution. This limit statement is nothing but the continuation of the classical ML paradigm, namely to make the dataset more "probable" under the fitted distribution in the model, or, equivalently, to fit the most "likely" distribution in the model to the dataset.

Section 3 states that given a divergence pseudo distance ϕ in CR the Minimum Divergence Estimator (MDE) is obtained as a proxy of the minimizer of the large deviation limit for some bootstrap version of the empirical distribution, which establishes that the MDE is MLE for bootstrapped samples defined in relation with the divergence. This fact is based on the strong relation which associates to any CR ϕ-divergence a specific RV W (see Section 1.1.2); this link is the cornerstone for the interpretation of the minimum ϕ-divergence estimators as MLEs for specific bootstrapped sampling schemes where W has a prominent rôle. Some specific remark explores the link between MDE and MLE in exponential families. As a by product, we also introduce a bootstrapped estimator of the divergence pseudo-distance ϕ between the distribution of the data and the model.

In Section 4, we specify the bootstrapped estimator of the divergence which can be used in order to perform an optimal test of fit. Due to the type of asymptotics handled in this paper, optimality is studied in terms of Bahadur efficiency. It is shown that tests of fit based on such estimators enjoy Bahadur optimality with respect to other bootstrap plans when the bootstrap is performed under the distribution associated with the divergence criterion itself.

The discussion held in this paper pertains to parametric estimation in a model $\mathcal{P}_\Theta$ whose elements P_θ are probability measures defined on the same finite space $\mathcal{Y} := \{d_1, \ldots, d_K\}$, and $\theta \in \Theta$ is an index space; we assume identifiability, namely different values of θ induce different probability laws P_θ's. Also all the entries of P_θ will be positive for all θ in Θ.

1.1. Notation

1.1.1. Divergences

We consider regular *divergence functions* φ which are non negative convex functions with values in $\overline{\mathbb{R}^+}$ which belong to $C^2(\mathbb{R})$ and satisfy $\varphi(1) = \varphi'(1) = 0$ and $\varphi''(1) = 1$; see [3,4] for properties and extensions. An important class of such functions is defined through the power divergence functions

$$\varphi_\gamma(x) := \frac{x^\gamma - \gamma x + \gamma - 1}{\gamma(\gamma - 1)} \qquad (1)$$

defined for all real $\gamma \neq 0, 1$ with $\varphi_0(x) := -\log x + x - 1$ (the likelihood divergence function) and $\varphi_1(x) := x \log x - x + 1$ (the Kullback-Leibler divergence function). This class is usually referred to as the Cressie-Read family of divergence functions (see [12]). It is a very simple class of functions (with the limits in $\gamma \to 0, 1$) which allows to represent nearly all commonly used statistical criterions. Parametric inference in commonly met situations including continuous models or some non-regular models can be performed with them; see [6]. The L_1 divergence function $\varphi(x) := |x - 1|$ is not captured by the CR family of functions. When undefined the function φ is declared to assume value $+\infty$.

Associated with a divergence function φ, ϕ is the *divergence* between a probability measure and a finite signed measure; see [14].

For $P := (p_1, \ldots, p_K)$ and $Q := (q_1, \ldots, q_K)$ in $\mathbb{S}^K$, the simplex of all probability measures on $\mathcal{Y}$, define, whenever Q and P have non-null entries

$$\phi(Q, P) := \sum_{k=1}^{K} p_k \varphi\left(\frac{q_k}{p_k}\right).$$

Indexing this pseudo-distance by γ and using φ_γ as divergence function yields the Kullback-Leibler divergence $KL(Q, P) := \phi_1(Q, P) := \sum q_k \log\left(\frac{q_k}{p_k}\right)$, the likelihood or modified Kullback-Leibler divergence

$$KL_m(Q, P) := \phi_0(Q, P) := -\sum p_k \log\left(\frac{q_k}{p_k}\right),$$

the Hellinger divergence

$$\phi_{1/2}(Q, P) := \frac{1}{2} \sum p_k \left(\sqrt{\frac{q_k}{p_k}} - 1\right)^2,$$

the modified (or Neyman) χ^2 divergence

$$\chi_m^2(Q, P) := \phi_{-1}(Q, P) := \frac{1}{2} \sum p_k \left(\frac{q_k}{p_k} - 1\right)^2 \left(\frac{q_k}{p_k}\right)^{-1}.$$

The χ^2 divergence

$$\phi_2(Q, P) := \frac{1}{2} \sum p_k \left(\frac{q_k}{p_k} - 1\right)^2$$

is defined between signed measures; see [15] for definitions in more general setting, and [6] for the advantage to extend the definition to possibly signed measures in the context of parametric inference for non-regular models. Also the present discussion which is restricted to finite spaces $\mathcal{Y}$ can be extended to general spaces.

The conjugate divergence function of φ is defined through

$$\widetilde{\varphi}(x) := x\varphi\left(\frac{1}{x}\right) \qquad (2)$$

and the corresponding divergence $\widetilde{\phi}(P, Q)$ is

$$\widetilde{\phi}(P, Q) := \sum_{k=1}^{K} q_k \widetilde{\varphi}\left(\frac{p_k}{q_k}\right)$$

which satisfies

$$\widetilde{\phi}(P, Q) = \phi(Q, P)$$

whenever defined, and equals $+\infty$ otherwise. When $\varphi = \varphi_\gamma$ then $\widetilde{\varphi} = \varphi_{1-\gamma}$ as follows by substitution. Pairs $(\varphi_\gamma, \varphi_{1-\gamma})$ are therefore *conjugate pairs*. Inside the Cressie-Read family, the Hellinger divergence function is self-conjugate.

For $P = P_\theta$ and $Q \in \mathbb{S}^K$ we denote $\phi(Q, P)$ by $\phi(Q, \theta)$ (resp $\phi(\theta, Q)$, or $\phi(\theta', \theta)$, etc. according to the context).

1.1.2. Weights

This paragraph introduces the special link which connects CR divergences with specific random variables, which we call weights. Those will be associated to the dataset and define what is usually referred to as a generalized bootstrap procedure. This is the setting which allows for an interpretation of the MDE's as generalized bootstrapped MLEs.

For a given real valued random variable (RV) W denote

$$M(t) := \log E[\exp(tW)] \quad (3)$$

its cumulant generating function which we assume to be finite in a non-void open neighborhood of 0. The Fenchel Legendre transform of M (also called the Chernoff function) is defined through

$$\varphi^W(x) = M^*(x) := \sup_t (tx - M(t)). \quad (4)$$

The function $x \to \varphi^W(x)$ is non-negative, is C^∞ and convex. We also assume that $EW = 1$ together with $VarW = 1$ which implies $\varphi^W(1) = (\varphi^W)'(1) = 0$ and $(\varphi^W)''(1) = 1$. Hence $\varphi^W(x)$ is a divergence function with corresponding divergence ϕ^W. Associated with φ^W is the conjugate divergence $\phi^{\widetilde{W}}$ with divergence function $\widetilde{\varphi^W}$, which therefore satisfies $\phi^W(Q, P) = \phi^{\widetilde{W}}(P, Q)$ whenever neither P nor Q have null entries.

It is of interest to note that the classical power divergences φ_γ can be represented through (4) for $\gamma \le 1$ or $\gamma \ge 2$. A first proof of this lays in the fact that when W has a distribution in a Natural Exponential Family (NEF) with power variance function with exponent $\alpha = 2 - \gamma$, then the Legendre transform φ^W of its cumulant generating function M is indeed of the form (1). See [16,17] for NEF's and power variance functions, and [18] for relation to the bootstrap. A general result of a different nature, including the former ones, can be seen in [19], Theorem 20. Correspondence between the various values of γ and the distribution of the respective weights can be found in [19], Example 39, and it can be summarized as presented now.

For $\gamma < 0$ the RV W is constructed as follows: Let Z be an auxiliary RV with density f_Z and support $[0, \infty)$ of a stable law with parameter triplet $\left(-\frac{\gamma}{1-\gamma}, 0, \frac{(1-\gamma)^{-\gamma/(1-\gamma)}}{\gamma}\right)$ in terms of the "form B notation" on p 12 in [20]; then W has an absolutely continuous distribution with density

$$f_W(y) := \frac{\exp(-y/(1-\gamma))}{\exp(1/\gamma)} f_Z(y) 1_{[0,\infty)}(y).$$

For $\gamma = 0$ (which amounts to consider the limit as $\gamma \to 0$ in (1)) then W has a standard exponential distribution $E(1)$ on $[0, \infty)$.

For $\gamma \in (0, 1)$ then W has a compound Gamma-Poisson distribution

$$C(POI(\theta), GAM(\alpha, \beta))$$

where

$$\theta = \frac{1}{\gamma}, \alpha = \frac{1}{1-\gamma}, \beta = \frac{\gamma}{1-\gamma}.$$

For $\gamma = 1$, W has a Poisson distribution with parameter 1, $POI(1)$.
For $\gamma = 2$, the RV W has normal distribution with expectation and variance equal to 1.

For $\gamma > 2$, the RV W is constructed as follows: Let Z be an auxiliary RV with density f_Z and support $(-\infty, \infty)$ of a stable law with parameter triplet $\left(\frac{\gamma}{\gamma-1}, 0, \frac{(\gamma-1)^{-\gamma/(\gamma-1)}}{\gamma}\right)$ in terms of the "form B notation" on p 12 in [20]; then W has an absolutely continuous distribution with density

$$f_W(y) := \frac{\exp(y/(\gamma-1))}{\exp(1/\gamma)} f_Z(-y), \quad y \in \mathbb{R}.$$

2. Maximum Likelihood under Finitely Supported Distributions and Simple Sampling

2.1. Standard Derivation

Let $X_1, \ldots X_n$ be a set of n independent random variables with common probability measure P_{θ_T} and consider the Maximum Likelihood estimator of θ_T. A common way to define the ML paradigm is as follows: For any θ consider independent random variables $(X_{1,\theta}, \ldots X_{n,\theta})$ with probability measure P_θ, thus *sampled in the same way as the X_i's, but under some alternative θ*.

Denote

$$P_n := \frac{1}{n}\sum_{i=1}^n \delta_{X_i}$$

and

$$P_{n,\theta} := \frac{1}{n}\sum_{i=1}^n \delta_{X_{i,\theta}}$$

the empirical measures pertaining respectively to $(X_1, \ldots X_n)$ and $(X_{1,\theta}, \ldots X_{n,\theta})$.

Define θ_{ML} as the value of the parameter θ for which the probability that, up to a permutation of the order of the $X_{i,\theta}$'s, the probability that $(X_{1,\theta}, \ldots X_{n,\theta})$ coincides with $X_1, \ldots X_n$ is maximal, conditionally on the observed sample $X_1, \ldots X_n$. In formula

$$\theta_{ML} := \arg\max_\theta P_\theta(P_{n,\theta} = P_n | P_n). \tag{5}$$

An explicit enumeration of the above expression $P_\theta(P_{n,\theta} = P_n | P_n)$ involves the quantities

$$n_j := card\{i : X_i = d_j\}$$

for $j = 1, \ldots, K$ and yields

$$P_\theta(P_{n,\theta} = P_{n,X} | P_{n,X}) = \frac{n! P_\theta(d_j)^{n_j}}{\prod_{j=1}^K n_j!} \tag{6}$$

as follows from the classical multinomial distribution. Optimizing on θ in (6) yields

$$\theta_{ML} = \arg\max_\theta \sum_{j=1}^K \frac{n_j}{n} \log P_\theta(d_j)$$

$$= \arg\max_\theta \frac{1}{n}\sum_{i=1}^n \log P_\theta(X_i).$$

It follows from direct evaluation that

$$\theta_{ML} = \arg\inf_\theta KL_m(P_\theta, P_n).$$

Introducing the Kullback-Leibler divergence $KL(P_n, P_\theta)$ it thus holds

$$\theta_{ML} = \arg\inf_\theta \widetilde{KL_m}(P_n, P_\theta) = \arg\inf_\theta KL(P_n, P_\theta).$$

We have recalled that minimizing the Kullback-Leibler divergence $KL(P_n, \theta)$ amounts to minimizing the Likelihood divergence $KL_m(\theta, P_n)$ and produces the ML estimate of θ_T.

2.2. Asymptotic Derivation

We assume that
$$\lim_{n \to \infty} P_n = P_{\theta_T} \quad \text{a.s.}$$

This holds for example when the X_i's are drawn as an i.i.d. sample with common law P_{θ_T} which we may assume in the present context. From an asymptotic standpoint, Kullback-Leibler divergence is related to the way P_n keeps away from P_θ when θ is not equal to the true value of the parameter θ_T generating the observations X_i's and is closely related with the type of sampling of the X_i's. In the present case, when i.i.d. sampling of the $X_{i,\theta}$'s under P_θ is performed, Sanov Large Deviation theorem leads to

$$\lim_{n \to \infty} \frac{1}{n} \log P_\theta(P_{n,\theta} = P_n | P_n) = -KL(\theta_T, \theta). \tag{7}$$

This result can easily be obtained from (6) using Stirling formula to handle the factorial terms and the law of large numbers which states that for all j's, n_j/n tends to $P_{\theta_T}(d_j)$ as n tends to infinity. We note that the MLE θ_{ML} is a proxy of the minimizer of the natural estimator θ_T of $KL(\theta_T, \theta)$ in θ, substituting the unknown measure generating the X_i's by its empirical counterpart P_n. Alternatively as will be used in the sequel, θ_{ML} minimizes upon θ the Likelihood divergence $KL_m(\theta, \theta_T)$ between P_θ and P_{θ_T} substituting the unknown measure P_{θ_T} generating the X_i's by its empirical counterpart P_n. Summarizing we have obtained:

The ML estimate can be obtained from a LDP statement as given in (7), optimizing in θ in the estimator of the LDP rate where the plug-in method of the empirical measure of the data is used instead of the unknown measure P_{θ_T}. Alternatively it holds

$$\theta_{ML} := \arg\min_\theta \widehat{KL_m}(\theta, \theta_T) \tag{8}$$

with
$$\widehat{KL_m}(\theta, \theta_T) := KL_m(\theta, P_n).$$

This principle will be kept throughout this paper: the estimator is defined as maximizing the probability that the simulated empirical measure be close to the empirical measure as observed on the sample, conditionally on it, following the same sampling scheme. This yields a maximum likelihood estimator, and its properties are then obtained when randomness is introduced as resulting from the sampling scheme.

3. Bootstrap and Weighted Sampling

The sampling scheme which we consider is commonly used in connection with the bootstrap and is referred to as the *weighted* or *generalized bootstrap*, sometimes called *wild bootstrap*, first introduced by Newton and Mason [21].

Let $X_1, \ldots, X_n$ with common distribution P on $\mathcal{Y} := \{d_1, \ldots, d_K\}$.

Consider a collection $W_1, \ldots, W_n$ of independent copies of W, whose distribution satisfies the conditions stated in Section 1. The weighted empirical measure P_n^W is defined through

$$P_n^W := \frac{1}{n} \sum_{i=1}^n W_i \delta_{X_i}.$$

This empirical measure need not be a probability measure, since its mass may not equal 1. Also it might not be positive, since the weights may take negative values. Therefore P_n^W can be identified with a random point in $\mathbb{R}^K$. The measure P_n^W converges almost surely to P when the weights W_i's satisfy the hypotheses stated in Section 1.

We also consider the normalized weighted empirical measure

$$\mathfrak{P}_n^W := \sum_{i=1}^n Z_i \delta_{X_i} \qquad (9)$$

where

$$Z_i := \frac{W_i}{\sum_{j=1}^n W_j} \qquad (10)$$

whenever $\sum_{j=1}^n W_j \neq 0$, and

$$\mathfrak{P}_n^W = \infty$$

when $\sum_{j=1}^n W_j = 0$, where $\mathfrak{P}_n^W = \infty$ means $\mathfrak{P}_n^W(d_k) = \infty$ for all d_k in $\mathcal{Y}$.

3.1. A Conditional Sanov Type Result for the Weighted Empirical Measure

We now state a conditional Sanov type result for the family of random measures $\mathfrak{P}_n^W$. It follows readily from a companion result pertaining to P_n^W and enjoys a simple form when the weights W_i are associated to power divergences, as defined in Section 1.1.2. We quote the following results, referring to [19].

Consider a set Ω in $\mathbb{R}^K$ such that

$$cl\Omega = cl[\text{Int}(\Omega)] \qquad (11)$$

which amounts to a regularity assumption (obviously met when Ω is an open set), and which allows for the replacement of the usual lim inf and lim sup by standard limits in usual LDP statements. We denote by P^W the probability measure of the random family of i.i.d. weights W_i.

It then holds

Proposition 1 (Theorem 9 in [19]). *The weighted empirical measure P_n^W satisfies a conditional Large Deviation Principle in $\mathbb{R}^K$ namely, denoting P the a.s. limit of P_n,*

$$\lim_{n \to \infty} \frac{1}{n} \log P^W \left(P_n^W \in \Omega \big| X_1^n \right) = -\phi^W(\Omega, P)$$

where $\phi^W(\Omega, P) := \inf_{Q \in \Omega} \phi^W(Q, P)$.

As a direct consequence of the former result, it holds, for any $\Omega \subset \mathbb{S}^K$ satisfying (11), where $\mathbb{S}^K$ designates the simplex of all pm's on $\mathcal{Y}$.

Theorem 1 (Theorem 12 in [19]). *The normalized weighted empirical measure $\mathfrak{P}_n^W$ satisfies a conditional Large Deviation Principle in $\mathbb{S}^K$*

$$\lim_{n \to \infty} \frac{1}{n} \log P^W \left(\mathfrak{P}_n^W \in \Omega \big| X_1^n \right) = - \inf_{m \neq 0} \phi^W(m\Omega, P). \qquad (12)$$

A flavour of the simple proofs of Proposition 1 and Theorem 1 is presented in Appendix A; see [19] for a detailed treatment; see also Theorem 3.2 and Corollary 3.3 in [22] where Theorem 1 is proved in a more abstract setting.

We will be interested in the pm's in Ω which minimize the RHS in the above display. The case when ϕ^W is a power divergence, namely $\phi^W = \phi_\gamma$ for some γ enjoys a special property with respect to the pm's Q achieving the infimum (upon Q in Ω) in (12). It holds

Proposition 2 (Lemma 14 in [19]). *Assume that ϕ^W is a power divergence. Then*

$$Q \in \arg\inf \left\{ \inf_{m \neq 0} \phi^W(mQ, P), Q \in \Omega \right\}$$

and

$$Q \in \arg\inf \left\{ \phi^W(Q, P), Q \in \Omega \right\}$$

are equivalent statements.

Indeed Proposition 2 holds as a consequence of the following results, to be used later on.

Lemma 1. *For Q and P two pm's such that the involved expressions are finite, it holds*
(i) *For $\gamma \neq 0$ and $\gamma \neq 1$ it holds that*

$$\inf_{m \neq 0} \phi_\gamma(mQ, P) = \frac{1}{\gamma} \left[1 - (1 + \gamma(\gamma - 1)\phi_\gamma(Q, P))^{-1/(\gamma - 1)} \right].$$

(ii) $\inf_{m \neq 0} \phi_1(mQ, P) = 1 - \exp(-KL(Q, P)) = 1 - \exp(-\phi_1(Q, P))$.
(iii) $\inf_{m \neq 0} \phi_0(mQ, P) = KL_m(Q, P) = \phi_0(Q, P)$

In the case where W is a RV with standard exponential distribution, then a link between the present approach and Bayesian inference can be drawn, since the normalized weighted empirical measure $\mathfrak{P}_n^W$ is a realization of the a posteriori distribution for the Dirichlet prior on the non parametric distribution of X. See [23].

The weighted empirical measure P_n^W has been used in the weighted bootstrap (or wild bootstrap) context, although it is not a pm. However, conditionally upon the sample points, its produces statistical estimators $T(P_n^W)$ whose weak behavior (conditionally upon the sample) converges to the same limit as does $T(P_n)$ when normalized on the classical CLT range; see eg Newton and Mason [21]. Large deviation theorem for the weighted empirical measure P_n^W has been obtained by [24]; for other contributions in line with those, see [22,25]. Normalizing the weights produces families of exchangeable weights Z_i, and the normalized weighted empirical measure $\mathfrak{P}_n^W$ is the cornerstone for the so-called non-parametric Bayesian bootstrap, initiated by [23], and further developed by [26] among others. Note however that in this context the RV's W_i's are chosen distributed as standard exponential variables. The link with spacings from a uniform distribution and the corresponding reproducibility of the Dirichlet distributions are the basic ingredients which justify the non parametric bootstrap approach; in the present context, the choice of the distribution of the W_i's is a natural extension of this paradigm, at least when those W_i's are positive RV's.

3.2. Maximum Likelihood for the Generalized Bootstrap

Let's turn back to the estimation of θ_T, assuming P_{θ_T} the common distribution of the independent observations $X_1, \ldots, X_n$. We will consider maximum likelihood in the same spirit as developed in Section 2.2, here in the context of the normalized weighted empirical measure; it amounts to justify minimum divergence estimators as appropriate MLEs under such bootstrap procedure.

We thus consider the same statistical model $\mathcal{P}_\Theta$ and keep in mind the ML principle as seen as resulting from a maximization of the conditional probability of getting simulated observations close to the initially observed data. Similarly as in Section 2 fix an arbitrary θ and simulate $X_{1,\theta}, \ldots, X_{n,\theta}$ with distribution P_θ. Define accordingly $P_{n,\theta}^W$ and $\mathfrak{P}_{n,\theta}^W$ making use of i.i.d. RV's $W_1, \ldots, W_n$. Now the event $\mathfrak{P}_{n,\theta}^W(k) = n_k/n$ has probability 0 in most cases (for example when W has a continuous distribution), and therefore we are led to consider events of the form $\mathfrak{P}_{n,\theta}^W \in V_\varepsilon(P_n)$, meaning $\max_k \left| \mathfrak{P}_{n,\theta}^W(d_k) - P_n(d_k) \right| \leq \varepsilon$ for some $\varepsilon > 0$; notice that $V_\varepsilon(P_n)$ defined through

$$V_\varepsilon(P_n) := \left\{ Q \in \mathbb{S}^K : \max_k |Q(d_k) - P_n(d_k)| \leq \varepsilon \right\}$$

has non-void interior.

For such a configuration consider

$$P^W \left(\mathfrak{P}_{n,\theta}^w \in V_\varepsilon(P_n) | X_{1,\theta}, \ldots, X_{n,\theta}, P_n \right) \tag{13}$$

where the $X_{i,\theta}$ are randomly drawn i.i.d. under P_θ. Obviously for θ far away from θ_T the sample $(X_{1,\theta}, \ldots, X_{n,\theta})$ is realized "far away" from $(X_1, \ldots, X_n)$, which has been generated under the truth, namely P_{θ_T}, and the probability in (13) is small, whatever the weights, for small ε.

We will now consider (13) for large n, since, in contrast with the first derivation of the standard MLE in Section 2.1, we cannot perform the same calculation for each n, which was based on multinomial counts. Note that we obtained a justification for the usual MLE through the asymptotic Sanov LDP, leading to the KL divergence and finally back to the MLE through an approximation step of this latest. From Theorem 12 together with the a.s. convergence of P_n to P_{θ_T} in $\mathbb{S}^K$ it follows that for some $\alpha < 1 < \beta$

$$- \inf_{m \neq 0} \phi^W(mV_{\alpha\varepsilon}(P_{\theta_T}), \theta) \tag{14}$$

$$\leq \lim_{n \to \infty} \frac{1}{n} \log P^W \left(\mathfrak{P}_{n,\theta}^W \in V_\varepsilon(P_n) | X_{1,\theta}, \ldots, X_{n,\theta}, P_n \right)$$

$$\leq - \inf_{m \neq 0} \phi^W(mV_{\beta\varepsilon}(P_{\theta_T}), \theta)$$

where $\phi^W(V_{c\varepsilon}(\theta_T), \theta) = \inf_{\mu \in V_{c\varepsilon}(P_{\theta_T})} \phi^W(\mu, \theta)$.

As $\varepsilon \to 0$, by continuity it holds that

$$\lim_{\varepsilon \to 0} \lim_{n \to \infty} \frac{1}{n} \log P^W \left(\mathfrak{P}_{n,\theta}^W \in V_\varepsilon(P_n) | X_{1,\theta}, \ldots, X_{n,\theta}, P_n \right) \tag{15}$$

$$= - \inf_{m \neq 0} \phi^W(mP_{\theta_T}, \theta).$$

The ML principle amounts to maximize

$$P^W \left(\mathfrak{P}_{n,\theta}^W \in V_\varepsilon(P_n) | X_{1,\theta}, \ldots, X_{n,\theta}, P_n \right) \tag{16}$$

over θ. Whenever Θ is a compact set we may insert this optimization in (14) which yields, following (15)

$$\lim_{\varepsilon \to 0} \lim_{n \to \infty} \frac{1}{n} \log \sup_\theta P^W \left(\mathfrak{P}_{n,\theta}^W \in V_\varepsilon(P_n) | X_{1,\theta}, \ldots, X_{n,\theta}, P_n \right)$$

$$= - \inf_{\theta \in \Theta} \inf_{m \neq 0} \phi^W(mP_{\theta_T}, \theta).$$

We consider weights W's such that there exists a power divergence function φ_γ satisfying (4), which amounts to $\phi^W = \phi_\gamma$; by the results quoted in Section 1.1.2 this holds when $\gamma \in (-\infty, 1] \cup [2, +\infty)$.

By Proposition 2 the argument of the infimum upon θ in the RHS of the above display coincides with the corresponding argument of $\phi^W(\theta_T, \theta)$, which obviously gets θ_T. This justifies to consider a proxy of this minimization problem as a "ML" estimator based on normalized weighted data.

A further interpretation of the MDE in the context of non-parametric Bayesian procedures may also be proposed; this is postponed to a next paper.

Since
$$\phi^W(\theta_T, \theta) = \widetilde{\phi}^W(\theta, \theta_T)$$
the ML estimator is obtained as in the conventional case by plug in the LDP rate. Obviously the "best" plug in consists in the substitution of P_{θ_T} by P_n, the empirical measure of the sample, since P_n achieves the best rate of convergence to P_{θ_T} when confronted to any bootstrapped version, which adds "noise" to the sampling. We may therefore call

$$\theta_{ML}^W := \arg\inf_{\theta \in \Theta} \widetilde{\phi}^W(\theta, P_n) := \arg\inf_{\theta \in \Theta} \sum_{k=1}^K P_n(d_k) \widetilde{\varphi}^W\left(\frac{P_\theta(d_k)}{P_n(d_k)}\right) \qquad (17)$$
$$= \arg\inf_{\theta \in \Theta} \sum_{k=1}^K P_\theta(d_k) \varphi^W\left(\frac{P_n(d_k)}{P_\theta(d_k)}\right)$$

the MLE for the bootstrap sampling; here $\widetilde{\phi}^W$ (with divergence function $\widetilde{\varphi}$) is the conjugate divergence of ϕ^W (with divergence function φ). Since $\phi^W = \phi_\gamma$ for some γ, it holds $\widetilde{\phi}^W = \phi_{1-\gamma}$.

We can also plug in the normalized weighted empirical measure, which also is a proxy of P_{θ_T} for each run of the weights. This produces a bootstrap estimate of θ_T through

$$\theta_B^W := \arg\inf_{\theta \in \Theta} \widetilde{\phi}^W(\theta, \mathfrak{P}_n^W) := \arg\inf_{\theta \in \Theta} \sum_{k=1}^K \mathfrak{P}_n^W(d_k) \widetilde{\varphi}^W\left(\frac{P_\theta(d_k)}{\mathfrak{P}_n^W(d_k)}\right) \qquad (18)$$
$$= \arg\inf_{\theta \in \Theta} \sum_{k=1}^K P_\theta(d_k) \varphi^W\left(\frac{\mathfrak{P}_n^W(d_k)}{P_\theta(d_k)}\right)$$

where $\mathfrak{P}_n^W$ is defined in (9), assuming n large enough such that the sum of the W_i's is not zero. Whenever $P(W=0) > 0$, these estimators are defined for large n in order that $\mathfrak{P}_n^W(d_k)$ be positive for all k. Since $E(W) = 1$, this occurs for large samples.

For a given weighted bootstrapped sample with weights $W_1, \ldots, W_n$ leading to the weighted normalized empirical measure $\mathfrak{P}_n^W$, θ_B^W is the MLE in the sense of (16), hence defined as a proxy of the maximizer of

$$P^{W'}\left(\mathfrak{P}_{n,\theta}^{W'} \in V_\epsilon(\mathfrak{P}_n^W) | X_{1,\theta}, \ldots, X_{n,\theta}, \mathfrak{P}_n^W\right)$$

where the vector $(W_1', \ldots, W_n')$ is an independent copy of $(W, \ldots, W_n)$. This estimator usually differs from the bootstrapped version of the MLE based on P_n (see (8)) which is defined for n large enough through

$$\theta_{ML}^B := \arg\inf_\theta KL_m(\theta, \mathfrak{P}_n^W).$$

When $\mathcal{Y}$ is not a finite space then an equivalent construction can be developed based on the variational form of the divergence; see [6].

Remark 1. *We may also consider cases when the MLE defined through θ_{ML}^W defined in (17) coincide with the standard MLE θ_{ML} under i.i.d. sampling, and when its bootstrapped counterparts θ_B^W defined in (18) coincides with the bootstrapped standard MLE θ_{ML}^b defined through the likelihood estimating equation where the factor $1/n$ is substituted by the weight Z_j. It is proved in Theorem 5 of [11] that whenever $\mathcal{P}_\Theta$ is an exponential family with natural parametrization $\theta \in \mathbb{R}^d$ and sufficient statistics T*

$$P_\theta(d_j) = \exp\left[T(d_j)'\theta - C(\theta)\right], \quad 1 \leq j \leq K$$

where the Hessian matrix of $C(\theta)$ is definite positive, then for all divergence pseudo distance ϕ satisfying regularity conditions (including therefore the present cases), θ_{ML}^W equals θ_{ML}, the classical MLE in $\mathcal{P}_\Theta$ defined as the solution of the normal equation

$$\frac{1}{n}\sum T(X_i) = \nabla C(\theta_{ML})$$

irrespectively upon ϕ. Therefore on regular exponential families, and under i.i.d. sampling, all minimum divergence estimators coincide with the MLE (which is indeed one of them). The proof of this result is based on the variational form of the estimated divergence $Q \to \phi(Q, P)$, which coincides with the plug in version in (17) when the common support of all distributions in $\mathcal{P}_\Theta$ is finite. Following verbatim the proof of Theorem 5 in [11] substituting P_n by $\mathfrak{P}_n^W$ it results that θ_B^W equals the weighted MLE (standard generalized bootstrapped MLE θ_{ML}^b) defined through the normal equation

$$\sum_{i=1}^n Z_i T(X_i) = \nabla C(\theta_{ML}^b),$$

where the Z_i's are defined in (10). This fact holds for any choice of the weights, irrespectively on the choice of the divergence function φ with the only restriction that it satisfies the mild conditions (RC) in [11]. It results that for those models any generalized bootstrapped MDE coincides with the corresponding standard bootstrapped MLE.

Example 1. *A-When W has a standard Poisson $POI(1)$ distribution then the resulting estimator is the minimum modified Kullback-Leibler one. which takes the usual weighted form of the standard generalized bootstrap MLE*

$$\theta_B^{POI(1)} := \arg\sup_\theta \sum_{k=1}^K \left(\frac{\sum_{i=1}^n W_i 1_k(X_i)}{\sum_{i=1}^n W_i}\right) \log P_\theta(k)$$

which is defined for n large enough. Also in this case θ_{ML}^W coincides with the standard MLE.

B-If W has an Inverse Gaussian distribution IG(1,1) then $\varphi(x) = \varphi_{-1}(x) = \frac{1}{2}(x-1)^2/x$ for $x > 0$ and the ML estimator minimizes the Pearson Chi-square divergence with generator function $\varphi_2(x) = \frac{1}{2}(x-1)^2$ which is defined on $\mathbb{R}$.

C-If W follows a normal distribution with expectation and variance 1, then the resulting divergence is the Pearson Chi-square divergence $\varphi_2(x)$ and the resulting estimator minimizes the Neyman Chi-square divergence with $\varphi(x) = \varphi_{-1}(x)$.

D-When W has a Compound Poisson Gamma distribution $C(POI(2), \Gamma(2,1))$ distribution then the corresponding divergence is $\varphi_{1/2}(x) = 2(\sqrt{x}-1)^2$ which is self conjugate, whence the ML estimator is the minimum Hellinger distance one.

4. Bahadur Efficiency of Minimum Divergence Tests under Generalized Bootstrap

In [27] Efron and Tibshirani suggest the bootstrap as a valuable approach for testing, based on bootstrapped samples. We show that bootstrap testing for parametric models based on appropriate divergence statistics enjoys maximal Bahadur efficiency with respect to any bootstrap test statistics.

The standard approach to Bahadur efficiency can be adapted for the present generalized Bootstrapped tests as follows.

Consider the test of some null hypothesis H0: $\theta_T = \theta$ versus a simple Hypothesis H1 $\theta_T = \theta'$.

We consider two competitive statistics for this problem. The first one is based on the bootstrap estimate of $\widetilde{\phi}^W(\theta, \theta_T)$ and

$$T_{n,X} := \widetilde{\Phi}\left(\theta, \mathfrak{P}_{n,X}^W\right) = T\left(\mathfrak{P}_{n,X}^W\right)$$

which allows to reject H0 for large values since $\lim_{n\to\infty} T_{n,X} = 0$ whenever H0 holds. In the above display we have emphasized in $\mathfrak{P}_{n,X}^W$ the fact that we have used the RV X_i's. Let

$$L_n(t) := P^W(T_{n,X} > t | X_1, \ldots, X_n).$$

We use P^W to emphasize that the hazard is due to the weights. Consider now a set of RVs $Z_1, \ldots, Z_n$ extracted from a sequence such that

$$\lim_{n\to\infty} P_{n,Z} = P_{\theta'}$$

a.s; we have denoted $P_{n,Z}$ the empirical measure of $(Z_1, \ldots, Z_n)$; accordingly define $\mathfrak{P}_{n,Z}^{W'}$, the normalized weighted empirical measure of the Z_i's making use of weights $(W_1', \ldots, W_n')$ which are i.i.d. copies of $(W_1, \ldots, W_n)$, drawn independently from $(W_1, \ldots, W_n)$. Define accordingly

$$T_{n,Z} := \widetilde{\Phi}\left(\theta, \mathfrak{P}_{n,Z}^{W'}\right) = T\left(\mathfrak{P}_{n,Z}^{W'}\right).$$

Define

$$L_n(T_{n,Z}) := P^W(T_{n,W} > T_{n,Z} | X_1, \ldots, X_n)$$

which is a RV (as a function of $T_{n,Z}$). It holds

$$\lim_{n\to\infty} T_{n,Z} = \widetilde{\Phi}(\theta, \theta') \quad \text{a.s}$$

and therefore the Bahadur slope for the test with statistics T_n is $\Phi(\theta', \theta)$ as follows from

$$\lim_{n\to\infty} \frac{1}{n} \log L_n(T_{n,Z}) = -\inf\{\Phi(Q, \theta_T) : \widetilde{\Phi}(\theta, Q) > \widetilde{\Phi}(\theta, \theta')\}$$
$$= -\inf\{\Phi(Q, \theta_T) : \Phi(Q, \theta) > \Phi(\theta', \theta)\}$$
$$= -\Phi(\theta', \theta)$$

If $\theta_T = \theta$. Under H0 the rate of decay of the p-value corresponding to a sampling under H1 is captured through the divergence $\Phi(\theta', \theta)$.

Consider now a competitive test statistics $S\left(\mathfrak{P}_{n,X}^W\right)$ and evaluate its Bahadur slope. Similarly as above it holds, assuming continuity of the functional S on $\mathbb{S}^K$

$$\lim_{n\to\infty} \frac{1}{n} \log P^W\left(S\left(\mathfrak{P}_{n,X}^W\right) > S\left(\mathfrak{P}_{n,Z}^{W'}\right) \Big| X_1, \ldots, X_n\right)$$
$$= -\inf\{\Phi(Q, \theta_T) : S(Q) > S(\theta')\}$$
$$\geq -\Phi(\theta', \theta_T)$$

as follows from the continuity of $Q \to \Phi(Q, \theta_T)$. Hence the Bahadur slope of the test based on $S\left(\mathfrak{P}_{n,X}^W\right)$ is larger or equal $\Phi(\theta', \theta)$.

We have proved that the chances under H0 for the statistics $T_{n,X}$ to exceed a value obtained under H1 are (asymptotically) less that the corresponding chances associated with any other statistics based on the same bootstrapped sample; as such it is most specific on this scale with respect to any competing ones. Namely the following result holds:

Proposition 3. *Under the weighted sampling the test statistics $T\left(\mathfrak{P}_{n,X}^W\right)$ is the most efficient among all tests which are empirical versions of continuous functionals on $\mathbb{S}^K$.*

Funding: This research received no external funding.

Institutional Review Board Statement: Not applicable.

Informed Consent Statement: Not applicable.

Acknowledgments: The author thanks the Editor and two anonymous referees for many remarks which helped to improve this paper.

Conflicts of Interest: The authors declare no conflict of interest.

Appendix A

A Heuristic Derivation of the Conditional LDP for the Normalized Weighted Empirical Measure

The following sketch of proof gives the core argument which yields to Proposition 1; a proof adapted to a more abstract setting can be found in [22], following their Theorem 3.2 and Corollary 3.3, but we find it useful to present a proof which reduces to simple arguments. We look at the probability of the event

$$P_n^W \in V(R) \tag{A1}$$

for a given vector R in $\mathbb{R}^K$, where $V(R)$ denotes a neighborhood of R, therefore defined through

$$(Q \in V(R)) \iff (Q(d_l) \approx R(d_l); 1 \leq l \leq k)$$

We denote by P the distribution of the RV X so that P_n converges to P a.s.

Evaluating loosely the probability of the event defined in (A1) yields, denoting $P_{X_1^n}$ the conditional distribution given $(X_1, \ldots, X_n)$

$$P_{X_1^n}\left(P_n^W \in V(R)\right) = P_{X_1^n}\left(\bigcap_{l=1}^K \left(\frac{1}{n}\sum_{i=1}^n W_i \delta_{X_i}(d_l) \approx R(d_l)\right)\right)$$
$$= P_{X_1^n}\left(\bigcap_{l=1}^K \left(\frac{1}{n}\sum_{i=1}^{n_l} W_{i,l} \approx R(d_l)\right)\right)$$
$$= \prod_{l=1}^K P_{X_1^n}\left(\frac{1}{n_l}\sum_{i=1}^{n_l} W_{i,l} \approx \frac{n}{n_l}R(d_l)\right)$$
$$= \prod_{l=1}^K P_{X_1^n}\left(\frac{1}{n_l}\sum_{i=1}^{n_l} W_{i,l} \approx \frac{R(d_l)}{P(d_l)}\right)$$

where we used repeatedly the fact that the r.v's W are i.i.d.. In the above display, from the second line on, the r.v's are independent copies of W_1 for all i and l. In the above displays n_l is the number of X_i's which equal d_l, and the $W_{i,l}$ are the weights corresponding to these X_i's. We used the convergence of n_l/n to $P(d_l)$ in the last display.

Now for each l in $\{1, 2, \ldots, K\}$ by the Cramer LDP for the empirical mean, it holds

$$\frac{1}{n_l}\log P\left(\frac{1}{n_l}\sum_{i=1}^{n_l} W_{i,l} \approx \frac{R(d_l)}{P(d_l)}\right) \approx -\varphi^W\left(\frac{R(d_l)}{P(d_l)}\right)$$

i.e.,

$$\frac{1}{n}\log P\left(\frac{1}{n_l}\sum_{i=1}^{n_l} W_{i,l} \approx \frac{R(l)}{P(l)}\right) \approx -\frac{R(d_l)}{P(d_l)}\varphi^W\left(\frac{R(d_l)}{P(d_l)}\right)$$

as follows from the classical Cramer LDP, and therefore

$$\frac{1}{n}\log P_{X_1^n}\left(P_n^W \in V(R)\right)$$
$$\approx \frac{1}{n}\log P_{X_1^n}\left(\bigcap_{l=1}^{K}\left(\frac{1}{n}\sum_{i=1}^{n_l} W_{i,l} \approx R(d_l)\right)\right)$$
$$\rightarrow -\sum_{l=1}^{K}\varphi^W\left(\frac{R(d_l)}{P(d_l)}\right)P(d_l) = -\phi^W(R,P)$$

where the limit in the last line applies to the case where we let $n \to \infty$.

A precise derivation of Proposition 1 involves two arguments: firstly for a set $\Omega \subset \mathbb{R}^K$ a covering procedure by small balls allowing to use the above derivation locally, and the regularity assumption (11) which allows to obtain proper limits in the standard LDP statement.

The argument leading from Proposition 1 to Theorem 1 can be summarized now. For some subset Ω in $\mathbb{S}^K$ with non-void interior it holds

$$\left(\mathfrak{P}_n^W \in \Omega\right) = \bigcup_{m \neq 0}\left(\left(P_n^W \in m\Omega\right) \cap \left(\sum_{i=1}^n W_i = m\right)\right)$$

and $\left(P_n^W \in m\Omega\right) \subset \left(\sum_{i=1}^n W_i = m\right)$ for all $m \neq 0$. Therefore

$$P_{X_1^n}\left(\mathfrak{P}_n^W \in \Omega\right) = P_{X_1^n}\left(\bigcup_{m \neq 0}\left(P_n^W \in m\Omega\right)\right).$$

Making use of Proposition 1

$$\lim_{n \to \infty}\frac{1}{n}\log P_{X_1^n}\left(\mathfrak{P}_n^W \in \Omega\right) = -\phi^W\left(\bigcup_{m \neq 0} m\Omega, P\right).$$

Now

$$\phi^W\left(\bigcup_{m \neq 0} m\Omega, P\right) = \inf_{m \neq 0}\inf_{Q \in \Omega}\phi^W(mQ,P).$$

We have sketched the arguments leading to Theorem 1; see [19] for details.

References

1. Ali, S.M.; Silvey, S.D. A general class of coefficients of divergence of one distribution from another. *J. Roy. Statist. Soc. Ser. B* **1966**, *28*, 131–142. [CrossRef]
2. Csiszár, I. Information-type measures of difference of probability distributions and indirect observations. *Studia Sci. Math. Hungar.* **1967**, *2*, 299–318.
3. Broniatowski, M.; Stummer, W. Some universal insights on divergences for statistics, machine learning and artificial intelligence. In *Geometric Structures of Information*; Springer: Cham, Switzerland, 2019; pp. 149–211.
4. Liese, F.; Vajda, I. *Convex Statistical Distances*; Teubner-Texte zur Mathematik [Teubner Texts in Mathematics], 95.; BSB B G. Teubner Verlagsgesellschaft: Leipzig, Germany, 1987.
5. Liese, F.; Vajda, I. On divergences and informations in statistics and information theory. *IEEE Trans. Inform. Theory* **2006**, *52*, 4394–4412. [CrossRef]
6. Broniatowski, M.; Keziou, A. Parametric estimation and tests through divergences and the duality technique. *J. Multivariate Anal.* **2009**, *100*, 16–36. [CrossRef]
7. Broniatowski, M.; Keziou, A. Divergences and duality for estimation and test under moment condition models. *J. Statist. Plann. Inference* **2012**, *142*, 2554–2573. [CrossRef]
8. Basu, A.; Shioya, H.C. *Statistical Inference*; The Minimum Distance Approach; Monographs on Statistics and Applied Probability, 120; CRC Press: Boca Raton, FL, USA, 2011; p. 409.

9. Pardo, L. *Statistical Inference Based on Divergence Measures*; Statistics: Textbooks and Monographs, 185; Chapman & Hall/CRC: Boca Raton, FL, USA, 2006; p. 492.
10. Csiszár, I. Why least squares and maximum entropy? An axiomatic approach to inference for linear inverse problems. *Ann. Statist.* **1991**, *4*, 2032–2066. [CrossRef]
11. Broniatowski, M. Minimum divergence estimators, maximum likelihood and exponential families. *Statist. Probab. Lett.* **2014**, *93*, 27–33. [CrossRef]
12. Read, T.R.C.; Cressie, N.A.C. *Goodness-of-Fit Statistics for Discrete Multivariate Data*; Springer Series in Statistics; Springer: New York, NY, USA, 1988; p. 211.
13. Basu, A.; Harris, I.R.; Hjort, N.L.; Jones, M.C. Robust and efficient estimation by minimizing a density power divergence. *Biometrika* **1998**, *85*, 549–559. [CrossRef]
14. Broniatowski, M.; Vajda, I. Several applications of divergence criteria in continuous families. *Kybernetika* **2012**, *48*, 600–636.
15. Broniatowski, M.; Keziou, A. Minimization of ϕ-divergences on sets of signed measures. *Studia Sci. Math. Hungar.* **2006**, *43*, 403–442.
16. Bar-Lev, S.K.; Enis, P. Reproducibility and natural exponential families with power variance functions. *Ann. Statist.* **1986**, *14*, 1507–1522. [CrossRef]
17. Letac, G.; Mora, M. Natural real exponential families with cubic variance functions. *Ann. Statist.* **1990**, *18*, 1–37. [CrossRef]
18. Broniatowski, M. A weighted bootstrap procedure for divergence minimization problems. In *Analytical Methods in Statistics*; Springer: Cham, Switzerland, 2017; pp. 1–22.
19. Broniatowski, M.; Stummer, W. A precise bare simulation approach to the minimization of some distances. *Foundations* **2021**. Preprint under preparation.
20. Zolotarev, V.M. *Modern Theory of Summation of Random Variables*; Modern Probability and Statistics; VSP: Utrecht, The Netherlands, 1997; p. 412.
21. Mason, D.M.; Newton, M.A. A rank statistic approach to the consistency of a general bootstrap. *Ann. Statist.* **1992**, *20*, 1611–1624. [CrossRef]
22. Trashorras, J.; Wintenberger, O. Large deviations for bootstrapped empirical measures. *Bernoulli* **2014**, *20*, 1845–1878. [CrossRef]
23. Rubin, D.B. The Bayesian bootstrap. *Ann. Stat.* **1981**, *9*, 130–134. [CrossRef]
24. Barbe, P.; Bertail, P. The Weighted Bootstrap. In *Lecture Notes in Statistics*; Springer: New York, NY, USA, 1995.
25. Najim, J. A Cramer type theorem for weighted random variables. *Electron. J. Probab.* **2002**, *7*, 32. [CrossRef]
26. Newton, M.A.; Raftery, A.E. Approximate Bayesian inference with the weighted likelihood bootstrap. With discussion and a reply by the authors. *J. Roy. Statist. Soc.* **1994**, *56*, 3–48.
27. Efron, B.; Tibshirani, R.J. *An Introduction to the Bootstrap*; Chapman and Hall: New York, NY, USA, 1993; p. 436.

Article
Error Exponents and α-Mutual Information

Sergio Verdú

Independent Researcher, Princeton, NJ 08540, USA; verdu@informationtheory.org

Abstract: Over the last six decades, the representation of error exponent functions for data transmission through noisy channels at rates below capacity has seen three distinct approaches: (1) Through Gallager's E_0 functions (with and without cost constraints); (2) large deviations form, in terms of conditional relative entropy and mutual information; (3) through the α-mutual information and the Augustin–Csiszár mutual information of order α derived from the Rényi divergence. While a fairly complete picture has emerged in the absence of cost constraints, there have remained gaps in the interrelationships between the three approaches in the general case of cost-constrained encoding. Furthermore, no systematic approach has been proposed to solve the attendant optimization problems by exploiting the specific structure of the information functions. This paper closes those gaps and proposes a simple method to maximize Augustin–Csiszár mutual information of order α under cost constraints by means of the maximization of the α-mutual information subject to an exponential average constraint.

Keywords: information measures; relative entropy; Rényi divergence; mutual information; α-mutual information; Augustin–Csiszár mutual information; data transmission; error exponents; large deviations

---

Citation: Verdú, S. Error Exponents and α-Mutual Information. *Entropy* **2021**, *23*, 199. https://doi.org/10.3390/e23020199

Received: 7 December 2020
Accepted: 28 January 2021
Published: 5 February 2021

Publisher's Note: MDPI stays neutral with regard to jurisdictional claims in published maps and institutional affiliations.

Copyright: © 2021 by the author. Licensee MDPI, Basel, Switzerland. This article is an open access article distributed under the terms and conditions of the Creative Commons Attribution (CC BY) license (https://creativecommons.org/licenses/by/4.0/).

1. Introduction
1.1. Phase 1: The MIT School

The capacity C of a stationary memoryless channel is equal to the maximal symbol-wise input–output mutual information. Not long after Shannon [1] established this result, Rice [2] observed that, when operating at any encoding rate $R < C$, there exist codes whose error probability vanishes exponentially with blocklength, with a speed of decay that decreases as R approaches C. This early observation moved the center of gravity of information theory research towards the quest for the reliability function, a term coined by Shannon [3] to refer to the maximal achievable exponential decay as a function of R. The MIT information theory school, and most notably, Elias [4], Feinstein [5], Shannon [3,6], Fano [7], Gallager [8,9], and Shannon, Gallager and Berlekamp [10,11], succeeded in upper/lower bounding the reliability function by the sphere-packing error exponent function and the random coding error exponent function, respectively. Fortunately, these functions coincide for rates between C and a certain value, called the critical rate, thereby determining the reliability function in that region. The influential 1968 textbook by Gallager [9] set down the major error exponent results obtained during Phase 1 of research on this topic, including the expurgation technique to improve upon the random coding error exponent lower bound. Two aspects of those early works (and of Dobrushin's contemporary papers [12,13] on the topic) stand out:

(a) The error exponent functions were expressed as the result of the Karush-Kuhn-Tucker optimization of ad-hoc functions which, unlike mutual information, carried little insight. In particular, during the first phase, center stage is occupied by the parametrized function of the input distribution P_X and the random transformation (or "channel") $P_{Y|X}$,

$$E_0(\rho, P_X) = -\log \sum_{y \in \mathcal{B}} \left(\sum_{x \in \mathcal{A}} P_X(x) P_{Y|X}^{\frac{1}{1+\rho}}(y|x) \right)^{1+\rho}, \tag{1}$$

introduced by Gallager in [8].

(b) Despite the large-deviations nature of the setup, none of the tools from that then-nascent field (other than the Chernoff bound) found their way to the first phase of the work on error exponents; in particular, relative entropy, introduced by Kullback and Leibler [14], failed to put in an appearance.

To this date, the reliability function remains open for low rates even for the binary symmetric channel, despite a number of refined converse and achievability results (e.g., [15–21]) obtained since [9]. Our focus in this paper is not on converse/achievability techniques but on the role played by various information measures in the formulation of error exponent results.

1.2. Phase 2: Relative Entropy

The second phase of the error exponent research was pioneered by Haroutunian [22] and Blahut [23], who infused the expressions for the error exponent functions with meaning by incorporating relative entropy. The sphere-packing error exponent function corresponding to a random transformation $P_{Y|X}$ is given as

$$E_{\text{sp}}(R) = \sup_{P_X} \min_{\substack{Q_{Y|X}:\,\mathcal{A} \to \mathcal{B} \\ I(P_X, Q_{Y|X}) \leq R}} D(Q_{Y|X} \| P_{Y|X} | P_X). \tag{2}$$

Roughly speaking, optimal codes of rate $R < C$ incur in errors due to atypical channel behavior, and large deviations establishes that the overwhelmingly most likely such behavior can be explained as if the channel would be supplanted by the one with mutual information bounded by R which is closest to the true channel in conditional relative entropy $D(Q_{Y|X} \| P_{Y|X} | P_X)$. Within the confines of finite-alphabet memoryless channels, this direction opened the possibility of using the combinatorial method of types to obtain refined results robustifying the choice of the optimal code against incomplete knowledge of the channel. The 1981 textbook by Csiszár and Körner [24] summarizes the main results obtained during Phase 2.

1.3. Phase 3: Rényi Information Measures

Entropy and relative entropy were generalized by Rényi [25], who introduced the notions of Rényi entropy and Rényi divergence of order α. He arrived at Rényi entropy by relaxing the axioms Shannon proposed in [1], and showed to be satisfied by no measure but entropy. Shortly after [25], Campbell [26] realized the operational role of Rényi entropy in variable-length data compression if the usual average encoding length criterion $\mathbb{E}[\ell(c(X))]$ is replaced by an exponential average $\alpha^{-1} \log \mathbb{E}[\exp(\alpha\, \ell(c(X))]$. Arimoto [27] put forward a generalized conditional entropy inspired by Rényi's measures (now known as Arimoto-Rényi conditional entropy) and proposed a generalized mutual information by taking the difference between Rényi entropy and the Arimoto-Rényi conditional entropy. The role of the Arimoto-Rényi conditional entropy in the analysis of the error probability of Bayesian M-ary hypothesis testing problems has been recently shown in [28], tightening and generalizing a number of results dating back to Fano's inequality [29].

Phase 3 of the error exponent research was pioneered by Csiszár [30] where he established a connection between Gallager's E_0 function and Rényi divergence by means of a Bayesian measure of the discrepancy among a finite collection of distributions introduced by Sibson [31]. Although [31] failed to realize its connection to mutual information, Csiszár [30,32] noticed that it could be viewed as a natural generalization of mutual information. Arimoto [27] also observed that the unconstrained maximization of his generalized mutual information measure with respect to the input distribution coincides with a scaled version of the maximal E_0 function. This resulted in an extension of the Arimoto-Blahut algorithm useful for the computation of error exponent functions [33] (see also [34]) for finite-alphabet memoryless channels.

Within Haroutunian's framework [22] applied in the context of the method of types, Poltyrev [35] proposed an alternative to Gallager's E_0 function, defined by means of a cumbersome maximization over a reverse random transformation. This measure turned out to coincide (modulo different parametrizations) with another generalized mutual information introduced four years earlier by Augustin in his unpublished thesis [36], by means of a minimization with respect to an output probability measure.

The key contribution in the development of this third phase is Csiszár's paper [32] where he makes a compelling case for the adoption of Rényi's information measures in the large deviations analysis of lossless data compression, hypothesis testing and data transmission. Recall that more than two decades earlier, Csiszár [30] had already established the connection of Gallager's E_0 function and the generalized mutual information inspired by Sibson [31], which, henceforth, we refer to as the α-mutual information. Therefore, its relevance to the error exponent analysis of error correcting codes had already been established. Incidentally, more recently, another operational role was found for α-mutual information in the context of the large deviations analysis of composite hypothesis testing [37]. In addition to α-mutual information, and always working with discrete alphabets, Csiszár [32] considers the generalized mutual informations due to Arimoto [27], and to Augustin [36], which we refer to as the Augustin–Csiszár mutual information of order α. Csiszár shows that all those three generalizations of mutual information coincide upon their unconstrained maximization with respect to the input distribution. Further relationships among those Rényi-based generalized mutual informations have been obtained in recent years in [38–45]. In [32] the maximal α-mutual information or generalized capacity of order α finds an operational characterization as a generalized cutoff rate–an equivalent way to express the reliability function. This would have been the final word on the topic if it weren't for its limitation to discrete-alphabet channels, and more importantly, encoding without cost constraints.

1.4. Cost Constraints

If the transmitted codebook is cost-constrained, i.e., every codeword $(c_1, \ldots, c_n)$ is forced to satisfy $\sum_{i=1}^{n} \mathsf{b}(c_i) \leq n\,\theta$ for some nonnegative cost function $\mathsf{b}(\cdot)$, then the channel capacity is equal to the input–output mutual information maximized over input probability measures restricted to satisfy $\mathbb{E}[\mathsf{b}(X)] \leq \theta$. Gallager [9] incorporated cost constraints in his treatment of error exponents by generalizing (1) to the function

$$E_0(\rho, P_X, r, \theta) = -\log \sum_{y \in \mathcal{B}} \left(\sum_{x \in \mathcal{A}} P_X(x) \exp(r\,\mathsf{b}(x) - r\,\theta) P_{Y|X}^{\frac{1}{1+\rho}}(y|x) \right)^{1+\rho}, \qquad (3)$$

with which he was able to prove an achievability result invoking Shannon's random coding technique [1]. Gallager also suggested in the footnote of page 329 of [9] that the converse technique of [10] is amenable to extension to prove a sphere-packing converse based on (3). However, an important limitation is that that technique only applies to constant-composition codes (all codewords have the same empirical distribution). A more powerful converse circumventing that limitation (at least for symmetric channels) was given by [46] also expressing the upper bound on the reliability function by optimizing (3) with respect to ρ, r and P_X. A notable success of the approach based on the optimization of (3) was the determination of the reliability function (for all rates below capacity) of the direct detection photon channel [47].

In contrast, the Phase Two expression (2) for the sphere-packing error exponent for cost-constrained channels is much more natural and similar to the way the expression for channel capacity is impacted by cost constraints, namely we simply constrain the maximization in (2) to satisfy $\mathbb{E}[b(X)] \leq \theta$. Unfortunately, no general methods to solve the ensuing optimization have been reported.

Once cost constraints are incorporated, the equivalence among the maximal α-mutual information, maximal order-α Augustin–Csiszár mutual information, and maximal Arimoto mutual information of order α breaks down. Of those three alternatives, it is the maximal Augustin–Csiszár mutual information under cost constraints that appears in the error exponent functions. The challenge is that Augustin–Csiszár mutual information is much harder to evaluate, let alone maximize, than α-mutual information. The Phase 3 effort to encompass cost constraints started by Augustin [36] and was continued recently by Nakiboglu [43]. Their focus was to find a way to express (3) in terms of Rényi information measures. Although, as we explain in Item 62, they did not quite succeed, their efforts were instrumental in developing key properties of the Augustin–Csiszár mutual information.

1.5. Organization

To enhance readability and ease of reference, the rest of this work is organized in 81 items, grouped into Section 13 and an appendix.

Basic notions and notation (including the key concept of α-response) are collected in Section 2. Unlike much of the literature on the topic, we do not restrict attention to discrete input/output alphabets, nor do we impose any topological structures on them.

The paper is essentially self-contained. Section 3 covers the required background material on relative entropy, Rényi divergence of order α, and their conditional versions, including a key representation of Rényi divergence in terms of relative entropies and a tilted probability measure, and additive decompositions of Rényi divergence involving the α-response.

Section 4 studies the basic properties of α-mutual information and order-α Augustin–Csiszár mutual information. This includes their variational representations in terms of conventional (non-Rényi) information measures such as conditional relative entropy and mutual information, which are particularly simple to show in the main range of interest in applications to error exponents, namely, $\alpha \in (0,1)$.

The interrelationships between α-mutual information and order-α Augustin–Csiszár mutual information are covered in Section 5, which introduces the dual notions of α-adjunct and $\langle \alpha \rangle$-adjunct of an input probability measure.

The maximizations with respect to the input distribution of α-mutual information and order-α Augustin–Csiszár mutual information account for their role in the fundamental limits in data transmission through noisy channels. Section 6 gives a brief review of the results in [45] for the maximization of α-mutual information. For Augustin–Csiszár mutual information, Section 7 covers its unconstrained maximization, which coincides with its α-mutual information counterpart. Section 8 proposes an approach to find $\mathbb{C}_\alpha^c(\theta)$, the maximal Augustin–Csiszár mutual information of order $\alpha \in (0,1)$ subject to $\mathbb{E}[b(X)] \leq \theta$. Instead of trying to identify directly the input distribution that maximizes Augustin–Csiszár mutual information, the method seeks its $\langle \alpha \rangle$-adjunct. This is tantamount to maximizing α-mutual information over a larger set of distributions.

Section 9 shows

$$\rho\, \mathbb{C}^c_{\frac{1}{1+\rho}}(\theta) = \min_{r \geq 0} \max_{P_X} E_0(\rho, P_X, r, \theta), \qquad (4)$$

where the maximization on the right side is unconstrained. In other words, the minimax of Gallager's E_0 function (3) with cost constraints is shown to be equal to the maximal

Augustin–Csiszár mutual information, thereby bridging the existing gap between the Phase 1 and Phase 3 representations alluded to earlier in this introduction.

As in [48], Section 10 defines the sphere-packing and random-coding error exponent functions in the natural canonical form of Phase 2 (e.g., (2)), and gives a very simple proof of the nexus between the Phase 2 and Phase 3 representations, namely,

$$E_{\text{sp}}(R) = \sup_{\rho \geq 0} \left\{ \rho\, \mathbb{C}^c_{\frac{1}{1+\rho}}(\theta) - \rho R \right\}, \tag{5}$$

with or without cost constraints. In this regard, we note that, although all the ingredients required were already present at the time the revised version of [24] was published three decades after the original, [48] does not cover the role of Rényi's information measures in channel error exponents.

Examples illustrating the proposed method are given in Sections 11 and 12 for the additive Gaussian noise channel under a quadratic cost function, and the additive exponential noise channel under a linear cost function, respectively. Simple parametric expressions are given for the error exponent functions, and the least favorable channels that account for the most likely error mechanism (Section 1.2) are identified in both cases.

2. Relative Information and Information Density

We begin with basic terminology and notation required for the subsequent development.

1. If $(\mathcal{A}, \mathscr{F}, P)$ is a probability space, $X \sim P$ indicates $\mathbb{P}[X \in \mathcal{F}] = P(\mathcal{F})$ for all $\mathcal{F} \in \mathscr{F}$.
2. If probability measures P and Q defined on the same measurable space $(\mathcal{A}, \mathscr{F})$ satisfy $P(A) = 0$ for all $A \in \mathscr{F}$ such that $Q(A) = 0$, we say that P is dominated by Q, denoted as $P \ll Q$. If P and Q dominate each other, we write $P \ll\gg Q$. If there is an event such that $P(A) = 0$ and $Q(A) = 1$, we say that P and Q are mutually singular, and we write $P \perp Q$.
3. If $P \ll Q$, then $\frac{dP}{dQ}$ is the Radon-Nikodym derivative of the dominated measure P with respect to the reference measure Q. Its logarithm is known as the relative information, namely, the random variable

$$\imath_{P\|Q}(a) = \log \frac{dP}{dQ}(a) \in [-\infty, +\infty), \quad a \in \mathcal{A}. \tag{6}$$

As with the Radon-Nikodym derivative, any identity involving relative informations can be changed on a set of measure zero under the reference measure without incurring in any contradiction. If $P \ll Q \ll R$, then the chain rule of Radon-Nikodym derivatives yields

$$\imath_{P\|Q}(a) + \imath_{Q\|R}(a) = \imath_{P\|R}(a), \quad a \in \mathcal{A}. \tag{7}$$

Throughout the paper, the base of exp and log is the same and chosen by the reader unless explicitly indicated otherwise. We frequently define a probability measure P from the specification of $\imath_{P\|Q}$ and $Q \gg P$ since

$$P(A) = \int_A \exp\left(\imath_{P\|Q}(a)\right) dQ(a), \quad A \in \mathscr{F}. \tag{8}$$

If $X \sim P$ and $Y \sim Q$, it is often convenient to write $\imath_{X\|Y}(x)$ instead of $\imath_{P\|Q}(x)$. Note that

$$\mathbb{E}\left[\exp\left(\imath_{X\|Y}(Y)\right)\right] = 1. \tag{9}$$

Example 1. If $X \sim \mathcal{N}(\mu_X, \sigma_X^2)$ (Gaussian with mean μ_X and variance σ_X^2) and $Y \sim \mathcal{N}(\mu_Y, \sigma_Y^2)$, then,

$$\iota_{X\|Y}(a) = \frac{1}{2}\log\frac{\sigma_Y^2}{\sigma_X^2} + \frac{1}{2}\left(\frac{(a-\mu_Y)^2}{\sigma_Y^2} - \frac{(a-\mu_X)^2}{\sigma_X^2}\right)\log e. \tag{10}$$

4. Let $(\mathcal{A}, \mathscr{F})$ and $(\mathcal{B}, \mathscr{G})$ be measurable spaces, known as the input and output spaces, respectively. Likewise, $\mathcal{A}$ and $\mathcal{B}$ are referred to as the input and output alphabets respectively. The simplified notation $P_{Y|X}: \mathcal{A} \to \mathcal{B}$ denotes a random transformation from $(\mathcal{A}, \mathscr{F})$ to $(\mathcal{B}, \mathscr{G})$, i.e. for any $x \in \mathcal{A}$, $P_{Y|X=x}(\cdot)$ is a probability measure on $(\mathcal{B}, \mathscr{G})$, and for any $B \in \mathscr{G}$, $P_{Y|X=\cdot}(B)$ is an $\mathscr{F}$-measurable function.

5. We abbreviate by $\mathcal{P}_\mathcal{A}$ the set of probability measures on $(\mathcal{A}, \mathscr{F})$, and by $\mathcal{P}_{\mathcal{A} \times \mathcal{B}}$ the set of probability measures on $(\mathcal{A} \times \mathcal{B}, \mathscr{F} \otimes \mathscr{G})$. If $P \in \mathcal{P}_\mathcal{A}$ and $P_{Y|X}: \mathcal{A} \to \mathcal{B}$ is a random transformation, the corresponding joint probability measure is denoted by $P P_{Y|X} \in \mathcal{P}_{\mathcal{A} \times \mathcal{B}}$ (or, interchangeably, $P_{Y|X}P$). The notation $P \to P_{Y|X} \to Q$ simply indicates that the output marginal of the joint probability measure $P P_{Y|X}$ is denoted by $Q \in \mathcal{P}_\mathcal{B}$, namely,

$$Q(B) = \int P_{Y|X}(B|x)\,dP_X(x) = \mathbb{E}\left[P_{Y|X}(B|X)\right], \quad B \in \mathscr{G}. \tag{11}$$

6. If $P_X \to P_{Y|X} \to P_Y$ and $P_{Y|X=a} \ll P_Y$, the information density $\iota_{X;Y}: \mathcal{A} \times \mathcal{B} \to [-\infty, \infty)$ is defined as

$$\iota_{X;Y}(a;b) = \iota_{P_{Y|X=a}\|P_Y}(b), \quad (a,b) \in \mathcal{A} \times \mathcal{B}. \tag{12}$$

Following Rényi's terminology [49], if $P_X P_{Y|X} \ll P_X \times P_Y$, the dependence between X and Y is said to be regular, and the information density can be defined on $(x,y) \in \mathcal{A} \times \mathcal{B}$. Henceforth, we assume that $P_{Y|X}$ is such that the dependence between its input and output is regular regardless of the input probability measure. For example, if $X = Y \in \mathbb{R}$, then $P_{Y|X=a}(A) = 1\{a \in A\}$, and their dependence is not regular, since for any P_X with non-discrete components $P_{XY} \not\ll P_X \times P_Y$.

7. Let $\alpha > 0$, and $P_X \to P_{Y|X} \to P_Y$. The α-response to $P_X \in \mathcal{P}_\mathcal{A}$ is the output probability measure $P_{Y[\alpha]} \ll P_Y$ with relative information given by

$$\iota_{Y[\alpha]\|Y}(y) = \frac{1}{\alpha}\log \mathbb{E}[\exp(\alpha\, \iota_{X;Y}(X;y) - \kappa_\alpha)], \quad X \sim P_X, \tag{13}$$

where κ_α is a scalar that guarantees that $P_{Y[\alpha]}$ is a probability measure. Invoking (9), we obtain

$$\kappa_\alpha = \alpha \log \mathbb{E}\left[\mathbb{E}^{\frac{1}{\alpha}}[\exp(\alpha\, \iota_{X;Y}(X;\bar{Y}))|\bar{Y}]\right], \quad (X,\bar{Y}) \sim P_X \times P_Y. \tag{14}$$

For brevity, the dependence of κ_α on P_X and $P_{Y|X}$ is omitted. Jensen's inequality applied to $(\cdot)^\alpha$ results in $\kappa_\alpha \leq 0$ for $\alpha \in (0,1)$ and $\kappa_\alpha \geq 0$ for $\alpha > 1$. Although the α-response has a long record of services to information theory, this terminology and notation were introduced recently in [45]. Alternative terminology and notation were proposed in [42], which refers to the α-response as the order α Rényi mean. Note that $\kappa_1 = 0$ and the 1-response to P_X is P_Y. If $p_{Y[\alpha]}$ and $p_{Y|X}$ denote the densities of $P_{Y[\alpha]}$ and $P_{Y|X}$ with respect to some common dominating measure, then (13) becomes

$$p_{Y[\alpha]}(y) = \exp\left(-\frac{\kappa_\alpha}{\alpha}\right)\mathbb{E}^{\frac{1}{\alpha}}\left[p_{Y|X}^\alpha(y|X)\right], \quad X \sim P_X. \tag{15}$$

For $\alpha > 1$ (resp. $\alpha < 1$) we can think of the normalized version of $p_{Y|X}^\alpha$ as a random transformation with less (resp. more) "noise" than $p_{Y|X}$.

8. We will have opportunity to apply the following examples.

Example 2. If $Y = X + N$, where $X \sim \mathcal{N}(\mu_X, \sigma_X^2)$ independent of $N \sim \mathcal{N}(\mu_N, \sigma_N^2)$, then the α-response to P_X is

$$Y[\alpha] \sim \mathcal{N}\left(\mu_X + \mu_N, \alpha\, \sigma_X^2 + \sigma_N^2\right). \tag{16}$$

Example 3. Suppose that $Y = X + N$, where N is exponential with mean ζ, independent of X, which is a mixed random variable with density

$$f_X(t) = \frac{\zeta}{\alpha\mu}\delta(t) + \left(1 - \frac{\zeta}{\alpha\mu}\right)\frac{1}{\mu}e^{-t/\mu}\mathbf{1}\{t > 0\}, \tag{17}$$

with $\alpha\mu \geq \zeta$. Then, $Y[\alpha]$, the α-response to P_X, is exponential with mean $\alpha\mu$.

3. Relative Entropy and Rényi Divergence

Given a pair of probability measures $(P, Q) \in \mathcal{P}_\mathcal{A}^2$, relative entropy and Rényi divergence gauge the distinctness between P and Q.

9. Provided $P \ll Q$, the relative entropy is the expectation of the relative information with respect to the dominated measure

$$D(P\|Q) = \mathbb{E}\left[\iota_{P\|Q}(X)\right], \quad X \sim P \tag{18}$$

$$= \mathbb{E}\left[\exp\left(\iota_{P\|Q}(Y)\right)\iota_{P\|Q}(Y)\right], \quad Y \sim Q \tag{19}$$

$$\geq 0, \tag{20}$$

with equality if and only if $P = Q$. If $P \not\ll Q$, then $D(P\|Q) = \infty$. As in Item 3, if $X \sim P$ and $Y \sim Q$, we may write $D(X\|Y)$ instead of $D(P\|Q)$, in the same spirit that the expectation and entropy of P are written as $\mathbb{E}[X]$ and $H(X)$, respectively.

10. Arising in the sequel, a common optimization in information theory finds, among the probability measures satisfying an average cost constraint, that which is closest to a given reference measure Q in the sense of $D(\cdot\|Q)$. For that purpose, the following result proves sufficient. Incidentally, we often refer to unconstrained maximizations over probability distributions. It should be understood that those optimizations are still constrained to the sets $\mathcal{P}_\mathcal{A}$ or $\mathcal{P}_\mathcal{B}$. As customary in information theory, we will abbreviate $\max_{P_X \in \mathcal{P}_\mathcal{A}}$ by $\max_X$ or $\max_{P_X}$.

Theorem 1. Let $P_Z \in \mathcal{P}_\mathcal{A}$ and suppose that $g: \mathcal{A} \to [0, \infty)$ is a Borel measurable mapping. Then,

$$\min_X \{D(X\|Z) + \mathbb{E}[g(X)]\} = -\log \mathbb{E}[\exp(-g(Z))], \tag{21}$$

achieved uniquely by $P_X^* \lll P_Z$ defined by

$$\iota_{X^*\|Z}(a) = -g(a) - \log \mathbb{E}[\exp(-g(Z))], \quad a \in \mathcal{A}. \tag{22}$$

Proof. Note that since g is nonnegative, $\eta = \mathbb{E}[\exp(-g(Z))] \in (0, 1]$. Furthermore,

$$\mathbb{E}[g(X^*)] = \frac{\int g(t)\exp(-g(t))\,\mathrm{d}P_Z(t)}{\mathbb{E}[\exp(-g(Z))]} \in \left[0, \frac{1}{e\eta}\right]. \tag{23}$$

Therefore, the subset of $\mathcal{P}_\mathcal{A}$ for which the term in $\{\cdot\}$ in (21) is finite is nonempty: Fix any P_X from that subset, (which therefore satisfies $P_X \ll P_Z \ll P_X^*$) and invoke the chain rule (7) to write

$$D(X\|Z) + \mathbb{E}[g(X)] = \mathbb{E}\Big[\imath_{X\|X^*}(X) + \imath_{X^*\|Z}(X) + g(X)\Big] \qquad (24)$$
$$= D(X\|X^*) - \log \mathbb{E}[\exp(-g(Z))], \quad X \sim P_X, \qquad (25)$$

which is uniquely minimized by letting $P_X = P_X^*$. Note that for typographical convenience we have denoted $X^* \sim P_X^*$. □

11. Let p and q denote the Radon-Nikodym derivatives of probability measures P and Q, respectively, with respect to a common dominating σ-finite measure μ. The Rényi divergence of order $\alpha \in (0,1) \cup (1,\infty)$ between P and Q is defined as [25,50]

$$D_\alpha(P\|Q) = \frac{1}{\alpha - 1} \log \int_\mathcal{A} p^\alpha q^{1-\alpha} d\mu \qquad (26)$$
$$= \frac{1}{\alpha - 1} \log \mathbb{E}\Big[\exp\Big(\alpha \imath_{P\|R}(Z) + (1-\alpha)\imath_{Q\|R}(Z)\Big)\Big], \quad Z \sim R \qquad (27)$$
$$= \frac{1}{\alpha - 1} \log \mathbb{E}\Big[\exp\Big(\alpha \imath_{P\|Q}(Y)\Big)\Big], \quad Y \sim Q \qquad (28)$$
$$= \frac{1}{\alpha - 1} \log \mathbb{E}\Big[\exp\Big((\alpha-1)\imath_{P\|Q}(X)\Big)\Big], \quad X \sim P, \qquad (29)$$

where (28) and (29) hold if $P \not\ll Q$, and in (27), R is a probability measure that dominates both P and Q. Note that (28) and (29) state that $(t-1)D_t(X\|Y)$ and $tD_{1+t}(X\|Y)$ are the cumulant generating functions of the random variables $\imath_{X\|Y}(Y)$ and $\imath_{X\|Y}(X)$, respectively. The relative entropy is the limit of $D_\alpha(P\|Q)$ as $\alpha \uparrow 1$, so it is customary to let $D_1(P\|Q) = D(P\|Q)$. For any $\alpha > 0$, $D_\alpha(P\|Q) \geq 0$ with equality if and only if $P = Q$. Furthermore, $D_\alpha(P\|Q)$ is non-decreasing in α, satisfies the skew-symmetric property

$$(1-\alpha)D_\alpha(P\|Q) = \alpha D_{1-\alpha}(Q\|P), \quad \alpha \in [0,1], \qquad (30)$$

and

$$\inf_{\alpha \in (0,1)} D_\alpha(P\|Q) = \infty \iff P \perp Q \implies \inf_{\alpha > 1} D_\alpha(P\|Q) = \infty. \qquad (31)$$

12. The expressions in the following pair of examples will come in handy in Sections 11 and 12.

Example 4. *Suppose that $\sigma_\alpha^2 = \alpha \sigma_1^2 + (1-\alpha)\sigma_0^2 > 0$ and $\alpha \in (0,1) \cup (1,\infty)$. Then,*

$$D_\alpha\Big(\mathcal{N}(\mu_0, \sigma_0^2)\,\|\,\mathcal{N}(\mu_1, \sigma_1^2)\Big) = \frac{1}{2}\log\frac{\sigma_1^2}{\sigma_0^2} + \frac{1}{2(\alpha-1)}\log\frac{\sigma_1^2}{\sigma_\alpha^2} + \frac{\alpha(\mu_1 - \mu_0)^2}{2\sigma_\alpha^2}\log e, \qquad (32)$$

$$D\Big(\mathcal{N}(\mu_0, \sigma_0^2)\,\|\,\mathcal{N}(\mu_1, \sigma_1^2)\Big) = \frac{1}{2}\log\frac{\sigma_1^2}{\sigma_0^2} + \frac{1}{2}\left(\frac{\sigma_0^2}{\sigma_1^2} - 1\right)\log e + \frac{(\mu_1 - \mu_0)^2}{2\sigma_1^2}\log e \qquad (33)$$
$$= \lim_{\alpha \to 1} D_\alpha\Big(\mathcal{N}(\mu_0, \sigma_0^2)\,\|\,\mathcal{N}(\mu_1, \sigma_1^2)\Big). \qquad (34)$$

Example 5. *Suppose Z is exponentially distributed with unit mean, i.e., its probability density function is $e^{-t}1\{t \geq 0\}$. For $d_0 \geq d_1$ and α such that $(1-\alpha)\mu_0 + \alpha\mu_1 > 0$ we obtain*

$$D_\alpha(\mu_0 Z + d_0 \| \mu_1 Z + d_1) = \frac{d_0 - d_1}{\mu_1} \log e + \log \frac{\mu_1}{\mu_0} + \frac{1}{1-\alpha} \log\left(\alpha + (1-\alpha)\frac{\mu_0}{\mu_1}\right),$$

$$D(\mu_0 Z + d_0 \| \mu_1 Z + d_1) = \left(\frac{\mu_0}{\mu_1} - 1 + \frac{d_0 - d_1}{\mu_1}\right) \log e + \log \frac{\mu_1}{\mu_0} \tag{35}$$

$$= \lim_{\alpha \to 1} D_\alpha(\mu_0 Z + d_0 \| \mu_1 Z + d_1). \tag{36}$$

13. Intimately connected with the notion of Rényi divergence is the tilted probability measure P_α defined, if $D_\alpha(P_1 \| P_0) < \infty$, by

$$\imath_{P_\alpha \| Q}(a) = \alpha\, \imath_{P_1 \| Q}(a) + (1-\alpha)\, \imath_{P_0 \| Q}(a) + (1-\alpha) D_\alpha(P_1 \| P_0), \tag{37}$$

where Q is any probability measure that dominates both P_0 and P_1. Although (37) is defined in general, our main emphasis is on the range $\alpha \in (0,1)$, in which, as long as $P_0 \not\perp P_1$, the tilted probability measure is defined and satisfies $P_\alpha \ll P_0$ and $P_\alpha \ll P_1$, with corresponding relative informations

$$\imath_{P_\alpha \| P_0}(a) = \imath_{P_\alpha \| Q}(a) - \imath_{P_0 \| Q}(a) \tag{38}$$

$$= (1-\alpha) D_\alpha(P_1 \| P_0) + \alpha \left(\imath_{P_1 \| Q}(a) - \imath_{P_0 \| Q}(a)\right), \tag{39}$$

$$\imath_{P_\alpha \| P_1}(a) = \imath_{P_\alpha \| Q}(a) - \imath_{P_1 \| Q}(a) \tag{40}$$

$$= (1-\alpha) D_\alpha(P_1 \| P_0) - (1-\alpha)\left(\imath_{P_1 \| Q}(a) - \imath_{P_0 \| Q}(a)\right), \tag{41}$$

where we have used the chain rule for $P_\alpha \ll P_0 \ll Q$ and $P_\alpha \ll P_1 \ll Q$. Taking a linear combination of (38)–(41) we conclude that, for all $a \in \mathcal{A}$,

$$(1-\alpha) D_\alpha(P_1 \| P_0) = (1-\alpha)\, \imath_{P_\alpha \| P_0}(a) + \alpha\, \imath_{P_\alpha \| P_1}(a). \tag{42}$$

Henceforth, we focus particular attention on the case $\alpha \in (0,1)$ since that is the region of interest in the application of Rényi information measures to the evaluation of error exponents in channel coding for codes whose rate is below capacity. In addition, often proofs simplify considerably for $\alpha \in (0,1)$.

14. Much of the interplay between relative entropy and Rényi divergence hinges on the following identity, which appears, without proof, in (3) of [51].

Theorem 2. *Let $\alpha \in (0,1)$ and assume that $P_0 \not\perp P_1$ are defined on the same measurable space. Then, for any $P \ll P_1$ and $P \ll P_0$,*

$$\alpha\, D(P \| P_1) + (1-\alpha)\, D(P \| P_0) = D(P \| P_\alpha) + (1-\alpha) D_\alpha(P_1 \| P_0), \tag{43}$$

where P_α is the tilted probability measure in (37) and (43) holds regardless of whether the relative entropies are finite. In particular,

$$D(P \| P_\alpha) < \infty \iff \max\{D(P \| P_0), D(P \| P_1)\} < \infty. \tag{44}$$

Proof. We distinguish three overlapping cases:

(1) $D(P \| P_\alpha) < \infty$: Taking expectation of (42) with respect to $a \leftarrow X \sim P$, yields (43) because

$$\mathbb{E}\left[\imath_{P_\alpha \| P_0}(X)\right] = D(P\|P_0) - D(P\|P_\alpha), \tag{45}$$

$$\mathbb{E}\left[\imath_{P_\alpha \| P_1}(X)\right] = D(P\|P_1) - D(P\|P_\alpha), \tag{46}$$

where, thanks to the assumption that $D(P \| P_\alpha) < \infty$, we have invoked Corollary A1 in the Appendix twice with $(P, Q, R) \leftarrow (P, P_\alpha, P_0)$ and $(P, Q, R) \leftarrow (P, P_\alpha, P_1)$, respectively;

(2) $\max\{D(P \| P_0), D(P \| P_1)\} < \infty$: The proof is identical since we are entitled to invoke Corollary A1 to show (45) (resp., (46)) because $D(P \| P_0) < \infty$ (resp., $D(P \| P_1) < \infty$).

(3) $D(P \| P_\alpha) = \infty$ and $\max\{D(P \| P_0), D(P \| P_1)\} = \infty$: both sides of (43) are equal to ∞.

Finally, to show that (44) follows from (43), simply recall from (31) that $D_\alpha(P_1 \| P_0) < \infty$. □

15. Relative entropy and Rényi divergence are related by the following fundamental variational representation.

Theorem 3. *Fix $\alpha \in (0, 1)$ and $(P_1, P_0) \in \mathcal{P}_\mathcal{A}^2$. Then, the Rényi divergence between P_1 and P_0 satisfies*

$$(1 - \alpha) D_\alpha(P_1 \| P_0) = \min_{P}\{\alpha D(P\|P_1) + (1 - \alpha) D(P\|P_0)\}, \tag{47}$$

where the minimum is over $\mathcal{P}_\mathcal{A}$. If $P_0 \not\perp P_1$, then the right side of (47) is attained by the tilted measure P_α, and the minimization can be restricted to the subset of probability measures which are dominated by both P_1 and P_0.

Proof. If $P_0 \perp P_1$, then both sides of (47) are $+\infty$ since there is no probability measure that is dominated by both P_0 and P_1. If $P_0 \not\perp P_1$, then minimizing both sides of (43) with respect to P yields (47) and the fact that the tilted probability measure attains the minimum therein. □

The variational representation in (47) was observed in [39] in the finite-alphabet case, and, contemporaneously, in full generality in [50]. Unlike Theorem 3, both of those references also deal with $\alpha > 1$. The function $d(\alpha) = (1 - \alpha) D_\alpha(P_1\|P_0)$, with $d(1) = \lim_{\alpha \uparrow 1} d(\alpha)$, is concave in α because the right side of (47) is a minimum of affine functions of α.

16. Given random transformations $P_{Y|X}: \mathcal{A} \to \mathcal{B}$, $Q_{Y|X}: \mathcal{A} \to \mathcal{B}$, and a probability measure $P_X \in \mathcal{P}_\mathcal{A}$ on the input space, the conditional relative entropy is

$$D(P_{Y|X} \| Q_{Y|X} \mid P_X) = D(P_{Y|X} P_X \| Q_{Y|X} P_X) \tag{48}$$

$$= \mathbb{E}\left[D\left(P_{Y|X}(\cdot|X) \| Q_{Y|X}(\cdot|X)\right)\right], \quad X \sim P_X. \tag{49}$$

Analogously, the conditional Rényi divergence is defined as

$$D_\alpha(P_{Y|X} \| Q_{Y|X} \mid P_X) = D_\alpha(P_{Y|X} P_X \| Q_{Y|X} P_X). \tag{50}$$

A word of caution: the notation in (50) conforms to that in [38,45] but it is not universally adopted, e.g., [43] uses the left side of (50) to denote the Rényi generalization of the right side of (49). We can express the conditional Rényi divergence as

$$D_\alpha(P_{Y|X} \| Q_{Y|X}|P_X)$$
$$= \frac{1}{\alpha-1} \log \mathbb{E}\left[\exp\left((\alpha-1)D_\alpha\left(P_{Y|X}(\cdot|X) \| Q_{Y|X}(\cdot|X)\right)\right)\right], \quad X \sim P_X, \quad (51)$$
$$= \frac{1}{\alpha-1} \log \mathbb{E}\left[\left(\frac{dP_{Y|X}}{dQ_{Y|X}}(Y|X)\right)^{\alpha-1}\right], \quad (X,Y) \sim P_X P_{Y|X}, \quad (52)$$

where (52) holds if $P_X P_{Y|X} \ll P_X Q_{Y|X}$. Jensen's inequality applied to (51) results in

$$D_\alpha(P_{Y|X} \| Q_{Y|X}|P_X) \leq \mathbb{E}\left[D_\alpha(P_{Y|X}(\cdot|X) \| Q_{Y|X}(\cdot|X))\right], \quad \alpha \in (0,1); \quad (53)$$
$$D_\alpha(P_{Y|X} \| Q_{Y|X}|P_X) \geq \mathbb{E}\left[D_\alpha(P_{Y|X}(\cdot|X) \| Q_{Y|X}(\cdot|X))\right], \quad \alpha > 1. \quad (54)$$

Nevertheless, an immediate and crucial observation we can draw from (51) is that the unconstrained maximizations of the sides of (53) and of (54) over P_X do coincide: for all $\alpha > 0$,

$$\sup_X D_\alpha(P_{Y|X} \| Q_{Y|X}|P_X) = \sup_X \mathbb{E}\left[D_\alpha(P_{Y|X}(\cdot|X) \| Q_{Y|X}(\cdot|X))\right] \quad (55)$$
$$= \sup_{a \in \mathcal{A}} D_\alpha(P_{Y|X=a} \| Q_{Y|X=a}). \quad (56)$$

17. Conditional Rényi divergence satisfies the following additive decomposition, originally pointed out, without proof, by Sibson [31] in the setting of finite $\mathcal{A}$.

Theorem 4. *Given $P_X \in \mathcal{P}_\mathcal{A}$, $Q_Y \in \mathcal{P}_\mathcal{B}$, $P_{Y|X} \colon \mathcal{A} \to \mathcal{B}$, and $\alpha \in (0,1) \cup (1,\infty)$, we have*

$$D_\alpha(P_{Y|X} \| Q_Y|P_X) = D_\alpha(P_{Y|X} \| P_{Y[\alpha]}|P_X) + D_\alpha(P_{Y[\alpha]} \| Q_Y). \quad (57)$$

Furthermore, with κ_α as in (14),

$$D_\alpha\left(P_{Y|X} \| P_{Y[\alpha]}|P_X\right) = \frac{\kappa_\alpha}{\alpha - 1}. \quad (58)$$

Proof. Select an arbitrary probability measure $R_Y \in \mathcal{P}_\mathcal{B}$ that dominates both Q_Y and P_Y, and, therefore, $P_{Y[\alpha]}$ too. Letting $(X,Z) \sim P_X \times R_Y$, we have

$$D_\alpha(P_{Y|X} \| Q_Y|P_X) = \frac{1}{\alpha-1} \log \mathbb{E}\left[\left(\frac{dP_{XY}}{dP_X \times R_Y}(X,Z)\right)^\alpha \left(\frac{dQ_Y}{dR_Y}(Z)\right)^{1-\alpha}\right] \quad (59)$$
$$= \frac{1}{\alpha-1} \log \mathbb{E}\left[\mathbb{E}[\exp(\alpha\, \imath_{X;Y}(X;Z))|Z]\left(\frac{dP_Y}{dR_Y}(Z)\right)^\alpha \left(\frac{dQ_Y}{dR_Y}(Z)\right)^{1-\alpha}\right] \quad (60)$$
$$= \frac{\kappa_\alpha}{\alpha-1} + \frac{1}{\alpha-1} \log \mathbb{E}\left[\left(\frac{dP_{Y[\alpha]}}{dP_Y}(Z)\right)^\alpha \left(\frac{dP_Y}{dR_Y}(Z)\right)^\alpha \left(\frac{dQ_Y}{dR_Y}(Z)\right)^{1-\alpha}\right] \quad (61)$$
$$= \frac{\kappa_\alpha}{\alpha-1} + \frac{1}{\alpha-1} \log \mathbb{E}\left[\left(\frac{dP_{Y[\alpha]}}{dR_Y}(Z)\right)^\alpha \left(\frac{dQ_Y}{dR_Y}(Z)\right)^{1-\alpha}\right] \quad (62)$$
$$= \frac{\kappa_\alpha}{\alpha-1} + D_\alpha(P_{Y[\alpha]} \| Q_Y), \quad (63)$$

where (61) follows from (13), and (62) follows from the chain rule of Radon-Nikodym derivatives applied to $P_{Y[\alpha]} \ll P_Y \ll R_Y$. Then, (58) follows by specializing $Q_Y = P_{Y[\alpha]}$, and the proof of (57) is complete, upon plugging (58) into the right side of (63). □

A proof of (57) in the discrete case can be found in Appendix A of [37].

18. For all $\alpha > 0$, given two inputs $(P_X, Q_X) \in \mathcal{P}_\mathcal{A}^2$ and one random transformation $P_{Y|X}: \mathcal{A} \to \mathcal{B}$, Rényi divergence (and, in particular, relative entropy) satisfies the data processing inequality,

$$D_\alpha(P_X \| Q_X) \geq D_\alpha(P_Y \| Q_Y), \tag{64}$$

where $P_X \to P_{Y|X} \to P_Y$, and $Q_X \to P_{Y|X} \to Q_Y$. The data processing inequality for Rényi divergence was observed by Csiszár [52] in the more general context of f-divergences. More recently it was stated in [39,50]. Furthermore, given one input $P_X \in \mathcal{P}_\mathcal{A}$ and two transformations $P_{Y|X}: \mathcal{A} \to \mathcal{B}$ and $Q_{Y|X}: \mathcal{A} \to \mathcal{B}$, conditioning cannot decrease Rényi divergence,

$$D_\alpha(P_{Y|X} \| Q_{Y|X} | P_X) \geq D_\alpha(P_Y \| Q_Y). \tag{65}$$

Since $D_\alpha(P_{Y|X} \| Q_{Y|X} | P_X) = D_\alpha(P_X P_{Y|X} \| P_X Q_{Y|X})$, (65) follows by applying (64) to a deterministic transformation which takes an input pair and outputs the second component. Inequalities (53) and (65) imply the convexity of $D_\alpha(P \| Q)$ in (P, Q) for $\alpha \in (0, 1]$.

4. Dependence Measures

In this paper we are interested in three information measures that quantify the dependence between random variables X and Y, such that $P_X \to P_{Y|X} \to P_Y$, namely, mutual information, and two of its generalizations, α- mutual information and Augustin–Csiszár mutual information of order α.

19. The mutual information is

$$I(X;Y) = I(P_X, P_{Y|X}) = D(P_{Y|X} \| P_Y | P_X) \tag{66}$$

$$= \min_{Q_Y} D(P_{Y|X} \| Q_Y | P_X) \tag{67}$$

$$= \min_{Q_Y} D(P_{XY} \| P_X \times Q_Y). \tag{68}$$

20. Given $\alpha \in (0,1) \cup (1, \infty)$, the α-mutual information is defined as (see [30–32,40,42,45])

$$I_\alpha(X;Y) = I_\alpha(P_X, P_{Y|X}) \tag{69}$$

$$= \min_{Q_Y} D_\alpha(P_{Y|X} \| Q_Y | P_X) \tag{70}$$

$$= \min_{Q_Y} D_\alpha(P_{XY} \| P_X \times Q_Y) \tag{71}$$

$$= D_\alpha\left(P_{Y|X} \| P_{Y[\alpha]} | P_X\right) \tag{72}$$

$$= \frac{1}{\alpha - 1} \log \mathbb{E}\left[\exp\left((\alpha - 1) D_\alpha\left(P_{Y|X}(\cdot|X) \| P_{Y[\alpha]}\right)\right)\right], \quad X \sim P_X \tag{73}$$

$$= D_\alpha\left(P_{Y|X} \| P_Y | P_X\right) - D_\alpha\left(P_{Y[\alpha]} \| P_Y\right) \tag{74}$$

$$= \frac{\kappa_\alpha}{\alpha - 1} \tag{75}$$

$$= \frac{\alpha}{\alpha - 1} \log \mathbb{E}[\mathbb{E}^{\frac{1}{\alpha}}[\exp(\alpha \imath_{X;Y}(X; \tilde{Y})) | \tilde{Y}]], \quad (X, \tilde{Y}) \sim P_X \times P_Y, \tag{76}$$

where (72) and (74) follow from (57); (73) is a special case of (51); (75) follows from Theorem 4; and, (76) is (14). In view of (67) and (69), we let $I_1(X;Y) = I(X;Y)$. The notation we use for α-mutual information conforms to that used in [40,42,45,53]. Other notations include K_α in [32,38,39] and I_α^g in [43]. $I_0(X;Y)$ and $I_\infty(X;Y)$ are defined by taking the corresponding limits.

21. Theorem 4 and (72) result in the additive decomposition

$$I_\alpha(X;Y) = D_\alpha(P_{Y|X} \| Q_Y | P_X) - D_\alpha(P_{Y[\alpha]} \| Q_Y), \tag{77}$$

for any Q_Y with $D_\alpha(P_{Y[\alpha]} \| Q_Y) < \infty$, thereby generalizing the well-known decomposition for mutual information,

$$I(X;Y) = D(P_{Y|X} \| Q_Y | P_X) - D(P_Y \| Q_Y), \tag{78}$$

which, in contrast to (77), is a simple consequence of the chain rule whenever the dependence between X and Y is regular, and of Lemma A1 in general.

22. **Example 6.** *Additive independent Gaussian noise.* If $Y = X + N$, where $X \sim \mathcal{N}(0, \sigma_X^2)$ independent of $N \sim \mathcal{N}(0, \sigma_N^2)$, then, for $\alpha > 0$,

$$Y[\alpha] \sim \mathcal{N}\left(0, \alpha \sigma_X^2 + \sigma_N^2\right), \tag{79}$$

$$I_\alpha(X; X+N) = I_\alpha(X+N;X) = \frac{1}{2}\log\left(1 + \alpha \frac{\sigma_X^2}{\sigma_N^2}\right). \tag{80}$$

23. If $\alpha \in (0,1)$, (47) and (69) result in

$$(1-\alpha) I_\alpha(P_X, P_{Y|X})$$
$$= \min_{Q_X Q_{Y|X}} \left\{ D(Q_X \| P_X) + \alpha\, D(Q_{Y|X} \| P_{Y|X} | Q_X) + (1-\alpha)\, I(Q_X, Q_{Y|X}) \right\}. \tag{81}$$

For $\alpha > 1$ a proof of (81) is given in [39] for finite alphabets.

24. Unlike $I(P_X, P_{Y|X})$, we can express $I_\alpha(P_X, P_{Y|X})$ directly in terms of its arguments without involving the corresponding output distribution or the α-response to P_X. This is most evident in the case of discrete alphabets, in which (76) becomes

$$I_\alpha(X;Y) = \frac{\alpha}{\alpha-1} \log \sum_{y \in \mathcal{B}} \left(\sum_{x \in \mathcal{A}} P_X(x) P_{Y|X=x}^\alpha(y) \right)^{\frac{1}{\alpha}}, \tag{82}$$

$$I_0(X;Y) = -\log \max_{y \in \mathcal{B}} \sum_{x \in \mathcal{A}} P_X(x) \mathbf{1}\{P_{Y|X}(y|x) > 0\}, \tag{83}$$

$$I_\infty(X;Y) = \log \left(\sum_{b \in \mathcal{Y}} \sup_{a:\, P_X(a) > 0} P_{Y|X}(b|a) \right). \tag{84}$$

For example, if X is discrete and $H_\alpha(X)$ denotes the Rényi entropy of order α, then for all $\alpha > 0$,

$$H_\alpha(X) = I_{\frac{1}{\alpha}}(X;X). \tag{85}$$

If X and Y are equiprobable with $\mathbb{P}[X \neq Y] = \delta$, then, in bits, $I_\alpha(X;Y) = 1 - h_\alpha(\delta)$, where $h_\alpha(\delta)$ denotes the binary Rényi entropy.

25. In the main region of interest, namely, $\alpha \in (0,1)$, frequently we use a different parametrization in terms of $\rho > 0$, with $\alpha = \frac{1}{1+\rho}$.

Theorem 5. *For any $\rho > 0$, we have the upper bound*

$$\rho I_{\frac{1}{1+\rho}}(X;Y) \leq \min_{Q_{Y|X}: \mathcal{A} \to \mathcal{B}} \left\{ D(Q_{Y|X} \| P_{Y|X} | P_X) + \rho I(P_X, Q_{Y|X}) \right\}. \tag{86}$$

Proof. Fix $Q_{Y|X}: \mathcal{A} \to \mathcal{B}$, and let $P_X \to Q_{Y|X} \to Q_Y$. Then,

$$I_{\frac{1}{1+\rho}}(X;Y) \leq D_{\frac{1}{1+\rho}}(P_{XY} \| P_X \times Q_Y) \tag{87}$$

$$= \frac{1+\rho}{\rho} \min_{R_{XY}} \left\{ \frac{1}{1+\rho} D(R_{XY} \| P_{XY}) + \frac{\rho}{1+\rho} D(R_{XY} \| P_X \times Q_Y) \right\} \tag{88}$$

$$\leq \frac{1}{\rho} D(Q_{Y|X} P_X \| P_{XY}) + D(Q_{Y|X} P_X \| P_X \times Q_Y) \tag{89}$$

$$= \frac{1}{\rho} D(Q_{Y|X} \| P_{Y|X} | P_X) + I(P_X, Q_{Y|X}), \tag{90}$$

where (87), (88) and (90) follow from (69), (47) and (66) respectively. □

Just like (53), we will show in Section 7 that (86) becomes an equality upon the unconstrained maximization of both sides.

26. Before introducing the last dependence measure in this section, recall from Definition 7 and (58) that $P_{Y[\alpha]} \ll P_Y$, the α-response (of $P_{Y|X}$) to P_X defined by

$$\iota_{Y[\alpha] \| Y}(y) = \frac{1}{\alpha} \log \mathbb{E}[\exp\left(\alpha \iota_{X;Y}(X;y) + (1-\alpha) D_\alpha \left(P_{Y|X} \| P_{Y[\alpha]} | P_X\right)\right)], \tag{91}$$

attains $\min_{Q_Y} D_\alpha(P_{Y|X} \| Q_Y | P_X)$, where the expectation is with respect to $X \sim P_X$. We proceed to define $P_{Y\langle\alpha\rangle} \ll P_Y$, the $\langle\alpha\rangle$-response (of $P_{Y|X}$) to P_X by means of

$$\iota_{Y\langle\alpha\rangle \| Y}(y) = \frac{1}{\alpha} \log \mathbb{E}\left[\exp(\alpha \iota_{X;Y}(X;y) + (1-\alpha) D_\alpha \left(P_{Y|X}(\cdot|X) \| P_{Y\langle\alpha\rangle}\right)\right], \tag{92}$$

with $X \sim P_X$. Note that $P_{Y\langle 1\rangle} = P_{Y[1]} = P_Y$.

27. In the case of discrete alphabets, (92) becomes the implicit equation

$$P^\alpha_{Y\langle\alpha\rangle}(y) = \sum_{a \in \mathcal{A}} P_X(a) \frac{P^\alpha_{Y|X}(y|a)}{\sum_{b \in \mathcal{B}} P^\alpha_{Y|X}(b|a) P^{1-\alpha}_{Y\langle\alpha\rangle}(b)}, \quad y \in \mathcal{B}, \tag{93}$$

which coincides with (9.24) in Fano's 1961 textbook [7], with $s \leftarrow 1 - \alpha$, and is also given by Haroutunian in (19) of [22]. For example, if $\mathcal{A} = \mathcal{B}$ is discrete and $Y = X$, then $P_{Y\langle\alpha\rangle} = P_X$, while $P^\alpha_{Y[\alpha]}(y) = c\, P_X(y), y \in \mathcal{A}$.

28. The $\langle\alpha\rangle$-response satisfies the following identity, which can be regarded as the counterpart of (57) satisfied by the α-response.

Theorem 6. *Fix $P_X \in \mathcal{P}_\mathcal{A}$, $P_{Y|X}: \mathcal{A} \to \mathcal{B}$ and $Q_Y \in \mathcal{P}_\mathcal{B}$. Then,*

$$D_\alpha(P_{Y\langle\alpha\rangle} \| Q_Y)$$

$$= \frac{1}{\alpha - 1} \log \mathbb{E}\left[\exp\left((1-\alpha)\left(D_\alpha(P_{Y|X}(\cdot|X) \| P_{Y\langle\alpha\rangle}) - D_\alpha(P_{Y|X}(\cdot|X) \| Q_Y)\right)\right)\right]. \tag{94}$$

Proof. For brevity we assume $Q_Y \ll P_Y$. Otherwise, the proof is similar adopting a reference measure that dominates both Q_Y and P_Y. The definition of unconditional

Rényi divergence in Item 11 implies that we can write $(\alpha - 1)$ times the exponential of the left side of (94) as

$$\exp\left((\alpha-1)D_\alpha(P_{Y\langle\alpha\rangle}\|Q_Y)\right) = \mathbb{E}\left[\left(\frac{dP_{Y\langle\alpha\rangle}}{dP_Y}(Y)\right)^\alpha \left(\frac{dQ_Y}{dP_Y}(Y)\right)^{1-\alpha}\right] \quad (95)$$

$$= \mathbb{E}\left[\exp\left(\alpha \imath_{X;Y}(X;Y) + (1-\alpha)D_\alpha\left(P_{Y|X}(\cdot|X)\|P_{Y\langle\alpha\rangle}\right)\right)\left(\frac{dQ_Y}{dP_Y}(Y)\right)^{1-\alpha}\right] \quad (96)$$

$$= \mathbb{E}\left[\mathbb{E}\left[\exp\left(\alpha \imath_{X;Y}(X;Y) + (1-\alpha)\left(\imath_{Q_Y\|P_Y}(Y) + D_\alpha\left(P_{Y|X}(\cdot|X)\|P_{Y\langle\alpha\rangle}\right)\right)\right)\Big|X\right]\right]$$

$$= \mathbb{E}\left[\exp\left((1-\alpha)\left(D_\alpha\left(P_{Y|X}(\cdot|X)\|P_{Y\langle\alpha\rangle}\right) - D_\alpha\left(P_{Y|X}(\cdot|X)\|Q_Y\right)\right)\right)\right], \quad (97)$$

where $(X,Y) \sim P_X \times P_Y$, (96) follows from (92), and (97) follows from the definition of unconditional Rényi divergence in (27). □

Theorem 7. *If $\alpha \in (0,1]$, then*

$$D_\alpha(P_{Y\langle\alpha\rangle}\|Q_Y) \leq \mathbb{E}\left[D_\alpha(P_{Y|X}(\cdot|X)\|Q_Y)\right] - \mathbb{E}\left[D_\alpha(P_{Y|X}(\cdot|X)\|P_{Y\langle\alpha\rangle})\right] \quad (98)$$

$$\leq D(P_{Y\langle\alpha\rangle}\|Q_Y). \quad (99)$$

If $\alpha \geq 1$, inequalities (98) and (99) are reversed.

Proof. Assume $\alpha \in (0,1]$. Jensen's inequality applied to the right side of (94) results in (98). To show (99), again we assume for brevity $Q_Y \ll P_Y$, and define the positive functions $V: \mathcal{A} \times \mathcal{B} \to (0,\infty)$ and $W: \mathcal{A} \times \mathcal{B} \to (0,\infty)$,

$$V(x,y) = \exp\left(\alpha \imath_{X;Y}(x;y) + (1-\alpha)\imath_{Y\langle\alpha\rangle\|Y}(y)\right), \quad (100)$$

$$W(x,y) = \exp\left(\alpha \imath_{X;Y}(x;y) + (1-\alpha)\imath_{Q_Y\|P_Y}(y)\right). \quad (101)$$

Note that, with $(X,Y) \sim P_X \times P_Y$, and $(x,y) \in \mathcal{A} \times \mathcal{B}$,

$$\mathbb{E}[V(x,Y)] = \exp\left((\alpha-1)D_\alpha(P_{Y|X=x}\|P_{Y\langle\alpha\rangle})\right), \quad (102)$$

$$\mathbb{E}[W(x,Y)] = \exp\left((\alpha-1)D_\alpha(P_{Y|X=x}\|Q_Y)\right), \quad (103)$$

$$\mathbb{E}\left[\frac{V(X,y)}{\mathbb{E}[V(X,Y)|X]}\right] = \exp\left((1-\alpha)\imath_{Y\langle\alpha\rangle\|Y}(y)\right) \cdot$$
$$\cdot \mathbb{E}\left[\exp\left(\alpha \imath_{X;Y}(X;y) + (1-\alpha)D_\alpha(P_{Y|X}(\cdot|X)\|P_{Y\langle\alpha\rangle})\right)\right] \quad (104)$$

$$= \frac{dP_{Y\langle\alpha\rangle}}{dP_Y}(y). \quad (105)$$

where (104) uses (100) and (102) and (105) follows from (92). Then,

$$D_\alpha(P_{Y|X=x}\|Q_Y) - D_\alpha(P_{Y|X=x}\|P_{Y\langle\alpha\rangle})$$
$$= \frac{1}{1-\alpha}\log\frac{\mathbb{E}[V(x,Y)]}{\mathbb{E}[W(x,Y)]} \quad (106)$$

$$\leq \frac{1}{1-\alpha}\mathbb{E}\left[\frac{V(x,Y)}{\mathbb{E}[V(x,Y)]}\log\frac{V(x,Y)}{W(x,Y)}\right] \quad (107)$$

$$= \mathbb{E}\left[\frac{V(x,Y)}{\mathbb{E}[V(x,Y)]}\left(\imath_{Y\langle\alpha\rangle\|Y}(Y) - \imath_{Q_Y\|P_Y}(Y)\right)\right], \quad (108)$$

where the expectations are with respect to $Y \sim P_Y$, and

- (107) follows from the log-sum inequality for integrable non-negative random variables,

$$\mathbb{E}[V] \log \frac{\mathbb{E}[V]}{\mathbb{E}[W]} \leq \mathbb{E}\left[V \log \frac{V}{W}\right]; \qquad (109)$$

- (108) ⇐ (100) and (101).

Taking expectation with respect to $X \sim P_X$ of (106)–(108) yields (99) because of Lemma A1 and (105). If $\alpha \geq 1$, then Jensen's inequality applied to the right side of (94) results in (98) but with the opposite inequality. Moreover, (107) is reversed and the remainder of the proof holds verbatim. □

In the case of finite input-alphabets, a different proof of (99) is given in Appendix B of [54].

29. Introduced in the unpublished dissertation [36] and rescued from oblivion in [32], the Augustin–Csiszár mutual information of order α is defined for $\alpha > 0$ as

$$I_\alpha^c(X;Y) = I_\alpha^c(P_X, P_{Y|X}) = \min_{Q_Y} \mathbb{E}\left[D_\alpha(P_{Y|X}(\cdot|X) \| Q_Y)\right] \qquad (110)$$

$$= \mathbb{E}\left[D_\alpha(P_{Y|X}(\cdot|X) \| P_{Y\langle\alpha\rangle})\right], \qquad (111)$$

where (111) follows from (98) if $\alpha \in (0,1]$, and from the reverse of (99) if $\alpha \geq 1$. We conform to the notation in [40], where I_α^a was used to denote the difference between entropy and Arimoto-Rényi conditional entropy. In [32,39,43] the Augustin–Csiszár mutual information of order α is denoted by I_α. In Augustin's original notation [36], $I^\rho(P_X)$ means $I_{1-\rho}^c(P_X, P_{Y|X})$, $\rho \in (0,1)$. Independently of [36], Poltyrev [35] introduced a functional (expressed as a maximization over a reverse random transformation) which turns out to be $\rho I_{\frac{1}{1+\rho}}^c(X;Y)$ and which he denoted by $E_0(\rho, P_X)$, although in Gallager's notation that corresponds to $\rho I_{\frac{1}{1+\rho}}(X;Y)$, as we will see in (233). $I_0^c(X;Y)$ and $I_\infty^c(X;Y)$ are defined by taking the corresponding limits.

30. In the discrete case, (110) boils down to

$$I_\alpha^c(X;Y) = \min_{Q_Y} \frac{1}{\alpha - 1} \sum_{x \in \mathcal{A}} P_X(x) \log \sum_{y \in \mathcal{B}} P_{Y|X}^\alpha(y|x) Q_Y^{1-\alpha}(y), \qquad (112)$$

which can be juxtaposed with the much easier expression in (82) for $I_\alpha(X;Y)$ involving no further optimization. Minimizing the Lagrangian, we can verify that the minimizer in (112) satisfies (93). With $(X, \bar{Y}) \sim P_X \times Q_Y$, we have

$$I_0^c(X;Y) = \min_{Q_Y} \mathbb{E}\left[\log \frac{1}{\mathbb{P}[P_{Y|X}(\bar{Y}|X) > 0 \mid X]}\right], \qquad (113)$$

$$I_\infty^c(X;Y) = \min_{Q_Y} \mathbb{E}\left[\log \left\| \frac{P_{Y|X}(\bar{Y}|X)}{Q_Y(\bar{Y})} \right\|_\infty\right], \qquad (114)$$

where the expectations are with respect to X.

31. The respective minimizers of (72) and (110), namely, the α-response and the $\langle\alpha\rangle$-response, are quite different. Most notably, in contrast to Item 7, an explicit expression for $P_{Y\langle\alpha\rangle}$ is unknown. Instead of defining $P_{Y\langle\alpha\rangle}$ through (92), [36] defines it, equivalently, as the fixed point of the operator (dubbed the Augustin operator in [43]) which maps the set of probability measures on the output space to itself,

$$\frac{d\mathbb{T}_\alpha(Q)}{dQ}(y) = \mathbb{E}\left[\left(\frac{dP_{Y|X}}{dQ}(y|X)\right)^\alpha \exp\left((1-\alpha)D_\alpha(P_{Y|X}(\cdot|X)\|Q)\right)\right], \qquad (115)$$

where $X \sim P_X$. Although we do not rely on them, Lemma 34.2 of ($\alpha \in (0,1)$) and Lemma 13 of [43] ($\alpha > 1$) claim that the minimizer in (110), referred to in [43] as the Augustin mean of order α, is unique and is a fixed point of the operator $\mathbb{T}_\alpha$ regardless of P_X. Moreover, Lemma 13(c) of [43] establishes that for $\alpha \in (0,1)$ and finite input alphabets, repeated iterations of the operator $\mathbb{T}_\alpha$ with initial argument $P_{Y[\alpha]}$ converge to $P_{Y\langle\alpha\rangle}$.

32. It is interesting to contrast the next example with the formulas in Examples 2 and 6.

Example 7. *Additive independent Gaussian noise. If $Y = X + N$, where $X \sim \mathcal{N}(0, \sigma_X^2)$ independent of $N \sim \mathcal{N}(0, \sigma_N^2)$, then*

$$Y\langle\alpha\rangle \sim \mathcal{N}\left(0, \frac{\sigma_N^2}{2}\left(2 - \frac{1}{\alpha} + \Delta + \mathrm{snr}\right)\right), \tag{116}$$

$$\mathrm{snr} = \frac{\sigma_X^2}{\sigma_N^2}, \tag{117}$$

$$\Delta = \sqrt{4\,\mathrm{snr} + \left(\frac{1}{\alpha} - \mathrm{snr}\right)^2}. \tag{118}$$

This result can be obtained by postulating a zero-mean Gaussian distribution with variance v_α^2 as $P_{Y\langle\alpha\rangle}$ and verifying that (92) is indeed satisfied if v_α^2 is chosen as in (116). The first step is to invoke (32), which yields

$$D_\alpha\left(P_{Y|X=x} \,\|\, P_{Y\langle\alpha\rangle}\right) = \frac{\lambda_\alpha}{2} + \frac{\alpha\,x^2}{2\,s_\alpha^2}\log e, \tag{119}$$

$$\lambda_\alpha = \log \frac{v_\alpha^2}{\sigma_N^2} + \frac{1}{\alpha - 1}\log \frac{v_\alpha^2}{s_\alpha^2}, \tag{120}$$

where we have denoted $s_\alpha^2 = \alpha v_\alpha^2 + (1-\alpha)\sigma_N^2$. Since $Y \sim \mathcal{N}(0, \sigma_X^2 + \sigma_N^2)$,

$$\imath_{X;Y}(x;y) = \frac{1}{2}\log \frac{\sigma_X^2 + \sigma_N^2}{\sigma_N^2} + \frac{1}{2}\left(\frac{y^2}{\sigma_X^2 + \sigma_N^2} - \frac{(y-x)^2}{\sigma_N^2}\right)\log e, \tag{121}$$

$$\imath_{Y\langle\alpha\rangle\|Y}(y) = \frac{1}{2}\log \frac{\sigma_X^2 + \sigma_N^2}{v_\alpha^2} + \frac{1}{2}\left(\frac{y^2}{\sigma_X^2 + \sigma_N^2} - \frac{y^2}{v_\alpha^2}\right)\log e. \tag{122}$$

Assembling (120) and (121), the right side of (92) becomes

$$\frac{1}{\alpha}\log \mathbb{E}\left[\exp(\alpha\,\imath_{X;Y}(X;y) + (1-\alpha)D_\alpha\left(P_{Y|X}(\cdot|X) \,\|\, P_{Y\langle\alpha\rangle}\right)\right]$$

$$= \frac{1}{2}\log \frac{\sigma_X^2 + \sigma_N^2}{\sigma_N^2} + \frac{1}{2}\frac{y^2 \log e}{\sigma_X^2 + \sigma_N^2} + \frac{1-\alpha}{2\alpha}\lambda_\alpha$$

$$+ \frac{1}{\alpha}\log \mathbb{E}\left[\exp_e\left(-\frac{\alpha(y-X)^2}{2\sigma_N^2} + \frac{\alpha(1-\alpha)X^2}{2s_\alpha^2}\right)\right] \tag{123}$$

$$= \frac{1}{2}\log \frac{\sigma_X^2 + \sigma_N^2}{\sigma_N^2} + \frac{1-\alpha}{2\alpha}\lambda_\alpha + \frac{y^2 \log e}{2}\left(\frac{1}{\sigma_X^2 + \sigma_N^2} - \frac{s_\alpha^2 - \alpha(1-\alpha)\sigma_X^2}{\sigma_N^2 s_\alpha^2 + \alpha^2 v_\alpha^2 \sigma_X^2}\right)$$

$$+ \frac{1}{2\alpha}\log \frac{\sigma_N^2 s_\alpha^2}{\sigma_N^2 s_\alpha^2 + \alpha^2 v_\alpha^2 \sigma_X^2} \tag{124}$$

$$= \frac{1}{2}\log \frac{\sigma_X^2 + \sigma_N^2}{v_\alpha^2} + \frac{1}{2}\left(\frac{y^2}{\sigma_X^2 + \sigma_N^2} - \frac{y^2}{v_\alpha^2}\right)\log e, \tag{125}$$

where (124) follows by Gaussian integration, and the marvelous simplification in (125) is satisfied provided that we choose

$$s_\alpha^2 = \frac{\alpha \, \sigma_X^2 \, v_\alpha^2}{v_\alpha^2 - \sigma_N^2}. \qquad (126)$$

Comparing (122) and (125), we see that (92) is indeed satisfied with $Y\langle\alpha\rangle \sim \mathcal{N}(0, v_\alpha^2)$ if v_α^2 satisfies the quadratic equation (126), whose solution is in (116)–(118). Invoking (32) and (116), we obtain

$$I_\alpha^c(X; X+N) = \frac{\alpha \, \text{snr}}{1 + \alpha \Delta + \alpha \, \text{snr}} \log e + \frac{1}{2} \log\left(1 + \frac{1}{2}\left(\Delta + \text{snr} - \frac{1}{\alpha}\right)\right)$$
$$- \frac{1}{2(1-\alpha)} \log \frac{2 - \frac{1}{\alpha} + \Delta + \text{snr}}{1 + \alpha \Delta + \alpha \, \text{snr}}. \qquad (127)$$

Beyond its role in evaluating the Augustin–Csiszár mutual information for Gaussian inputs, the Gaussian distribution in (116) has found some utility in the analysis of finite blocklength fundamental limits for data transmission [55].

33. This item gives a variational representation for the Augustin–Csiszár mutual information in terms of mutual information and conditional relative entropy (i.e., non-Rényi information measures). As we will see in Section 10, this representation accounts for the role played by Augustin–Csiszár mutual information in expressing error exponent functions.

Theorem 8. *For $\alpha \in (0,1)$, the Augustin–Csiszár mutual information satisfies the variational representation in terms of conditional relative entropy and mutual information,*

$$(1-\alpha) \, I_\alpha^c(P_X, P_{Y|X}) = \min_{Q_{Y|X}} \left\{ \alpha \, D(Q_{Y|X} \| P_{Y|X} | P_X) + (1-\alpha) \, I(P_X, Q_{Y|X}) \right\}, \qquad (128)$$

where the minimum is over all the random transformations from the input to the output spaces.

Proof. Invoking (47) with $(P_1, P_0) \leftarrow (P_{Y|X=x}, Q_Y)$ we obtain

$$(1-\alpha) \, D_\alpha(P_{Y|X=x} \| Q_Y) = \min_{R_Y} \left\{ \alpha \, D(R_Y \| P_{Y|X=x}) + (1-\alpha) \, D(R_Y \| Q_Y) \right\} \qquad (129)$$

$$= \min_{R_{Y|X=x}} \left\{ \alpha \, D(R_{Y|X=x} \| P_{Y|X=x}) + (1-\alpha) \, D(R_{Y|X=x} \| Q_Y) \right\}. \qquad (130)$$

Averaging over $x \sim P_X$, followed by minimization with respect to Q_Y yields (128) upon recalling (67). □

In the finite-alphabet case with $\alpha \in (0,1) \cup (1, \infty)$, the representation in (128) is implicit in the appendix of [32], and stated explicitly in [39], where it is shown by means of a minimax theorem. This is one of the instances in which the proof of the result is considerably easier for $\alpha \in (0,1)$; we can take the following route to show (128) for $\alpha > 1$. Neglecting to emphasize its dependence on P_X, denote

$$f_\alpha(Q_Y, R_{Y|X}) = \frac{\alpha}{1-\alpha} D(R_{Y|X} \| P_{Y|X} | P_X) + D(R_{Y|X} \| Q_Y | P_X). \qquad (131)$$

Invoking (47) we obtain

$$D_\alpha(P_{Y|X=x} \| Q_Y) = \max_{R_{Y|X=x}} \left\{ \frac{\alpha}{1-\alpha} D(R_{Y|X=x} \| P_{Y|X=x}) + D(R_{Y|X=x} \| Q_Y) \right\}. \qquad (132)$$

Averaging (132) with respect to P_X followed by minimization over Q_Y, results in

$$I_\alpha^c(P_X, P_{Y|X}) = \min_{Q_Y} \max_{R_{Y|X}} f_\alpha(Q_Y, R_{Y|X}) \tag{133}$$

$$\geq \max_{R_{Y|X}} \min_{Q_Y} f_\alpha(Q_Y, R_{Y|X}) \tag{134}$$

$$= \max_{R_{Y|X}} \left\{ \frac{\alpha}{1-\alpha} D(R_{Y|X} \| P_{Y|X} | P_X) + I(P_X, R_{Y|X}) \right\}, \tag{135}$$

which shows $\geq$ in (128). If a minimax theorem can be invoked to show equality in (134), then (128) is established for $\alpha > 1$. For that purpose, for fixed $R_{Y|X}$, $f(\cdot, R_{Y|X})$ is convex and lower semicontinuous in Q_Y on the set where it is finite. Rewriting

$$f(Q_Y, R_{Y|X})$$
$$= \frac{1}{1-\alpha} D(R_{Y|X} \| P_{Y|X} | P_X) + D(R_{Y|X} \| Q_Y | P_X) - D(R_{Y|X} \| P_{Y|X} | P_X), \tag{136}$$

it can be seen that $f(Q_Y, \cdot)$ is upper semicontinuous and concave (if $\alpha > 1$). A different, and considerably more intricate route is taken in Lemma 13(d) of [43], which also gives (128) for $\alpha > 1$ assuming finite input alphabets.

34. Unlike mutual information, neither $I_\alpha(X;Y) = I_\alpha(Y;X)$ nor $I_\alpha^c(X;Y) = I_\alpha^c(Y;X)$ hold in general.

Example 8. *Erasure transformation. Let* $\mathcal{A} = \{0,1\}, \mathcal{B} = \{0,1,\mathsf{e}\}$,

$$P_{Y|X}(b|a) = \begin{cases} 1-\delta, & a=b; \\ \delta, & b=\mathsf{e}; \\ 0, & a \neq b \neq \mathsf{e}, \end{cases} \tag{137}$$

with $\delta \in (0,1)$, *and* $P_X(0) = \frac{1}{2}$. *Then, we obtain, for* $\alpha \in (0,1) \cup (1,\infty)$,

$$I_\alpha(X;Y) = I_\alpha^c(X;Y) = \frac{\alpha}{\alpha-1} \log\left(\delta + (1-\delta) 2^{\left(1-\frac{1}{\alpha}\right)}\right), \tag{138}$$

$$I_\alpha(Y;X) = \frac{1}{\alpha-1} \log\left(\delta + (1-\delta) 2^{\alpha-1}\right), \tag{139}$$

$$I_\alpha^c(Y;X) = I(X;Y) = 1-\delta \text{ bits.} \tag{140}$$

35. It was shown in Theorem 5.2 of [38] that α-mutual information satisfies the data processing lemma, namely, if X and Z are conditionally independent given Y, then

$$I_\alpha(X;Z) \leq \min\{I_\alpha(X;Y), I_\alpha(Y;Z)\}, \tag{141}$$

$$I_\alpha(Z;X) \leq \min\{I_\alpha(Z;Y), I_\alpha(Y;X)\}. \tag{142}$$

As shown by Csiszár [32] using the data processing inequality for Rényi divergence, the data processing lemma also holds for I_α^c.

36. From (53), (54) and the monotonicity of $D_\alpha(P\|Q)$ in α, we obtain the ordering

$$I_\beta(X;Y) \leq I_\alpha(X;Y) \leq I_\alpha^c(X;Y) \leq I_\nu^c(X;Y) \leq I(X;Y), \quad 0 < \beta \leq \alpha \leq \nu < 1; \tag{143}$$

$$I(X;Y) \leq I_\nu^c(X;Y) \leq I_\alpha^c(X;Y) \leq I_\alpha(X;Y) \leq I_\beta(X;Y), \quad 1 < \nu \leq \alpha \leq \beta. \tag{144}$$

37. The convexity/concavity properties of the generalized mutual informations are summarized next.

Theorem 9.
(a) $\rho I_{\frac{1}{1+\rho}}(X;Y)$ and $\rho I^c_{\frac{1}{1+\rho}}(X;Y)$ are concave and monotonically non-decreasing in $\rho \geq 0$.
(b) $I(\cdot, P_{Y|X})$ and $I^c_\alpha(\cdot, P_{Y|X})$ are concave functions. The same holds for $I_\alpha(\cdot, P_{Y|X})$ if $\alpha > 1$.
(c) If $\alpha \in (0,1)$, then $I(P_X, \cdot)$, $I_\alpha(P_X, \cdot)$ and $I^c_\alpha(P_X, \cdot)$ are convex functions.

Proof.
(a) According to (81) and (128), respectively, with $\alpha = \frac{1}{1+\rho} \in (0,1)$, $\rho I_{\frac{1}{1+\rho}}(X;Y)$ and $\rho I^c_{\frac{1}{1+\rho}}(X;Y)$ are the infima of affine functions with nonnegative slopes.

(b) For mutual information the result goes back to [56] in the finite-alphabet case. In general, it holds since (67) is the infimum of linear functions of P_X. The same reasoning applies to Augustin–Csiszár mutual information in view of (110). For α-mutual information with $\alpha > 1$, notice from (51) that $D_\alpha(P_{Y|X} \| Q_Y | P_X)$ is concave in P_X if $\alpha > 1$. Therefore,

$$I_\alpha(\lambda P_X^1 + (1-\lambda) P_X^0, P_{Y|X}) \tag{145}$$

$$= \inf_{Q_Y} D_\alpha(P_{Y|X} \| Q_Y | \lambda P_X^1 + (1-\lambda) P_X^0) \tag{146}$$

$$\geq \inf_{Q_Y} \lambda D_\alpha(P_{Y|X} \| Q_Y | P_X^1) + (1-\lambda) D_\alpha(P_{Y|X} \| Q_Y | P_X^0) \tag{147}$$

$$\geq \lambda I_\alpha(P_X^1, P_{Y|X}) + (1-\lambda) I_\alpha(P_X^0, P_{Y|X}). \tag{148}$$

(c) The convexity of $I(P_X, \cdot)$ and $I_\alpha(P_X, \cdot)$ follow from the convexity of $D_\alpha(P\|Q)$ in (P,Q) for $\alpha \in (0,1]$ as we saw in Item 18. To show convexity of $I^c_\alpha(P_X, \cdot)$ if $\alpha \in (0,1)$, we apply (169) in Item 45 with $P_{Y|X} = \lambda P^1_{Y|X} + (1-\lambda) P^0_{Y|X}$, and invoke the convexity of $I_\alpha(P_X, \cdot)$:

$$(1-\alpha) I^c_\alpha(P_X, P_{Y|X})$$

$$= \max_{Q_X} \{(1-\alpha) I_\alpha(Q_X, \lambda P^1_{Y|X} + (1-\lambda) P^0_{Y|X}) - D(P_X \| Q_X)\}, \tag{149}$$

$$\leq \max_{Q_X} \{\lambda \left(1-\alpha\right) I_\alpha(Q_X, P^1_{Y|X}) - D(P_X \| Q_X)\right)$$

$$+ (1-\lambda)\left(1-\alpha\right) I_\alpha(Q_X, P^0_{Y|X}) - D(P_X \| Q_X)\right)\} \tag{150}$$

$$\leq (1-\alpha)\left(\lambda I^c_\alpha(P_X, P^1_{Y|X}) + (1-\lambda) I^c_\alpha(P_X, P^0_{Y|X})\right). \tag{151}$$

□

Although not used in the sequel, we note, for completeness, that if $\alpha \in (0,1) \cup (1,\infty)$, [38] (see corrected version in [41]) shows that $\exp\left(\left(1 - \frac{1}{\alpha}\right) I_\alpha(\cdot, P_{Y|X})\right)/(\alpha-1)$ is concave.

5. Interplay between $I_\alpha(P_X, P_{Y|X})$ and $I^c_\alpha(P_X, P_{Y|X})$

In this section we study the interplay between both notions of mutual informations of order α, and, in particular, various variational representations of these information measures.

38. For given $\alpha \in (0,1) \cup (1,\infty)$ and $P_{Y|X}: \mathcal{A} \to \mathcal{B}$, define $Q_{X[\alpha]} \lll P_X$, the α-adjunct of P_X by

$$\imath_{Q_{X[\alpha]} \| P_X}(x) = (\alpha-1) D_\alpha\left(P_{Y|X=x} \| P_{Y[\alpha]}\right) - \kappa_\alpha, \tag{152}$$

with κ_α the constant in (14) and $P_{Y[\alpha]}$, the α-response to P_X.

39. **Example 9.** Let $Y = X + N$ with $X \sim \mathcal{N}(0, \sigma_X^2)$ independent of $N \sim \mathcal{N}(0, \sigma_N^2)$, and snr $= \frac{\sigma_X^2}{\sigma_N^2}$. The α-adjunct of the input is

$$Q_{X[\alpha]} = \mathcal{N}\left(0, \sigma_X^2 \frac{1 + \alpha^2 \, \mathrm{snr}}{1 + \alpha \, \mathrm{snr}}\right). \tag{153}$$

40. **Theorem 10.** *The $\langle \alpha \rangle$-response to $Q_{X[\alpha]}$ is $P_{Y[\alpha]}$, the α-response to P_X.*

    Proof. We just need to verify that (92) is satisfied if we substitute $Y\langle \alpha \rangle$ by $Y[\alpha]$, and instead of taking the expectation in the right side with respect to $X \sim P_X$ we take it with respect to $\widetilde{X} \sim Q_{X[\alpha]}$. Then,

$$\mathbb{E}\left[\exp(\alpha \, \imath_{X;Y}(\widetilde{X}; y) + (1-\alpha) D_\alpha\left(P_{Y|X}(\cdot|\widetilde{X}) \,\|\, P_{Y[\alpha]}\right)\right)\right]$$
$$= \mathbb{E}\left[\exp\left(\imath_{Q_{X[\alpha]}\|P_X}(X) + \alpha \, \imath_{X;Y}(X; y) + (1-\alpha) D_\alpha\left(P_{Y|X}(\cdot|X) \,\|\, P_{Y[\alpha]}\right)\right)\right] \tag{154}$$
$$= \mathbb{E}\left[\exp(\alpha \, \imath_{X;Y}(X; y) - \kappa_\alpha)\right] \tag{155}$$
$$= \exp\left(\alpha \, \imath_{Y[\alpha]\|Y}(y)\right), \tag{156}$$

where (154) is by change of measure, (155) follows by substitution of (152), and (156) is the same as (13). □

41. For given $\alpha \in (0,1) \cup (1, \infty)$ and $P_{Y|X} \colon \mathcal{A} \to \mathcal{B}$, we define $Q_{X\langle\alpha\rangle} \ll\gg P_X$, the $\langle\alpha\rangle$-adjunct of an input probability measure P_X through

$$\imath_{Q_{X\langle\alpha\rangle}\|P_X}(x) = (1-\alpha) \, D_\alpha\left(P_{Y|X=x} \,\|\, P_{Y\langle\alpha\rangle}\right) + v_\alpha, \tag{157}$$

where $P_{Y\langle\alpha\rangle}$ is the $\langle\alpha\rangle$-response to P_X and v_α is a normalizing constant so that $Q_{X\langle\alpha\rangle}$ is a probability measure. According to (9), we must have

$$\mathbb{E}\left[\exp\left(\imath_{Q_{X\langle\alpha\rangle}\|P_X}(X)\right)\right] = 1, \quad X \sim P_X. \tag{158}$$

Hence,

$$v_\alpha = (\alpha - 1) \, D_\alpha\left(P_{Y|X} \,\|\, P_{Y\langle\alpha\rangle} \,|\, Q_{X\langle\alpha\rangle}\right). \tag{159}$$

42. With the aid of the expression in Example 7, we obtain

    Example 10. Let $Y = X + N$ with $X \sim \mathcal{N}(0, \sigma_X^2)$ independent of $N \sim \mathcal{N}(0, \sigma_N^2)$, and snr $= \frac{\sigma_X^2}{\sigma_N^2}$. Then, the $\langle\alpha\rangle$-adjunct of the input is

$$Q_{X\langle\alpha\rangle} = \mathcal{N}\left(0, \sigma_X^2 \frac{1 + \alpha(\Delta + \mathrm{snr})}{1 + \alpha(\Delta - \mathrm{snr}) + 2\alpha^2 \, \mathrm{snr}}\right), \tag{160}$$

which, in contrast to $Q_{X[\alpha]}$, has larger variance than σ_X^2 if $\alpha \in (0,1)$.

43. The following result is the dual of Theorem 10.

    Theorem 11. *The α-response to $Q_{X\langle\alpha\rangle}$ is $P_{Y\langle\alpha\rangle}$, the $\langle\alpha\rangle$-response to P_X. Therefore,*

$$v_\alpha = (\alpha - 1) \, I_\alpha\left(Q_{X\langle\alpha\rangle}, P_{Y|X}\right). \tag{161}$$

Proof. The proof is similar to that of Theorem 10. We just need to verify that we obtain the right side of (92) if on the right side of (91) we substitute P_X by $Q_{X\langle\alpha\rangle}$ and $P_{Y[\alpha]}$ by $P_{Y\langle\alpha\rangle}$. Let $\bar{X} \sim Q_{X\langle\alpha\rangle}$. Then,

$$\frac{1}{\alpha} \log \mathbb{E}\left[\exp\left(\alpha \imath_{X;Y}(\bar{X};y) + (1-\alpha)D_\alpha\left(P_{Y|X} \| P_{Y\langle\alpha\rangle}|Q_{X\langle\alpha\rangle}\right)\right)\right]$$
$$= \frac{1}{\alpha} \log \mathbb{E}\left[\exp\left(\imath_{Q_{X\langle\alpha\rangle}\|P_X}(X) + \alpha \imath_{X;Y}(X;y) - v_\alpha\right)\right] \tag{162}$$
$$= \frac{1}{\alpha} \log \mathbb{E}\left[\exp\left(\alpha \imath_{X;Y}(X;y) + (1-\alpha)D_\alpha\left(P_{Y|X}(\cdot|X) \| P_{Y\langle\alpha\rangle}\right)\right)\right] \tag{163}$$
$$= \imath_{Y\langle\alpha\rangle\|Y}(y), \tag{164}$$

where (162)–(164) follow by change of measure, (157), and (92), respectively. □

44. By recourse to a minimax theorem, the following representation is given for $\alpha \in (0,1) \cup (1,\infty)$ in the case of finite alphabets in [39], and dropping the restriction on the finiteness of the output space in [43]. As we show, a very simple and general proof is possible for $\alpha \in (0,1)$.

Theorem 12. *Fix* $\alpha \in (0,1)$, $P_X \in \mathcal{P}_\mathcal{A}$ *and* $P_{Y|X}: \mathcal{A} \to \mathcal{B}$. *Then,*

$$(1-\alpha) I_\alpha(X;Y) = \min_{Q_X}\left\{(1-\alpha) I_\alpha^c(Q_X, P_{Y|X}) + D(Q_X \| P_X)\right\}, \tag{165}$$

where the minimum is attained by $Q_{X[\alpha]}$, *the α-adjunct of* P_X *defined in (152).*

Proof. The variational representations in (81) and (128) result in (165). To show that the minimum is indeed attained by $Q_{X[\alpha]}$, recall from Theorem 10 that the $\langle\alpha\rangle$-response to $Q_{X[\alpha]}$ is $P_{Y[\alpha]}$. Therefore, evaluating the term in {} in (165) for $Q_X \leftarrow Q_{X[\alpha]}$ yields, with $\tilde{X} \sim Q_{X[\alpha]}$,

$$(1-\alpha) I_\alpha^c(Q_{X[\alpha]}, P_{Y|X}) + D(Q_{X[\alpha]} \| P_X)$$
$$= (1-\alpha) \mathbb{E}\left[D_\alpha(P_{Y|X}(\cdot|\tilde{X}) \| P_{Y[\alpha]})\right] + D(Q_{X[\alpha]} \| P_X) \tag{166}$$
$$= -\kappa_\alpha \tag{167}$$
$$= (1-\alpha) I_\alpha(X;Y), \tag{168}$$

where (167) follows from (152) and (168) results from (69)–(75). □

45. For finite-input alphabets, Lemma 18(b) of [43] (earlier Theorem 3.4 of [35]) gave an equivalent variational characterization assuming, in addition, finite output alphabets) established the following dual to Theorem 12.

Theorem 13. *Fix* $\alpha \in (0,1)$, $P_X \in \mathcal{P}_\mathcal{A}$ *and* $P_{Y|X}: \mathcal{A} \to \mathcal{B}$. *Then,*

$$(1-\alpha) I_\alpha^c(X;Y) = \max_{Q_X}\left\{(1-\alpha) I_\alpha(Q_X, P_{Y|X}) - D(P_X \| Q_X)\right\}. \tag{169}$$

The maximum is attained by $Q_{X\langle\alpha\rangle}$, *the $\langle\alpha\rangle$-adjunct of* P_X *defined by (157).*

Proof. First observe that (165) implies that $\geqslant$ holds in (169). Second, the term in {} on the right side of (169) evaluated at $Q_X \leftarrow Q_{X\langle\alpha\rangle}$ becomes

$$(1-\alpha) I_\alpha(Q_{X\langle\alpha\rangle}, P_{Y|X}) - D(P_X \| Q_{X\langle\alpha\rangle})$$
$$= (1-\alpha) I_\alpha(Q_{X\langle\alpha\rangle}, P_{Y|X}) + (1-\alpha)I_\alpha^c(P_X, P_{Y|X}) + v_\alpha \tag{170}$$
$$= (1-\alpha)I_\alpha^c(P_X, P_{Y|X}), \tag{171}$$

where (170) follows by taking the expectation of minus (157) with respect to P_X. Therefore, $\leq$ also holds in (169) and the maximum is attained by $Q_{X\langle\alpha\rangle}$, as we wanted to show. □

Hinging on Theorem 8, Theorems 12 and 13 are given for $\alpha \in (0,1)$ which is the region of interest in the analysis of error exponents. Whenever, as in the finite-alphabet case, (128) holds for $\alpha > 1$, Theorems 12 and 13 also hold for $\alpha > 1$.

Notice that since the definition of $Q_{X\langle\alpha\rangle}$ involves $P_{Y\langle\alpha\rangle}$, the fact that it attains the maximum in (169) does not bring us any closer to finding $I_\alpha^c(X;Y)$ for a specific input probability measure P_X. Fortunately, as we will see in Section 8, (169) proves to be the gateway to the maximization of $I_\alpha^c(X;Y)$ in the presence of input-cost constraints.

46. Focusing on the main range of interest, $\alpha \in (0,1)$, we can express (169) as

$$I_\alpha^c(P_X, P_{Y|X}) = \max_{Q_X}\left\{I_\alpha(Q_X, P_{Y|X}) - \frac{1}{1-\alpha}D(P_X \| Q_X)\right\} \quad (172)$$

$$= \max_{\xi \geq 0}\left\{\mathbb{I}(\xi) - \frac{\xi}{1-\alpha}\right\} \quad (173)$$

$$= \mathbb{I}(\xi_\alpha) - \frac{\xi_\alpha}{1-\alpha}, \quad (174)$$

where we have defined the function (dependent on α, P_X, and $P_{Y|X}$)

$$\mathbb{I}(\xi) = \max_{\substack{Q_X: \\ D(P_X \| Q_X) \leq \xi}} I_\alpha(Q_X, P_{Y|X}), \quad (175)$$

and ξ_α is the solution to

$$\dot{\mathbb{I}}(\xi_\alpha) = \frac{1}{1-\alpha}. \quad (176)$$

Recall that the maxima over the input distribution in (172) and (175) are attained by the $\langle\alpha\rangle$-adjunct $Q_{X\langle\alpha\rangle}$ defined in Item 41.

47. At this point it is convenient to summarize the notions of input and output probability measures that we have defined for a given α, random transformation $P_{Y|X}$, and input probability measure P_X:

- P_Y: The familiar output probability measure $P_X \to P_{Y|X} \to P_Y$, defined in Item 5.
- $P_{Y[\alpha]}$: The α-response to P_X, defined in Item 7. It is the unique achiever of the minimization in the definition of α-mutual information in (67).
- $P_{Y\langle\alpha\rangle}$: The $\langle\alpha\rangle$-response to P_X defined in Item 26. It is the unique achiever of the minimization in the definition of Augustin–Csiszár α-mutual information in (110).
- $Q_{X[\alpha]}$: The α-adjunct of P_X, defined in (152). The $\langle\alpha\rangle$-response to $Q_{X[\alpha]}$ is $P_{Y[\alpha]}$. Furthermore, $Q_{X[\alpha]}$ achieves the minimum in (165).
- $Q_{X\langle\alpha\rangle}$: The $\langle\alpha\rangle$-adjunct of P_X, defined in (157). The α-response to $Q_{X\langle\alpha\rangle}$ is $P_{Y\langle\alpha\rangle}$. Furthermore, $Q_{X\langle\alpha\rangle}$ achieves the maximum in (169).

6. Maximization of $I_\alpha(X;Y)$

Just like the maximization of mutual information with respect to the input distribution yields the channel capacity (of course, subject to conditions [57]), the maximization of $I_\alpha(X;Y)$ and of $I_\alpha^c(X;Y)$ arises in the analysis of error exponents, as we will see in Section 10. A recent in-depth treatment of the maximization of α-mutual information is given in [45]. As we see most clearly in (82) for the discrete case, when it comes to its optimization, one advantage of $I_\alpha(X;Y)$ over $I(X;Y)$ is that the input distribution does not affect the expression through its influence on the output distribution.

48. The maximization of α-mutual information is facilitated by the following result.

Theorem 14 ([45]). *Given $\alpha \in (0,1) \cup (1, \infty)$; a random transformation $P_{Y|X} \colon \mathcal{A} \to \mathcal{B}$; and, a convex set $\mathcal{P} \subset \mathcal{P}_\mathcal{A}$, the following are equivalent.*

(a) $P_X^* \in \mathcal{P}$ *attains the maximal α-mutual information on $\mathcal{P}$,*

$$I_\alpha(P_X^*, P_{Y|X}) = \max_{P \in \mathcal{P}} I_\alpha(P, P_{Y|X}) < \infty. \tag{177}$$

(b) *For any $P_X \in \mathcal{P}$, and any output distribution $Q_Y \in \mathcal{P}_\mathcal{B}$,*

$$D_\alpha(P_{Y|X} \| P_{Y[\alpha]}^* | P_X) \leqslant D_\alpha(P_{Y|X} \| P_{Y[\alpha]}^* | P_X^*) \tag{178}$$

$$\leqslant D_\alpha(P_{Y|X} \| Q_Y | P_X^*), \tag{179}$$

where $P_{Y[\alpha]}^*$ is the α-response to P_X^*.

Moreover, if $P_{Y[\alpha]}$ denotes the α-response to P_X, then

$$D_\alpha(P_{Y[\alpha]} \| P_{Y[\alpha]}^*) \leqslant I_\alpha(P_X^*, P_{Y|X}) - I_\alpha(P_X, P_{Y|X}) < \infty. \tag{180}$$

Note that, while $I_\alpha(\cdot, P_{Y|X})$ may not be maximized by a unique (or, in fact, by any) input distribution, the resulting α-response $P_{Y[\alpha]}^*$ is indeed unique. If $\mathcal{P}$ is such that none of its elements attain the maximal I_α, it is known [42,45] that the α-response to any asymptotically optimal sequence of input distributions converges to $P_{Y[\alpha]}^*$. This is the counterpart of a result by Kemperman [58] concerning mutual information.

49. The following example appears in [45].

Example 11. Let $Y = X + N$ where $N \sim \mathcal{N}(0, \sigma_N^2)$ independent of X. Fix $\alpha \in (0,1)$ and $P > 0$. Suppose that the set, $\mathcal{P} \subset \mathcal{P}_\mathcal{A}$, of allowable input probability measures consists of those that satisfy the constraint

$$\mathbb{E}\left[\exp_e\left(-\frac{\alpha(1-\alpha)X^2}{2(\alpha^2 P + \sigma_N^2)}\right)\right] \geqslant \sqrt{\frac{\alpha^2 P + \sigma_N^2}{\alpha P + \sigma_N^2}}. \tag{181}$$

We can readily check that $X^* \sim \mathcal{N}(0, P)$ satisfies (181) with equality, and as we saw in Example 2, its α-response is $P_{Y[\alpha]}^* = \mathcal{N}(0, \alpha P + \sigma^2)$. Theorem 14 establishes that P_X^* does indeed maximize the α-mutual information among all the distributions in $\mathcal{P}$, yielding (recall Example 6)

$$\max_{P_X \in \mathcal{P}} I_\alpha(X; Y) = \frac{1}{2} \log\left(1 + \frac{\alpha P}{\sigma^2}\right). \tag{182}$$

Curiously, if, instead of $\mathcal{P}$ defined by the constraint (181), we consider the more conventional $\mathcal{P} = \{X \colon \mathbb{E}[X^2] \leqslant P\}$, then the left side of (182) is unknown at present. Numerical evidence shows that it can exceed the right side by employing non-Gaussian inputs.

50. Recalling (56) and (178) implies that if P_X^* attains the finite maximal unconstrained α-mutual information and its α-response is denoted by $P_{Y[\alpha]}^*$, then,

$$\max_X I_\alpha(X;Y) = \max_{P \in \mathcal{P}} I_\alpha(P, P_{Y|X}) = \max_{a \in \mathcal{A}} D_\alpha(P_{Y|X=a} \| P_{Y[\alpha]}^*), \tag{183}$$

which requires that $P_X^*(\mathcal{A}_\alpha^*) = 1$, with

$$\mathcal{A}_\alpha^* = \left\{x \in \mathcal{A} \colon D_\alpha(P_{Y|X=x} \| P_{Y[\alpha]}^*) = \max_{a \in \mathcal{A}} D_\alpha(P_{Y|X=a} \| P_{Y[\alpha]}^*)\right\}. \tag{184}$$

For discrete alphabets, this requires that if $x \notin \mathcal{A}_\alpha^*$, then $P_X^*(x) = 0$, which is tantamount to

$$\sum_{y \in \mathcal{B}} P_{Y|X}^\alpha(y|x) \, \mathbb{E}^{\frac{1-\alpha}{\alpha}}\left[P_{Y|X}^\alpha(y|X^*)\right] \geq \exp\left(\frac{\alpha-1}{\alpha} I_\alpha(X^*; Y^*)\right), \tag{185}$$

with equality for all $x \in \mathcal{A}$ such that $P_X^*(x) > 0$. For finite-alphabet random transformations this observation is equivalent to Theorem 5.6.5 in [9].

51. Getting slightly ahead of ourselves, we note that, in view of (128), an important consequence of Theorem 15 below, is that, as anticipated in Item 25, the unconstrained maximization of $I_\alpha(X; Y)$ for $\alpha \in (0, 1)$ can be expressed in terms of the solution to an optimization problem involving only conventional mutual information and conditional relative entropy. For $\rho \geq 0$,

$$\rho \sup_X I_{\frac{1}{1+\rho}}(X; Y) = \sup_X \min_{Q_{Y|X}: \mathcal{A} \to \mathcal{B}} \left\{ D(Q_{Y|X} \| P_{Y|X} | P_X) + \rho \, I(P_X, Q_{Y|X}) \right\}. \tag{186}$$

7. Unconstrained Maximization of $I_\alpha^c(X;Y)$

52. In view of the fact that it is much easier to determine the α-mutual information than the order-α Augustin–Csiszár information, it would be advantageous to show that the unconstrained maximum of $I_\alpha^c(X; Y)$ equals the unconstrained maximum of $I_\alpha(X; Y)$. In the finite-alphabet setting, in which it is possible to invoke a "minisup" theorem (e.g., see Section 7.1.7 of [59]), Csiszár [32] showed this result for $\alpha > 0$. The assumption of finite output alphabets was dropped in Theorem 1 of [42], and further generalized in Theorem 3 of the same reference. As we see next, for $\alpha \in (0, 1)$, it is possible to give an elementary proof without restrictions on the alphabets.

Theorem 15. *Let $\alpha \in (0, 1)$. If the suprema are over $\mathcal{P}_\mathcal{A}$, the set of all probability measures defined on the input space, then*

$$\sup_X I_\alpha^c(X; Y) = \sup_X I_\alpha(X; Y). \tag{187}$$

Proof. In view of (143), $\geq$ holds in (187). To show $\leq$, we assume $\sup_X I_\alpha(X; Y) < \infty$ as, otherwise, there is nothing left to prove. The unconstrained maximization identity in (183) implies

$$\sup_X I_\alpha(X; Y) = \sup_{a \in \mathcal{A}} D_\alpha(P_{Y|X=a} \| P_{Y[\alpha]}^*) \tag{188}$$

$$= \sup_{P_X \in \mathcal{P}} \mathbb{E}\left[D_\alpha(P_{Y|X}(\cdot|X) \| P_{Y[\alpha]}^*)\right] \tag{189}$$

$$\geq \inf_{Q \in \mathcal{Q}} \sup_{P_X \in \mathcal{P}} \mathbb{E}\left[D_\alpha(P_{Y|X}(\cdot|X) \| Q)\right] \tag{190}$$

$$\geq \sup_{P_X \in \mathcal{P}} \inf_{Q \in \mathcal{Q}} \mathbb{E}\left[D_\alpha(P_{Y|X}(\cdot|X) \| Q)\right] \tag{191}$$

$$= \sup_X I_\alpha^c(X; Y), \tag{192}$$

where $P_{Y[\alpha]}^*$ is the unique α-response to any input that achieves the maximal α-mutual information, and if there is no such input, it is the limit of the α-responses to any asymptotically optimal input sequence (Item 48). □

Furthermore, if $\{X_n\}$ is asymptotically optimal for I_α, i.e., $\lim_{n\to\infty} I_\alpha(X_n;Y_n) = \sup_X I_\alpha(X;Y)$, then $\{X_n\}$ is also asymptotically optimal for I_α^c because for any $\delta > 0$, we can find N, such that for all $n > N$,

$$I_\alpha(X_n;Y_n) + \delta \geq \sup_{a\in\mathcal{A}} D_\alpha(P_{Y|X=a}\|P^*_{Y[\alpha]}) \tag{193}$$

$$\geq \mathbb{E}\left[D_\alpha(P_{Y|X}(\cdot|X_n)\|P^*_{Y[\alpha]})\right] \tag{194}$$

$$\geq I_\alpha^c(X_n;Y_n) \tag{195}$$

$$\geq I_\alpha(X_n;Y_n). \tag{196}$$

8. Maximization of $I_\alpha^c(X;Y)$ Subject to Average Cost Constraints

This section is at the heart of the relevance of Rényi information measures to error exponent functions.

53. Given $\alpha \in (0,1)$, $P_{Y|X}\colon \mathcal{A} \to \mathcal{B}$, a cost function $b\colon \mathcal{A} \to [0,\infty)$ and real scalar $\theta \geq 0$, the objective is to maximize the Augustin–Csiszár mutual information allowing only those probability measures that satisfy $\mathbb{E}[b(X)] \leq \theta$, namely,

$$\mathbb{C}_\alpha^c(\theta) = \sup_{\substack{P_X:\\ \mathbb{E}[b(X)] \leq \theta}} I_\alpha^c(P_X, P_{Y|X}). \tag{197}$$

Unfortunately, identity (187) no longer holds when the maximizations over the input probability measure are cost-constrained, and, in general, we can only claim

$$\mathbb{C}_\alpha^c(\theta) \geq \sup_{\substack{P_X:\\ \mathbb{E}[b(X)] \leq \theta}} I_\alpha(P_X, P_{Y|X}). \tag{198}$$

A conceptually simple approach to solve for $\mathbb{C}_\alpha^c(\theta)$ is to

(a) postulate an input probability measure P_X^* that achieves the supremum in (197);
(b) solve for its $\langle\alpha\rangle$-response P_Y^* using (92);
(c) show that (P_X^*, P_Y^*) is a saddle point for the game with payoff function

$$B(P_X, Q_Y) = \int D_\alpha\left(P_{Y|X=x}\|Q_Y\right) dP_X, \tag{199}$$

where $Q_Y \in \mathcal{P}_\mathcal{A}$ and P_X is chosen from the convex subset of $\mathcal{P}_\mathcal{A}$ of probability measures which satisfy $\mathbb{E}[b(X)] \leq \theta$.

Since P_Y^* is already known, by definition, to be the $\langle\alpha\rangle$-response to P_X^*, verifying the saddle point is tantamount to showing that $B(P_X, P_Y^*)$ is maximized by P_X^* among $\{P_X \in \mathcal{P}_\mathcal{A}\colon \mathbb{E}[b(X)] \leq \theta\}$. Theorem 1 of [43] guarantees the existence of a saddle point in the case of finite input alphabets. In addition to the fact that it is not always easy to guess the optimum input P_X^* (see e.g., Section 12), the main stumbling block is the difficulty in determining the $\langle\alpha\rangle$-response to any candidate input distribution, although sometimes this is indeed feasible as we saw in Example 7.

54. Naturally, Theorem 15 implies

$$\mathbb{C}_\alpha^c(\theta) \leq \sup_X I_\alpha(X;Y). \tag{200}$$

If the unconstrained maximization of $I_\alpha^c(\cdot, P_{Y|X})$ is achieved by an input distribution $X^\star$ that satisfies $\mathbb{E}[b(X^\star)] \leq \theta$, then equality holds in (200), which, in turn, is equal to $I_\alpha^c(P_X^\star, P_{Y|X})$. In that case, the average cost constraint is said to be inactive. For most cost functions and random transformations of practical interest, the cost constraint is active for all $\theta > 0$. To ascertain whether it is, we simply verify whether there exists an input achieving the right side of (200), which happens to satisfy the constraint.

If so, $\mathbb{C}_\alpha^c(\theta)$ has been found. The same holds if we can find a sequence $\{X_n\}$ such that $\mathbb{E}[b(X_n)] \leq \theta$ and $I_\alpha(X_n;Y_n) \to \sup_X I_\alpha(X;Y)$. Otherwise, we proceed with the method described below. Thus, henceforth, we assume that the cost constraint is active.

55. The approach proposed in this paper to solve for $\mathbb{C}_\alpha^c(\theta)$ for $\alpha \in (0,1)$ hinges on the variational representation in (172), which allows us to sidestep having to find any $\langle \alpha \rangle$-response. Note that once we set out to maximize $I_\alpha^c(P_X, P_{Y|X})$ over $\mathcal{P} = \{P_X \in \mathcal{P}_\mathcal{A}: \mathbb{E}[b(X)] \leq \theta\}$, the allowable Q_X in the maximization in (175) range over a ξ-blow-up of $\mathcal{P}$ defined by

$$\Gamma_\xi(\mathcal{P}) = \{Q_X \in \mathcal{P}_\mathcal{A}: \exists P_X \in \mathcal{P}, \text{ such that } D(P_X \| Q_X) \leq \xi\}. \tag{201}$$

As we show in Item 56, we can accomplish such an optimization by solving an unconstrained maximization of the sum of α-mutual information and a term suitably derived from the cost function.

56. It will not be necessary to solve for (176), as our goal is to further maximize (172) over P_X subject to an average cost constraint. The Lagrangian corresponding to the constrained optimization in (197) is

$$\mathbb{L}_\alpha(\nu, P_X) = I_\alpha^c(X;Y) - \nu \, \mathbb{E}[b(X)] + \nu \theta, \tag{202}$$

where on the left side we have omitted, for brevity, the dependence on θ stemming from the last term on the right side. The Lagrange multiplier method (e.g., [60]) implies that if X^* achieves the supremum in (197), then there exists $\nu^* \geq 0$ such that for all P_X on $\mathcal{A}$ and $\nu \geq 0$,

$$\mathbb{L}_\alpha(\nu^*, P_X) \leq \mathbb{L}_\alpha(\nu^*, P_X^*) \leq \mathbb{L}_\alpha(\nu, P_X^*). \tag{203}$$

Note from (202) that the right inequality in (203) can only be achieved if

$$\mathbb{E}[b(X^*)] = \theta, \tag{204}$$

and, consequently,

$$\mathbb{C}_\alpha^c(\theta) = \mathbb{L}_\alpha(\nu^*, P_X^*) = \min_{\nu \geq 0} \max_{P_X} \mathbb{L}_\alpha(\nu, P_X) = \max_{P_X} \min_{\nu \geq 0} \mathbb{L}_\alpha(\nu, P_X). \tag{205}$$

The pivotal result enabling us to obtain $\mathbb{C}_\alpha^c(\theta)$ without the need to deal with Augustin–Csiszár mutual information is the following.

Theorem 16. *Given $\alpha \in (0,1)$, $\nu \geq 0$, $P_{Y|X}: \mathcal{A} \to \mathcal{B}$, and $b: \mathcal{A} \to [0,\infty)$, denote the function*

$$\mathbb{A}_\alpha(\nu) = \max_X \left\{ I_\alpha(X;Y) + \frac{1}{1-\alpha} \log \mathbb{E}[\exp(-(1-\alpha)\nu \, b(X))] \right\}. \tag{206}$$

Then,

$$\sup_{P_X \in \mathcal{P}_\mathcal{A}} \mathbb{L}_\alpha(\nu, P_X) = \nu \theta + \mathbb{A}_\alpha(\nu), \tag{207}$$

and

$$\mathbb{C}_\alpha^c(\theta) = \min_{\nu \geq 0} \{\nu \theta + \mathbb{A}_\alpha(\nu)\}. \tag{208}$$

Proof. Plugging (172) into (197) we obtain, with $X \sim P_X$, and $\hat{X} \sim Q_X$,

$$\sup_{P_X \in \mathcal{P}_A} \mathbb{L}_\alpha(\nu, P_X) = \sup_{P_X} \{I_\alpha^c(X;Y) - \nu\, \mathbb{E}[b(X)] + \nu\theta\} \qquad (209)$$

$$= \sup_{P_X \in \mathcal{P}_A} \left\{ \max_{Q_X \in \mathcal{P}_A} \left\{ I_\alpha(Q_X, P_{Y|X}) - \frac{1}{1-\alpha} D(P_X \| Q_X) \right\} - \nu\, \mathbb{E}[b(X)] + \nu\theta \right\} \qquad (210)$$

$$= \nu\theta + \max_{Q_X \in \mathcal{P}_A} \left\{ I_\alpha(Q_X, P_{Y|X}) - \frac{1}{1-\alpha} \inf_{P_X} \{D(P_X \| Q_X) + \nu(1-\alpha)\mathbb{E}[b(X)]\} \right\} \qquad (211)$$

$$= \nu\theta + \max_{Q_X \in \mathcal{P}_A} \left\{ I_\alpha(Q_X, P_{Y|X}) + \frac{1}{1-\alpha} \log \mathbb{E}\!\left[\exp\!\big(-\nu(1-\alpha)b(\hat{X})\big)\right] \right\} \qquad (212)$$

$$= \nu\theta + \mathbb{A}_\alpha(\nu), \qquad (213)$$

where (209) and (213) follow from (202) and (206), respectively, and (212) follows by invoking Theorem 1 with $Z \sim Q_X$ and

$$g(a) = (1-\alpha)\nu\, b(a), \qquad (214)$$

which is nonnegative since $\alpha \in (0,1)$ and $\nu > 0$. Finally, (208) follows from (205) and (207). □

In conclusion, we have shown that the maximization of Augustin–Csiszár mutual information of order α subject to $\mathbb{E}[b(X)] \leq \theta$ boils down to the unconstrained maximization of a Lagrangian consisting of the sum of α-mutual information and an exponential average of the cost function. Circumventing the need to deal with $\langle\alpha\rangle$-responses and with Augustin–Csiszár mutual information of order α leads to a particularly simple optimization, as illustrated in Sections 11 and 12.

57. Theorem 16 solves for the maximal Augustin–Csiszár mutual information of order α under an average cost constraint without having to find out the input probability measure P_X^* that attains it nor its $\langle\alpha\rangle$-response P_Y^* (using the notation in Item 53). Instead, it gives the solution as

$$\mathbb{C}_\alpha^c(\theta) = \min_{\nu \geq 0} \left\{ \nu\theta + \max_X \left\{ I_\alpha(X;Y) + \frac{1}{1-\alpha} \log \mathbb{E}[\exp(-(1-\alpha)\nu\, b(X))] \right\} \right\}. \qquad (215)$$

Although we are not going to invoke a minimax theorem, with the aid of Theorem 9-(b) we can see that the functional within the inner brackets is concave in P_X; Furthermore, if $V \in (0,1]$, then $\log \mathbb{E}[V^\nu]$ is easily seen to be convex in ν with the aid of the Cauchy-Schwarz inequality. Before we characterize the saddle point (ν^*, Q_X^*) of the game in (215) we note that (P_X^*, P_Y^*) can be readily obtained from (ν^*, Q_X^*).

Theorem 17. *Fix $\alpha \in (0,1)$. Let $\nu^* > 0$ denote the minimizer on the right side of (215), and Q_X^* the input probability measure that attains the maximum in (206) (or (215)) for $\nu = \nu^*$. Then,*

(a) Q_X^* is the $\langle\alpha\rangle$-adjunct of P_X^*.
(b) $P_Y^* = Q_{Y[\alpha]}^*$, the α-response to Q_X^*.

(c) $P_X^* \ll\gg Q_X^*$ with

$$\imath_{P_X^* \| Q_X^*}(a) = -(1-\alpha)\nu^*\, b(a) + \tau_\alpha, \quad a \in \mathcal{A}, \qquad (216)$$

where τ_α is a normalizing constant ensuring that P_X^* is a probability measure.

Proof.

(a) We had already established in Theorem 13 that the maximum on the right side of (210) is achieved by the $\langle\alpha\rangle$-adjunct of P_X. In the special case $\nu = \nu^*$, such

P_X is P_X^*. Therefore, Q_X^*, the argument that achieves the maximum in (206) for $\nu = \nu^*$, is the $\langle\alpha\rangle$-adjunct of P_X^*.

(b) According to Theorem 11, the α-response to Q_X^* is the $\langle\alpha\rangle$-response to P_X^*, which is P_Y^* by definition.

(c) For $\nu = \nu^*$, P_X^* achieves the supremum in (209) and the infimum in (211). Therefore, (216) follows from Theorem 1 with $Z \sim Q_X^*$ and $g(\cdot)$ given by (214) particularized to $\nu = \nu^*$.

□

The saddle point of (215) admits the following characterization.

Theorem 18. *If $\alpha \in (0,1)$, the saddle point (ν^*, Q_X^*) of (215) satisfies*

$$\mathbb{E}\big[\mathsf{b}(\bar{X}^*)\exp\big(-(1-\alpha)\nu^*\mathsf{b}(\bar{X}^*)\big)\big] = \theta\,\mathbb{E}\big[\exp\big(-(1-\alpha)\nu^*\mathsf{b}(\bar{X}^*)\big)\big], \quad \bar{X}^* \sim Q_X^*; \quad (217)$$

$$D_\alpha\big(P_{Y|X=a} \,\|\, Q^*_{Y[\alpha]}\big) = \nu^*\mathsf{b}(a) + c_\alpha(\nu^*), \quad a \in \mathcal{A}, \quad (218)$$

where $Q^*_{Y[\alpha]}$ is the α-response to Q_X^*, and $c_\alpha(\nu^*)$ does not depend on $a \in \mathcal{A}$. Furthermore,

$$\mathbb{A}_\alpha(\nu^*) = c_\alpha(\nu^*), \quad (219)$$

$$\mathbb{C}^c_\alpha(\theta) = \nu^*\theta + c_\alpha(\nu^*). \quad (220)$$

Proof. First, we show that the scalar $\nu^* \geq 0$ that minimizes

$$f(\nu) = \nu\theta + I_\alpha(Q_X^*, P_{Y|X}) + \frac{1}{1-\alpha}\log\mathbb{E}\big[\exp\big(-(1-\alpha)\nu\mathsf{b}(\bar{X}^*)\big)\big] \quad (221)$$

satisfies (217). If we abbreviate $V = \exp\big(-(1-\alpha)\mathsf{b}(\bar{X}^*)\big) \in (0,1]$, then the dominated convergence theorem results in

$$\frac{d}{d\nu}\left\{\nu\theta + \frac{1}{1-\alpha}\log\mathbb{E}[V^\nu]\right\} = \theta + \frac{1}{1-\alpha}\frac{\mathbb{E}[V^\nu \log V]}{\mathbb{E}[V^\nu]}. \quad (222)$$

Therefore, (217) is equivalent to $\dot{f}(\nu^*) = 0$, which is all we need on account of the convexity of $f(\cdot)$. To show (218), notice that for all $a \in \mathcal{A}$,

$$(1-\alpha)\nu^*\mathsf{b}(a) - \tau_\alpha = \imath_{Q_X^* \| P_X^*}(a) \quad (223)$$

$$= (1-\alpha)D_\alpha(P_{Y|X=a} \,\|\, P_Y^*) + \nu_\alpha, \quad (224)$$

where (223) is (216) and (224) is (157) with $P_{Y\langle\alpha\rangle} \leftarrow P_Y^*$ in view of Theorem 17-(b). In conclusion, (218) holds with

$$c_\alpha(\nu^*) = \frac{\nu_\alpha + \tau_\alpha}{\alpha - 1}. \quad (225)$$

Finally, (206) implies

$$\mathbb{A}_\alpha(\nu^*) = I_\alpha(Q_X^*, P_{Y|X}) + \frac{1}{1-\alpha}\log\mathbb{E}\big[\exp\big(-(1-\alpha)\nu^*\, b(\tilde{X}^*)\big)\big] \qquad (226)$$

$$= \frac{1}{\alpha-1}\log\mathbb{E}\big[\exp\big((\alpha-1)D_\alpha\big(P_{Y|X}(\cdot|\tilde{X}^*)\,\|\,P_Y^*\big)\big)\big]$$

$$+ \frac{1}{1-\alpha}\log\mathbb{E}\big[\exp((\alpha-1)\nu^*\, b(\tilde{X}^*))\big] \qquad (227)$$

$$= \frac{1}{\alpha-1}\log\mathbb{E}\big[\exp((\alpha-1)(\nu^*\, b(\tilde{X}^*) + c_\alpha(\nu^*)))\big]$$

$$+ \frac{1}{1-\alpha}\log\mathbb{E}\big[\exp((\alpha-1)\nu^*\, b(\tilde{X}^*))\big] \qquad (228)$$

$$= c_\alpha(\nu^*), \qquad (229)$$

where (227) follows from the definition of α-mutual information and Theorem 17-(b), and (228) follows from (218). Plugging (219) into (208) results in (220). □

58. Typically, the application of Theorem 18 involves
    (a) guessing the form of the auxiliary input Q_X^* (modulo some unknown parameter),
    (b) obtaining its α-response $Q_{Y[\alpha]}^*$, and
    (c) verifying that (217) and (218) are satisfied for some specific choice of the unknown parameter.

With the same approach, we can postulate, for every $\nu \geq 0$, an input distribution R_X^ν, whose α-response $R_{Y[\alpha]}^\nu$ satisfies

$$D_\alpha\big(P_{Y|X=a}\,\|\,R_{Y[\alpha]}^\nu\big) = \nu\, b(a) + c_\alpha(\nu), \quad a \in \mathcal{A}, \qquad (230)$$

where the only condition we place on $c_\alpha(\nu)$ is that it not depend on $a \in \mathcal{A}$. If this is indeed the case, then the same derivation in (226)–(229) results in

$$\mathbb{A}_\alpha(\nu) = c_\alpha(\nu), \qquad (231)$$

and we determine ν^* as the solution to $\theta = -\dot{c}_\alpha(\nu^*)$, in lieu of (217). Sections 11 and 12 illustrate the effortless nature of this approach to solve for $\mathbb{A}_\alpha(\nu)$. Incidentally, (230) can be seen as the α-generalization of the condition in Problem 8.2 of [48], elaborated later in [61].

9. Gallager's E_0 Functions and the Maximal Augustin–Csiszár Mutual Information

In keeping with Gallager's setting [9], we stick to discrete alphabets throughout this section.

59. In his derivation of an achievability result for discrete memoryless channels, Gallager [8] introduced the function (1), which we repeat for convenience,

$$E_0(\rho, P_X) = -\log \sum_{y \in \mathcal{B}} \left(\sum_{x \in \mathcal{A}} P_X(x) P_{Y|X}^{\frac{1}{1+\rho}}(y|x)\right)^{1+\rho}. \qquad (232)$$

Comparing (82) and (232), we obtain

$$E_0(\rho, P_X) = \rho\, I_{\frac{1}{1+\rho}}(X;Y), \qquad (233)$$

which, as we mentioned in Section 1, is the observation by Csiszár in [30] that triggered the third phase in the representation of error exponents. Popularized in [9], the E_0 function was employed by Shannon, Gallager and Berlekamp [10] for $\rho \geq 0$

and by Arimoto [62] for $\rho \in (-1, 0)$ in the derivation of converse results in data transmission, the latter of which considers rates above capacity, a region in which error probability increases with blocklength, approaching one at an exponential rate. For the achievability part, [8] showed upper bounds on the error probability involving $E_0(\rho, P_X)$ for $\rho \in [0, 1]$. Therefore, for rates below capacity, the α-mutual information only enters the picture for $\alpha \in (0, 1)$. One exception in which Rényi divergence of order greater than 1 plays a role at rates below capacity was found by Sason [63], where a refined achievability result is shown for binary linear codes for output symmetric channels (a case in which equiprobable P_X maximizes (233)), as a function of their Hamming weight distribution.

Although Gallager did not have the benefit of the insight provided by the Rényi information measures, he did notice certain behaviors of E_0 reminiscent of mutual information. For example, the derivative of (233) with respect to ρ, at $\rho \leftarrow 0$ is equal to $I(X; Y)$. As pointed out by Csiszár in [32], in the absence of cost constraints, Gallager's E_0 function in (232) satisfies

$$\max_{P_X} E_0(\rho, P_X) = \rho \max_X I_{\frac{1}{1+\rho}}(X; Y) = \rho \max_X I^c_{\frac{1}{1+\rho}}(X; Y), \tag{234}$$

in view of (233) and (187).

Recall that Gallager's modified E_0 function in the case of cost constraints is

$$E_0(\rho, P_X, r, \theta) = -\log \sum_{y \in \mathcal{B}} \left(\sum_{x \in \mathcal{A}} P_X(x) \exp(r \, \mathsf{b}(x) - r\theta) P_{Y|X}^{\frac{1}{1+\rho}}(y|x) \right)^{1+\rho}, \tag{235}$$

which, like (232) he introduced in order to show an achievability result. Up until now, no counterpart to (234) has been found with cost constraints and (235). This is accomplished in the remainder of this section.

60. In the finite alphabet case the following result is useful to obtain a numerical solution for the functional in (206). More importantly, it is relevant to the discussion in Item 61.

Theorem 19. *In the special case of discrete alphabets, the function in (206) is equal to*

$$\mathbb{A}_\alpha(\nu) = \max_G \frac{\alpha}{\alpha - 1} \log \sum_{y \in \mathcal{B}} \left(\sum_{a \in \mathcal{A}} G(a) \, P^\alpha_{Y|X}(y|a) \right)^{\frac{1}{\alpha}}, \tag{236}$$

where the maximization is over all $G \colon \mathcal{A} \to [0, \infty)$ *such that*

$$\sum_{a \in \mathcal{A}} G(a) \exp(-(1 - \alpha)\nu \mathsf{b}(a)) = 1. \tag{237}$$

Proof. Recalling (82) we have

$$I_\alpha(X; Y) + \frac{1}{1 - \alpha} \log \mathbb{E}[\exp(-(1 - \alpha)\nu \, \mathsf{b}(X))]$$

$$= \frac{\alpha}{\alpha - 1} \log \sum_{y \in \mathcal{B}} \left(\sum_{x \in \mathcal{A}} P_X(x) P^\alpha_{Y|X=x}(y) \right)^{\frac{1}{\alpha}}$$

$$+ \frac{1}{1 - \alpha} \log \mathbb{E}[\exp(-(1 - \alpha)\nu \, \mathsf{b}(X))] \tag{238}$$

$$= \frac{\alpha}{\alpha - 1} \log \sum_{y \in \mathcal{B}} \left(\frac{\mathbb{E}\left[P^\alpha_{Y|X}(y|X) \right]}{\mathbb{E}[\exp(-(1 - \alpha)\nu \mathsf{b}(X))]} \right)^{\frac{1}{\alpha}} \tag{239}$$

$$= \frac{\alpha}{\alpha - 1} \log \sum_{y \in \mathcal{B}} \left(\sum_{a \in \mathcal{A}} G(a) \, P^\alpha_{Y|X}(y|a) \right)^{\frac{1}{\alpha}}, \tag{240}$$

where

$$G(x) = \frac{P_X(x)}{\sum_{a \in \mathcal{A}} P_X(a) \exp(-(1-\alpha)\nu\, b(a))}. \tag{241}$$

□

61. We can now proceed to close the circle between the maximization of Augustin–Csiszár mutual information subject to average cost constraints (Phase 3 in Section 1) and Gallager's approach (Phase 1 in Section 1).

Theorem 20. *In the discrete alphabet case, recalling the definitions in (202) and (235), for $\rho > 0$,*

$$\max_{P_X} E_0(\rho, P_X, r, \theta) = \rho \max_{P_X} \mathbb{L}_{\frac{1}{1+\rho}}\left(r + \frac{r}{\rho}, P_X\right), \quad r > 0; \tag{242}$$

$$\min_{r \geq 0} \max_{P_X} E_0(\rho, P_X, r, \theta) = \rho\, \mathbb{C}^c_{\frac{1}{1+\rho}}(\theta), \tag{243}$$

where the maximizations are over $\mathcal{P}_\mathcal{A}$.

Proof. With

$$\alpha = \frac{1}{1+\rho} \quad \text{and} \quad \nu = r\frac{1+\rho}{\rho} = \frac{r}{1-\alpha'} \tag{244}$$

the maximization of (235) with the respect to the input probability measure yields

$$\max_{P_X} E_0(\rho, P_X, r, \theta)$$

$$= \max_{P_X}\left\{(1+\rho)\, r\theta - \log \sum_{y \in \mathcal{B}}\left(\sum_{x \in \mathcal{A}} P_X(x) \exp(r\, b(x)) P_{Y|X}^{\frac{1}{1+\rho}}(y|x)\right)^{1+\rho}\right\} \tag{245}$$

$$= \rho \nu \theta + \rho \max_{P_X} \frac{\alpha}{\alpha-1} \log \sum_{y \in \mathcal{B}}\left(\sum_{x \in \mathcal{A}} P_X(x) \exp((1-\alpha)\, \nu\, b(x)) P_{Y|X}^{\alpha}(y|x)\right)^{\frac{1}{\alpha}} \tag{246}$$

$$= \rho \nu \theta + \rho \max_{G} \frac{\alpha}{\alpha-1} \log \sum_{y \in \mathcal{B}}\left(\sum_{x \in \mathcal{A}} G(x) P_{Y|X}^{\alpha}(y|x)\right)^{\frac{1}{\alpha}} \tag{247}$$

$$= \rho \nu \theta + \rho \mathbb{A}_\alpha(\nu) \tag{248}$$

$$= \rho \max_{P_X} \mathbb{L}_\alpha(\nu, P_X), \tag{249}$$

where
- the maximization on the right side of (247) is over all $G\colon \mathcal{A} \to [0, \infty)$ that satisfy (237), since that constraint is tantamount to enforcing the constraint that $P_X \in \mathcal{P}_\mathcal{A}$ on the left side of (247);
- (248) ⟸ Theorem 19;
- (249) ⟸ Theorem 16.

The proof of (242) is complete once (244) is invoked to substitute α and ν from the right side of (249). If we now minimize the outer sides of (245)–(249) with respect to r we obtain, using (205) and (244),

$$\min_{r\geq 0}\max_{P_X} E_0(\rho, P_X, r, \theta) = \rho \min_{r\geq 0}\max_{P_X} \mathbb{L}_\alpha\left(\frac{r}{1-\alpha}, P_X\right) \qquad (250)$$

$$= \rho \min_{\nu\geq 0}\max_{P_X} \mathbb{L}_\alpha(\nu, P_X) \qquad (251)$$

$$= \rho\, \mathbb{C}^c_{\frac{1}{1+\rho}}(\theta). \qquad (252)$$

□

In p. 329 of [9], Gallager poses the unconstrained maximization (i.e., over $P_X \in \mathcal{P}_A$) of the Lagrangian

$$E_0(\rho, P_X, r, \theta) + \gamma \sum_{a\in\mathcal{A}} P_X(a)\mathsf{b}(a) - \gamma\theta. \qquad (253)$$

Note the apparent discrepancy between the optimizations in (243) and (253): the latter is parametrized by r and γ (in addition to ρ and θ), while the maximization on the right side of (243) does not enforce any average cost constraint. In fact, there is no disparity since Gallager loc. cit. finds serendipitously that $\gamma = 0$ regardless of r and θ, and, therefore, just one parameter is enough.

62. The raison d'être for Augustin's introduction of I^c_α in [36] was his quest to view Gallager's approach with average cost constraints under the optic of Rényi information measures. Contrasting (232) and (235) and inspired by the fact that, in the absence of cost constraints, (232) satisfies a variational characterization in view of (69) and (233), Augustin [36] dealt, not with (235), but with

$$\min_{Q_Y} D_\alpha(\tilde{P}_{Y|X}\|Q_Y|P_X), \quad \text{where } \tilde{P}_{Y|X=x} = P_{Y|X=x}\exp(r'\mathsf{b}(x)).$$

Assuming finite alphabets, Augustin was able to connect this quantity with the maximal $I^c_\alpha(X;Y)$ under cost constraints in an arcane analysis that invokes a minimax theorem. This line of work was continued in Section 5 of [43], which refers to $\min_{Q_Y} D_\alpha(\tilde{P}_{Y|X}\|Q_Y|P_X)$ as the Rényi-Gallager information. Unfortunately, since $\tilde{P}_{Y|X}$ is not a random transformation, the conditional pseudo-Rényi divergence $D_\alpha(\tilde{P}_{Y|X}\|Q_Y|P_X)$ need not satisfy the key additive decomposition in Theorem 4 so the approach of [36,43] fails to establish an identity equating the maximization of Gallager's function (235) with the maximization of Augustin–Csiszár mutual information, which is what we have accomplished through a crisp and elementary analysis.

10. Error Exponent Functions

The central objects of interest in the error exponent analysis of data transmission are the functions $E_{\mathrm{sp}}(R, P_X)$ and $E_{\mathrm{r}}(R, P_X)$ of a random transformation $P_{Y|X}\colon \mathcal{A} \to \mathcal{B}$. Reflecting the three different phases referred to in Section 1, there is no unanimity in the definition of those functions. Following [48], we adopt the standard canonical Phase 2 (Section 1.2) definitions of those functions, which are given in Items 63 and 67.

63. If $R \geq 0$ and $P_X \in \mathcal{P}_A$, the sphere-packing error exponent function is (e.g., (10.19) of [48])

$$E_{\mathrm{sp}}(R, P_X) = \min_{\substack{Q_{Y|X}\colon \mathcal{A}\to\mathcal{B}\\ I(P_X, Q_{Y|X})\leq R}} D(Q_{Y|X}\|P_{Y|X}|P_X). \qquad (254)$$

64. As a function of $R \geq 0$, the basic properties of (254) for fixed $(P_X, P_{Y|X})$ are as follows.

(a) If $R \geq I(P_X, P_{Y|X})$, then $E_{\mathrm{sp}}(R, P_X) = 0$;
(b) If $R < I(P_X, P_{Y|X})$, then $E_{\mathrm{sp}}(R, P_X) > 0$;
(c) The infimum of the arguments for which the sphere-packing error exponent function is finite is denoted by $R_\infty(P_X)$;
(d) On the interval $R \in (R_\infty(P_X), I(P_X, P_{Y|X}))$, $E_{\mathrm{sp}}(R, P_X)$ is convex, strictly decreasing, continuous, and equal to (254) where the constraint is satisfied with equality. This implies that for R belonging to that interval, we can find $\rho_R \geq 0$ so that for all $r \geq 0$,

$$E_{\mathrm{sp}}(r, P_X) \geq E_{\mathrm{sp}}(R, P_X) - \rho_R r + \rho_R R. \tag{255}$$

65. In view of Theorem 8 and its definition in (254), it is not surprising that $E_{\mathrm{sp}}(R, P_X)$ is intimately related to the Augustin–Csiszár mutual information, through the following key identity.

Theorem 21.

$$E_{\mathrm{sp}}(R, P_X) = \sup_{\rho \geq 0} \left\{ \rho\, I^c_{\frac{1}{1+\rho}}(X;Y) - \rho R \right\}, \quad R \geq 0; \tag{256}$$

$$R_\infty(P_X) = I^c_0(X;Y). \tag{257}$$

Proof. First note that $\geq$ holds in (256) because from (128) we obtain, for all $\rho \geq 0$,

$$\rho\, I^c_{\frac{1}{1+\rho}}(X;Y) = \min_{Q_{Y|X}} \left\{ D(Q_{Y|X} \| P_{Y|X} | P_X) + \rho\, I(P_X, Q_{Y|X}) \right\} \tag{258}$$

$$\leq \min_{\substack{Q_{Y|X}:\\ I(P_X, Q_{Y|X}) \leq R}} \left\{ D(Q_{Y|X} \| P_{Y|X} | P_X) + \rho\, I(P_X, Q_{Y|X}) \right\} \tag{259}$$

$$\leq E_{\mathrm{sp}}(R, P_X) + \rho R, \tag{260}$$

where (260) follows from the definition in (254). To show $\leq$ in (256) for those R such that $0 < E_{\mathrm{sp}}(R, P_X) < \infty$, Property (d) in Item 64 allows us to write

$$\min_{Q_{Y|X}} \left\{ D(Q_{Y|X} \| P_{Y|X} | P_X) + \rho_R\, I(P_X, Q_{Y|X}) \right\} = \min_{r \geq 0} \left\{ E_{\mathrm{sp}}(r, P_X) + \rho_R r \right\} \tag{261}$$

$$\geq E_{\mathrm{sp}}(R, P_X) + \rho_R R, \tag{262}$$

where (262) follows from (255).

To determine the region where the sphere-packing error exponent is infinite and show (257), first note that if $R < I^c_0(X;Y) = \lim_{\alpha \downarrow 0} I^c_\alpha(X;Y)$, then $E_{\mathrm{sp}}(R, P_X) = \infty$ because for any $\rho \geq 0$, the function in $\{\}$ on the right side of (256) satisfies

$$\rho\, I^c_{\frac{1}{1+\rho}}(X;Y) - \rho R = \rho\, I^c_{\frac{1}{1+\rho}}(X;Y) - \rho\, I^c_0(X;Y) + \rho\, I^c_0(X;Y) - \rho R \tag{263}$$

$$\geq \rho\, I^c_0(X;Y) - \rho R, \tag{264}$$

where (264) follows from the monotonicity of $I^c_\alpha(X;Y)$ in α we saw in (143). Conversely, if $I^c_0(X;Y) < R < \infty$, there exists $\epsilon \in (0,1)$ such that $I^c_\epsilon(X;Y) < R$, which implies that in the minimization

$$I^c_\epsilon(X;Y) = \min_{Q_{Y|X}} \left\{ \frac{\epsilon}{1-\epsilon} D(Q_{Y|X} \| P_{Y|X} | P_X) + I(P_X, Q_{Y|X}) \right\} \tag{265}$$

we may restrict to those $Q_{Y|X}$ such that $I(P_X, Q_{Y|X}) \leq R$, and consequently, $I^c_\epsilon(X;Y) \geq \frac{\epsilon}{1-\epsilon} E_{\mathrm{sp}}(R, P_X)$. Therefore, to avoid a contradiction, we must have $E_{\mathrm{sp}}(R, P_X) < \infty$.

The remaining case is $I_0^c(X;Y) = \infty$. Again, the monotonicity of the Augustin–Csiszár mutual information implies that $I_\alpha^c(X;Y) = \infty$ for all $\alpha > 0$. So, (128) prescribes $D(Q_{Y|X}\|P_{Y|X}|P_X) = \infty$ for any $Q_{Y|X}$ is such that $I(P_X, Q_{Y|X}) < \infty$. Therefore, $E_{\mathrm{sp}}(R, P_X) = \infty$ for all $R \geqslant 0$, as we wanted to show. □

Augustin [36] provided lower bounds on error probability for codes of type P_X as a function of $I_\alpha^c(X;Y)$ but did not state (256); neither did Csiszár in [32] as he was interested in a non-conventional parametrization (generalized cutoff rates) of the reliability function. As pointed out in p. 5605 of [64], the ingredients for the proof of (256) were already present in the hint of Problem 23 of Section II.5 of [24]. In the discrete case, an exponential lower bound on error probability for codes with constant composition P_X is given as a function of $I^c_{\frac{1}{1+\rho}}(P_X, P_{Y|X})$ in [44,64]. As in [64], Nakiboglu [65] gives (256) as the definition of the sphere-packing function and connects it with (254) in Lemma 3 therein, within the context of discrete input alphabets.

In the discrete case, (257) is well-known (e.g., [66]), and given by (83). As pointed out in [40], $\max_X I_0^c(X;Y)$ is the zero-error capacity with noiseless feedback found by Shannon [67], provided there is at least a pair $(a_1, a_2) \in \mathcal{A}^2$ such that $P_{Y|X=a_1} \perp P_{Y|X=a_2}$. Otherwise, the zero-error capacity with feedback is zero.

66. The critical rate, $R_c(P_X)$, is defined as the smallest abscissa at which the convex function $E_{\mathrm{sp}}(\cdot, P_X)$ meets its supporting line of slope -1. According to (256),

$$I^c_{\frac{1}{2}}(X;Y) = R_c(P_X) + E_{\mathrm{sp}}(R_c(P_X), P_X). \tag{266}$$

67. If $R \geqslant 0$ and $P_X \in \mathcal{P}_A$, the random-coding exponent function is (e.g., (10.15) of [48])

$$E_{\mathrm{r}}(R, P_X) = \min_{Q_{Y|X}:\, \mathcal{A} \to \mathcal{B}} \left\{ D(Q_{Y|X}\|P_{Y|X}|P_X) + [I(P_X, Q_{Y|X}) - R]^+ \right\}, \tag{267}$$

with $[t]^+ = \max\{0, t\}$.

68. The random-coding error exponent function is determined by the sphere-packing error exponent function through the following relation, illustrated in Figure 1.

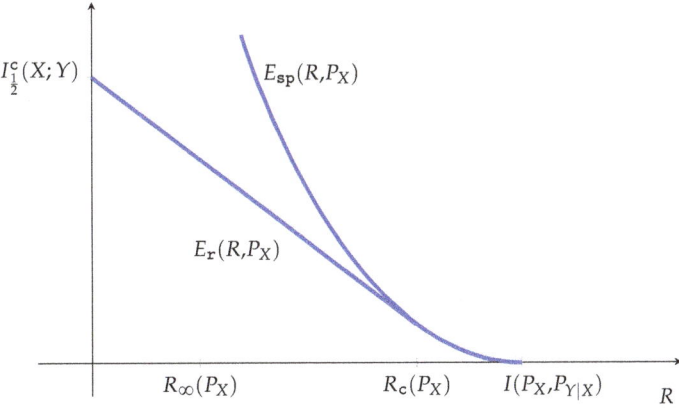

Figure 1. $E_{\mathrm{sp}}(\cdot, P_X)$ and $E_{\mathrm{r}}(\cdot, P_X)$.

Theorem 22.

$$E_{\mathbf{r}}(R, P_X) = \min_{r \geq R}\{E_{\mathbf{sp}}(r, P_X) + r - R\} \tag{268}$$

$$= \begin{cases} 0, & R \geq I(P_X, P_{Y|X}); \\ E_{\mathbf{sp}}(R, P_X), & R \in [R_c(P_X), I(P_X, P_{Y|X})]; \\ I^c_{\frac{1}{2}}(X;Y) - R, & R \in [0, R_c(P_X)]. \end{cases} \tag{269}$$

$$= \sup_{\rho \in [0,1]}\left\{\rho I^c_{\frac{1}{1+\rho}}(X;Y) - \rho R\right\}. \tag{270}$$

Proof. Identities (268) and (269) are well-known (e.g. Lemma 10.4 and Corollary 10.4 in [48]). To show (270), note that (256) expresses $E_{\mathbf{sp}}(\cdot, P_X)$ as the supremum of supporting lines parametrized by their slope $-\rho$. By definition of critical rate (for brevity, we do not show explicitly its dependence on P_X), if $R \in [R_c, I(P_X, P_{Y|X})]$, then $E_{\mathbf{sp}}(R, P_X)$ can be obtained by restricting the optimization in (256) to $\rho \in [0, 1]$. In that segment of values of R, $E_{\mathbf{sp}}(R, P_X) = E_r(R, P_X)$ according to (269). Moreover, on the interval $R \in [0, R_c]$, we have

$$\max_{\rho \in [0,1]}\left\{\rho I^c_{\frac{1}{1+\rho}}(X;Y) - \rho R\right\} = I^c_{\frac{1}{2}}(X;Y) - R \tag{271}$$

$$= E_{\mathbf{sp}}(R_c, P_X) + R_c - R \tag{272}$$

$$= E_{\mathbf{r}}(R, P_X), \tag{273}$$

where we have used (266) and (269). □

The first explicit connection between $E_{\mathbf{r}}(R, P_X)$ and the Augustin–Csiszár mutual information was made by Poltyrev [35] although he used a different form for $I^c_\alpha(X;Y)$, as we discussed in (29).

69. The unconstrained maximizations over the input distribution of the sphere-packing and random coding error exponent functions are denoted, respectively, by

$$E_{\mathbf{sp}}(R) = \sup_{P_X} E_{\mathbf{sp}}(R, P_X), \tag{274}$$

$$E_{\mathbf{r}}(R) = \sup_{P_X} E_{\mathbf{r}}(R, P_X). \tag{275}$$

Coding theorems [8–10,22,48] have shown that when these functions coincide they yield the reliability function (optimum speed at which the error probability vanishes with blocklength) as a function of the rate $R < \max_X I(X;Y)$. The intuition is that, for the most favorable input distribution, errors occur when the channel behaves so atypically that codes of rate R are not reliable. There are many ways in which the channel may exhibit such behavior and they are all unlikely, but the most likely among them is the one that achieves (254).

It follows from (187), (256) and (270) that (274) and (275) can be expressed as

$$E_{\mathbf{sp}}(R) = \sup_{\rho \geq 0}\left\{\rho \sup_X I_{\frac{1}{1+\rho}}(X;Y) - \rho R\right\}, \tag{276}$$

$$E_{\mathbf{r}}(R) = \sup_{\rho \in [0,1]}\left\{\rho \sup_X I_{\frac{1}{1+\rho}}(X;Y) - \rho R\right\}. \tag{277}$$

Therefore, we can sidestep working with the Augustin–Csiszár mutual information in the absence of cost constraints.

70. Shannon [1] showed that, operating at rates below maximal mutual information, it is possible to find codes whose error probability vanishes with blocklength; for the

converse, instead of error probability, Shannon measured reliability by the conditional entropy of the message given the channel output. That alternative reliability measure, as well as its generalization to Arimoto-Rényi conditional entropy, is also useful analyzing the average performance over code ensembles. It turns out (see e.g., [28,68]) that, below capacity, those conditional entropies also vanish exponentially fast in much the same way as error probability with bounds that are governed by $E_{\mathrm{sp}}(R)$ and $E_{\mathrm{r}}(R)$ thereby lending additional operational significance to those functions.

71. We now introduce a cost function b: $\mathcal{A} \to [0, \infty)$ and real scalar $\theta \geq 0$, and reexamine the optimizations in (274) and (275) allowing only those probability measures that satisfy $\mathbb{E}[b(X)] \leq \theta$. With a patent, but unavoidable, abuse of notation we define

$$E_{\mathrm{sp}}(R, \theta) = \sup_{\substack{P_X: \\ \mathbb{E}[b(X)] \leq \theta}} E_{\mathrm{sp}}(R, P_X) \qquad (278)$$

$$= \sup_{\rho \geq 0} \left\{ \rho \sup_{\substack{P_X: \\ \mathbb{E}[b(X)] \leq \theta}} I^c_{\frac{1}{1+\rho}}(X;Y) - \rho R \right\} \qquad (279)$$

$$= \sup_{\rho \geq 0} \left\{ \rho \, \mathbb{C}^c_{\frac{1}{1+\rho}}(\theta) - \rho R \right\} \qquad (280)$$

$$= \sup_{\rho \geq 0} \left\{ -\rho R + \rho \min_{\nu \geq 0} \left\{ \nu \theta + \mathbb{A}_{\frac{1}{1+\rho}}(\nu) \right\} \right\} \qquad (281)$$

$$= \sup_{\rho \geq 0} \left\{ -\rho R + \min_{\nu \geq 0} \left\{ \rho \nu \theta + \max_X \left\{ \rho I_{\frac{1}{1+\rho}}(X;Y) + (1+\rho) \log \mathbb{E}\left[\exp\left(-\frac{\rho \nu}{1+\rho} b(X)\right)\right] \right\} \right\} \right\}, \qquad (282)$$

where (279), (281) and (282) follow from (256), (208) and (206), respectively.

72. In parallel to (278)–(281),

$$E_{\mathrm{r}}(R, \theta) = \sup_{\substack{P_X: \\ \mathbb{E}[b(X)] \leq \theta}} E_{\mathrm{r}}(R, P_X) \qquad (283)$$

$$= \sup_{\rho \in [0,1]} \left\{ \rho \sup_{\substack{P_X: \\ \mathbb{E}[b(X)] \leq \theta}} I^c_{\frac{1}{1+\rho}}(X;Y) - \rho R \right\} \qquad (284)$$

$$= \sup_{\rho \in [0,1]} \left\{ \rho \, \mathbb{C}^c_{\frac{1}{1+\rho}}(\theta) - \rho R \right\}, \qquad (285)$$

where (284) follows from (270). In particular, if we define the critical rate and the cutoff rate as

$$R_{\mathrm{c}} = \sup_{\substack{P_X: \\ \mathbb{E}[b(X)] \leq \theta}} R_{\mathrm{c}}(P_X), \qquad (286)$$

$$R_0 = \sup_{\substack{P_X: \\ \mathbb{E}[b(X)] \leq \theta}} I^c_{\frac{1}{2}}(X;Y), \qquad (287)$$

respectively, then it follows from (270) that

$$E_{\mathrm{r}}(R) = R_0 - R, \quad R \in [0, R_{\mathrm{c}}]. \qquad (288)$$

Summarizing, the evaluation of $E_{\text{sp}}(R,\theta)$ and $E_{\text{r}}(R,\theta)$ can be accomplished by the method proposed in Section 8, at the heart of which is the maximization in (206) involving α-mutual information instead of Augustin–Csiszár mutual information. In Sections 11 and 12, we illustrate the evaluation of the error exponent functions with two important additive-noise examples.

11. Additive Independent Gaussian Noise; Input Power Constraint

We illustrate the procedure in Item 58 by taking Example 6 considerably further.

73. Suppose $\mathcal{A} = \mathcal{B} = \mathbb{R}$, $b(x) = x^2$, and $P_{Y|X=a} = \mathcal{N}(a, \sigma_N^2)$. We start by testing whether we can find $R_X^\nu \in \mathcal{P}_{\mathcal{A}}$ such that its α-response satisfies (230). Naturally, it makes sense to try $R_X^\nu = \mathcal{N}(0, \sigma^2)$ for some yet to be determined σ^2. As we saw in Example 6, this choice implies that its α-response is $R_{Y[\alpha]}^\nu = \mathcal{N}(0, \alpha \sigma^2 + \sigma_N^2)$. Specializing Example 4, we obtain

$$D_\alpha\left(P_{Y|X=x} \| R_{Y[\alpha]}^\nu\right) = D_\alpha\left(\mathcal{N}(x, \sigma_N^2) \| \mathcal{N}(0, \alpha\sigma^2 + \sigma_N^2)\right) \tag{289}$$

$$= \frac{1}{2}\log\left(1 + \frac{\alpha\sigma^2}{\sigma_N^2}\right) - \frac{1}{2(1-\alpha)}\log\left(1 + \frac{\alpha(1-\alpha)\sigma^2}{\alpha^2\sigma^2 + \sigma_N^2}\right) + \frac{1}{2}\frac{\alpha x^2}{\alpha^2\sigma^2 + \sigma_N^2}\log e. \tag{290}$$

Therefore, (230) is indeed satisfied with

$$c_\alpha(\nu) = \frac{1}{2}\log\left(1 + \frac{\alpha\sigma^2}{\sigma_N^2}\right) - \frac{1}{2(1-\alpha)}\log\left(1 + \frac{\alpha(1-\alpha)\sigma^2}{\alpha^2\sigma^2 + \sigma_N^2}\right), \tag{291}$$

$$\nu = \frac{1}{2}\frac{\alpha}{\alpha^2\sigma^2 + \sigma_N^2}\log e, \tag{292}$$

where (292) follows if we choose the variance of the auxiliary input as

$$\sigma^2 = \frac{\log e}{2\alpha \nu} - \frac{\sigma_N^2}{\alpha^2} \tag{293}$$

$$= \frac{\sigma_N^2}{\alpha^2}\left(\frac{\alpha}{\lambda} - 1\right). \tag{294}$$

In (294) we have introduced an alternative, more convenient, parametrization for the Lagrange multiplier

$$\lambda = \frac{2\nu\sigma_N^2}{\log e} \in (0,\alpha). \tag{295}$$

In conclusion, with the choice in (293), $\mathcal{N}(0,\sigma^2)$ attains the maximum in (206), and in view of (231), $\mathbb{A}_\alpha(\nu)$ is given by the right side of (291) substituting σ^2 by (293). Therefore, we have

$$\nu\theta + \mathbb{A}_\alpha(\nu) = \frac{\lambda}{2}\text{snr}\log e + c_\alpha\left(\frac{\lambda \log e}{2\sigma_N^2}\right) \tag{296}$$

$$= \frac{\lambda}{2}\text{snr}\log e + \frac{1}{2}\log\left(1 + \frac{1}{\lambda} - \frac{1}{\alpha}\right) - \frac{1}{2(1-\alpha)}\log(\alpha - \lambda(1-\alpha)) + \frac{\log \alpha}{1-\alpha}, \tag{297}$$

where we denoted $\text{snr} = \frac{\theta}{\sigma_N^2}$.

In accordance with Theorem 16 all that remains is to minimize (297) with respect to ν, or equivalently, with respect to λ. Differentiating (297) with respect to λ, the minimum is achieved at λ^* satisfying

$$\text{snr} = \frac{1}{\lambda^*} \frac{\alpha - \lambda^*}{\alpha - \lambda^* + \alpha \lambda^*}, \tag{298}$$

whose only valid root (obtained by solving a quadratic equation) is

$$\lambda^* = \frac{1 + \alpha\,\text{snr} - \alpha\Delta}{2\,\text{snr}\,(1-\alpha)} \in (0, \alpha), \tag{299}$$

with Δ defined in (118). So, for $\alpha \in (0,1)$, (208) becomes

$$\mathbb{C}^c_\alpha(\text{snr}\,\sigma_N^2) = \frac{1 + \alpha\,\text{snr} - \alpha\Delta}{4(1-\alpha)} \log e + \frac{1}{2} \log\left(1 + \frac{2\,\text{snr}\,(1-\alpha)}{1 + \alpha\,\text{snr} - \alpha\Delta} - \frac{1}{\alpha}\right)$$
$$- \frac{1}{2(1-\alpha)} \log\left(\frac{\alpha\,\text{snr} + \alpha\Delta - 1}{2\,\text{snr}\,\alpha^2}\right). \tag{300}$$

Letting $\alpha = \frac{1}{1+\rho}$, we obtain

$$\mathbb{C}^c_{\frac{1}{1+\rho}}(\text{snr}\,\sigma_N^2) = \frac{\text{snr}}{2\rho}(1-\beta)\log e + \frac{1}{2}\log(1+\beta\,\text{snr}) - \frac{1+\rho}{2\rho}\log((1+\rho)\beta), \tag{301}$$

with

$$\beta = \frac{1}{2}\left(1 - \frac{1}{\alpha\,\text{snr}} + \frac{\Delta}{\text{snr}}\right) = \frac{1}{2}\left(1 - \frac{1+\rho}{\text{snr}} + \sqrt{\frac{4}{\text{snr}} + \left(\frac{1+\rho}{\text{snr}} - 1\right)^2}\right). \tag{302}$$

74. Alternatively, it is instructive to apply Theorem 18 to the current Gaussian/quadratic cost setting. Suppose we let $Q_X^* = \mathcal{N}(0, \sigma^{*2})$, where σ^{*2} is to be determined. With the aid of the formulas

$$\mathbb{E}\left[X^2 e^{-\mu X^2}\right] = \frac{\sigma^2}{(1 + 2\mu\sigma^2)^{\frac{3}{2}}}, \tag{303}$$

$$\mathbb{E}\left[e^{-\mu X^2}\right] = \frac{1}{\sqrt{1 + 2\mu\sigma^2}}, \tag{304}$$

where $\mu \geq 0$, and $X \sim \mathcal{N}(0, \sigma^2)$, (217) becomes

$$\frac{1}{\text{snr}} = \frac{\sigma_N^2}{\sigma^{*2}} + (1-\alpha)\lambda^*, \tag{305}$$

upon substituting $\sigma^2 \leftarrow \sigma^{*2}$ and

$$\mu \leftarrow \nu^* \frac{1-\alpha}{\log e} = \lambda^* \frac{1-\alpha}{2\sigma_N^2}. \tag{306}$$

Likewise (218) translates into (291) and (292) with $(\nu, \sigma^2) \leftarrow (\nu^*, \sigma^{*2})$, namely,

$$c_\alpha(\nu^*) = \frac{1}{2}\log\left(1 + \frac{\alpha\sigma^{*2}}{\sigma_N^2}\right) - \frac{1}{2(1-\alpha)}\log\left(1 + \frac{\alpha(1-\alpha)\sigma^{*2}}{\alpha^2\sigma^{*2} + \sigma_N^2}\right), \tag{307}$$

$$\lambda^* = \frac{\alpha\sigma_N^2}{\alpha^2\sigma^{*2} + \sigma_N^2}. \tag{308}$$

Eliminating σ^{*2} from (305) by means of (308) results in (299) and the same derivation that led to (300) shows that it is equal to $\nu^*\theta + c_\alpha(\nu^*)$.

75. Applying Theorem 17, we can readily find the input distribution, P_X^*, that attains $\mathbb{C}_\alpha^c(\theta)$ as well as its $\langle\alpha\rangle$-response P_Y^* (recall the notation in Item 53). According to Example 2, P_Y^*, the α-response to Q_X^* is Gaussian with zero mean and variance

$$\sigma_N^2 + \alpha \sigma^{*2} = \sigma_N^2 \left(1 + \frac{1}{\lambda^*} - \frac{1}{\alpha}\right) \tag{309}$$

$$= \frac{\sigma_N^2}{2}\left(2 - \frac{1}{\alpha} + \Delta + \text{snr}\right), \tag{310}$$

where (309) follows from (308) and (310) follows by using the expression for Δ in (118). Note from Example 7 that P_Y^* is nothing but the $\langle\alpha\rangle$-response to $\mathcal{N}(0,\text{snr}\,\sigma_N^2)$. We can easily verify from Theorem 17 that indeed $P_X^* = \mathcal{N}(0,\text{snr}\,\sigma_N^2)$ since in this case (216) becomes

$$\iota_{P_X^* \| Q_X^*}(a) = -(1-\alpha)\nu^* a^2 + \tau_\alpha, \tag{311}$$

which can only be satisfied by $P_X^* = \mathcal{N}(0,\text{snr}\,\sigma_N^2)$ in view of (305). As an independent confirmation, we can verify, after some algebra, that the right sides of (127) and (300) are identical.

In fact, in the current Gaussian setting, we could start by postulating that the distribution that maximizes the Augustin–Csiszár mutual information under the second moment constraint does not depend on α and is given by $P_X^* = \mathcal{N}(0,\theta)$. Its $\langle\alpha\rangle$-response $P_{Y\langle\alpha\rangle}^*$ was already obtained in Example 7. Then, an alternative method to find $\mathbb{C}_\alpha^c(\theta)$, given in Section 6.2 of [43], is to follow the approach outlined in Item 53. To validate the choice of P_X^* we must show that it maximizes $B(P_X, P_{Y\langle\alpha\rangle}^*)$ (in the notation introduced in (199)) among the subset of $\mathcal{P}_\mathcal{A}$ which satisfies $\mathbb{E}[X^2] \leq \theta$. This follows from the fact that $D_\alpha\left(P_{Y|X=x}\|P_{Y\langle\alpha\rangle}^*\right)$ is an affine function of x^2.

76. Let's now use the result in Item 73 to evaluate, with a novel parametrization, the error exponent functions for the Gaussian channel under an average power constraint.

Theorem 23. Let $\mathcal{A} = \mathcal{B} = \mathbb{R}$, $b(x) = x^2$, and $P_{Y|X=a} = \mathcal{N}(a,\sigma_N^2)$. Then, for $\beta \in [0,1]$,

$$E_{\text{sp}}(R, \text{snr}\,\sigma_N^2) = \frac{\text{snr}}{2}(1-\beta)\log e - \frac{1}{2}\log(1 + \text{snr}\,\beta(1-\beta)), \tag{312}$$

$$R = \frac{1}{2}\log\left(1 + \frac{\beta^2}{\beta(1-\beta) + \frac{1}{\text{snr}}}\right). \tag{313}$$

The critical rate and cutoff rate are, respectively,

$$R_c = \frac{1}{2}\log\left(\frac{1}{2} + \frac{\text{snr}}{4} + \frac{1}{2}\sqrt{1 + \frac{\text{snr}^2}{4}}\right), \tag{314}$$

$$R_0 = \frac{1}{2}\left(1 + \frac{\text{snr}}{2} - \sqrt{1 + \frac{\text{snr}^2}{4}}\right)\log e + \frac{1}{2}\log\left(\frac{1}{2} + \frac{1}{2}\sqrt{1 + \frac{\text{snr}^2}{4}}\right). \tag{315}$$

Proof. Expression (315) for the cutoff rate follows by letting $\rho = 1$ in (301) and (302). The supremum in (281) is attained by $\rho^* \geq 0$ that satisfies (recall the concavity result in Theorem 9-(a))

$$R = \frac{d}{d\rho} \rho \, \mathbb{C}^c_{\frac{1}{1+\rho}}(\text{snr} \, \sigma_N^2)\bigg|_{\rho \leftarrow \rho^*} \tag{316}$$

$$= \frac{1}{2} \log\left(\text{snr} + \frac{1}{\beta}\right) - \frac{1}{2} \log(1 + \rho^*), \tag{317}$$

obtained after a dose of symbolic computation working with (301). In particular, letting $\rho^* = 1$, we obtain the critical rate in (314). Note that if in (302) we substitute $\rho \leftarrow \rho^*$, with ρ^* given as a function of R, snr and β by (317), we end up with an equation involving R, snr, and β. We proceed to verify that that equation is, in fact, (312). By solving a quadratic equation, we can readily check that (302) is the positive root of

$$1 + \rho = \text{snr}(1 - \beta) + \frac{1}{\beta}. \tag{318}$$

If we particularize (318) to $\rho \leftarrow \rho^*$, with ρ^* given by (317), namely,

$$\rho^* = -1 + \exp(-2R)\left(\text{snr} + \frac{1}{\beta}\right), \tag{319}$$

we obtain

$$\exp(2R) = \frac{\text{snr} \, \beta + 1}{\text{snr} \, \beta(1 - \beta) + 1}, \tag{320}$$

which is (313). Notice that the right side of (320) is monotonic increasing in $\beta > 0$ ranging from 1 (for $\beta = 0$) to $1 + \text{snr}$ (for $\beta = 1$). Therefore, $\beta \in [0, 1]$ spans the whole gamut of values of R of interest.

Assembling (281), (301) and (317), we obtain

$$E_{\text{sp}}(R, \text{snr} \, \sigma_N^2)$$

$$= -\rho^* R + \frac{\text{snr}}{2}(1 - \beta) \log e + \frac{\rho^*}{2} \log(1 + \beta \, \text{snr}) - \frac{1 + \rho^*}{2} \log((1 + \rho^*)\beta) \tag{321}$$

$$= -\rho^* R + \frac{\text{snr}}{2}(1 - \beta) \log e + \frac{\rho^*}{2} \log(1 + \beta \, \text{snr}) - \frac{1 + \rho^*}{2} \log \beta$$

$$+ (1 + \rho^*)R - \frac{1 + \rho^*}{2} \log\left(\text{snr} + \frac{1}{\beta}\right) \tag{322}$$

$$= R + \frac{\text{snr}}{2}(1 - \beta) \log e - \frac{1}{2} \log(1 + \beta \, \text{snr}) \tag{323}$$

$$= \frac{\text{snr}}{2}(1 - \beta) \log e - \frac{1}{2} \log(1 + \text{snr} \, \beta(1 - \beta)), \tag{324}$$

where (324) follows by substituting (313) on the left side. □

Note that the parametric expression in (312) and (313) (shown in Figure 2) is, in fact, a closed-form expression for $E_{\text{sp}}(R, \text{snr} \, \sigma_N^2)$ since we can invert (313) to obtain

$$\beta = \frac{1}{2}(1 - \exp(-2R))\left(1 + \sqrt{1 + \frac{4}{\text{snr} \, (1 - \exp(-2R))}}\right). \tag{325}$$

The random coding error exponent is

$$E_r(R, \theta) = \begin{cases} E_{\text{sp}}(R, \theta), & R \in (R_c, \frac{1}{2}\log(1 + \text{snr})); \\ R_0 - R, & R \in [0, R_c], \end{cases} \qquad (326)$$

with the critical rate R_c and cutoff rate R_0 in (314) and (315), respectively. It can be checked that (326) coincides with the expression given by Gallager [9] (p. 340) where he optimizes (235) with respect to ρ and r, but not P_X, which he just assumes to be $P_X = \mathcal{N}(0, \theta)$. The expression for R_c in (314) can be found in (7.4.34) of [9]; R_0 in (314) is implicit in p. 340 of [9], and explicit in e.g., [69].

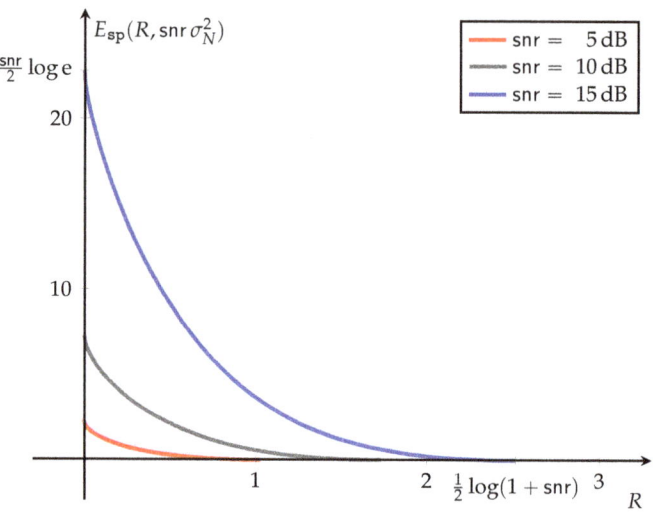

Figure 2. $E_{\text{sp}}(R, \text{snr}\,\sigma_N^2)$ in (312) and (313); logarithms in base 2.

77. The expression for $E_{\text{sp}}(R, \theta)$ in Theorem 23 has more structure than meets the eye. The analysis in Item 73 has shown that $E_{\text{sp}}(R, P_X)$ is maximized over P_X with second moment not exceeding θ by $P_X^* = \mathcal{N}(0, \theta)$ regardless of $R \in \left(0, \frac{1}{2}\log(1 + \text{snr})\right)$. The fact that we have found a closed-form expression for (254) when evaluated at such input probability measure and $P_{Y|X=a} = \mathcal{N}(a, \sigma_N^2)$ is indicative that the minimum therein is attained by a Gaussian random transformation $Q_{Y|X}^*$. This is indeed the case: define the random transformation

$$Q_{Y|X=a}^* = \mathcal{N}\left(\beta a, \sigma_1^2\right), \qquad (327)$$

$$\frac{\sigma_1^2}{\sigma_N^2} = 1 + \text{snr}\,\beta(1 - \beta). \qquad (328)$$

In comparison with the nominal random transformation $P_{Y|X=a} = \mathcal{N}(a, \sigma_N^2)$, this channel attenuates the input and contaminates it with a more powerful noise. Then,

$$I(P_X^*, Q_{Y|X}^*) = \frac{1}{2}\log\left(1 + \frac{\beta^2}{\beta(1 - \beta) + \frac{1}{\text{snr}}}\right) = R. \qquad (329)$$

Furthermore, invoking (33), we get

$$D(Q^*_{Y|X} \| P_{Y|X} | P^*_X) = \mathbb{E}\left[D\left(\mathcal{N}(\beta X^*, \sigma_1^2) \| \mathcal{N}(X^*, \sigma_N^2)\right)\right] \quad (330)$$

$$= \frac{1}{2}\left((\beta-1)^2 \mathrm{snr} + \frac{\sigma_1^2}{\sigma_N^2} - 1\right)\log e - \frac{1}{2}\log\frac{\sigma_1^2}{\sigma_N^2} \quad (331)$$

$$= \frac{\mathrm{snr}}{2}(1-\beta)\log e - \frac{1}{2}\log(1+\mathrm{snr}\,\beta(1-\beta)) \quad (332)$$

$$= E_{\mathrm{sp}}(R, \mathrm{snr}\,\sigma_N^2), \quad (333)$$

where (333) is (312). Therefore, $Q^*_{Y|X}$ does indeed achieve the minimum in (254) if $P_{Y|X=a} = \mathcal{N}(a, \sigma_N^2)$ and $P^*_X = \mathcal{N}(0, \theta)$. So, the most likely error mechanism is the result of atypically large noise strength and an attenuated received signal. Both effects cannot be combined into additional noise variance: there is no $\sigma^2 > 0$ such that $Q_{Y|X=a} = \mathcal{N}(a, \sigma^2)$ achieves the minimum in (254).

12. Additive Independent Exponential Noise; Input-Mean Constraint

This section finds the sphere-packing error exponent for the additive independent exponential noise channel under an input-mean constraint.

78. Suppose that $\mathcal{A} = \mathcal{B} = [0, \infty)$, $b(x) = x$, and

$$Y = X + N, \quad (334)$$

where N is exponentially distributed, independent of X, and $\mathbb{E}[N] = \zeta$. Therefore $P_{Y|X=a}$ has density

$$p_{Y|X=a}(t) = \frac{1}{\zeta} e^{-\frac{t-a}{\zeta}} 1\{t \geq a\}. \quad (335)$$

It is shown in [70,71] that

$$\max_{X:\, \mathbb{E}[X] \leq \theta} I(X; X+N) = \log(1+\mathrm{snr}), \quad (336)$$

$$\mathrm{snr} = \frac{\theta}{\zeta}, \quad (337)$$

achieved by a mixed random variable with density

$$f^*_X(t) = \frac{\zeta}{\zeta + \theta}\delta(t) + \frac{\theta}{(\zeta+\theta)^2} e^{-t/(\zeta+\theta)} 1\{t > 0\}. \quad (338)$$

To determine $\mathbb{C}^c_\alpha(\mathrm{snr}\,\zeta)$, $\alpha \in (0,1)$, we invoke Theorem 18. A sensible candidate for the auxiliary input distribution Q^*_X is a mixed random variable with density

$$q^*_X(t) = \Gamma^* \delta(t) + (1 - \Gamma^*) \frac{1}{\mu} e^{-t/\mu} 1\{t > 0\}, \quad (339)$$

$$\mu = \frac{\zeta}{\alpha\,\Gamma^*}, \quad (340)$$

where $\Gamma^* \in (0,1)$ is yet to be determined. This is an attractive choice because its α-response, $Q^*_{Y[\alpha]}$, is particularly simple: exponential with mean $\alpha\mu = \frac{\zeta}{\Gamma^*}$, as we can verify using Laplace transforms. Then, if Z is exponential with unit mean, with the aid of Example 5, we can write

$$D_\alpha\left(P_{Y|X=x} \| Q^*_{Y[\alpha]}\right) = D_\alpha(\zeta Z + x \| \alpha \mu Z) \tag{341}$$

$$= \frac{x}{\alpha \mu} \log e + \log \frac{\alpha \mu}{\zeta} + \frac{1}{1-\alpha} \log\left(\alpha + (1-\alpha)\frac{\zeta}{\alpha \mu}\right) \tag{342}$$

$$= \frac{\Gamma^* x}{\zeta} \log e - \log \Gamma^* + \frac{1}{1-\alpha} \log(\alpha + (1-\alpha)\Gamma^*). \tag{343}$$

So, (218) is satisfied with

$$\nu^* = \frac{\Gamma^*}{\zeta} \log e, \tag{344}$$

$$c_\alpha(\nu^*) = \frac{1}{1-\alpha} \log(\alpha + (1-\alpha)\Gamma^*) - \log \Gamma^*. \tag{345}$$

To evaluate (217), it is useful to note that if $\gamma > -1$, then

$$\mathbb{E}\left[Z e^{-\gamma Z}\right] = \frac{1}{(1+\gamma)^2}, \tag{346}$$

$$\mathbb{E}\left[e^{-\gamma Z}\right] = \frac{1}{1+\gamma}. \tag{347}$$

Therefore, the left side of (217) specializes to, with $\bar{X}^* \sim Q^*_X$,

$$\mathbb{E}\left[b(\bar{X}^*) \exp\left(-(1-\alpha)\nu^* b(\bar{X}^*)\right)\right] = \frac{\mu(1-\Gamma^*)}{\left(1+\mu(1-\alpha)\frac{\nu^*}{\log e}\right)^2} \tag{348}$$

$$= \zeta \alpha \left(\frac{1}{\Gamma^*} - 1\right), \tag{349}$$

while the expectation on the right side of (217) is given by

$$\mathbb{E}\left[\exp\left(-(1-\alpha)\nu^* b(\bar{X}^*)\right)\right] = \alpha + \Gamma^* - \alpha \Gamma^*. \tag{350}$$

Therefore, (217) yields

$$\text{snr} = \frac{1}{\Gamma^*} - \frac{1}{\alpha + (1-\alpha)\Gamma^*} \tag{351}$$

whose solution is

$$\Gamma^* = \frac{1}{2\rho \,\text{snr}}\left(\sqrt{(1+\text{snr})^2 + 4\rho \,\text{snr}} - 1 - \text{snr}\right), \tag{352}$$

with $\rho = \frac{1-\alpha}{\alpha}$. So, finally, (220), (344) and (345) give the closed-form expression

$$\mathbb{C}^c_\alpha(\theta) = \text{snr}\, \Gamma^* \log e - \log \Gamma^* + \frac{1}{1-\alpha} \log(\alpha + (1-\alpha)\Gamma^*). \tag{353}$$

As in Item 73, we can postulate an auxiliary distribution that satisfies (230) for every $\nu \geq 0$. This is identical to what we did in (341)–(343) except that now (344) and (345) hold for generic ν and Γ. Then, (351) is the result of solving $\theta = -\dot{c}_\alpha(\nu^*)$, which is, in fact, somewhat simpler than obtaining it through (217).

79. We proceed to get a very simple parametric expression for $E_{\text{sp}}(R,\theta)$.

Theorem 24. *Let $\mathcal{A} = \mathcal{B} = [0, \infty)$, $b(x) = x$, and $Y = X + N$, with N exponentially distributed, independent of X, and $\mathbb{E}[N] = \zeta$. Then, under the average cost constraint $\mathbb{E}[b(X)] \leq \zeta \, \mathrm{snr}$,*

$$E_{\mathrm{sp}}(R, \zeta \, \mathrm{snr}) = \left(\frac{1}{\eta} - 1\right) \log e + \log \eta, \tag{354}$$

$$R = \log(1 + \eta \, \mathrm{snr}), \tag{355}$$

where $\eta \in (0, 1]$.

Proof. Rewriting (353), results in

$$\rho \, \mathbb{C}^c_{\frac{1}{1+\rho}}(\theta) = \rho \, \mathrm{snr} \, \Gamma^* \log e - \rho \log \Gamma^* + (1+\rho) \log \frac{1 + \rho \Gamma^*}{1 + \rho}, \tag{356}$$

which is monotonically decreasing with ρ. With $\dot{\Gamma}^* = \frac{\partial}{\partial \rho} \Gamma^*(\rho, \mathrm{snr})$, the counterpart of (317) is now

$$R = \frac{d}{d\rho} \rho \, \mathbb{C}^c_{\frac{1}{1+\rho}}(\theta) \bigg|_{\rho \leftarrow \rho^*} \tag{357}$$

$$= (\Gamma^* + \rho^* \dot{\Gamma}^*) \left(\mathrm{snr} - \frac{1}{\Gamma^*} + \frac{1 + \rho^*}{1 + \rho^* \Gamma^*} \right) \log e + \log \frac{1 + \rho^* \Gamma^*}{\Gamma^* + \rho^* \Gamma^*} \tag{358}$$

$$= (\Gamma^* + \rho^* \dot{\Gamma}^*) \left(\mathrm{snr} + \frac{1}{\Gamma^*} \frac{\Gamma^* - 1}{1 + \rho^* \Gamma^*} \right) \log e + \log \frac{1 + \rho^* \Gamma^*}{\Gamma^* + \rho^* \Gamma^*} \tag{359}$$

$$= \log \frac{1 + \rho^* \Gamma^*}{\Gamma^* + \rho^* \Gamma^*}, \tag{360}$$

where the drastic simplification in (360) occurs because, with the current parametrization, (351) becomes

$$1 - \Gamma^* = (1 + \rho^* \Gamma^*) \Gamma^* \, \mathrm{snr}. \tag{361}$$

Now we go ahead and express both ρ^* and Γ^* as functions of snr and R exclusively. We may rewrite (357)–(360) as

$$\rho^* \Gamma^* = \frac{\exp(-R) - \Gamma^*}{1 - \exp(-R)}, \tag{362}$$

which, when plugged in (361), results in

$$\Gamma^* = \frac{1}{\mathrm{snr}} (1 - \exp(-R)) < 1, \tag{363}$$

$$\rho^* = \frac{(1 + \mathrm{snr}) \exp(-R) - 1}{(1 - \exp(-R))^2} > 0, \tag{364}$$

where the inequalities in (363) and (364) follow from $R < \log(1+\text{snr})$. So, in conclusion,

$$E_{\text{sp}}(R,\theta) = \max_{\rho \geq 0} \left\{ \rho\, \mathbb{C}^c_{\frac{1}{1+\rho}}(\theta) - \rho R \right\} \tag{365}$$

$$= \rho^*\, \mathbb{C}^c_{\frac{1}{1+\rho^*}}(\theta) - \rho^* R \tag{366}$$

$$= \rho^*\, \text{snr}\, \Gamma^* \log e - \rho^* \log \Gamma^* + (1+\rho^*) \log \frac{1+\rho^*\Gamma^*}{1+\rho^*} - \rho^* R \tag{367}$$

$$= \rho^*\, \text{snr}\, \Gamma^* \log e - \rho^* \log \Gamma^* + (1+\rho^*)(R + \log \Gamma^*) - \rho^* R \tag{368}$$

$$= \rho^*\, \text{snr}\, \Gamma^* \log e + \log \Gamma^* + R \tag{369}$$

$$= \left(\frac{\text{snr}}{\exp(R)-1} - 1 \right) \log e + \log \frac{\exp(R)-1}{\text{snr}} \tag{370}$$

$$= \left(\frac{1}{\eta} - 1 \right) \log e + \log \eta, \tag{371}$$

where we have introduced

$$\eta = \frac{\exp(R)-1}{\text{snr}} = \frac{\Gamma^*}{1-\text{snr}\,\Gamma^*}. \tag{372}$$

Evidently, the left identity in (372) is the same as (355). □

The critical rate and the cutoff rate are obtained by particularizing (360) and (356) to $\rho^* = 1$ and $\rho = 1$, respectively. This yields

$$R_{\text{c}} = \log \frac{1+\Gamma_1^*}{2\Gamma_1^*}, \tag{373}$$

$$R_0 = \text{snr}\, \Gamma_1^* \log e - \log(4\Gamma_1^*) + 2\log(1+\Gamma_1^*), \tag{374}$$

$$\Gamma_1^* = \frac{\sqrt{(1+\text{snr})^2 + 4\,\text{snr}} - 1 - \text{snr}}{2\,\text{snr}}. \tag{375}$$

As in (326), the random coding error exponent is

$$E_{\text{r}}(R,\zeta\,\text{snr}) = \begin{cases} E_{\text{sp}}(R,\zeta\,\text{snr}), & R \in (R_{\text{c}}, \log(1+\text{snr})); \\ R_0 - R, & R \in [0, R_{\text{c}}], \end{cases} \tag{376}$$

with the critical rate R_{c} and cutoff rate R_0 in (373) and (375), respectively. This function is shown along with $E_{\text{sp}}(R, \zeta\,\text{snr})$ in Figure 3 for snr = 3.

80. In parallel to Item 77, we find the random transformation that explains the most likely mechanism to produce errors at every rate R, namely the minimizer of (254) when $P_X = P_X^*$, the maximizer of the Augustin–Csiszár mutual information of order α. In this case, P_X^* is not as trivial to guess as in Section 11, but since we already found Q_X^* in (339) with $\Gamma = \Gamma^*$, we can invoke Theorem 17 to show that the density of P_X^* achieving the maximal order-α Augustin–Csiszár mutual information is

$$p_X^*(t) = \frac{\Gamma^*}{\alpha + (1-\alpha)\Gamma^*} \delta(t) + \frac{1-\Gamma^*}{\alpha + (1-\alpha)\Gamma^*} \frac{\alpha \Gamma^*}{\zeta} e^{-t\Gamma^*/\zeta} 1\{t > 0\}, \tag{377}$$

whose mean is, as it should,

$$\frac{\alpha \zeta}{\Gamma^*} \frac{1-\Gamma^*}{\alpha + (1-\alpha)\Gamma^*} = \zeta\,\text{snr} = \theta. \tag{378}$$

Let Q_Y^* be exponential with mean $\theta + \kappa$, and $Q_{Y|X=a}^*$ have density

$$q_{Y|X=a}^*(t) = \frac{1}{\kappa} e^{-\frac{t-a}{\kappa}} 1\{t \geq a\}, \tag{379}$$

with

$$\kappa = \frac{\zeta}{\eta}, \tag{380}$$

and η as defined in (372). Using Laplace transforms, we can verify that $P_X^* \to Q_{Y|X}^* \to Q_Y^*$ where P_X^* is the probability measure with density in (377). Let Z be unit-mean exponentially distributed. Writing mutual information as the difference between the output differential entropy and the noise differential entropy we get

$$I(P_X^*, Q_{Y|X}^*) = h((\theta + \kappa)Z) - h(\kappa Z) \tag{381}$$

$$= \log\left(1 + \frac{\theta}{\kappa}\right) \tag{382}$$

$$= R, \tag{383}$$

in view of (363). Furthermore, using (335) and (379),

$$D(Q_{Y|X}^* \| P_{Y|X} | P_X^*) = \log \frac{\zeta}{\kappa} + \left(\frac{\kappa}{\zeta} - 1\right) \log e \tag{384}$$

$$= \log \eta + \left(\frac{1}{\eta} - 1\right) \log e \tag{385}$$

$$= E_{\text{sp}}(R, \zeta \, \text{snr}), \tag{386}$$

where we have used (380) and (354). Therefore, we have shown that $Q_{Y|X}^*$ is indeed the minimizer of (254). In this case, the most likely mechanism for errors to happen is that the channel adds independent exponential noise with mean ζ/η, instead of the nominal mean ζ. In this respect, the behavior is reminiscent of that of the exponential timing channel for which the error exponent is dominated (at least above critical rate) by an exponential server which is slower than the nominal [72].

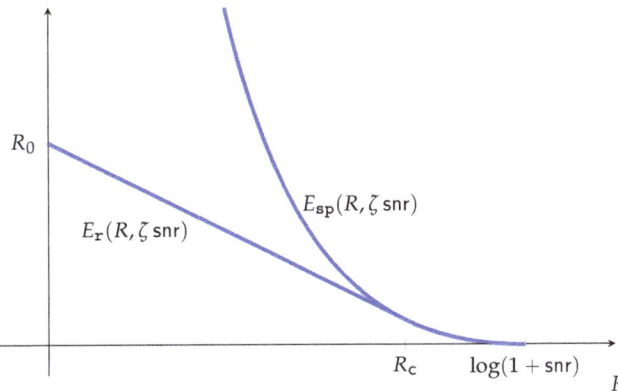

Figure 3. Error exponent functions in (354), (355) and (376).

13. Recap

81. The analysis of the fundamental limits of noisy channels in the regime of vanishing error probability with blocklength growing without bound expresses channel capacity

in terms of a basic information measure: the input–output mutual information maximized over the input distribution. In the regime of fixed nonzero error probability, the asymptotic fundamental limit is a function of not only capacity but channel dispersion [73], which is also expressible in terms of an information measure: the variance of the information density obtained with the capacity-achieving distribution. In the regime of exponentially decreasing error probability (at fixed rate below capacity) the analysis of the fundamental limits has gone through three distinct phases. No information measures were involved during the first phase and any optimization with respect to various auxiliary parameters and input distribution had to rely on standard convex optimization techniques, such as Karush-Kuhn-Tucker conditions, which not only are cumbersome to solve in this particular setting, but shed little light on the structure of the solution. The second phase firmly anchored the problem in a large deviations foundation, with the fundamental limits expressed in terms of conditional relative entropy as well as mutual information. Unfortunately, the associated maximinimization in (2) did not immediately lend itself to analytical progress. Thanks to Csiszár's realization of the relevance of Rényi's information measures to this problem, the third phase has found a way to, not only express the error exponent functions as a function of information measures, but to solve the associated optimization problems in a systematic way. While, in the absence of cost constraints, the problem reduces to finding the maximal α-mutual information, cost constraints make the problem much more challenging because of the difficulty in determining the order-α Augustin–Csiszár mutual information. Fortunately, thanks to the introduction of an auxiliary input distribution (the $\langle \alpha \rangle$-adjunct of the distribution that maximizes I_α^c), we have shown that α-mutual information also comes to the rescue in the maximization of the order-α Augustin–Csiszár mutual information in the presence of average cost constraints. We have also finally ended the isolation of Gallager's E_0 function with cost constraints from the representations in Phases 2 and 3. The pursuit of such a link is what motivated Augustin in 1978 to define a generalized mutual information measure. Overall, the analysis has given yet another instance of the benefits of variational representations of information measures, leading to solutions based on saddle points. However, we have steered clear of off-the-shelf minimax theorems and their associated topological constraints.

We have worked out two channels/cost constraints (additive Gaussian noise with quadratic cost, and additive exponential noise with a linear cost) that admit closed-form error-exponent functions, most easily expressed in parametric form. Furthermore, in Items 77 and 80 we have illuminated the structure of those closed-form expressions by identifying the anomalous channel behavior responsible for most errors at every given rate. In the exponential noise case, the solution is simply a noisier exponential channel, while in the Gaussian case it is the result of both a noisier Gaussian channel and an attenuated input.

These observations prompt the question of whether there might be an alternative general approach that eschews Rényi's information measures to arrive at not only the most likely anomalous channel behavior, but the error exponent functions themselves.

Funding: This research received no external funding.

Acknowledgments: The manuscript incorporates constructive suggestions by Academic Editor Igal Sason and the anonymous referees.

Data Availability Statement: Not applicable.

Conflicts of Interest: The author declares no conflict of interest.

Appendix A

Recall that the relative information $\iota_{P\|Q}$ is defined only if $P \ll Q$, while $D(P\|Q) \in [0, +\infty]$ is always defined and equal to $+\infty$ if (but not only if) $P \not\ll Q$.

Lemma A1. *If $Q \ll R$ and $X \sim P \ll R$, then*

$$\mathbb{E}\left[\imath_{P\|R}(X) - \imath_{Q\|R}(X)\right] = D(P \| Q), \tag{A1}$$

regardless of whether the right side is finite.

Proof. If $P \ll Q \ll R$, we may invoke the chain rule (7) to decompose

$$\imath_{P\|R}(a) - \imath_{Q\|R}(a) = \imath_{P\|Q}(a). \tag{A2}$$

Then, the result follows by taking expectations of (A2) when $a \leftarrow X \sim P$.

To show that (A1) also holds when $P \not\ll Q$, i.e., that the expectation on the left side is $+\infty$, we invoke the Lebesgue decomposition theorem (e.g. p. 384 of [74]), which ensures that we can find $\alpha \in [0,1)$, $P_0 \perp Q$ and $P_1 \ll Q$, such that

$$P = \alpha P_1 + (1 - \alpha) P_0. \tag{A3}$$

Since $P_1 \perp P_0$, we have

$$D(P_1 \| P) = \log \frac{1}{\alpha}, \tag{A4}$$

$$D(P_0 \| P) = \log \frac{1}{1 - \alpha}. \tag{A5}$$

If $X_1 \sim P_1$, then

$$\mathbb{E}\left[\imath_{P\|R}(X_1) - \imath_{Q\|R}(X_1)\right] = \mathbb{E}\left[\imath_{P_1\|R}(X_1) - \imath_{Q\|R}(X_1)\right] - \mathbb{E}\left[\imath_{P_1\|R}(X_1) - \imath_{P\|R}(X_1)\right] \tag{A6}$$

$$= D(P_1 \| Q) - D(P_1 \| P) \tag{A7}$$

$$= D(P_1 \| Q) - \log \frac{1}{\alpha}, \tag{A8}$$

where

- (A7) $\Longleftarrow$ (A1) with $(P,Q,R) \leftarrow (P_1,Q,R)$ and (A1) with $(P,Q,R) \leftarrow (P_1,P,R)$, which we are entitled to invoke since P_1 is dominated by both Q and R;
- (A8) $\Longleftarrow$ (A4).

Analogously, if $X_0 \sim P_0$, then

$$\mathbb{E}\left[\imath_{P\|R}(X_0)\right] = \mathbb{E}\left[\imath_{P_0\|R}(X_0)\right] - \mathbb{E}\left[\imath_{P_0\|R}(X_0) - \imath_{P\|R}(X_0)\right] \tag{A9}$$

$$= D(P_0 \| R) - D(P_0 \| P) \tag{A10}$$

$$= D(P_0 \| R) - \log \frac{1}{1 - \alpha}. \tag{A11}$$

Therefore, we are ready to conclude that

$$\mathbb{E}\left[\imath_{P\|R}(X) - \imath_{Q\|R}(X)\right]$$

$$= \alpha \mathbb{E}\left[\imath_{P\|R}(X_1) - \imath_{Q\|R}(X_1)\right] + (1 - \alpha) \mathbb{E}\left[\imath_{P\|R}(X_0) - \imath_{Q\|R}(X_0)\right] \tag{A12}$$

$$= \alpha D(P_1 \| Q) + (1 - \alpha) D(P_0 \| R) - (1 - \alpha) \mathbb{E}\left[\imath_{Q\|R}(X_0)\right] - h(\alpha) \tag{A13}$$

$$= +\infty, \tag{A14}$$

where

- (A12) $\Longleftarrow$ (A3);
- (A13) $\Longleftarrow$ $h(\cdot)$ is the binary entropy function, (A8) and (A11);

- (A14) $\impliedby \mathbb{E}\left[\iota_{Q\|R}(X_0)\right] = -\infty \impliedby P_0\left(x \in \mathcal{A}: \frac{dQ}{dR}(x) = 0\right) = 1 \impliedby P_0 \perp Q$.

□

Corollary A1. *Suppose that $Q \ll R$ and $X \sim P \ll R$. Then,*

$$\mathbb{E}\left[\iota_{Q\|R}(X)\right] = D(P \| R) - D(P \| Q), \tag{A15}$$

as long as at least one of the relative entropies on the right side is finite.

References

1. Shannon, C.E. A Mathematical Theory of Communication. *Bell Syst. Tech. J.* **1948**, *27*, 379–423. [CrossRef]
2. Rice, S.O. Communication in the Presence of Noise–Probability of Error for Two Encoding Schemes. *Bell Syst. Tech. J.* **1950**, *29*, 60–93. [CrossRef]
3. Shannon, C.E. Probability of Error for Optimal Codes in a Gaussian Channel. *Bell Syst. Tech. J.* **1959**, *38*, 611–656. [CrossRef]
4. Elias, P. Coding for Noisy Channels. *IRE Conv. Rec.* **1955**, *4*, 37–46.
5. Feinstein, A. Error Bounds in Noisy Channels without Memory. *IRE Trans. Inf. Theory* **1955**, *1*, 13–14. [CrossRef]
6. Shannon, C.E. Certain Results in Coding Theory for Noisy Channels. *Inf. Control* **1957**, *1*, 6–25. [CrossRef]
7. Fano, R.M. *Transmission of Information*; Wiley: New York, NY, USA, 1961.
8. Gallager, R.G. A Simple Derivation of the Coding Theorem and Some Applications. *IEEE Trans. Inf. Theory* **1965**, *11*, 3–18. [CrossRef]
9. Gallager, R.G. *Information Theory and Reliable Communication*; Wiley: New York, NY, USA, 1968.
10. Shannon, C.E.; Gallager, R.G.; Berlekamp, E. Lower Bounds to Error Probability for Coding on Discrete Memoryless Channels, I. *Inf. Control* **1967**, *10*, 65–103. [CrossRef]
11. Shannon, C.E.; Gallager, R.G.; Berlekamp, E. Lower Bounds to Error Probability for Coding on Discrete Memoryless Channels, II. *Inf. Control* **1967**, *10*, 522–552. [CrossRef]
12. Dobrushin, R.L. Asymptotic Estimates of the Error Probability for Transmission of Messages over a Discrete Memoryless Communication Channel with a Symmetric Transition Probability Matrix. *Theory Probab. Appl.* **1962**, *7*, 270–300. [CrossRef]
13. Dobrushin, R.L. Optimal Binary Codes for Low Rates of Information Transmission. *Theory Probab. Appl.* **1962**, *7*, 208–213. [CrossRef]
14. Kullback, S.; Leibler, R.A. On Information and Sufficiency. *Ann. Math. Stat.* **1951**, *22*, 79–86. [CrossRef]
15. Csiszár, I.; Körner, J. Graph Decomposition: A New Key to Coding Theorems. *IEEE Trans. Inf. Theory* **1981**, *27*, 5–11. [CrossRef]
16. Barg, A.; Forney Jr., G.D. Random codes: Minimum Distances and Error Exponents. *IEEE Trans. Inf. Theory* **2002**, *48*, 2568–2573. [CrossRef]
17. Sason, I.; Shamai, S. Performance Analysis of Linear Codes under Maximum-likelihood Decoding: A Tutorial. *Found. Trends Commun. Inf. Theory* **2006**, *3*, 1–222. [CrossRef]
18. Ashikhmin, A.E.; Barg, A.; Litsyn, S.N. A New Upper Bound on the Reliability Function of the Gaussian Channel. *IEEE Trans. Inf. Theory* **2000**, *46*, 1945–1961. [CrossRef]
19. Haroutunian, E.A.; Haroutunian, M.E.; Harutyunyan, A.N. Reliability Criteria in Information Theory and in Statistical Hypothesis Testing. *Found. Trends Commun. Inf. Theory* **2007**, *4*, 97–263. [CrossRef]
20. Scarlett, J.; Peng, L.; Merhav, N.; Martinez, A.; Guillén i Fàbregas, A. Expurgated Random-coding Ensembles: Exponents, Refinements, and Connections. *IEEE Trans. Inf. Theory* **2014**, *60*, 4449–4462. [CrossRef]
21. Somekh-Baruch, A.; Scarlett, J.; Guillén i Fàbregas, A. A Recursive Cost-Constrained Construction that Attains the Expurgated Exponent. In Proceedings of the 2019 IEEE International Symposium on Information Theory, Paris, France, 7–12 July 2019; pp. 2938–2942.
22. Haroutunian, E.A. Estimates of the Exponent of the Error Probability for a Semicontinuous Memoryless Channel. *Probl. Inf. Transm.* **1968**, *4*, 29–39.
23. Blahut, R.E. Hypothesis Testing and Information Theory. *IEEE Trans. Inf. Theory* **1974**, *20*, 405–417. [CrossRef]
24. Csiszár, I.; Körner, J. *Information Theory: Coding Theorems for Discrete Memoryless Systems*; Academic: New York, NY, USA, 1981.
25. Rényi, A. On Measures of Information and Entropy. In *Berkeley Symposium on Mathematical Statistics and Probability*; Neyman, J., Ed.; University of California Press: Berkeley, CA, USA, 1961; pp. 547–561.
26. Campbell, L.L. A Coding Theorem and Rényi's Entropy. *Inf. Control* **1965**, *8*, 423–429. [CrossRef]
27. Arimoto, S. Information Measures and Capacity of Order α for Discrete Memoryless Channels. In *Topics in Information Theory*; Bolyai: Keszthely, Hungary, 1975; pp. 41–52.
28. Sason, I.; Verdú, S. Arimoto-Rényi conditional entropy and Bayesian M-ary hypothesis testing. *IEEE Trans. Inf. Theory* **2018**, *64*, 4–25. [CrossRef]
29. Fano, R.M. *Class Notes for Course 6.574: Statistical Theory of Information*; Massachusetts Institute of Technology: Cambridge, MA, USA, 1953.

30. Csiszár, I. A Class of Measures of Informativity of Observation Channels. *Period. Mat. Hung.* **1972**, *2*, 191–213. [CrossRef]
31. Sibson, R. Information Radius. *Z. Wahrscheinlichkeitstheorie Und Verw. Geb.* **1969**, *14*, 149–161. [CrossRef]
32. Csiszár, I. Generalized Cutoff Rates and Rényi's Information Measures. *IEEE Trans. Inf. Theory* **1995**, *41*, 26–34. [CrossRef]
33. Arimoto, S. Computation of Random Coding Exponent Functions. *IEEE Trans. Inf. Theory* **1976**, *22*, 665–671. [CrossRef]
34. Candan, C. Chebyshev Center Computation on Probability Simplex with α-divergence Measure. *IEEE Signal Process. Lett.* **2020**, *27*, 1515–1519. [CrossRef]
35. Poltyrev, G.S. Random Coding Bounds for Discrete Memoryless Channels. *Probl. Inf. Transm.* **1982**, *18*, 9–21.
36. Augustin, U. Noisy Channels. Ph.D. Thesis, Universität Erlangen-Nürnberg, Erlangen, Germany, 1978.
37. Tomamichel, M.; Hayashi, M. Operational Interpretation of Rényi Information Measures via Composite Hypothesis Testing against Product and Markov Distributions. *IEEE Trans. Inf. Theory* **2018**, *64*, 1064–1082. [CrossRef]
38. Polyanskiy, Y.; Verdú, S. Arimoto Channel Coding Converse and Rényi Divergence. In Proceedings of the 48th Annual Allerton Conference on Communication, Control, and Computing, Monticello, IL, USA, 29 September–1 October 2010; pp. 1327–1333.
39. Shayevitz, O. On Rényi Measures and Hypothesis Testing. In Proceedings of the 2011 IEEE International Symposium on Information Theory, St. Petersburg, Russia, 31 July–5 August 2011; pp. 894–898.
40. Verdú, S. α-Mutual Information. In Proceedings of the 2015 Information Theory and Applications Workshop (ITA), San Diego, CA, USA, 1–6 February 2015.
41. Ho, S.W.; Verdú, S. Convexity/Concavity of Rényi Entropy and α-Mutual Information. In Proceedings of the 2015 IEEE International Symposium on Information Theory, Hong Kong, China, 15–19 June 2015; pp. 745–749.
42. Nakiboglu, B. The Rényi Capacity and Center. *IEEE Trans. Inf. Theory* **2019**, *65*, 841–860. [CrossRef]
43. Nakiboglu, B. The Augustin Capacity and Center. *arXiv* **2018**, arXiv:1803.07937.
44. Dalai, M. Some Remarks on Classical and Classical-Quantum Sphere Packing Bounds: Rényi vs. Kullback–Leibler. *Entropy* **2017**, *19*, 355. [CrossRef]
45. Cai, C.; Verdú, S. Conditional Rényi Divergence Saddlepoint and the Maximization of α-Mutual Information. *Entropy* **2019**, *21*, 969. [CrossRef]
46. Vázquez-Vilar, G.; Martinez, A.; Guillén i Fàbregas, A. A Derivation of the Cost-constrained Sphere-Packing Exponent. In Proceedings of the 2015 IEEE International Symposium on Information Theory, Hong Kong, China, 15–19 June 2015; pp. 929–933.
47. Wyner, A.D. Capacity and Error Exponent for the Direct Detection Photon Channel. *IEEE Trans. Inf. Theory* **1988**, *34*, 1449–1471. [CrossRef]
48. Csiszár, I.; Körner, J. *Information Theory: Coding Theorems for Discrete Memoryless Systems*, 2nd ed.; Cambridge University Press: Cambridge, UK, 2011.
49. Rényi, A. On Measures of Dependence. *Acta Math. Hung.* **1959**, *10*, 441–451. [CrossRef]
50. van Erven, T.; Harremoës, P. Rényi Divergence and Kullback-Leibler Divergence. *IEEE Trans. Inf. Theory* **2014**, *60*, 3797–3820. [CrossRef]
51. Csiszár, I.; Matúš, F. Information Projections Revisited. *IEEE Trans. Inf. Theory* **2003**, *49*, 1474–1490. [CrossRef]
52. Csiszár, I. Information-type Measures of Difference of Probability Distributions and Indirect Observations. *Stud. Sci. Math. Hung.* **1967**, *2*, 299–318.
53. Nakiboglu, B. The Sphere Packing Bound via Augustin's Method. *IEEE Trans. Inf. Theory* **2019**, *65*, 816–840. [CrossRef]
54. Nakiboglu, B. The Augustin Capacity and Center. *Probl. Inf. Transm.* **2019**, *55*, 299–342 [CrossRef]
55. Vázquez-Vilar, G. Error Probability Bounds for Gaussian Channels under Maximal and Average Power Constraints. *arXiv* **2019**, arXiv:1907.03163.
56. Shannon, C.E. Geometrische Deutung einiger Ergebnisse bei der Berechnung der Kanalkapazität. *Nachrichtentechnische Z.* **1957**, *10*, 1–4.
57. Verdú, S.; Han, T.S. A General Formula for Channel Capacity. *IEEE Trans. Inf. Theory* **1994**, *40*, 1147–1157. [CrossRef]
58. Kemperman, J.H.B. On the Shannon Capacity of an Arbitrary Channel. *K. Ned. Akad. Van Wet. Indag. Math.* **1974**, *77*, 101–115. [CrossRef]
59. Aubin, J.P. *Mathematical Methods of Game and Economic Theory*; North-Holland: Amsterdam, The Netherlands, 1979.
60. Luenberger, D.G. *Optimization by Vector Space Methods*; Wiley: New York, NY, USA, 1969.
61. Gastpar, M.; Rimoldi, B.; Vetterli, M. To Code, or Not to Code: Lossy Source–Channel Communication Revisited. *IEEE Trans. Inf. Theory* **2003**, *49*, 1147–1158. [CrossRef]
62. Arimoto, S. On the Converse to the Coding Theorem for Discrete Memoryless Channels. *IEEE Trans. Inf. Theory* **1973**, *19*, 357–359. [CrossRef]
63. Sason, I. On the Rényi Divergence, Joint Range of Relative Entropies, Measures and a Channel Coding Theorem. *IEEE Trans. Inf. Theory* **2016**, *62*, 23–34. [CrossRef]
64. Dalai, M.; Winter, A. Constant Compositions in the Sphere Packing Bound for Classical-quantum Channels. *IEEE Trans. Inf. Theory* **2017**, *63*, 5603–5617. [CrossRef]
65. Nakiboglu, B. The Sphere Packing Bound for Memoryless Channels. *Probl. Inf. Transm.* **2020**, *56*, 201–244. [CrossRef]
66. Dalai, M. Lower Bounds on the Probability of Error for Classical and Classical-quantum Channels. *IEEE Trans. Inf. Theory* **2013**, *59*, 8027–8056. [CrossRef]
67. Shannon, C.E. The Zero Error Capacity of a Noisy Channel. *IRE Trans. Inf. Theory* **1956**, *2*, 8–19. [CrossRef]

68. Feder, M.; Merhav, N. Relations Between Entropy and Error Probability. *IEEE Trans. Inf. Theory* **1994**, *40*, 259–266. [CrossRef]
69. Einarsson, G. Signal Design for the Amplitude-limited Gaussian Channel by Error Bound Optimization. *IEEE Trans. Commun.* **1979**, *27*, 152–158. [CrossRef]
70. Anantharam, V.; Verdú, S. Bits through Queues. *IEEE Trans. Inf. Theory* **1996**, *42*, 4–18. [CrossRef]
71. Verdú, S. The Exponential Distribution in Information Theory. *Probl. Inf. Transm.* **1996**, *32*, 86–95.
72. Arikan, E. On the Reliability Exponent of the Exponential Timing Channel. *IEEE Trans. Inf. Theory* **1996**, *48*, 1681–1689. [CrossRef]
73. Polyanskiy, Y.; Poor, H.V.; Verdú, S. Channel Coding Rate in the Finite Blocklength Regime. *IEEE Trans. Inf. Theory* **2010**, *56*, 2307–2359. [CrossRef]
74. Royden, H.L.; Fitzpatrick, P. *Real Analysis*, 4th ed.; Prentice Hall: Boston, FL, USA, 2010.

Article
Discriminant Analysis under f-Divergence Measures

Anmol Dwivedi, Sihui Wang and Ali Tajer *

Department of Electrical, Computer, and Systems Engineering, Rensselaer Polytechnic Institute,
Troy, NY 12180, USA; dwivea2@rpi.edu (A.D.); scottwon@bupt.edu.cn (S.W.)
* Correspondence: tajer@ecse.rpi.edu; Tel.: +1-518-276-8237

Abstract: In statistical inference, the information-theoretic performance limits can often be expressed in terms of a statistical divergence between the underlying statistical models (e.g., in binary hypothesis testing, the error probability is related to the total variation distance between the statistical models). As the data dimension grows, computing the statistics involved in decision-making and the attendant performance limits (divergence measures) face complexity and stability challenges. Dimensionality reduction addresses these challenges at the expense of compromising the performance (the divergence reduces by the data-processing inequality). This paper considers linear dimensionality reduction such that the divergence between the models is maximally preserved. Specifically, this paper focuses on Gaussian models where we investigate discriminant analysis under five f-divergence measures (Kullback–Leibler, symmetrized Kullback–Leibler, Hellinger, total variation, and χ^2). We characterize the optimal design of the linear transformation of the data onto a lower-dimensional subspace for zero-mean Gaussian models and employ numerical algorithms to find the design for general Gaussian models with non-zero means. There are two key observations for zero-mean Gaussian models. First, projections are not necessarily along the largest modes of the covariance matrix of the data, and, in some situations, they can even be along the smallest modes. Secondly, under specific regimes, the optimal design of subspace projection is identical under all the f-divergence measures considered, rendering a degree of universality to the design, independent of the inference problem of interest.

Keywords: dimensionality reduction; discriminant analysis; f-divergence; statistical inference

1. Introduction
1.1. Motivation

Consider a simple binary hypothesis testing problem in which we observe an n-dimensional sample X and aim to discern the underlying model according to:

$$H_0 : X \sim \mathbb{P} \quad \text{vs.} \quad H_1 : X \sim \mathbb{Q} . \qquad (1)$$

The optimal decision rule (in the Neyman-Pearson sense) involves computing the likelihood ratio $\frac{d\mathbb{P}}{d\mathbb{Q}}(X)$ and the performance limit (sum of type I and type II errors) is related to the total variation distance between $\mathbb{P}$ and $\mathbb{Q}$. We emphasize that our focus is on the settings in which the n elements of X are not statistically independent, in which case the likelihood ratio $\frac{d\mathbb{P}}{d\mathbb{Q}}(X)$ cannot be decomposed into the product of the coordinate-level likelihood ratios. One of the key practical obstacles to solve such problems pertains to the computational cost of finding and performing the statistical tests. This renders a gap between the performance that is information-theoretically viable (unbounded complexity) versus a performance possible under bounded computational complexity [1,2].

Dimensionality reduction techniques have become an integral part of statistical analysis in high dimensions [3–6]. In particular, linear dimensionality reduction methods have been developed and used for over a century for various reasons, such as their low computational complexity and simple geometric interpretation, as well as for a multitude of applications, such as data compression, storage, and visualization, to name only a few.

These methods linearly map the high-dimensional data to lower dimensions while ensuring that the desired features of the data are preserved. There exist two broad sets of approaches to linear dimensionality reduction in one dataset X, which we review next.

1.2. Related Literature

(1) **Feature extraction**: In one set of approaches, the objective is to select and extract informative and non-redundant features in the dataset X. These approaches are generally unsupervised. These widely-used approaches are principal component analysis (PCA), and its variations [7–9], multidimensional scaling (MDS) [10–13], and sufficient dimensionality reduction (SDR) [14]. The objective of PCA is to retain as much variation in the data in a lower dimension by minimizing the reconstruction error. In contrast, MDS aims to maximize the scatter of the projection and maximizes an aggregate scatter metric. Finally, the objective of SDR is to design an orthogonal mapping of the data that makes the data X and the responses conditionally independent (given the projected data). There exist extensive variations to the three approaches, and we refer the reader to Reference [6] for more discussions.

(2) **Class separation**: In another set of approaches, the objective is to perform classification in the lower dimensional space. These approaches are supervised. Depending on the problem formulation and the underlying assumptions, the resulting decision boundaries between the models can be linear or non-linear. One approach pertinent to this paper's scope is discriminant analysis (DA), that leverages the distinction between given models and designs a mapping such that its lower-dimensional output exhibits maximum separation across different models [15–20]. In general, this approach generates two matrices: within-class and between-class scatter matrices. The within-class scatter matrix shows the scatter of the samples around their respective class means, whereas, in contrast, the between-class scatter matrix captures the scatter of the samples around the mixture mean of all the models. Subsequently, a univariate function of these matrices is formed such that it increases when the between-class scatter becomes larger, or when the within-class scatter becomes smaller. Examples of such a function of between-class and within-class matrices is a classification index that includes the ratio of their determinants, difference of their determinants, and ratio of their traces [17]. These approaches focus on reducing the dimension to one and maximize separability between the two classes. There exist, however, studies that consider reducing to dimensions higher than one and separation across more than two classes. Finally, depending on the structure of the class-conditional densities, the resulting shape of the decision boundaries give rise to linear and quadratic DA.

The f-divergences between a pair of probability measures quantifies the similarity between them. Shannon [21] introduced the mutual information as a divergence measure, which was later studied comprehensively by Kullback and Leibler [22] and Kolmogorov [23], establishing the importance of such measures in information theory, probability theory, and related disciplines. The family of f-divergences, independently introduced by Csiszár [24], Ali and Silvey [25], and Morimoto [26], generalize the Kullback–Leibler divergence which enable characterizing the information-theoretic performance limits of a wide range of inference, learning, source coding, and channel coding problems. For instance, References [27–30] consider their application to various statistical decision-making problems [31–34]. More recent developments on the properties of f-divergence measures can be found in Reference [31,35–37].

1.3. Contributions

The contribution of this paper has two main distinctions from the existing literature on DA. First, DA generally focuses on the classification problem for determining the underlying model of the data. Secondly, motivated by the complexities of finding the optimal decision rules for classification (e.g., density estimation), the existing criteria used for separation are selected heuristically. In this paper, we study this problem by referring to the family of f-divergences as measures of the distinction between a pair of probability distributions. Such a choice has three main features: (i) it enables designing linear mappings for a wider range of inference problems (beyond classification); (ii) it provides the designs that are optimal for the inference problem at hand; and (iii) it enables characterizing the information-theoretic performance limits after linear mapping. Our analyses are focused on Gaussian models. Even though we observe that the design of the linear mapping has differences under different f-divergence measures, we have two main observations in the case of zero-mean Gaussian models: (i) the optimal design of the linear mapping is not necessarily along the most dominant components of the data matrix; and (ii) in certain regimes, irrespective of the choice of the f-divergence measure, the design of the linear map that retains the maximal divergence between the two models is robust. In such cases, this makes the optimal design of the linear map independent of the inference problem at hand rendering a degree of universality (in the considered space of the Gaussian probability measures).

The remainder of the paper is organized as follows. Section 2 provides the linear dimensionality reduction model, and it provides an overview of the f-divergence measures considered in this paper. Section 3 formulates the problem, and it helps to facilitate the mathematical analysis in subsequent sections. In Section 4, we provide a motivating operational interpretation for each f-divergence measure and then characterize an optimal design of the linear mapping for zero-mean Gaussian models. Section 5 considers numerical simulations for inference problems associated with the f-divergence measure of interest for zero-mean Gaussian models. Section 6 generalizes the theory to non-zero mean Gaussian models and discusses numerical algorithms that help characterize the design of the linear map, and Section 7 concludes the paper. A list of abbreviations used in this paper is provided on page 22.

2. Preliminaries

Consider a pair of n-dimensional Gaussian models:

$$\mathbb{P}: \mathcal{N}(\mu_\mathbb{P}, \Sigma_\mathbb{P}), \quad \text{and} \quad \mathbb{Q}: \mathcal{N}(\mu_\mathbb{Q}, \Sigma_\mathbb{Q}), \tag{2}$$

where $\mu_\mathbb{P}, \mu_\mathbb{Q}$ and $\Sigma_\mathbb{P}, \Sigma_\mathbb{Q}$ are two distinct mean vectors and covariance matrices, respectively, and $\mathbb{P}$ and $\mathbb{Q}$ denote their associated probability measures. The nature selects one model and generates a random variable $X \in \mathbb{R}^n$. We perform linear dimensionality reduction on X via matrix $\mathbf{A} \in \mathbb{R}^{r \times n}$, where $r < n$, rendering

$$Y \triangleq \mathbf{A} \cdot X. \tag{3}$$

After linear mapping, the two possible distributions of Y induced by matrix $\mathbf{A}$ are denoted by $\mathbb{P}_\mathbf{A}$ and $\mathbb{Q}_\mathbf{A}$, where

$$\begin{array}{l} \mathbb{P}_\mathbf{A}: \mathcal{N}(\mathbf{A} \cdot \mu_\mathbb{P}, \mathbf{A} \cdot \Sigma_\mathbb{P} \cdot \mathbf{A}^\top) \\ \mathbb{Q}_\mathbf{A}: \mathcal{N}(\mathbf{A} \cdot \mu_\mathbb{Q}, \mathbf{A} \cdot \Sigma_\mathbb{Q} \cdot \mathbf{A}^\top) \end{array}. \tag{4}$$

Motivated by inference problems that we discuss in Section 3, our objective is to design the linear mapping parameterized by matrix $\mathbf{A}$ that ensures that the two possible distributions of Y, i.e., $\mathbb{P}_\mathbf{A}$ and $\mathbb{Q}_\mathbf{A}$, are maximally distinguishable. That is, to design $\mathbf{A}$ as a function of the statistical models (i.e., $\mu_\mathbb{P}, \mu_\mathbb{Q}, \Sigma_\mathbb{P}$ and $\Sigma_\mathbb{Q}$) such that relevant notions of f-divergences between $\mathbb{P}_\mathbf{A}$ and $\mathbb{Q}_\mathbf{A}$ are maximized. We use a number of f-divergence measures for capturing the distinction between $\mathbb{P}_\mathbf{A}$ and $\mathbb{Q}_\mathbf{A}$, each with a distinct operational meaning under specific inference problems. For this purpose, we denote the f-divergence of $\mathbb{Q}_\mathbf{A}$ from $\mathbb{P}_\mathbf{A}$ by $D_f(\mathbf{A})$, where

$$D_f(\mathbf{A}) \triangleq \mathbb{E}_{\mathbb{P}_\mathbf{A}}\left[f\left(\frac{d\mathbb{Q}_\mathbf{A}}{d\mathbb{P}_\mathbf{A}}\right)\right]. \tag{5}$$

We use the shorthand $D_f(\mathbf{A})$ for the canonical notation $D_f(\mathbb{Q}_\mathbf{A} \parallel \mathbb{P}_\mathbf{A})$ for emphasizing the dependence on $\mathbf{A}$ and for the simplicity in notations. $\mathbb{E}_{\mathbb{P}_\mathbf{A}}$ denotes the expectation with respect to $\mathbb{P}_\mathbf{A}$, and $f : (0, +\infty) \to \mathbb{R}$ is a convex function that is strictly convex at 1 and $f(1) = 0$. Strict convexity at 1 ensures that the f-divergence between a pair of probability measures is zero if and only if the probability measures are identical. Given the linear dimensionality reduction model in (3), the objective is to solve

$$\mathcal{P}: \max_{\mathbf{A} \in \mathbb{R}^{r \times n}} D_f(\mathbf{A}), \tag{6}$$

for the following choices of the f-divergence measures.

1. *Kullback–Leibler (KL) divergence* for $f(t) = t \log t$:

$$D_{\mathsf{KL}}(\mathbf{A}) \triangleq \mathbb{E}_{\mathbb{Q}_\mathbf{A}} \left[\log \frac{d\mathbb{Q}_\mathbf{A}}{d\mathbb{P}_\mathbf{A}} \right]. \tag{7}$$

   We also denote the KL divergence from $\mathbb{P}_\mathbf{A}$ to $\mathbb{Q}_\mathbf{A}$ by $D_{\mathsf{KL}}(\mathbb{P}_\mathbf{A} \parallel \mathbb{Q}_\mathbf{A})$.

2. *Symmetric KL divergence* for $f(t) = (t-1)\log t$:

$$D_{\mathsf{SKL}}(\mathbf{A}) \triangleq D_{\mathsf{KL}}(\mathbb{Q}_\mathbf{A} \parallel \mathbb{P}_\mathbf{A}) + D_{\mathsf{KL}}(\mathbb{P}_\mathbf{A} \parallel \mathbb{Q}_\mathbf{A}). \tag{8}$$

3. *Squared Hellinger distance* for $f(t) = (1 - \sqrt{t})^2$:

$$\mathsf{H}^2(\mathbf{A}) \triangleq \int_{\mathbb{R}^r} \left(\sqrt{d\mathbb{Q}_\mathbf{A}} - \sqrt{d\mathbb{P}_\mathbf{A}} \right)^2. \tag{9}$$

4. *Total variation distance* for $f(t) = \frac{1}{2} \cdot |t - 1|$:

$$d_{\mathsf{TV}}(\mathbf{A}) \triangleq \frac{1}{2} \int_{\mathbb{R}^r} |d\mathbb{Q}_\mathbf{A} - d\mathbb{P}_\mathbf{A}|. \tag{10}$$

5. χ^2-*divergence* for $f(t) = (t-1)^2$:

$$\chi^2(\mathbf{A}) \triangleq \int_{\mathbb{R}^r} \frac{(d\mathbb{Q}_\mathbf{A} - d\mathbb{P}_\mathbf{A})^2}{d\mathbb{P}_\mathbf{A}}. \tag{11}$$

   We also denote the χ^2-divergence from $\mathbb{P}_\mathbf{A}$ to $\mathbb{Q}_\mathbf{A}$ by $\chi^2(\mathbb{P}_\mathbf{A} \parallel \mathbb{Q}_\mathbf{A})$.

3. Problem Formulation

In this section, without loss of generality, we focus on the setting where one of the covariance matrices is the identity matrix, and the other one has a covariance matrix Σ in order to avoid complex representations. One key observation is that the design of $\mathbf{A}$ under different measures has strong similarities. We first note that, by defining $\bar{\mathbf{A}} \triangleq \mathbf{A} \cdot \Sigma_{\mathbb{P}}^{1/2}$, $\mu \triangleq \Sigma_{\mathbb{P}}^{-1/2} \cdot (\mu_{\mathbb{Q}} - \mu_{\mathbb{P}})$, and $\Sigma \triangleq \Sigma_{\mathbb{P}}^{-1/2} \cdot \Sigma_{\mathbb{Q}} \cdot \Sigma_{\mathbb{P}}^{-1/2}$, designing $\mathbf{A}$ for maximally distinguishing

$$\mathcal{N}(\mathbf{A} \cdot \mu_{\mathbb{P}}, \mathbf{A} \cdot \Sigma_{\mathbb{P}} \cdot \mathbf{A}^\top) \quad \text{and} \quad \mathcal{N}(\mathbf{A} \cdot \mu_{\mathbb{Q}}, \mathbf{A} \cdot \Sigma_{\mathbb{Q}} \cdot \mathbf{A}^\top) \tag{12}$$

is equivalent to designing $\bar{\mathbf{A}}$ for maximally distinguishing

$$\mathcal{N}(\mathbf{0}, \bar{\mathbf{A}} \cdot \bar{\mathbf{A}}^\top) \quad \text{and} \quad \mathcal{N}(\bar{\mathbf{A}} \cdot \mu, \bar{\mathbf{A}} \cdot \Sigma \cdot \bar{\mathbf{A}}^\top). \tag{13}$$

Hence, without loss of generality, we focus on the setting where $\mu_{\mathbb{P}} = \mathbf{0}$, $\Sigma_{\mathbb{P}} = \mathbf{I}_n$, and $\Sigma_{\mathbb{Q}} = \Sigma$. Next, we show that determining an optimal design for $\mathbf{A}$ can be confined to the class of semi-orthogonal matrices.

Theorem 1. *For every $\mathbf{A}$, there exists a semi-orthogonal matrix $\bar{\mathbf{A}}$ such that $D_f(\bar{\mathbf{A}}) = D_f(\mathbf{A})$.*

Proof. See Appendix A. □

This observation indicates that we can reduce the unconstrained problem in (6) to the following constrained problem:

$$\mathcal{Q}: \max_{\mathbf{A} \in \mathbb{R}^{r \times n}} D_f(\mathbf{A}) \quad \text{s.t.} \quad \mathbf{A} \cdot \mathbf{A}^\top = \mathbf{I}_r. \tag{14}$$

We show that the design of $\mathbf{A}$ in the case of $\boldsymbol{\mu} = \mathbf{0}$, under the considered f-divergence measures, directly relates to analyzing the eigenspace of matrix $\boldsymbol{\Sigma}$. For this purpose, we denote the non-negative eigenvalues of $\boldsymbol{\Sigma}$ ordered in the descending order by $\{\lambda_i : i \in [n]\}$, where for an integer m we have defined $[m] = \{1, \ldots, m\}$. For an arbitrary permutation function $\pi : [n] \to [n]$, we denote the permutation of $\{\lambda_i : i \in [n]\}$ with respect to π by $\{\lambda_{\pi(i)} : i \in [n]\}$. We also denote the eigenvalues of $\mathbf{A} \cdot \boldsymbol{\Sigma} \cdot \mathbf{A}^\top$ ordered in the descending order by $\{\gamma_i : i \in [r]\}$. Throughout the analysis, we frequently use Poincaré separation theorem [38] for finding the row space of matrix $\mathbf{A}$ with respect to the eigenvalues of $\boldsymbol{\Sigma}$.

Theorem 2 (Poincaré Separation Theorem). *Let $\boldsymbol{\Sigma}$ be a real symmetric $n \times n$ matrix and $\mathbf{A}$ be a semi-orthogonal $r \times n$ matrix. The eigenvalues of $\boldsymbol{\Sigma}$ denoted by $\{\lambda_i : i \in [n]\}$ (sorted in the descending order) and the eigenvalues of $\mathbf{A} \cdot \boldsymbol{\Sigma} \cdot \mathbf{A}^\top$ denoted by $\{\gamma_i : i \in [r]\}$ (sorted in the descending order) satisfy*

$$\lambda_{n-(r-i)} \leq \gamma_i \leq \lambda_i, \quad \forall i \in [r]. \tag{15}$$

Finally, we define the following functions, which we will refer to frequently throughout the paper:

$$h_1(\mathbf{A}) \triangleq \mathbf{A} \cdot \boldsymbol{\Sigma} \cdot \mathbf{A}^\top, \tag{16}$$

$$h_2(\mathbf{A}) \triangleq \boldsymbol{\mu}^\top \cdot \mathbf{A}^\top \cdot \mathbf{A} \cdot \boldsymbol{\mu}, \tag{17}$$

$$h_3(\mathbf{A}) \triangleq \boldsymbol{\mu}^\top \cdot \mathbf{A}^\top \cdot [h_1(\mathbf{A})]^{-1} \cdot \mathbf{A} \cdot \boldsymbol{\mu}. \tag{18}$$

In the next sections, we analyze the design of $\mathbf{A}$ under different f-divergence measures. In particular, in Sections 4 and 5, we focus on zero-mean Gaussian models for $\mathbb{P}$ and $\mathbb{Q}$ where we provide an operational interpretation of the measure in the dichotomous mode in (4). Subsequently, we will discuss the generalization to non-zero mean Gaussian models in Section 6.

4. Main Results for Zero-Mean Gaussian Models

In this section, we analyze problem $\mathcal{Q}$ defined in (14) for each of the f-divergence measures separately. Specifically, for each case, we briefly provide an inference problem as a motivating example, in the context of which we relate the optimal performance limit of that inference problem to the f-divergence of interest. These analyses are provided in Sections 4.1–4.5. Subsequently, we provide the main results on the optimal design of the linear mapping matrix $\mathbf{A}$ in Section 4.6.

4.1. Kullback–Leibler Divergence

4.1.1. Motivation

The KL divergence, being the expected value of the log-likelihood ratio, captures, at least partially, the performance of a wide range of inference problems. One specific problem whose performance is completely captured by $D_{\mathsf{KL}}(\mathbf{A})$ is the quickest change-point detection. Consider an observation process (time-series) $\{X_t : t \in \mathbb{N}\}$ in which the observations $X_t \in \mathbb{R}^n$ are generated by a distribution with probability measure $\mathbb{P}$ specified in (2). This distribution changes to $\mathbb{Q}$ at an unknown (random or deterministic) time κ, i.e.,

$$X_t \sim \mathbb{P} \quad t < \kappa, \quad \text{and} \quad X_t \sim \mathbb{Q} \quad t \geq \kappa. \tag{19}$$

Change-point detection algorithms sample the observation process sequentially and aim to detect the change point with the minimal delay after it occurs subject to a false alarm constraint. Hence, the two key figures of merit capturing the performance of a sequential change-point detection algorithm are the average detection delay (ADD) and the rate of false alarms. Whether the change-point κ is random or deterministic gives rise to two broad classes of quickest change-point detection problems, namely the Bayesian setting (κ is random) and minimax setting (κ is deterministic). Irrespective of their discrepancies in settings and the nature of performance guarantees, the ADD for the (asymptotically) optimal algorithms are in the form [39]:

$$\text{ADD} \sim \frac{c_1}{D_{\mathsf{KL}}(\mathbb{Q} \parallel \mathbb{P})} . \tag{20}$$

Hence, after the linear mapping induced by matrix $\mathbf{A}$, for the ADD, we have

$$\text{ADD} \sim \frac{c_2}{D_{\mathsf{KL}}(\mathbb{Q}_\mathbf{A} \parallel \mathbb{P}_\mathbf{A})}, \tag{21}$$

where c_1 and c_2 are constants specified by the false alarm constraints. Clearly, the design of $\mathbf{A}$ that minimizes the ADD will be maximizing the disparity between the pre- and post-change distributions $\mathbb{P}_\mathbf{A}$ and $\mathbb{Q}_\mathbf{A}$, respectively.

4.1.2. Connection between D_{KL} and $\mathbf{A}$

By noting that $\mathbf{A}$ is a semi-orthogonal matrix and recalling that the eigenvalues of $h_1(\mathbf{A})$ are denoted by $\{\gamma_i : i \in [r]\}$, simple algebraic manipulations simplify $D_{\mathsf{KL}}(\mathbb{Q}_\mathbf{A} \parallel \mathbb{P}_\mathbf{A})$ to:

$$D_{\mathsf{KL}}(\mathbb{Q}_\mathbf{A} \parallel \mathbb{P}_\mathbf{A}) = \frac{1}{2}\left[\log \frac{1}{|h_1(\mathbf{A})|} - r + \text{Tr}[h_1(\mathbf{A})] + h_2(\mathbf{A})\right]. \tag{22}$$

By setting, and leveraging, Theorem 2, the problem of finding an optimal design for $\mathbf{A}$ that solves (14) can be found as the solution to:

$$\max_{\{\gamma_i \,:\, i \in [r]\}} \sum_{i=1}^{r} g_{\mathsf{KL}}(\gamma_i) \quad \text{s.t.} \quad \lambda_{n-(r-i)} \le \gamma_i \le \lambda_i \ \forall i \in [r], \tag{23}$$

where we have defined

$$g_{\mathsf{KL}}(x) \triangleq \frac{1}{2}(x - \log x - 1). \tag{24}$$

Likewise, finding the optimal design for $\mathbf{A}$ that optimizes $D_{\mathsf{KL}}(\mathbb{P}_\mathbf{A} \parallel \mathbb{Q}_\mathbf{A})$ when $\mu = 0$ can be found by replacing $g_{\mathsf{KL}}(\gamma_i)$ by $g_{\mathsf{KL}}\left(\frac{1}{\gamma_i}\right)$ in (23). In either case, the optimal design of $\mathbf{A}$ is constructed by choosing r eigenvectors of Σ as the rows of $\mathbf{A}$. The results and observations are formalized in Section 4.6.

4.2. Symmetric KL Divergence

4.2.1. Motivation

The KL divergence discussed in Section 4.1 is an asymmetric measure of separation between two probability measures. It is symmetrized by adding two directed divergence measures in reverse directions. The symmetric KL divergence has applications in model selection problems in which the model selection criteria is based on a measure of disparity between the true model and the approximating models. As shown in Reference [40], using the symmetric KL divergence outperforms the individual directed KL divergences since it better reflects the risks associated with underfitting and overfitting of the models, respectively.

4.2.2. Connection between D_{SKL} and $\mathbf{A}$

For a given $\mathbf{A}$, the symmetric KL divergence of interest specified in (8) is given by

$$D_{\text{SKL}}(\mathbf{A}) = \frac{1}{2} \cdot \left[\text{Tr}\left([h_1(\mathbf{A})]^{-1} + h_1(\mathbf{A}) \right) + h_2(\mathbf{A}) + h_3(\mathbf{A}) \right] - r . \qquad (25)$$

By setting $\mu = 0$, and leveraging Theorem 2, the problem of finding an optimal design for $\mathbf{A}$ that solves (14) can be found as the solution to:

$$\max_{\{\gamma_i : i \in [r]\}} \sum_{i=1}^{r} g_{\text{SKL}}(\gamma_i) \quad \text{s.t.} \quad \lambda_{n-(r-i)} \leq \gamma_i \leq \lambda_i \ \forall i \in [r] , \qquad (26)$$

where we have defined

$$g_{\text{SKL}}(x) \triangleq \frac{1}{2}\left(x + \frac{1}{x} - 2 \right) . \qquad (27)$$

4.3. Squared Hellinger Distance
4.3.1. Motivation

Squared Hellinger distance facilitates analysis in high dimensions, especially when other measures fail to take closed-form expressions. We will discuss an important instance of this in the next subsection in the analysis of d_{TV}. Squared Hellinger distance is symmetric, and it is confined in the range $[0, 2]$.

4.3.2. Connection between H^2 and $\mathbf{A}$

For a given matrix $\mathbf{A}$, we have the following closed-form expression:

$$\text{H}^2(\mathbf{A}) = 2 - 2 \frac{|4 \cdot h_1(\mathbf{A})|^{\frac{1}{4}}}{|h_1(\mathbf{A}) + \mathbf{I}_r|^{\frac{1}{2}}} \cdot \exp\left(-\frac{\mu^\top \cdot \mathbf{A}^\top \cdot [h_1(\mathbf{A}) + \mathbf{I}_r]^{-1} \cdot \mathbf{A} \cdot \mu}{4} \right) . \qquad (28)$$

By setting $\mu = 0$, and leveraging Theorem 2, the problem of finding an optimal design for $\mathbf{A}$ that solves (14) can be found as the solution to:

$$\max_{\{\gamma_i : i \in [r]\}} \prod_{i=1}^{r} g_{\text{H}}(\gamma_i) \quad \text{s.t.} \quad \lambda_{n-(r-i)} \leq \gamma_i \leq \lambda_i \ \forall i \in [r] , \qquad (29)$$

where we have defined

$$g_{\text{H}}(x) \triangleq \frac{(x+1)^2}{x} . \qquad (30)$$

4.4. Total Variation Distance
4.4.1. Motivation

The total variation distance appears as the key performance metric in binary hypothesis testing and in high-dimensional inference, e.g., Le Cam's method for the binary quantization and testing of the individual dimensions (which is in essence binary hypothesis testing). In particular, for the simple binary hypothesis testing model in (65), the minimum total probability of error (sum of type-I and type-II error probabilities) is related to the total variation $d_{\text{TV}}(\mathbf{A})$. Specifically, for a decision rule $d : \mathcal{X} \to \{\text{H}_0, \text{H}_1\}$, the following holds:

$$\inf_d \left[\mathbb{P}_{\mathbf{A}}(d = \text{H}_1) + \mathbb{Q}_{\mathbf{A}}(d = \text{H}_0) \right] = 1 - d_{\text{TV}}(\mathbf{A}) . \qquad (31)$$

The total variation between two Gaussian distributions does not have a closed-form expression. Hence, unlike the other settings, an optimal solution to (6) in this context cannot be obtained analytically. Alternatively, in order to gain intuition into the structure of a near optimal matrix **A**, we design **A** such that it optimizes known bounds on $d_{TV}(\mathbf{A})$. In particular, we use two sets of bounds on $d_{TV}(\mathbf{A})$. One set is due to bounding it via the Hellinger distance, and another set is due to a recent study that established upper and lower bounds that are identical up to a constant factor [41].

4.4.2. Connection between d_{TV} and **A**

(1) Bounding by Hellinger Distance: The total variation distance can be bounded by the Hellinger distance according to

$$\frac{1}{2}H^2(\mathbf{A}) \leq d_{TV}(\mathbf{A}) \leq H(\mathbf{A})\sqrt{1 - \frac{H^2(\mathbf{A})}{4}}. \tag{32}$$

It can be readily verified that these bounds are monotonically increasing with $H^2(\mathbf{A})$ in the interval $[0,2]$. Hence, they are maximized simultaneously by maximizing the squared Hellinger distance as discussed in Section 4.3. We refer to this bound as the Hellinger bound.

(2) Matching Bounds up to a Constant: The second set of bounds that we used are provided in Reference [41]. These bounds relate the total variation between two Gaussian models to the Frobenius norm (FB) of a matrix related to their covariance matrices. Specifically, these FB-based bounds on the total variation $d_{TV}(\mathbf{A})$ are given by

$$\frac{1}{100} \leq \frac{d_{TV}(\mathbf{A})}{\min\{1, \sqrt{\sum_{i=1}^{r} g_{TV}(\gamma_i)}\}} \leq \frac{3}{2}, \tag{33}$$

where we have defined

$$g_{TV}(x) \triangleq \left(\frac{1}{x} - 1\right)^2. \tag{34}$$

Since the lower and upper bounds on $d_{TV}(\mathbf{A})$ are identical up to a constant, they will be maximized by the same design of **A**.

4.5. χ^2-Divergence

4.5.1. Motivation

χ^2-divergence appears in a wide range of statistical estimation problems for the purpose of finding a lower bound on the estimation noise variance. For instance, consider the canonical problem of estimating a latent variable θ from the observed data X, and denote two candidate estimates by $p(X)$ and $q(X)$. Define $\mathbb{P}$ and $\mathbb{Q}$ as the probability measures of $p(X)$ and $q(X)$, respectively. According to the Hammersly-Chapman-Robbins (HCR) bound on the quadratic loss function, for any estimator $\hat{\theta}$, we have

$$\text{var}_\theta(\hat{\theta}) \geq \sup_{p \neq q} \frac{[\mathbb{E}_\mathbb{Q}[q(X)] - \mathbb{E}_\mathbb{P}[p(X)]]^2}{\chi^2(\mathbb{Q} \| \mathbb{P})}, \tag{35}$$

which, for unbiased estimators p and q, simplifies to the Cramér-Rao lower bound

$$\text{var}_\theta(\hat{\theta}) \geq \sup_{p \neq q} \frac{(q-p)^2}{\chi^2(\mathbb{Q} \| \mathbb{P})}, \tag{36}$$

depending on $\mathbb{P}$ and $\mathbb{Q}$ through their χ^2-divergence. Besides the applications to estimation problems, χ^2 is easier to compute compared to some of other f-divergence measures (e.g., total variation). Specifically, for product distributions χ^2 tensorizes to be expressed in terms of the one-dimensional components that are easier to compute than the KL divergence and TV variation distance. Hence, a combination of bounding other measures with χ^2 and then analyzing χ^2 appears in a wide range of inference problems.

4.5.2. Connection between χ^2 and $\mathbf{A}$

By setting $\mu = 0$, for a given matrix $\mathbf{A}$, from (11), we have the following closed-form expression:

$$\chi^2(\mathbf{A}) = \frac{1}{|h_1(\mathbf{A})|\sqrt{|2(h_1(\mathbf{A}))^{-1} - \mathbf{I}_r|}} - 1 \tag{37}$$

$$= \prod_{i=1}^{r} g_{\chi_1}(\gamma_i) - 1, \tag{38}$$

where we have defined

$$g_{\chi_1}(x) \triangleq \frac{1}{\sqrt{x(2-x)}}. \tag{39}$$

As we show in Appendix C, for $\chi^2(\mathbf{A})$ to exist (i.e., be finite), all the eigenvalues $\{\lambda_i : i \in [r]\}$ should fall in the interval $(0,2)$. Subsequently, finding the optimal design for $\mathbf{A}$ that optimizes $\chi^2(\mathbb{P}_\mathbf{A} \parallel \mathbb{Q}_\mathbf{A})$ when $\mu = 0$ can be done by replacing g_{χ_1} in (38) by g_{χ_2}, which is given by

$$g_{\chi_2}(x) \triangleq \sqrt{\frac{x^2}{2x-1}}. \tag{40}$$

Based on this, and by following a similar line of argument as in the case of the KL divergence, designing an optimal $\mathbf{A}$ reduces to identifying a subset of the eigenvalues of $\mathbf{\Sigma}$ and assigning their associated eigenvectors as the rows of matrix $\mathbf{A}$. These observations are formalized in Section 4.6.

4.6. Main Results

In this section, we provide analytical closed-form solutions to design optimal matrices $\mathbf{A}$ for the following f-divergence measures: D_{KL}, D_{SKL}, H^2, and χ^2. The total variation measure d_{TV} does not admit a closed-form for Gaussian models. In this case, we provide a design for $\mathbf{A}$ that optimizes the bound we have provided for d_{TV} in Section 4.4. Due to their structural similarities of the results, we group and treat D_{KL}, D_{SKL}, and d_{TV} in Theorem 3. Similarly, we group and treat H^2 and χ^2 in Theorem 4.

Theorem 3 (D_{KL}, D_{SKL}, d_{TV}). *For a given function* $g : \mathbb{R} \to \mathbb{R}$, *define the permutations:*

$$\pi^* \triangleq \arg\max_\pi \sum_{i=1}^{r} g(\lambda_{\pi(i)}). \tag{41}$$

Then, for $D_f(\mathbf{A}) \in \{D_{\mathsf{KL}}(\mathbf{A}), D_{\mathsf{SKL}}(\mathbf{A}), d_{\mathsf{TV}}(\mathbf{A})\}$ *and functions* $g_f \in \{g_{\mathsf{KL}}, g_{\mathsf{SKL}}, g_{\mathsf{TV}}\}$:

1. *For maximizing* D_f, *set* $g = g_f$ *and select the eigenvalues of* $\mathbf{A}\mathbf{\Sigma}\mathbf{A}^\top$ *as*

$$\gamma_i = \lambda_{\pi^*(i)}, \quad \text{for} \quad i \in [r]. \tag{42}$$

2. *Row* $i \in [r]$ *of matrix* $\mathbf{A}$ *is the eigenvector of* $\mathbf{\Sigma}$ *associated with the eigenvalue* γ_i.

Proof. See Appendix B. □

By further leveraging the structures of functions $g_{\mathsf{KL}}, g_{\mathsf{SKL}}$, and g_{TV}, we can simplify approaches for designing the matrix $\mathbf{A}$. Specifically, note that the functions $g_{\mathsf{KL}}, g_{\mathsf{SKL}}$, and g_{TV} are all strictly convex functions taking their global minima at $x = 1$. Based on this, we have the following observations.

Corollary 1 (D_{KL}, D_{SKL}, d_{TV}). *For maximizing $D_f(\mathbf{A}) \in \{D_{\mathsf{KL}}(\mathbf{A}), D_{\mathsf{SKL}}(\mathbf{A}), d_{\mathsf{TV}}(\mathbf{A})\}$, when $\lambda_n \geq 1$, we have $\gamma_i = \lambda_i$ for all $i \in [r]$, and the rows of $\mathbf{A}$ are eigenvectors of Σ associated with its r largest eigenvalues, i.e., $\{\lambda_i : i \in [r]\}$.*

Corollary 2 (D_{KL}, D_{SKL}, d_{TV}). *For maximizing $D_f(\mathbf{A}) \in \{D_{\mathsf{KL}}(\mathbf{A}), D_{\mathsf{SKL}}(\mathbf{A}), d_{\mathsf{TV}}(\mathbf{A})\}$, when $\lambda_1 \leq 1$, we have $\gamma_i = \lambda_{n-r+i}$ for all $i \in [r]$, and the rows of $\mathbf{A}$ are eigenvectors of Σ associated with its r smallest eigenvalues, i.e., $\{\lambda_i : i \in \{n-r+1,\ldots,n\}\}$.*

Remark 1. *In order to maximize $D_f(\mathbf{A}) \in \{D_{\mathsf{KL}}(\mathbf{A}), D_{\mathsf{SKL}}(\mathbf{A}), d_{\mathsf{TV}}(\mathbf{A})\}$ when $\lambda_n \leq 1 \leq \lambda_1$, finding the best permutation of eigenvalues involves sorting all the n eigenvalues λ_i's and subsequently performing r comparisons as illustrated in Algorithm 1. This amounts to $\mathcal{O}(n \cdot \log(n))$ time complexity instead of $\mathcal{O}(n \cdot \log(r))$ time complexity involved in determining the design for $\mathbf{A}$ in the case of Corollaries 1 and 2, which require finding the r extreme eigenvalues in determining the design for π^*.*

Remark 2. *The optimal design of $\mathbf{A}$ often does not involve being aligned with the largest eigenvalues of the covariance matrix Σ, which is in contrast to some of the key approaches to linear dimensionality reduction that generally perform linear mapping along the eigenvectors associated with the largest eigenvalues of the covariance matrix. When the eigenvalues of Σ are all smaller than 1, in particular, $\mathbf{A}$ will be designed by choosing eigenvectors associated with the smallest eigenvalues of Σ in order to preserve largest separability.*

Next, we provide the counterpart results for the H^2 and χ^2-divergence measures. Their major distinction from the previous three measures is that, for these two, $D_f(\mathbf{A})$ can be decomposed into a product of individual functions of the eigenvalues $\{\gamma_i : i \in [r]\}$. Next, we provide the counterparts of Theorem 3 and Corollaries 1 and 2 for H^2 and χ^2.

Theorem 4 (H^2, χ^2). *For a given function $g : \mathbb{R} \to \mathbb{R}$, define the permutations:*

$$\pi^* \triangleq \arg\max_{\pi} \prod_{i=1}^{r} g(\lambda_{\pi(i)}) . \tag{43}$$

Then, for $D_f(\mathbf{A}) \in \{\mathsf{H}^2(\mathbf{A}), \chi^2(\mathbf{A}), \chi^2(\mathbb{P}_\mathbf{A} \parallel \mathbb{Q}_\mathbf{A})\}$ and functions $g_f \in \{g_\mathsf{H}, g_{\chi_1}, g_{\chi_2}\}$:

1. *For maximizing D_f, set $g = g_f$ and select the eigenvalues of $\mathbf{A}\Sigma\mathbf{A}^\top$ as*

$$\gamma_i = \lambda_{\pi^*(i)}, \quad \text{for} \quad i \in [r] . \tag{44}$$

2. *Row $i \in [r]$ of matrix $\mathbf{A}$ is the eigenvector of Σ associated with the eigenvalue γ_i.*

Proof. See Appendix C. □

Next, note that g_H is a strictly convex function taking its global minimum at $x = 1$. Furthermore, g_{χ_i} for $i \in [2]$ are strictly convex over $(0, 2)$ and take their global minimum at $x = 1$.

Corollary 3 (H^2, χ^2). *For maximizing $D_f(\mathbf{A}) \in \{\mathsf{H}^2(\mathbf{A}), \chi^2(\mathbf{A}), \chi^2(\mathbb{P}_\mathbf{A} \parallel \mathbb{Q}_\mathbf{A})\}$, when $\lambda_n \geq 1$, we have $\gamma_i = \lambda_i$ for all $i \in [r]$, and the rows of $\mathbf{A}$ are eigenvectors of Σ associated with its r largest eigenvalues, i.e., $\{\lambda_i : i \in [r]\}$.*

Corollary 4 (H^2, χ^2). *For maximizing $D_f(\mathbf{A}) \in \{\mathsf{H}^2(\mathbf{A}), \chi^2(\mathbf{A}), \chi^2(\mathbb{P}_\mathbf{A} \parallel \mathbb{Q}_\mathbf{A})\}$, when $\lambda_1 \leq 1$, we have $\gamma_i = \lambda_{n-r+i}$ for all $i \in [r]$, and the rows of $\mathbf{A}$ are eigenvectors of Σ associated with its r smallest eigenvalues, i.e., $\{\lambda_i : i \in \{n-r+1,\ldots,n\}\}$.*

Algorithm 1 Optimal Permutation π^* When $\lambda_n \leq 1 \leq \lambda_1$

1: Initialize $i \leftarrow n, j \leftarrow 1, p_k \leftarrow \lambda_k \ \forall k \in \{i,j\}, \pi^* \leftarrow \emptyset$
2: Sort the eigenvalues of Σ in descending order $\{\lambda_k : k \in [n]\}$
3: **while** $|\pi^*| \neq r$ **do**
4:     **if** $g_f(p_i) > g_f(p_j)$ **then**
5:         $\pi^* \leftarrow \pi^* \cup \{p_i\}$
6:         $i \leftarrow i - 1$
7:     **else**
8:         $\pi^* \leftarrow \pi^* \cup \{p_j\}$
9:         $j \leftarrow j + 1$
10:     **end if**
11: **end while**
12: **return** π^*

Finally, we remark that, unlike the other measures, total variation does not admit a closed-form, and we used two sets of tractable bounds to analyze this case of total variations. By comparing the design of **A** based on different bounds, we have the following observation.

Remark 3. *We note that both sets of bounds lead to the same design of **A** when either $\lambda_1 \leq 1$ or $\lambda_n \geq 1$. Otherwise, each will be selecting a different set of the eigenvectors of Σ to construct **A** according to the functions*

$$g_H(x) = \frac{(x+1)^2}{x} \quad \text{versus} \quad g_{TV}(x) = \left(\frac{1}{x} - 1\right)^2. \tag{45}$$

5. Zero-Mean Gaussian Models–Simulations

5.1. KL Divergence

In this section, we show gains of the above analysis for the KL divergence measure $D_{KL}(\mathbf{A})$ through simulations on a change-point detection problem. We focus on the minimax setting in which the change-point κ is deterministic. The objective is to detect a change in the stochastic process X_t with minimal delay after the change in the probability measure occurs at κ and define $\tau \in \mathbb{N}$ as the time that we can form a confident decision. A canonical model to quantify the decision delay is the conditional average detection delay (CADD) due to Pollak [42]

$$\text{CADD}(\tau) \triangleq \sup_{\kappa \geq 1} \mathbb{E}_\kappa \left[\tau - \kappa \mid \tau \geq \kappa\right], \tag{46}$$

where $\mathbb{E}_\kappa$ is the expectation with respect to the probability distribution when the change happens at time κ. The objective of this formulation is to optimize the decision delay for the worst-case realization of the random change-point κ (that is, the change-point realization that leads to the maximum decision delay), while the constraints on the false alarm rate are satisfied. In this formulation, this worst-case realization is $\kappa = 1$, in which case all the data points are generated from the post-change distribution. In the minimax setting, a reasonable measure of false alarms is the mean-time to false alarm, or its reciprocal, which is the false alarm rate (FAR) defined as

$$\text{FAR}(\tau) \triangleq \frac{1}{\mathbb{E}_\infty[\tau]}, \tag{47}$$

where $\mathbb{E}_\infty$ is the expectation with respect to the distribution when a change never occurs, i.e., $\kappa \triangleq \infty$. A standard approach to balance the trade-off between decision delay and false alarm rates involves solving [42]

$$\min_{\tau} \text{CADD}(\tau) \quad \text{s.t.} \quad \text{FAR}(\tau) \leq \alpha, \tag{48}$$

where $\alpha \in \mathbb{R}_+$ controls the rate of false alarms. For the quickest change-point detection formulation in (48), the popular cumulative sum (CuSum) test generates the optimal solutions, involving computing the following test statistic:

$$W[t] \triangleq \max_{1 \leq k \leq t+1} \sum_{i=k}^{t} \log\left(\frac{d\mathbb{Q}_\mathbf{A}(X_i)}{d\mathbb{P}_\mathbf{A}(X_i)}\right). \tag{49}$$

Computing $W[t]$ follows a convenient recursion given by

$$W[t] \triangleq \left(W[t-1] + \log\left(\frac{d\mathbb{Q}_\mathbf{A}(X_t)}{d\mathbb{P}_\mathbf{A}(X_t)}\right)\right)^+, \tag{50}$$

where $W[0] = 0$. The CuSum statistic declares a change at a stopping time τ given by

$$\tau \triangleq \inf\{t \geq 1 : W[t] > C\}, \tag{51}$$

where C is chosen such that the constraint on $\text{FAR}(\tau)$ in (48) is satisfied.

In this setting, we consider two zero-mean Gaussian models with the following pre- and post-linear dimensionality reduction structures:

$$\begin{aligned} \mathbb{P} : & \quad \mathcal{N}(\mathbf{0}, \mathbf{I}_n) \quad \text{and} \quad \mathbb{Q} : \quad \mathcal{N}(\mathbf{0}, \mathbf{\Sigma}) \\ \mathbb{P}_\mathbf{A} : & \quad \mathcal{N}(\mathbf{0}, \mathbf{I}_r) \quad \text{and} \quad \mathbb{Q}_\mathbf{A} : \quad \mathcal{N}(\mathbf{0}, h_1(\mathbf{A})) \end{aligned}, \tag{52}$$

where the covariance matrix $\mathbf{\Sigma}$ is generated randomly, and its eigenvalues are sampled from a uniform distribution. In particular, for the original data dimension n, $\lceil 0.9n \rceil$ eigenvalues are sampled such that $\{\lambda_i \sim \mathcal{U}(0.064, 1)\}$, and the remaining eigenvalues are sampled such that $\{\lambda_i \sim \mathcal{U}(1, 4.24)\}$. We note that this is done since the objective function lies in the same range for the eigenvalues within the range $[0.0649, 1]$ and $[1, 4.24]$. In order to consider the worst case detection delay, we set $\kappa = 1$ and generate stochastic observations according to the model described in (52) that follows the change-point detection model in (19). For every random realization of covariance matrix $\mathbf{\Sigma}$, we run the CuSum statistic (50), where we generate $\mathbf{A}$ according to the following two schemes:

(1) Largest eigen modes: In this scheme, the linear map $\mathbf{A}$ is designed such that its rows are eigenvectors associated with the r largest eigenvalues of $\mathbf{\Sigma}$.

(2) Optimal design: In this scheme, the linear map $\mathbf{A}$ is designed such that its rows are eigenvectors associated with r eigenvalues of $\mathbf{\Sigma}$ that maximize $D_{\text{KL}}(\mathbf{A})$ according to Theorem 3.

In order to evaluate and compare the performance of the two schemes, we compute the ADD obtained by running a Monte-Carlo simulation over 5000 random realizations of the stochastic process X_t following the change-point detection model in (19) for every random realization of $\mathbf{\Sigma}$ and for each reduced dimension $1 \leq r \leq 9$. The detection delays obtained are then averaged again over 100 random realizations of covariance matrices $\mathbf{\Sigma}$ for each reduced dimension r. Figure 1 shows the plot for ADD versus r for multiple initial data dimension n and for a fixed $\text{FAR} = \frac{1}{5000}$. Owing to the dependence on $D_{\text{KL}}(\mathbf{A})$ given in (21), the delay associated with the optimal linear mapping in Theorem 3 achieves better performance.

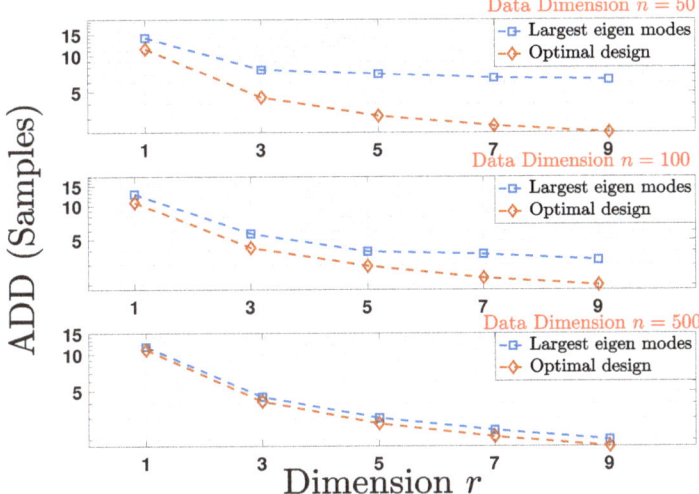

Figure 1. Comparison of the average detection delay (ADD) under the optimal design and largest eigen modes schemes for multiple reduced data dimensions r as a function of original data dimension n for a fixed false alarm rate (FAR) which is equal to $1/5000$.

5.2. Symmetric KL Divergence

In this section, we show the gains of the analysis by numerically computing $D_{\mathsf{SKL}}(\mathbf{A})$. We follow the pre- and post-linear dimensionality reduction structures given in (52), where the covariance matrix $\mathbf{\Sigma}$ is randomly generated following the setup used in Section 5.1. As plotted in Figure 2, by choosing the design scheme for $D_{\mathsf{SKL}}(\mathbf{A})$ according to Theorem 3, the optimal design outperforms other schemes.

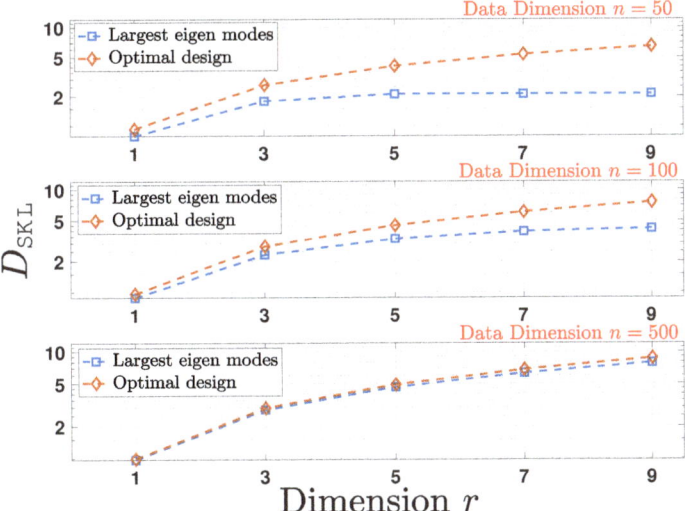

Figure 2. Comparison of the empirical average computed for the optimal design and largest eigen modes schemes for multiple reduced data dimensions r as a function of original data dimension n.

5.3. Squared Hellinger Distance

We consider a Bayesian hypothesis testing problem given class a priori parameters $p_{\mathbb{P}_A}, p_{\mathbb{Q}_A}$ and Gaussian class conditional densities for the linear dimensionality reduction model in (52). Without loss of generality, we assume a 0–1 loss function associated with misclassification for the hypothesis test. In order to quantify the performance of the Bayes decision rule, it is imperative to compute the associated probability of error, also known as the Bayes error, which we denote by P_e. Since, in general, computing P_e for the optimal decision rule for multivariate Gaussian conditional densities is intractable, numerous techniques have been devised to bound P_e. Owing to its simplicity, one of the most commonly employed metric is the Bhattacharyya coefficient given by

$$\mathrm{BC}(\mathbf{A}) \triangleq \int_{\mathbb{R}^r} \sqrt{\mathrm{d}\mathbb{P}_\mathbf{A} \cdot \mathrm{d}\mathbb{Q}_\mathbf{A}} \,. \tag{53}$$

The metric in (53) facilitates upper bounding the error probability as

$$P_e \leq \sqrt{p_{\mathbb{P}_A} \, p_{\mathbb{Q}_A}} \cdot \mathrm{BC}(\mathbf{A}) \,, \tag{54}$$

which is widely referred to as the Bhattacharrya bound. Relevant to this study is that the squared Hellinger distance is related to the Bhattacharyya coefficient in (53) through

$$\mathrm{H}^2(\mathbf{A}) = 2 - \mathrm{BC}(\mathbf{A}) \,. \tag{55}$$

Hence, maximizing the Hellinger distance $\mathrm{H}^2(\mathbf{A})$ results in a tighter bound on P_e from (54). To show the performance numerically, we compute the $\mathrm{BC}(\mathbf{A})$ via (55). For the pre- and post-linear dimensionality reduction structures as given in (52), the covariance matrix $\mathbf{\Sigma}$ is randomly generated following the setup used in Section 5.1. As plotted in Figure 3, by employing the design scheme according to Theorem 4, the optimal design results in a smaller $\mathrm{BC}(\mathbf{A})$ and, hence, a tighter upper bound on P_e in comparison to other schemes.

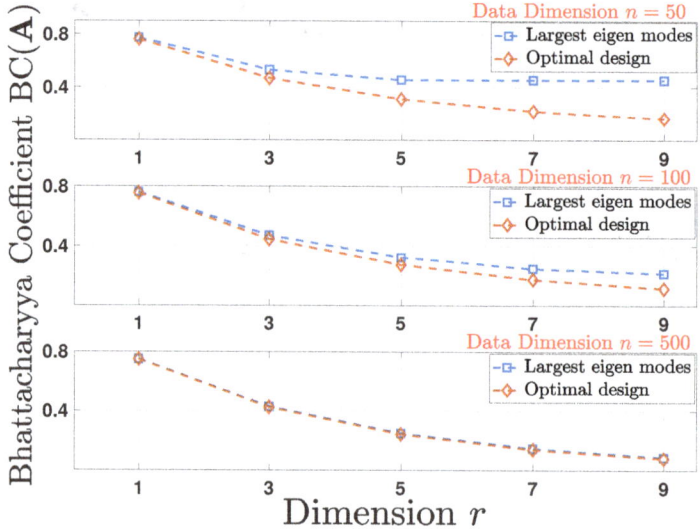

Figure 3. Comparison of the empirical average of the Bhattacharyya coefficient $\mathrm{BC}(\mathbf{A})$ under optimal design and largest eigen modes schemes for multiple reduced data dimensions r as a function of original data dimension n.

5.4. Total Variation Distance

Consider a binary hypothesis test with Gaussian class conditional densities following the model in (52) and equal class a priori probabilities, i.e., $p_{\mathbb{P}_A} = p_{\mathbb{Q}_A}$. We define c_{ij} as the cost associated with deciding in favor of H_i when the true hypothesis is H_j such that $0 \leq i, j \leq 1$, and denote the densities associated with measures $\mathbb{P}_A$, $\mathbb{Q}_A$ by $f_{\mathbb{P}_A}$ and $f_{\mathbb{Q}_A}$, respectively. Without loss of generality, we assume a 0–1 loss function such that $c_{ij} = 1 \ \forall \ i \neq j$ and $c_{ii} = 0 \ \forall \ i$. The optimal Bayes decision rule that minimizes the error probability is given by

$$\frac{f_{\mathbb{P}_A}(x)}{f_{\mathbb{Q}_A}(x)} \overset{d=H_1}{\underset{d=H_0}{\lessgtr}} 1 . \tag{56}$$

Since the total variation distance cannot be computed in closed-form, we numerically compute the error probability P_e under the two bounds (Hellinger-based and FB-based) introduced in Section 4.4.2 to quantify the performance of the design of matrix **A** for the underlying inference problem. The covariance matrix Σ is randomly generated following the setup used in Section 5.1. As plotted in Figure 4, by optimizing the Hellinger-based bound according to Theorem 4 and optimizing the FB-based bound according to Theorem 3, the two design schemes achieve a smaller P_e. We further observe that the bounds due to FB-based are loose in comparison to Hellinger-based bounds. Therefore, we choose not to plot the lower bound on P_e for the FB-based bounds in Figure 4.

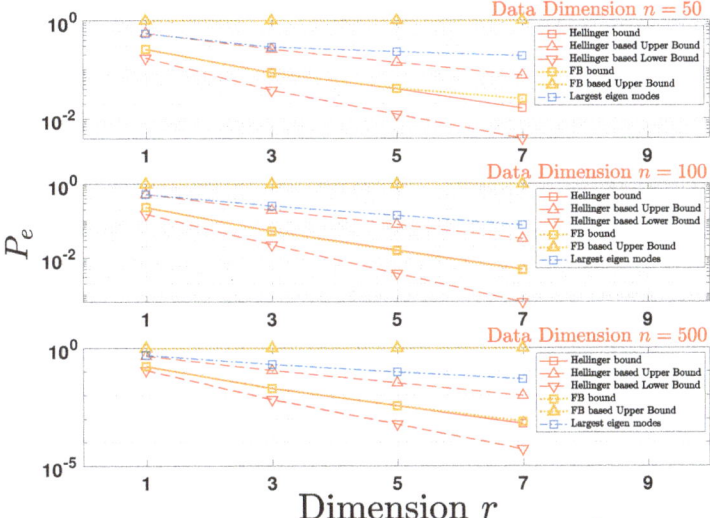

Figure 4. Comparing the logarithm of the empirical average value for P_e under the two bounds on $d_{TV}(\mathbf{A})$ (Hellinger-based and Frobenius norm (FB)-based) with the largest eigen modes scheme for multiple projected data dimensions r as a function of initial data dimension n.

5.5. χ^2-Divergence

In this section, we show the gains of the proposed analysis through numerical evaluations by numerically computing $\chi^2(\mathbf{A})$, to find a lower bound on the noise variance $\text{var}_\theta(\hat{\theta})$ up to a constant. Following the pre- and post-linear dimensionality reduction structures given in (52), the covariance matrix Σ is randomly generated following the setup used in Section 5.1. As shown in Figure 5, constructing the optimal design according to Theorem 4 achieves a tighter lower bound in comparison to the other scheme.

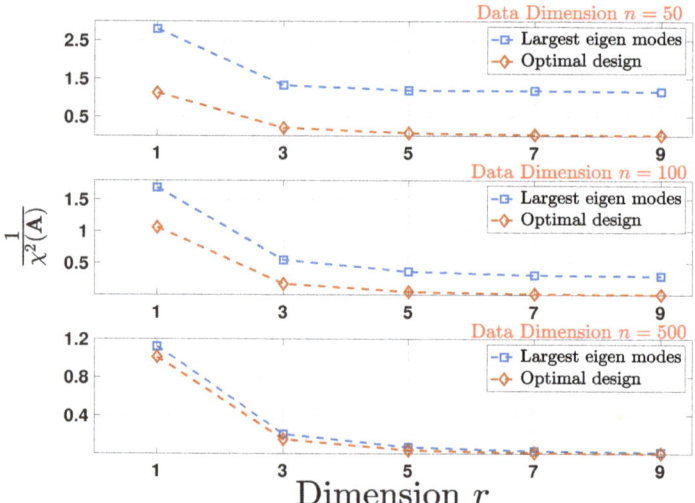

Figure 5. Comparison of the lower bound on noise variance given by $\frac{1}{\chi^2(\mathbf{A})}$ under the optimal and largest eigen modes schemes for multiple reduced data dimensions r as a function of original data dimension n.

6. General Gaussian Models

In the previous section, we focused on $\boldsymbol{\mu} = \mathbf{0}$. When $\boldsymbol{\mu} \neq \mathbf{0}$, optimizing each f-divergence measure under the semi-orthogonality constraint does not render closed-form expressions. Nevertheless, to provide some intuitions, we provide a numerical approach to the optimal design of $\mathbf{A}$, which might also enjoy some *local* optimality guarantees. To start, note that the feasible set of solutions given by $\mathcal{M}_n^r \triangleq \{\mathbf{A} \in \mathbb{R}^{r \times n} : \mathbf{A} \cdot \mathbf{A}^\top = \mathbf{I}_r\}$ owing to the orthogonality constraints in $\mathcal{Q}$ is often referred to as the Stiefel manifold. Therefore, solving $\mathcal{Q}$ requires designing algorithms that optimize the objective while preserving manifold constraints during iterations.

We employ the method of Lagrange multipliers to formulate the Lagrangian function. By denoting the matrix of Lagrangian multipliers by $\mathbf{L} \in \mathbb{R}^{r \times r}$, the Lagrangian function of problem (14) is given by

$$\mathcal{L}(\mathbf{A}, \mathbf{L}) = D_f(\mathbf{A}) + \langle \mathbf{L}, \mathbf{A} \cdot \mathbf{A}^\top - \mathbf{I}_r \rangle . \tag{57}$$

From the first order optimality condition, for any local maximizer $\mathbf{A}^*$ of (14), there exists a Lagrange multiplier $\mathbf{L}^*$ such that

$$\nabla_{\mathbf{A}} \mathcal{L}(\mathbf{A}, \mathbf{L}) \Big|_{\mathbf{A}^*, \mathbf{L}^*} = 0 , \tag{58}$$

where we denote the partial derivative with respect to $\mathbf{A}$ by $\nabla_{\mathbf{A}}$. In what follows, we iterate the design mapping $\mathbf{A}$ using the gradient ascent algorithm in order to find a solution for $\mathbf{A}$. As discussed in the next subsection, this solution is guaranteed to be at least locally optimal.

6.1. Optimizing via Gradient Ascent

We use an iterative gradient ascent-based algorithm to find the local maximizer of $D_f(\mathbf{A})$ such that $\mathbf{A} \in \mathcal{M}_n^r$. The gradient ascent update at any given iteration $k \in \mathbb{N}$ is given by

$$\mathbf{A}^{k+1} = \mathbf{A}^k + \alpha \cdot \nabla_{\mathbf{A}} \mathcal{L}(\mathbf{A}, \mathbf{L}) \Big|_{\mathbf{A}^k} . \tag{59}$$

Note that, following this update, since the new point $\mathbf{A}^{k+1}$ in (59) may not satisfy the semi-orthogonality, i.e., $\mathbf{A}^{k+1} \notin \mathcal{M}_n^r$, it is imperative to establish a relation between the multipliers $\mathbf{L}$ and $\mathbf{A}^k$ in every iteration k to ensure a constraint-preserving update scheme. In particular, to enforce the semi-orthogonality constraint on $\mathbf{A}^{k+1}$, a relationship between the multipliers and the gradients in every iteration k is derived. Following a similar line of analysis for gradient descent in Reference [43], the relationship between multipliers and the gradients is provided in Appendix E. More details on the analysis of the update scheme can be found in Reference [43], and a detailed discussion on the convergence guarantees of classical steepest descent update schemes adapted to semi-orthogonality constraints can be found in Reference [44].

In order to simplify $\nabla_\mathbf{A} \mathcal{L}(\mathbf{A}, \mathbf{L})$ and state the relationships, we define $\mathbf{\Lambda} \triangleq \mathbf{L} + \mathbf{L}^\top$ and subsequently find a relationship between $\mathbf{\Lambda}$ and $\mathbf{A}^k$ in every iteration k. This is obtained by right-multiplying (59) by $\mathbf{A}^{k+1}$ and solving for $\mathbf{\Lambda}$ that enforces the semi-orthogonality constraint on $\mathbf{A}^{k+1}$. To simplify the analysis, we take a finite Taylor series expansion of $\mathbf{\Lambda}$ around $\alpha = 0$ and choose α such that the error in forcing the constraint is a good approximation of the gradient of the objective subjected to $\mathbf{A} \cdot \mathbf{A}^\top = \mathbf{I}_r$. As derived in the Appendix E, by simple algebraic manipulations, it can be shown that the matrices $\mathbf{\Lambda}_0$, $\mathbf{\Lambda}_1$, and $\mathbf{\Lambda}_2$, for which the finite Taylor series expansion of $\mathbf{\Lambda} \approx \mathbf{\Lambda}_0 + \alpha \cdot \mathbf{\Lambda}_1 + \alpha^2 \cdot \mathbf{\Lambda}_2$ is a good approximation of the constraint, are given by

$$\mathbf{\Lambda}_0 \triangleq -\frac{1}{2}\left[\nabla_\mathbf{A} D_f(\mathbf{A}) \cdot (\mathbf{A})^\top + \mathbf{A} \cdot \nabla_\mathbf{A} D_f(\mathbf{A})^\top\right], \tag{60}$$

$$\mathbf{\Lambda}_1 \triangleq -\frac{1}{2}\left[\left(\nabla_\mathbf{A} D_f(\mathbf{A}) + \mathbf{\Lambda}_0 \mathbf{A}\right) \cdot \left(\nabla_\mathbf{A} D_f(\mathbf{A}) + \mathbf{\Lambda}_0 \mathbf{A}\right)^\top\right], \tag{61}$$

$$\mathbf{\Lambda}_2 \triangleq -\frac{1}{2}\left[\mathbf{\Lambda}_1 \cdot \mathbf{A} \cdot \nabla_\mathbf{A} D_f(\mathbf{A})^\top + \nabla_\mathbf{A} D_f(\mathbf{A}) \cdot (\mathbf{A})^\top \cdot \mathbf{\Lambda}_1 + \mathbf{\Lambda}_0 \cdot \mathbf{\Lambda}_1 + \mathbf{\Lambda}_1 \cdot \mathbf{\Lambda}_0\right]. \tag{62}$$

Additionally, we note that, since finding the global maximum is not guaranteed, it is imperative to initialize $\mathbf{A}^0$ close to the estimated maximum. In this regard, we leverage the structure of the objective function for each f-divergence measure as given in Appendix D. In particular, we observe that the objective of each f-divergence measure can be decomposed into two objectives: the first not involving μ (making this objective a convex problem as shown in Section 4), and the second objective a function of μ. Hence, leveraging the structure of the solution from Section 4, we initialize $\mathbf{A}^0$ such that it maximizes the objective in the case of zero-mean Gaussian models. We further note that, while there are more sophisticated orthogonality constraint-preserving algorithms [45], we find that our method adopted from Reference [43] is sufficient for our purpose, as we show next through numerical simulations.

6.2. Results and Discussion

The design of $\mathbf{A}$ when $\mu \neq 0$ is not characterized analytically. Therefore, we resort to numerical simulations to show the gains of optimizing f-divergence measures when $\mu \neq 0$. In particular, we consider the linear discriminant analysis (LDA) problem where the goal is to design a mapping $\mathbf{A}$ and perform classification in the lower dimensional space (of dimension r). Without loss of generality, we assume $n = 10$ and consider Gaussian densities with the following pre- and post-linear dimensionality reduction structures:

$$\begin{array}{ll} \mathbb{P}: & \mathcal{N}(\mathbf{0}, \mathbf{I}_n) \quad \text{and} \quad \mathbb{Q}: \mathcal{N}(\mu, \mathbf{\Sigma}) \\ \mathbb{P}_\mathbf{A}: & \mathcal{N}(\mathbf{0}, \mathbf{I}_r) \quad \text{and} \quad \mathbb{Q}_\mathbf{A}: \mathcal{N}(\mathbf{A} \cdot \mu, h_1(\mathbf{A})) \end{array}, \tag{63}$$

where the covariance matrix $\mathbf{\Sigma}$ is generated randomly the eigenvalues of which are sampled from a uniform distribution $\{\lambda_i \sim \mathcal{U}(0,1)\}_{i=1}^{10}$. For the model in (63), we consider two kinds of performance metrics that have information-theoretic performance interpretations: (i) the total probability of error related to the $d_{\mathsf{TV}}(\mathbf{A})$, and (ii) the exponential decay of error probability related to $D_{\mathsf{KL}}(\mathbb{P}_\mathbf{A} \parallel \mathbb{Q}_\mathbf{A})$. In what follows, we demonstrate that optimizing appropriate f-divergence measures between $\mathbb{P}_\mathbf{A}$ and $\mathbb{Q}_\mathbf{A}$ lead to better performance when compared to the performance of the popular Fisher's quadratic discriminant analysis (QDA) classifier [20]. In particular, the Fisher's approach sets $r = 1$ and designs $\mathbf{A}$ by solving

$$\arg\max_{\mathbf{A} \in \mathbb{R}^{1 \times n}} \frac{(\boldsymbol{\mu} \cdot \mathbf{A}^\top)^2}{\mathbf{A} \cdot (\mathbf{I}_n + \boldsymbol{\Sigma}) \cdot \mathbf{A}^\top} . \tag{64}$$

In contrast, we design $\mathbf{A}$ such that the information-theoretic objective functions associated with the total probability of error (captured by $d_{\mathsf{TV}}(\mathbf{A})$) and the exponential decay of error probability (captured by $D_{\mathsf{KL}}(\mathbb{P}_\mathbf{A} \parallel \mathbb{Q}_\mathbf{A})$) are minimized. The structure of the objective functions is discussed in Total probability of error and Type-II error subjected to type-I error constraints. Both methods and Fisher's method, after projecting the data into a lower dimension, deploy optimal detectors to discern the true model. It is noteworthy that, in both methods the data in the lower dimensions has a Gaussian model, and the conventional QDA [20] classifier is the optimal detector. Hence, we emphasize that our approach aims to have a design for $\mathbf{A}$ that maximizes the distance between the probability measures after reducing the dimensions, i.e., the distance between $\mathbb{P}_\mathbf{A}$ and $\mathbb{Q}_\mathbf{A}$. Since this distance captures the quality of the decisions, our design of $\mathbf{A}$ outperforms that of Fisher's. For each comparison, we consider various values for $\boldsymbol{\mu}$ and compare the appropriate performance metrics with that of Fisher's QDA for each. In all cases, the data is synthetically generated, i.e., sampled from a Gaussian distribution where we consider 2000 data points associated with each measure $\mathbb{P}$ and $\mathbb{Q}$.

6.2.1. Schemes for Linear Map

(1) Total Probability of Error: In this scheme, the linear map $\mathbf{A}$ is designed such that $d_{\mathsf{TV}}(\mathbf{A})$ is optimized via gradient ascent iterations until convergence. As discussed in Section 4.4.1, since the total probability of error is the key performance metric that arises while optimizing $d_{\mathsf{TV}}(\mathbf{A})$, it is expected that optimizing $d_{\mathsf{TV}}(\mathbf{A})$ will result in a smaller total error in comparison to other schemes that optimize other objective functions (e.g., Fisher's QDA). We note that, since there do not exist closed-form expressions for the total variation distance, we maximize bounds on $d_{\mathsf{TV}}(\mathbf{A})$ instead via the Hellinger bound in (33) as a proxy to minimize the total probability of error. The corresponding gradient expression to optimize $\mathsf{H}^2(\mathbf{A})$ (to perform iterative updates as in (59)) is derived in closed-form and is given in Appendix D.

(2) Type-II Error Subjected to Type-I Error Constraints: In this scheme, the linear map $\mathbf{A}$ is designed such that $D_{\mathsf{KL}}(\mathbb{P}_\mathbf{A} \parallel \mathbb{Q}_\mathbf{A})$ is optimized via gradient ascent iterations until convergence. In order to establish a relation, consider the following binary hypothesis test:

$$\mathsf{H}_0 : X \sim \mathbb{P}_\mathbf{A} \quad \text{versus} \quad \mathsf{H}_1 : X \sim \mathbb{Q}_\mathbf{A} . \tag{65}$$

When minimizing the probability of type-II error subjected to type-I error constraints, the optimal test guarantees that the probability of type-II error decays exponentially as

$$\lim_{s \to \infty} \frac{-\log(\mathbb{Q}_\mathbf{A}(d = \mathsf{H}_0))}{s} = D_{\mathsf{KL}}(\mathbb{P}_\mathbf{A} \parallel \mathbb{Q}_\mathbf{A}) , \tag{66}$$

where we have define $d : X \to \{\mathsf{H}_0, \mathsf{H}_1\}$ as the decision rule for the hypothesis test, and s denotes the sample size. As a result, $D_{\mathsf{KL}}(\mathbb{P}_\mathbf{A} \parallel \mathbb{Q}_\mathbf{A})$ appears as the error exponent for hypothesis test in (65). Hence, it is expected that optimizing $D_{\mathsf{KL}}(\mathbb{P}_\mathbf{A} \parallel \mathbb{Q}_\mathbf{A})$ will result in a smaller type-II error for the same type-I error when comparing with a method that optimizes other objectives (e.g., Fisher's QDA). The corresponding gradient expression to optimize the $D_{\mathsf{KL}}(\mathbb{P}_\mathbf{A} \parallel \mathbb{Q}_\mathbf{A})$ is derived in closed-form and is given in Appendix D.

For the sake of comparison and reference, we also consider schemes in which $\mathbf{A}$ is designed to optimize the objectives $D_{\mathsf{KL}}(\mathbf{A})$, the largest eigen modes (LEM), and the smallest eigen modes (SEM), which carry no specific operational significance in the context

of the binary classification problem. In the case of LEM and SEM schemes, the linear map
A is designed such that the rows of **A** are the eigenvector associated with the largest and
smallest modes of the matrix Σ, respectively. Furthermore, we define $\mathbb{1}$ as the vector of all
those of appropriate dimension.

6.2.2. Performance Comparison

After learning the linear map **A** for each scheme described in Section 6.2.1, we perform
classification in the lower dimensional space of dimension r to find the type-I, type-II,
and total probability of error for each scheme. Tables 1–4 tabulate the results for various
choices of the mean parameter μ. We have the following important observations: (i) we
observe that optimizing $H^2(\mathbf{A})$ results in a smaller total probability of error in comparison
to the total error obtained by optimizing the Fisher's objective; it is important to note that
the superior performance is observed despite maximizing bounds on $d_{TV}(\mathbf{A})$ (that is sub-
optimal) and not the distance itself; and (ii) we observe that except for the case of $\mu = 0.8 \cdot \mathbb{1}$,
optimizing $D_{KL}(\mathbb{P}_\mathbf{A} \parallel \mathbb{Q}_\mathbf{A})$ results in a smaller type-II error in comparison to that obtained
by optimizing the Fisher's objective indicating a gain in optimizing $D_{KL}(\mathbb{P}_\mathbf{A} \parallel \mathbb{Q}_\mathbf{A})$ in
comparison to the Fisher's objective in (64).

Table 1. $\mu = 0.2 \cdot \mathbb{1}, r = 1$.

	Fisher's QDA	$D_{KL}(\mathbb{P}_\mathbf{A} \parallel \mathbb{Q}_\mathbf{A})$	$H^2(\mathbf{A})$	$D_{KL}(\mathbf{A})$	SEM	LEM
$\mathbb{P}_\mathbf{A}(d = H_1)$	331/2000	331/2000	331/2000	331/2000	337/2000	915/2000
$\mathbb{Q}_\mathbf{A}(d = H_0)$	1226/2000	63/2000	63/2000	63/2000	64/2000	811/2000
Total Error	1557/4000	394/4000	394/4000	394/4000	401/4000	1726/4000

Table 2. $\mu = 0.4 \cdot \mathbb{1}, r = 1$.

	Fisher's QDA	$D_{KL}(\mathbb{P}_\mathbf{A} \parallel \mathbb{Q}_\mathbf{A})$	$H^2(\mathbf{A})$	$D_{KL}(\mathbf{A})$	SEM	LEM
$\mathbb{P}_\mathbf{A}(d = H_1)$	344/2000	344/2000	344/2000	345/2000	347/2000	782/2000
$\mathbb{Q}_\mathbf{A}(d = H_0)$	594/2000	63/2000	63/2000	63/2000	64/2000	739/2000
Total Error	938/4000	407/4000	407/4000	408/4000	411/4000	1521/4000

Table 3. $\mu = 0.6 \cdot \mathbb{1}, r = 1$.

	Fisher's QDA	$D_{KL}(\mathbb{P}_\mathbf{A} \parallel \mathbb{Q}_\mathbf{A})$	$H^2(\mathbf{A})$	$D_{KL}(\mathbf{A})$	SEM	LEM
$\mathbb{P}_\mathbf{A}(d = H_1)$	326/2000	326/2000	335/2000	318/2000	335/2000	638/2000
$\mathbb{Q}_\mathbf{A}(d = H_0)$	137/2000	55/2000	108/2000	57/2000	61/2000	669/2000
Total Error	463/4000	381/4000	443/4000	375/4000	396/4000	1307/4000

Table 4. $\mu = 0.8 \cdot \mathbb{1}, r = 1$.

	Fisher's QDA	$D_{KL}(\mathbb{P}_\mathbf{A} \parallel \mathbb{Q}_\mathbf{A})$	$H^2(\mathbf{A})$	$D_{KL}(\mathbf{A})$	SEM	LEM
$\mathbb{P}_\mathbf{A}(d = H_1)$	264/2000	264/2000	159/2000	255/2000	307/2000	561/2000
$\mathbb{Q}_\mathbf{A}(d = H_0)$	25/2000	53/2000	64/2000	55/2000	60/2000	580/2000
Total Error	289/4000	317/4000	214/4000	310/4000	367/4000	1141/4000

It is important to note that the convergence of the gradient ascent algorithm only
guarantees a locally optimal solution. While we have restricted the results that consider
a maximum separation of $\mu = 0.8 \cdot \mathbb{1}$, we have performed additional simulations for
larger separation between models (greater $\mu > 0.8$). We have the following observations:
(i) solution for the linear map **A** obtained through gradient ascent becomes highly sensitive
to the initialization $\mathbf{A}^0$; specifically, it was observed that optimizing the Fisher's objective
outperforms optimizing $H^2(\mathbf{A})$ for various initializations $\mathbf{A}^0$, and vice versa, for other
random initializations; and (ii) the gradient ascent solver becomes more prone to getting
stuck at the local maxima for larger separations between the models. We conjecture that
the odd observation in the case of $\mu = 0.8 \cdot \mathbb{1}$ when optimizing $D_{KL}(\mathbb{P}_\mathbf{A} \parallel \mathbb{Q}_\mathbf{A})$ (where
optimizing the Fisher's objective outperforms optimizing $D_{KL}(\mathbb{P}_\mathbf{A} \parallel \mathbb{Q}_\mathbf{A})$) supports this

observation. Furthermore, we note that, since the problem is convex for $\mu = 0$, a deviation from this assumption moves the problem further from being convex, making the solver prone to getting stuck at the locally optimal solutions for larger separation between the Gaussian models.

6.2.3. Subspace Representation

In order to gain more intuition towards the learned representations, we illustrate the 2-dimensional projections of the original 10-dimensional data obtained after optimizing the corresponding f-divergence measures. For brevity, we only show the plots for $D_{KL}(\mathbb{P}_\mathbf{A} \parallel \mathbb{Q}_\mathbf{A})$ and $H^2(\mathbf{A})$. Figures 6 and 7 plot the two-dimensional projections of the synthetic dataset that optimize $D_{KL}(\mathbb{P}_\mathbf{A} \parallel \mathbb{Q}_\mathbf{A})$ and $H^2(\mathbf{A})$, respectively. As expected, it is observed that the total probability of error is smaller when optimizing $H^2(\mathbf{A})$. Figure 8 shows the variation in the objective function as a function of gradient ascent iterations. As the iterations grow, the objective functions eventually converges to a locally optimal solution.

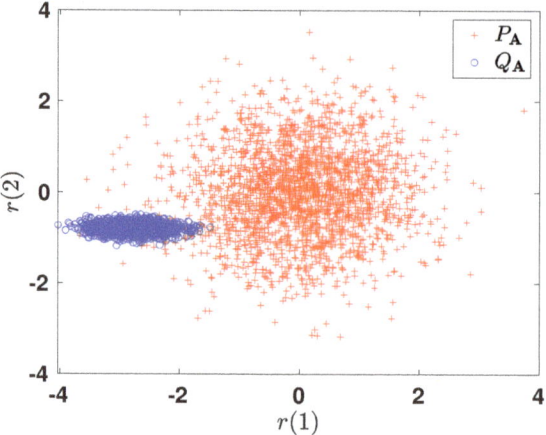

Figure 6. Two-dimensional projected data obtained by optimizing $D_{KL}(\mathbb{P}_\mathbf{A} \parallel \mathbb{Q}_\mathbf{A})$.

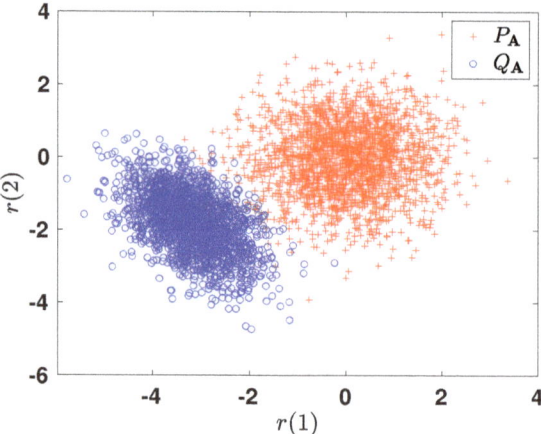

Figure 7. Two-dimensional projected data obtained by optimizing $H^2(\mathbf{A})$.

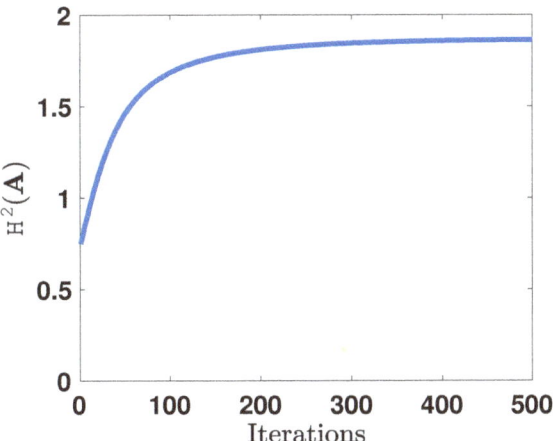

Figure 8. Convergence of the gradient ascent algorithm as a result of optimizing $H^2(\mathbf{A})$.

7. Conclusions

In this paper, we have considered the problem of discriminant analysis such that separation between the classes is maximized under f-divergence measures. This approach is motivated by dimensionality reduction for inference problems, where we have investigated discriminant analysis under Kullback–Leibler, symmetrized Kullback–Leibler, Hellinger, χ^2, and total variation measures. We have characterized the optimal design for the linear transformation of the data onto a lower-dimensional subspace for each in the case of zero-mean Gaussian models and adopted numerical algorithms to find the design of the linear transformation in the case of general Gaussian models with non-zero means. We have shown that, in the case of zero-mean Gaussian models, the row space of the mapping matrix lies in the eigenspace of a matrix associated with the covariance matrix of the Gaussian models involved. While each f-divergence measure favors specific eigenvector components, we have shown that all the designs become identical in certain regimes, making the design of the linear mapping independent of the inference problem of interest.

Author Contributions: A.D., S.W. and A.T. contributed equally. All authors have read and agreed to the published version of the manuscript.

Funding: This research was supported in part by the U. S. National Science Foundation under grants CAREER Award ECCS-1554482 and ECCS-1933107, and RPI-IBM Artificial Intelligence Research Collaboration (AIRC).

Institutional Review Board Statement: Not applicable.

Informed Consent Statement: Not applicable.

Data Availability Statement: Not applicable.

Conflicts of Interest: The authors declare no conflict of interest.

Abbreviations

The following abbreviations are used in this manuscript:

PCA	Principal Component Analysis
MDS	Multidimensional Scaling
SDR	Sufficient Dimension Reduction
DA	Discriminant Analysis
KL	Kullback Leibler
TV	Total Variation
ADD	Average Detection Delay

FAR	False Alarm Rate
CuSum	Cumulative Sum
BC	Bhattacharyya Coefficient
LEM	Largest Eigen Modes
SEM	Smallest Eigen Modes
LDA	Linear Discriminant Analysis
QDA	Quadratic Discriminant Analysis

Appendix A. Proof of Theorem 1

Consider two pairs of probability measures $(\mathbb{P}_\mathbf{A}, \mathbb{Q}_\mathbf{A})$ and $(\mathbb{P}_{\bar{\mathbf{A}}}, \mathbb{Q}_{\bar{\mathbf{A}}})$ associated with the mapping $\mathbf{A}$ in space $\mathcal{X}$ and $\bar{\mathbf{A}}$ in space $\mathcal{Y}$, respectively. Let $g : \mathcal{X} \to \mathcal{Y}$ denote any invertible transformation. Under the invertible map, we have

$$d\mathbb{Q}_{\bar{\mathbf{A}}} = d\mathbb{Q}_\mathbf{A} \cdot |\mathcal{T}|^{-1}, \quad \text{and} \quad d\mathbb{P}_{\bar{\mathbf{A}}} = d\mathbb{P}_\mathbf{A} \cdot |\mathcal{T}|^{-1}, \tag{A1}$$

where $|\mathcal{T}|$ denotes the determinant of the Jacobian matrix associated with g. Leveraging (A1), the f-divergence measure $D_f(\bar{\mathbf{A}})$ simplifies as follows.

$$D_f(\bar{\mathbf{A}}) \triangleq \mathbb{E}_{\mathbb{P}_{\bar{\mathbf{A}}}}\left[f\left(\frac{d\mathbb{Q}_{\bar{\mathbf{A}}}}{d\mathbb{P}_{\bar{\mathbf{A}}}}\right)\right] \tag{A2}$$

$$= \int_\mathcal{Y} f\left(\frac{d\mathbb{Q}_{\bar{\mathbf{A}}}}{d\mathbb{P}_{\bar{\mathbf{A}}}}\right) d\mathbb{P}_{\bar{\mathbf{A}}}(y) \tag{A3}$$

$$= \int_\mathcal{X} |\mathcal{T}(x)|^{-1} \cdot f\left(\frac{d\mathbb{Q}_\mathbf{A} \cdot |\mathcal{T}(x)|^{-1}}{d\mathbb{P}_\mathbf{A} \cdot |\mathcal{T}(x)|^{-1}}\right) \cdot |\mathcal{T}(x)| \, d\mathbb{P}_\mathbf{A}(x) \tag{A4}$$

$$= \int_\mathcal{X} f\left(\frac{d\mathbb{Q}_\mathbf{A}}{d\mathbb{P}_\mathbf{A}}\right) d\mathbb{P}_\mathbf{A}(x) \tag{A5}$$

$$= D_f(\mathbf{A}). \tag{A6}$$

Therefore, f-divergence measures are invariant under invertible transformations (both linear and non-linear) ensuring the existence of $\bar{\mathbf{A}}$ for every $\mathbf{A}$ as a special case for linear transformations.

Appendix B. Proof of Theorem 3

We observe that $D_{\mathsf{KL}}(\mathbf{A})$, $D_{\mathsf{SKL}}(\mathbf{A})$, and the objective to be optimized through the matching bound Section 4.4.2, Matching Bounds up to a Constant on $d_{\mathsf{TV}}(\mathbf{A})$ can be decomposed as the summation of strictly convex functions involving $g_{\mathsf{KL}}(x)$, $g_{\mathsf{SKL}}(x)$, and $g_{\mathsf{TV}}(x)$, respectively. Since the summation of strictly convex functions is strictly convex, we conclude that each objective $D_f \in \{D_{\mathsf{KL}}(\mathbf{A}), D_{\mathsf{SKL}}(\mathbf{A}), d_{\mathsf{TV}}(\mathbf{A})\}$ is strictly convex.

Next, the goal is to choose $\{\gamma_i\}_{i=1}^r$ such that $D_f \in \{D_{\mathsf{KL}}(\mathbf{A}), D_{\mathsf{SKL}}(\mathbf{A}), d_{\mathsf{TV}}(\mathbf{A})\}$ is maximized subjected to spectral constraints given by $\lambda_{n-(r-i)} \leq \gamma_i \leq \lambda_i$. In order to choose appropriate γ_i's, we first note that the global minimizer for functions $g_f \in \{g_{\mathsf{KL}}, g_{\mathsf{SKL}}, g_{\mathsf{TV}}\}$ appears at $x = 1$. By noting that each g_f is strictly convex, it can be readily verified that $g_f(x)$ is monotonically increasing for $x > 1$ and monotonically decreasing for $x < 1$. This will guide selecting $\{\gamma_i\}_{i=1}^r$, as explained next.

In the case of $\lambda_n \geq 1$, i.e., when all the eigenvalues are larger than or equal to 1, the objective of maximizing each $D_f \in \{D_{\mathsf{KL}}(\mathbf{A}), D_{\mathsf{SKL}}(\mathbf{A}), d_{\mathsf{TV}}(\mathbf{A})\}$ boils down to maximizing a monotonically increasing function (considering the domain). This is trivially done by choosing $\gamma_i = \lambda_i$ for $i \in [r]$, proving Corollary 1. On the other hand, when $\lambda_1 \leq 1$, i.e., when all the eigenvalues are smaller than or equal to 1, following the same line of argument, the objective boils down to maximizing each $D_f \in \{D_{\mathsf{KL}}(\mathbf{A}), D_{\mathsf{SKL}}(\mathbf{A}), d_{\mathsf{TV}}(\mathbf{A})\}$, where each D_f is a monotonically decreasing function (considering the domain). This is trivially done by choosing $\gamma_i = \lambda_{n-r+i}$ for $i \in [r]$.

When $\lambda_n \leq 1 \leq \lambda_1$, the selection process is not trivial. Rather, an iterative algorithm can be followed, where we start from the eigenvalues farthest away from 1 on both sides and, subsequently, choose the one in every iteration that achieves a higher objective. This procedure can be repeated recursively until r eigenvalues are chosen. This procedure is also discussed in Algorithm 1 in Section 4.6.

Finally, constructing the optimal matrix $\mathbf{A}$, which maximizes D_f for any data matrix $\mathbf{\Sigma}$, becomes equivalent to choosing eigenvectors as the rows of $\mathbf{A}$ associated with the chosen permutation of eigenvalues for each of the aforementioned cases.

Appendix C. Proof for Theorem 4

We first find a closed-form expression for $\chi^2(\mathbf{A})$ and $\chi^2(\mathbb{P}_\mathbf{A} \parallel \mathbb{Q}_\mathbf{A})$. From the definition, we have

$$\chi^2(\mathbf{A}) \triangleq \frac{|\mathbf{I}_r|^{\frac{1}{2}}}{(2\pi)^{\frac{r}{2}} \cdot |h_1(\mathbf{A})|} \cdot \int_{\mathbb{R}^r} \exp\left[-\frac{1}{2} \cdot \left(Y^\top \cdot \mathbf{K}_1 \cdot Y\right)\right] dY - 1, \tag{A7}$$

where we defined $\mathbf{K}_1 \triangleq 2 \cdot h_1(\mathbf{A})^{-1} - \mathbf{I}_r$. We note that $\mathbf{K}_1$ is a real symmetric matrix since $h_1(\mathbf{A})$ is a real symmetric matrix. We denote the eigen decomposition of $\mathbf{K}_1$ as $\mathbf{K}_1 = \mathbf{U} \cdot \mathbf{\Theta} \cdot \mathbf{U}^\top$, where the matrix $\mathbf{\Theta}$ is a diagonal matrix with the eigenvalues $\{\theta_i\}_{i=1}^r$ as its elements. Based on this decomposition, we have

$$\chi^2(\mathbf{A}) = \frac{1}{(2\pi)^{\frac{r}{2}} \cdot |h_1(\mathbf{A})|} \cdot \int_{\mathbb{R}^r} \exp\left[-\frac{1}{2}\left(Y^\top \cdot \mathbf{U}\mathbf{\Theta}\mathbf{U}^\top \cdot Y\right)\right] dY - 1 \tag{A8}$$

$$= \frac{1}{(2\pi)^{\frac{r}{2}} \cdot |h_1(\mathbf{A})|} \cdot \int_{\mathbb{R}^r} \exp\left[-\frac{1}{2}\left(W^\top \cdot \mathbf{\Theta} \cdot W\right)\right] dW - 1 \tag{A9}$$

$$= \frac{1}{(2\pi)^{\frac{r}{2}} \cdot |h_1(\mathbf{A})|} \cdot \prod_{i=1}^r \int_{-\infty}^{\infty} \exp\left[-\frac{1}{2}\left(\theta_i \cdot w_i^2\right)\right] dw_i - 1, \tag{A10}$$

where we have defined $W \triangleq \mathbf{U}^\top \cdot Y$. We note that, in order for $\chi^2(\mathbf{A})$ to be finite, it is required that the eigenvalues $\{\theta_i\}_{i=1}^r$ be non-negative. Hence, based on the definition of $\mathbf{K}_1$, all the eigenvalues λ_i should fall in the interval $(0, 2)$. Hence, we obtain:

$$\chi^2(\mathbf{A}) = \frac{1}{(2\pi)^{\frac{r}{2}} \cdot |h_1(\mathbf{A})|} \cdot \prod_{i=1}^r \int_{-\infty}^{\infty} \exp\left[-\frac{1}{2}\left(\theta_i \cdot w_i^2\right)\right] dw_i - 1 \tag{A11}$$

$$= \frac{1}{(2\pi)^{\frac{r}{2}} \cdot |h_1(\mathbf{A})|} \cdot \prod_{i=1}^r \sqrt{\frac{2\pi}{\theta_i}} - 1 \tag{A12}$$

$$= \frac{1}{|h_1(\mathbf{A})|} \cdot \sqrt{\frac{1}{|\mathbf{K}_1|}} - 1. \tag{A13}$$

Recall that the eigenvalues of $h_1(\mathbf{A})$ are given by $\{\gamma_i\}_{i=1}^r$ in the descending order. Therefore, (A13) simplifies to:

$$\chi^2(\mathbf{A}) = \prod_{i=1}^r \sqrt{\frac{1}{\gamma_i \cdot (2 - \gamma_i)}} - 1 = \prod_{i=1}^r g_{\chi_1}(\gamma_i) - 1. \tag{A14}$$

Hence, from (A14), maximizing $\chi^2(\mathbf{A})$ is equivalent to choosing the eigenvalues $\{\gamma_i\}_{i=1}^r$ such that they maximize $g_{\chi_1}(x)$. Similarly, the closed-form expression for $\chi^2(\mathbb{P}_\mathbf{A} \parallel \mathbb{Q}_\mathbf{A})$ can be derived as follows:

$$\chi^2(\mathbb{P}_\mathbf{A} \parallel \mathbb{Q}_\mathbf{A}) = \frac{|h_1(\mathbf{A})|^{\frac{1}{2}}}{(2\pi)^{\frac{r}{2}} \cdot |\mathbf{I}_r|} \cdot \int_{\mathbb{R}^r} \exp\left[-\frac{1}{2} \cdot \left(Y^\top \cdot \mathbf{K}_2 \cdot Y\right)\right] dY - 1, \tag{A15}$$

where we defined $\mathbf{K}_2 \triangleq 2 \cdot \mathbf{I}_r - h_1(\mathbf{A})^{-1}$. We note that $\mathbf{K}_2$ is a real symmetric matrix due to $h_1(\mathbf{A})$ being a real symmetric matrix. Hence, following a similar line of argument as in the case of $\chi^2(\mathbf{A})$, and as a consequence of Theorem 2, we conclude that all the eigenvalues λ_i should fall in the interval $(0.5, \infty)$ to ensure a finite value for $\chi^2(\mathbb{P}_\mathbf{A} \| \mathbb{Q}_\mathbf{A})$. Following this requirement, since the integrands are bounded, we obtain the following closed-form expression:

$$\chi^2(\mathbb{P}_\mathbf{A} \| \mathbb{Q}_\mathbf{A}) = \frac{|h_1(\mathbf{A})|^{\frac{1}{2}}}{1} \cdot \sqrt{\frac{1}{|\mathbf{K}_2|}} - 1. \tag{A16}$$

Recall that the eigenvalues of $h_1(\mathbf{A})$ are given by $\{\gamma_i\}_{i=1}^r$; then, (A16) simplifies to

$$\chi^2(\mathbb{P}_\mathbf{A} \| \mathbb{Q}_\mathbf{A}) = \prod_{i=1}^r \sqrt{\frac{\gamma_i^2}{(2\gamma_i - 1)}} - 1 = \prod_{i=1}^r g_{\chi_2}(\gamma_i) - 1. \tag{A17}$$

Hence, from (A17), maximizing $\chi^2(\mathbb{P}_\mathbf{A} \| \mathbb{Q}_\mathbf{A})$ is equivalent to choosing the eigenvalues $\{\gamma_i\}_{i=1}^r$ such that they maximize $g_{\chi_2}(x)$.

We observe that $\mathsf{H}^2(\mathbf{A})$, $\chi^2(\mathbf{A})$, and $\chi^2(\mathbb{P}_\mathbf{A} \| \mathbb{Q}_\mathbf{A})$ can be decomposed as the product of r non-negative identical convex functions involving $g_\mathsf{H}(x)$, $g_{\chi_1}(x)$, and $g_{\chi_2}(x)$, respectively. Hence, the goal is to choose $\{\gamma_i\}_{i=1}^r$ such that $D_f \in \{\mathsf{H}^2(\mathbf{A}), \chi^2(\mathbf{A}), \chi^2(\mathbb{P}_\mathbf{A} \| \mathbb{Q}_\mathbf{A})\}$ is maximized subjected to spectral constraints given by $\lambda_{n-(r-i)} \le \gamma_i \le \lambda_i$. In order to choose appropriate γ_i's, we first note that the global minimizer for each $g_f \in \{g_\mathsf{H}, g_{\chi_1}, g_{\chi_2}\}$ is attained at $x = 1$. Leveraging this observation, along with the structure that each g_f is convex, it is easy to infer that each $g_f(x)$ is monotonically increasing for $x > 1$ and monotonically decreasing $x < 1$. From the exact same argument in Appendix B, we obtain Corollaries 3 and 4.

Therefore, similar to Appendix B, constructing the linear map $\mathbf{A}$ that maximizes $D_f \in \{\mathsf{H}^2(\mathbf{A}), \chi^2(\mathbf{A}), \chi^2(\mathbb{P}_\mathbf{A} \| \mathbb{Q}_\mathbf{A})\}$ for any data matrix Σ boils down to choosing eigenvectors as rows of $\mathbf{A}$ associated with the chosen permutation of eigenvalues for each of the aforementioned cases.

Appendix D. Gradient Expressions for f-Divergence Measures

For clarity in analysis, we define the following functions:

$$h_2(\mathbf{A}) \triangleq \boldsymbol{\mu}^\top \cdot \mathbf{A}^\top \cdot \mathbf{A} \cdot \boldsymbol{\mu}, \tag{A18}$$

$$h_3(\mathbf{A}) \triangleq \boldsymbol{\mu}^\top \cdot \mathbf{A}^\top \cdot [h_1(\mathbf{A})]^{-1} \cdot \mathbf{A} \cdot \boldsymbol{\mu}. \tag{A19}$$

Based on these definitions, we have the following representations for the divergence measures and their associated gradients:

$$D_{\mathsf{KL}}(\mathbf{A}) = \frac{1}{2}\left[\log \frac{1}{|h_1(\mathbf{A})|} - r + \text{Tr}[h_1(\mathbf{A})] + h_2(\mathbf{A})\right], \tag{A20}$$

$$\nabla_\mathbf{A} D_{\mathsf{KL}}(\mathbf{A}) = [h_1(\mathbf{A})]^{-1} \cdot \left[\mathbf{I}_r - [h_1(\mathbf{A})]^{-1} - \mathbf{A} \cdot \boldsymbol{\mu} \cdot \boldsymbol{\mu}^\top \cdot \mathbf{A}^\top \cdot [h_1(\mathbf{A})]^{-1}\right] \cdot \mathbf{A} \cdot \Sigma$$
$$+ [h_1(\mathbf{A})]^{-1} \cdot \mathbf{A} \cdot \boldsymbol{\mu} \cdot \boldsymbol{\mu}^\top.$$

$$D_{\mathsf{KL}}(\mathbb{P}_\mathbf{A} \| \mathbb{Q}_\mathbf{A}) = \frac{1}{2}\left[\log |h_1(\mathbf{A})| - r + \text{Tr}\left[h_1(\mathbf{A})^{-1}\right] + h_3(\mathbf{A})\right], \tag{A21}$$

$$\nabla_\mathbf{A} D_{\mathsf{KL}}(\mathbb{P}_\mathbf{A} \| \mathbb{Q}_\mathbf{A}) = \left(\mathbf{I}_r - [h_1(\mathbf{A})]^{-1}\right) \cdot \mathbf{A} \cdot \Sigma + \mathbf{A} \cdot \boldsymbol{\mu} \cdot \boldsymbol{\mu}^\top.$$

$$D_{\mathsf{SKL}}(\mathbf{A}) = \frac{1}{2} \cdot \left[\text{Tr}\left([h_1(\mathbf{A})]^{-1} + h_1(\mathbf{A})\right) + h_2(\mathbf{A}) + h_3(\mathbf{A})\right] - r, \tag{A22}$$

$$\nabla_\mathbf{A} D_{\mathsf{SKL}}(\mathbf{A}) = \left[\mathbf{I}_r - [h_1(\mathbf{A})]^{-2} - [h_1(\mathbf{A})]^{-1} \cdot \mathbf{A} \cdot \boldsymbol{\mu} \cdot \boldsymbol{\mu}^\top \cdot \mathbf{A}^\top \cdot [h_1(\mathbf{A})]^{-1}\right] \cdot \mathbf{A} \cdot \Sigma$$
$$+ \left(\mathbf{I}_r + [h_1(\mathbf{A})]^{-1}\right) \cdot \mathbf{A} \cdot \boldsymbol{\mu} \cdot \boldsymbol{\mu}^\top. \tag{A23}$$

$$H^2(\mathbf{A}) = 2 - 2 \frac{|4 \cdot h_1(\mathbf{A})|^{\frac{1}{4}}}{|h_1(\mathbf{A}) + \mathbf{I}_r|^{\frac{1}{2}}} \cdot \exp\left(-\frac{\mu^\top \cdot \mathbf{A}^\top \cdot [h_1(\mathbf{A}) + \mathbf{I}_r]^{-1} \cdot \mathbf{A} \cdot \mu}{4}\right), \quad \text{(A24)}$$

$$\frac{\nabla_\mathbf{A} H^2(\mathbf{A})}{-[1 - H^2(\mathbf{A})]} = \frac{1}{2} \cdot [h_1(\mathbf{A})]^{-1} \cdot \mathbf{A} \cdot \mathbf{\Sigma} + [h_1(\mathbf{A}) + \mathbf{I}_r]^{-1} \cdot \left[-\mathbf{A} \cdot [\mathbf{\Sigma} + \mathbf{I}_n] - \frac{1}{2} \cdot \mathbf{A} \cdot \mu \cdot \mu^\top \right.$$
$$\left. + \frac{1}{2} \cdot \mathbf{A} \cdot \mu \cdot \mu^\top \cdot \mathbf{A}^\top \cdot [h_1(\mathbf{A}) + \mathbf{I}_r]^{-1} \cdot \mathbf{A} \cdot [\mathbf{\Sigma} + \mathbf{I}_n]\right].$$

Appendix E. Proof for Lagrange Multipliers

Denoting $\nabla_\mathbf{A} \mathcal{L}$ by $\tilde{\Delta}$ and $\nabla_\mathbf{A} D_f$ by Δ, and further post-multiplying (59) by $\mathbf{A}^{k+1}$, we have:

$$\mathbf{A}^{k+1} \cdot (\mathbf{A}^{k+1})^\top = \mathbf{A}^k \cdot (\mathbf{A}^{k+1})^\top + \alpha \cdot \tilde{\Delta} \cdot (\mathbf{A}^{k+1})^\top, \quad \text{(A25)}$$

$$\mathbf{I}_r = \mathbf{A}^k \cdot (\mathbf{A}^k + \alpha \cdot \tilde{\Delta})^\top + \alpha \cdot \tilde{\Delta} \cdot (\mathbf{A}^k + \alpha \cdot \tilde{\Delta})^\top, \quad \text{(A26)}$$

$$0 = \mathbf{A}^k \cdot \tilde{\Delta}^\top + \tilde{\Delta} \cdot (\mathbf{A}^k)^\top + \alpha \cdot \tilde{\Delta} \cdot \tilde{\Delta}^\top. \quad \text{(A27)}$$

Substituting $\tilde{\Delta} = \Delta + \Lambda \cdot \mathbf{A}$ in (A27) and simplifying the expression, we obtain:

$$2 \cdot \Lambda + \mathbf{A}^k \cdot \Delta^\top + \Delta \cdot (\mathbf{A}^k)^\top = -\alpha \cdot (\Delta \cdot \Delta^\top + \Delta \cdot (\mathbf{A}^k)^\top \Lambda + \Lambda \cdot \mathbf{A}^k \cdot \Delta^\top + \Lambda \cdot \Lambda^\top). \quad \text{(A28)}$$

By noting that Λ is symmetric, taking the Taylor series expansions of Λ around $\alpha = 0$ and equating the terms of α in both sides, we obtain the relationships in (60)–(62).

References

1. Kunisky, D.; Wein, A.S.; Bandeira, A.S. Notes on computational hardness of hypothesis testing: Predictions using the low-degree likelihood ratio. *arXiv* **2019**, arXiv:1907.11636.
2. Gamarnik, D.; Jagannath, A.; Wein, A.S. Low-degree hardness of random optimization problems. *arXiv* **2020**, arXiv:2004.12063.
3. van der Maaten, L.; Postma, E.; van den Herik, J. Dimensionality reduction: A comparative review. *J. Mach. Learn. Res.* **2009**, *10*, 66–71.
4. Lee, J.A.; Verleysen, M. *Nonlinear Dimensionality Reduction*; Springer Science: Berlin/Heidelberg, Germany, 2007.
5. DeMers, D.; Cottrell, G.W. Non-linear dimensionality reduction. In Proceedings of the Advances in Neural Information Processing Systems, Denver, CO, USA, 3–6 November 1993; pp. 580–587.
6. Cunningham, J.P.; Ghahramani, Z. Linear dimensionality reduction: Survey, insights, and generalizations. *J. Mach. Learn. Res.* **2015**, *16*, 2859–2900.
7. Pearson, K. On lines and planes of closest fit to systems of points in space. *Philos. Mag.* **1901**, *2*, 559–572. [CrossRef]
8. Eckart, C.; Young, G. The approximation of one matrix by another of lower rank. *Psychometrika* **1936**, *1*, 211–218. [CrossRef]
9. Jolliffe, I., *Principal Component Analysis*; Springer: Berlin/Heidelberg, Germany, 2002.
10. Torgerson, W.S. Multidimensional scaling: I. Theory and method. *Psychometrika* **1952**, *17*, 401–419. [CrossRef]
11. Cox, T.F.; Cox, M.A. Multidimensional scaling. In *Handbook of Data Visualization*; Springer: Berlin/Heidelberg, Germany, 2008.
12. Borg, I.; Groenen, P.J. *Modern Multidimensional Scaling: Theory and Applications*; Springer: Berlin/Heidelberg, Germany, 2005.
13. Izenman, A.J. Linear discriminant analysis. *Modern Multivariate Statistical Techniques*; Springer: New York, NY, USA, 2013; pp. 237–280.
14. Globerson, A.; Tishby, N. Sufficient dimensionality reduction. *J. Mach. Learn. Res.* **2003**, *3*, 1307–1331.
15. Fisher, R.A. The use of multiple measurements in taxonomic problems. *Ann. Eugen.* **1936**, *7*, 179–188. [CrossRef]
16. Rao, C.R. The utilization of multiple measurements in problems of biological classification. *J. R. Stat. Soc. Ser. B* **1948**, *10*, 159–203. [CrossRef]
17. Fukunaga, K. *Introduction to Statistical Pattern Recognition*; Elsevier: Amsterdam, The Netherlands, 2013.
18. Suresh, B.; Ganapathiraju, A. Linear discriminant analysis—A brief tutorial. *Inst. Signal Inf. Process.* **1998**, *18*, 1–8.
19. Bishop, C.M. *Pattern Recognition and Machine Learning*; Springer: Berlin/Heidelberg, Germany, 2006.
20. Hastie, T.; Tibshirani, R.; Friedman, J. *The Elements of Statistical Learning: Data Mining, Inference, and Prediction*; Springer Science & Business Media: Berlin/Heidelberg, Germany, 2009.
21. Shannon, C.E. A mathematical theory of communication. *Bell Syst. Tech. J.* **1948**, *27*, 379–423. [CrossRef]
22. Kullback, S.; Leibler, R.A. On information and sufficiency. *Ann. Math. Stat.* **1951**, *22*, 79–86. [CrossRef]
23. Gelfand, I.M.; Kolmogorov, A.N.; Yaglom, A.M. On the general definition of the amount of information. *Dokl. Akad. Nauk SSSR* **1956**, *11*, 745–748.

24. Csiszár, I. Eine Informationstheoretische Ungleichung und ihre Anwendung auf den Bewis der Ergodizität von Markhoffschen Ketten. *Magy. Tudományos Akad. Mat. Kut. Intézetének Közleményei* **1948**, *8*, 379–423.
25. Ali, S.M.; Silvey, S.D. General Class of Coefficients of Divergence of One Distribution from Another. *J. R. Stat. Soc.* **1966**, *28*, 131–142. [CrossRef]
26. Morimoto, T. Markov Processes and the H-Theorem. *J. Phys. Soc. Jpn.* **1963**, *18*, 328–331. [CrossRef]
27. Arimoto, S. Information-theoretical considerations on estimation problems. *Inf. Control* **1971**, *19*, 181–194. [CrossRef]
28. Barron, A.R.; Gyorfi, L.; Meulen, E.C. Distribution estimation consistent in total variation and in two types of information divergence. *IEEE Trans. Inf. Theory* **1992**, *38*, 1437–1454. [CrossRef]
29. Berlinet, A.; Vajda, I.; Meulen, E.C. About the asymptotic accuracy of Barron density estimates. *IEEE Trans. Inf. Theory* **1998**, *44*, 999–1009. [CrossRef]
30. Gyorfi, L.; Morvai, G.; Vajda, I. Information-theoretic methods in testing the goodness of fit. In Proceedings of the IEEE International Symposium on Information Theory, Sorrento, Italy, 25–30 June 2000.
31. Liese, F.; Vajda, I. On Divergences and Informations in Statistics and Information Theory. *IEEE Trans. Inf. Theory* **2006**, *52*, 4394–4412. [CrossRef]
32. Kailath, T. The Divergence and Bhattacharyya Distance Measures in Signal Selection. *IEEE Trans. Commun. Technol.* **1967**, *15*, 52–60. [CrossRef]
33. Poor, H. Robust decision design using a distance criterion. *IEEE Trans. Inf. Theory* **1980**, *26*, 575–587. [CrossRef]
34. Clarke, B.S.; Barron, A.R. Information-theoretic asymptotics of Bayes methods. *IEEE Trans. Inf. Theory* **1990**, *36*, 453–471. [CrossRef]
35. Harremoes, P.; Vajda, I. On Pairs of f-divergences and their joint range. *IEEE Trans. Inf. Theory* **2011**, *57*, 3230–3235. [CrossRef]
36. Sason, I.; Verdú, S. f-Divergence Inequalities. *IEEE Trans. Inf. Theory* **2016**, *62*, 5973–6006. [CrossRef]
37. Sason, I. On f-divergence: Integral representations, local behavior, and inequalities. *Entropy* **2018**, *20*, 383. [CrossRef]
38. Rao, C.R.; Statistiker, M. *Linear Statistical Inference and Its Applications*; Wiley: New York, NY, USA, 1973.
39. Poor, H.V.; Hadjiliadis, O. *Quickest Detection*; Cambridge University Press: Cambridge, UK, 2008.
40. Cavanaugh, J.E. Criteria for linear model selection based on Kullback's symmetric divergence. *Aust. N. Z. J. Stat.* **2004**, *46*, 257–274. [CrossRef]
41. Devroye, L.; Mehrabian, A.; Reddad, T. The total variation distance between high-dimensional Gaussians. *arXiv* **2020**, arXiv:1810.08693.
42. Pollak, M. Optimal detection of a change in distribution. *Ann. Stat.* **1985**, *13*, 206–227. [CrossRef]
43. Carter, K.M.; Raich, R.; Finn, W.G.; Hero, A.O. Information preserving component analysis: Data projections for flow cytometry analysis. *IEEE J. Sel. Top. Signal Process.* **2009**, *3*, 148–158. [CrossRef]
44. Wen, Z.; Yin, W. A feasible method for optimization with orthogonality constraints. *Math. Program.* **2013**, *142*, 397–434. [CrossRef]
45. Edelman, A.; Arias, T.; Smith, S. The geometry of algorithms with orthogonality constraints. *SIAM J. Matrix Anal. Appl.* **1998**, *20*, 303–353. [CrossRef]

MDPI
St. Alban-Anlage 66
4052 Basel
Switzerland
Tel. +41 61 683 77 34
Fax +41 61 302 89 18
www.mdpi.com

Entropy Editorial Office
E-mail: entropy@mdpi.com
www.mdpi.com/journal/entropy

www.ingramcontent.com/pod-product-compliance
Lightning Source LLC
LaVergne TN
LVHW070446100526
838202LV00014B/1675